TV BOOK

THE ULTIMATE TELEVISION BOOK
EDITED BY JUDY FIREMAN

TV BOOK

THE ULTIMATE TELEVISION BOOK
EDITED BY JUDY FIREMAN

WORKMAN PUBLISHING COMPANY
NEW YORK, NEW YORK

Library of Congress Cataloging in Publication Data

Main entry under title:

TV book.

Includes index.
1. Television broadcasting—Addresses, essays, lectures.
I. Fireman, Judy.
PN 1992.5.T13   791.45'0973   77-5303
ISBN 0-89480-001-9
ISBN 0-89480-002-7 pbk.

Art Director: Paul Hanson
Designers: Bob Fitzpatrick, Gabrielle Maubrie
Assistants to the Editor: Barbara Reiss, David Trainer
Cover photo: Jerry Darvin

Workman Publishing Company, Inc.
231 East 51 Street
New York, New York 10022
Manufactured in the United States of America
First printing September 1977
10 9 8 7 6 5 4 3 2 1

Acknowledgments:

Workman Publishing thanks the following for their cooperation in research and obtaining photographs:

John Abramson; John Robert Christopher; General Electric; John F. Kennedy Library; KHJ-TV, Los Angeles; KTLA-TV, Los Angeles; Madison Square Garden; Helen Manasian; N.A.S.A.; Nam June Paik; Judith A. Posner; R.C.A.; Paul Scharfman; Lee Silvian; Vincent Terrace; Kent Warner; Warner Brothers; Wisconsin Center for Theatre Research.

Workman Publishing thanks the following for permission to include copyrighted material:

Arlen, Michael, "TV War Coverage: The View From Highway 1," adapted from THE VIEW FROM HIGHWAY 1, pp. 146–162. Copyright © 1974, 1975, 1976, by Michael Arlen. Reprinted by permission of the author and Farrar, Straus & Giroux, Inc. This article appeared originally in *The New Yorker*.

Blake, Howard, "The Worst Program in TV History," appeared under the title of "An Apologia from the Man Who Produced the Worst Program in TV History," *Fact* magazine, January–February 1966, pp. 41–45. Reprinted by permission.

Crown, Peter, "The Electronic Fireplace," adapted from an article of the same title, *Videography*, March 1977, pp. 17–19. Reprinted by permission.

Jaffe, Louis, "Videotape Versus Film," adapted from "Videotape Versus Film, Half-Inch, 16 mm and Super 8," *Radical Software #3*, Spring 1971. Reprinted by permission.

Leonard, John, "Reflections of a TV Critic," excerpted from "Reflections on My Seven Years of Being at Swords' Points," The New York *Times*, April 17, 1977. Copyright © 1977 by The New York Times Company. Reprinted by permission.

Newell, David, "Memoirs of Speedy Delivery," adapted from an article of the same title, *Pittsburgh* magazine, February 1971. Reprinted by permission.

Nimoy, Leonard, "My Life with Spock," excerpted from I AM NOT SPOCK, pp. 22–31. Copyright © 1975 by Leonard Nimoy. Reprinted by permission of the author and Celestial Arts.

Thorburn, David, "Homage to David Janssen," adapted from "Is TV Acting A Distinctive Art Form?" The New York *Times*, August 14, 1977. Copyright © 1977 by The New York Times Company. Reprinted by permission.

Winn, Marie, "TV: The Children's Drug," adapted from THE PLUG-IN DRUG, pp. 3–11. Copyright © 1977 by Marie Winn Miller. Reprinted by permission of the author and The Viking Press, Inc.

CONTENTS
I. THE REVOLUTIONARY MACHINE

In 1939, RCA intended to mass produce the TRK-12, but World War II caused a cancelation in the manufacturing of commercial sets.

II. THE CREATIVE MACHINE

No one used live television as expertly as the multi-talented Sid Caesar and Imogene Coca, the top comedians of television's "Golden Age."

III. THE COMPANION MACHINE

Game shows like Concentration *provide vicarious thrills and companionship for daytime viewers.*

IV. THE ENTERTAINMENT MACHINE

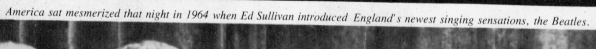

America sat mesmerized that night in 1964 when Ed Sullivan introduced England's newest singing sensations, the Beatles.

V. THE INFORMATION MACHINE

Television news is distinguished by informal conversations like this one at the 1976 Democratic convention between Edward Kennedy and Walter Cronkite.

VI. THE SELLING MACHINE

In 1970 NBC painted Inga Nielsen to advertise its sports programming.

VII. THE CONTROVERSIAL MACHINE

In Happy Anniversary
*David Niven demonstrates
one of the possible
responses to the controversy
about television's quality.*

INTRODUCTION

Television has changed the way we think, spend our leisure time, see reality. Clearly, it is the most important invention since the printing press. The claims made for it are enormous; its effects are far–reaching and still unmeasured. But what we can know about TV is much more than what we do know. TV BOOK answers the questions we all have about TV, or would have if we thought about it at all.

This is not a book about the controversial effects of television, although that subject is discussed. This is not a book about the vast technological breakthrough represented by satellite transmission and portable TV cameras, although these and other innovations are explained. Nor is this a book specifically about the expanding multi-million dollar industry which creates, packages, and profits from television programming, although the industry is analyzed here.

Rather, this is a book to help us understand and enjoy what appears on our screens. TV BOOK is a real guide to television, a book full of the kind of information that makes day-to-day TV watching more informed, more entertaining, more fun. I have invited one hundred and fifty experts, critics, stars, fans, writers, and producers to come together in one book and explain. And remember. And analyze. And criticize. And praise.

TV BOOK is a compilation of one hundred and fifty points of view; it is a collection of facts, theories, gossip, stories, and memories. TV BOOK will answer your questions about TV, and give you information you didn't realize you were lacking. It will tell you who invented TV. And who chooses the programs you watch. It will tell you what gets censored. And why Lucy is eternally popular. TV BOOK will answer these questions and more; it will remind you of your favorite shows and stars, your happiest and your saddest moments as a TV viewer.

Television has put us all on schedule together. In Seattle or Atlanta, Los Angeles or New York, at seven in the morning we stagger to consciousness listening to Tom and Jane or David and whomever. At seven in the evening we sit hushed or muttering, watching the network news. Because of television, many of us no longer read the papers, and certainly none of us relies on books and magazines for entertainment or information to the same extent anymore. We cannot think of the moon walk without recalling our eyewitness experience of it on the TV screen. We cannot remember John Kennedy without recalling our communal experience of his death and funeral in front of our TV sets. We cannot think of Elvis Presley or the Beatles without associating them with their formal introductions to us on *The Ed Sullivan Show*. We cannot remember a political convention, a peace march, the war in Viet Nam, or Zsa Zsa without realizing that it is television which brings us the world—live, on tape, and in color.

TV BOOK is a book for all of us who watch television. For those of us who love it, hate it, shake our fists at it and talk back to it when it is or isn't giving us what we want. TV BOOK is for the TV watchers who like talk shows, game shows, sports shows, news programs, soaps, movies, cop shows, and sitcoms. TV BOOK tells us what is going on behind the screen and in front of it, then and now. TV BOOK tells all about this marvelous machine that changed the world, and created for us a new world, television.

Judy Fireman

A Photo History of Television

Compiled and Written by Danny Peary

In the beginning television was no more a source of amusement than the telegraph. Television was simply a device used in the transmission of pictures from one place to another. Television as an entertainment came later; its definition changed with the decades, and eventually with the seasons.

To understand today's television we must look back at the topical comedies and cop shows of the early seventies; the rural comedies and private eye dramas of the sixties; the quiz shows and adult westerns of the late fifties; the live dramas and comedy of TV's "Golden Age"; the primitive broadcasts of the thirties and forties; and the experiments of the early twenties when inventors worked on a dream they had for a new communications system.

This photo history records chronologically the highlights of more than fifty years in the life of television, the "revolutionary machine."

I. THE REVOLUTIONARY MACHINE

1923. Vladimir Zworykin, funded by Westinghouse, invents the iconoscope. The photocell "eye" of the early TV cameras is the first element necessary in the development of an all-electronic television system.

In England, John L. Baird forms the first company exclusively devoted to television. Here Baird looks at the receiver of his first experimental television apparatus.

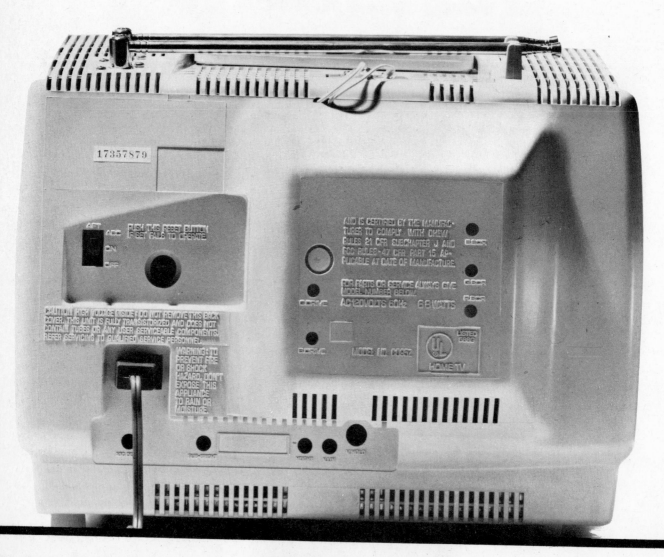

An early radiovisor in which the image is caught from a hole in the box by the mirror and reflected through a magnifying glass. Its inventor, C. Francis Jenkins, transmits a mechanically scanned photo of President Harding from Washington to Philadelphia. In 1925, Jenkins will be the first to transmit the image of a moving object.

1925. Baird makes the first demonstration of wireless television. In 1929, he will begin daily transmissions over the BBC.

The back of Bell Telephone's 1927 receiver used in the first "live" intercity broadcast, which is also the first time both sound and image have been sent together over a long distance.

THE HISTORY OF TV TECHNOLOGY

JOHN P. TAYLOR

Television was not invented by any one man. Nor did it spring into being overnight. It evolved gradually, over a long period, from the ideas of many men—each one building on the work of his predecessors. The process began in 1873, when it was accidentally discovered that the electrical resistance of the element selenium varied in proportion to the intensity of the light shining on it. Scientists quickly recognized that this provided a way of transforming light variations into electrical signals. Almost immediately a number of schemes were proposed for sending pictures by wire (it was, of course, before radio).

Early Systems

One of the earliest of these schemes was patterned on the human eye. Suggested by G. R. Carey in 1875, it envisioned a mosaic of selenium cells on which the picture to be transmitted would be focused by a lens system. At the receiving end there would be a similarly arranged mosaic made up of electric lights. Each selenium cell would be connected by an individual wire to the similarly placed light in the receiving mosaic. Light falling on the selenium cell would cause the associated electric light to shine in proportion. Thus the mosaic of lights would reproduce the original picture. Had the necessary amplifiers, and the right kind of lights, been available this system would have worked. But it also would have required an impractical number of connecting wires. Carey recognized this and in a second scheme proposed to "scan" the cells—transmitting the signal from each cell to its associated light, in turn, over a single wire. If this were

Ray D. Kell and Dr. E. F. W. Alexanderson, early television pioneers, pose with the mechanical scanning disk.

done fast enough, the retentive power of the eye would cause the resultant images to be seen as a complete picture.

The next forward step was to eliminate the selenium mosaic by scanning the image directly. In 1881 Shelford Bidwell, in England, demonstrated one way this could be done. He mounted a single selenium cell in a box with a pinhole. A motor-driven cam moved the box rapidly up and down and across the plane of the image. The system worked but the scanning speed

3

1928. E.F.W. Alexanderson, chief television consultant at General Electric, demonstrates the first home TV set. It has a three-by-four-inch screen; the control in Alexanderson's hand keeps the mechanical receiving apparatus in pace with the signal.

Alexanderson poses with his television receiver, an intricate device for projecting images on a screen from a position backstage. GE's station WGY in Schenectady, New York, begins the first regular programming, three times a week, on May 10, 1928.

FELIX THE CAT: STAR OF EARLY TELEVISION

The first "star" of television was Felix the Cat, a well-known cartoon character of the twenties. He made his debut before the TV cameras in 1929. RCA engineers needed someone to focus their camera on while they experimented with their equipment. They soon ran out of human volunteers—no one could stand the lights and the tedium for very long. So they mounted a foot-high statuette of Felix on a turntable and placed that in front of their camera. There he went round and round, hour after hour, day after day—and, in fact, year after year. What began as a temporary expedient became a fixture. Felix's career spanned most of the 1930's. His smiling visage became not only a symbol of early television, but also a sort of test pattern by which the engineers measured their progress. The pictures below illustrate this. At Felix's debut in 1929, the RCA engineers were using a 60-line scanning speed and the image appears as if seen through a venetian blind. The 120-line picture of 1932 is much better, although still very fuzzy. The 441-line picture—typical of television as introduced at the 1939 World's Fair—is quite sharp. These, of course, are just three of the steps in television's progress. There were many in-between steps—and Felix appeared in most of them.

was very limited. Soon afterward Maurice LeBlanc, in France, suggested that the image could be scanned by an oscillating mirror which would reflect the light variations onto a fixed selenium cell.

The Nipkow Disk

A number of other mechanical scanning arrangements were proposed at about this time. But it remained for a German, Paul Nipkow, to devise the simplest and most workable one. In 1884 he filed a patent on a system which used a scanning disk that had small holes spaced around the outer circumference in a spiral pattern. This disk rotated at high speed in front of the selenium cell at the sending end. As it did so, each hole scanned a line across the image to be transmitted. Because of the spiral pattern each scan line was slightly below the preceding line—until the whole image, top to bottom, had been scanned. An identical disk—rotating in synchronization—was placed in front of the light source at the receiving end. This produced lines of varying light intensity which reproduced the original image.

Nipkow never had the money to build a working model of his concept. But many who came after him did, and the "Nipkow Disk"—or a variation of it—was used in most television systems until the early thirties.

Electronic Experimentation

There were some early experimenters who were not satisfied with mechanical scanning. The cathode-ray tube had been developed by K. F. Braun in 1897, and soon after there were attempts to adapt it for television. In 1902 Boris Rosing, a Russian, started experimenting with cathode-ray tubes for image reproduction. In 1907 he described and actually built a system in which the picture was viewed on a cathode-ray tube in which the beam was deflected in synchronization with the sending signal. Rosing was a professor at the Technological Institute of Saint Petersburg, and one of his greatest legacies, perhaps, is that among his young pupils was Vladimir K. Zworykin.

4

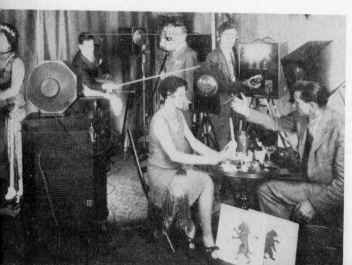

September 11, 1928. WGY Schenectady, broadcasts the first TV drama, *The Queen's Messenger.* There is an individual camera for each performer and also one for props being manipulated by the two people at the table. The actors dress for their parts, although the small picture can show only their faces.

NBC has its first TV personality. Felix the Cat is transmitted from New York to Kansas during a series of 1928 experiments. His image is picked up on primitive 60-line viewers. Eventually, sophisticated viewers will have 525 lines.

"Television was not invented by any one man."

Others were working along the same lines. In Germany a system using a cathode ray tube at the receiving end (much like Rosing's) was described by Dieckman in 1906. Neither he nor Rosing knew of the other's work. In 1918 A. A. Campbell Swinton, in England, suggested a system which would use cathode-ray tubes at both sending and receiving ends. He never built such a system but he is usually credited with being the first to suggest the idea of all-electronic television. In 1911 A. Sinding-Larsen suggested the use of radio as a carrier for picture signals. Thus, well before World War I, all of the concepts of what we think of as "modern television" had been put forward. But the onset of the war interrupted the early experiments, and for almost a decade television was forgotten.

Public Demonstrations Begin

In the early twenties there was a new burst of television activity. C. F. Jenkins, J. L. Baird, Zworykin, Philo T. Farnsworth and others were busy in their laboratories. And then there began to be public demonstrations. In 1925 Jenkins, in the United States, and Baird, in England, publicly demonstrated working (albeit crude) television systems using the Nipkow disk. Other experimenters were working behind locked doors.

This activity inevitably drew the attention of the big corporations. And with that came a marked change. The first fifty years of television development (from 1875 to 1925) had seen lonely inventors working by themselves or in small laboratories. But starting

The image in this Jenkins radiovisor is reflected by the mirror onto the magnifying glass where it is viewed.

about 1925 the big radio companies undertook major television development programs. Public demonstrations of operating television systems were made by AT&T (1927), General Electric (1928), RCA (1930), Dumont (1930), and Philco (1931).

All of these systems used mechanical scanning systems employing either the Nipkow disk or something similar. The very earliest were 30-line systems—that is, the scene to be transmitted was scanned by 30 horizontal lines. Later systems increased this to 60 lines, to 120 lines and, in one case, to 243 lines. But even then the pictures were not sharp and the large disks required (some four feet in diameter) were obviously not practical for home use.

Beginning of the Electronic Age

Fortunately, a better system was on the horizon. In 1919, Zworykin had emigrated to the United States

1929. Now working for RCA, Vladimir Zworykin demonstrates the kinescope, a cathode-ray TV receiver, which along with the iconoscope completes an all-electronic TV system.

C. Francis Jenkins's receiver with a round screen.

1930. NBC projects a picture from W2XBS, its experimental TV station in New York, onto a six-by-eight-foot screen at a midtown theater.

"The process began in 1873..."

and gone to work for the Westinghouse Company where he continued the study of electronic television which he had begun (under Professor Rosing) some ten years before. In 1923 he filed his first patent on the iconoscope, the first camera pickup tube. In the iconoscope the picture to be transmitted was focused on a photosensitive mosaic mounted in the tube. The mosaic was scanned, line-for-line, by an electron beam which released a small electric charge from each tiny photoelement as the beam passed over it. Thus the basic concept of scanning was continued. But now there was an important difference. The speed of the beam and the number of lines scanned were no longer limited by mechanical considerations.

In November 1929, Zworykin demonstrated the kinescope—a greatly improved cathode-ray television picture tube. Now, with an iconoscope at the sending end and a kinescope at the receiving end, an all-electronic system was a practical possibility.

RCA Backs Electronic Television

Zworykin took his ideas for developing such a system to David Sarnoff, then vice-president and general manager of RCA. Sarnoff was enthralled. Within months Zworykin transferred to RCA where he was made director of electronic research. He was provided with the money and manpower he needed to carry out his project. Equally important, other groups within RCA engineering and research were set up to develop needed system elements (cameras, transmitters, receivers). RCA had decided to place all its bets on electronic television.

During all of the 1930's RCA (and other companies, too) worked continuously to improve television quality. The measure of their progress is indicated by the increasing number of scanning lines employed in the successive demonstrations which RCA made during this period:

DATE OF DEMONSTRATION	NO. OF PICTURE LINES
1930	60 lines
1931	120 lines
1933	240 lines
1936	343 lines
1939	441 lines
1941	525 lines

In 1939, RCA announced that coincident with the opening of the New York World's Fair it would start regular television broadcasting, and would offer receivers for sale to the public. It did—but not for long. Other manufacturers complained and the FCC rescinded its approval for commercial television while an industry committee reviewed the standards. In the end, this committee recommended the basic RCA system, but changed the number of lines from 441 to 525. The FCC then approved the start of commercial television. RCA quickly changed its equipment to 525 lines and went back on the air. But within months came Pearl Harbor, and television once again went into mothballs.

The Postwar Boom

Shortly after World War II ended RCA introduced a new television receiver—the famous "630"—which was a tremendous advance over prewar receivers. And, to stimulate production, it gave other companies the manufacturing drawings. The market exploded. New television stations came on the air at a fast pace. Some interference problems cropped up and the FCC

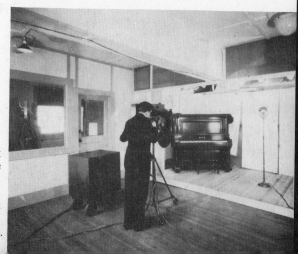

Once again, a model of Felix the Cat is used in an early broadcast demonstration at W2XBS. For hours, Felix revolves on a phonograph turntable while tests are made. Felix is used because humans cannot tolerate the hot TV lights for long periods.

1931. A program promoting home TV is broadcast from the Dumont station WXCD in Passaic, New Jersey. In 1938, Dumont will place the first all-electronic home television set on the market.

"froze" new station construction for a time. But not even this could stop the boom. Television receivers continued to sell and sets in use increased at a phenomenal rate:

YEAR	SETS IN USE
1946	6,000
1947	142,000
1948	977,000
1949	3,660,000
1950	9,732,000
1951	15,637,000
1952	21,782,000

(Source: *Television Factbook*, Television Digest Inc., 1977)

The Debate Over Color

All of the receivers sold until this time were, of course, monochrome—black-and-white. But meantime the push for color was starting. In 1939 CBS had shown a color TV system in which a wheel with three color segments (filters) rotated at high speed in front of the camera lens. A similar wheel was used in the receiver. This system produced three picture fields (red, blue, and green) in rapid succession (hence the name "field sequential" system). Persistence of vision in the eye caused the viewer to see a single full-color picture. After the war CBS resumed work on this system and made a number of impressive demonstrations.

In 1949 the FCC started a series of hearings on proposed color TV standards. The commission viewed demonstrations of the CBS field sequential system, which worked very well, and of a new RCA all-electronic color system, which did not work quite so well. The RCA system used three separate pickup tubes in the camera and three kinescopes (one for each color) in the receiver. These required exact—and hard

This public advertisement announced the formation of the National Broadcasting Company by RCA in 1926.

to maintain—alignment. However, this system had the big advantage of being "compatible" (i.e., a monochrome receiver tuned to the color transmission produced a good monochrome picture).

NBC places a TV antenna atop the Empire State Building in 1931. Picture definition improves dramatically.

1936. Bell Telephone engineers construct a coaxial cable between New York and Philadelphia with the capacity to carry simultaneous electrical impulses of different frequencies. In 1948, the East and Midwest will be linked; it will take until 1951 to link both coasts.

1937. NBC initiates the first mobile TV unit. It uses a microwave transmitter in a truck to relay images to the Empire State Building. In 1938, this unit will unexpectedly come upon and film a fire at Ward's Island, New York, the first unscheduled TV news event.

In 1930, David Sarnoff, a Russian immigrant, was elected president of the Radio Corporation of America.

The FCC chose the CBS system, and in 1950 gave the go-ahead for color on this basis. RCA sued, but lost, and in July 1951 CBS went on the air with color transmission. The industry did not follow. It did not like the idea of a color wheel in every receiver, and it wanted compatibility. Moreover, by this time RCA had developed the tri-color kinescope. In a few months CBS gave up on the field sequential system.

Meantime the industry formed another committee—the second NTSC (National Television Standards Committee). It deliberated for many months and eventually recommended a set of standards based on the RCA system (with some changes suggested by other manufacturers). On December 17, 1953, the FCC approved the start of color television broadcasting based on the NTSC-recommended standards.

Color Telecasting Begins

It was the final approval needed. NBC began telecasting many of its programs in color. RCA started selling cameras and transmitting equipment to television stations, and color television receivers to the public. Other manufacturers soon followed. But color TV did not explode as monochrome had earlier. It turned out that producing programs in color was much more expensive than in monochrome. With only a few color receivers in use, advertisers were reluctant to pay the extra cost. And the public was slow to buy color receivers when only a few programs were in color. It was a classic chicken-and-egg situation. For awhile it looked as if color would fail. But RCA persevered, pouring millions of dollars into color promotion and subsidizing, in part, the extra cost of color production on NBC and on independent stations. Slowly the number of color receivers rose. By 1962 there were about one million color sets in use—sufficient to make the extra cost of color worthwhile to the advertiser. By 1965 there were five million color sets, and all the networks had gone to full-color. Color bloomed! By 1970 there were 37 million color sets.

Further Improvements

Since 1953 there have been no further changes in the system used in the United States. But there have been tremendous changes in both home receivers and telecasting equipment. Increasing use of solid-state components (transistors, diodes) and of integrated circuits has made today's receivers smaller, lighter, more reliable—and they require far less power.

In telecasting equipment there have been corresponding advances. For example, RCA's 1954 color camera used 35 tubes, weighed 280 pounds and required 375 watts of power. RCA's newest comparable camera (studio type) uses just 3 tubes (the pickup

January 1, 1939. Vladimir Zworykin is granted a patent on his iconoscope, seen here, and his kinescope. Television will quickly become totally electronic; its growth is thus assured.

April 20, 1939. RCA President David Sarnoff dedicates the RCA pavilion at the New York World's Fair in the first scheduled news event covered by television. In his speech, Sarnoff predicts a great future for the new medium.

April 30, 1939. President Franklin D. Roosevelt speaks at the World's Fair, the first head of state to appear on television.

1939

HOW TELEVISION WORKS

Television works by a process called "scanning." At the sending end (the studio, or an outside pickup point) the image to be transmitted is scanned by an exploring element which travels across the image in a succession of descending horizontal lines (see illustration). This scanning process generates an electrical current (signal) which varies in proportion to the light intensity at each point in the image. The signal is sent over a communications channel (wire, cable, or over-the-air) to the receiving point. There a reproducing element generates a spot of light whose intensity varies in proportion to the signal received. Synchronizing signals, which are sent with the picture signal, cause the light spot to travel over the viewing screen in exactly the same pattern as the exploring element travels over the image field. If the spot travels fast enough, the persistence of vision in the human eye will cause the viewer to see a picture on the viewing screen that matches the image at the sending end.

The principle of scanning was suggested by G. R. Carey in 1875, and every television system built to this day has employed scanning in one form or another. The earliest systems were mechanical and used a light-sensitive element for pickup and a light beam for reproduction. Today's systems are all-electronic and use electron beams for scanning, both in the camera pickup tube and in the picture tube. The electronic system provides sharper and brighter pictures. But basically it operates the same way as the early mechanical systems.

For color transmission, three pickup tubes are used (in most systems). Three signals are transmitted (for red, green, and blue images). In an incredibly complex process the receiver separates out the three signals and reproduces them as dots of the three colors. The eye blends these into a single color.

tubes), weighs 45 pounds, and uses only 100 watts of power. Color cameras designed for news gathering are even smaller—the Thompson-CSF Microcam weighs only 8 pounds. In other equipment areas—for example, in studio switchers and in transmitting equipment—there have been equally important (though less visible) advances.

There have been other technological developments which have appreciably affected production and operating procedures. For instance the introduction by Ampex in 1956 of quadruplex videotape recording. Before then all TV programs (except films) were produced live, and usually in the studios of the networks or stations. Today almost all TV programs (except film and news) are taped, and the taping may be done by production companies, in the field, or almost anywhere.

Another development, less spectacular but important, was the introduction—by Philips in 1962—of the Plumbicon®, a new type of camera pickup tube. It

June 20, 1939. TV's first opera, Gilbert and Sullivan's *The Pirates of Penzance*, is the first musical production in NBC's regular TV programming.

September 30, 1939. Fordham defeats Waynesburg State 34–7 in the first televised football game. Baseball, boxing, and tennis will also make their TV debuts this year.

Maverick inventor Peter Goldmark was founder and president of CBS's technological research division. He contributed to the development of color TV, the LP record, a video cassette system, and live photo reception from the moon.

was considerably smaller (1¼-inch diameter) than the previously used Image-Orthicons (3-inch diameter) so

that much smaller cameras became possible. And it had other technical advantages. The Plumbicon® led to a whole new generation of color cameras providing easier portability and greater production flexibility.

Recently a ⅔-inch diameter Plumbicon® was developed and this made possible the very small ENG (for Electronic News Gathering) cameras now coming into widespread use. These have already revolutionized television news by making it possible to get live news pickups of events that previously could be covered only by filming (with consequent delay for developing). Moreover these cameras are also being used increasingly for live and tape program production in the field. For such use their mobility and economical operating costs are an important advantage.

In the Future

In the future, we can see numerous technological developments on the horizon. Satellites will be used increasingly—and perhaps in new ways. Circularly polarized antennae (recently approved by FCC) will reduce ghosting problems. New high-density methods of recording, using disks or perhaps "bubble" memories, will make today's videotape recorders look cumbersome. There also will be another new generation of still smaller cameras that will probably employ miniature "charge-coupled" devices (postage stamp size units in which half a million tiny sensors each transmit one element of the picture) instead of pickup tubes. Digital techniques (as used in computer data transmission) will be used increasingly—in fact, the whole TV system conceivably could be digital. And if it is entirely new methods of scanning and picture transmission may evolve. But whatever the direction, it is likely that technological advances in the next twenty-five years will equal those of the past twenty-five.

A 1939 RCA Model TRK-9 designed for home viewing. Sarnoff plans to flood the market with TV sets.

In 1939, RCA also manufactures its TRK-12 model. World War II will curtail most TV production and thwart the plans of both Sarnoff and CBS president William Paley to initiate mass commercial programming.

RCA experimenters with a small, solid state camera.

GLOSSARY

Coaxial cable. A special kind of cable consisting of a small inner conductor separated by insulation from a concentric outer conductor. It is capable of carrying the wide band-width required to transmit television signals over long distances.

Film camera. A device used to convert the optical images on a motion picture film (or on slides) to a television signal.

Hookup. A system of coaxial cable, microwave, or satellite connections between two or more stations that allows them simultaneously to telecast a program originating at one point.

Iconoscope. The very first type of pickup tube. Invented by V. K. Zworykin in 1923, used in most prewar television systems.

Image orthicon. Later type of pickup tube. Used in most systems from 1947 to the mid-1960's.

Kinescope. Technical term for the picture tube in the home receiver (or monitor). In this tube an electron scanning beam causes the color dots on the kinescope face to fluoresce in accordance with the received signal and thus to reproduce the scene at the transmitting point.

Live camera. A device used to pick up the optical image of a live event (sports, news, studio program) and convert it to a television signal. It includes a lens system, a pickup tube (or tubes), an amplifier, and control circuits.

Microwave system. A chain of relay stations, located about twenty-five miles apart, which are used to send television signals over long distances (e.g., coast-to-coast).

Pickup Tube. An electron tube in the camera which electronically scans the image and generates an electrical signal proportioned to the light intensity at each spot in the picture.

Plumbicon®. An improved pickup tube introduced in 1962 and used in most broadcast TV systems today.

Receiving antenna. An arrangement of rodlike elements (usually mounted on the house top) that picks up signal radiated from the transmitting antenna and feeds it to the receiver.

Satellite. A relay station in the sky located in geosynchronous orbit, it receives signals from one point on earth and relays (retransmits) them to another point a continent, or an ocean, away.

STL (Studio Transmitter Link). A special telephone line, coaxial cable, or microwave system used to send the television signal from the studio to the transmitter site.

Studio switcher. A large console with monitors, indicator lights, and rows of push-button switches. Used for observing pictures from various sources (remote points, various studios, VTR's, film cameras) and selecting one to be sent to the transmitter for telecast.

Transmitter. A large piece of equipment that amplifies the television signal received from the studio to high power, converts it to VHF (very high frequency) or UHF (ultra high frequency) and feeds it to the antenna.

During the war, Dumont is the only network to continue extensive commercial programming. Paul Winchell and Jerry Mahoney appear on WABD, New York.

1946. The war over, television begins to dominate domestic life. Within the next five years the total number of home TV sets in America will rise from ten thousand to twelve million. In the 1950's, forty million Americans will be born and seventy million sets built.

Heavyweight boxer Ezzard Charles poses with Gorgeous George, the man chiefly responsible for "modernizing" wrestling. Spectator sports that demand sophisticated camera work must take a back seat to boxing and wrestling on early TV.

THE DREAMERS
WHO MADE TELEVISION

Modern television is the creation of many men. But two names stand out above all others—Vladimir Zworykin and David Sarnoff. Both were born in Russia, came to this country as youths, became U.S. citizens, and flourished under the American system. In 1923 Zworykin invented the iconoscope, the first camera tube, and in 1928 the kinescope, the first picture tube. In 1929 he described to David Sarnoff his idea for using these as the basis of an all-electronic television system. Sarnoff, then vice-president and general manager of RCA, was a man of great prescience. He quickly grasped the possibilities of electronic television and agreed to provide the money and manpower to develop it.

The vision that Zworykin and Sarnoff shared came true. But not until numerous obstacles had been surmounted. It took many years and millions of dollars. Sarnoff was acutely conscious of the protracted struggle, and often spoke of it. One such occasion was at the 1944 convention of the Television Broadcasters Association, when both he and Dr. Zworykin were given awards. Zworykin, who received his first, was hailed as the man who made television possible. In accepting, Zworykin said, "I was just the dreamer. I went to David Sarnoff with my idea and he agreed to back me. It was he who made television possible." When it became Sarnoff's turn he referred to Zworykin's statement and said, "as I remember it, Dr. Zworykin came to me with his idea for an electronic system. I asked him how much it would cost and how long it would take. He said it would cost about a hundred thousand dollars and might take a year and a half. That was fifteen years, and ten million dollars, ago—and I believed him! Who was the dreamer?"

As things turned out they were both still dreaming. It was to be another five years, and cost RCA some $40 million more, before black-and-white television became profitable in 1949. And it took an additional sixteen years (until 1965), and another $100 million of RCA's money, before color television was fully established.

Transmitting antenna. A turnstilelike arrangement of pipes and rods (usually mounted on a tall tower) that radiates the high-power television signal in all directions.

TV receiver. The device in the home that amplifies the received signals, decodes them, and displays the program on the picture tube that it houses.

Vidicon. A less expensive type pickup tube used in many industrial and educational type TV cameras.

VTR (Video Tape Recorder). A device used to record a television signal on magnetic tape so that it can be telecast at a later time or sent to other stations, as in syndication.

By the end of the decade, wrestling will become so popular that it runs every night in some cities. *TV Guide* will set up a department to compile match results. Dumont announcer Dennis James and wrestlers such as Gorgeous George, Baron Leone, the Zebra Kid, Ricki Starr, and Antonino Rocca become household words.

Inexpensively produced game shows, often with children as panelists, fill television schedules in the late 1940's.

A VISIT WITH VLADIMIR ZWORYKIN, THE FATHER OF TELEVISION

JOHN P. TAYLOR

How does it feel to be a legend in one's own time? Dr. Zworykin simply shrugged off the question. He doesn't think of himself that way. He is aware, of course, that many refer to him as the father of television—the man who made it possible—the inventer of the iconoscope and the kinescope, and so on. But he pays little heed. And, unless prompted, he seldom refers to the past. His consuming interest is the present—and, even more, the future. It is symptomatic of this remarkable man.

But Vladimir Kosma Zworykin, whether he recognizes it or not, is a legendary figure in electronics. Born in Murom, Russia, in 1889, his life has paralleled—and been closely entwined with—the long evolution of television. His interest in electronic television began in 1907, when he became a laboratory assistant to the famous Professor Boris Rosing. He graduated from the Technological Institute of St. Petersburg in 1912, served as a communications officer in the Czarist army during World War I, came to the United States in 1919. In 1923, he patented the iconoscope—the breakthrough that made electronic television possible. In the thirties he played a major role in RCA's long struggle to bring television to the public. During World War II his group worked on infrared devices (the snooperscope, etc.) and on television-guided missiles. In 1954—having reached the mandatory age—he officially retired from RCA and immediately began a new career with the Medical

Electronics Center of the Rockefeller Institute.

Today, at age 88, one might expect to find him rocking on his porch and musing on the past. Not Dr. Zworykin! We found him in his office at RCA laboratories in Princeton, where he spends almost every morning. Afternoons he is apt to be at the Fusion Energy Corporation, also in Princeton, where he is active as a consultant. He is also a consultant on medical electronics to several organizations. And, from December to April, he is a "visiting scientist" at the University of Miami.

Dr. Zworykin does not consider all this activity unusual. He says, "When you work all your life you can't stop. What can you do, play golf? It's too late for me. Drinking I never did, just a little stuff. I don't smoke. You have to occupy yourself." And he does!

His office at RCA (where he is an honorary vice president) is very much a working office. None of his fifty or so awards adorn the walls. There is only one picture—a small photo of B. J. Thompson, a brilliant associate who was killed while testing radar over occupied Italy. But there are papers and reports and books in great profusion. Most are in the area of theoretical physics, which has been Dr. Zworykin's

13

In 1947, Jack Barry begins a seven-year stint as host of the entertaining children's program, *Juvenile Jury*. In the fifties, he will also moderate another kiddie show, *Winky Dink and You*.

December 27, 1947. "What time is it, boys and girls?" *Howdy Doody* begins a thirteen-year run on NBC as a daily fifteen-minute program.

Puppet shows abound from coast to coast. *Kukla, Fran, and Ollie* debuts locally on WBKB in Chicago in 1947. Burr Tillstrom is the puppeteer for the Kuklapolitans who visit Fran Allison.

Dr. Vladimir Zworykin poses in his office at RCA in Princeton, New Jersey with his 1923 invention, the iconoscope.

love since he was a very young man, and which he still follows avidly.

Fortunately for us, Dr. Zworykin, despite his preoccupied air and his imposing presence, is a warm and kindly man. He greeted us in the friendliest fashion and patiently tried to answer our mundane (for him) questions.

How does Dr. Zworykin feel about what has happened to the miracle he wrought? "I feel elated," he says, "especially at times when I see things like the moon landings and, even more, the pictures which the Viking lander sent back from Mars. Without television this would not have been possible."

Has television worked out the way he thought it would back in 1923? "Not exactly," he says. "In those days when they asked me, 'what are you going to do with it?' I said, with television you can supplement your eyes. Television will help the eye where the eye cannot give us the information—too far, too

dangerous, too small, and so forth."

The closeups of the moon are a good example of what Dr. Zworykin was thinking of fifty years ago. So too is the use of television to observe nuclear operations, to explore the ocean bottom, to see particles of molecular size (through the electron scanning microscope). Today there are many applications of television in industry, medicine, and education that fit his original concept of "extending man's sight."

Apparently entertainment programs were not an important part of Zworykin's early thinking on television. Even today he is equivocal about them. "I don't use television myself," he says. "My wife looks at it and calls my attention to programs I like—news, wildlife programs, things like that. But when they put on an old story about Amos and Andy as a whole program. . . !"

What does Dr. Zworykin foresee in the future for television? "I think the Moon and Mars telecasts

John Cameron Swayze becomes TV's first big newscaster in 1947 on NBC's *The Camel News Camera*. In 1948, Swayze will also host a panel show called *Who Said That?* and in the fifties he will even do a little acting. Ironically, Swayze will gain TV immortality by losing a Timex watch he is testing for durability in a large tank of water on a live commercial.

Douglas Edwards is shifted from CBS-radio to CBS-TV to do daily fifteen-minute broadcasts. Edwards will remain the top CBS newscaster until 1962. Because of their lack of popularity with viewers, there will be fewer news programs in 1952 than in 1948.

Gene Autry, the movies' first singing cowboy in the 1930's, leads his horse, Champion, onto the TV screen in 1947. Already wealthy from his numerous Saturday morning matinees and recordings of such songs as "Silver Haired Daddy of Mine" and "Rudolph the Red-Nosed Reindeer," Autry will make it big in television as well.

"I said with television you can supplement your eyes . . ."

open—even for commercial people—tremendous new fields for television. I visualize an international educational and technological library using television and satellites—and perhaps video disks, which can be produced at very low cost, almost the same as music." He thinks satellites will be much less expensive when they are launched from the space shuttle; that possibly they will be battery-operated, with the battery being recharged by the shuttle. At some time in the not-too-distant future he believes all TV will be by satellite.

What about the use of fiber optics for television transmission? "But why?" says Dr. Zworykin. "That won't change the situation. Maybe in the next ten years they will put in cable with fiber optics. But that is just improving the technique which already exists, for specific reasons—cheaper, less cable, etc. It's a good development, but it is not fundamental. What I'm trying to do is something that is fundamental."

What is Zworykin working on? "Nothing. I'm retired," he says, eyes twinkling. "If you ask what am I doing—reading, reading till I'm going half crazy." And, one might add—thinking, thinking, and spouting new ideas faster than anyone can keep up with him.

One of the things Dr. Zworykin has been thinking about is the energy crisis. He believes fusion power is the right long-term answer (*fusion* is the combining of atomic nuclei, as contrasted to *fission*, the splitting of atoms, which is the process used in present nuclear plants). But he believes present efforts to develop fusion power are wrongly directed.

As Dr. Zworykin explains it, "At present they are going to bigger and bigger stations and getting bigger and bigger difficulties. I think that is the wrong way. My idea is to build the generator on a very small scale—something like the laundromat or the electric heater in the house. Make it small, like we do in the laboratory. Why is this possible? Because the energy of particles is tremendous. Some of the work we are doing in television, like the electron multiplier, can be used for ion multiplication on a small scale—like a television tube. Even if you release only one kilowatt, it will be a small device and you can multiply the power by placing several in parallel. Recent figures show that the average family consumption of power is under eight kilowatts, so if you produce up to ten kilowatts then we are independent of the big power stations. Imagine such a device in every family kitchen—all our social order will change.

"It's a dream all right," Zworykin concedes, "but a dream which is based on what is going on right now, and where it is going to."

Actually, fusion has been accomplished in the laboratory on a very small scale. The process is still inefficient—more power in than out. But the possibility is there. And, as Dr. Zworykin points out, if the goal were a small home-type generator (instead of a mammoth power station), probably many small experimenters would be working on it. They would face many problems, but no more than electronic television seemed to face before Zworykin's breakthrough invention of the iconoscope in 1923.

A nuclear generator in every kitchen is only one of Dr. Zworykin's current interests. There are many others—all far-out. For, as Robert Sarnoff said of him at his eightieth birthday party, "His brilliant mind has never waited for others."

John P. Taylor is a free-lance writer and contributing editor to Television/Radio Age.

15

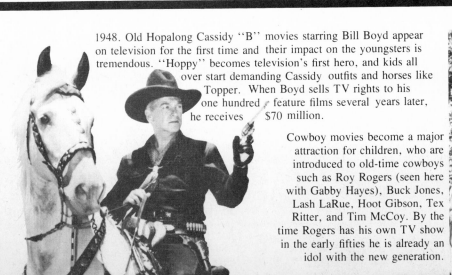

1948. Old Hopalong Cassidy "B" movies starring Bill Boyd appear on television for the first time and their impact on the youngsters is tremendous. "Hoppy" becomes television's first hero, and kids all over start demanding Cassidy outfits and horses like Topper. When Boyd sells TV rights to his one hundred feature films several years later, he receives $70 million.

Cowboy movies become a major attraction for children, who are introduced to old-time cowboys such as Roy Rogers (seen here with Gabby Hayes), Buck Jones, Lash LaRue, Hoot Gibson, Tex Ritter, and Tim McCoy. By the time Rogers has his own TV show in the early fifties he is already an idol with the new generation.

OUR FIRST TV SET
MICHAEL LAULETTA

We bought our first television set in 1951. It was a General Electric with a fifteen-inch screen, two doors, four big knobs, and a giant speaker covered with brown mesh. It must have weighed more than a hundred pounds. What a set!

Railroad flats in Brooklyn were perfect for a GE. The set fit quite comfortably between the two parlor windows that faced the street, and a seven-year-old could actually sit at the kitchen table and watch the screen four rooms down the long hallway. The one drawback was the lack of an outdoor antenna. We had to buy a pair of those "rabbit ears," and carefully position the base, and delicately adjust the antennae every time we changed channels. Precision tuning depended on the time of day, the weather and where my father was sitting that evening.

We weren't the first ones in the family to get a TV. We weren't even the first ones on our block. But I'll bet we're the last family to get rid of our set. To this day, that old General Electric sits under the cellar stairs, waiting patiently to be plugged in again.

Once that television arrived, my whole life changed. I don't think I ever listened to *The Lone Ranger* or *Straight Arrow* on the radio ever again. They just didn't stand a chance against the likes of *Six-Gun Playhouse, Howdy Doody,* or *Beat the Clock.* Suddenly I hated to go to my grandmother's house because it no longer made a difference that the kid across the street from her had a television set. I had my own.

Of course, not all the changes were for the better. It must have been coincidence, but I seemed to catch

> "The best thing about that General Electric was that it never showed a bad program."

cold a lot more easily after we got that set, and my attendance at school was less than perfect. My mother must have seen a connection, though. Whenever I stayed home with a cold, she would leave the set off until three o'clock when my health began to improve again.

Back in the 1950's, of course, people would never admit that they *didn't* watch TV. Conversations at school began with, "Did you see . . . ?" I would immediately jump in with, "Yea . . ." whether I saw the show or not, and hope against hope that the inevitable "How'd you like the part . . . ?" question wouldn't follow.

It's difficult to remember every show I used to watch and impossible to pick a favorite. I do remember my favorite test pattern, though. It was the one with the Indian's head in the middle, on Channel 13 from New Jersey. After Bob Crosby signed off every afternoon, I immediately switched to 13 for that test pattern until the next show started. Maybe that's what's wrong with today's television. Not enough test patterns.

That GE was the first in what was to become a long line of television sets, all progressively bigger, fancier, more expensive to fix—and less fun to watch.

16

The Lone Ranger, for years a popular radio series, moves to television in 1948. The masked man, played by Clayton Moore (and briefly by John Hart), and his loyal companion Tonto, played by real-life Indian Jay Silverheels, will successfully battle bandits, cheap sets, and cliché-ridden scripts for four years.

Early TV programming is viewed on receivers like this 1948 Pilot set with an optional bubble that magnifies the screen.

Texaco Star Theatre, a wild variety show starring Milton Berle, becomes the most-watched program on television in 1948, its debut season. It will keep Americans glued to their sets on Tuesday nights for five years. "Mr. Television" will be offered a lucrative lifetime contract by NBC.

RCA manufactured this 12-inch TV set with doors in 1950. The retail price of the set in walnut or mahogany finish was $299.95; in limed oak it sold for $319.95. It featured a "jewel light" at the base to indicate when it was turned on.

The television we have now doesn't even have a little white dot to watch disappear after you turn it off.

The best thing about that General Electric was that it never showed a bad program. Whether it was Jackie Gleason in the role of Loudmouth Bratton, or a housewife admitting to the world that her husband was an alcoholic dwarf who'd just run off with her sister and the new dishwasher on *Queen for a Day,* every program was sheer entertainment.

One of these days I'm going back to that cellar and I'm going to pull that old friend out from under the stairs, plug it in, and watch an Indian-head test pattern. Then I'll go back upstairs—after the white dot disappears—and see if my mother remembers to ask that all-important question, "Did you close the doors?"

Michael Lauletta is a writer who still watches more than the average amount of television.

17

June 20, 1948. Ed Sullivan's *Toast of the Town* debuts. Comedy team Dean Martin and Jerry Lewis make their first TV appearance on this first "really big show." Sullivan will be a Sunday night fixture on CBS for twenty-three years.

The Original Amateur Hour comes to television. Host Ted Mack, following in the footsteps of longtime radio MC Major Bowes, chats here with drummer Burton Hurley, a four-year-old contestant.

COLLECTING VINTAGE TELEVISION SETS

KENT WARNER

When I lived in New York City, back in the late 1950's, there was a small area of second-hand radio and TV shops in lower Manhattan known as "Radio Row." Within the battered confines of these decrepit stores one could find masses of vintage radio and television sets of every shape, size, and description. Because I was quite young at the time, and did not have much money, I couldn't even consider buying any of these "talking-seeing" pieces of furniture. But I was curious nonetheless, and after I moved to California in 1962, I became an active collector of radio and television sets.

I returned to visit New York in the winter of 1975, and of course I headed directly (cash in hand) for that packed, electronic paradise I remembered from the 1950's. Much to my shock and disappointment, however, the entire area had been cleared and replaced by the 110-story World Trade Center. I asked around, but no one seemed to know or care about what had become of all those old radio and TV store owners, or their merchandise. It was all gone—just disappeared. Do you suppose the World Trade Center is delicately perched on an RCA TT5 or a McMurdo Silver chassis, or a Brunswick Panatrope? Whatever the case, I realized *now is the time. We must preserve television's past.*

Contrary to a popular belief, television is not a product of post–World War II American technology. The combined efforts of many minds, working in many countries, over many years, created television

Kent Warner poses with his prized 1939 RCA TRK-12 receiver.

18

On January 25, 1949, the first Emmy Awards are presented and KTLA in Los Angeles is chosen best station. Its top show, Mike Stokey's *Pantomime Quiz,* wins as TV's most popular program.

The Spade Cooley Show is one of KTLA's earliest successes. It attracts such guests as Frank Sinatra, Jerry Lewis, and Sarah Vaughan and remains on the air until 1956. In 1961, Cooley is sentenced to life in prison for killing his wife. In 1969, just prior to his parole, he performs for the first time in eight years. Backstage, after the show, Spade Cooley dies from a heart attack.

as we know it today. In 1847, in England, Frederick Bakewell was experimenting with sending line drawings by wire. In Germany, Paul Nipkow was granted a patent for sending moving pictures by wire in 1884. He employed a mechanical, or scanning-disk system that was further developed by John Baird in England in 1925, and simultaneously in America by C. Francis Jenkins and the Bell Telephone Laboratories. Early in the 1930's, scanning-disk television was developed to its fullest potential, but it soon became evident that its flickering picture and low definition would not be acceptable to a public that was then accustomed to the better quality of motion picture film.

It was the work of two Americans, Philo T. Farnsworth and Dr. Vladimir Zworykin, that finally enabled television to come of age. Their television tube patents provided the basic elements for the wholly electronic system that we use today. By 1936 the scanning-disk system was outdated and fully electronic television was being experimentally broadcast in England, Germany, and the United States.

By late 1938 and 1939, many American radio manufacturers were introducing television sets to the public with major campaigns to encourage buyers. Sales were slow. Receivers were expensive and there was minimum daily programming available. There were only twenty-one licensed television stations in the United States in 1941, when World War II temporarily halted television's advance. But after the war, television quickly regained momentum, and by the end of 1948 there were over one million television sets in the United States.

Sadly, little remains of those early television receivers. New developments in electronic technology rendered them outdated, and people were quick to discard their old friends for new models that boasted increased dependability and larger screens. Electronically gutted, the superior cabinetry of those early sets

still survives here and there and examples of it can sometimes be found hiding in used-furniture stores disguised as record cupboards and liquor cabinets.

One of the first relics of progress that I was able to save from the junk pile was a 1948 Pilot-Radio Candid TV receiver. My discovery was still in its original shipping carton and sported a magnifying bubble over its three-inch picture tube. This primitive-looking receiver sparked my interest in early television and marked the beginning of a fascinating hobby.

I soon learned that there were some publications on television from the 1930's and 1940's that could be found by those who were willing to plough through dusty bookstores with perseverance. A little such background material is very helpful in revealing the differences between a rare 1936 RCA set and a mass-produced model of the early 1950's. I also discovered that some clubs and current publications primarily de-

19

KTLA's *Space Patrol* is one of television's first space adventure series. Standing are Ken Mayer, Virginia Hewitt, and Nina Bara. Seated are Lynn Osborne and Ed Kemmer, who plays commander Buzz Corey. For eight years, these actors will do a fifteen-minute, live local show five days a week; a thirty-minute, live network show three times a week; and a live, weekly radio show.

Network daytime TV began in the late forties with Bert Parks hosting a game show called *What's My Name?* from Chicago. Parks will establish himself further by hosting the popular *Break the Bank* and other game shows in the 1940's and 1950's.

Captain Video and His Video Rangers, with Al Hodge (who replaced Richard Coogan as Captain Video) and young Don Hastings, ushers in a wave of TV sci-fi shows. Dumont broadcasts this serial on a daily basis from 1949 to 1953, when it becomes a weekly series for three more action-packed years.

voted to antique radio collecting are now beginning to show an interest in early television too. Many of the sets in my collection were obtained through these publications, as well as by hunting through swap-meets and at second-hand stores.

Although pre-1950 television sets can still be found at discount prices, it is very unlikely you will find them in working condition. Admirers of your newest acquisition will inevitably expect a demonstration, but unless you are electronically adept, repairs can be costly.

Extraordinary finds are not impossible, as a friend of mine proved recently by purchasing a 1936 RCA experimental receiver for forty dollars. My latest acquisition required exhausting legwork and a larger investment, but the result was a rewarding addition to my collection. It is an RCA model TRK-12 receiver

A 1946 television receiving set, the RCA 621 TS.

that was used as a demonstration set for television's public debut at the 1939 New York World's Fair.

20

"Extraordinary finds are not impossible."

A 1948 Pilot-Candid TV receiver rescued from a junk pile.

These early RCA receivers are distinctive in appearance because the screen is in a horizontal position; it was viewed through a reflecting mirror positioned above, on the lid of the cabinet.

Aspiring collectors should note that these early television sets, manufactured before World War II, are not easy to find. I know of only a handful, most of which are in the hands of a very few devoted owners.

It is my hope that by increasing public awareness and interest in early television, many sets still hiding in garages and basements will surface and be saved from destruction. Perhaps you may be the next to locate a rare 1930's television set, or one of the elusive scanning-disk receivers of the 1920's, and thereby preserve a long neglected part of our American heritage.

Kent Warner is a TV costume designer who thinks museums should take an interest in television.

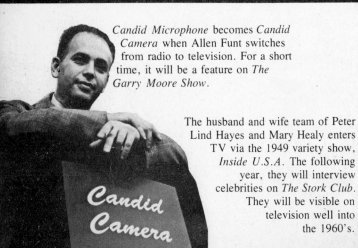

Candid Microphone becomes *Candid Camera* when Allen Funt switches from radio to television. For a short time, it will be a feature on *The Garry Moore Show.*

The husband and wife team of Peter Lind Hayes and Mary Healy enters TV via the 1949 variety show, *Inside U.S.A.* The following year, they will interview celebrities on *The Stork Club.* They will be visible on television well into the 1960's.

Candid Camera

CABLE TV: AN ALTERNATIVE

CAROL F. BROWN

If you haven't already got the picture, there are a few things you ought to know about cable TV. It's a highly seductive medium, and, ironically, the less enamored you are with the traditional boob tube, the more susceptible you'll be once you discover what's on "the other television."

When you subscribe to cable TV, you pay a monthly fee to keep your set hooked up to a system of wires owned by your local cable company. Through these wires you receive the usual broadcast channels very clearly, because the signals coming through them have been picked up by a powerful community antenna. But more interesting are the extra channels many cable systems offer. Subscribers can tune in "imported" channels from distant cities, weather reports, news wire headlines, live sports events, community meetings, special movies, and even foreign language programming. Ordinarily, these features come at no additional cost. But once communities get "hooked," complain some critics of the industry, what will prevent cable companies from charging for these extras?

In Columbus, Ohio, one of the country's largest cable chains has already begun to develop an experiment through which subscribers can order—for a per-program fee—operas, ballets, concerts, local sports events, numerous video games, and college courses for credit. Many viewers everywhere will no doubt be willing to pay for the luxury or convenience of receiving first-run films at home, viewing ticker tape direct from Wall Street, or tuning in a computerized partner for a game of chess. But there are other cable consumers who would rather organize their communities to fill up the extra channel space with local fare. The broadcast media have never been able to offer the public effective access to the airwaves. But most cable systems with over thirty-five hundred subscribers are required by the FCC to set aside at least one channel for local programming. Part of this unique provision requires cable companies to give at least five minutes of *free* TV time, on a "first-come, first-served, non-discriminatory" basis to *anyone* who asks for it.

Some cable operators have expanded this idea and encouraged local viewers to come up with full-scale productions of their own. In New York City, where the concept of designating "public access" channels originated in the late 1960's, local rules require cable franchises to provide two entire channels exclusively for TV shows produced by the public at large. Any afternoon or evening, you can find these channels filled with videotapes and live shows put together by such unlikely TV producers as taxi drivers, housewives, stockbrokers, Chinese immigrants, Israelis, Arabs, Irish freedom fighters, film buffs, and self-styled talk show hosts of all ages. Their "narrowcasts" lack the slick professional look of broadcast television, but they fulfill the need most special interest groups have to communicate with their neighbors, and they give creative individuals a chance to try out their ideas.

One producer in Manhattan has devised a game show during which viewers with push-button telephones can play pinball over TV by simply pushing

Ted Steele hosts a syndicated variety show in the late 1940's.

Radio's *Martin Kane, Private Eye,* is the first successful TV detective show. During its five-year run, beginning in 1949, four different actors play Kane. Here William Gargan repeats his radio role.

Lee Tracy is *Martin Kane* in this episode. With Tracy is Gene Lyons.

certain digits on their phones to operate certain levers on a televised pinball machine. An astrologer hosts a show on which he takes phone calls from viewers and gives out on-the-spot horoscopes. And for awhile an animal lover was using public access time to show off stray cats and dogs in the hope that viewers would call in and adopt them.

Because New York state's cable rules forbid censorship of public access shows, one of Manhattan's franchises ran into some problems when the publisher of *Screw* newspaper began producing the now infamous *Midnight Blue,* a late-night sex show. Some politicians and citizen groups alleged the show was pornographic and therefore in violation of FCC regulations that obligate cable operators to keep pornography and obscenity off the screen. But at this writing, state and federal rules still conflict, and a toned-down version of the program is still being cablecast. Those cable operators who oppose the financial "burden" of maintaining public access channels have tried to use Manhattan's legal snag as an example of why the public access programming concept "can't work." But the majority of public access programs in New York and elsewhere go on week after week without controversy.

In Reading, Pennsylvania, where public access television has been popular for years, cable TV has moved in still another new direction: "interactive," or two-way, television. A grant of about $1.2 million from the National Science Foundation to a consortium of Reading city agencies, researchers from New York University, and the local cable franchise, facilitated the production of two hours a day of two-way TV last year. The experiment worked so well that local groups have been raising their own funds to perpetuate the programming since the grant expired.

When the interactive shows are on, two apartment houses for the elderly, a recreation center, and various classrooms and offices in town become "live" TV studios. People at these different locations can talk to one another on TV, not only verbally, but *visually!* The mayor might appear on TV from his office to talk about a tax bill. If a retired businessman in one of the apartment houses disagrees with the mayor, he can argue back by stepping in front of the camera in his apartment lobby to express his own view. Perhaps a woman viewing from the recreation center nearby thinks both the mayor and the businessman are wrong. Viewers will soon see her presenting her viewpoint, because the recreation center can also become an instant studio. The Reading experiment and others like it may lead to a time when we can all talk to each other through our television sets.

But the cable innovation closest to most viewers' fantasies is probably neither public access TV nor interactive programming, but "TV on demand." This idea is already working in a cabled area just outside Montreal, where a catalogue distributed to viewers lists four thousand cartoons, documentaries, replays of prize fights and team sports, and entertainment features available by phone request. As soon as one of the eight channels reserved for those special interest programs is available, a technician at the cable company will broadcast the tape. In more technologically sophisticated systems, such as the one in Columbus, Ohio, viewers can order shows simply by pushing buttons on a computerized device the size of a cigar box.

Once such computerized devices are installed in people's homes, the viewer's privacy is potentially endangered. The same kinds of devices that enable a subscriber to pick his own programs could also be designed to supply data banks with information about his viewing habits—and maybe even his buying habits, too—if the company that installed them so desired. In several states, including New York, California, Florida, and Texas, surveillance channels have

22

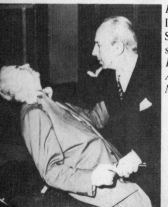

Movie character actor, Lloyd Nolan (on the right) becomes the hero when he takes over the role of *Martin Kane, Private Eye.* In 1953, Mark Stevens will star in *The Further Adventures of Martin Kane.*

Arthur Godfrey begins to challenge Milton Berle's supremacy as the top television personality. Both *Arthur Godfrey's Talent Scouts* and *Arthur Godfrey and His Friends* are immediate hits in the late forties. They will remain popular for a decade each.

Likable humorist Herb Shriner hosts a variety show in 1949 for CBS. It will only last two seasons, but by that time the drawling "Hoosier Hotshot" will be an established TV star.

From the videotape library of a cable company outside of Montreal, the operator broadcasts tapes upon phone requests.

"The next step, fear opponents of this new technology, could be Big Brother peeking into our living spaces."

intruded on people's privacy, and policemen and security guards have kept an eye on streets, school buildings, and apartment lobbies over cable hookups. The next step, fear opponents of this new technology, could be Big Brother peeking into our private living spaces.

Are the futuristic advantages of cable TV worth the price of personal freedom? The answer is obviously "no," but any potential threat by cable to a community's right to privacy is heavily offset by the fact that cable companies can't exist without subscribers. Cable systems aren't licensed by the FCC like broadcasters. They receive franchises from the communities or states in which they operate. Because of this arrangement and the fact that cable revenues are generated by subscription fees, cable companies have to be more directly responsive to their viewers than do broadcasters. If concerned citizens maintain a running dialogue with their local cable management, they ought to arrive at a happy medium.

Carol F. Brown teaches journalism at Pace University, writes about video for the Village Voice, *and is working on a book about public access television.*

Gertrude Berg is the creator and writer of the radio classic, *The Goldbergs,* which she brings to CBS-TV in 1949. Pressure from anti-Communist groups will result in Berg's firing of Philip Loeb (Jake). Loeb's subsequent suicide will serve as the grimmest reminder of television's blacklisting during the McCarthy era, and will taint fond memories of the show Loeb had helped make funny.

Mama, a light comedy starring (L-R) Judson Laire, Robin Morgan, Peggy Wood (Mama), Rosemary Rice, and Dick Van Patten as a Norwegian family living in San Francisco around 1910, begins a healthy run on CBS in 1949. The show, like the 1949 movie, is based on John Van Druten's play, *I Remember Mama,* which was, in turn, based on Kathryn Forbes's book, *Mama's Bank Account.*

PAY TV: AN ALTERNATIVE
WALTER TROY SPENCER

After several decades of speculation and inconclusive experimentation, pay television began to realize its potential and become an important communications and entertainment form in the second half of the 1970's. The concept of pay TV is almost as old as the practical technology of television itself. As early as 1938, only ten years after General Electric's first television broadcast, viewers in England could buy tickets to watch prize fights telecast in theaters—a process that, of course, continues today.

The first over-the-air-broadcast pay TV system started in New York in 1950. It folded shortly thereafter, but a variety of broadcast pay TV systems were subsequently attempted. In 1971, a New Jersey firm began using the master-antenna systems of hotels for pay TV, charging guests for movies, and in 1972 pay TV had its first commercial try on cable television.

That was the year Home Box Office, a wholly-owned subsidiary of Time, Inc., piped its first pay TV movie into 365 homes in Wilkes-Barre, Pennsylvania. The Paul Newman film *Sometimes a Great Notion* had been released six months earlier to less than enthusiastic box office response. However, within four years, pay TV showings of theatrical motion pictures had become a major success in many parts of the nation, stirring anger among theater owners, apprehension and some optimism among film studio executives, and confusion among lawmakers and government regulatory agencies in Washington. The movie industry, however, is only one segment of the entertainment field, including sports, nighclubs, and opera, which began to feel the force of pay TV in the late 1970's.

> ## "The concept of pay TV is almost as old as . . . television itself."

In the fall of 1975, Home Box Office began daily transmissions of its programming by satellite. It can now show any event, live or on film, to subscribers in two hundred communities in thirty-two states that are served by cable TV systems that have entered into partnership with Home Box Office or one of the other, smaller cable TV program suppliers. At the beginning of 1977, about nine hundred thousand homes nationwide were hooked into this system.

A number of firms, including movie company subsidiaries, have entered the pay TV distribution or programming field. Movie companies and theater owners are particularly concerned about the increasing impact of pay TV on the film industry, since it would clearly seem to provide the greatest challenge and potential for change in the movie business since the cataclysmic onset of free television in the 1940's and 1950's, which permanently changed the nature of the movie business.

In 1976, theater owners mounted a major, but unsuccessful, battle before a subcommittee of the Senate Communications Committee to half—or at least delay until after theatrical showing—the sale of motion pictures to pay TV. This campaign was a direct reflection of the impact pay TV had on movie theaters, whose casual weekend audiences were decreased by

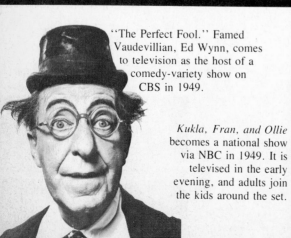

"The Perfect Fool." Famed Vaudevillian, Ed Wynn, comes to television as the host of a comedy-variety show on CBS in 1949.

Kukla, Fran, and Ollie becomes a national show via NBC in 1949. It is televised in the early evening, and adults join the kids around the set.

RCA's Satcom II, 22,300 miles above the equator, transmits Home Box Office programming to various cable television systems across the country. About 900,000 American homes are hooked into this live or film satellite system.

the availability of second-rank films on pay TV shortly after expensive theatrical showing and long before showing on free TV. The reluctance of the public to attend "average" films in their original theatrical runs accelerated a trend in Hollywood to create fewer films, but ones of blockbuster status. Distributors never even bother to book some movies into some areas at all. For example, numbers of films with regional appeal are

December 28, 1949. *The Admiral Broadway Revue* showcases the wild and wonderful comedic talents of Sid Caesar and Imogene Coca (who first appeared on TV back in 1939). The show is produced by Max Liebman. After thirteen weeks Admiral withdraws its sponsorship.

NBC vice-president Sylvester "Pat" Weaver makes one of his monumental programming maneuvers. He convinces Liebman to produce a live one-and-a-half-hour Caesar-Coca show each week as part of a two-hour program called *Saturday Night Revue.* The first half hour is hosted by Jack Carter from Chicago.

From the beginning Caesar and Coca center numerous sketches around the dinner table. In fact, many of their best routines were conceived while they ate together off-camera.

played to drive-in audiences, but never shown in metropolitan New York theaters, where advertising and opening costs can run as high as $150,000; the films make their money in the rest of the country and the sales to pay TV are gravy.

In May 1977, a federal appeals court in Washington struck down major portions of the Federal Communications Commission's restrictions on pay TV programming, including limitations on when feature films and sporting events could be shown. Previously, films could be shown on pay TV only if they had been released theatrically within the previous three years. Features older than ten years could also be shown on pay TV under certain conditions.

While motion pictures and sporting events have been the mainstay of present pay TV programming, cultural attractions with more limited appeal have expressed serious interest in representation. New York City's Lincoln Center has been actively seeking a pay TV outlet. John Mazzola, managing director of Lincoln Center, said: "We do about two hundred fifty different productions a year for a total of more than three thousand performances. If we had a box office pay TV television system that charged viewers for each event they watched, we'd offer every single performance on television. That would be ideal."

A decade ago, communications expert Sylvester L. "Pat" Weaver presented officials in Washington with a system for using pay television by satellite in which the individual citizen would pay the government for the right to receive cultural programming, and the government would in turn use the funds for program development. But so far pay TV has remained a free enterprise operation with little government participation, except in regulation.

On March 1, 1977, the first over-the-air pay television service began in the New York City metropolitan area. Some two hundred homes served by a Newark, New Jersey, station were given their choice of a number of relatively recent motion pictures for a monthly fee of $12.95. The system was unlike most other forms of pay TV in that it did not require prior subscription to cable television to buy the pay programming.

As pay TV grows, there is expected to be a broad split in the two basic types of service available: the current subscription system where viewers pay a monthly fee and watch as much or as little as they wish; and the per-program system, where the viewers select and pay for programs they want to watch on an individual basis.

In the futuristic vision of communications speculators, home television systems will be plugged into computer retrieval systems so that a viewer could literally dial up almost any one of millions of pretaped programs. For live entertainment, the subscriber could dial a device similar to a telephone exchange which would then connect his cable to an appropriate program trunk. Components of this system have been in use in England for the past several years.

Long anticipated, but still to come on any widespread practical basis, are a variety of potential pay TV offerings: electronic home security systems; direct shopping from home to local department store, with goods displayed on the screen and orders dialed directly to the store; and even home delivery of the daily newspaper by means of a printed facsimile which drops out of the TV set. Technology for each of these innovations has been around for some time. Someday we will take them all for granted.

Walter Troy Spencer is the film critic for WOR Radio in New York City and writes about the arts and the media for a variety of publications.

Caesar and Coca watch television in one of their early sketches. They obviously realize the hypnotic effect of the new medium.

Kraft Theatre, Studio One, and *Philco Playhouse* upgrade the level of live drama, and television in general. Movie star Robert Montgomery agrees to produce, host, and sometimes star in a live anthology series of his own. *Robert Montgomery Presents* (also called *The Lucky Strike Theatre*) will be a fixture at NBC for seven years. Other Hollywood celebrities soon will follow Montgomery's lead.

Funnyman Morey Amsterdam is host of a syndicated variety show in 1949. In 1950, he will be the first host of the nightly 11:00–12:00 P.M. *Broadway Open House,* the forerunner of *The Tonight Show.*

THE MINICAM REVOLUTION

ED HERSH

It's 4:15 P.M., and at Channel 3 they're putting the finishing touches on the order of events for tonight's six o'clock news. It is a routine day; nothing special. But then a call comes over the police radio—hostage situation at a downtown bank building. . . .

Five years ago, coverage of that event for the six o'clock news would have meant a reporter in the field relaying the story to an announcer in the studio who would have concluded his aural report with an apologetic, "We'll have film at eleven." There was just no time to get film on the air in an hour.

But all that has changed now. We're in the age of the minicam—a technical advancement that is transforming the news programs you see every day. A truck with a camera crew and transmitter can get to that downtown bank, set up shop, and start transmitting live reports back to the station. You can see news whenever, wherever it happens; no need to wait.

Stations around the country promote their minicam capabilities in different ways, calling them everything from "Insta-Cam" to "Action-Cam" to "Live Eye," but they're all talking about basically the same technical process. It is a miniaturized process which replaces bulky film gear with lightweight electronic videotape equipment that can also transmit live back to the station.

Until recently, the stories you watched on the news were shot with sound film, not unlike that used in home movies you might shoot yourself. And, like those movies, the film was not ready for viewing as soon as it was taken out of the camera; it had to be processed.

"We're in the age of the minicam."

Stations didn't have to take it to the drugstore to be developed; most had their own processing machines, but the processing could take up to half an hour after the film got back to the station. Then a reporter and film editor had to sit down and put the story together. Even with the best hands and equipment, there was a delay between the time a story was covered and when it got on the air.

The technology that gave us digital watches and twenty-dollar calculators has changed all that. Minicams and their adjunct videotape machines don't work like movie cameras. They are comparable to the small cassette tape recorders you may have, except they are larger and record both picture and sound. Like cassette recorders, minicams record images on magnetic tape. The tape is ready to be played back as soon as it is recorded, so there is no processing time involved. If the tape is unsatisfactory, it can be reshot on the spot—a luxury never enjoyed by film crews who had to wait hours to see their results.

The same technology that developed the small, reliable minicam has also improved what is called microwave transmission. Now the equivalent of a whole television studio can be packed into a vehicle the size of a bread truck.

From a transmitting "dish" on top of a truck to a receiver on top of a tall building, a crew can send

27

Jerry Lester, here being kissed by Norma Kaiser, succeeds Amsterdam on *Broadway Open House* in 1950. During the next year, Lester, announcer Wayne Howell, orchestra leader Milton DeLugg, and the inimitable Dagmar will build up a large, devoted following, proving that late-night shows can attract a significant audience. In 1951 the show will disband amid much confusion, with Lester going on to host his own program for a year.

Red Channels is published in 1950 by three former FBI agents. It lists 151 people in the entertainment field who are "reported" to have Communist leanings. Many on the list, and many others whose politics networks and sponsors consider questionable, become victims of widespread blacklisting. CBS institutes a loyalty oath.

Red Channels

The Report of
COMMUNIST INFLUENCE IN RADIO AND TELEVISION

Published By
COUNTERATTACK
THE NEWSLETTER OF FACTS TO COMBAT COMMUNISM
55 West 42 Street, New York 18, N. Y.
$1.00 per copy

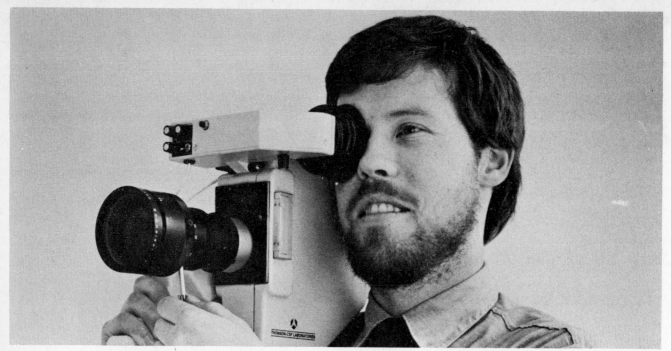

The minicam replaces bulky film gear with lightweight electronic videotape equipment that can transmit live.

either live pictures or tape back to the station to be put on the air instantly, or edited for later use.

The results are obvious. The 4:00 P.M. deadline for the six o'clock news is now a thing of the past. News can—and does—happen anytime up to and during a newscast. And minicam technology means you can see news as it happens, or at least as fast as the station can get someone there to cover it.

The system has its critics. Film can be cut apart, hung on a peg, and edited physically. Tape can't. It is an electronic process, the splicing block replaced by an elaborate editing console. The abstract quality of the process rankles some film editors, bred to appreciate the tactile sense of film. And lest you think these technical developments have all occurred in the name of better journalism, station managements have

another reason for going all minicam: It is cheaper. The electronics cost more up front, but, unlike film, tape can be reused. And a minicam crew is made up of two technicians—not the three required by film.

The virtues of the process clearly outweigh the problems, and the minicam is not the "wave of the future" anymore; it is here now. By the time this book appears, most major stations and the three networks will be largely out of the film business. But the zenith hasn't been reached yet; an electronics firm has already begun a second generation of even smaller cameras, aptly called "the microcams."

Ed Hersh is video producer at KYW-TV, Philadelphia. He taught the use of the minicam at the Columbia University School of Journalism.

Meanwhile, the frivolity continues. Master game show producers Mark Goodson and Bill Todman introduce *Beat the Clock* into the CBS schedule on March 23, 1950. After eight years, it will switch to ABC for another four seasons. Bud Collyer (R), radio's Superman, will MC throughout.

February 2, 1950. Goodson and Todman's *What's My Line?* makes its debut on CBS. The show is moderated by John Daly, the head of ABC's news department from 1949 to 1961. Regular panelists, who must guess the occupations of guests and the names of mystery celebrities, are Arlene Francis, Louis Untermeyer, and Hal Block. Absent is columnist Dorothy Kilgallen.

Famous playwright Moss Hart takes the strange role of host on a show called *Answer Yes or No*, which lasts only one season. Hart's infatuation with game shows runs in the family: his wife, Kitty Carlisle, becomes a long-time panelist on *To Tell The Truth*, which will begin in two years. Seated next to Hart is panelist Arlene Francis.

VIDEOTAPE VERSUS FILM

LOUIS JAFFE

All TV that is not live is reproduced from film or videotape. Most television professionals and many home viewers can tell which medium is being used, and most agree that each has a different "feel" as perceived over the tube. Would exactly the same script, performances, camera angles, etc. "look" different on film from the way it looks on tape?

What are the differences between videotape and film as perceived by viewers? Dramatic shows produced on tape are usually described as "flat" or "wooden" compared to similar material on film. Often film is said to be "mellower" and "more human." Conversely, the substitution of videotape for film in news gathering has led to "immediacy."

This "immediacy" of tape seems to enhance documentary TV, but can sometimes work against the sense of fantasy in drama. By contrast, film seems to have a certain "distance" from the reality of the viewer that makes shaky drama more believable.

Scientific study will be necessary to determine whether varying effects of tape and film are due to differences in the way they are received by the human senses. The two do use fundamentally different means to store and retrieve picture and sound. Videotape is an electronic and film a chemical process. Video translates the picture to electronic impulses, which are recorded on magnetic tape; film stores the images directly as a sequence of photographs.

Watching sound film we see twenty-four different pictures a second, interspersed with instants of darkness. In fact, the screen is dark about half the time but the flicker rate meshes with retinal image retention in the human eye and we perceive a persistent picture. This picture is an optical enlargement of the image on the film. Grays in the film image are the light of the projection lamp being blocked by a barrier of silver grains in the film. The light that does get through projects the pattern of the grain which is the fabric of the image. The brightest part of the film image is light passing through clear areas of the film.

In video, the picture is traced by the tip of a moving electron beam, which uses the same scanning pattern the reader's eye uses on a page. Phosphorescence is excited by the passage of the beam in 525 geometrically exact lines. The lines are drawn in two trips from top to bottom of the screen—one for the odd lines, one for the evens. Each 1/60 second trip is called a "field." As one field fades, a second is being drawn. The constantly-regenerating image on the screen is an exact reproduction of how motion is scanned in the camera. The brightest part of this image is the flash set off by the strongest electronic pulse.

Sound is also reproduced by different means in film and tape. On film, the sound is stored as variations of light and dark which are read by a light-sensing device. Videotape sound is played back magnetically, as in an audio tape recorder. Whether the viewer can hear the difference is, like the question of whether or not he can see the difference between tape and film, a matter of individual sensitivity and professional knowledge.

Louis Jaffe, a New York–based independent producer, works under the name Videotape Projects.

The most unlikely TV game show host is the hilarious Groucho Marx, who begins an eleven-year stint on NBC's *You Bet Your Life,* which he has transferred from radio. The program is enormously popular because of the interplay between Groucho, his strange assortment of guests, and his announcer–straight man, George Fenneman. Groucho calls TV educational: "When it's on, I go into the other room and read a book."

Ralph Edwards is seen on several audience-participation shows in the early fifties. He becomes well known as the first host of the game show *Truth or Consequences* when it appears on NBC in 1950. In two years Edwards will begin his pet project, *This Is Your Life,* which will run for nine years.

TV VIDEO GAMES
TIM ONOSKO

Video games were probably born on some forgotten day during the 1950's when a computer operator discovered that his machine could be taught to play "tic-tac-toe." Since then, the games have become an industry of more than $200 million in sales annually and made possible an entirely new way of using the traditional TV set. The fact that some viewers are turning off *Laverne and Shirley* to chase electronic blips of light across their screens even has a few network officials worried.

The credit for starting the video game craze must be given to Magnavox, Incorporated, a manufacturer of TV sets, and to Atari, Incorporated, one of the bright young electronics firms inhabiting the area south of San Francisco, nicknamed "silicon gulch" after the area's main product, silicon integrated-circuit "chips." Atari (whose name is the Japanese word meaning "charge") was founded in 1972 by computer whiz-kid Nolan Bushnell, the originator of the first TV tennis game, Pong.

While Atari was the first to introduce video games to the public via its line of quarter-per-play arcade games, Magnavox first went to market with a home game, Odyssey, in 1973. The first Odyssey game was a primitive device that was not only limited in the number of games it could play, but necessitated the use of plastic screen overlays (like the 1950's TV show for children, *Winky Dink and You,* which featured a kit with a transparent screen for children to draw on.)

The video game "boom" of 1976, in which dozens of different models of game devices battled each other for the consumer dollar, was the result of a technological breakthrough. That breakthrough was the consolidation, by one parts manufacturer, of all of the electronics necessary for TV tennis, hockey, and handball onto a single chip. This allowed a great number of toymakers and electronics firms, without any research-and-development programs, to build video game sets around the chips. Unhappily, though, the market became glutted with games that all did exactly the same things. Today, these ball-and-paddle games have dropped in price (some are under twenty dollars), and are being de-emphasized in favor of more complex and colorful games.

Atari's current line of home video games, for instance, offers virtually every arcade game that the company makes. In *Stunt Cycle,* a player can control an on-screen motorcycle to "jump" up to thirty-two school buses. With a *Tank* game, players can fire heavy artillery at each other while trying to avoid an explosive minefield. *Video Pinball* offers seven visually exciting games in which the "ball" follows all the laws of physics of an actual pinball rolling around a table.

The most intriguing developments are the recent programmable games, now being made by Atari, and Fairchild Instrument. These are microcomputers—essentially "blank" machines—which can be taught to play almost an infinite number of different games by inserting various program cartridges, each of which can hold up to fifty game variations. The most important aspect of these programmable games is that they represent the introduction of full-fledged microcom-

Variety shows flourish. Jackie Gleason, already a TV favorite after a year starring in *The Life of Riley,* hosts *The Cavalcade of Stars.* It features regulars Art Carney, Audrey Meadows, Joyce Randolph, and Pert Kelton. In 1952 the program will move from Dumont to CBS, where it will be retitled *The Jackie Gleason Show.*

Among the most popular characters Gleason creates is bus driver Ralph Kramden, who plays opposite Alice (Pert Kelton) in *The Honeymooners* sketches.

The Video Computer System developed by Atari for home use.

puters into America's living rooms. Essentially, the computers are using the home TV set as a graphic display terminal. Similar, more sophisticated computers that not only play games, but do anything from maintain a recipe file to fill out federal income tax forms are, literally, just around the corner, and will probably be developed by some of the same companies now making video games.

Furthermore, it's now technically possible, if not economically feasible, to play video games across town, over a cable television system, or cross-country, using a standard telephone. Who knows? Someday there may be a nationwide Pong tournament in which none of the players leave their living rooms.

Tim Onosko is writing a book about amusement parks.

31

Emmy Award–winning variety program for 1950, *The Alan Young Show* successfully combines comedy vignettes with visually interesting musical numbers. It runs from 1950 to 1953.

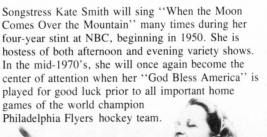

Songstress Kate Smith will sing "When the Moon Comes Over the Mountain" many times during her four-year stint at NBC, beginning in 1950. She is hostess of both afternoon and evening variety shows. In the mid-1970's, she will once again become the center of attention when her "God Bless America" is played for good luck prior to all important home games of the world champion Philadelphia Flyers hockey team.

Frank Sinatra hosts his own half-hour musical program for CBS in 1950. It will last only two years.

UNDERGROUND TELEVISION

Christopher Newman

Ed Norton would never believe it, but Bruce Waterman is a TV cameraman—in the sewer. Bruce works for Video Pipe Grouting, Inc. of Newfield, New Jersey, a company that cleans, videotapes, and repairs any type of buried or hidden pipe that is too small for a man to crawl through. The scene of Bruce's latest subterranean TV production was the sewer systems of Cape May and several other South Jersey shore towns, where overworked and faulty mains have been dumping raw sewage directly into the ocean.

Bruce works for one of a number of teams operated by Video Pipe Grouting. Each team consists of several men who operate a complex hydraulic device called a Meyers apparatus. This is basically a heavy-duty garden hose through which water is pumped from a tank on a truck at a pressure of two thousand pounds per square inch. Driven by the powerful spray, the hose threads itself through an underground pipe from one manhole to another. If there is any blockage in the pipe, a cutting nozzle can be activated to blow a clear path.

After the pipe is thoroughly clean, a small cylindrical television camera equipped with two tiny headlights is attached to the end of the hose and pulled back slowly through the pipe. The resulting picture of the pipe interior is transmitted to a monitor in a control van, where it is carefully scrutinized by a foreman, or videotaped for closer examination later. Any crack in the pipe will show up as a shadow on the tape. If cracks or faulty joints are discovered, the hose is threaded back through the pipe with a grouting apparatus attached behind the camera. The grouter fills each crack or joint with two chemicals which, when exposed to each other in the presence of oxygen, form a rubber sealant. The operation continues until all cracks are repaired, and the pipe is certified sound.

The use of television in pipe maintenance is only about seven years old. Before the process was invented, the only way to examine or repair a small underground pipe was to tear it up—often a disruptive job, and always an expensive one. But Video Pipe Grouting charges about a dollar a foot to survey mains, and can pinpoint precisely the location of those breaks that it cannot repair on the spot. The saving in blacktop alone is immense. But Ed Norton would be jealous—Bruce Waterman and the employees of Video Pipe Grouting spend all day in the sewer without ever getting their feet wet!

Christopher Newman is a writer who is interested in new ways to solve old problems.

December 2, 1950. Milton Berle plays a dentist on *The Frank Sinatra Show*.

"Banjo Eyes" Eddie Cantor caps an illustrious career in show business by appearing numerous times as host of *The Colgate Comedy Hour*.

Bud Abbott and Lou Costello also host *The Colgate Comedy Hour* on several occasions during its five years on NBC. The veteran comedy team of burlesque theater and radio, whose films saved financially-troubled Universal Studios in the forties, finds a new home on television. From 1952 to 1954, they will star in their own series on CBS.

VIDEO ART
JOHN G. HANHARDT

The history of video art reads as a continual challenge to the traditional definition of the medium offered by broadcast television. Since its introduction in the late 1940's, commercial television has rapidly become a mass medium, plugged into virtually every household, and playing an active role in shaping the public's consciousness. The television set is a central piece of household furniture around which the family organizes its schedule and movements. Like a giant electronic night-light, the television set offers a kind of security, playing for hours on end, its screen emitting a glow that requires little concentration yet demands passive acceptance of its messages. Commercial television sells its air time to advertisers, and its programming provides a context and support for commercial messages. Even public television primarily presents traditional narratives and seldom takes risks except in specific issues of content and subject matter. The presentation of a visual abstraction, time of silence, or avant-garde narrative devices, is considered too high a risk.

The term *video art* describes a wide range of work produced in this electronic medium independent of the restrictions in form and content of commercial television. Video as a medium for personal creative expression was largely made possible by the introduction of the Sony Portapak video system in 1968. This system utilizes a handheld video camera and a portable, battery-powered, tape recorder. Unlike studio equipment which uses two-inch videotape, the portable unit employs one-half inch tape. The resulting lightweight and relatively inexpensive video system

"Video as an art form . . . exists within the context of the contemporary, modernist, and post-modernist art scene."

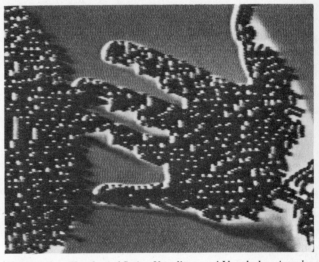

Video artists Woody and Steina Vasulka taped Vocabulary *in color in 1973–74. It uses representational and abstract images to create a mysterious electronic experience.*

has changed the previously held notion that television was the exclusive preserve of what we traditionally see on our home TV sets. Beginning in the 1940's, when 16-mm film and cameras were developed and mar-

33

The Arthur Murray Dance Party, featuring dance contests and instruction, with hostess Kathryn Murray and choreographer June Taylor, debuts on Dumont in 1950. From 1952 to 1957, it will serve as a summer replacement show, and will resume as a weekly show from 1958 to 1960 on NBC.

Saturday Night Revue changes its name to *Your Show of Shows,* a title it will keep until it goes off the air in 1954.

keted a similar situation occurred in filmmaking. Since then independent filmmaking has grown rich and varied; it is now a personal film art created outside the production, distribution, and exhibition network of the commercial Hollywood entertainment film.

Video as an art form essentially was created in the late 1960's, and exists within the context of the contemporary, modernist, and post-modernist art scene. This means that video shares many concepts with painting, sculpture, music, performance, theater, film, and the recent mutations, permutations, and breakdowns of these traditional categories. But the situation for the video artist is complicated by the fact that, unlike the other arts, video does not have a past to develop from or react against. Rather it has the definition of the medium imposed by the dominant "presence" of commercial television. Furthermore, while video art is strongly influenced by and is an integral part of the contemporary visual arts, it does not enjoy extensive economic and critical support, and is not a commodity in the art market, like a painting or work of sculpture. Except for some pieces produced by artists in conjunction with public television "experimental laboratories," and an occasional showing on public and cable television, video art is largely shown in an increasing number of museums, colleges and universities, galleries, independent exhibition spaces, and artists' lofts.

The range of work and quality of achievement of contemporary video is enormous. One area of experimentation has been the use of multiple monitors to create an environment of video images. Juan Downey's *Video Trans Americas,* for example, created a metaphor in video for the process of communication between cultures. Upon entering the exhibition space, the viewer saw monitors grouped at specific points representing the north-south, east-west axes, displaying images of cultures and places that alternated in a

"Video art challenges . . . the viewer by opening up new ways of perceiving . . . the world."

rhythmic pattern between the screens. In the center of the room a film image of a group of monitors was projected onto the floor from the ceiling. The viewer could walk onto the "screen" on the floor, and be seen live on one of the monitors placed in the room. Thus the viewer participated in the piece and actually became part of it as the video camera placed him in the video environment.

Woody and Steina Vasulka's video uses a single monitor to display a wide range of strong and mysterious abstract and representational images created out of the electronic process itself. Brian Connell's *La Lucha Final,* a single-channel video piece, is a treatment of the illusion in images we think we understand, namely commercial television's interpretation of news events. A political work employing modernist narrative devices, this videotape combines commentary with images to create a displacement of meaning, confounding fact and fiction. It ultimately asks questions about how we perceive the world through television's recording and interpretation of events.

Unlike broadcast television, the best of video art demands that viewers concentrate and reflect upon what they have experienced. Video art challenges and ultimately satisfies the viewer by opening up new ways of perceiving and new perceptions of the world. It takes nothing for granted, least of all the medium of video and the way we relate to it.

John G. Hanhardt is curator of Film and Video at the Whitney Museum of American Art in New York City.

CBS deals its competitors a crushing blow when it makes a deal with several big-name radio stars. Jack Benny arrives in 1950 and stays fourteen years. Here Benny is with his wife, Mary Livingston, a semi-regular on his program.

Benny's close friends, the great vaudeville team George Burns and Gracie Allen, bring their radio show to CBS where it will delight viewers for eight years. Here Burns tricks his announcer, Harry Von Zell.

Amos 'n' Andy, which started as an NBC radio show in 1929, is sold to CBS-TV in 1951. Freeman Gosden and Charles Correll, the white men who starred in and created the radio version, give way to Spencer Williams and Alvin Childress in the title roles. *Amos 'n' Andy* is the first TV show to have an all-black cast.

THE VIDEO ART OF NAM JUNE PAIK

Peter Moore

Nam June Paik is perhaps this country's leading video artist. Born in Korea in 1932, Paik was studying music in Germany in 1958 when he met John Cage, the avant-garde American composer, an event that was the turning point of his life. Paik's musical compositions became more and more experimental, and eventually led him to television as an artistic medium. "I knew there was something to be done in television and nobody else was doing it, so I said why not make it my job?" In 1963, he presented his first video show in Germany.

Paik, working with engineer-inventor Shuya Abe, went on to develop the Paik-Abe videosynthesizer, a mechanism that converts video images into an infinite number of color patterns and configurations. Examples of Paik's video pieces—"portraits" of poet Allen Ginsberg and former President Richard Nixon—and some of Paik's thoughts follow.

35

Television experimentation persists. Russell Law (L) and Dr. H. B. Law examine an RCA all-electronic compatible color TV set demonstrated to the industry and the FCC in 1950.

June 25, 1951. CBS presents the first commercial color program. Sponsored by sixteen companies, it is fed from New York to Boston, Philadelphia, Baltimore, and Washington. The show is highlighted by the appearances of Arthur Godfrey, Faye Emerson, Garry Moore, and Ed Sullivan. Here Robert Alda and Isabel Bigley of the Broadway smash, *Guys and Dolls*, sing "You're Just In Love."

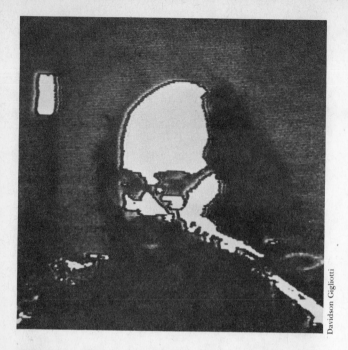

Davidson Gigliotti

Davidson Gigliotti

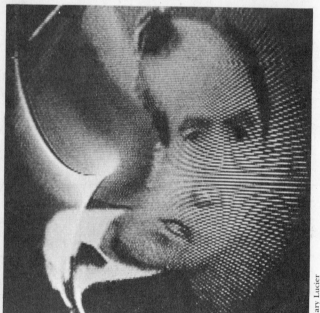

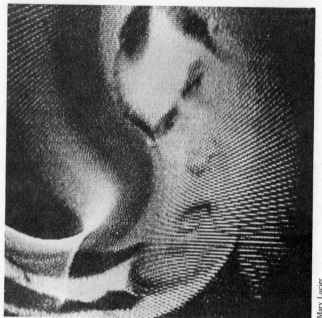

Mary Lucier

Mary Lucier

In 1951 *You Asked For It*, one of the most peculiar shows in television history, comes on the air. Each week, host Art Baker introduces viewers to some of the most unusual sights and people found around the world. Here, for instance, Baker visits with a strange man and his dog.

Art Baker chats with
Archie Gayer (L)
and Alga Hessler,
the "headless woman."
You Asked For It
will last eight years.

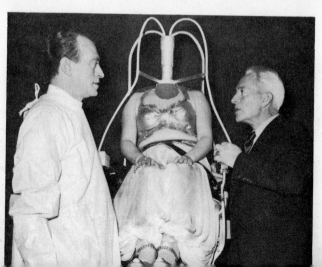

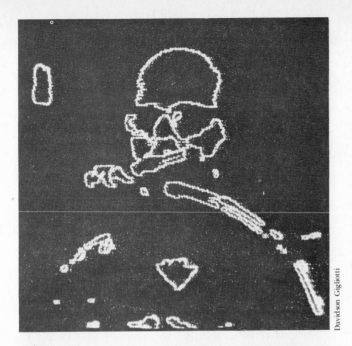

Davidson Gigliotti

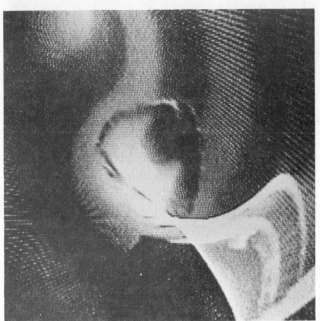

Mary Lucier

Nam June Paik Comments:

"I have treated the TV screen as a canvas, and proved it can be a superior canvas. From now on, I will treat the cathode ray as a paper and pen. . . . If Joyce lived today, surely he would have written *Finnegan's Wake* on videotape, because of the vast possibility of manipulation in magnetic information storage."

"Plato thought the word, or the conceptual, expresses the deepest thing. St. Augustine thought the sound, or the audible, expresses the deepest thing. Spinoza thought the vision, or the visible, expresses the deepest thing. This argument is settled for good. TV commercials have all three."

"Tolstoy spent 20 pages for the description of Anna Karenina and Flaubert 30 pages for Madame Bovary. . . . What they needed was simply a Polaroid camera."

"TV cameras are following so busily the latest spots of violence that kids, who receive most of their education from TV, think that such noble countries as Switzerland and Norway are chunks of real estate lying somewhere in the Milky Way or at best beyond Madagascar. How can we teach about peace while blocking out one of the few existing examples from the screen?"

"My experimental TV is not always interesting but not always uninteresting. [It is] like nature, which is beautiful not because it changes beautifully but simply because it changes."

"Nobody had put two frequencies into one place, so (in 1962) I do just that, horizontal and vertical, and this absolutely new thing comes out. I make mistake after mistake, and it comes out positive. That is the story of my whole life."

37

Strike It Rich provides luckless contestants with a forum to explain why they could use donations from home viewers. The contestant with the most pitiful tale of the day is also awarded the "heartline," a large cash prize, by host Warren Hull (R). Sailor B. M. Frazer seems too happy for this show.

Jacqueline Susann hosts her own thirty-minute talk show for Dumont in 1951. In 1953 she will do the same for ABC.

March 5, 1951. *Mr. Wizard* debuts, and at last there is an educational program that is truly popular with the junior set. For the next fourteen years, Don Herbert will prove to boys and girls that science can be fun as well as interesting.

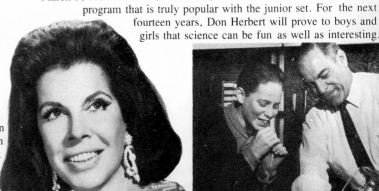

THE FUTURE OF TV
ISAAC ASIMOV

As long as there are no more channels than now exist, as long as the distribution of television is limited to the few commercial stations, the future of television will consist largely of embroidery on present technology.

If civilization survives, however, the time will soon come when the earth will be surrounded by communications satellites more versatile and capable than now exist. They will be interconnected by laser beams of light, with wavelengths less than a millionth as long as those of radio waves, and therefore with over a million times more room for channels.

In the age of laser-connected communications satellites, and of optical fiber transmitting laser-light on Earth, it will be possible for each person to have his own TV channel, as he now has his own telephone number. Each person will be able to take advantage of closed-circuit television as he or she now takes advantage of a closed telephone conversation.

You will, for instance, be able to subscribe to a news service which will allow you to tune the equivalent of a newspaper onto your screen, adjusting it for the sports, financial, or the comic page, or whatever you choose, and you will be able to make a facsimile of any item you want for more permanent reference. (The saving on paper will be enormous, since no one would want to copy an entire newspaper.)

You will be able to do your shopping by television, since you will be able not only to "dial for advertising" so to speak, but you will be able to view the shelves of a supermarket, or the items in a department store, and either order on the basis of that, or at least narrow matters down so that your actual trip will be shorter and more effectively concentrated.

You will still be able to listen to the commercial stations, of course, and enough people will do so to keep them in business, but you will also be able to lease cassettes on any subject that might be of interest to you, from chess instruction to old movies (or pornography?), and run them at your convenience.

For that matter, you could hook your personal wavelength into a computerized, centralized world library, which could transmit to you any book, periodical, or document that you want to read or copy. (Working out the royalty problem will be difficult.)

In combination with complex computers, the television screen will become a teaching machine and the prime educational process of the future. Each child will be taught at his own speed according to his own curiosities.

Since closed circuit viewing will be holographic (that is, three-dimensional), television could be used by supervisors to check and control machinery, factories, and automated offices; to receive and transmit documents; and to hold conferences without leaving home. In short, information will be transferred directly, instead of by way of paper or people. A great deal of the shuffling of matter back and forth will be transformed into a whizzing of laser beams at the speed of light, with incredible gains in convenience and conservation of energy.

Isaac Asimov is the author of 185 books of science fiction, history, science, and literature.

March 14, 1951. And there is education for adults. Senator Estes Kefauver conducts his Senate Crime Committee Investigation in front of both CBS and NBC cameras. Eventually 20 million people will watch the live daily broadcasts and become experts on the Fifth Amendment. Kefauver will emerge a presidential contender; Frank Costello, who permits only his hands to be televised, is revealed as a powerful ganglord.

Crime drama also captures the TV viewer's fancy. Producer Hal Roach's *Racket Squad* is added to CBS's schedule in 1951 after a year in syndication. Reed Hadley narrates and plays police captain John Braddock of the bunco squad. In 1954 Hadley will star in CBS's *Public Defender*.

Ken Taylor (R) is *Boston Blackie*, master thief turned detective. Blackie, who was portrayed in several 1940's movies by Chester Morris, will walk the television streets of New York for three years.

THE LOOK OF THE FUTURE

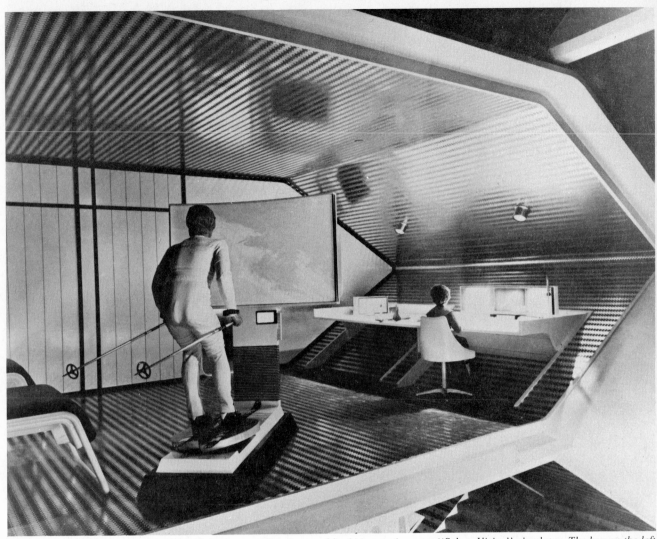

A sports and hobby center in the home of the future will make possible ski instruction on a "SelectaVision" simulator. The boy on the left can practice on a tilting platform while viewing video tapes of mountain slopes. The boy on the right constructs a model rocket with instructions from his TV system. This display (and the two on the following page) is on view at RCA's Space Mountain in Walt Disney World, Orlando, Florida.

Meanwhile in L.A.—dum de dum dum. Jack Webb as Sergeant Joe Friday and Ben Alexander as Frank Smith appear in *Dragnet*. Webb is the producer, director, and top writer of this low-key, realistic police drama based on actual criminal cases. His clever use of music, snappy dialogue, and sharp editing is so impressive that *Dragnet* will serve as a model for most future television drama. In December 1953 *Dragnet* will become the first series to use color regularly.

Ziv Productions' *The Cisco Kid*, starring Duncan Rinaldo (R) and Leo Carillo as his partner Pancho, is widely distributed in 1951. Its first season had been filmed in color, although there is no way to telecast color at the time.

The home of the future may include a nursery with a TV camera (here held by the toy clown) that functions as an electronic baby-sitter. The baby can be viewed from monitors throughout the house.

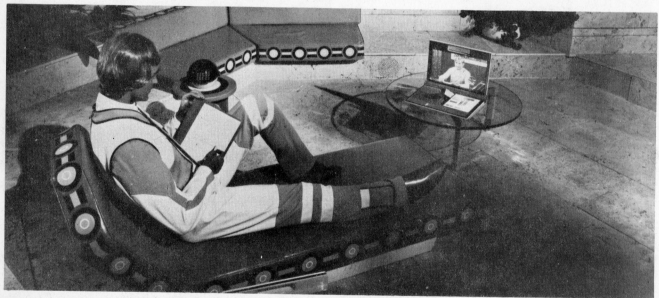

Business will be conducted from the home through this portable attache case TV set. People will see and talk to each other from any place in the world through a two-way TV system.

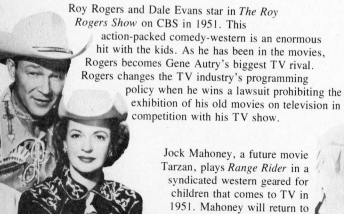

Roy Rogers and Dale Evans star in *The Roy Rogers Show* on CBS in 1951. This action-packed comedy-western is an enormous hit with the kids. As he has been in the movies, Rogers becomes Gene Autry's biggest TV rival. Rogers changes the TV industry's programming policy when he wins a lawsuit prohibiting the exhibition of his old movies on television in competition with his TV show.

Jock Mahoney, a future movie Tarzan, plays *Range Rider* in a syndicated western geared for children that comes to TV in 1951. Mahoney will return to television as *Yancy Derringer* in 1958.

Eugene O'Neill's "Ah Wilderness!" is presented on ABC's acclaimed *Celanese Theatre* on October 3, 1951. Thomas Mitchell costars with Dorothy Peterson.

II. THE CREATIVE MACHINE

Lippert Pictures releases to theaters *Superman and the Mole Men*, starring George Reeves as the mighty comic book hero. It is re-edited into *Unknown People* and is used as a television pilot.

Lon Chaney, Jr. appears on *Tales of Tomorrow*. The son of ''the man with a thousand faces'' has been typecast as a monster since starring in *The Wolf Man*, a movie in 1940. Finally in 1957, he will break out somewhat as Chingachgook in *Hawkeye and the Last of the Mohicans*, a TV series.

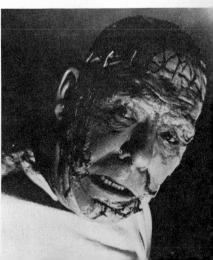

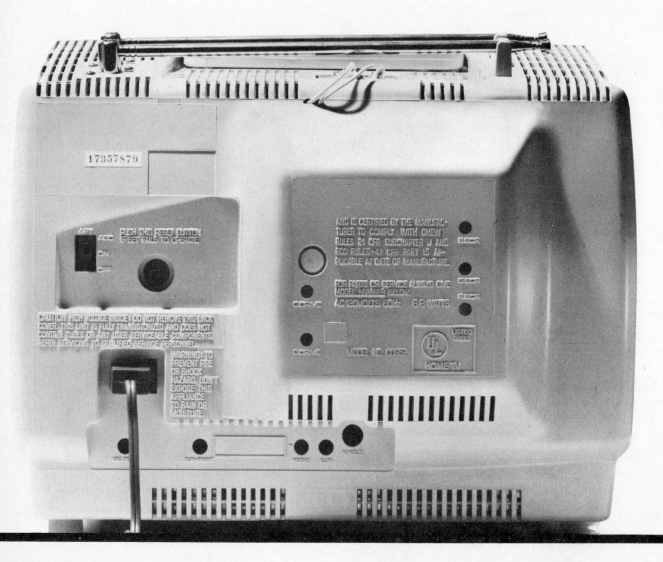

17357879

Rosemary Clooney, vocalist on CBS's 1951 musical contest show, *Songs for Sale,* joins Frank Sinatra, another CBS star.

September 31, 1951. *The Red Skelton Show* debuts. After only four months, Skelton will carry off Emmys for both the best comedy show of the year and for best comedian. This versatile comic, master of everything from slapstick to pantomime, will delight TV viewers for the next twenty years.

October 15, 1951. *I Love Lucy,* starring Lucille Ball and husband Desi Arnaz as Lucy and Ricky Ricardo, and William Frawley and Vivian Vance as their neighbors Fred and Ethel Mertz, debuts on CBS. It is filmed in front of a live studio audience. This madcap comedy, loosely based on Ball's hit radio series *My Favorite Husband,* quickly becomes TV's most popular show, and goes on to establish itself as the most successful television comedy of all time.

THE STUDIO AUDIENCE

ROBERT ORBEN

The first thing you notice when you enter a TV studio is—it's cold. There are various technological reasons for this, but the audience is an important one too. A chilled audience is an active one. It laughs, it applauds, it reacts. Turn up the heat and they start addressing postcards to the folks back home.

Once inside this meat locker with ushers, the audience is warmed up psychologically. The show's announcer or some other staff member with a sense of humor goes to work on them. A few time-tested, PG-rated jokes are told. The audience members are encouraged to relax and enjoy themselves, to laugh when the spirit moves them, and applaud when the flashing electric sign tells them to do so. The announcer repeats Fred Allen's warning about what happens when you stifle a laugh: "It backs up, goes the other way and spreads your hips!" This one never misses. A salvo of overweight laughter, the star is introduced, and the show begins.

Nobody really knows how an audience will respond or why. The late Edward Everett Horton used to tour in a tried and true comedy called *Springtime for Henry*. One night the company played a town in Maine and nothing seemed to work. Every big laugh line went into the ground. You could have sold the silence to libraries. The last-act curtain came down, and Horton went back to his dressing room thoroughly depressed. A few minutes later a group of townspeople knocked on the door to say they had enjoyed the evening. One Down Easter said, "Mr. Horton, your play was so funny, there were times when I could hardly keep from laughing out loud."

> ## "Nobody really knows how an audience will respond or why."

Enthusiasm is contagious. If the TV networks could salt every audience with extroverts, audience reaction would skyrocket. They have succeeded in doing this with game shows, but in most audiences, someone dressed as a banana split would be something of a distraction.

And packing an audience can have some unexpected, boomerang effects. Ed Sullivan used to feature the hottest pop singers and rock groups, and in the early days of the show the fan clubs of these stars were invited to be a part of the studio audience. These masses of screaming teenagers proved to be a great audience—but only for their favorites. The fan clubs despised every other act on the show, because it kept them from seeing more of the stars they worshiped. Try to do a comedy routine about home ownership in the suburbs to a thousand kids who regard "ooba-dooba-wah-wah-yeah!" as the ultimate in communication. It's not easy.

Most studio audiences today are hit-or-miss in composition. They represent a fair cross-section of America and react accordingly. Top-rated shows distribute their tickets a few months in advance, but it's still not unusual to see tourists shanghaied on Hollywood Boulevard or in the Farmers' Market to fill empty seats. These last-minute starters tend to be good

In 1952 NBC answers *I Love Lucy* with *I Married Joan*. It stars comedienne Joan Davis as the unpredictable wife of Judge Bradley Stevens, played by Jim Backus. Although the show doesn't achieve Lucy's overwhelming success, Davis proves herself adept at getting into nutty predicaments.

Eve Arden moves her radio comedy series *Our Miss Brooks* to CBS in 1952. Gale Gordon (L), Richard Crenna, and Robert Rockwell costar in this comedy about the staff and students at Madison High. It becomes so popular during its five-year TV stretch that it spawns a film.

additions. The sudden change in their sight-seeing plans fills them with a sense of adventure. There isn't enough time for expectations to rise to unrealistic levels. In short, they're laughing on their way in.

Rainy-day audiences also tend to be good ones. The theory is that they braved the bad weather to see the show and come hell or high water, they're going to enjoy it. Perhaps the best audiences of all are those made up of senior citizens. Some people dare a performer to succeed. There is no such combativeness in senior citizens. They have fought the good fight. They know who they are and where they are. They savor each day. They want to laugh, and so they do laugh. The only possible complaint against older audiences is that the women wear gloves. Their applause sounds like caterpillars running over a Persian rug.

Do we really need studio audiences? More and more, television is saying "no." At present, only two types of shows call for live audiences—game shows and some comedies. Eventually, game show audiences may give hysteria a bad name, but right now they are as necessary as the participants onstage.

Many comedy shows, however, are doing quite well without live audiences. In fact, the only ones who really miss the studio audience are the actors and comedy performers who are psyched up by a living response. They play to the audience. They depend on it for timing. They begin their next line at the precise moment the laughter for the previous joke starts to fade. Without a live audience to cue them, TV comedians and comediennes have to estimate what a realistic response to a joke would be. Then they have to mug or do a bit of business to provide sufficient time for the insertion of laugh track.

Like the computer that does the work of fifty mathematicians, the laugh track does the work of thousands of ecstatic audiences. It giggles, it chuck-

"Eventually, game show audiences may give hysteria a bad name . . ."

les, it roars, it applauds, it cries "Bravo" and calls for more. A collection of tapes embodying every conceivable type of audience reaction, and the electronic equipment to employ them at will—laugh track has become the perfect audience. Undemanding, sure, but enthusiastic? You better believe it!

There are very few comedy shows on television that do not employ laugh track to some extent. The situation comedies and variety shows that are shot without audiences rely on it 100 percent. Even the shows that work to studio audiences will often enhance the live reaction with an overlay of laugh track. It's called "sweetening." As a result, nothing in television ever misses. The small joke always gets a big laugh. The modest talent always gets an extravagant hand. The laugh track loves them all and, in time, the laugh track becomes its own reality.

I once heard a story about a major comedian who did his show in front of a live audience, but when the response to a line or a bit wasn't up to his expectation, it was sweetened with laugh track. The star did this personally with the electronic engineer. As they were working on one show, they came to a mild little joke and the engineer started to push the "chuckle" button. The comedian said, "What do you mean, chuckle? That's a big laugh. That's a scream!" Well, one of the first things you learn in television is that the boss may not always be right, but he's always the boss. So the engineer put in a scream.

Three weeks later they were working together again, when they stopped to watch this same episode

Gale Storm begins a three-year run in *My Little Margie* in 1952 with one-time matinee idol Charles Farrell as her father Vernon Albright. Never a success in films, Storm becomes a valuable TV property as well as a million-selling recording artist.

Women make advances in variety shows as well. Jane Froman, with a song in her heart, stars in the fifteen-minute *Jane Froman's U.S.A. Canteen* in 1952. Other women who hostess variety shows are Kate Smith, Dinah Shore, Roberta Quinlan, Martha Raye, and Dagmar.

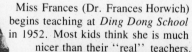

Miss Frances (Dr. Frances Horwich) begins teaching at *Ding Dong School* in 1952. Most kids think she is much nicer than their "real" teachers.

Steve Allen, an early pioneer in talk shows, was one of the first hosts to take his mike out into the audience and ad lib.

as it was actually being shown on television. The show progressed to the point of the mild little joke, and it got a tremendous belly laugh—the one that had been inserted. Whereupon the comedian turned to the engineer and said, "See, I told you it would get a scream." In Hollywood, it is not at all unusual for the conners to be conned by the con.

The replacement of audiences with laugh track may bring about a much more serious problem. We learn by observation and through experience. A budding comedy writer will hear a joke told to a live audience, and his sense of what is and isn't funny will be conditioned by the response. But there is very little live show business left in America. Consequently, the humor writers of tomorrow may be turning to television to learn their craft and using the laugh track as a gauge of audience reaction. Now, as we all know from watching years of situation comedies, when a TV father comes down to breakfast and says "good morning," the laugh track has already started to giggle. The novice comedy writer watching all this says to himself: "Aha! 'Good morning.' That's a pretty funny line!"

I can't even guess where all this may lead, but one further disturbing thought presents itself. In addition to fledgling comedy writers, tens of millions of young Americans are also having their individual senses of humor molded, shaped, and conditioned by the laugh track. I leave you to draw your own conclusions. Meanwhile, to end this piece on a somewhat brighter and more cheerful note, let me pass on one of the sharpest, funniest lines I've heard in a long time: "Good morning!"

Robert Orben is a comedy writer who has written for Red Skelton, Dick Gregory, Red Buttons, and Jack Paar.

Precocious children are highlighted in *The Quiz Kids,* based on the famous radio program in which brilliant children answer dificult questions. Joe Kelly is host when the show goes on in 1952; Clifton Fadiman later takes over for the show's four-year run.

Game shows continue to thrive in 1952. *The Big Payoff* is a daily program in which men win prizes for their ladies. Viewers tune in as much to see former Miss America Bess Myerson model clothes as they do for the game activities. Randy Merriman is later replaced by Bert Parks.

HOW TO WRITE A SITCOM

ED BURNHAM

Whether you know it or not, you're already an expert. Having watched hundreds, maybe thousands, of situation comedy half-hours, each of you possesses more knowledge and greater understanding of the sitcom form than you probably realize. You have seen some shows survive for ten years, and you've watched comedy change from the slapstick shenanigans of *I Love Lucy* to the soapy satire of *Mary Hartman, Mary Hartman*. You have a huge assortment of joke formats and situations at your subconscious fingertips. All that's necessary to design and/or write your own sitcom is to reflect on what you've already seen, and identify the various elements of this popular comic form.

For the purpose of this article, let's assume that you'd like to design a sitcom treatment from scratch. A treatment is a well-developed written idea that describes, to varying degrees, the many aspects of your proposed show. This is not easy. On the one hand, your sitcom must satisfy the formulas that have withstood the test of time, and on the other, it must be new and different enough to interest a network executive or producer. This fine line is a mile wide.

The first thing you need is a setting for your sitcom. In the past, shows have taken place everywhere from living rooms to police stations, from haunted houses to doctors' offices. Almost any setting is possible; all you have to do is find one you like. But be careful. It can be a trap to look for an inherently comic setting. Certainly there isn't anything funny about a doctor's office, for example, or being stranded on a desert island. Or is there? Humor can exist any-

> ## "Whether you know it or not, you're already an expert."

where; it's a point of view. The comedy will originate more from the characters' personalities and conflicts than from the location. The main function of the setting is to act as the *glue* for situations and setups. It is the *vehicle* that allows your characters to interact, make jokes and resolve their problems.

For the most part, sitcoms take place in contemporary settings; they thrive on being current and accessible. The contemporary atmosphere binds us together as a viewing audience, serving as a mirror and helping us to laugh at our own hang-ups. Most good sitcoms succeed because they keep us from taking present-day life, and ourselves, too seriously.

Once you have your setting, people must be placed in it. A group of characters must be invented who will interact, laugh, cry, argue, support, scold, love, hate, and grow. In short—you need a *family*. But not necessarily a literal one. The cops in Barney Miller's station house are as much a family as the Jeffersons; the inhabitants of Gilligan's Island are as close in kinship as the bloodlessly-related Munsters.

Within this family of players you may want to identify some roles as major, and some as minor. Or your show may be built on the "star concept"—one central figure around whom the entire series revolves. Just remember: the more characters a show has, the

Masquerade Party debuts in 1952 and lasts until 1958. Here Eddie Bracken, the second of six hosts the show will employ, sits with a famous masked lady.

By 1952, *Burns and Allen* is a top TV show. Here military police question George while Gracie and neighbors Fred Clark and Bea Benaderet (Harry and Blanche Morton) look on. Clark will later be replaced by Larry Keating.

Little Ricky wanted a horse so Lucy entered a "Name the Horse" contest and won. Harry James and Betty Grable join the regular I Love Lucy crowd for one of their thirteen hour-long specials. the Lucille Ball-Desi Arnaz Show in 1958.

In April of 1952, the two-year-old variety show *Life with Linkletter* goes off ABC. Five months later CBS adds *Art Linkletter's House Party* to its daytime schedule where it will remain for seventeen years. Meanwhile, Linkletter moves into the second year of his ten-year stint on NBC's *People Are Funny*.

Country-and-western music shows are popular on many local stations around the country. *Hometown Jamboree,* hosted by Cliffie Stone (L) is a top program on KTLA on Los Angeles. It introduces the comic and singing talents of Tennessee Ernie Ford to TV audiences. In 1954, Ford will replace Kay Kyser as host of NBC's *Kay Kyser's Kollege of Musical Knowledge.*

The Grand Ole Opry, hosted by Red Foley, is the first country music show to have widespread national exposure. Among its most celebrated weekly performers are Les Paul and Mary Ford, Lonzo and Oscar, and singer-comedienne Minnie Pearl.

more it will cost to produce. Bit players can be introduced from time to time, but basically your central family must have most of the action and dialogue. It is their show, and they must carry the load.

Contrast your characters' personalities. Archie is hot-tempered and intolerant; Edith, scattered and naively honest; Gloria, super-emotional and vulnerable; Michael is argumentative and idealistic. Contrast makes for strong story lines—for absorbing and outrageous dialogue. The attributes bestowed on your characters should be diverse ones, and, once you begin putting words in their mouths, you'll notice that some lines can *only* be spoken by certain characters. Your characters will begin to breathe. The more character development you do in the early stages, the easier it will be to write dialogue later. Describe your characters, give them strengths and weaknesses, physical and emotional traits, verbal mannerisms, and show how they might react to varied situations. If you can't see the characters in your own mind, others won't either.

It's often helpful to use people you know as character models. If you're stuck while trying to get the handle on a character, go outside and look around—and take your pad and pencil with you. The character type you're seeking may be just around the corner, or sitting in your local coffee shop.

Comedy springs from the way in which characters relate, the punch of their lines, and their manner of delivery. If Ted Baxter is held up on the street and merely raises his hands, that isn't funny. But if he throws up his arms and runs behind a car yelling, "Don't shoot, I'm an anchor man," it's a different story. And the modes of comedy are changing; the slapstick of twenty years ago is quickly disappearing.

Adversary relationships make for strong comedy. But don't overdo it. Lucy argued with Ricky; Fred Sanford scolds his son; Kotter battles with the kids;

Archie berates *everyone*. Sarcasm is a rich source of humor, and whether the quips are biting or subtle (or both), a little tension can go a long way.

And what about the humor itself? Making people laugh isn't easy. You can kill comedy by overanalyzing it, but the following are some commonly used elements: *Exaggeration*—when Horshak laughs on *Welcome Back Kotter,* his "hee-haw" cracks up the audience every time. A straight laugh wouldn't do the job. *Understatement*—one of the keys to Bob Newhart's sense of comedy is his matter-of-factness. *Foot-in-mouth syndrome*—this is Archie Bunker's downfall. *Victim as hero*—Fish's melancholy makes us laugh *with* him. *The smart alec*—CPO Sharkey's insults are designed to make us laugh. *Mishaps and schemes*—audiences laughed just as hard when Lucy's washing machine literally filled the apartment with soapsuds, as they did when Mary Hartman's visitor

48

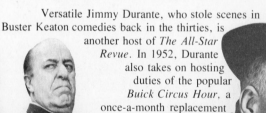

Dennis Day, tenor and comic for Jack Benny, also stars in *The Dennis Day Show,* a half-hour comedy-variety show that will last until 1954.

Ed Wynn, seen here with Bert Lahr, continues to be a popular variety show star. Until 1953, he will be an alternating host of *The All-Star Revue* (formerly called *The Four-Star Revue*). Then he will vanish from television.

Versatile Jimmy Durante, who stole scenes in Buster Keaton comedies back in the thirties, is another host of *The All-Star Revue.* In 1952, Durante also takes on hosting duties of the popular *Buick Circus Hour,* a once-a-month replacement for Milton Berle's *Texaco Star Theatre.*

drowned in a bowl of chicken soup. *Unlikely elements*—Ted Baxter wins a writing contest.

It should be noted that sitcoms do not contain wall-to-wall comedy. Perhaps the most striking development in the comtemporary sitcom form is the use of pathos. Lucy threw us a laugh every eight seconds, but the new shows are exploring everything from breast cancer to homosexuality to fidelity in marriage. In fact, this trend has brought comedy to a refreshing state of believability. The old axiom "keep 'em laughing," is slowly being replaced by "keep 'em feeling." Not only is this good for the integrity of drama, but it allows writers and actors to develop whole characters who are capable of displaying the entire range of their emotions. The biggest winner is the viewer. Of course, the main objective of the sitcom, still, is to provide fun-filled entertainment.

Now that you've described your characters and setting, it's time to begin thinking about situations and story ideas—circumstances in which your characters can reveal their follies, dreams and vulnerabilities. Virtually any story idea can work, but real-life experiences and emotions are the heart of the best ones. Of course, a vital ingredient in any story is comic tension. Some traditional plot categories are: *Everyday "catastrophes"*—the Bunkers were recently victims of a fire in their bathroom, with Archie unsuccessfully trying to dupe the insurance company. *Crimes*—believe it or not, they are fertile ground for humor. Bob Newhart was held hostage in his office by a robber and the invasion of Barney Miller's station house by a suicidal demolitions expert made for a wonderful mix of humor and social commentary. *Love relationships*—bruised egos, jealousy, the "other woman" (or man) syndrome, marital problems, flirtatiousness, are all possible subjects of comedy. *On the job*—Ralph Cramdon forever complained about his work, and this was the key to his explosive behavior; on the other hand, egomaniacal Ted Baxter *loves* his work dearly, and that's his problem. *Self assertion*—Marion, from *Happy Days*, decided to assert herself by getting a job as a waitress in her son's hangout, which led to understandably "disastrous" results. *Money problems*—the threat of foreclosure on Fred Sanford's mortgage sent him into a panic.

The list is endless, and these are only suggestions. The important thing is that you *make up your own situations*.

Finally, you may want to go a step further and write a sample scene or two for your principle characters, or even a full script. Choose scenes from your story ideas that stimulate your concept of humor. The only way to write good dialogue is to jump in. You must give yourself to your characters. *They* will know when you're resisting, and consequently will not be able to give their best. You are the medium through which your characters express themselves. If you're blocked, you'll cut off the flow. Test out lines, go for jokes, understand your characters' weaknesses and hang-ups, draw on their idiosyncrasies. Bring them alive with words and actions and—most important —make us love them.

Ed Burnham is a TV writer and program developer.

Keep *in mind that the networks are constantly being deluged with scripts and proposals of all kinds, so getting an idea accepted isn't easy. The trend is away from submitting a property directly to a network. Rather, try to submit to an agent, TV packager or producer. If an agent or producer approaches a network with your idea, you'll be in a much stronger position.*

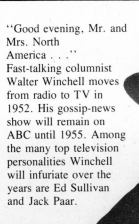

"Good evening, Mr. and Mrs. North America . . ." Fast-talking columnist Walter Winchell moves from radio to TV in 1952. His gossip-news show will remain on ABC until 1955. Among the many top television personalities Winchell will infuriate over the years are Ed Sullivan and Jack Paar.

For those interested in a more "serious" approach to the news there is ABC's ace woman reporter Pauline Frederick, top United Nations correspondent, who will be given her own daily news program.

HOW TO SELL A SCRIPT

ELIO ZARMATI

Los Angeles Canyon Road—Exterior Day

A 1961 convertible Triumph TR3 with Connecticut license plates speeds through a canyon road heading toward the San Fernando Valley. Its sleek body is in dire need of repair—the left fender is hanging close to the road despite the miles of tape and string that surround it and the back is dented all the way to the front seat. Nevertheless, the Writer is very obviously proud of his vehicle. Notice the look of contempt on his face as he passes the nondescript air-conditioned dinosaurs on the road. He is a man in a hurry, on his way to "take" a meeting.

Next to him, on the passenger seat, a heavy 152-page mass of paper neatly typed, expensively Xeroxed and bound—the Script. As he speeds towards the studio, he leafs through the Script. God, it's good. No doubt the studio will love the Script and it will express such love in the form of a check that will help the Writer repair the fender on his TR3, buy a truckload of typewriter ribbon, and stop by the supermarket.

As he slows down at the studio gate, the Writer crosses the fingers of both hands and, in the process, almost runs over a cat.

CUT TO: ***Studio Gate—Exterior Day***

The Guard at the gate motions him to stop. The Writer has an important look on his face. Marcello Mastroianni in Fellini's La Dolce Vita.

WRITER
Bungalow 117½. I'm going to see Mr. Executive Story Consultant of Tip-Top Productions, Inc.

GUARD *(indifferent)*
What's your name, sir? Do you have an appointment?

WRITER
Sure do. We're taking a meeting at eleven.

The Guard checks his list. He doesn't pay any attention to the boasting tone of the Writer. He's been around the studio for thirty-five years and he's seen it all. He finds the name on the list and lifts the gate. The Writer revs up his engine and drives into the sanctuary.

CUT TO: ***Studio Street—Exterior Day***

As the Writer drives through the studio street, a series of quick flashes fly through his mind—the endless parade of writers and directors and stars who have driven through this same gate in the past half-century. And now him. Unconsciously, he sits up, stretches his shoulders and holds his breath.

A moment later, he gets out of his car, holding the Script as though it were the original Dead Sea Scrolls. A wave of panic almost paralyzes him as he enters the bungalow.

CUT TO: ***Executive Office—Interior Day***

It's a small office, unimpressive, cluttered with mimeographed scripts stacked on all desks, chairs, and even on the wastepaper basket. The Executive Story Consultant is a balding man in his late forties who chain-smokes and chain-drinks cold coffee from

An up-and-coming newscaster at NBC in 1952 is Edwin Newman.

Another NBC newscaster is John K. M. McCaffery, former moderator of *The Author Meets the Critics*. In 1953, he will host a CBS game show.

CBS-TV's Washington correspondent in 1952 is Walter Cronkite, seated here with Senator Edward Morton. Cronkite will help Edward R. Murrow cover the 1952 political conventions for CBS. In 1953 he will host *You Are There*, a show in which historical events are restaged, with reporters in modern dress providing on-the-spot coverage.

Styrofoam cups. He speaks with a strong New York accent and it takes the Writer a while to understand that "stowy," "pictchah," and "telplie" mean respectively story, picture, and teleplay.

EXEC

You're a good strong writer and I'm sure that your stowy would make a good strong pictchah if you rewrite the telplie. But I can't use it. It's too controversial, you know what I mean? I mean there are too many Jews, blacks, and chicanos in your stowy. And homosexuals. Networks will never buy that stuff. No sir.

WRITER *(mumbling)*

But my agent said you were interested in taking it to the networks. He said that you liked it.

EXEC

Sure I like it. Did I say I didn't like it? It's a good script. I love it. I told your agent, what'shisname? . . . Oh yeah, Murray. I told Murray that I love it. I told him this kid can sure as hell write, but I can't use this. Unless he rewrites it. And I mean rewrite it.

WRITER

It's been rewritten seventeen times.

EXEC

So one more rewrite won't hurt. That's life in the studio, kid. You write and you rewrite until your stowy's picked up. Then you've got it made.

A moment of silence. The writer starts to gather the Script and is about to get up, when the Executive motions him to stay put.

EXEC

Now you go home and do that rewrite and take out the Jews and the blacks and the homos. Give me a neat, family-type piece of noncontroversial entertainment and I'll take it to the networks. As a pilot.

WRITER *(surprised)*

You mean for a series?

EXEC

What else? You got a series there. You got two strong characters. People that the audience can root for. Only trouble is that they're the villains. Make them the good guys. Give them more action, a little physical jeopardy, a chase or two—you know what I mean.

WRITER *(down)*

I know what you mean. But Murray said that you wanted to do it as a movie. As is.

EXEC

Forget the movies. That's like shooting crap at Vegas. Series is where it's at.

WRITER

But I don't know anything about series. I never watch them.

EXEC

You East Coast novelists are all the same. You all go for the glory, not for the bucks. *(pause)* Now you go on home, watch a coupla episodes and give me a good telplie—a ninety-minute commercial for a potential series and you've got it made and—*if* the network gives us a go ahead and *if* we produce it and *if* the ratings are good and *if* it gets good reviews in the trade papers and *if* the right people at the network decide to pick it up as a series. . . . Got it?

WRITER

Sort of, but I'm still not clear on what you want me to do.

EXEC

Go home and write the Bible.

June 25, 1952. Legendary CBS news journalist Edward R. Murrow participates in a program depicting the simulated bombing of New York City on the innovative current-events series *See It Now*. Between November 1951 and 1958, Murrow and his producer Fred Friendly will explore the potential of television to the fullest. In 1954 Murrow will use the program as a forum to challenge Senator Joseph McCarthy and initiate his political downfall.

For the first time, in 1952, television is a major factor in the national elections. Here, Estes Kefauver makes an unsuccessful bid to win the Democratic presidential nomination. Adlai Stevenson wins that nomination, but loses the election. Dwight Eisenhower's campaign is highlighted by twenty-second TV ads. Vice-Presidential candidate Richard Nixon comes on TV to deny accepting any illegal contributions other than a cocker spaniel named Checkers. The Eisenhower-Nixon inauguration will be the first carried live on television, January 20, 1953.

WRITER
Beg your pardon?

EXEC
The Bible. Don't you know what the Bible is?
The Writer shakes his head.

EXEC
It's a ten- to 30-page document outlining the format of
the series, the style, the themes, the main characters.
Who they are, what they like, what they don't like,
what kind of dressing they use on their salad—all that.
When you write it, think of all the other writers who'll
be churning out every weekly episode.

WRITER
But all that's already in the script.

EXEC
Sweetheart, network people don't read scripts. Network people don't even read the papers, except the
trades—for the ratings.

*He points to the stacks of scripts spread all over the
office.*

EXEC
Look around you. See all these scripts. I got people
sending me garbage all the way from Kalamazoo.
Who has time to read all this? No, you got to show a
few pages, even if you have the whole script written
out.

*He takes a last sip from his Styrofoam cup, then
crunches the cup and throws it on the floor.*

EXEC
Also, networks don't buy scripts like you buy oranges.
They like to be in on the creative process. Which is
why they like to commission scripts rather than buy
them ready made. They want to see a writer earn his
money before their eyes.

52

WRITER
All right, so I'll do a sort of outline of the story, right?

EXEC
Right. If they like it, they'll give you a step deal:
outline, stowy, telplie. They'll pay you to write a
stowy in forty or fifty pages, then they'll decide
whether they want to bring in another writer, or not.

WRITER *(stunned)*
Bring in . . . *WHAT?*

EXEC
Take it easy, kid. It's done all the time. Guy writes
script. Network rewrites script. It keeps the industry
busy.

WRITER
But the script doesn't even need a rewrite.

EXEC
All scripts always need a rewrite. That's a cardinal
rule of this industry. You rewrite for the producer, you
rewrite for the network, you rewrite for the stars, you
rewrite for the set designer, you rewrite even for the
location scout.

WRITER
I'll be damned if I do—

EXEC
You'll be damned if you don't. Lookit, you gotta understand this—for a writer, to be the "creator" of a
series is a gold mine. You'll be getting a royalty check
for every show that goes on the air, for every rerun,
every foreign sale, *everything.* If the show goes on for
six or seven years, you'll be a rich man even if you
never write another line for the show.

WRITER
Sounds great but why can't *I* do the rewrite?

EXEC
You're not on the list of network-approved writers.

An ex-President appears on television. Herbert Hoover,
who, as secretary of commerce, had been the subject of
C. Francis Jenkins's first intercity transmission in
the twenties, is seen on CBS on January 27, 1952.

7:00 A.M., January 14,
1952. *The Today Show*
debuts shakily on NBC.
This daily early-morning
information program is
hosted by Dave Garroway
(R), whose
Chicago-based *Garroway
at Large* (1949–1951)
variety show had earned
the easy-going moderator
a devoted following.
Sportscaster Jack
Lescoulie is in the
foreground.

How can I sell a show with you as the sole writer? You haven't even got a name.

WRITER

What do you mean, I haven't got a name?

EXEC
(condescendingly patient)

A name that means something to somebody up there at the network. That's what I need. What's a matter with you kid, don't you need money? Splitting a royalty check is better than nothing ain't it?

WRITER

I guess it is.

EXEC

All right, now you go on home and write the Bible, then do a little polish on the script and come back in three weeks. Remember—a lot of jeopardy, a coupla chases.

WRITER

What happens in three weeks?

EXEC

I'll take the script upstairs. I need the producers' approval. Then the producer will take it to the network. Then the network will decide whether they want to produce it and if they do . . . whether they want to bring in another writer . . . then we'll take meetings on the cast and the directors. Then the show will go into production . . . then we'll sit back and wait for the ratings.

WRITER

What if the ratings aren't so good?

EXEC

That's it. The project goes down the drain. Finito. Dead. We start all over again with another project and another and another. Until we hit the jackpot. Or we get ulcers. Or whatever. Now get out of here and get down to work. Remember, a lot of jeopardy and a coupla chases.

CUT TO: *Studio Lot—Exterior Day*

The Writer, feeling dejected, slowly walks to his car. He inspects the taped fender, which is about to fall off. It will be a while before it can get repaired. A rewrite. Maybe two rewrites. And the network's approval. And good ratings.

CUT TO: *Studio Gate—Exterior Day*

As he drives through the gate, the guard smiles at him.

GUARD

How did it go?

WRITER

So, so.

GUARD

Don't you worry none. Been in this business thirty-five years. Seen them come and seen them go. If it don't go this season, it'll go next season. Just gotta keep on truckin'.

CUT TO: *Los Angeles Boulevard—Exterior Day*

The TR3 speeds out of the canyon, heading toward the sunset on Sunset Boulevard.

THE END
(to be rewritten)

Elio Zarmati is a screenwriter and director who lives in Hollywood and spends 55 percent of his time taking meetings, 22 percent of his time bitching about it and 23 percent writing and directing films and hopes that someday the figures will be different.

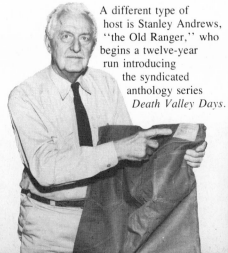

A different type of host is Stanley Andrews, "the Old Ranger," who begins a twelve-year run introducing the syndicated anthology series *Death Valley Days*.

Suspense anthologies, popular TV fare since CBS introduced *Suspense, Danger,* and *The Web* (all live) in 1949 and 1950, continue to spring up. Herbert Marshall is host of NBC's *The Unexpected,* a 1952 suspense series.

Mr. and Mrs. North returns to television in 1952. Richard Denning and Barbara Britton assume the roles played by Joseph Allen and Mary Lou Taylor three years earlier.

THE CENSORSHIP GAME
STEVEN BOCHCO

There is a very weighty debate raging these days about the relative effects of television violence upon the viewing public, young and old. I admit with refreshing candor that I have absolutely no new light to shed on the subject, though I am not without bias in the matter. On the contrary, I am very biased. I believe that if entertainment is by and large a reflection of our real world, then certainly violence has a place in our popular entertainment. This is not to say that it should rage ungoverned. Television shows that are intrinsically violent should be programmed for late-night viewing. Additionally, violence should never be depicted casually—there are emotional and psychic realities attendant upon violence that should be dramatized as well. Even in a cop's world, violence is not something that is accepted with equanimity, no matter which end of the .38 a person is on.

Questions abound. Are we spawning a generation of mindless ax murderers, or do our young assimilate TV violence the way older generations assimilated Saturday afternoon local movie house violence? Is constant exposure to TV violence turning young people into passive onlookers, unable to react emotionally to the violence in the real world? (Don't tell that to the millions of young people in the late sixties who protested—sometimes violently—everything from the war to the bra). And who, finally, owns responsibility for censoring what is seen on TV? The government? The networks? The producers of prime time fare? Or the viewer, whose right it is to turn the damn thing off altogether and read a book, or make love to a wife, or a friend, or a friend's wife.

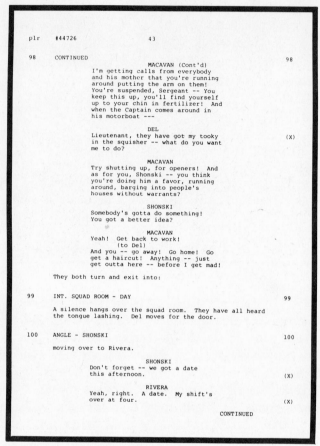

The disputed dialogue in its final script form.

These and many other pertinent questions are being hotly debated by parents, doctors, psychologists, and the general population. None of these experts has come up with the definitive answer. Cer-

54

In *Biff Baker, U.S.A.*, Randy Stuart (L) and Alan Hale (R) play a married couple who work as undercover agents for the U.S. government inside the Soviet Union.

The popular comic strip *Terry and the Pirates* comes to TV on Dumont in 1952. John Baer plays Terry Lee, an aviator searching for a lost gold mine in the Orient. Each week he must resist the treacherous seductress Lai Choi San, the Dragon Lady, played by Gloria Saunders.

Judd Hirsch, who plays the outspoken and sometimes controversial Delvecchio, is joined here by his partner, Charles Haid, disguised as a priest. No inappropriate language was exchanged in this episode of the show.

"I receive a memo . . . telling me . . . that Delvecchio may not say his cookies are in a squisher."

tainly, I don't have one. However, as a writer-producer of a sometimes-violent police series (*Delvecchio*, which has recently been canceled), I have found myself dealing with the profound issue of censorship in television on a very different—and far less lofty—plane.

It is my responsibility to submit each of my scripts to the network's Broadcast Standards Department before it is shot. The representative I work with from that department is a very nice lady performing a difficult task. She has, however, several powerful weapons at her disposal: an elaborate set of ground rules that have been established by higher-ups in her department; the ultimate authority to deny me the right to make any given episode if it does not meet certain broadcast standards as set forth in the aforementioned elaborate ground rules; and the ability to cry at me over the phone any time I raise my voice at her. But these weapons are offset by some weaponry of my own: I'm older than she is, I shout louder, I am not

Another pilot arriving on television in 1952 is *Sky King*. Kirby Grant flies *The Songbird* after bad guys on horses in this modern western for children.

Sky King's spirited niece Penny, who lives with him on the Flying Crown Ranch, is played by Gloria Winters. In 1949, Winters was Gleason's daughter Babs on *The Life of Riley*.

Jon Hall, a former romantic lead opposite such exotic movie heroines as Dorothy Lamour and Maria Montez, stars as a "white witch doctor" in *Ramar of the Jungle*, which begins a lengthy run in syndication in 1952.

"... one last directive: 'reduce the use of casual profanity (hells and damns) by at least half.'"

intimidated by cheap trickery (such as crying on the phone), and, ultimately, I am a better negotiator. For that is what censorship, in the real world, is all about—negotiating. For example:

There is a scene in a *Delvecchio* script I have submitted to Broadcast Standards wherein Delvecchio is angrily telling his lieutenant that he will *not* obey an order to butt out of a particular situation, since it is Delvecchio's "cookies that are in a squisher." I receive a memo on pink paper from Broadcast Standards, telling me, among other things, that Delvecchio may not say his cookies are in a squisher. I call Broadcast Standards to complain, and am told that the word "cookies," in the plural, strongly suggests the male genitalia. This is an unacceptable reference. I suggest changing cookies to cookie. After all, everyone knows that genitalia (by and large) come in matched sets. The word "cookie," I am told, whether singular, plural, or chocolate chip is deemed unacceptable. I have a fallback position, however: I suggest that perhaps a euphemism for "backside" might be less offensive. There is a pause on the other end of the line as my Broadcast Standards person considers this counter-proposal. Sensing a possible victory here, I suggest the word "buns." (As in: "Lieutenant, they've got my buns in a squisher!") No good, I am told. It's plural, and therefore a no-no. I remind her that she let me use the word "flapjacks" in a similar context in an earlier show. She is now on the defensive, and quickly

I suggest using the word *tuchus*. This is acceptable to her. But on second thought I veto the suggestion, since Delvecchio is an Italian Catholic and thinks a *briss* is some kind of French cheese. We split the difference, finally, and settle on the word "tookie." "Lieutenant! They've got my tookie in a squisher!" Bingo! And we move on to the next point. We spend the next ten minutes debating how many gunshots should be fired in one scene, how much cleavage (as opposed to carnage) should be exposed in another scene, how hard Delvecchio should frisk a suspect in a third scene, and in yet a fourth scene we dicker over the phrase "rat doo-doo," finally agreeing on "rat-doo." And at the bottom of this rather lengthy memo is one last directive: "Reduce the use of casual profanity (hells and damns) by at least half." As a matter of course, I agree, since I have padded the script with those oaths on the assumption that eight will yield me four, whereas six will only yield me three. In this particular case, I have seven hells and damns. I decide to live dangerously and delete only three. This is the kind of courageous executive decision for which producers get paid large salaries.

If all the above sounds false, believe me—it is not. If it sounds silly, believe me—it is. But my point in relating these events is not so much to poke fun at TV censorship as to point out that the realities of day-to-day production virtually obscure the most important aspect of the whole issue of television censorship. And that is, *not* whether violence or sex or anything else is "good" or "bad" for the viewer, but more importantly, with whom does the right to make those judgments reside? With the networks? With the government? Or with the traditional arbiter of American taste, the people?

Steven Bochco has spent his entire adult life writing and producing at Universal City Television Studios.

November 9, 1952. *Omnibus* begins a seven-year television journey, during which it will treat viewers to live presentations in theater, dance, and opera. In its first season, Royal Dano appears in James Agee's "Mr. Lincoln."

Bishop Fulton J. Sheen, whose religious discourse *Life Is Worth Living* is broadcast on the Dumont network, is the Emmy Awards' surprise victor over Lucille Ball, Jimmy Durante, Edward R. Murrow, and Arthur Godfrey as "Most Outstanding Television Personality" of 1952.

January 19, 1953. The birth of little Ricky on *I Love Lucy* makes national headlines, deflecting much of the limelight from Eisenhower's inauguration. The show, which coincides exactly with the birth of Lucille Ball's own baby, wins astronomical ratings.

CONFESSIONS OF A STORY EDITOR

DAVID JACOBS

The Blue Knight appeared as a television series early in 1976—a midseason replacement—and when it was picked up late by the network for the next season, there was a mad dash to order scripts. I had never written one, but I knew I could. Understandably, the producer hired experienced hands, but around Labor Day he called and asked it I would be interested in doing a rewrite. If the rewrite was good, I could then do an original. Sure, I said. I did the rewrite over the holiday weekend, handed it in on Tuesday. He called on Wednesday morning: could I come in? I went. He was in a meeting when I got there. I sat outside his office, and while I waited I heard the location scout discussing the script that would be shot next week. The one I had just rewritten. I guessed that meant I'd done all right.

The producer confirmed that when he greeted me a few minutes later. Thanks for the good job, he said, and by the way, how would you like to be story editor of *The Blue Knight?* The salary would be some number I'd never heard of before. I said sure.

Only . . .what's a story editor?

Episodic television is a demanding medium. The script for a one hour show must be between fifty-five and sixty pages, must show in forty-eight minutes, must be shot in six or seven days—with so many days preallocated for exteriors and so many days for interiors on the sound stage. The star has certain preferences regarding dialogue; he must work so many hours and be given so many hours of rest. The principal guest stars must have enough to do to earn a weekly fee; the smaller parts must be limited to one or two

> "The days were ten, eleven, twelve hours long, and they flew by."

days. Juveniles, if any, must not have to work more than four hours in any one day.

It is impossible to expect free-lance writers to write the best possible scripts within the many production limitations. It is also impossible for each writer to know exactly what is happening in every other episode. Therefore, the scripts submitted by the writers are essentially road maps, points of departure. The story editor is the person who refashions the scripts to conform with production demands, cast idiosyncracies, and the special requirements caused by weather or locations. He is also responsible for the show's overall continuity. Bumper Morgan—the aging cop hero of *The Blue Knight*—could not detest liver-and-onions in episode 3, and then order liver-and-onions on a dinner break in episode 8. Bumper's dialogue as written by Writer A may be as realistic as his dialogue according to Writer B—but it is up to the story editor to make sure that A's and B's jargon sounds the same on screen.

The story editor makes set calls. Some things that look fine on paper won't "play." A call comes from the set, and down to the set the story editor goes, adjusting and readjusting the script until it plays right.

The story editor works hard and has fun.

Peg Lynch and Alan Bunce play *Ethel and Albert.* This domestic situation comedy series started as a segment on the *Kate Smith Hour*. It will appear on three networks, disappearing finally in 1956.

Topper, the classic comedy movie about a mild-mannered man whose life is disrupted by two friendly but mischievous ghosts, comes to television. Seated are Leo G. Carroll (Cosmo Topper), and Lee Patrick (Henrietta). Standing are ghosts Anne Jeffreys (Miriam Kirby), Robert Sterling (George Kirby), and Buck as the alcoholic Neil.

Gary Frank, Sada Thompson, James Broderick, Meredith Baxter-Birney, and Kristy McNichol pose for a Family *portrait.*

The Blue Knight was shot at the Burbank Studios—the old Warner Brothers lot. Don't think I wasn't aware of that as I drove through the gate on that first day. The Gate. Bette Davis drove through this gate. And Jimmy Cagney. And Bogart. And me.

There were names painted on parking spaces. Names of stars. I did not yet have my name on one, but it was only a matter of time.

58

The old William Powell film *Life with Father* appears on television in 1953. Leon Ames (L) plays Clarence Day whose behind-the-times values make it difficult for his large family to adjust to the newly arrived twentieth century. Lurene Tuttle is his wife.

A contemporary family comedy is *The Life of Riley*, which returns to television in 1953 for a five-year stretch on NBC. William Bendix is the dumb but lovable Chester A. Riley; Marjorie Reynolds is his practical wife Peg. Jackie Gleason and Rosemary DeCamp played the original Rileys in the Dumont series of 1949–1950.

We were way behind. The day I started, we started shooting the script I'd rewritten. We still didn't have a script ready for the following week. I went right to work—a massive rewrite of a script based on a good idea, but which had been very poorly executed.

Time out for dailies—a showing of the film shot the day before. On my second day, the dailies were from my rewrite. Actors on the screen were speaking lines I had written. The thrill was indescribable. By the end of the week I'd learned better. What is he *doing?* That's not how those lines are supposed to be delivered. Stupid actors.

The days were ten, eleven, twelve hours long, and they flew by.

The Blue Knight premiered; its opposition on the other networks were new: *The Quest,* (a western) and *Charlie's Angels,* (a who-knows-what). *Charlie's Angels* pulled in about half the viewing audience; we split the difference with *The Quest.*

It can't last, we said. People will watch *Charlie's Angels* once, maybe twice, and then the novelty of three gorgeous women skateboarding as they escape from Southern chain gangs will wear off. A 50 share of the viewers? Never again.

We were right. The next week *Charlie's Angels* reached a 55 share. *The Quest* dropped a little; we stayed the same. Okay, now we're getting mad; that's it for *Charlie's Angels* and 55 shares. Week three and *C.A.* hit 60—but we did go up a little as *The Quest* dwindled. But we were in trouble.

Then the network shut us down. Not a cancellation—just an on-salary hiatus while the network made up its mind about *The Blue Knight.* It was awful. We played darts, exchanged rumors about our future, based on the expert testimony of people's aunts and cleaning persons. All of us were from New York. We talked about egg creams and decent corned beef. One day we walked over to Warner Brothers' celeb-

---

"After four weeks we were cancelled."

rated New York Street (on every inch of which James Cagney had at one time or another died) and played punchball. It was funny, but it didn't help.

After four weeks we were canceled. Only four episodes had reached the television screen. Everybody was relieved—up to a point. They'd all been through it before; that's TV for you, they said. I had had no previous experience, and I felt terrible. I knew the others did, too, underneath it all. Television reality or not, it hurts to fail.

I had functioned as a story editor for four weeks; my name had never appeared on screen in that capacity. Nevertheless, getting work was no problem. A story editor is after all someone who knows what it's all about. I promptly got three assignments writing episodes of three different shows. Two of them asked me to be story editor.

I took the offer from *Family.*

Like *The Blue Knight, Family* had premiered early in 1976 as a mini-series. It had done well—not like *Charlie's Angels* (which is a product of the same production company that turns out *Family*)—but well enough to influence the network into considering it as a permanent series for the 1976–77 season. And, as was the case with *The Blue Knight,* the network made its decision late. There had been a mad rush to get scripts, and when I started work on *Family* in January, 1977, there were eight shows left to shoot—and only one script ready to go.

The last several episodes of the series were not nearly as good as the earlier ones because the best scripts had been shot already; and, given the time

59

1953. *Mr. Peepers,* starring Wally Cox as a timid high school biology teacher, moves into its second season. Also in the cast are Tony Randall, Marion Lorne, and Patricia Benoit, Mr. Peepers' girlfriend.

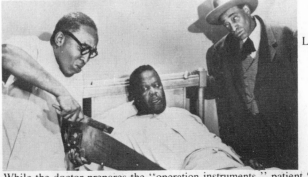

While the doctor prepares the "operation instruments," patient Spencer Williams looks on nervously and his friend, Tim Moore (The Kingfish), looks on sympathetically. On June 11, 1953, *Amos 'n' Andy* will leave the air. In 1966, because of continued pressure from the NAACP, reruns will be withdrawn from syndication.

Beulah will also leave the air in 1953. And it too will later be withdrawn from syndication. Louise Beavers is the third actress to play Beulah, succeeding Ethel Waters and Hattie McDaniel in 1952.

"I started work on 'Family' in January, 1977; there were eight shows left to shoot—and only one script ready to go."

pressure, there was not enough time to whip the others into the best possible shape. My contribution was mixed: I was, to be sure, another body to help out; but I was also new to the behavior of the characters. The decline in quality probably wasn't as sharp as I thought, but it was real. Nevertheless, as the series wound down toward the end of its first season, its ratings climbed. People had gotten used to *Family*, and decided it was the sort of program they would like to watch regularly.

The other networks responded. *Family* had never had easy competition—the excellent *Police Story* and the popular *Switch*. But *Switch* was moved, and *Kojak* replaced it. *Family* continued to climb, despite the fact that it now occupied one of the most competitive time slots in television.

The network was impressed. *Family* was the first show renewed for the 1977–78 season.

Very nice, only that didn't help us with the remaining scripts for the season still in progress. The low point came in February, when we suddenly found ourselves with no script to be shot the following week. (The script scheduled for shooting that week featured Nancy's ex-husband, and the actor who played that part was unexpectedly unavailable.) It was Thursday morning; shooting would begin on the nonexistent script on Monday. To complicate matters, I was getting married on Saturday—so I couldn't work over the weekend unless I were prepared to live with an ex-

tremely guilty conscience. The producer, the executive story consultant, and I talked briefly, and then I sat down at the typewriter.

As I finished each yellow page, I dropped it on the floor. Every half hour or so, the executive story consultant would come in, collect the pages, edit, and rewrite as needed. The script went off to be mimeoed an act at a time. By Friday afternoon the script was done. Shooting started on schedule, Monday. I was no longer new to the characters or the show.

I write this as shooting has stopped. The last show of the season will be aired next week. The producer and executive story consultant, who are husband and wife, are away on vacation. I have talked to approximately sixty writers about next season's scripts. Almost all of the twenty-two shows have been assigned. Some of the scripts have started coming in, and they're much better than last year. By the time we start shooting, in mid-June, we expect to have half of our scripts mimeoed and ready to shoot. Emergencies will arise, no doubt, but there's no way the pressure can come close to what it was last year. That of course is good news, but . . .

The producer said it all during that two-day script-writing marathon in February. Yellow paper was heaped on the floor. I had just spilled coffee on my desk and wouldn't take the time to clean it up. I hadn't stopped for lunch and had just called out to the secretary to put no more calls through. I was typing faster than I thought I could. The producer stuck his head into my office; I didn't turn around to see what he wanted. He watched me for a moment, then turned and said something to his wife, which I overheard: "I've never seen him so happy."

David Jacobs was once a prolific writer of fiction and non-fiction in New York. In 1976 he moved to Hollywood to sell out.

60

"Thank you, Julie, and that, folks, was Julie's swan song." Another television exit is made in 1953 when singer Julius LaRosa is fired on the air by Arthur Godfrey during *Arthur Godfrey and His Friends*.

It's "Four for the Money" when the Perriconi quadruplets visit host Herb Shriner on CBS's new game show, *Two For the Money*.

CREATING "RYAN'S HOPE"

PAUL MAYER

St. Patrick's Day is celebrated with warmth and conviviality in the Ryan family bar in New York City.

In 1973 my partner Claire Labine and I were working at another network when ABC invited us to create a new daytime serial for them. We were promised a free hand to do as we liked, and we took it. We drew on our own roots to some extent, and proposed to write about a real family that lived in a real place. The place was New York City and the Irish, Roman Catholic family kept a bar. To our great delight, ABC encouraged us to go forward, so we began to explore our fantasy family, the Ryans.

We started with their beginnings. Johnny Ryan, paterfamilias and head of the family, was born in New York City in 1918. His mother died in the influenza epidemic of 1919, and his policeman father was killed in the line of duty in 1929. Johnny was taken in by a stern and pious maiden aunt and then . . .

In its third year on television *Your Hit Parade* settles on a permanent troupe. Dorothy Collins, Snooky Lanson, Russell Arms, and Gisele Mackenzie will sing the nation's top songs until 1958 when the rock 'n' roll craze will make their style seem outdated.

The Today Show is a television fixture by 1953 thanks in part to famous chimpanzee J. Fred Muggs (L), who has become a regular on the program. Muggs establishes himself as one of TV's most popular entertainers.

July 27, 1953. *The Tonight Show* debuts as a local 11:20 P.M.-to-midnight show in New York. Steve Allen is the host of this live, anything-goes talk show, which expands to 105 minutes when it becomes a network show on November 27, 1954.

"We wanted to create a fantasy world that was entirely new to the audience . . ."

In the original "bible"—the name given to the 100-page document in which we worked out the history of Johnny Ryan and his family and their friends—we traced the life of each character from long ago to the present time. When we then began to plan the future story, it was solidly grounded in concrete events. Before our first show went on the air in July 1975, we had laid out what would happen for the next two years.

Since we were fortunate enough to be invited to produce as well as write the show, we had the opportunity to oversee casting, scenic and costume design, makeup, hairstyles, and all the other elements of physical production. We wanted to create a world that was entirely new to the audience, so we looked for performers who had not had heavy daytime exposure (approximately half our cast had never appeared on television at all). Then our designer set out to create rooms that would truly reflect the lives of the people they contained. (Claire and I once had worked on another show that had three married couples and three living rooms; we noted that it didn't matter which couple was in which living room, because all were so totally without character.) When we first saw *Ryan's* kitchen with its huge old-fashioned iron stove, great ancient refrigerator, and terrible/wonderful rose-patterned linoleum, we felt we had the kind of reality in which our stories could grow. We worked for further realism by using a minimum of makeup on the actors, no hair spray, and costumes that reflected accurately the tastes and pocketbooks of the characters.

When we prepare individual episodes, we use our future story as a guide. We write outlines in groups of five—one week at a time—and from these outlines, five dialogue scripts are written. We do two ourselves, and other writers are hired to do the rest. Outlines and scripts are usually written about four to six weeks ahead of air date, and the actual taping takes place a week or two before the show appears.

We have one basic guideline: We try to write scenes that we want to see, and desperately try to avoid scenes that would bore us. Whenever we feel that some proposed incident or confrontation is dull, we look for another, better way to advance the story. If we were able to write *Ryan's Hope* as well as we'd like, each daily episode would have the emotional intensity of *Wuthering Heights*, the strong characterizations and unforgettable story lines of Dickens, and the stylistic delights of Jane Austen. We can't do that of course, but we do take the challenge seriously and do the very best we can. Our biggest enemy is time, or the lack of it. Two hundred fifty half-hour episodes a year would test the invention of Brontë, Dickens, and Austen put together.

There is a theory that writers draw heavily upon their unconscious fantasies, and if this is true then perhaps one of the things that makes writing *Ryan's Hope* such fun is that Claire Labine and I share a common fantasy life. We both enjoy the same kinds of sentimental, upbeat, love stories. The title of the show reflects our attitude—we are hopeful, and so are the Ryans. We love our characters and the fantasy they inhabit, so the whole experience of the show—while exhausting—is for us very much a labor of love.

Paul Mayer writes, produces, and collects Emmies with his partner, Claire Labine, for their soap, Ryan's Hope.

June 2, 1953. Queen Elizabeth II is crowned. ABC scoops CBS and NBC by broadcasting tapes flown in from England that cover the coronation. CBS and NBC, which were waiting to televise highlights only, follow suit when they realize that ABC is grabbing their audience.

The Queen of the West, *Annie Oakley,* comes to ABC in 1953 for a five-year run. Gail Davis is the legendary sharpshooter; Brad Johnson is her friend, Sheriff Lofty Craig.

CBS picks up *The Lone Ranger* in 1953, after four years of syndication. The 221 episodes will be shown on network television until 1961 when the reruns will be sold back into syndication. With Clayton Moore is the incredible Silver.

ON THE SET OF "THE DOCTORS"

DEBRA WEINER

Maybe people watch them because the actors are handsome and the actresses are pretty and it is difficult to resist almost any cliff-hanging serial; or maybe people watch them because they enjoy stories that go on endlessly, like life, with just as many twists and turns. For thirteen years Dr. Matt Powers of *The Doctors* never so much as sneezed without saying "God bless you." Now he has been charged with murder—pulling the plug from a patient's respirator. Who would have suspected? But then, that's life. Maybe soap operas are for people who like life.

It is 7:45 A.M. at the Seven Arts Room in the Hotel Edison in New York City. The actors know their lines, because they have had the script for three days. Norman Hall, director of *The Doctors,* knows the stage blocking, because he has had the script for one week. He steers the players around clusters of chairs that represent the scenery and sets, and in a soft voice explains the motivation behind the lines. They rehearse each scene several times, then run through the entire show once. Hall's assistant uses a stopwatch to time the scenes down to the number of seconds.

In NBC's Studio 3B at 30 Rockefeller Plaza, the technical crew is building two living rooms, a room with a window and Andre's, the all-purpose nightclub/restaurant/bar. The only permanent set is the nurse's station, and it includes an elevator door.

A three-camera setup is used to videotape *The Doctors.* The production crew rehearses the camera blocking. They practice moving the cameras, the sound equipment, and the lights from one set to the

Lydia Bruce, the fourth actress to play Dr. Maggie Fielding since the show's beginning in 1963, and James Pritchett, who plays Dr. Matt Powers, have a serious conversation.

63

The Adventures of Superman comes to television in 1953. One of the first shows filmed in color, it immediately becomes the top children's program. George Reeves, who played one of Scarlett O'Hara's suitors in *Gone With the Wind,* stars. Phyllis Coates is Lois Lane. In 1954, Coates will be replaced by Noel Neill.

Superman bends Jeff Corey's rifle in "The Unknown People," a two-part edited version of the *Superman and the Mole Men* feature film. People will complain through the years that TV's Superman causes too much needless damage to cars, doors, and guns in order to show off.

CUE CARD COMPANY

Although they are fifty-one and fifty-three years old respectively, Don Stewart and Carl Marlow call themselves The Card Boys. For twenty-three years they have been holding cue cards for performers on television. Even now, when teleprompter machines have usurped much of the hand-held business, the "boys" still work regularly on variety, news, and music specials, and five days a week on the soap opera *The Doctors*. Armed with their sets of hand-printed 22- by 24-inch cards, on which each actor's part is written in a different color, Don and Carl extend a personal and professional service. They stand where the cards can be easily read. They never cast shadows. And they pull used cards away quickly.

Of course accidents can happen—upside-down cards, or erroneous dialogue, have been known to occur. Once Carl dropped a card, and it slid in front of the camera. Still, The Card Boys maintain that their customized cues are better than the mechanical ones. Whole conversations, rather than the teleprompter's single lines, are visible at a glance. The cards can be flipped forward to show an entire scene. And letters can be printed in any size.

The Card Boys started as would-be actors who found themselves working as ushers at the CBS studio in 1954. They made their prompting debut on the hour-long Perry Como show. Still "boys," they are now the grand old men of the East Coast cue card business.

next, as quickly as possible.

Wardrobe supervisor, Mildred Packard, is in a closet filled with nurses' uniforms. The uniforms can be worn for many years. Street clothes must be updated. Most of these are designer fashions, and each female lead has a closetful. Packard—short, gray-haired, and grandmotherly—is looking for a uniform with a V neckline. It needs to be altered.

John Geller is the music director. He is in the music library along with four hours of original music. He is trying to find nine minutes' worth to intersperse throughout the script. Some of the measures should sound mysterious. Others evil. Each character needs his or her theme song. And, of course, there must be

plenty of love music. Geller has been with the show many years. He knows the music as he knows his family.

Soaps may be popular among college students, but they are intended to please people over the age of twenty-five—housewives and mothers, husbands and fathers who are at home during the day. That is why the commercials concentrate on family items like underwear, cleansers, and baby products, and why the story lines concentrate on all varieties of family conflict.

There wasn't much sex on TV when *The Doctors* began in 1964—unlike today's soaps in which everyone sleeps with everyone else, even blood relatives. But

64

Another hit with youngsters and adults alike is *Zoo Parade*. Marlin Perkins is director of Chicago's Lincoln Park Zoo, point of origin of his weekly telecasts.

It is the time of McCarthy and the Cold War. The syndicated *I Led Three Lives*, based on the Herbert Philbrick book *I Was a Communist for the FBI*, is popular all across America in 1953. Richard Carlson plays FBI agent Philbrick who sabotages Communist plots each week.

"There wasn't much sex when 'The Doctors' began in 1964."

then today nothing is taboo. Child abuse, abortion, drugs, euthanasia, alcohol, and rape are all acceptable subjects for soaps. "Play out the headlines," say the producers, who have been told by the sponsors (Colgate-Palmolive in the case of *The Doctors*) to provide entertainment.

Usually that has meant melodrama, but *The Doctors'* head writer, Douglas Marland (a former soap opera actor), believes that can change. He plans to elevate *The Doctors* to a plausible, realistic, and possibly even enlightening level. He wants to make the characters more human.

"Soaps are about people with problems and the ways they try to solve them," he says. "They may not be the right ways or the ways you would solve them, but at least the viewer sees that he is not the only person in the world with problems." Marland's primary source for material is his family. He takes their problems and puts them under a microscope when he writes the show.

By 11:15 A.M. everyone and everything is in Studio 3B ready for the "run-thru." Hall is in the control room, and as he eats his lunch he watches the rehearsal on several tiny television screens. He instructs by way of a microphone, which sits next to his cottage cheese, telling the actors things like, "Don't move so fast. You're anticipating everything"; "Look at your wife. She's the one who is important"; and "Don't kiss so passionately. You have your coats on." He doesn't have to worry about the actors forgetting their lines, because two men with cue cards are present on the set.

During the break between the run-thru and the dress rehearsal, the actors slip into costume, put on their makeup, and watch television in the actors' lounge. They turn on the competition: *As the World Turns* and *The Young and the Restless,* which they call *As the Stomach Turns* and *The Young and the Breastless.* Finally, after a long day of preparation, the latest episode of *The Doctors* goes before the cameras.

Welcome to Hope Memorial Hospital in Madison, Wisconsin. It is the never-ending present as the story unfolds, and we meet Dr. Ann who likes Dr. Steve. But he is married to Carolee, who has contracted catatonia, so Ann has hidden her in a sanitarium. Steve, believing Carolee is gone forever, proposes to Ann.

We meet Dr. Paul who hates Dr. Matt. Paul's wife, Stacy, has killed one of Matt's patients. But it is Matt who has resigned from his job, Matt who has turned to drink, Matt who is crumbling, and Matt who refuses to discuss any of it with his wife. Matt's wife is upset.

And we meet middle-aged Eleanor, friend of the doctors, who was married to a man who committed suicide. Through a mutual acquaintance she meets Luke Dancy, the young and disreputable fortune-hunter/gigolo. Can they make a go of it? Will they make a go of it? And if so, what then?

We also catch a glimpse of the ill-starred marriage of Jerry, the young lawyer, and Penny, the young medical student, and of Steve's child's bout with pneumonia. But more of them on another day in the life of *The Doctors* of Hope Memorial Hospital in Madison, Wisconsin.

Debra Weiner, who writes frequently about the arts for various publications, once wanted to be a doctor.

Alan Mowbray (R) is Humphrey Flack and Frank Jenks is Uthas P. Garvey in *Colonel Flack,* the story of an amiable con man and his assistant who travel around the world relieving the wealthy of money.

David Brian (R) is Paul Garrett, *Mr. District Attorney,* "champion of the people, defender of truth, guardian of our fundamental rights to life, liberty, and the pursuit of happiness." Brian had replaced Jay Jostyn as the D.A. when the old radio show came to TV in 1951.

September 29, 1953. *Make Room For Daddy* debuts. This comedy, starring Danny Thomas (R), Jean Hagen (L), Sherry Jackson, and Rusty Hamer, wins an Emmy as 1953's "Best New Series." It is ABC's first genuine hit show.

WRITING A TV PLAY
DAVID TRAINER

"**D**o you think you could write a play for television?" my agent wondered in the fall of 1974, because until then I had only written plays for the stage.

"I can certainly try!" I replied enthusiastically.

He sent me to see a producer named Barbara Schultz, who was visiting New York to commission original scripts for the Los Angeles public television station KCET's new series, *Visions*. Barbara had funding from several large foundations as well as from the Public Broadcasting System itself, and was looking for work by writers with little or no experience in television. The purpose of her project was to introduce new people to the medium, in hopes that they would want to write more for it. Barbara and I chatted pleasantly for awhile, and then she said, "What would you like to do?"

I said I wanted to write a play about a prosperous family that has fallen on hard times. I wanted to show what happens to the family's teenaged daughter when, in order to save money, her parents are forced to spend the winter in a deserted beach town.

Barbara was thoughtful for a moment. One of her many virtues as a producer is her ability to decide quickly whether or not she likes an idea. She has strong instincts, and she trusts them. "I like it," she said. "We've got a deal." I was delighted. I had never written a television play before, and here at last was my chance.

According to the contract that was drawn up on the basis of a brief written statement of my idea, I had to write a detailed outline, and then two drafts of the play, for which I would be paid upon delivery. If at any time Barbara decided that she didn't like the play, she could cancel the contract. This meant that for the first time in my writing career, I had to please someone else as well as myself. I finished the outline and sent it to Barbara. Then I waited nervously for her response. As always, it came quickly, and as always, she was explicit about both what she liked and what she disliked. Chief among her criticisms was that I wasn't taking sufficient advantage of the amazing flexibility of television tape. All my previous experience had been in the theater, where it is often difficult to change settings. As a result I tended to write long scenes in which the characters came and went while the setting stayed the same. Barbara taught me that in television the scenes should be set where the characters go, and reminded me that with tape the characters could go anywhere. She also reminded me that while the theater is primarily a verbal medium, television is a visual one. She urged me to show rather than tell whenever possible.

It took me about a month to write the first draft of the play, and then another month to incorporate Barbara's critical advice into a second draft. In general, the play became more airy and expansive as I worked on it. I added tiny scenes that would be impractical on stage, and encouraged the characters to wander about wherever they wanted. When I was finished, Barbara and I were both pleased with the results. My initial enthusiasm was not misplaced. I *could* write a television play.

The next step was to see it produced. In the fall of

The biggest event on television in 1954 is the Army-McCarthy Hearings. From April to June, more than twenty million viewers tune in ABC. Roy Cohn (L), McCarthy's attorney, can do little to help his client protect his crumbling image.

Perhaps the second biggest TV event of 1954 is Wally Cox's marriage to Patricia Benoit on *Mr. Peepers*.

1975, about a year after I began work on the script, I flew to Los Angeles for the first day of rehearsal. The actors had already been chosen by Barbara and the director, Rick Bennewitz. The interior sets were already being built in the studio, and the exterior locations had already been selected on the island of Catalina.

While I was very happy with all the choices that had been made, it became clear that the writer has very little to contribute to a television play once the script is done. In the early stages of rehearsal I cut and rewrote brief sections of the text, but because complex and expensive arrangements had been made on the basis of what I'd written in New York, major changes, even if they had been needed, would have been nearly impossible. Still, at first it was hard to see how television was much different from the theater. The actors read through the play while sitting around a table smoking cigarettes and drinking coffee as actors everywhere do. Soon they got up on their feet and began to wander around playing with make-believe props in make-believe rooms marked by chalk on the floor of the rehearsal hall. Then one afternoon I got my first glimpse of what is undeniably the magnificent flexibility of tape.

The company drove down to the harbor and boarded a forty-foot sport fishing boat, which sped several miles out into the ocean where it was met by a small helicopter. Out of the side door of this helicopter hung a man strapped to a television camera. My stage-bound imagination was staggered. A year before, urged to take advantage of television's flexibility, I had casually written the word "boat" in a script. Now I stood on the deck of that boat, and shaded my eyes from the sun as I peered up at a helicopter that it had never occurred to me to mention at all. The brief scene that resulted from this wonderful excursion into the ocean expresses better and faster and more com-

David Trainer on location: "The brief scene that resulted from this wonderful excursion into the ocean expresses better . . . than words ever could the exhilaration felt by the heroine."

pletely than words ever could the exhilaration felt by the teenaged heroine when she finally breaks away from her conservative family stuck in the deserted town. I know how the girl feels in the scene on the

67

December Bride debuts in 1954. This witty situation comedy stars veteran character actress Spring Byington as the adventurous widow Lily Ruskin, Harry Morgan as neighbor Pete, Dean Miller as Matt Henshaw, and Frances Rafferty as his wife Ruth, Lily's daughter.

Chick Young's comic strip "Blondie" makes an uneven transition to television. The Bumsteads are played for one year by Arthur Lake (Dagwood), Pamela Britton (Blondie), Stuffy Singer (Alexander), and Ann Barnes (Cookie).

Ann Sothern appears on television in 1954 as Susie McNamara in the comedy hit *Private Secretary*. It will last three seasons on CBS.

"A great deal of work and care and worry was over in an hour."

boat surging through the sea, because I felt just the same way while we were taping it.

Everyone who works on a television production has a specific job to do. Only the writer, whose work is done when production begins, is free to stand around and watch. Sometimes I stood by the cameras during taping, other times I sat in front of a monitor and gazed at the images of my play framed for the first time by a television screen. The afternoon on the boat taught me how expansive television could be, but the view on the monitor taught me that television is equally intimate. Words, inflections, gestures, and looks take on new intensity, power, and meaning when isolated on the screen.

I liked the actors in the cast, and got to know them well in the course of the production, but when I saw their faces close up on the monitor, I felt that I was seeing *into* them for the first time. I also realized that while I had created the characters and the story, the entire apparatus of production was really the true author of the show. For, in an immensely technical medium such as television, the technicians are as important as the writer, director, and producer. When all the scenes had been taped, I returned to New York. In a month or so the show would be edited, and Barbara promised to send a copy of it east for me to see.

When the show arrived in New York, it was played for me in a little room not much bigger than a closet. For the first time I saw the title of the play on the screen: WINTER TOUR, WRITTEN BY DAVID TRAINER. I was very proud. Then the play began, and for an hour I experienced a peculiar kind of mental stress. Words, scenes, pictures and ideas that I had imagined occurring in a certain rhythm occurred—differently. Everything was there as I had written and rehearsed it, but the play flowed with a life of its own rather than mine. It was as if I had come home after a long day to discover that all the furniture in my living room had been slightly rearranged. All the objects were there, but the relationships were different. As I watched the show, I was fascinated by all the subtle changes that had taken place in the editing, but I felt somewhat forlorn and left out too, because it had all been done without me. When the show was over, I walked out of the little room dazed and a bit uncertain of what I'd seen. I recognized the play as my own, but at the same time I realized that what had started as a personal expression had grown in stages to be the product and ultimately the property of a very large group of other people as well.

In December 1976 the play was shown on television. I sat in my apartment and watched the finished product broadcast back to the very place where it had originated as an idea over two years before. The play seemed something at once very distant from me in time, and yet very close to me in feeling. I followed the story avidly, and when it ended I was sorry. Some friends in the building gathered outside my door to applaud. The phone rang a few times. And then there was silence. A great deal of work, and care, and worry, was over in an hour. I wondered how many people had seen the show, and whether they liked it.

For a few weeks I kept meeting people who had seen the play. Their comments kept it alive in my mind, but soon, of course, the show was forgotten. That is the thing about television: it passes. But I just heard that the play may be rebroadcast next summer. I liked it and will be sure to watch.

David Trainer is a playwright in New York.

68

Ham Fisher's comic strip hero *Joe Palooka* comes to television, with Joe Kirkwood, Jr. (C) playing the naïve, true-blue boxing champion.

Movie favorite *Lassie* comes home via television in 1954. The collie's first TV owner is Tommy Rettig (Jeff Miller).

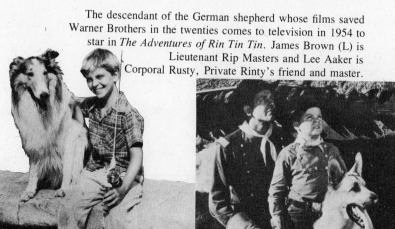

The descendant of the German shepherd whose films saved Warner Brothers in the twenties comes to television in 1954 to star in *The Adventures of Rin Tin Tin*. James Brown (L) is Lieutenant Rip Masters and Lee Aaker is Corporal Rusty, Private Rinty's friend and master.

A TV ACTOR'S INITIATION
RICHARD LARSON

My big break had come. After a year of frustration, odd jobs, and threatening letters from my landlord, I had finally been rewarded with my first role in a TV dramatic series. The part was that of an impassioned union organizer recently arrived from the old sod. It certainly wasn't *Hamlet,* but it was a start.

Nervously I paced the floor of my dressing room cubicle rehearsing my lines. "There comes a time when a man has got to look himself in the mirror," rolled from my lips in an Irish brogue. It was my favorite line. The exact meaning of it in the context of the scene escaped me, but it had a ring of profundity.

"Mr. Larson, makeup is ready for you now," said a voice from outside my door.

"One minute." I quickly put on my costume and reached for my bottle of Tranzene. This, my doctor insisted, was not a tranquilizer but a calming agent usually given to hyperactive children. He had prescribed it to help control the hypertension I had recently developed due to the stress of *not* working in my chosen profession. I forced the dry capsule down my throat, and looked in the mirror. An intense young actor stared back at me. "There comes a time when a man has got to look himself in the mirror," he said convincingly. A smug smile erupted on his face.

A brisk assistant director ushered me to a makeup table and chair set up in a grassy courtyard of the studio lot. As the makeup man dabbed at my face, the director and the young star of the series joined me. It alarmed me to see the director looking tense and disheveled; he had seemed so composed when I auditioned for him in the producer's office two days

Richard Larson triumphant after his television initiation.

before. When he failed to remember my name, I reminded him who I was and introduced myself to the star, who shook my hand perfunctorily.

"Did you get the script changes?" the director asked. I informed him that I had picked up the script late the day before in revised form.

"Good," he said. "Let's rehearse the scene."

I delivered my first line. There was an awkward silence. The star looked at me vacantly. I repeated the line. The director riffled through his script.

"I don't see that line here." He thrust the script under my nose. There wasn't a line on the page that I

69

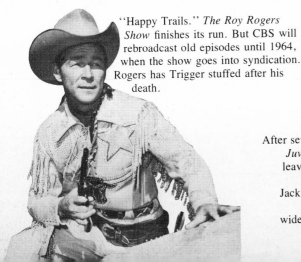

"Happy Trails." *The Roy Rogers Show* finishes its run. But CBS will rebroadcast old episodes until 1964, when the show goes into syndication. Rogers has Trigger stuffed after his death.

After seven years, *Juvenile Jury* leaves the air. Here host Jack Barry sits with three wide-eyed jury members.

recognized. My heart pounded mercilessly. The makeup man blotted the beads of perspiration that burst from my forehead. I wished I had taken two Tranzenes instead of one.

"This isn't the scene I learned," I stammered.

"You said you got the changes!"

"Not these changes," I protested. "I had a line about a man looking himself in the mirror."

"What man? What mirror? What the hell are you talking about?" His eyes seemed to bulge from his head as he shook the unfamiliar script at me. I could feel my face turning bright crimson under my pancake base. The makeup man continued mopping my brow.

"I'm sorry," I said, "but I never saw this scene before now."

"Well, you'd better learn it. And damned fast." He threw the script in my lap and stormed off. I looked to my fellow actor for an encouraging word; he offered only a blank stare.

A few minutes later we were before the cameras blocking the scene. The urgency of the situation helped me to retain my new lines quickly. Unfortunately, the young star had great difficulty retaining his. In fact, it seemed that he knew very little about acting at all. The director worked hard to improve his performance, but all efforts failed. Desperately trying to create dramatic tension in the scene, the director pumped up my energy to twice that of the star. Having spent ten years in the theater, I was well aware that my acting was approaching stage level and that it would be excessive for the camera. This was what TV producers feared most from a stage actor making his transition to the screen. I tried to cut back, but the director wouldn't allow it. "Give me more," he demanded. When the scene reached the point where I was shouting and the star was barely whispering, I stopped in the middle of a line.

"Are you sure," I appealed to the director, "that what I'm doing isn't too stagy?"

"Stagy? No. The scene is working now," he replied.

Shooting the scene took the entire morning. The star kept fluffing his lines or his blocking. After every fluff, the director would vent his anger by yelling at me. But we muddled through it, and after the final take the director pulled me aside. He thanked me for rescuing the scene and complimented me on my work. I asked him once again if I hadn't been too stagy. He assured me I hadn't, and that I could look ahead to a successful career in TV. We parted warmly.

That afternoon my agent called me at my apartment. "How did the shooting go?" he asked.

"I'm not sure. I couldn't stay to see the rushes."

"I'll call the producers and find out and call you right back," he said, and hung up.

A few minutes later I snatched up the receiver on the first ring. My agent hesitated on the other end; my heart began to thump against my chest.

"What did they say?" I asked.

"They thought it was a little . . . stagy."

"Stagy," I repeated in a controlled rage.

"Yeah. When are you actors going to learn to use less energy for TV?"

I didn't try to explain, but told him I'd do better next time. Completely dejected, I set down the receiver. I listened to my heart pound. A faint sound began to reverberate in my ears. At first I assumed it was caused by stroke-level blood pressure. But as the sound grew louder, I realized it was a voice, a voice with a slight Irish brogue. It kept repeating the favorite line I had never gotten to say: "There comes a time when a man has got to look himself in the mirror."

Richard Larson is a Los Angeles-based actor and writer who will continue to persevere.

Jack Bailey takes over *Truth or Consequences* on May 18, 1954.

Here Jack Bailey hosts *Place the Face,* a game show in which contestants must identify someone from their past.

Another host of *Place the Face* is the bright, moody Jack Paar. In 1954, Paar is host of two morning variety-talk shows for CBS, *The Morning Show* and *The Jack Paar Show,* which eventually moves into the afternoon schedule.

THE GOLDEN AGE OF TV DRAMA
IRA AVERY

Maybe in retrospect we've gilded it a little. The Golden Age of television wasn't all that rich in quality, but the challenge, freedom and excitement of the fifties made it a very special time nonetheless, a time never again to be revived. At the beginning of the decade five of the vanishing big bands were on the tube. There were a handful of game shows, a little news and sports, a single film series *(Hopalong Cassidy),* about two dozen talking, clowning, or singing "personalities" (not including Uncle Miltie, who was to come and go later), and eighteen, count 'em, *eighteen* "live anthology dramas"—the term applied to a dramatic series with an original play and a different cast every week. What became of them, and why?

For the answer it's necessary to go back a quarter of a century and examine why the anthologies existed in the first place. There was the form itself, flexible, varied, and inviting experimentation—a vehicle that could be shaped by an advertiser into a suitable climate for his commercial messages, a selective mounting for his corporate image and, most of all, a type of entertainment that could be tailored to reach the desired segment of the public. (Please note the quaintly archaic innocence of the word "desired," not "largest.") And note that *advertisers* were doing the deciding.

It would be fatuous to contend that all clients and their agencies were high-minded innovators then any more than now, or that banality was a later invention, but the point is that sheer numbers and differing tastes guaranteed a variety of fare that has never been seen since on commercial television. The life story of one

"Dramatic series which failed to pull a rating were systematically demolished . . ."

anthology series may serve to illustrate who throttled the goose that laid the Golden Age.

The Armstrong Cork Company and its agency, BBDO, decided to enter television with a live dramatic series for all the reasons cited earlier, and because Armstrong had pioneered very successfully with the form in radio. The networks competed vigorously in offering favorable time periods, and NBC was ultimately selected on the basis of studio facilities, the size and type of audience promised, and the number of stations that would be made available. A number of existing shows were considered, but it was finally decided that Armstrong and BBDO could exert better control and achieve greater impact by creating an entirely new series under the sponsor's own name.

This was 1950. The advertising director of the Armstrong Cork Company was E. Cameron Hawley, whose concept of his new show embraced original scripts, a well-known stage or film star each week, and a framework that would simulate a theater lobby where a large number of Armstrong products would be displayed in arcade fashion. The title he proposed was *Armstrong's Circle A Theatre,* referring to the familiar company logo, but the *A* was dropped when someone suggested that the program listing might suggest a series of horse operas.

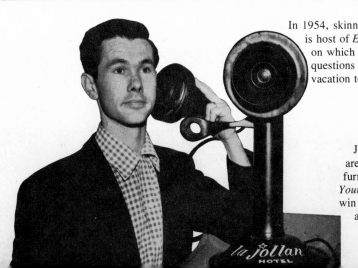

In 1954, skinny comic Johnny Carson is host of *Earn Your Vacation,* a show on which contestants must answer questions to win an all-expenses-paid vacation to the place of their dreams.

Janis Carter and Bud Collyer are MC's of NBC's new home furnishings quiz show, *Feather Your Nest,* on which people can win anything from an ashtray to a completely furnished ranch house.

Barbara Baxley, John Stephen, and Darren McGavin in a dramatic episode of Armstrong Circle Theatre, *an early anthology series.*

72

The first telecast of the Academy Awards takes place in 1954. Running too long, it is cut off before the end of the ceremonies. Future broadcasts will invariably be too long or too short. Bob Hope hosts the event more than fifteen times.

Bing Crosby makes his television debut in 1954 with two specials. Bob Hope and Frank Sinatra guest on one show, sponsored by Edsel, the one product even television cannot sell. In time, the sound track for this historical program is erased accidentally and lost forever.

Respighi's opera ''Sleeping Beauty'' makes its American debut on *Omnibus*. Jim Hawthorne (Prince Charming) and Jo Sullivan sing the principal roles.

Harold Levey, a former arranger for Victor Herbert and a veteran radio conductor, was to compose and direct the theme and background music. The company's commercials would be presented by the attractive team of Kay Campbell and Nelson Case. The search for scripts and stars was to be conducted by BBDO, and NBC provided a producer and a director.

Two early, unsuccessful candidates were quickly replaced by Hudson Faussett as producer and Garry Simpson (now head of Vermont University's television department) as director. The star of the opening program was Brian Aherne, the second major film personality after Robert Montgomery to agree to tackle live television. There were, in fact, no scripts submitted which met the exacting standards set for the show until the program was in its ninth week. Accordingly, the first eight scripts to go on the air (one of which was later the first television drama to be sold as a feature film) were my virgin television efforts, three of them in collaboration with E. Cameron Hawley, all of them but one credited to imaginary writers.

This, obviously, could not continue, and a vigorous search for *new* writers was instituted by BBDO editor Edward B. Roberts, himself a former playwright. In 1950 a writer's only hope of seeing his material aired was to submit a complete script, which became the sole property of the sponsor. Contracts amounted to a one-page release form drawn by BBDO, a far cry from today's lengthy (and necessary) documents dealing with step deals, residuals, secondary rights, limited rewrites, and assorted guarantees.

Armstrong, however, paid top money for all material, regardless of authorship, and among the more than twenty *new* writers whose first New York television exposure was on *The Armstrong Circle Theatre* were names that now read like a TV Hall of Fame, Rod Serling, Frank Gilroy, Anne Howard Bailey, Carey Wilber, and Michelle Cousin.

During the run of the original *Circle Theatre*, Cam Hawley retired and was succeeded by Max Banzhaf as manager of advertising, promotion, and publicity. Banzhaf not only continued the open-door policy for scripts, but considerably broadened the boundaries of subject matter and experimentation, even to commissioning an original television opera, this despite a painfully tightening budget squeeze.

By 1955 practical considerations made it necessary to abandon the star system. Banzhaf made the bold decision to change emphasis from pure entertainment to show biz-cum-public service by means of "actuals," dramas based on issues and events he felt the public should be interested in. The network, so far content to stand by while agencies and sponsors poured money and manpower into developing programs, began to see dollar signs and became interested.

Network control was still some distance off, but network influence became a force to reckon with. NBC's first move in Armstrong's case was to insist on shifting the program to a new time slot more to its advantage and less to the sponsor's. The network also foresaw the superior rating strength of a show with *permanent* stars and applied pressure on Armstrong to revamp the *Circle Theatre*'s format in that direction.

Max Banzhaf resisted. Thus the Armstrong Cork Company became one of the earliest sponsors to reject the dollar-sign syndrome in favor of the company's integrity and established television image. The products advertised were a "considered purchase," not impulse items, and the *right* audience counted more than the *biggest* audience. Two significant decisions ensued—to expand the *Circle Theatre* to a full hour and to move it to CBS, the network that was clearly in its ascendancy.

The behind-the-scenes battle between sponsors and agencies on one hand and networks on the other reached its climax in an FCC public hearing in 1961.

CBS's *The Best of Broadway* spares no expense in bringing top dramatic specials to television. Its first presentation is "The Royal Family" starring Nancy Olson, Fredric March, Helen Hayes, Claudette Colbert, and Kent Smith. This television experiment will be discontinued after one year.

June 5, 1954. *Your Show of Shows* goes off the air. It has made Sid Caesar and Imogene Coca the king and queen of live TV and it has made stars of regulars Carl Reiner and Howard Morris. It has also been the perfect vehicle for such offbeat writers as Neil Simon, Mel Brooks, and Woody Allen. Among the show's most memorable sketches is this spoof of *From Here to Eternity*.

Orson Welles rehearses "King Lear" for Omnibus, *an anthology series hosted by Alistair Cooke, which ran from 1952 to 1959 and presented some of the best programming in TV history.*

This was the Waterloo of the Golden Age. The jubilant networks' test of their new strength was to begin denying time periods to programs that they felt were insufficiently competitive and profitable. Dramatic series that failed to pull a rating were systematically demolished—no matter how effective for their sponsors—by the simple denial of time on the air.

In fairness it must be stated that many advertising agencies had already learned that they could reduce their own overhead by turning more and more shows over to independent outside producers, and this was a concomitant trend. Costs rose to a point where only a handful of advertisers could realistically consider the full sponsorship of a television program even if the option were open to them. Control was partly lost, partly given away, and today the selection of what we may see or not see on television is firmly in the hands of three men whose single purpose is to achieve the greatest possible circulation, which can then be reflected in the rates charged to advertisers.

So—we had our fun, and nobody in the fifties called it a rat race. Mainly because sponsors like Armstrong, U. S. Steel, General Electric, Lux, Goodyear, Philco, Ford, Bigelow, Kraft, Magnavox, Texaco, General Motors, Lucky Strike, Colgate, Pontiac, and Nash were less concerned with the numbers game than with finding fresh talent, less interested in competitive violence than in pleasure. This is not to denigrate the excellence of a *Kojak* or *Mary Tyler Moore,* and certainly not to deny the genius of a Freddy Silverman, but one wistfully wishes from time to time that there could be a few more of him—or that some Cam Hawleys or Max Banzhafs could be in the control room again.

Ira Avery is a former vice-president of BBDO, a television writer and the author of five novels which are not about Madison Avenue.

Newton Minow, then chairman of the FCC but new to television, had openly stated his aversion to what he discovered on the tube, and declared that the obvious cure for the medium's terminal ills was to wrest control from the greedy sponsors and transfer it to the benign embrace of the networks. It was so decreed.

74

While Coca goes off to do an unsuccessful variety program, Caesar stars in *Caesar's Hour,* a show in the *Your Show of Shows* tradition. Nanette Fabray replaces Coca as Caesar's partner; Carl Reiner and Howard Morris stay on as regulars.

Storyteller Somerset Winterset is one of Caesar's most popular characters.

"Well, I'll be a dirty bird." Mild-mannered comic George Gobel begins a five-year stint as host of his own NBC variety show that features Jeff Donnell as his wife Alice and singer Peggy King. It will alternate with the *Eddie Fisher Show* from 1957 to 1959. Here Gobel is visited by Fred MacMurray.

COSTUMING FOR LIVE TV

BILL JOBE

In the early 1950's television was performed live. It is no longer live or lively or alive; it is on film or tape and has become homogenized. In the live days, I was the costume designer on the nation's number one rated program, *The George Gobel Show*. We performed before a live audience every Saturday at 5:00 PM, Pacific Time. In New York, viewers saw the show at the same time at 8:00 PM, Eastern Time. In California, we saw a kinescope of the broadcast at 8:00 PM, our time. Then, we would see our mistakes. Every night was opening night, with fluffed lines, ties askew, flys open, and overstuffed merry widows. It was exciting, immediate, and to do it one had to be young and agile.

We often made costume changes in a minute or less. I remember a suit for Lou Costello on *The Colgate Comedy Hour* that was fastened together like coveralls. The tie hid a zipper and when it was pulled, the entire costume came off and the next change was underneath. The audiences at the El Capitan Theatre thought we were magic.

Those were the days of black and white—no color. However, black couldn't be photographed and white couldn't be photographed. If anyone wore something white next to their face, the reflection created the appearance of needing a shave. Once Sarah Churchill told Tallulah Bankhead that she had been invited to appear on television, and wondered what she should do? Tallulah's baritone advised, "Shave."

The costume department was called the Department of Cleavages and Crotches. The network didn't seem to care what anyone wore as long as there was no

Your Show of Shows, which ran from 1950 to 1954, regularly included elaborate costume sketches. Here Sid Caesar and Imogene Coca spoof "The Sheik," Rudolph Valentino's famous costume movie of the 1920's. Caesar and Coca probably had to make this costume change in two minutes flat.

75

Back in 1951, the radio hit *Meet Corliss Archer,* a comedy about a wacky teenage girl, had come to television as a live show. In 1954 it returns as a filmed series, indicative of the trend in television toward filmed programs. Starring as Corliss is Ann Baker; Bobby Ellis is her boyfriend and John Eldridge is her father.

Love That Bob, a comedy starring movie star Robert Cummings as a photographer with romance on his mind, debuts in 1954. It will play on all three networks before leaving the air in 1961. Dwayne Hickman and Rosemary DeCamp costar.

"The network didn't seem to care what anyone wore as long as there was no cleavage."

Vicki Lawrence as a gambling casino on The Carol Burnett Show.

cleavage. The slightest shadow on bare skin could cause a panic. We always had flowers and bits of lace standing by to add to the fronts of lady performers. It was the period of the merry widow, and ladies were so corseted and the skin so pushed up and around that everyone had curves. Bra cups were stuffed with foam rubber, Kleenex, sweat socks, or whatever was handy. Those flying buttresses looked like the grotesque shape of '53 Cadillac bumpers; it didn't matter as long as no skin showed.

Designer Bob Campel complained of a Durante girl with cleavage starting at the cleft in her chin. (It wasn't Mary Tyler Moore.) Perhaps one of the worst moments was on a Milton Berle show. Ann Sheridan was the guest star. The finale was a South American number. Miss Sheridan had a minute to change from her previous costume to a rumba outfit. In the rush, her right breast was left out of the ruffled top. Before the dresser could check her, impetuous Uncle Miltie pulled her on stage. We stood in the wings and agonized. On the monitor, the fuzzy camera work was on our side, and you couldn't tell the bare bosom from the ruffles.

Dress rehearsal was on-camera, and we could watch the show on a monitor to see what the camera was distorting. On a Steve Allen show, designer Grady Hunt dressed chorus girls in striped panties, with the stripes making a diamond design at the crotch. When the girls came down slides toward the camera, the skirts flew up and the diamonds seemed to wink. Unacceptable. For the actual show, dark panties were used. As they used to say when they didn't know how to get out of a sequence, go to black!

Bill Jobe, a costume designer for Universal Studios, has recently designed for Testimony of Two Men *and* Jaws II.

76

October 3, 1954. *Father Knows Best* debuts. Billy Gray, Lauren Chapin, Elinor Donahue, Jane Wyatt, and Robert Young, who had been in the radio show, comprise the Anderson family of Springfield. CBS announces the show's cancellation but public outcry keeps it on the air.

Preston Foster plays tugboat captain John Herrick on the popular syndicated series *Waterfront,* an adventure show distinguished by the fact that its hero is married.

Richard Boone is Dr. Konrad Styner in *Medic,* which debuts on NBC in 1954. Television's first medical drama is filmed in various Los Angeles hospitals.

THE ZIV TRADITION

TIM ONOSKO

The traditional alternative to network television has always been syndication—an arrangement by which programs are sold or traded directly to independent stations and network affiliates. Today syndication is considered primarily a way for network producers to dump their titles following successful prime time runs. (The most shining example of this is the 179 episodes of *I Love Lucy* which will run, as they say, forever.) But TV syndication has its roots in newspaper syndication, and really began with radio where it predated the network practice of putting old programming out to pasture. If anyone can be called the "father" of TV syndication, it is Frederic W. Ziv, whose last name has often been mistaken for some strange acronym when it appears in his company's log at the tail end of such shows as *Sea Hunt*, *Boston Blackie*, and *Science Fiction Theatre*.

Ziv was a Cincinnati-based producer and distributor of radio programming who, starting in 1937, eventually marketed 37 radio series, including Goodman Ace's *Easy Aces* and Humphrey Bogart's *Bold Venture*, directly to station owners, big and small. Beginning in the early forties, while television was still a dream being kicked around on the pages of *Popular Science*, Ziv began purchasing TV rights simultaneously with radio rights to programs like *The Cisco Kid*. His theory was that, since the development of TV would be slow and limited by federal control, stations would have little choice other than to operate in accordance with the whims of the broadcasting giants whose growth Ziv witnessed in the 1930's. He was the alternative.

> ## "The Cisco Kid is not a corpse. He was alive and well on television this morning."

In February, 1948, Ziv began the TV syndication business with the purchase of the General Film Library of New York—10 million feet of film—for $240,000. In July of that year, another 3.5 million feet of newsreel-style footage was purchased from General Film Library of California, for the price of $100,000, making Ziv Television the largest television film library in the world. The fifteen-minute compilation programs edited from these purchases and packaged under the title *Yesterday's Newsreel* are still being seen on television.

Network officials told Ziv that television was a *live* medium, that he was in the wrong business, and that the medium had little or no use for filmed programming. The prediction, of course, was false. At the start of the 1976 network prime time season, 72 percent of programming was on film. In 1949, disregarding the warnings of the networks, Ziv began production of *The Cisco Kid*, and further flabbergasted the industry by producing the first season in color, despite the lack of a viable way to telecast color film, and the greatly increased cost of production. In 1956, however, Ziv's risk paid off. Early color installations did not yet have color studio cameras and had to depend on film to originate color broadcasts.

Produced by *Studio One* veteran Worthington Miner and written by James Moser, who will later create *Ben Casey*, *Medic* strives for authenticity. One episode even shows the birth of a baby. Blood is often part of the wardrobe.

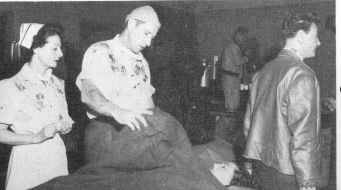

Occasionally, *Medic* tries too hard to show the uglier side of life.

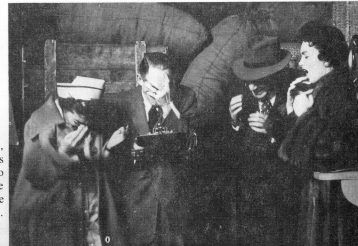

Ziv's Tombstone Territory *professed to be about a newspaper editor, but the real star was Pat Conway, who used his sheriff's guns to tame "the town too tough to die."*

In fact, many of the Ziv series became models for programs in their genres that would follow. Is *Highway Patrol*, for instance, really any different from *Kojak*, *Police Story*, or *Adam-12*, twenty years later? Weren't the Ziv westerns *The Cisco Kid* or *MacKenzies' Raiders* the forerunners of the fifties' and sixties' network western boom? In 1957, beginning with the sale of *Tombstone Territory* to ABC, Ziv even began to supply the networks with shows.

The Ziv quality was behind the camera, as well as in front of it, and the company gave opportunities to many unknown names that are now familiar to viewers. *Star Trek*'s Gene Roddenberry cut his TV teeth on a dozen or so best-forgotten episodes of *I Led Three Lives*. Ziv series figured prominently in the early careers of both John Rich, the director of *All in the Family*, and film producer-director William Castle. Rich was writer-director of the Broderick Crawford vehicle *King of Diamonds* and Castle produced and directed *Men of Annapolis*. Sam Peckinpah, today regarded as a brilliant film director with a brutal style, was the writer on a sometimes poignant episode of *Tombstone Territory*, "Johnny Ringo's Last Ride."

Maybe the best thing that can be said of the Ziv titles is that they are durable. Since 1960, when Frederic Ziv sold out to United Artists Television, most of the Ziv films have consistently been on the air. Occasionally, one of the "big three" will devote an hour or so of its time to a retrospective of television, in the hope that younger viewers will get a taste of what the early days of the medium were like. Fragments of those old programs are dusted off so we can all look at the corpses. But *The Cisco Kid* is not a corpse. He was alive and well on television this morning.

Tim Onosko is a writer with a particular interest in the early days of television.

Perhaps the hallmark of the Ziv series was their look. While the films were not cheap to produce, they had a certain low-budget quality that was reminiscent of the best of the Hollywood "B" dramas. This quality, a somewhat more realistic patina than, say, the average MGM studio production, lent itself well to action dramas, westerns, and cop shows.

78

March 25, 1954. The first commercial RCA color television receivers come off the production line at the company's plant in Bloomington, Indiana.

One of the first shows to emphasize color is *Disneyland*, which debuts on ABC on October 27, 1954. The agreement by Walt Disney Studios (followed by an ABC agreement with Warner Brothers) to produce programs for television changes the industry. The other major movie studios will quickly start TV production as well.

December 15, 1954. "Born on a mountaintop in Tennessee," *Davy Crockett, Indian Fighter* appears as the first of a three-part series about the legendary frontiersman on *Disneyland*. Unknown movie actor Fess Parker, receiving a small salary, stars as the buckskin-clad pioneer. Helene Stanley is Polly Crockett, who dies off-screen in the second episode.

THE SYNDICATION GAME

JOYCE JAFFE

If you are ever selected to appear as a contestant on a game show and are told that your program will be seen in New York and Los Angeles three weeks later and in Miami two weeks after that, then you are most likely appearing on a syndicated television program. So don't be surprised if you are asked to report to NBC studios for the taping and are advised that the show plays on ABC in New York and CBS in Baltimore. And, to confuse matters further, even though you will see yourself at 7:30 P.M., your parents in Miami will have to take the day off from work to see it at 4:00 P.M.

Network programs are fed at a designated date and time via telephone lines or microwave to all stations across the country that are affiliated with a particular network. Syndicated programs, on the other hand, are sold to individual stations regardless of network affiliation. For example, *To Tell the Truth* is produced by Goodson-Todman Enterprises, and sold to local stations by the Firestone Program Syndication Company in return for a commission paid by the producers.

Firestone and his sales force sell *To Tell the Truth* in as many "markets" as possible. The amount of money received depends on the demand for the program, the size of the market and the time of day the show will be aired. Deals are usually made for a year's worth of programming, with a specified number of first runs and reruns. A station will begin broadcasting the series when the desired time slot is available.

Each episode of *To Tell the Truth* is assigned a "show number" and is incorporated into a particular year's programming. New York may be already playing that year's series at the time of the taping, but Minneapolis may not be starting for several months; and perhaps Firestone was not able to make a sale at all in Chicago.

After the show is taped, the master tape is sent to the distributor. Since the stations that have bought the show do not belong to a network, each must receive its own copy of the program. The distributor of *To Tell the Truth* is EUE/Screen Gems, which has been advised what stations are going to play the show and is equipped to make copies ("dubs") of the master tape. As it would be extraordinarily expensive to make dubs for all stations playing the show, and it is not necessary for all stations to play the show on the same date, one dub is used to service several stations. This process is called "bicycling." A program may be sent to WABC in New York which will send it on to WBZ in Boston for airing later and so on until the last station returns it to EUE.

Sometimes it can take as long as two years for a particular show to appear in any given city. As with most syndication, a series of *To Tell the Truth* programs may be sold in any market as long as it has never played in that market before. Syndication may be confusing, but it does enable most of your friends and relatives across the country to catch your appearance as a game show contestant at one time or another—the bicycling phenomenon and the syndication sale insure your national reputation.

Joyce Jaffe has been in the syndication game for about eight years, most recently as manager of Syndication Operations for Goodson-Todman Productions.

February 23, 1955. By the time the final episode, "Davy Crockett at The Alamo" is presented, the country has gone Davy Crockett crazy. Davy Crockett outfits, coonskin caps, bubble gum cards, books, and records flood the market. Kids learn the twenty-verse song. *Davy Crockett, King of the Wild Frontier*, a movie edited from the TV shows, becomes one of 1955's top moneymakers. Joining the now-famous Parker at the Alamo's last stand are (L to R) Hans Conried, Nick Cravat, and Buddy Ebsen, who plays Davy's partner George Russell.

Walt Disney's *The Mickey Mouse Club* debuts in 1955. Featuring songs and dances and exclusive films from the Walt Disney library, this daily show quickly becomes the top-rated after-school children's program. Kids all over America want to be Mouseketeers and sing with host Jimmie Dodd.

AN OPEN LETTER TO THE NETWORKS

Once upon a time, in order to save money and fill insignificant time slots, the television networks ran and reran old standard sitcoms and series over and over again until finally these classics had been run into the ground. Then there was a dry spell, and a good many of the best old standards were not to be seen at all. Eventually, the rumor goes, some far-thinking TV executive decided it was time to get shows like *Our Miss Brooks* back on the air—not because they could be replayed without further payment of royalties to the casts, but because they were classics that remained funny despite the passage of years. Unfortunately, this idea was ahead of its time. Viewers still resented reruns simply because they were reruns, and perhaps because they remembered the days when it was virtually *My Little Margie, Amos 'n' Andy,* and *I Married Joan* from dawn to dusk. Not only did the initial classic rerun campaign flop, but it evidently established an ironclad rule that the public could never be made to swallow another campaign like it. Only *The Honeymooners* and *I Love Lucy* have been able to break through this embargo on the past. I have even begun to fear that, as a result of this programming decision and in order to make more storage space in warehouses, film for a number of TV's true classics has been discarded or even destroyed. If so, the loss to the television viewers of America is immense.

Now, I know that the networks have had occasional ninety-minute and two-hour specials covering the past few decades of TV, but I don't think this is enough. Even so, I will admit that a number of shows I would love to see again (not in two-minute seg-

Although Mr. Peepers, *starring Wally Cox as Robinson J. Peepers and Tony Randall as Harvey Weskitt, ran from 1952 to 1955, it was a classic comedy, and yet many of today's viewers have not had an opportunity to see it.*

ments, but in their entirety), I would not want to watch with fervent devotion for months on end. The solution, it appears, falls somewhere between these two extremes. It could be the basis for a summer TV festival.

If each network selected some half-hour Monday-through-Friday time slot, and ran five episodes of a different series every week, the result would be a fabulously entertaining summer of one great show after another. This format would permit the showing of all the true TV classics; it would also make possible the showing of "collectors' items," that, although somewhat dated, would be great fun to see for a little while.

Tall Clint Walker plays the title role in *Cheyenne* in one of four rotating series on *Warner Brothers Presents* on ABC. While the three other segments, *Casablanca, King's Row,* and *Conflict* fall by the wayside, the first hour-long adult western builds an audience.

Another adult western that begins in 1955 on ABC is *The Life and Legend of Wyatt Earp,* starring Hugh O'Brian (usually without an eye patch). It will last until 1961, during which time the scripts that tell the story of the man who supposedly cleaned up Dodge City and Tombstone will rely more on legend than life and will cater more and more to children.

Guest Raymond Burr defends accused murderer Jack Benny on The Jack Benny Program *in 1964. Excellent shows like these ought to be available to contemporary viewers.*

Of the series that were naturally delightful, the most obvious would be *Our Miss Brooks,* followed by *Amos 'n' Andy; I Married Joan; Mr. Peepers; The Adventures of Hiram Holliday: Maverick; Fair Exchange;* and *The Thin Man,* to name a few.

". . . the loss to the television viewers of America is immense."

Of the "collectors' items," less well-remembered shows come to mine—*Stanley,* if only to see Buddy Hackett and Carol Burnett when they were just making their reputations; *Heaven for Betsy,* to see Jack Lemmon in a sitcom; *Pride of the Family* for an adolescent Natalie Wood and a post–*King Kong* Fay Wray; *The Buccaneers,* to see a swashbuckling Robert Shaw; and, for the real connoisseurs, *Bonino* (with Ezio Pinza) and *The Halls of Ivy* (with Ronald Colman and Benita Hume).

Indeed, if each network had more than a half-hour slot to spare—and if live broadcasts were preserved on film for posterity—the mind boggles at the treasures to be seen: Margot Fonteyn in *The Sleeping Beauty* ballet; Paul Newman, Frank Sinatra, and Eva Marie Saint in *Our Town;* Rod Steiger in *Marty;* Humphrey Bogart, Lauren Bacall, and Henry Fonda in *The Petrified Forest;* Alfred Lunt and Lynn Fontanne in *The Great Sebastians;* and Laurence Olivier and Judith Anderson leading an all-star cast in *The Moon and Sixpence.*

I cannot believe that the networks have never thought of this. There may be reasons why doing it would be impossible, or uneconomical, or incredibly stupid. However, if what the networks have been waiting for is encouragement from the viewer at home, there *are* ways to run a survey—to which, I suspect, the response would be overwhelmingly positive.

A Viewer At Home

81

September 10, 1955. Marshall Matt Dillon and the longtime radio hit, *Gunsmoke,* comes to television on CBS. James Arness stars in the role John Wayne rejected. Amanda Blake plays Kitty Russell; Milburn Stone plays Doc Adams; and Dennis Weaver plays the limping Chester Goode.

Another popular television animal is Yukon King, who co-stars with Richard Simmons in the colorful adventure series for kids, *Sergeant Preston of the Yukon.*

Fury is a modern-day western for kids on Saturday mornings. It stars James Arness's brother Peter Graves, young Bobby Diamond as the orphan Graves takes home to his Broken Wheel Ranch, and William Fawcett. The brave stallion, Fury, is played by Gypsy.

THE NEW TREND IN TV PROGRAMMING

MICHAEL SHAMBERG AND MEGAN WILLIAMS

In the mid-1970's, network news switched from film to videotape. Handheld TV cameras and portable video recorders replaced 16-mm film. This new system was given the rather unimaginative name ENG—an acronym for "electronic news gathering."

ENG is more than just a different way to "gather" news. It means different news can be gathered. Various terrorist groups have gotten into TV programming because ENG can go virtually anywhere to cover them live. Because videotape is cheap and reusable, reporters can spend the same amount of time on a story while shooting more footage. This means more thorough coverage, more natural behavior to edit from, and fewer "talking heads."

The next big change in TV style will be in dramatic and entertainment programming. As with ENG, the change will be brought about by new techniques made possible by a new technology. That technology consists of the same minicams used for news, combined with newly designed one-inch videotape recorders manufactured by Sony, Ampex, and others.

Two-inch videotape has been the industry standard for the last twenty-five years. But at $150,000 per recorder it is too expensive to encourage experimentation. Two-inch video is also difficult to edit because the image cannot be seen when the tape is played in reverse or at high speed. Expensive,

computer-controlled editing equipment is needed to work with two-inch tape, whereas film can be edited on relatively inexpensive equipment on which an image is visible at all times.

One-inch videotape allows for hands-on, Movieola-style editing similar to the film editing process. Handheld minicams permit film-style shooting in video. The quality of this hybrid system matches both two-inch videotape and 35-mm film and it is about two-thirds cheaper.

The three networks have already begun to convert their soundstages to one-inch video. But its real impact will come in moving TV entertainment—particularly comedy—outdoors and on location.

Most sitcoms are really drawing room comedies that depend exclusively on dialogue because they are shot on sound stages with static cameras. The new video will mean more "reality based" characters who act in the real world and don't just talk about it. Their lifestyles will be based on mobility rather than staying home. The next Archie Bunker, for example, will probably be a retiree who drives around the country in a Winnebago rec-vee in search of people to dislike. The next Mary Tyler Moore will actually go out and cover a news story.

The look of "reality base" shows will totally blur the line between fiction and nonfiction TV. Ac-

Sergeant Ernie Bilko of Fort Baxter in Roseville, Kansas. Phil Silvers stars as the army's most ingenious, money-hungry con man in *You'll Never Get Rich*, which debuts in 1955 on CBS. On its way to becoming a TV comedy classic, the show will win Emmys in 1955 for Best Comedy Series, Best Actor (Silvers), Best Comedian (Silvers), Best Writing, and Best Director (creator Nat Hiken).

Paul Ford plays Colonel Hall who likes to pretend that he, and not Sergeant Bilko, is running Fort Baxter.

The people of TVTV, an independent TV production company.

tors like Archie Bunker already serve as dramatic newscasters. You read about something in the paper one week; next week it's the subject of *All in the Family*. Because television is about people, and people are not facts and not myths but a mixture of both, it's just a matter of time before fictional characters are dropped into nonfiction situations.

CBS's *60 Minutes*, a news show, is already an entertainment hit. In the future, we can expect to see "information sitcoms" which mix the content of news with the context of scripted situation comedy. Imagine a fictional news team, whose "off-camera" lives are presented as subplots woven into the real events they cover. Or gonzo camera crews like so many video Hunter Thompsons who use the news as a premise for their own improvisation.

In TVTV's documentary "Super Bowl" (1976), we experimented with an actor who played a football fan whose wife had run off with a Pittsburgh Steeler.

In "TVTV Looks at the Oscars," about the 1976 Academy Awards, Lily Tomlin played a fictional TV viewer who watched and commented on the Oscars telecast. We call these characters "super fans." In the future, we imagine that the super fan format can be applied to any event requiring a character with the access of a commentator and the mentality of a spectator.

At the other end of the spectrum, real people playing *themselves* will enter the entertainment marketplace. Already, former presidents Ford and Nixon, along with Henry Kissinger, have sold themselves to the highest bidding network. The President recently made himself available for "A Day in the Life of Jimmy Carter," but the next step is for the networks to option the lives of public figures even before they step back into private life. Every two years, for example, there might be a congressional draft, just as there is in football, where new congressmen and senators sell their career stories to ABC, NBC, or CBS.

Comedy acting will be more visual and less verbal because the richness of locations will decrease the need for forcing dialogue to support performances. Very little of Ernie Kovacs's work had much dialogue, and it was all shot on video. If he were still alive he would undoubtedly be using the new video on location for even more extreme sight gags.

Finally, low-cost versions of the new video equipment are already available for home use. Just as kids make home movies and want to be filmmakers, the upcoming TV generation will probably infiltrate commercial television with new stories and styles based on growing up in the age of media.

Michael Shamberg and Megan Williams, co-founders of TVTV, an independent TV production house, are currently at work developing new forms for commercial broadcasting.

March 15, 1955. Andy Griffith (L) is naïve country boy Will Stockdale in the TV adaptation of the comedy-play, "No Time For Sergeants," on *The United States Steel Hour*. He will later repeat the role on Broadway and in the movies. Also in the cast are (L-R) Eddie LeRoy, Bob Hastings, and Arthur Storch.

Greer Garson and Peter Lorre star in Robert Sherwood's "Reunion in Vienna" on NBC's prestigious monthly live telecast *Producers' Showcase*. It is produced by Fred Coe who also produced *The Philco-Goodyear Television Playhouse*.

March 7, 1955. Mary Martin and her daughter Heller Halliday sing "I've Gotta Crow" in "Peter Pan" on *Producers' Showcase*. Sixty-five million viewers watch this first TV network presentation of a complete Broadway production, which is 1955's top program.

CHALLENGING THE NETWORKS

RICHARD GOLDSTEIN

The year 1976 is remembered as the year ABC, the maverick among networks, dislodged its competition to become the most powerful force in television; 1977 will be remembered as the year the other networks scrambled to recoup their losses, belching out mini-novels and extravaganzas to little avail; and 1978 may be remembered as the year the networks realized it didn't matter who was on top—they were all being rendered obsolete.

Forces at work in television today—independent investment, technological innovation, rebelliousness among advertisers—are conspiring to open up America's most sheltered form of entertainment. No film studio or record company exercises the kind of control over the form and content of its productions that the TV networks do. In defense, they cry necessity: no medium is subject to such a variety of pressures, they claim—from the trepidation of advertisers to the hand of government, which is alleged to be ever-poised for the strike. In fact, aside from assailing the independence of TV news, the FCC has done little to fulfill its mandate, which is to assure responsibility among those who seek to profit from the airwaves, which actually are held, by law, to belong to the people.

But the legislation which has regulated broadcasting since the 1930's is about to be rewritten, and many in Congress are pressing for greater competition within television, especially from the burgeoning cable industry. At present, cable is forbidden to bid against networks for entertainment events. But under new legislation, the networks may find themselves wearing hollow crowns, as cable syndicates offer

> "What the record industry learned from rock 'n' roll . . . is beginning to haunt TV."

first-run movies and R-rated variety shows, *without commercials,* through the magic of pay TV.

But even those who resent paying for TV are losing their allegiance to the networks. David Frost's decision to broadcast his Nixon interviews on independent stations did not hurt his ratings at all. Nixon beat the networks cold, as he always wanted to do, and the lesson has not been lost on syndicators. There is definitely a growing market for syndicated programming, independently produced.

Not long ago, the largest supplier of TV shows, MCA-TV, entered into an agreement with ninety-five unaffiliated stations to finance and distribute entertainment outside network hands. Its first effort, a mini-series called *Testimony of Two Men,* turned a profit for everyone, accelerating talk of a "fourth network." Though that is unlikely, it is certainly true that viewer dissatisfaction has given independents a wedge into the huge programming competition being run by the networks. As Norman Lear discovered when he sold *Mary Hartman, Mary Hartman* into syndication after the networks had rejected it, viewers respond to anything that breaks with the rigid insensibility of the prime time mold.

And the quality of that response may be more

September 11, 1955. Mary Martin (R) also stars in Thornton Wilder's "The Skin of Our Teeth," the premiere presentation of NBC's *Color Spread.* Also in the cast are (L-R) Helen Hayes, Heller Halliday, and George Abbott.

September 24, 1955. Judy Garland makes her television debut, on CBS's *Ford Star Jubilee,* singing the songs she has made famous. Here she dances with The Escorts.

MH, MH, *rejected by the networks, brought a new young look to syndicated programming.*

Corn-fed cuties are portrayed by *Those Whiting Girls,* Margaret (R), her sister Barbara (C) and Mabel Albertson, who plays their mother, in a song-and-dance routine in an episode of their summer series in 1955

Jackie Gleason decides to concentrate exclusively on *The Honeymooners* in 1955. Audrey Meadows replaces Pert Kelton as Alice Kramden. Art Carney and Joyce Randolph play Ed and Trixie Norton.

Child movie star Jackie Cooper comes to TV in 1955 as Sock Miller in the popular comedy *The People's Choice,* which will stay on CBS until 1958. Patricia Breslin plays Mandy Peoples whom Miller will secretly marry. Cleo, the dog, comments on all activities through voice-over dubbing.

Space: 1999 *offers syndicated sci-fi fun to young audiences being neglected by the networks.*

important than its quantity. TV programmers have always striven for the broadest possible appeal, but in the 1970's, the fallacy of that quest is becoming clear, as shows that appeal to *no one* beyond surface tolerance drive great numbers of viewers into the arms of the independents. What the record industry learned from rock 'n' roll—that a sub-genre could emerge as the dominant form in popular culture, simply because it expressed itself in a personal way—is beginning to haunt TV. If the networks are to hold their own, they must acknowledge the heterogeneity of their audience. Urban people are not like rural people; blacks are not like whites; after rock, the young are not like the old.

When Newton Minow, FCC commissioner,

warned in 1961 that TV was a "vast wasteland," it was feared that television's ubiquity would destroy regional America, that everyone would come to speak and think alike. Now we see how persistent is the American affection for variety. And it is that affection, even more than the anger of sponsors or the snippiness of government, that is finally forcing television to change. The people and their desire for better television are the straw that will break the camel's back.

Richard Goldstein is a senior editor of the Village Voice *and the author of* The Poetry of Rock.

86

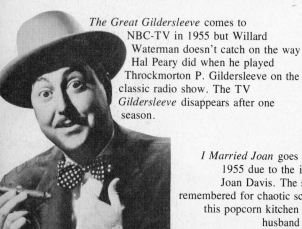

The Great Gildersleeve comes to NBC-TV in 1955 but Willard Waterman doesn't catch on the way Hal Peary did when he played Throckmorton P. Gildersleeve on the classic radio show. The TV *Gildersleeve* disappears after one season.

I Married Joan goes off the air in 1955 due to the illness of star Joan Davis. The show will be remembered for chaotic scenes such as this popcorn kitchen debacle with husband Jim Backus.

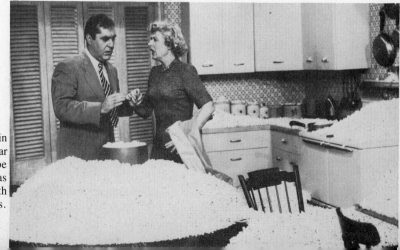

III. THE COMPANION MACHINE

October 3, 1955. *Captain Kangaroo* moves into CBS's *Treasure House*. Bob Keeshan, who had played the clown Clarabell on *Howdy Doody,* delights and educates kids with songs, puppets, animals, cartoons, and stories.

The old Hal Roach movie shorts *The Little Rascals* are syndicated nationwide in 1955. And, like the Laurel and Hardy shorts Roach brought to TV in 1948, these films are great discoveries for children and adults. The most popular "our gang" ensemble consists of (L-R) Alfalfa, Buckwheat, Spanky, Petey, and Porky.

Although Jim Backus is visible in *I Married Joan,* his main claim to fame is as the voice of Mr. Magoo. In 1955, few cartoons are shown on television; most of those shown originally ran in theaters.

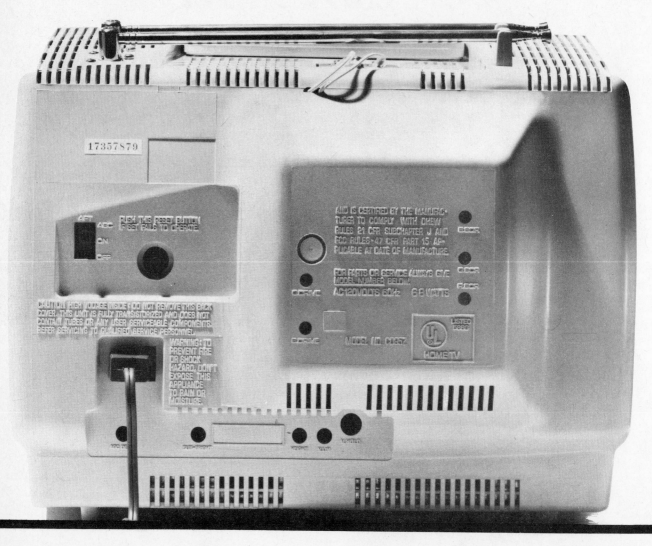

Johnny Weissmuller, the most famous Tarzan of them all, comes to TV in the syndicated kids' program *Jungle Jim*, re-creating another of his movie characters. Here he exchanges looks with guest Anita Lhoest while Dick Vallin is ignored.

Irish McCalla will become a cult favorite as the female answer to Tarzan, *Sheena, Queen of the Jungle.*

Although Davy Crockett, "King of the Wild Frontier," was killed off at the Alamo, his popularity necessitates his rebirth in "Davy Crockett's Keelboat Race" and "Davy Crockett and the River Pirates" on *Disneyland* in late 1955. Here Davy competes with Big Foot Mason (Mike Mazurki) in a shooting contest.

THE GAME SHOW HABIT
MAXENE FABE

I am one of 40 million fully-grown Americans who are addicted to game shows that ring, buzz, gong, klunk, and zonk from the TV set every morning and afternoon and now into the early evening hours as well.

What makes the shows so popular? They command 40 percent of the entire daytime viewing audience of housewives, college students, retirees, shut-ins, night shift workers, kids home from school with the sniffles, and me. They occupied a key place in the careers of Groucho Marx, Johnny Carson, Mike Wallace, Jack Paar, Merv Griffin, Bert Parks, Walter Cronkite, Jackie Gleason, and even Jacqueline Susann. They have made culture heroes out of Monty Hall, Ralph Edwards, Bill Cullen, Allen Ludden, Gene Rayburn, Jan Murray, and Peter Marshall, and saved a slew of aging and/or faltering celebrities from the Hollywood glue factory. They have weathered scandals in the past, and continue to survive periodic glut and *As the World Turns*. The networks love them too because they are the most inexpensive form of television to produce. The profit margin from game show advertising revenues runs between 500 and 800 percent. Quite simply, game shows finance all of prime time television: on all three networks, they generate over $600 million a year, or 60 percent of the networks' total gross income, with plenty left over for successful packagers like Goodson-Todman, Heatter-Quigley, Hatos-Hall, and Chuck Barris to have become multimillionaires.

Still, without the viewers there would be no games. For when ratings dip, sponsors with their

Beat the Clock, *a game show classic, pitted contestants against a ticking clock as they performed zany stunts.*

Vega hatchbacks and Broyhill dining rooms, Rice-a-roni, and Chapstick, swiftly steal away. Just what *is* it then that appeals to us game show addicts?

"Greed," the popular press is quick to say. But it's not greed or envy or crassness or veniality. With-

89

More and more, science fiction shows stress technical devices. *Science Fiction Theatre,* a fairly sober sci-fi program hosted by Truman Bradley, often uses elaborate sets to sustain viewer interest.

Queen for a Day debuts on ABC in 1955 with Jack Bailey hosting. Each day several women tell heartbreaking stories. The audience elects the most pathetic "queen," and she wins prizes galore. The others go home.

What's My Line *kept its panelists guessing for 17 years.*

"... if the game's any good, you'll find yourself talking to your television set."

out question, the vision of someone's winning $25,000 or a new car or a trip to Paris for half an hour's fun is an arresting one, motivation perhaps to keep watching or even to try to get on a show oneself. But is that greed?

No, people watch games for another reason entirely. For one thing, they are practically impossible not to watch, and are deliberately designed with that wonderfully insidious goal in mind. The secret of a successful game show's popularity is simplicity itself and can be summed up in one word: kibbitzing. You, as viewer, must be able to play along, to test yourself against the game, to yell advice when a contestant finds him or herself in a dilemma, to care about who wins and be sorry for who doesn't. The ultimate index: if the same is any good, you'll find yourself talking to your television.

This happens to be a totally original concept. The game show is a genre unique to television, without antecedents and untranslatable elsewhere. To be sure, there were "quiz shows" dating back to radio. But, a quiz is not a game. It has a static question-and-answer format that not even such suspense-injecting elements as sympathetic contestants, huge stakes, and blatant tampering can disguise forever. Ultimately, viewer boredom, not the scandals, killed the TV quiz. But devise a successful game, involve your audience, and the novelty never wears off. You will have invented an *institution* that will last ten, fifteen, and in the case of *What's My Line* (a show whose top prize was all of $50), seventeen years.

But game shows are far more than an audience of home viewers talking to their television. They touch on something deeper. Day after day they reveal the sight of people just like us being tested in real-life dramas whose outcome is unknown, and where behind Door Number 3 lies not only a refrigerator but the literal chance to change their lives. We watch because we must, to see how people act when it matters desperately what choice they make. And we ask: if it were *me* at this Judgment, before these pearly gates, offered this Reward, could *I* cut it? Would I be graceful under pressure? If I lost, would I be as good a sport? If I won, *would I be changed?* On television, game shows come and go and endure—their contestants, hosts, prizes, and riddles interchangeable—not out of greed, not out of mediocrity, but because of the larger riddle they pose.

Jan Murray, a former host of *Songs for Sale Dollar a Second,* has his own fifteen-minute variety show in 1955 following the NBC fights. His most successful giveaway show, *Treasure Hunt,* lasts from 1956 to 1960.

June 7, 1955. *The $64,000 Question* debuts on CBS, with Hal March as MC. It will temporarily dislodge *I Love Lucy* as television's top-rated program, and it will start a whole wave of big-money game shows broadcast in prime time. Within a year, CBS will televise *The $64,000 Challenge* with past winners from *The $64,000 Question* competing.

Marvin Miller is not a game show host. He plays Michael Anthony who gives away one million dollars of John Beresford Tipton's fortune each week on *The Millionaire,* which runs on CBS from 1955 to 1960.

THE BIG QUIZ SCANDALS

MAXENE FABE

January 1955: Louis G. Cowan, a forty-five-year-old TV packager, and father of long-time radio hits *Quiz Kids* and *Stop the Music,* is sitting in his Park Avenue study one morning, and dreams up a quiz show that will showcase the common man with uncommon knowledge. The figure $64,000 pops into his head—a quantum leap from the $64 question once offered on a radio quiz, *Take It or Leave It.* Cowan experiences a decided feeling of euphoria, rushes out to line up a sponsor: Revlon.

June 5, 1955: Tuesday night at 10:00 P.M. *The $64,000 Question* airs on CBS, complete with cool MC Hal March, an IBM question selector, isolation booth, Ben Feit, a New York Manufacturer's Trust bank officer, and catchy "think music." The show is an immediate smash. While it's on, the nation's crime rate drops. So do movie, baseball, and bingo attendance, water consumption and long distance calls. The night that shoemaker Gino Prato decides to keep the $32,000 and not go for the $64,000 question in opera, 55 million Americans are watching. The show receives a 57.1 Trendex rating and an 84.8 percent share. Revlon stock soars and women completely deplete the nation's drugstore shelves of Living Lipstick. Louis G. Cowan is made a vice-president of CBS.

April 8, 1956. A Sunday night. *The $64,000 Challenge* premieres on CBS. Champions from *The $64,000 Question* face adversaries in twin isolation booths who are asked the same questions. The show features celebrity contestants, such as Vincent Price who challenges Edward G. Robinson on art.

By July 1956: *The $64,000 Question* and *The*

> ## " 'I was told by the producers of *Twenty-One* to purposely lose to Van Doren . . .' "

$64,000 Challenge are the number one and two rated shows on television.

September 12, 1956: A Wednesday night. NBC enters the big money sweepstakes with *Twenty-One.* The show is a Jack Barry–Dan Enright production, sponsored by Geritol and Serutan ("That's nature's spelled backwards"). Like *The $64,000 Challenge, Twenty-One* pits two contestants against each other in twin isolation booths. But there is a bonus: they have the opportunity to win an *unlimited* amount of money.

Spring 1957: *Twenty-One's* ratings have remained desultory until the appearance of a most attractive contestant. His name is Charles Van Doren. A modest young graduate student and scion of a distinguished literary family, Van Doren defeats Herbert Stempel, whose arrogant brilliance has been irritating viewers. Van Doren goes on to win $129,000 before being defeated by Vivienne Nearing. The photogenic Van Doren becomes a household word, achieving over the next few years the cover of *Time,* guest appearances on *The Steve Allen Show,* love and marriage, and a $50,000-a-year contract with NBC on *The Today Show.* So popular does *Twenty-One* become that NBC purchases it from Barry-Enright from $2.2 million dollars to ensure that it will continue cutting

Gary Crosby (Bing's boy) and Cathy Crosby (Bob's girl) prepare a duet for the *Bob Crosby Show* shown weekdays on CBS.

Singer-impressionist Edie Adams is a regular on her husband's *The Ernie Kovacs Show* on NBC in 1955. Comedian Kovacs, who has had several short-lived local and network satirical revue programs since 1950, will have several more once this program goes off in six months. Kovacs is the first television comedy director to experiment with untried camera and sound techniques.

Charles Van Doren, in isolation booth, won $129,000 on 21 before testifying to a House Subcommittee that he had cheated.

into the ratings of *I Love Lucy.*

Meanwhile, to bolster their now sagging ratings and increasing viewer boredom, *The $64,000 Question* and *Challenge* announce they will quadruple their stakes. Contestant Teddy Nadler wins $264,000, the highest amount ever won on a quiz show, higher even than *Twenty-One* contestant Elfrida von Nardroff's $220,500.

Still, though the public will not fully realize it for another year-and-a-half, trouble is brewing in Quiz Show Land. Stempel has cried foul. "I was told by the producers of *Twenty-One* to purposely lose to Van Doren," he attests, "and I can prove it." He approaches the newspapers. It's a juicy story, all right, but *Twenty-One* producer Dan Enright denies the allegation, and the papers, fearing libel, decline to print it.

August 1957: *Look* and *Time* magazines both publish stories about how quiz shows, including *The $64,000 Question* and *Challenge* are "controlled." The stories are not specific and fail to make waves.

May 1958: The first serious rumblings of rigging come not from the big quizzes but from a peripheral NBC show called *Dotto,* which requires contestants to guess famous caricatures by filling in the dots. Waiting backstage, standby contestant Edward Hilgemeier chances to witness *Dotto*'s current champion studying a notebook. It contains the show's answers, furnished to the champion by the producers. Hilgemeier calls the New York *Post,* which cautiously first informs the FCC and the New York City district attorney's office. When *Dotto* is abruptly canceled, the *Post* prints Hilgemeier's story. The impact on the public is instan-

92

Oscar Levant—musician, wit, and intellectual—is often a guest on talk shows in the 1950's. He and his wife June have their own relaxed program on KTLA in Los Angeles.

KTLA veteran Lawrence Welk brings "champagne music" to ABC in 1955. The most popular of his many regulars are The Lennon Sisters—(L - R) Dianne, Janet, Peggy, and Cathy—who will soon be featured in comic books. Along with "champagne lady" Alice Lon, The Lennon Sisters will eventually have a falling out with Welk and go off on their own.

Jack Narz was host of Dotto, *the first quiz show canceled for cheating.* $64,000 Question *and* 21 *soon followed.*

taneous and serves to give focus to the rumors long circulating about *The $64,000 Question, The $64,000 Challenge,* and *Twenty-One.* Quiz show ratings plummet. And finally, at long last, the New York *Journal-American* prints Herbert Stempel's story.

August 1958: New York district attorney Frank Hogan responds to the mounting demand for hard information about quiz shows by opening a grand jury. It will sit nine months and hear two hundred witnesses. Barry and Enright resign from their posts to devote their full time to "disproving the unfounded charges against the integrity of our programs." *Twenty-One* producer Albert Freedman is indicted on two counts of perjury and led away in handcuffs.

Hogan declares that one hundred fifty of his witnesses have also perjured themselves. Still, there is no law on the books making it illegal to rig a quiz show and at first it looks as if the matter will die when the grand jury's findings are impounded by the judge and no indictments are forthcoming.

October 1959: The matter does not die. The grand jury foreman publicly declares his indignation over the suppression of the information. Now, Congress enters the picture. Oren Harris, Democratic congressman from Arkansas, calls the House Legislative Oversight Committee to probe the big money quizzes and, later, the use of "payola" on radio and TV. For now, however, national attention focuses on Charles Van Doren, who continues steadfastly to maintain his innocence. Subpoenaed, Van Doren hides for several days, then decides to bare his soul.

November 2, 1959: Charles Van Doren faces the subcommittee and testifies, "I was deeply involved in a deception." He reveals that he was provided with answers and ad-libs, and coached to hesitate, stammer, return to parts of questions later, and pat his brow to build suspense. The nation is stunned. President Eisenhower declares the deception "a terrible thing to do to the American public." Dave Garroway cries on *The Today Show.* The networks, declaring their ignorance of what has been going on, cancel all remaining big money quizzes and refuse to hire anyone connected with them, including new NBC anchor man, Charles Van Doren. Louis G. Cowan, president of CBS, is fired. Rigging a quiz show becomes a felony. The vigilant network standards and practices departments are born to guarantee that nothing like the quiz show scandals will ever happen again.

Maxene Fabe, a former contestant on Jeopardy, *is the author of a forthcoming book,* Game Shows!

93

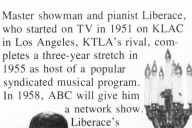

Master showman and pianist Liberace, who started on TV in 1951 on KLAC in Los Angeles, KTLA's rival, completes a three-year stretch in 1955 as host of a popular syndicated musical program. In 1958, ABC will give him a network show. Liberace's orchestra is conducted by his brother George.

In 1955, Tennessee Ernie Ford will host his own musical-variety show. He will remain on NBC until 1960, during which time his hit record "Sixteen Tons" will sell millions of copies. In 1960, Ford will move to ABC for a year.

Red Foley hosts *Jubilee U.S.A.* on ABC beginning in 1955; it lasts until 1961.

THE CONTESTANT CONTEST
WILLIAM MORRIS

I tried to become a contestant on a couple of quiz shows, but never managed to weather the selection process. A certain type of contestant is desired, and apparently I am not it. My experience was instructive, however. Here's what happened.

In 1975 my wife and I were the proprietors of a quietly floundering jewelry store in Manhattan Beach, California. Since we had no customers, we had plenty of time to read the Los Angeles *Times* every day. One day I noticed a small ad under "announcements." It said, "Quiz show contestants needed. *The Joker's Wild*. Call Evelyn. 880-4051."

Since my wife and I occasionally watched this show while malingering around the house, we knew perfectly well that contestants were winning cash prizes of up to $25,000. Also, from everything we'd ever heard, appearing on quiz programs was supposed to be a lot of fun. So we decided to respond to the ad. We would split the responsibilities. My wife would call the number. I would go on the show.

Two weeks later I found myself waiting with several other nervous, but ordinary, people in a corridor on the fourteenth floor of a Century City office building. A chain-smoking secretary of thirty-five or so ran the selection process. She led us into a testing room.

"Are you Evelyn?" someone asked.

"There is no Evelyn," the woman replied ominously.

Suddenly all the prospective contestants relaxed and started to smile. We introduced ourselves to each other. There were housewives, a teacher, and a glib shoe salesman from Orange County. A frazzled young girl sat next to me. She had split ends and no job.

Tests were distributed with instructions. Questions on the actual show usually concerned matters of general knowledge, which bordered on the trivial. The test of our ability to compete was ridiculously easy. One question asked: "Which of the following is not a country? . . . England, France, catsup." I noticed that the unemployed girl was struggling.

After the tests were collected, we were each given a piece of paper and asked to write down our most embarrassing experience. As contestants are introduced on the show, some embarrassing moment in their lives is revealed by the MC, Jack Barrie. This gives Barrie a chance to do a little leering, and get a few easy laughs at each guest's expense.

I thought for awhile, and then wrote down an episode I once had with a Mexican epileptic in Baja California. Meanwhile I noticed that "split ends" had written, "Being stuck in a pay toilet without the money and having to pee."

"Listen," I told her paternally, "you'll have to do better than that if you want to get on the show."

"No talking!" snapped the woman who was not Evelyn.

After pictures, and then a short break, some of us were asked to remain. I waited in vain for my name to be called. Split ends smiled wryly. She was the first one chosen to stay.

I had made several mistakes. I appeared too smart. It would have been better to miss a few questions intentionally than to get them all right. I hadn't

Perry Como is the one person even Ginger Rogers can't teach to dance. The relaxed, unassuming singer had begun in TV in 1948 on *The Chesterfield Supper Club*, and had hosted a fifteen-minute show since 1950. His new hour-long series that debuts on NBC in 1955 quickly takes over television on Saturday nights. Already popular with adults, his new songs for the younger generation move to the top of the charts.

Como's top comedy writer is Goodman Ace, who had co-starred with his wife Jane in the hit radio series *Easy Aces* as well as a TV version on Dumont in 1949, and had written for Milton Berle between 1952 and 1954.

In 1955 Milton Berle's star begins to fade. The three-year-old *Milton Berle Show* (which followed *Texaco Star Theatre*) changes its format in September in an attempt to boost ratings. But on June 5, 1956, Berle's show will be dropped. Here Berle is visited by Henny Youngman.

Host Monty Hall makes a deal with hopeful contestant.

smiled enough, and my embarrassing experience wasn't embarrassing enough.

I have subsequently learned that different shows look for different things in their contestants. All shows want people who are good at playing their particular game, or answering their particular kinds of questions, or relating to their particular kinds of guest stars. But some shows want conventionally attractive people whom viewers would like to spend time with, while others also take vulnerable and even stupid types with whom audiences can empathize. The girl with split ends was a good example of this category. And, of course, excitable people who jump and scream a lot are popular on almost all quiz and game shows. I was not daunted by rejection on *The Joker's Wild,* and the lure of the loot was still strong. I decided to learn from my experience and try to get on another show.

At the recommendation of a friend who had won a few small prizes on the show, *Concentration,* I called the number given at the end of that show. Two weeks later I found myself with ten more or less ordinary-looking people in the corridor on the fourteenth floor of

a Hollywood office building. A chain-smoking secretary of about thirty-five led us into an inner room. The approach was a little different here.

"Listen," she said, "we're not like some of those other game shows. We don't want you to go wild out there, but we do want you to look like you're enjoying yourselves. So smile, be happy, have fun."

Everyone got the message. The smiles were flying thick and fast. I hadn't seen that many teeth since *Jaws.* I tried to be as affable as I could. The only problem was, my smile kept breaking down.

We played the game of *Concentration* in the office for awhile. Suddenly the secretary turned to me. "You play the game very well," she said, "but you don't seem to know all the rules. Do you watch the game at home?"

"Well, I used to," I replied hesitantly.

That's when I realized I had blown it. The secretary's reaction was chilling. The other contestants nodded pitifully to each other. *Look at this jerk,* they seemed to say, *he doesn't even watch the show!* Everything else was futile, and I knew it.

I no longer desire to go on television. Still, when the moon is full, and the wind whistles through the Hollywood hills, sometimes I feel a wild burning in my chest, and a crazed look comes into my eye. . . . It's all my wife can do to keep me from trying to go on *The Gong Show* with my Chuck Barris imitation.

William Morris is a humorist in Los Angeles.

Raymond Massey portrays Prospero and Joan Chandler is Miranda in "The Tempest," which is presented on *Toast of the Town* directly from the Shakespeare Festival Theatre in Stratford, Connecticut.

The top dramatic program of 1955 is the *Kraft Theatre* showing of "Patterns" written by Rod Serling, who along with Paddy Chayefsky ("Marty," 1953), Gore Vidal ("Visit to a Small Planet," 1955), and Reginald Rose ("Twelve Angry Men," 1954), form the first generation of excellent live television scriptwriters.

THE WORST PROGRAM IN TV HISTORY

HOWARD BLAKE

What *Gone With the Wind* is to the American novel and *Life with Father* is to the American stage, *Queen for a Day,* I would guess, is to American broadcasting. *Queen* was one of the most popular of all radio-TV programs, and certainly the undisputed queen of the tearjerkers. Having been born on April 29, 1945, and having died on October 2, 1964, *Queen* lived to be nearly twenty. Money poured in (sponsors paid $4,000 for a one-minute commercial) and listeners tuned in (in 1955–56, *Queen* was daytime TV's all-time biggest hit: thirteen million Americans watched it every day). And just because of its phenomenal commercial and popular success, a close look at this program, I am convinced, reveals with shining clarity the essential, sobering truth about radio and TV in these United States.

The format of *Queen for a Day* was simple but brilliant: get believable women to tell their hard-luck stories over the air; let the audience choose the woman they think is most deserving; and then shower the winner with gifts. (Only be sure that the show doesn't pay for the gifts. Just let everybody *think* it does.)

The program would begin with its star, Jack Bailey, pointing straight into the camera and shouting, "Would *you* like to be Queen for a Day?" Then a parade of beautiful girls trots by, each showing off a different gift (furs, dresses, TV set, et cetera) to be presented to that day's Queen while an off-camera announcer extols how wonderful each gift is. Next,

". . . there was never a show like it."

Jack Bailey interviews the day's candidates, asking each one what her personal wish is and why she wants whatever she wants. The last candidate makes her tearful plea, and then comes the voting—by audience applause. The applause meter appears on the screen. Jack stands behind the first candidate and recaps: "Candidate number one, who wants a trousseau for her daugher's wedding." Mild applause. "Candidate number two, who badly needs repair for her leaky roof before the rainy season starts." The applause is a little louder. "Candidate number three, whose mother is coming to spend her few remaining years with her, and she desperately needs a bed." The applause is tumultuous. Jack Bailey shouts, "It's number three!" The house comes down. Later, if number three beats out two other contestants, a sable-collared red-velvet robe is placed around her shoulders, a jeweled crown is gently lowered onto her head, and Jack Bailey roars, "I now pronounce you—Queen for a Day!" Then, *ad infinitum* and *ad nauseam,* the Queen is shown all her gifts—not only the bed, but sheets, pillows, blankets, bedspreads, lamps, chaise lounge, bureau, and so forth. The Queen dissolves into tears. Jack puts his

October 11, 1956. Ed Wynn, seen here rehearsing with son Keenan, returns to television to appear in Serling's tense drama "Requiem For a Heavyweight," starring Jack Palance, which is broadcast on *Playhouse 90* during its debut season.

It wins the Emmy as 1956's Best Program, and Serling wins an Emmy for Best Original Teleplay for the second consecutive year. Both "Requiem" and "Patterns" are made into movies.

Cloris Leachman tries to persuade Henry Hull to leave his doomed house on "Mr. Finchley v. the Bomb," which is presented on NBC's *Kaiser Aluminum Hour* in 1956.

February 1, 1956. Broadway star Kim Stanley plays the lead in "Flight," the drama of a young girl's first love on NBC's *Playwrights 56.*

arm around her. Women in the audience faint and ushers carry them to the rear of the theater. Finally Jack faces the camera, smiles his kindest smile, and says to the viewer, ''Be with us again tomorrow when we'll elect another Queen. This is Jack Bailey, wishing we could make *every* woman Queen for a Day!''

For sheer psychological perfection, there was never a show like it.

When *Queen* made its debut on TV on January 1, 1955, *New York Times* critic Jack Gould shrieked, ''What hath Sarnoff wrought?!'' Critics all over the country howled in similar protest, and the result was that the show became number one in the ratings within three months.

Queen was hardly on the air six months when the network expanded it from thirty minutes to forty-five minutes, a very unusual length for a show, yet in this instance quite logical. At $4,000 for a one-minute commercial, it brought NBC's potential annual take from the program up from $9 million.

The money didn't come only from advertisers like Procter & Gamble and Alka-Seltzer. It also came from the companies that gave us free merchandise in return for plugs. For in addition to the merchandise they forked over, they had to cover the salaries of the beautiful girls who modeled the clothes we gave away and who displayed the other gifts. Oddly enough, the money paid for these models' fees also managed to be used for other expenses, like contributing to owner Ray Morgan's weekly $5,000.

And so it came to pass that the more gifts we gave the Queen, the more money we made. We *loaded* the Queens with gifts—at the rate of a million dollars a year. Eventually what with the regular commercials and the gift plugs, only about fifteen of the forty-five minutes were left for the actual show—for Jack Bailey's interviews with the candidates and the voting for the Queen. The other thirty minutes were nothing but commercials and plugs.

But we had our integrity, I'll have you know. Other audience participation shows chose their contestants after intensive interviews, wrote scripts for them to memorize, told them what answers to give the quiz questions, rehearsed them thoroughly in *how* to give those answers, and absolutely controlled who won and how much. None of this did we ever do. No candidate for Queen was ever planted, prompted, or rehearsed. Every candidate came from that day's walk-in audience. The Queen was chosen entirely by audience applause and this was never faked, or ''sweetened,'' as the trade calls it, although that's easy to do. And it was a strict rule that the Queen was to be treated like a queen during her one-day reign and given everything the show promised her.

How holy can you get?

Our integrity, however, had limits. Our holiness had holes. When it came to picking the women to appear on the show, the general assumption was that we chose the most needy and deserving. But the most needy and deserving usually had to be dumped. A lot of the women desperately needed a doctor or a lawyer, for instance. We could never provide either because there was no way of telling what it might eventually cost. And no doctor or lawyer would work for free in return for a plug (we investigated). A candidate had to want something we *could* plug—a stove, a carpet, a plane trip, an artificial leg, a detective agency, a year's supply of baby food. And the reason she needed whatever it was had to make a good story. Some of the women were ugly, some were incoherent. They had to be dumped too, deserving or not. A woman with a wish like a wish any other woman had had recently was also out of luck. We had only one aim—to pick the woman who would provide the best entertainment.

Before the show, every candidate was given a ''wish card'' to fill out. The cards were numbered.

97

A Night to Remember, about the sinking of the *Titanic,* is presented in 1956 on *Kraft Theatre.* Utilizing over one hundred actors and numerous sets, it is the most ambitious live presentation on television to date. It is directed by George Roy Hill, who will make *Butch Cassidy and the Sundance Kid* and *The Sting* in later years.

March 10, 1956. New British star Julie Andrews appears on U.S. TV for the first time when she costars with Bing Crosby in a musical version of Maxwell Anderson's ''High Tor'' on *Ford Star Jubilee.* The first ninety-minute film made for TV will eventually be the first unedited telefilm booked into theaters as a regular feature.

Three of four members of the staff went through them before the show and passed likely ones to me. I picked twenty-five. The twenty-five women were called on stage a few minutes before air time, and interviewed for a few seconds by Jack Bailey. Jack then chose the five with the best stories, and the best personalities, to be on the show. Complete phonies showed up once in a while, but Jack could smell a phony story almost every time.

The show had an embarrassing weakness. Only one of the five daily candidates could be elected Queen and have her wish granted. The other four, no matter how desperate their needs, supplied their share of the entertainment but had to settle for a small consolation prize—a radio, a toaster, a dozen pairs of stockings. Sometimes they would burst into tears, but we never let the camera see that. Once the Queen was elected, the losers were deliberately ignored.

Occasionally a really good liar would get past Jack's sensitive nose and fool the audience as well. But we were protected. A clause in the release every candidate had to sign specified that if her story proved untrue she'd get nothing, and we had to exercise that clause a number of times.

For instance, one woman's wish was for round-trip tickets to Miami for herself and her fourteen-year-old-son. Her mother was dying of cancer, the woman said, and had never seen her grandson. Tears rolled down her cheeks as she told all the heartbreaking details. Tears puddled the audience's seats too, and when it was time to vote, the applause for her almost broke the applause machine. It was a great show. But a neighbor of hers saw it and told the Queen's husband about it. The husband phoned us and said (1) they didn't have a son and (2) his wife's mother had been dead for ten years. His wife, he informed us, was having an affair with a friend of his, and she had been trying to find a way for the lovers to spend two weeks together in Miami. The husband wanted us to know that he wasn't in favor of it. We hated to buck a romance, but they didn't get to go.

We also had trouble whenever Jack went on vacation. Interviewing people is a most difficult art, and Jack had no peers. He learned his trade through years of work as a circus-carnival barker, an actor in stock, and a department-store salesman. The fact is that keeping an interview going without hesitating and stalling to think of appropriate questions takes experience—and innate genius to boot. Adolphe Menjou did the show for a couple of weeks and loved it. But he never knew the torture he put us through. He asked one woman about her husband's occupation. She replied, "He died in an automobile accident four months ago." Adolphe responded, "Wonderful! What kind of work did he do?" ("Wonderful!" is a stall word.)

Two imitations of *Queen* also turned out to be very successful—*Strike It Rich!* and Ralph Edwards's *It Could Be You*. But both expired long before *Queen* did. *Queen's* death was a lingering one and took years. The show started to breathe hard a few months after I got fired the first time (1956). (What a coincidence!) I got fired because I wanted to make daring experiments with the format, convinced that we needed new surprises to keep boredom from descending over our audiences. Jack Bailey disagreed and quoted Lucille Ball. Once one of Lucy's writers suggested some radical changes in her show, and she ordered: "Don't f--- around with success." So I left. I came back in 1957, thinking I would *now* be able to make innovations, but again Jack chickened out, and again I left. Ratings continued to drop. In the fall of 1959 ABC took over the show, and it lingered there for five years before finally giving up the ghost in October, 1964. If you want to be nasty about it, you can draw whatever conclusions you like from the fact that the show managed to last six more years without me.

November 3, 1956. *The Wizard of Oz,* the 1939 movie classic, appears for the first time as a special on *Ford Star Jubilee.* Accompanying Judy Garland down the yellow brick road are Jack Haley (L) and Ray Bolger. They are about to meet Bert Lahr.

The Steve Allen Show is placed on NBC's Sunday night schedule opposite Ed Sullivan. Wild comedy is provided by regulars (L-R) Bill Dana, Dayton Allen, Pat Harrington, Jr., and the "men on the street," Louis Nye and Tom Poston. Skitch Henderson conducts the orchestra. Gabe Dell and Don Knotts (not shown) also appear regularly.

Jack Bailey, queen-maker, usurps the throne.

Throughout my years with *Queen* I collected the "wish cards" that contestants submitted. I still have all the originals, and I read them over every once in a while.

Some of the wishes were pathetic:

● A bird for an old lady 94. She had one but it died. She does not realize it is dead. She keeps it in a cage, talks to it and takes it out and kisses its head.

● Some kind of car or hot rod or something to make my blind brother and crippled brother happy.

● A typewriter or a recording machine. Because my husband hit me over the head with a shoe and completely paralyzed me for 7½ months. It left me with my right side paralyzed & I am a writer.

● An artificial eye for my husband. Last winter his artificial eye (which he keeps in a small glass at night) froze and cracked. I have 16 children and No. 17 is coming up in the spring.

● Services of a detective. My sister was murdered and I have been told she left money. Since it was in another state I have no way of knowing without help.

● Urn to bury my mother. Her ashes have been in a vault and must be buried or they will throw them on the rose bush.

● Have my front teeth put in. I am unmarried and have 1 child 10½ months. If I had my teeth fixed maybe I could get a husband to take care of my kid.

● $100 for a divorce. Husband attempted rape on my 6 year old daughter, then left with money and car. Must be divorced so I can testify against him in court.

● Mattress. My husband died on our bed April 28 and ruined our mattress.

● Get a divorce. I want to divorce the man who ruined my life by taking me away from my home. He was 45 and I 14. Today I am on the street with 5 children and no husband. If I could divorce that monster perhaps the father of my 5 children would marry me.

● Celotex sheets and carpenter. Due to a brain tumor, my husband went into a seizure and took his life with a deer rifle. The high-powered bullets pierced the ceiling and wall of the bedroom. I'd like to have it repaired.

Some of the wishes were not so pathetic:

● To get "falsies" that won't blow up in the plane.

● 3 cases of I.W. Harper. My mother had heart trouble and her Dr. told her to take 2 jiggers every nite & she's always out of whiskey.

● Bra for my daughter. Can't find one to fit or hold them up. I guess you know what I mean. She don't take after me.

● I want a gun.

● A parakeet that will talk. I have a husband but

Toast of the Town becomes *The Ed Sullivan Show* in 1956. Sullivan pays rock 'n' roll idol Elvis Presley an unprecedented $50,000 to make a long-awaited television appearance and sing "Hound Dog." But when Elvis gyrates his pelvis, the camera moves above his waist.

Elvis Presley is not the only singer to have long hair. Carl Reiner, Sid Caesar, and Howard Morris are "The Haircuts."

Nanette Fabray wins an Emmy as Best Comedienne in a Series for her work in *Caesar's Hour*, but leaves the show to appear in such specials as "High Button Shoes."

he won't talk. I am on my third husband; have my eyes open.

• 100 pounds corn sugar. 50 lbs. hops. My husband drinks too much regular beer & this would be cheaper if he made it himself.

• Twin beds. My doctor said "Take it easy."

• To be mother of our country. There is so much misunderstanding among us. I want my address & phone no. before the nation, so any one needing help with problems I will donate my services for free. I am just a usual lady & have time to help man kind.

• To have my sister and her family analyzed, so the rest of us can live in peace.

• A ticket to the Art Linkletter Show.

• A Rolls-Royce with balloon tires for me. I'm *not* selfish.

All of these wishes, I want to emphasize, were *typical,* not unusual. Sure, *Queen* was vulgar and sleazy and filled with bathos and bad taste. That was why it was so successful: it was exactly what the general public wanted. After all, the average American voted Warren G. Harding into office, reads the *Reader's Digest,* and made *Hercules Unchained* a smash movie. In the slightly amended words of H. L. Mencken, "Nobody ever lost money underestimating the taste of the American public."

To be honest, a few intellectual friends used to ask me, "Aren't you ashamed of producing a show like that?" I was never ashamed for a second. Somebody once asked novelist John P. Marquand how he could lower himself to write all those lightweight Mr. Moto mysteries for the *Saturday Evening Post.* Marquand pointed out that the stories obviously brought pleasure to many people, he got very good money for them, and he thoroughly enjoyed writing them. That's how I felt about producing *Queen for a Day.* I knew the show for what it was, but it seemed to bring pleasure to millions, helped a few (all right, mighty few),

and it paid me a very good living. If all Americans —ad men, insurance brokers, lawyers—examined closely just how *they* make their livings, I think a high percentage would soon be on analysts' couches.

No, the show did not prove that there are good guys and bad guys, and the bad guys always eat up the good guys. I don't think there *were* any good guys. *Everybody* was on the make—we on the show, NBC and later ABC, the sponsors and the suppliers of gifts. And how about all the down-on-their-luck women who used to further our money-grubbing ends? Weren't they all on the make? Weren't they after something for nothing? Weren't they willing to wash their dirty linen on coast-to-coast TV for a chance at big money, for a chance to ride in our chauffeured Cadillac for the free tour of Disneyland and the Hollywood nightclubs? What about one of the most common wishes they turned in? "I'd like to pay back my mother for all the wonderful things she's done for me." The women who made that wish didn't want to pay back their mothers at all. They wanted *us* to.

You *bet* they were on the make.

We got what we were after. Five thousand Queens got what they were after. And the TV audience cried their eyes out, morbidly delighted to find there were people even worse off than they were, and so *they* got what they were after.

Queen for a Day was a typical American success story. And if you don't like it, either try to change the rules of the game—or go back where you come from.

This article originally appeared in Fact (January–February 1966).

Janet Blair replaces Nanette Fabray on *Caesar's Hour.* She will remain Caesar's partner until the show goes off the air a year later.

"Mmmm-wah." Dinah Shore, who first appeared on TV in 1939, delivers her famous weekly good-night kiss on the popular *Dinah Shore Show.* This variety show—Shore's third on NBC since 1950—is popular not only for the songs and sketches, but also for Dinah's magnificent wardrobe. The show will last six years.

THE SOAP OPERA FORMULA
MADELEINE EDMONDSON

Soap operas have been a part of American life for almost fifty years now, and from the beginning they have been very much what they are today: stories about women, largely invented by women, intended for—and enthusiastically accepted by—a huge audience of women. Essentially, the classic soap tells the life story of a heroine, an intimate biography presented in such vivid and bounteous detail that the audience can get to know the characters well enough to identify with them. This, after all, is what soap opera was designed to offer—a daily opportunity to participate imaginatively in the intimate lives of other people. Would an audience eagerly tune in to identify with domestic drudges and prisoners of convention? Women who endure repressed, unsatisfying, insignificant lives? Of course not. The audience is looking for lives more exciting than their own to share; they want to identify with women who are stronger, more interesting, more exciting than themselves.

The three people who most clearly imprinted their personalities on the soaps, determining the elements that would compose them and the direction they would take, were all gifted and ambitious women: Irna Phillips, who was writing a radio soap, *Painted Dreams*, as early as 1932 and continued to exert enormous influence on television soaps until her death in 1973; Elaine Carrington, creator of such durable hits as the thirties' *Pepper Young's Family* and *When a Girl Marries;* and Anne Hummert, the more creative partner in the legendary team of Frank and Anne Hummert, whose names were synonymous with radio soap opera for the many years during which they pro-

duced, among countless others, those favorites of today's parodists: *Our Gal Sunday, Stella Dallas,* and *John's Other Wife.*

In view of these origins, it should come as no surprise that the soaps' view of woman, her potential, and her role, is by no means an unflattering one. Soapland teems, as it always has, with exciting women. Many are heroines in the full dictionary sense (''a woman admired for her achievements and noble qualities and considered a model or ideal''), but there is plenty of variety. In order to enlarge the potential for identification, the soaps include a full spectrum of feminine possibility, from the murderous psychopath to that Other Woman who has always prowled the air waves in stealthy, but determined, quest of the heroine's husband. As persons to identify with (up to a point), villainesses can be very satisfying, since they tend to be outstandingly attractive, bold, unscrupulous, and seductive. In the end, of course, the mysterious and immutable laws of Soapland decree that the wicked shall be unmasked or reformed and their evil schemes come to naught, but then the audience can return to identifying with the wronged heroine.

She too, of course, is attractive. The average soap heroine has almost a superfluity of talents, accomplishments, strengths, and virtues. She has a deep understanding of character as well as innate sympathy and intuitiveness, and her man (she always has at least one adorer) depends on her for guidance in any difficult situation. The spiritual superiority of soap opera's women is unquestionable.

Nor is superiority confined to the moral and intel-

Broadway star Gwen Verdon guests on *The Dinah Shore Show*.

Singer Rosemary Clooney, a long-time television personality, gets her own syndicated show in 1956. In 1957, it will be on NBC.

Pop singer Nat King Cole is the first black to host a network variety show when *The Nat King Cole Show* appears on NBC in 1956. It lasts for only one year, because sponsors shy away.

General Hospital *staff consult a patient's chart.*

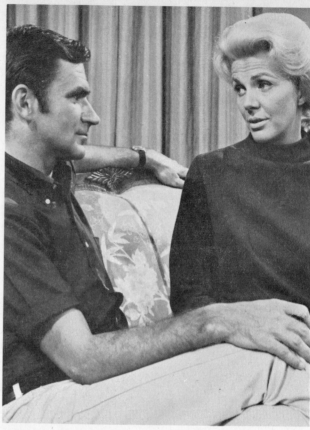

A Love of Life *couple have a heart-to-heart.*

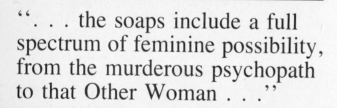

"... the soaps include a full spectrum of feminine possibility, from the murderous psychopath to that Other Woman ..."

lectual sphere. True, it is possible to be a heroine without ever leaving the kitchen, but the ladies rarely sacrifice their ambitions on the domestic altar. From radio soap's earliest days, glamorous careers for women have been the rule, not the exception. Helen Trent, the widow who set out to prove that romance can exist at thirty-five ("and even beyond"), was a dress designer. Young Widder Brown supported herself and her children by managing a tearoom. Ma Perkins ran a lumber yard. Mary Marlin took over her husband's seat in the Senate (when he disappeared in Asia) and became the President's most trusted adviser. And such radio soap titles as *Joyce Jordan, Girl In-*

102

Zany Jonathan Winters, possessor of one of the most creative comic minds in the business, has his own fifteen-minute variety show on NBC in 1956.

Famous actor-writer-director Orson Welles (R) guests on *The Herb Shriner Show.* Shriner's first variety show in several years will only last one season.

Former schoolteacher Sam Levenson (L) replaces Shriner (R) for the summer as host of Goodson-Todman's *Two for the Money* during the last year of its three-year run.

"The men and women of Soapland may look modern . . ."

tern and *Her Honor, Nancy James* suggest that the professional woman is no recent arrival on the soap scene.

Even the most successful of Soapland's career women (an astonishing percentage of whom are doctors these days) plan to keep house and raise children when they marry, but they do this only because they enjoy it. They often keep at least a part-time job, and they always maintain the option of rejoining the work force whenever their financial situation (or some new plot twist) warrants it. They are talented, versatile, and efficient, and any man with the temerity to compete with them is likely to come out a poor second. This effortless combination of the demands of home and career may lack something in realism, but it confirms the status of soap opera's women as the stronger sex.

A quick survey of the male population of Soapland completes the demonstration: without their womenfolk, these fellows could not survive a week. Attractive and charming they may be—one might shyly suggest that on soaps men tend to be seen as sex objects—but their inadequacy is basic. One loving soap heroine of radio days summed up the underlying attitude of all when she confided to her mother that her worst fear was that her husband might, in one of his vaguely demented states, wander in front of a car.

It is this weakness in men that usually leads the women into active adventure. If a husband dies or disappears (as husbands in Soapland so often do), the woman must struggle on alone, assuming (and triumphantly coping with) all kinds of traditionally masculine responsibilities. And if the husband is present and alive but in some way incapacitated (which is another typical life adjustment of soap husbands, who fall frequent prey to amnesia, paralysis, and blindness), the heroine has no choice but to swing into action.

It is not absolutely required, of course, that the husband be disabled or unavailable: he may be physically competent to deal with an emergency, but mentally unprepared. Perhaps he fails to understand the urgency of the threat, or, muster the requisite faith in the innocence of the victim, and in such cases the woman (with that well-established moral superiority of hers) takes over.

In short, the men and women of Soapland may look very modern, wearing the latest fashions, using current jargon, playing the guitar, or even lallygagging about in their waterbeds—but they have hardly changed at all in fifty years of soap opera. The inhabitants of all those "average" little towns still pursue the same old dream of love and happiness, still beset by the same old problems. Lovers are inevitably from two different worlds; love is fleeting; men will stray. In the background hovers the threat of bigamy, impotence, rape, illegitimacy, paralysis from the waist down, incest, hysterical blindness, whatever.

Nowadays these problems need not be darkly implied or sketched in shadowy outline—they can be discussed in clinical detail—but nothing said or done on any of today's soaps would shock or even surprise Irna Phillips, Elaine Carrington, or Anne Hummert. The world of soap operas is still the world they invented.

Madeleine Edmondson is co-author of From Mary Noble to Mary Hartman: The Complete Soap Opera Book. *She is still waiting for the right opportunity to say, casually,* "Plus ça change, plus c'est la même soap."

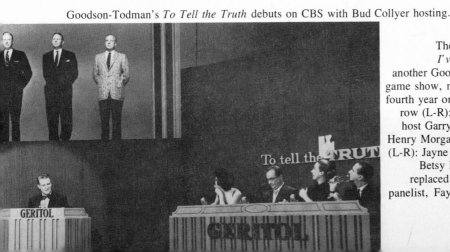

Goodson-Todman's *To Tell the Truth* debuts on CBS with Bud Collyer hosting.

The immensely popular *I've Got a Secret,* another Goodson-Todman game show, moves into its fourth year on CBS. Back row (L-R): Bill Cullen, host Garry Moore, and Henry Morgan. Front row (L-R): Jayne Meadows, and Betsy Palmer who has replaced the original panelist, Faye Emerson.

TV RECIPES
ALICE LOCKE

With a little forethought and minimal preparation, mundane TV snacking can be transformed into serious gourmet feasting. It's easy to unleash your imagination, tantalize your tastebuds, and be back in front of the set in time for your favorite show. Here's how to satisfy the cravings and ravings of those special sensations, the TV munchies.

Soap Opera Soup and Sandwich Special

If *Search for Tomorrow* leaves you hunting the refrigerator shelves for today's lunch, you might try this deliciously simple soup:

1 can cream of tomato soup
1 can cream of pea soup
1 small can crabmeat
½ to ¾ cup milk
2 to 4 tablespoons sweet sherry

Combine soups, crabmeat, and milk in saucepan. Add sherry and stir over low flame for five minutes, or until warm. Sprinkle with chopped parsley and serve with this protein-rich, open-faced sandwich:

Spread piece of toasted rye bread
with cream cheese or peanut butter.
Top with a banana sliced lengthwise
and sprinkle with cinnamon.

Top-Rated TV Dinners

With the twist of a cap or the shake of a spice jar, handy—but often horrible—frozen dinners can make evening news headlines.

A sprinkle of white wine makes sliced turkey in gravy, and swiss steak or veal parmigiana in tomato sauce positively haute.

Add vigor to brown gravy over meat loaf or roast beef dinners with a squirt of Worcestershire.

A veil of Parmesan cheese dresses up spaghetti and meat balls or macaroni and cheese.

Franks and beans snap to with a pinch of brown sugar and the tiniest dab of dry mustard.

Paprika on pale mashed potatoes can excite the eye and tingle a taste bud or two.

A touch of oregano or marjoram revives tired peas and carrots.

Green beans find their former flavor in the company of dill.

A shower of chopped parsley refreshes most meats and vegetables.

Pizza with Pizzazz

Spice up slices of the always-on-hand American snack, frozen pizza:

Five minutes before show time, preheat the oven and sprinkle pizza with one or all of these ingredients:

a few drops of olive oil
canned tomato sauce
minced garlic cloves or garlic powder
thinly sliced green pepper
slivers of onion
canned or fresh sliced mushrooms
pitted black olives, halved
dried or fresh chopped parsley

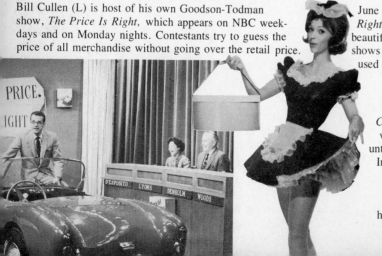

Bill Cullen (L) is host of his own Goodson-Todman show, *The Price Is Right*, which appears on NBC weekdays and on Monday nights. Contestants try to guess the price of all merchandise without going over the retail price.

June Ferguson of *The Price Is Right* is one of the many beautiful models on game shows who display merchandise used for prizes.

Bob Barker (R) becomes host of *Truth or Consequences* in 1956. He will remain with the show until it leaves NBC in 1965. In 1967, he will resume as host of the syndicated version. Then in the late seventies, he will MC an hour-long daytime version of *The Price Is Right*.

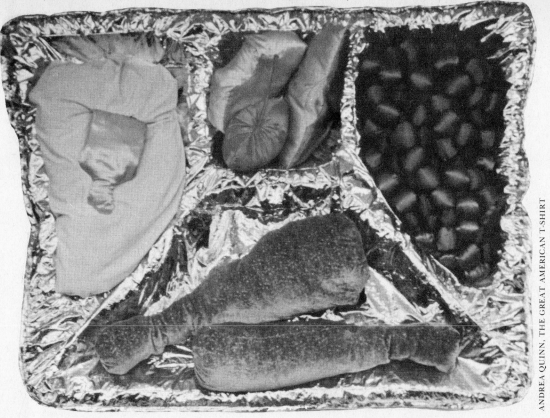

Linda Lou White's soft sculpture of a TV dinner is 4 × 6 feet and looks good enough to eat.

browned chopped meat
salami
pepperoni
anchovies
oregano, basil

Pop pizza into oven; let it bake eight to twelve minutes (according to instructions on box), and sit back until the first commercial. If the networks and your oven are on time, your pizza should be bubbling to be eaten.

Popcorn Showstoppers

What movie—classic or made-for-TV—would be complete without fresh popcorn and one of these tangy toppings? Pop your corn according to directions on package; in small saucepan melt half a stick of butter and add *one* of the following extras:

a sprinkle of garlic or *onion powder*
a teaspoon of anchovie paste
a dash of chili powder (be cautious)
a couple of shakes of oregano

Pour over popcorn and enjoy!

Alice Locke coauthored and illustrated The Munchies Eat Book *and is working on another cookbook.*

105

Radio greats, ventriloquist Edgar Bergen and Charlie McCarthy (L), moderate the daytime quiz show, *Do You Trust Your Wife?* Here they are visited by Mortimer Snerd. When the show switches from CBS to ABC, it will be retitled *Who Do You Trust?* and Johnny Carson will become the host.

August 17, 1956. Jack Barry launches a new big-money quiz show, *Twenty-One*, NBC's nighttime answer to the *$64,000 Question*. In 1958, former contestant Herbert Stempel will announce that answers are being provided to contestants such as the former champion, audience-favorite Charles Van Doren. A scandal will shake up the industry, and all major quiz shows—including *$64,000 Question* and *Twenty-One*—will be removed from the air.

VISITING "HOUSE PARTY"
NANCY MARSDEN

At the age of six I faced my first difficult decision. Marsha Levin said this could be my big chance. I might be discovered and become a movie star. Surveying my somewhat skimpy braids, unruly teeth, and the enormous white collar on my favorite dress, I thought that was unlikely. Why didn't the teacher choose Marsha to go on television—Marsha, with her pierced ears and already coy expression?

"Because you," my mother told me, "are articulate. You talk a lot."

True. But maybe I didn't want to be a movie star. Maybe I didn't want to go on Art Linkletter's show. I worried for several days and arrived at an impulsive decision. Weeks later a chauffeured limousine called for me at Monlux Elementary School.

It was 1953. The baby boom was in full swing. Art Linkletter had discovered what everyone already knew: *Kids say the darndest things*. The idea sold big on his daytime variety show and later in a best-selling book.

During the twenty-minute ride to Hollywood, a warm, reassuring woman chatted with me and the three other children in the car about our families, career aspirations, pet peeves. This was our initial screening. We were bound to come up with something that would tickle American housewives, especially against the backdrop of 1950's propriety.

The limousine glided up to the studio. Like small celebrities, we passed through the restricted areas into the bowels of television. There were no cowboys, no cartoon characters—just equipment and a few men working in the empty stage sets. For our amusement

---

" 'Be sure to tell Mr. Linkletter about those bad words. . . .' "

they lifted some Hollywood bricks with one finger.

Art Linkletter interviewed us in a small waiting room. Sitting beside me on a wide Naugahyde chair, he consulted notes our hostess had prepared. Even then, I knew I was being prompted. "Be sure to tell Mr. Linkletter about those bad words," his assistant smiled, as she led me onstage.

I nodded vaguely, climbing onto what seemed like a very tall stool. Stranded on that high rock, I was soon lost in the sea of light. There was music, applause, and the announcing voice of Jack Slattery. The cameras wheeled toward me, and I looked for my mother's face in the audience.

The conversation went something like this:

"You have a little brother, don't you?"

"Uh-huh."

"And how old is he?"

I held up four fingers.

"Is he a pretty nice brother?"

"Yes," I said, then added confidentially, "except he says bad words."

"Bad words?" tsked Art Linkletter. He raised his eyebrows at the audience. "How bad—sort of bad, or *really* bad?"

"Really bad!" I declared, trying to figure out why everyone was laughing.

Another victim of the quiz show scandals will be *Tic Tac Dough*, which debuts in 1956 on NBC. Here host Jay Jackson congratulates the show's biggest winner.

"Ten-Four." Broderick Crawford, who won an Academy Award for his performance in *All the King's Men*, is the star of the low-budget crime drama, *Highway Patrol*, which debuts in 1956.

Neville Brand, next to Audie Murphy, America's top WW II hero, terrorizes Academy Award–winning actress Jane Wyman on the "Ride With the Executioner" episode of the popular *Jane Wyman's Fireside Theater*.

Kids do say the darndest things!

When the cameras finally moved on to the next child, I was disappointed. I waited alone in my small sphere. Then someone put a doll in my arms, I waved good-bye, and it was over.

Our limousine left CBS loaded with treasure. There were roller skates, Tiny Tears dolls, cases of root beer, and a radio for our school. I never saw the radio, but Tiny Tears became a constant, if whimpering, companion.

We were taken to a French restaurant, where we dined on that old Continental favorite, Chicken a la King. It was late afternoon when our car returned to school. My brother was waiting. "I don't say bad words!" he claimed. Even then I thought he was probably right.

"We must go directly to Eric's house and apologize," Mother insisted, loading my gifts into the Chevy. "What on earth made you say a thing like that?"

I wasn't sure. But standing on the Walkers' front porch, I certainly regretted it. Fortunately, they took my comments humorously. And Eric was jubilant at hearing his name on TV. Bad words or good, the plug was all he cared about—and my already famous case of root beer.

During the next month, Marsha Levin and I waited patiently for my ascent to stardom. She was triumphant when, in early May, I received a call from CBS. They wanted me to return to *House Party* again that summer.

This time I had no doubts. The root beer was running low, and one skate was lost. But Mother was hesitant. "I don't know," she told me. "I just don't know. I'll have to think about it."

As an elementary school teacher in Los Angeles, Nancy Marsden now knows what Art Linkletter was up against.

"Now, where does he learn words like that?" Whispering: "You don't say bad words, do you?"

I looked at him in surprise. "No, *I* don't. He learns them from Eric Walker, down the street. He says *really* bad words."

"How old did you say Eric was?"

I held up three fingers, while Mother shuddered in the audience. Eric, his family, and our whole neighborhood were watching. As for me, I was beginning to enjoy myself. What a powerful sensation!

107

Gale Storm (R) tries to wrestle a plaid bag away from her sons Peter (L) and Paul on *Oh! Susanna,* which debuts on CBS in 1956. ZaSu Pitts co-stars.

MacDonald Carey plays a small-town M.D. in *Dr. Christian* when the old radio favorite comes to television in 1956. Carey will star in *Lock Up,* another syndicated series, in 1959.

REMEMBERING FRAN ALLISON: WHY I DON'T WATCH TV

GORDON LISH

Now that I am forty-three, I figure I am too old to lie. That's a mile and a half more than I could have figured for myself at forty-two, I can tell you. Who knows how old I'll be by the time you get to read this? But my bet is by then, one way or the terrible other, I'll be paying through the nose.

Which is why I have just this minute decided to spill all my beans—before a lousy old age extorts them from me one huge embarrassment at a time. Oh, sure, I know right along with the rest of the prudent boys and girls how a fellow is supposed to salt away a few beans for his failing years. But since nobody's giving me any guarantee that forty-three is *not* the only one of those years I'll ever see, I'm coming across right now.

Stand back, playmates! Here's the first big bean I've been saving for a rainy day:

Fran Allison, I hope your're watching, honey, because they're all coming off right now! Tie, shirt, trousers! Shoes and one-size-fits-all socks!

Fran Allison, I know you're not going to mind this because you've got a heart as wide as all outdoors. It's just there's no other way to do this but naked as the day I was born.

I love you, Fran Allison!

Not a man going ever loved you more! No boy, either! And I know you've had your share in that department too.

Listen, Fran Allison, this is no kid thing I've got for you. It goes back, believe me—back to before

Kukla and Ollie came out of the sewing machine. I'm talking about back to *Aunt* Frannie.

Now that's really back. When you're talking about *Don McNeill's Breakfast Club,* you're talking about really *back,* am I right? If anything's *back*, radio is—right?

Which proves it was your voice that did it to me first. And in my book that's a critical foreword in the authorized lexicon of love. Oh, voice! Who knows from voices, I ask you? Not many, I am prepared to tell you.

Listen, Frannie, here are the voices I loved—but none more than yours—and I'm getting this list out there because you tell me a better way to show you what you're dealing with? You're going to hear a list from a fellow who knows what to list.

Jane Ace, Jackson Beck, Barbara Luddy, Mandel Kramer, Larry Haines, Joseph Julian, Anne Seymour, Ken Lynch, John Doucette, Ralph Bell.

Just feature those, Fran Allison! Ten humdingers, right?

Are you dealing with a fellow who knows a thing or two, or are you dealing with a fellow who knows a

Robert Shaw, several years away from movie stardom, stars as ex-pirate Dan Tempest in *The Buccaneers,* an early-evening adventure series for children.

Robert Newton (R) repeats his movie role as the peg-legged buccaneer in *The Adventures of Long John Silver.* Kit Taylor is once again Jim Hawkins in this series, roughly adapted from Stevenson's *Treasure Island.*

Oddly cast Philip Carey (L) and Warren Stevens are officers in Screen Gems' new adventure series, *The 77th Bengal Lancers.*

Those lovable Kuklapolitans turn on the charm.

Fran Allison, for you I could have done it! If they hadn't invented mirrors, you could've counted on me to get up there on the ceiling and stay put until that *man*, that Burr Tillstrom (Burr, indeed!), came out from hiding and rudely kissed you off.

Oh, Frannie—how it hurt me when I saw him. And the agony that seized up my vitals when my boy's worrying swept me into wondering if what you felt for Kukla and what you felt for Ollie you felt for Burr as well. Was it *his* lips you blessed with yours when you touched yours to Kukla's hairless head? And when your hand smoothed Ollie's fur, was it Burr's crew cut that blazed with the flash of your fingers?

Frannie, Frannie, passion pure—I don't like to talk like this. If there were a jot of reproach in anything I said, I take it back, I swear! I know how things are. I'm a big fellow now, and I guess I know what the world is made of. Let's forget I ever mentioned a thing. Let's just wipe the slate clean and start all over.

I'm sitting up here, up here on the ceiling where I've always been, forty-three and still up here all crazy in love with you. And you, Fran Allison, are standing there forever and ever, that little playhouse where puppets capered for your favor all the human theater my heart will ever need.

It is a serene place, where I, maddened with longing, sit insanely upside down, and where you, endlessly patient and abiding, stand and stand and stand. Even your scolding is a fathomless benevolence. It is a kiss on my false, bald head.

I am not kidding, Fran Allison. You ruined me for real love because you were a lesson in true love. And since I have television to thank for it, the teaching and the unavailing seeking thereafter, you can see why I quit watching a long, cruel time ago.

Gordon Lish is fiction editor at Esquire *and a visiting fellow at Yale University.*

thing or two? Let's face it—in my particular case, I know *ten*. But in my particular case, what came up from the bellies and out of the mouths of those ten beauties was a bucket of nails knocked over on linoleum alongside the melody that came out of you.

My sweet mother would say, ''Get the hell away from that goddamn radio and get the hell outside and get some air!'' And I could do it—even when it was *Let's Pretend* and Daisy Alden that had me there. But when Don McNeill was on and a safe guess Aunt Frannie wouldn't be far behind, I wasn't budging for nothing!

Then came jet planes and frozen stringbeans and—Jesus God!—*you*, Fran Allison, on our first TV.

I saw you in a mirror first. Well, I guess you haven't forgotten how the screen used to be up there on the top of the set and there was a mirror up there too, so a person wouldn't have to sit on the ceiling to see what was what.

Scott Forbes stars in *The Adventures of Jim Bowie,* a fictional account of the hero who died with Davy Crockett at the Alamo. This show will run from 1956 to 1958.

Character actor Edgar Buchanan (L) plays the title role in Dumont's *Judge Roy Bean,* based on the exploits of the violent self-proclaimed judge of Langtry, Texas, in the 1870's. Paul Newman will play the same role in the movies.

FAN FARE:
LOVING OLLIE
LOUIS SCHAEFER

Because we were all supposed to have perfectly straight, braced, brushed teeth and you had the longest, ugliest tooth in the world . . .

Because you bellowed gustily when you sang while we had to mince words and clip our breath even in church, even in the bathtub . . .

Because you said "jolly" and "gee whiz" and kid stuff that even we didn't say, especially on the softball diamond . . .

Because you could nuzzle and cuddle while we had to shake hands and sit still . . .

Because you hurled yourself into games and shows and Gilbert and Sullivan, and had friends you knew were friends no matter what . . .

Because you laughed and guffawed and roared as if it were always recess, and loved a disaster whenever you met one . . .

Because you were never a dragon . . . we loved you.

Louis Schaefer is an actor and a writer in New York City.

Gee whiz, Ollie, stealing the show again!

Michael Ansara plays Apache chief Cochise in *Broken Arrow,* which begins a four-year stint on NBC in 1956. Based more on the Jimmy Stewart movie than on history, *Broken Arrow* co-stars John Lupton as Indian agent Tom Jeffords. It is one of the few westerns sympathetic to Indians.

Allen "Rocky" Lane, one-time movie cowboy idol, becomes TV's *Red Ryder* in 1956. Lane will later provide the voice of Alan Young's TV horse in *Mr. Ed.*

My Friend Flicka, based on Mary O'Hara's juvenile stories, comes to CBS for three years. Flicka's owners are (L-R): Gene Evans, Johnny Washbrook, and Anita Louise.

MEMOIRS OF SPEEDY DELIVERY

DAVID NEWELL

Having always been an incurable show biz buff, I spent a good part of my childhood going to the movies, listening to the radio, and persuading my grandfather to take me to the stage plays at the old Nixon Theatre in Pittsburgh. Then television invaded every household and put radio and the movie houses out of business. It was the answer to a young show biz buff's dreams. All that entertainment for nothing, and best of all, right in my own living room. I even considered giving up my paper route, since I no longer had to worry about bus fares and admission prices.

Television was the marijuana of the early 1950's. Everyone in the seventh grade seemed to live for their next television turn-on. I, of course, probably chalked up more television "flying time" than anyone in the class. Mornings, lunch hours, afternoons, evenings and weekends I spent watching the sign-on, noon news, *Howdy Doody, Captain Video, The Goldbergs, Your Hit Parade,* and *Jackie Gleason.*

I was ecstatic when I found out that Pittsburgh would soon be getting still another television station. It was going to be an educational station—WQED. I anxiously awaited the day when I would be able to add another channel to my viewing repertoire and at last—in April, 1954—WQED came on the air. I remember watching programs about how to make steel and the life of George Eliot. These were not exactly the topic of discussion by my fellow seventh graders, but there was one program that everyone in the school talked about and that program was called *The Children's Corner.* It was hosted by a pert young woman named Josie Carey and was written and produced by a

man named Fred Rogers.

Although no upstanding seventh grader would admit watching for his own pleasure, it was surprising how many just happened to catch it every day over the shoulders of the younger children in their families. To me, *The Children's Corner* was different from the other programs I saw on television. It was different because it didn't show any Hopalong Cassidy films, and nobody was ever hit with a custard pie or squirted with a seltzer bottle. And because it seemed, in a warm and informal way, to involve the viewer himself. For example, Josie and her puppet friends encouraged the audience to learn an incredible banquet of skills, from French conversation to Morse code. To this day I can spell my first name in Morse code, and juggle three oranges at the same time. At age thirteen, I even joined the Tame Tiger Torganization and, much to my surprise, actually received my Tame Tiger Pin in the mail. (I am still waiting for my Lone Ranger Ring.)

Although Josie Carey was the on-camera talent, Fred Rogers was the talent behind the scenes. Besides being the producer and staff musician, he also did the voices and manipulated all the puppets on the program. And, as report has it, whenever a musical interlude or an accompaniment for a song was needed, Fred would put down the puppets and make a running dash to the organ at the other end of the studio, arriving just in time to play. The musical moment concluded, he'd sprint back to the waiting puppets and continue with the next sequence.

Back in 1954, most of the programs I can re-

111

Mickey Braddock (L) stars as Corky in Screen Gem's *Circus Boy,* which debuts on CBS in 1956. Braddock will become more famous years later as Mickey Dolenz, singer-drummer of The Monkees. Here Andy Clyde feeds Bimbo, Jr., newly arrived at Big Tim Champion's circus.

Cheyenne becomes a weekly ABC series in 1956 with Clint Walker continuing as Cheyenne Bodie, here trying to convince Jean Byron to return his gun. *Cheyenne* will usher in a whole series of adult westerns that will soon dominate television. Despite contract disputes with Warner Brothers, Walker will play Cheyenne on and off until 1960.

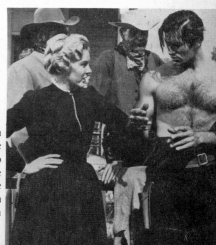

David Newell, in his role as Mr. McFeely, makes a delivery to his neighbor, Mister Rogers.

member were done live. *The Children's Corner* was no exception. In fact, this was part of the fun—at least for the viewer—because one never knew when some television personality might stop in at WQED and visit the program. I remember watching one afternoon when Gertrude Berg (Molly Goldberg) appeared, though what she actually said escapes me. Fred Ro-

gers reports that Molly just dropped by to give Henrietta Pussycat her recipe for blintzes. Molly stayed to linger awhile with King Friday XIII. King Friday asked if she had ever been presented at Court before and Molly answered, "Only at night court." Molly's visit was the highlight of my televiewing week.

Occasionally Josie had a mysterious visitor to

ABC's true-life adventure series, *Bold Journey*, debuts on prime time and is quite successful. Here John Stewart (R) visits a Polynesian pearl diver in "The Pearls of Tuomota." Jack Douglas will host the syndicated version of the series.

Sports has two big moments on television in 1956. Yankee Don Larson pitches a perfect game against Brooklyn in the World Series, and underdog Floyd Patterson (seen here) knocks out Archie Moore to win the heavyweight boxing championship vacated by Rocky Marciano.

Sugar Ray Robinson, who will be a five-time middleweight boxing champion, is a top television attraction.

"Many years later I learned that the prince was Fred Rogers . . ."

the *Corner*. It was a tall man in princely black cape and mask, a royal figure who waltzed with Josie and then left. Many years later I learned that the prince was Fred Rogers. who had once again put down his puppets and donned a costume for a rare on-camera appearance.

After a while, I managed to get out of the seventh grade and gradually became unfaithful to *The Children's Corner*. Meanwhile, Fred, Josie, and company continued their television work and garnered many kudos, including the 1955 Sylvania Award for the best locally-produced children's program in the country.

When *The Children's Corner* completed a seven-year run, Fred joined the Canadian Broadcasting Corporation in Toronto and began a fifteen-minute program called *Misterogers*. In 1964–65 he returned to Pittsburgh and established a half-hour version of the *Misterogers* program over the Eastern Educational Network. When the funds ran out, threatening the demise of *Misterogers,* the audience demand was so strong that new funds were sought to sustain the program. Fortunately, the Sears-Roebuck Foundation came to the rescue.

That was in 1967, the same year I was reacquainted with a familiar television friend, Fred Rogers. As fate would have it, I had been preparing for a career in theater arts (thanks to my grandfather's early encouragement) and one day found myself being interviewed by Fred Rogers for a position as a production assistant on *Mister Rogers' Neighborhood*. Because of the Sears-Roebuck grant and a matching one by the Public Broadcasting Service, the program was soon to be launched nationally on most of the PBS stations and a staff was being assembled.

Not only did I get the job as production assistant, but also the opportunity to play the part of Mr. McFeely, the Speedy Delivery man in *Mister Rogers' Neighborhood*. Mr. McFeely is an elderly but rather vigorous neighbor who makes his delivery rounds through the neighborhood on a bicycle.

McFeely is a collector. He collects everything from model trains to old movies. He is also somewhat of a show biz buff, because he is ready at a moment's notice to perform a tap dance in the neighborhood variety show or attempt to sing in one of King Friday's operas. And there is probably an Abbott and Costello movie somewhere in his home movie collection. I would say that Mr. McFeely is a composite of the childhood memories of my grandfather and our many afternoons spent theater-hopping all over Pittsburgh.

I like playing the role of Mr. McFeely, but what is also satisfying to me is observing how skillfully and sensitively Fred Rogers uses the medium of television to communicate with children. While some children's programs might use television to sell cereal, Fred Rogers uses it to help children to feel good about themselves. He uses television to interpret for children what a word like "assassination" means. And he uses television to encourage children to talk about their feelings. Fred Rogers has been in children's television for well over twenty years. Little did I realize when I was watching *The Children's Corner* long ago that I would become one of his most devoted neighbors.

David Newell, who is the associate producer of the PBS children's program, Mister Rogers' Neighborhood, *also portrays one of the neighbors, Mr. McFeely, the Speedy Delivery Man. This article originally appeared in* Pittsburgh Magazine *(February 1974).*

Chet Huntley and David Brinkley are so successful working as a team covering the 1956 political conventions that they are given their own daily fifteen-minute NBC newscast. They replace John Cameron Swayze.

Innovative Pat Weaver, who has been responsible for such important shows as *Today, Tonight, Home, Wide Wide World,* and many NBC "spectaculars" is forced to resign as NBC's chairman of the board. Robert Sarnoff takes over.

COMMUNICATING WITH CHILDREN

FRED ROGERS

Mister Rogers, creator of the neighborhood of make-believe.

There is no scientific or technological advance that is either good or bad in itself. Just because we hear sad news over the telephone doesn't mean that the invention of the telephone was a bad thing. It's only as we human beings give *meaning* to science or technology that they will have a positive or negative thrust.

A good friend of mine is using the splitting of the atom for medical diagnosis. Others we know have used it for destruction.

Television to me was a challenging new instrument. I wanted to use it the way I had used the piano and drama as a child to communicate some things that I felt were positive—and important—in our world. Since one can't be a communicator with equal impact on all segments of society, my early decision was clearly one to communicate with children. I wanted to help as many as I could to feel good about themselves and what they could become. I wanted to show them a wide range of artistry and feeling that make up a varied culture like ours. I wanted to help children learn to discover worth in little things, in things that had no price tag, in people who might have outer handicaps and great inner strengths. I wanted every child to know that he or she had something lovable and worth expressing, that everyone has limits as well as possibilities. I wanted to engender feelings of responsibility to oneself as well as others.

Public television has given me the sustained opportunity to work at these goals for twenty years. Any one year of planning and creating would have been simply frustrating, if there had not been the confidence of succeeding years to work out the creation. We must not waste money on short-term investments. Television programs, like everything else, need time to grow.

Public television has been an instrument for me to be a professional worker for families with young children. It must always be an expression of our highest idealism as well as an instrument for our positive creative powers.

Fred Rogers is creator, host, writer, and producer of Mister Rogers' Neighborhood, *the longest-running children's program on PBS.*

114

In October, 1956, Ernie Kovacs begins hosting *The Tonight Show* two nights a week, with Steve Allen continuing on the other three nights.

January 1957. *The Tonight Show* changes its format and becomes *Tonight! America After Dark.* Here people on the street look in as host Jack Lescoulie interviews a guest. The show, which also features on-the-spot news coverage, proves unpopular and is scrapped in July.

January 14, 1957. J. Fred Muggs helps Dave Garroway decorate a birthday cake marking *The Today Show's* fifth anniversary. After the sixth anniversary, Muggs will be taken off the show (for biting people, it is rumored).

FAN FARE:
DEAR ANDY'S GANG:

My whole life has been shaped by one single TV show—*Andy's Gang*. Because of Gunga and his elephant, India and adventure have always been synonymous for me. When *Andy's Gang* went off the air I was in agony until the networks started showing Sabu movies. That settled it. I swore I would someday travel to India and the Far East—the land of adventure!

When I applied to college, I answered the entrance exam essay question "What one person had the most influence on your life's development?" with "Sabu." The dean called me into his office to ask me to explain this most unusual choice. But I had no patience for school. Soon I dropped out and traveled around the world, just as I had sworn I would. When I returned I was excited to discover that there was a new show on television, *Maya,* featuring another young Indian boy, his elephant Maya, and a young white boy searching for his lost father. Except for a few minor alterations, I thought I was watching *Andy's Gang* again.

Everything about that show amused and delighted me, and it remains vividly alive in my imagination. I can still see Midnight the Black Cat standing on his rear paws playing the violin and saying "Nice, nice," while Squeaky the Hamster circles him on his motorcycle. I still believe they were real animals. I remember Froggie the Gremlin, whom Andy Devine introduced each week with, "Plunk your magic twanger, Froggie," as the frog appeared in a puff of smoke. I always watched the eager anticipation as the Italian professor would try to lecture the audience

From 1955 to 1960 Andy Devine led Andy's Gang *on NBC.*

about some chemicals and Froggie would interject some devious suggestion to completely devastate the scholar. Take this example:

> PROFESSOR: Now children, you must carefully take the ink . . .
> FROGGIE: And put it in your mouth.
> PROFESSOR: And put it in your mouth like so. . . . Oh! (spits) Oh, you monster!
> FROGGIE: Ha, ha, ha, ha.

I'm still laughing, too.

Love,
Paul Scharfman

Paul Scharfman is a memorabilia addict living in Los Angeles.

July 29, 1957. *The Tonight Show* returns with Jack Paar hosting. Hugh Downs (R), the ex-host of Pat Weaver's *Home,* acts as Paar's announcer and assistant. Zsa Zsa Gabor is a frequent guest.

April 5, 1957. Edward R. Murrow's acclaimed talk show, *Person to Person,* moves into its fifth year on CBS. Here Murrow visits the home of Elizabeth Taylor and Mike Todd, producer of *Around the World in Eighty Days.*

SATURDAY MORNING CARTOONS

MARK NARDONE

A champion can be found for almost everything on television, no matter how unpopular, obscure, or unimportant, yet one would be hard pressed to discover a serious, rational defender of the Saturday morning cartoon. The reason for this is quite obvious; as voice specialist June Foray (Rocky the Flying Squirrel) states matter-of-factly: "Saturday morning cartoons are garbage."

Each Saturday morning, our children's senses are bombarded by unrelenting, piercing sounds, dreadful characters and story lines, and unbelievably ugly images. There is no reprieve. All the cartoons blend into one another; they all look the same—there is no depth, there is no detail; every character looks like another from the previous cartoon—they all walk, talk, and react identically. Film cartoonist Ralph Bakshi correctly comments: "Television cartoon characters remind one of Levittown."

For several years the most popular cartoon characters have been superheroes (Aquaman, Spiderman, Wonder Woman, Birdman), monsters, and rock groups (the Beatles, the Jackson Five). To capitalize on all popular trends, the cartoonists have taken rock groups and placed them in the future *(The Partridge Family, 2200 A.D.)* and have taken monsters and put them in rock groups *(Frankenstein, Jr. and The Impossibles)*. Almost every character fights evil while riding on a screeching motorcycle or in a booming space rocket or a supercar with no muffler. As for the animal characters in the "funny" cartoons—for twenty years they have been poor imitations of Yogi Bear and Boo Boo who, while inoffen-

Batman and Superman appeared throughout the 1960's in crude, cheap animation—only their jaws seemed to move.

116

Networks devote much of their Sunday afternoon schedule to educational programming in 1957. Here Dr. Frank Baxter explains "The Thread of Life" in terms that both adults and children can understand. Baxter will give many lectures on Bell Telephone's science series on NBC.

Sunday September 15, 1957. Pablo Picasso, seventy-seven-year-old Spanish painter and sculptor, is the first subject of NBC's *Wisdom,* which will visit a total of twenty-six outstanding figures before leaving the air.

Dr. C. Walton Lillehei (R) tells *Conquest* reporter, Harry Reasoner, how medical science's newest discovery—the heart-lung machine— works in saving lives. On Sunday March 9, 1957, between 5:00 P.M. and 6:00 P.M., Lillehei will save the life of a six-year-old heart patient on the show.

All cartoons mentioned in this article were not made specifically for Saturday mornings, but eventually that's where they all wound up. It is interesting to note that some of the better cartoons were made for evening viewing, while the trash was automatically given to the children.

Journey to the Center of the Earth, *a cartoon based on the classic sci-fi novel by Jules Verne, appeared in 1967.*

sive enough, have no business being the ultimate TV cartoon stars.

Each year, the more prominent animation studios will present up to thirty new proposals to the net-

works. They will unveil an elaborate storyboard and may show the debut film of a new character. (They may only sell a couple, but each sale is worth between $60,000 and $100,000.) And over and over again, they will assure the networks that they can turn out their cartoons quick as a bunny. Of course, the faster the cartoon is produced, the lower the quality. Networks do not care if a cartoon is good as long as it meets their deadline, but many of the animators—usually veterans who made some of the best theatrical cartoons in the forties and fifties—regret the waste of their talents.

Robert McKimson directed many of the best Bugs Bunny and Daffy Duck cartoons at Warner Brothers thirty years ago. Today he does free-lance work for Depatie-Freleng (Fritz Freleng was also an old Warner's director. He was an original, beginning in the early thirties.), a studio whose main contribution to TV animation is the mediocre Pink Panther series. He is one of many who laments the virtual disappearance of the theatrical cartoon since the early fifties: "Limited animation is all we can do nowadays because of economics. We used to do a different drawing for each frame when we did full animation and that drawing was detailed; but today we use the same undetailed drawing many times. You don't get any personality into your characters. You're just concerned with getting things out quickly and economically. There is not much pride or satisfaction in this kind of work. We're really not creating anything."

Hanna-Barbera has been the major producer of television cartoons since the late fifties, when they introduced Ruff and Ready and Huckleberry Hound, still the top Hanna-Barbera TV characters to date. If any studio is to blame for setting trends in television cartooning, it is Hanna-Barbera—for pioneering the excessive use of violence; copying live-action shows (e.g., using *The Honeymooners* as a model for *The*

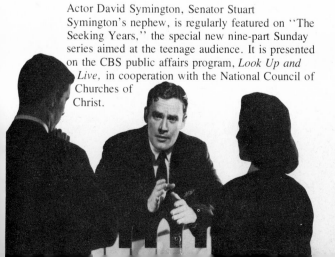

Actor David Symington, Senator Stuart Symington's nephew, is regularly featured on "The Seeking Years," the special new nine-part Sunday series aimed at the teenage audience. It is presented on the CBS public affairs program, *Look Up and Live,* in cooperation with the National Council of Churches of Christ.

October 7, 1957. "I give this record an 85, because it has a good beat and it's easy to dance to." Another show aimed at the teenage audience is *American Bandstand,* which ABC broadcasts daily from Philadelphia where it has been a local sensation since 1952. This is the show that will teach American youth how to dance everything from the jitterbug to the stroll to the twist to the hustle.

Josie and the Pussycats—*teenagers, outer space, and cats.*

Flintstones); using superheroes as cartoon stars; and using every available raucous noise to enliven shows. June Foray states: "To be hired by Joe Barbera, you have to sound loud and gravelly; you have to ruin your voice." But Hanna-Barbera proved to the networks that by cutting corners (actually chunks), it was possible to make cartoons cheaply enough for television's needs. They deserve thanks for nothing.

Bill Hanna defends his product as being the best that is possible considering the economic demands of TV: "When we did Tom and Jerry at MGM in the forties, we did one and a half minutes a week. Now we produce thirty or thirty-five minutes per week. Every phase of cartoon making could be handled more carefully. It is unfortunate that more money can't be spent. As it is, I think we do a fair job in character design, we do a decent job in background, and I think where we fall short is in the actual animation."

Actually, Hanna-Barbera falls short in everything. You see, TV cartoons—despite financial concerns—can have some originality at least. Wild, wacky *Beany and Cecil,* created by Bob Clampett, another Warner's alumnus, back in 1961 (from his early fifties live puppet show *A Time for Beany*) was uneven at best, but it is certainly preferable to the Hanna-Barbera assembly-line product. And, of course, we still cherish the reruns of Jay Ward's *Rocky and His Friends (Bullwinkle)* and *George of the Jungle,* the best cartoons ever made for television. Why is Ward not courted by the networks to give them inventive new material? Ward layout-man Lou Kessler is of the opinion that Ward will never get another cartoon show: "As Jay Ward says, 'CBS doesn't like us. ABC hates us. NBC despises us.' "

So the networks continue to go to Hanna-Barbera and its imitators (from as far away as Japan) for their cartoons. Meanwhile the best animation on TV is found in commercials, because it is in that area that those such as Jay Ward and the great Tex Avery (who created Bugs Bunny) must work to maintain their creative control. Veteran cartoonist Herb Klynn, today with Format Productions, sums up the distress animators feel because they are not being allowed to experiment on television: "We can create so much through animation, but try to show the networks. Most people I bring ideas to have no creative insight at all. I have so much personal frustration trying to deal with them." Klynn is someone who obviously understands what we who remember good animation are griping about.

During the last few years, there has been a gradual introduction of live-action Saturday morning shows. Soon ABC may try its luck at serializing children's books. But the undiscerning child still seems to prefer cartoons. And if the production schedule for next year's Saturday morning lineup is any indication, limited animation in the Hanna-Barbera mold will be even more prevalent than it is now.

Mark Nardone is a young screenwriter in Los Angeles.

Ageless Dick Clark will host *American Bandstand* through the fifties, sixties, and seventies, introducing many rock music stars and records to the American public for the first time. He will become fabulously wealthy and form his own production company.

Patti Page, "the Singing Rage," America's most successful female pop singer in the fifties, is hostess of 1957's hour-long *The Big Record,* on which guests perform their big hit songs. Dennis James is the announcer.

Comic-musician Spike Jones and The City Slickers come to CBS in 1957 for a four-month run on *The Spike Jones Show.* Jones had been host of NBC variety shows in 1951 and 1954.

SATURDAY MORNING SCI-FI PROGRAMS

JOHN DAVIS

It can reasonably be asked if there would be any space program or any NASA today without the television space shows of the fifties. Unlike Hollywood's science fiction films of the same period, which were usually concerned with catastrophic threats to the earth either directly or indirectly caused by ''the bomb,'' TV space shows presented a basically optimistic view of the future and the benefits of technology. In most cases, the heroes were members of military groups serving organizations called United Planets, or the United Solar System. In any event, for members of the postwar baby boom, the first generation to grow up with television, it was certainly the Saturday morning space operas that captured our imaginations and got us excited about the concept of man traveling through the inky reaches of outer space. It was also fitting that the wonders of tomorrow should be shown to us on the greatest scientific wonder of the day—as was attested by the appropriate title of the first of the television space shows, *Captain Video.*

Of course, there was nothing even remotely educational about most of these series. Even an eleven-year-old could catch scores of ridiculous inaccuracies, things like smoke rising from a rocket's exhaust, ray guns making nice sizzling sounds in what was supposed to be the vacuum of space, or a giant hole being blown in the side of a spaceship without everything inside being instantly sucked out. *Captain Video* was

> ## ''TV space shows presented a basically optimistic view of the future . . .''

one of the most notorious in this regard. Starting locally in New York City on the Dumont network, it quickly became a national phenomenon hampered only slightly by negligible production values (the uniforms the actors wore were obviously army surplus). Even so, Captain Video handled all sorts of dangers to the ''safety of the universe'' until 1956 when he was reduced to introducing a cartoon show.

Although some of the writers on shows like *Captain Video* and *Commando Cody* must have gotten their scientific training from watching old *Flash Gordon* and *Rocketman* serials, other shows did at least make a stab at believability. *Tom Corbett, Space Cadet,* on NBC from 1950 to 1956, had a rocketship (the Polaris) with a crew of three who actually looked as though they performed some function in getting their craft from one area of the cosmic frontier to another. Their space suits looked pretty convincing too, except for the large holes in the fronts of their clear plastic helmets. Perhaps the show that made the greatest effort to look up-to-date was *Rocky Jones,*

Although by 1957 *The Honeymooners* is no longer a series in itself, Jackie Gleason and Audrey Meadows continue to play Ralph and Alice Kramden many times on *The Jackie Gleason Show.*

Art Carney, an early Gleason discovery, remains part of Gleason's cast. Here, Carney bawls out Gleason's ''Poor Fool.''

Space Ranger. Its spaceship, the Orbit Jet, looked like a scaled-up version of a V-2, the space stations used the Werner von Braun concept of the revolving wheel, and the ships used some sort of hyperspace drive to account for traversing immense distances in short periods of time. Two other positive attributes of this show were the nice theme music that always accompanied rocket landings, and the scanty costume worn by Vena Ray, the female member of the crew.

However, the most ambitious Saturday morning sci-fi program, and one of the longest-running, was *Space Patrol.* It was so successful that, alone among these shows, it was at one point expanded to a full-hour format. Like most of the other space operas of the early fifties, *Space Patrol* was done live. Even its commercials were live, with members of the cast—usually Major Robertson—extolling the virtues of Rice Chex and Wheat Chex and offering an endless stream of items available for a cereal box-top and a small fee. In addition to superior promotion, *Space Patrol* had a superior cast, headed by Ed Kemmer as Commander Buzz Corey and Lynn Osborne as Cadet Happy, and stories that at times approached real science fiction. One series of episodes, for example, featured a planet whose inhabitants had been reduced to stone-age savagery by nuclear war; another series had for its villain a thinking crystal that believed it was God. But for all its class, the show still had its problems—like the morning a cast member walked into what was supposed to be a stone wall and knocked it over, along with a good deal of the rest of the set as well.

One other space show that had good production (it was shot on film) and interesting stories was *Flash Gordon,* starring Steve Holland as Alex Raymond's famous comic strip hero. It seemed much more genuinely other-wordly than the other space shows. Some stories featured such advanced concepts as an

Rocky Jones, Space Ranger made a great effort to look scientific. Richard Crane and Sally Mansfield starred.

120

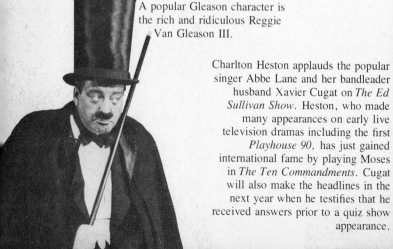

A popular Gleason character is the rich and ridiculous Reggie Van Gleason III.

Charlton Heston applauds the popular singer Abbe Lane and her bandleader husband Xavier Cugat on *The Ed Sullivan Show.* Heston, who made many appearances on early live television dramas including the first *Playhouse 90,* has just gained international fame by playing Moses in *The Ten Commandments.* Cugat will also make the headlines in the next year when he testifies that he received answers prior to a quiz show appearance.

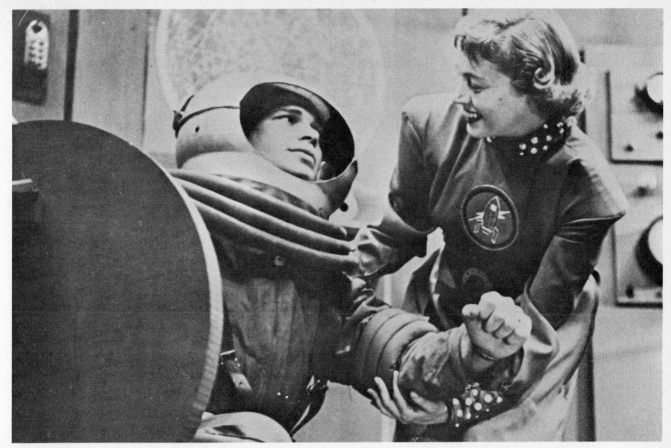

"Space Academy, U.S.A., in the world beyond tomorrow." Tom Corbett, Space Cadet, *one of the best of the fifties lot.*

army of clones, and civilizations destroyed by religious fanaticism. There was generally a gloomy atmosphere to the series, and some episodes had sado-masochistic overtones, such as the one in which a beautiful space witch had Flash tied to a pillar and played weird music on a harp which forced Dale to perform a sensual dance that was supposed to end with her stabbing Flash. The creators of this "children's entertainment" also seemed to enjoy strapping Dale to whirling tables and sinking platforms—but than *Flash Gordon* had a unique space show tone.

The genre lasted from 1950 to 1957, with 1954 and 1955 as the peak years. After the passing of the space operas, there were fewer and fewer quality live-action shows on Saturday mornings, and eventually even these were completely driven off the air by the advent of the cheaply-produced cartoon programs.

John Davis is the editor of The Velvet Light Trap, *an international film magazine.*

In September 1957, Jimmy Durante, who has been one of the most active performers on live television during the fifties, completes his last show. "Goodnight Mrs. Calabash, wherever you are."

A great cast is assembled for an hour on NBC's *The Kay Starr Show* in 1957. Tony Bennett, Harpo Marx, Kay Starr, and Louis Armstrong listen to pianist George Shearing.

Harpo Marx and Louis Armstrong perform a duet on *The Kay Starr Show.*

FAN FARE:
DEAR PERRY WHITE:

Once again, Superman staunchly protects Lois Lane.

This is to inform you that that jerk working for you at the *Daily Planet,* Clark Kent, is really Superman. That's why Clark has to go to the bathroom every time that even bigger jerk, Jimmy Olsen, manages to get himself trapped at the bottom of an abandoned uranium mine with only a poison gas bomb to talk to. Speaking of jerks, how is it that week after week Clark K. opens that phony door neatly labeled Store Room, goes inside, and jumps out the window, while you, Perry White, chief of a great metropolitan newspaper, never suspect a thing? You've been pulling the white hairs out of your head and screaming, ''Great Caesar's ghost'' for years just because nobody can figure out Superman's secret identity, and yet you don't seem to give a speeding bullet about why it takes Clark five and a half hours to find a dozen No. 2 pencils in that infamous phony storeroom.

In fact, it always happens the same way. You call Clark, Lois Lane, and your ace cub reporter Jimmy Olsen into your office to meet with that 24-karat incompetent, Inspector Henderson. Henderson says a crime wave is sweeping the city; the phone rings (it's always for the good inspector); Henderson very seriously reports the bad news that the First National Bank is being robbed; and our man Clark says, ''Excuse me, I gotta go find some 'While You Were Out' memo pads in the storeroom, heh heh.'' Then, Jimmy ''The Jerk'' Olsen says, ''Yes, Chief.'' You say, ''Don't call me Chief!'' Lovely Lois says, ''I wonder what happened to Clark?'' And I sit in front of my TV set screaming at the top of my lungs, ''He's in that ridiculous storeroom taking off his clothes and jumping out the window!!!'' Geez, Perry, come to think of it, you're the biggest jerk of all.

Your loyal fan,
Peter Odabashian

Disguised as a mild-mannered film editor, Peter Odabashian is a major motion picture director.

The Marge and Gower Champion Show appears on CBS in 1957 for a short time. Marge Champion had been the model for Disney's Snow White.

Singer-actress-game show panelist Polly Bergen hostesses her own musical-variety show in 1957 on CBS. This comes months after her Emmy-winning dramatic performance in ''The Helen Morgan Story'' on *Playhouse 90.*

The Gisele MacKenzie Show starring the popular singer from *Your Hit Parade* debuts on NBC in 1957 and lasts one season.

REMEMBERING LASSIE

KATHRYN LICHTER

Like most children of the fifties, I watched *Lassie* every Sunday night. There was never any dog as great as Lassie. All week I waited impatiently to savor every minute of her splendor.

For those of you who are not familiar with her, she was only the greatest dog on earth, a collie like no other collie, a canine like no other canine. She lived with the Millers on a farm and she slept with their son, Jeff. If necessary, in the dead of a winter night she would force the window open with her nose and leap out into the cold to run for miles to save a dog friend of hers who had accidentally fallen into an abandoned well and was lying there dying of fright. Many was the time she would disappear from the farm, only to return barking frantically and turning in a particular direction. The whole family would drop whatever they were doing, jump into the pickup truck, and follow her down the road where she would lead them to their best friend who had fallen out of a tree while he was trying to save his neighbor's cat and had broken his leg and couldn't move. At the end of each show Lassie would be hugged by the family and everyone was happy.

I thought my dog Spot was an awful lot like Lassie. She looked like Lassie, except that she was a trifle smaller. She was wonderful and very smart. I had been so inspired by her TV counterpart that I had trained her to perfection. The only drawback that I can recall was that she used to bite my nose. It was her very ingenious way of telling me she had had enough.

Since she was so much like Lassie, I decided to give her the ultimate test. One afternoon we headed into the woods. We stopped at nothing: poison ivy, poison oak, imaginary monsters—nothing could get in our way. Finally we were ready. I feigned a fall and screamed a lot. I said, "Spot, go home. I broke my leg. Wah! Wah!"

She stood there.

Again I insisted, "Spot, go home!"

Well, I had to repeat it many many times. I screamed and thrashed about. Finally she looked at me pathetically (she must have been thinking that this time the kid had really flipped) and trotted off downhill at a lively pace. And I thought, "Whew, she finally got it."

So I waited. And waited. It started to get dark. I started to get scared, so I decided to go home. Then I got lost. I fell down and twisted my ankle. Still, no one came to my rescue. Finally, after lots of praying (all I knew was, "Now I lay me down to sleep") and hysteria, I found my way home. My mother was so relieved that she spanked me and sent me to my room without any supper. (I didn't care. It was Tuesday and we were having frogs' legs.) When everyone was asleep, I sneaked out of my room and found Spot, the traitor. I reprimanded her for her negligence but it didn't work. She bit my nose.

Many years later, when Spot and I were both thirteen, I was with my family living in Mexico, and I was still a faithful Lassie watcher, even though the Millers were speaking Spanish. I didn't care. Lassie was the same. But then I started to get wise, about Lassie and life. There were rumors circulating, like the one about Lassie being a boy. No! Then there was the one about there really being thirteen Lassies, not

Gisele MacKenzie is a frequent guest on CBS's *The Jack Benny Program*. An often-repeated comic bit has the slow-playing Benny unable to keep up on the violin with the speedy MacKenzie who keeps stealing his spotlight.

Red Skelton visits *The Eve Arden Show* which debuts on CBS in 1957, soon after the final episode of *Our Miss Brooks*. Arden's new comedy will be less successful and only last one year.

Kathryn Lichter and her faithful but unresourceful dog, Spot.

Tommy Rettig and his faithful and resourceful dog, Lassie.

one. And the rumors stretched on and on, as rumors do. Boy, was I disillusioned. But disillusionment soon turned into acceptance. Lassie was, after all, an actress. Just doing her job. She was a very well-trained dog. When her trainer, off screen, said speak, she barked. When he said cry, she cried. On screen, Lassie displayed a full range of emotions. They were not

hers. They belonged to the character she was playing.

So now that I have figured it all out, this is what I have to say. Lassie, I still love you. You were the best. Spot, forgive me.

Kathryn Lichter, still an animal lover, trains dogs in New York City.

124

Three-time Oscar winner Walter Brennan comes to television in 1957 to star as Grampa Amos McCoy in ABC's *The Real McCoys*, a comedy about a poor West Virginia farming family transplanted to the fields of California.

The Real McCoys, Walter Brennan, Michael Winkleman, Lydia Reed, Kathy Nolan, and *Our Miss Brooks* alumnus Richard Crenna, rehearse with guest star Minerva Urecal.

Make Room for Daddy moves to CBS in 1957 and is retitled *The Danny Thomas Show*. Marjorie Lord (Kathy) replaces Jean Hagen as Danny Williams's wife, and little Angela Cartwright (Linda, not shown) joins Rusty Hamer (Rusty) and Sherry Jackson (Terry), as the Williams children. Within a short time this will become television's top comedy.

REMEMBERING GENE AUTRY

JOHN BUSKIN

When I was in the first grade my older brother convinced me that he was Gene Autry. It wasn't just that I was dumb or gullible. Even now when I look back upon it I realize that there was an overwhelming weight of evidence supporting the hypothesis. There was the fact that my brother had an uncanny talent for describing the action of a particular show before it began. (I was at the time unaware of *TV Guide* or encapsulated plot summaries in the newspaper.) There was the show's intricate shooting schedule that always took place after I was asleep. There was my own inability to refute any of his arguments. It did not matter that my brother bore not even the slightest resemblance to our cowboy hero—he convinced me that he was Gene. The crusher occurred one morning on the George Washington Bridge.

We often traveled to see relatives in New Jersey. For some reason which has since eluded me, my brother and I vied for the chance to reach over the back seat and through the driver's window to hand the toll collector the quarter. My uncle had worked out an alternating system but somehow it was never my turn. On the morning in question my brother was wearing his six-guns, western shirt, and cowboy hat. I remember the clothes vividly because when he grew out of them I got a hold of them myself for a few years. The shirt pockets had arrows on their ends and the cuffs and shoulders were different colors from the body. The hat, when new, had had cloth balls suspended all around the edge of the brim, suggesting a south-of-the-border motif. By the fateful morning, however, all the cloth balls had been pulled or bitten

"I felt strange about my brother being Gene Autry . . ."

off leaving ragged gaps in the brown plastic strip that edged the brim. This was the full regalia, and when my brother stuck his hand out the window with the quarter, he looked sharp. The toll collector glanced down at him for no more than a second. Then he turned his head back to his cash drawer and said, "Thanks, Gene." That was all I needed to hear.

I felt strange about my brother being Gene Autry. I didn't know whether to be proud or jealous. I asked if our mother knew and he said that she didn't and not to tell her. He said that to her he was only her young son and to know he was someone else would break her heart. My next conclusion was that if he wasn't her son then perhaps he wasn't my brother. He told me that this was true as well and if I divulged his real identity he would stop posing as one of my family and move elsewhere. A star of Gene Autry's magnitude had to preserve his anonymity.

I lived with the secret for awhile but in the end it was all too much for me. I was the kind of kid who liked Juicy Fruit gum but never knew whether or not to buy it because Gene chewed Doublemint. Life was confusing enough without being entrusted with sensitive information as well. One day after returning to school from lunch I blurted it out to David Katz. He stood behind me in our column of twos. Just before

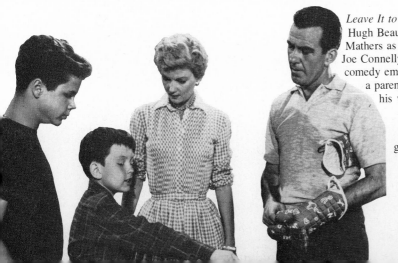

Leave It to Beaver stars Barbara Billingsley, Hugh Beaumont (R), Tony Dow, and Jerry Mathers as the Beaver. Created and written by Joe Connelly and Bob Mosher, this clever comedy emphasizes that it is hard to be a kid or a parent. Here, as usual, Beaver tries to talk his way out of trouble.

Beaver's worst fears are realized when a girl (!), Veronica Cartwright, gives him a kiss. *Leave It to Beaver* will remain on the air until 1963, but Beaver will not change his feelings about girls. Mathers will stop acting after the show's cancellation and eventually become a bank teller.

Gene Autry always got the bad guy, particularly when the bad guy was a scalawag disguised as a sheriff.

Mrs. Hoder had us lock our mouths, I turned around to David and told him that my brother was Gene Autry. "Oh no he's not," he said. "My brother is."

That night on TV Gene was receiving fire from five or six outlaws in a shack. He grabbed Champion's saddle blanket, climbed to the shack roof and draped the blanket over a smoking chimney. Within seconds the bad guys came out coughing. Gene had the drop on them. I'd always felt that the saddle blanket on the chimney was one of Gene's greatest ploys. My brother knew this and smugly asked me how I'd liked it. I just grunted. I told him it was my day for the green chair

and he was sitting in it. He said that as Gene Autry he got to sit where he wanted. I said, "No you don't."

It wasn't that I had started believing that David Katz's brother was Gene Autry. I was just a little wiser. I got up when Gene started singing, "I'm back in the saddle again," and was in my place at the kitchen table by the time he got to, "Out where a friend is a friend."

John Buskin, a writer, is grown up now and doesn't watch TV westerns anymore. He lives just down the block from his brother, Lieutenant Theo Kojak.

March 17, 1957. *Mama,* which CBS had given a one-year reprieve in 1956 because of viewer loyalty, is canceled. Here Toni Campbell (the second Dagmar) learns long division from Judson Laire while Rosemary Rice looks on. Mama (Peggy Wood), concentrates on her needlepoint for nearly the last time.

John Forsythe hugs Noreen Corcoran who plays his thirteen-year-old niece Kelly when the comedy *Bachelor Father* debuts on CBS in 1957. The show will also play on NBC and ABC before leaving television in 1962.

FAN FARE:
DEAR ADDAMS FAMILY:

I'm eleven years old, and it's early on a Friday evening in 1965. My mother and I have been out shopping—since the stores are open late tonight—and it's raining. We're almost home now, driving down a winding road below a steep hill on which, I never fail to think, your house would look right at home, especially on a rainy night. This macabre scene is enhanced by the fact that my mother is about to kill me, or at least run the car off the road and into a tree, because I'm bouncing up and down among the bags from Bamberger's hollering, "Come on, Mom, hurry up! *The Addams Family* is on in two minutes!"

It isn't hard to explain why physical force was the only way to keep me from watching you every Friday night when I was eleven. For one thing, you were refreshingly weird. As a fairly offbeat child locked into a world of normal parents, normal siblings, normal teachers, and normal boredom, I was fascinated by a family whose pets included a grown lion and an overgrown Venus's flytrap—a family where the parents almost never passed a negative judgment on an outsider, unless it was to wish that someone weren't quite so nervous. Unlike my pragmatic younger sister, who once asked my mother why she didn't "install" a Thing to help her around the house, I thought that everything that happened around your house made perfect sense. I drove my poor parents crazy with questions about why we couldn't have a lion (at the end of the television season, my folks came through with a lovable, but at the time prosaic, dog), and certain anatomical queries about Cousin Itt.

You also had style, years ahead of your time.

You had plants in your house back then that Californians are now growing in one-room apartments. You had chairs that collectors kill for today. You had wonderful names and a really terrific doorbell. You were rich and pleasure-loving and romantic. (Why didn't my father ever kiss my mother's arm clear up to the shoulder? He never even kissed her hand.) You had a lot more class than your neighbors over at the other network, the Munsters, who always came off looking like poor relations. You did everything with a certain grace and finesse, and hardly anyone in your family ever yelled. I went on a diet because I knew you had to be thin to dress like Morticia.

And you were funny, back when you didn't have to display social consciousness to be funny, and no one ever seemed to get hurt at your house.

At this point, I have to reveal that I had a big crush on Lurch. This is a secret I have carried around for years. Lurch was intelligent, strong, and not unattractive to a lovesick seventh-grader who was already five feet eight inches tall. He was a lot cuter than Pugsley, that's for sure.

Well, I had to outgrow you. But back in 1965, you were a lot more fun than reality and better than most fantasies, too. And twelve years later, I still know all the words to your theme song. And Lurch, I still have a thing for tall, intelligent men with bass voices.

Ellen Jaffe

Ellen Jaffe is a Los Angeles comedy writer trapped in the body of a receptionist.

127

September 21, 1957. Erle Stanley Gardner's *Perry Mason* hits the air on CBS. Raymond Burr is the famous attorney who never, except once, loses a case. Barbara Hale plays Della Street. The show is highlighted by a weekly courtroom confession scene.

David Janssen plays *Richard Diamond, Private Detective* on CBS from 1957 to 1959. Mary Tyler Moore, whose legs are the only part of her ever shown, is his secretary Sam, and Barbara Bain is his girlfriend Karen. Here Charles Bronson guest stars. Bronson will have his own crime series *Man With a Camera* on ABC from 1958 to 1960.

Rugged Lee Marvin stars as Chicago cop Lieutenant Frank Ballinger in *M Squad*, which debuts on NBC in 1957. It will stay on for three seasons.

TV SPORTS IN THE 1970'S

ROBERT RIGER

This year will mark the tenth anniversary of color television in the United States, as well as the electronic gifts of instant replay and slow motion, stop-action, and multiple screen images achieved *live* as the event is in progress at home or anywhere in the world. Now we are about to enter the second decade of electronic wizardry which will mark the extended use of the portable electronic (ENG) camera. In sports we must set up our studio in many remote stadiums and arenas in the world. We must make a studio at the top of a mountain or in the ocean to cover an event, no matter how large or small, whether it is a chess match in Reykjavik, or an Olympic decathlon in Mexico, or a high jump in Moscow.

The production of a television sports program is as competitive as the event—in different ways. There is strong competition between sports departments of the three major networks, and NBC and CBS are constantly bidding against ABC (the largest sports programmer) on all major world events. This brutal competition has caused the escalation of TV rights fees to the organizers of the events, to individual promoters, leagues, and world sporting organizations. This, in turn, has provoked in the 1970's the advent of synthetic sports competition, staged miniature athletic events between athletes and between nonathletes. These improvised events are organized for television and are grass roots affairs with little or no audience present, given shape and dramatic continuity in the cutting room. I call them synthetic because the results are never recorded in the record books of organized amateur or professional sports, and they would not

"We must make a studio at the top of a mountain . . ."

exist without the television exposure. I personally do not like these events and never watch them, but they have attracted a large audience. I believe, however, that they will not last, except for one or two events a year, as we approach the end of the seventies.

The TV sports executives who shape these synthetic sports and recruit the performers feel that they are good sporting entertainment, because it is more exciting to watch a famous athlete perform adequately or ridiculously than to watch unknown athletes in lesser sports perform for regional or national championships. This position will change within the next five years as television sports moves into the exciting decade of portable video tape cameras that can report live or on the same day of the event. We will then see a wealth of sports on TV that have had little or no exposure to date and have until now been covered by portable film cameras, edited, and then run on television as film shows. This is costly, and there is a delay of a week or two or months before the post-production work can be completed on these filmed events. When film shows are rushed to air the costs are very high.

In the coming era of portable tape and the miniaturization of the video recording units, we will see a television sports unit move from event to event in a panel truck or a station wagon and record with color

128

Dashiell Hammett's *The Thin Man* begins a two-year stint on NBC. Peter Lawford is the dashing ex-private eye Nick Charles and Phyllis Kirk is his wife Nora, who is forever getting him involved in crime investigations. The roles had been played by William Powell and Myrna Loy in a series of films. The Charles's famous dog is Asta.

A more famous dog, *Lassie*, gets her second owner on television when Jeff moves to the city and leaves the collie with Timmy (Jon Provost).

Walter Lantz brings all of his cartoon characters to television for the first time when *The Woody Woodpecker Show* debuts on ABC in 1957. Although the show will only last one year, Lantz's cartoons featuring Woody, Andy Panda, Chilly Willy and the others will continue to be shown on TV.

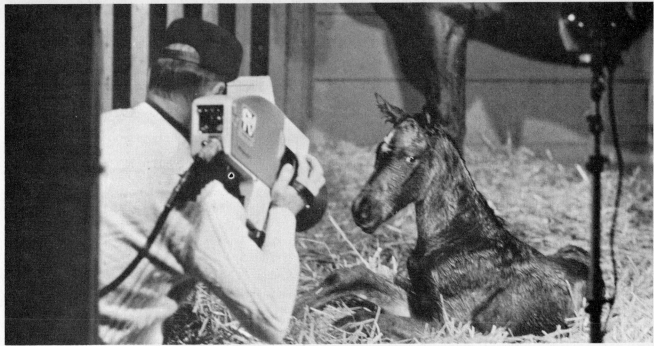

An ABC portable camera records the birth of a foal—but not for prime time viewing.

and fidelity which will prove amazing. We will see video tape units covering sailing from boats, sky diving from the air, underwater sports from underwater, and other sports from terrain that is inaccessible to the huge six-ton television trucks that you now see parked outside of football stadiums. Then, alpine and cross-country skiing, motocross, road racing, sailing and powerboat racing, ballooning, diving marathons, cycling, and cross-country equestrian events will all get the complete video coverage they deserve. These will broaden the base for television sports programming and alleviate the need for synthetic sports.

For example, as part of ABC's Kentucky Derby coverage this year, I directed an ENG portable tape unit on the horse farms in the bluegrass country and was permitted to take our video camera into the stall of a great race mare to record the birth of a foal. The brilliant picture in low light, the quietness of the hand-held video camera, inches from the newborn thoroughbred, proved an unforgettable experience for all who watched. The next morning our portable camera followed the foal and his mother into the paddock as it ran free on the first day of its life. It was decided, because of the delicate subject, to air the birth of a foal as part of our late night Derby Eve program with about five million viewers, instead of including it as part of our Derby coverage with thirty-eight million viewers. Eventually, original pieces such as this, done hours before or *live,* will help bring sports coverage into thrilling new areas.

Robert Riger is a producer for ABC Sports.

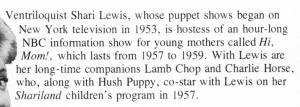

Ventriloquist Shari Lewis, whose puppet shows began on New York television in 1953, is hostess of an hour-long NBC information show for young mothers called *Hi, Mom!,* which lasts from 1957 to 1959. With Lewis are her long-time companions Lamb Chop and Charlie Horse, who, along with Hush Puppy, co-star with Lewis on her *Shariland* children's program in 1957.

December 27, 1957. *The Howdy Doody Show* celebrates its tenth anniversary. Although it will leave NBC in 1960 after more than 2,500 broadcasts, it will return in the 1970's as a syndicated series. For nostalgia buffs, it becomes one of early television's landmark shows.

SPORTS TAKES A PLUNGE

DANNY PEARY

I'm sorry, Mario Bisioni, I still remember you. To me you will always be the one person who best personifies the tremendous oversaturation of sports on television. You made a fool of yourself—but it was not your fault that millions of people were witness to it. Blame it on the networks.

It has become increasingly evident over the last few years that television knows few surer ways of earning advertising revenues than by programming sports. Saturday and Sunday afternoons in particular have been turned over almost completely to network sports departments. In turn, the sports departments have had to come up with events to fill a large number of hours. On occasion they will travel to distant parts of the world in order to present us with the most exciting athletic contests on earth, but too often they have walked down to the local gym and have tried to pass off whatever they found there as ''sports at its best.'' Consequently, we have been presented with such sorry attractions as arm wrestling, congressional baseball games, and body building, as well as many fabricated, totally meaningless (revenue-winning) events: *CBS Sports Challenge; Basketball Slam-Dunk Competition; Superstars; Celebrity Bowling; Celebrity Tennis;* and even *Celebrity Superstars.* How low can we go? You know the answer, Mario Bisioni, because you participated in what was probably the worst single sports event in the history of television: ''Target Diving from Miami Beach.''

The First Annual Target Diving Championships took place about 1970 at a small swimming pool behind what looked to be a $5-a-day Miami motel. I

''Blame it on the networks.''

---

think ABC's *Wide World of Sports* crew got the contestants—you included—by running into the lounge and asking the men at the bar, ''Hey, do any of you wanna be on TV?'' I guess they found enough guys who had swimming suits handy, and who needed extra cash, because ABC started rolling its cameras.

The object of the contest: each participant had to dive off a thirty-foot-high diving board and try to pass through a small circle of balloons—that's correct—floating in the water. The balloons were held apart from each other and kept in a circle by several swimmers—that's correct—who were constantly treading water. What made the water treaders' task extremely difficult were the powerful winds that continually pushed them and the balloons all over the pool.

The first contestant climbed the ladder and confidently made a perfect thirty-foot dive through the circle of balloons without smashing a single one. So far so good. But so much for good diving.

The second contestant used his only opportunity ever to appear on TV to display his million muscles. He was truly gorgeous. And so was his bikini-clad wife who took advantage of her husband's television break by joining him in front of the camera. Together, they smiled and posed. (They were definitely the

In 1957, such series as *The Adventures of Robin Hood, The Adventures of Sir Lancelot,* and *The Adventures of William Tell* fill the early evening hours. Another adventure series for the kids about the days of yore is *Ivanhoe,* a British-produced series starring Roger Moore as Sir Walter Scott's hero.

The Adventures of Superman ceases production in 1957. In 1959, star George Reeves, a fine actor who became so identified with Superman that no one would hire him to play anyone else, will commit suicide.

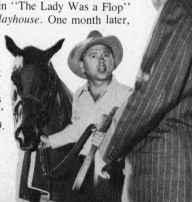

In his first dramatic starring role on television, Mickey Rooney plays a crippled former jockey who backs a filly with cold feet in ''The Lady Was a Flop'' on *Schlitz Playhouse.* One month later, on February 14, 1957, Rooney will give an Emmy-winning dramatic performance as ''The Comedian'' on *Playhouse 90.*

best-looking couple I have ever seen.) At last, the husband climbed the ladder. (I'm sure his wife wanted to follow.) He flexed his muscles and dove. Broken balloons everywhere. The cameras showed us the disqualified, disappointed muscleman as he rejoined his wife for consolation.

You were the third diver, Mario Bisioni. By this time the winds were really whirling about and drops of rain fell lightly from the black sky. Nevertheless, you completed your dive. You, too, struck the balloons. While you were crawling out of the pool with apparent difficulty, the ABC sportscaster told us that you had been eliminated. But your time was yet to come.

Minutes later you were stoical as you stood poolside with the sportscaster. He wore his new suit and you were still in your dripping swimming suit. The sportscaster tried to cheer you up. He said that the wind had blown the balloons into your path. He smiled as he told you, "The judges have decided to let you do your dive over!" He waited for what he and we were sure was going to be a happy response. We expected to hear you say: "Gee, that's great! What a break for me! I won't blow my second chance. That sure was swell of those judges. . . ." But instead you grimaced in pain, and in a voice that recalled Bill Dana's José Jimenez character you said angrily, "I don't care! My leg—I think it's broken!" Whereupon, without another word, you turned and hobbled away from the stunned sportscaster and your public. Jack Paar's walkout couldn't compare to this.

Oh, yes. The fourth contestant had the misfortune of trying to dive while the winds reached hurricane strength. He climbed the ladder and stood on the board waiting to muster up enough courage to make his attempt. The board swayed back and forth and the unhappy man had to hang on for dear life. Then—unbelievably—he chickened out! (Has such an occurrence been seen on TV sports before or since?)

"Mario Bisioni, I still remember you."

He carefully climbed down the long ladder while the camera unmercifully captured his entire humiliating trip. Neat, but anticlimactic after you, Mario Bisioni.

The treacherous weather made it impossible for any more diving attempts. So that was it: One guy did a good dive; the second broke some balloons and was disqualified; your dive, Mario Bisioni, didn't count but you probably fractured your leg doing it; and the fourth and final contestant was too scared to even attempt his dive. ABC had this event on *film*. They could have junked it, but no: they considered it topflight sports entertainment—or rather they thought that no one would know the difference between this event and real sports.

Nowadays, when *Wide World of Sports* has target diving we are usually transported to some exotic tropical locale where icy-eyed professional divers from around the world perform somersaults off what seem to be mile-high cliffs. These divers dodge the jagged rocks on their endless plunge into the mysterious ocean below. We are usually told that if they miss their small, small, small target area they will be taken by the wicked current out to sea where they will be devoured by starving sharks. I firmly believe that ABC has gone to such a spectacular format to make us forget that initial target diving contest, a classic example of condescending sports programming. But I'm sorry, Mario Bisioni, I still remember you.

Danny Peary is co-editor of a forthcoming book, The Cartoon: A Critical Anthology.

October 31, 1957. In a climactic courtroom scene, Joseph Cotten (L) pleads the case of a millionaire on trial in "The Edge of Innocence" on *Playhouse 90*. Also starring are Lorne Greene and Maureen O'Sullivan, who was Jane to Johnny Weissmuller's movie Tarzan in the thirties and forties.

Police officer Paul Douglas presses witness John Lupton for a truthful answer in a scene from "The Edge of Truth," a 1957 episode of CBS's *Studio One*.

THE GRIFFITH-PARET FIGHT
DAVID TRAINER

Back in the fifties and early sixties, my father used to like to watch boxing on television. One of the most vivid memories of my early childhood is lying in bed supposedly asleep while listening to the distant bell starting and ending every round, the roar of the crowd, and the chipper notes of the *Gillette Cavalcade of Sports* jingle that punctuated every bout. Sometimes when the match seemed especially exciting, I would slip out of bed, glide downstairs, and climb into my father's lap while he watched. He was usually too engaged in the fight to do anything but shift comfortably under me and say, "This is really a good one." He used to drink Labatt's India Pale ale on these occasions, and the heady aroma that arose when he poured the brew from the bottle to his glass often made me sleepier than I had been upstairs in bed.

When I got older I would sometimes ask for and get permission to stay up and watch a fight with my father from the beginning. We would read all the newspaper articles about the match ahead of time and make our own personal predictions. We usually made up scorecards, too, and awarded each round as we saw fit. After the bout we compared our scores to those of the officials. If we were in a particularly gamy mood, we would each put a quarter on the round in which we thought the fight would end. Whichever one of us was closer won twenty-five cents.

Unfortunately, part of growing up is getting beaten up once in awhile. This distressed my father just as much as it distressed me, especially because he was such a peaceful man, but he recognized his unpleasant obligation as a father to teach his son how to

defend himself. I don't believe my father really knew how to fight, but he would point out measures taken by the boxers on television and urge me to employ them the next time I was challenged on the way home from school.

There was one fight in 1962 which we looked forward to seeing. It was the third welterweight championship bout between Benny ("Kid") Paret and Emile Griffith, who had won the first but lost the second on a questionable decision. At the weigh-in for the second fight, Paret had called Griffith an insulting name. Griffith warned Paret to shut up and never call him that name again. On Saturday morning at the weigh-in for the third fight, however, Paret once again called Griffith a *maricón,* which is Spanish slang for homosexual. Paret also touched Griffith on the back, which made the challenger very angry. Fighters often make slighting remarks about each other before a bout in hopes of gaining some psychological advantage, but Paret's particularly pointed and galling insults were prompted by the fact that Griffith had a high-pitched voice and once designed ladies' hats for a living. These fairly electrifying background matters were thoroughly reported in the evening paper and served to heighten the already considerable drama of the fight.

Griffith battled hard and seemed to be well ahead through the first five rounds, but in the sixth Paret decked him with a left hook. Suddenly, with Griffith dazed, the fight seemed up for grabs. But in the tenth round Griffith caught Paret against the ropes and pounded him so long and hard that Paret couldn't even

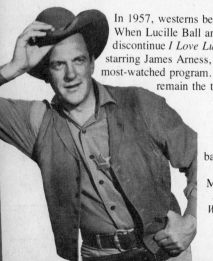

In 1957, westerns begin to dominate television. When Lucille Ball and Desi Arnaz decide to discontinue *I Love Lucy* in the spring, *Gunsmoke,* starring James Arness, becomes television's most-watched program. For four years, it will remain the top-rated show.

Wagon Train, an hour-long adult western, debuts on NBC. Loosely based on the movie *Wagonmaster* with Ward Bond, this show stars Bond as Major Seth Adams and Robert Horton as Scout Flint McCullough. In 1961, *Wagon Train* will usurp *Gunsmoke* as the highest-rated TV program.

Attendants minister to fatally-wounded "Kid" Paret.

Charles Hoff, New York Daily News

fall down. In the twelfth round, Griffith again slammed Paret into a corner and started pummeling him against the turnbuckle until Paret's head slipped out between the top and middle ropes. The referee kept trying to pull the enraged and maniacal Griffith off his now unconscious opponent, but Griffith seemed determined to annihilate the man who had insulted him so cruelly that morning. When at last the referee managed to halt the ferocious assault and pull Griffith away, Paret slipped off the ropes, where he had dangled seemingly forever, and slumped to the mat.

"It all happened so fast, and was so brutal and savage."

"He's dead," my father said in a chilled and distant voice. He was staring blankly at the screen where doctors now gathered around the inert body. I felt sick. It all happened so fast and was so brutal and savage. We had witnessed the destruction of a human life, as surely as if Paret had been hit by a speeding truck.

"How do you know he's dead?" I asked my father in a scared voice. I didn't want to believe it. And I had no idea that he had ever seen a dead person before, or could recognize one so surely in an instant.

"Look at him," my father said. "He's dead."

In fact Paret lived for ten more days, but he never came out of the coma, so my father was right—he was as good as dead. The event was like nothing we had ever seen on television before, and it provoked a lot of debate about the sport of boxing in general. I don't think we watched many more fights after that one, and pretty soon they disappeared from the air. Griffith and Paret were certainly not the sole cause of this decline in television boxing, but what happened between them didn't do much to arouse interest in the game.

I grew older and got interested in other things. I don't like boxing, and I would say I never have—except that I remember I used to sit and watch it with my father when I was a boy. The Griffith-Paret fight taught me more about my father than about boxing. He recognized death. That knowledge comes with age, whether you watch boxing on television or not.

David Trainer writes stories and plays.

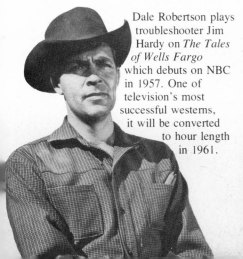

Dale Robertson plays troubleshooter Jim Hardy on *The Tales of Wells Fargo* which debuts on NBC in 1957. One of television's most successful westerns, it will be converted to hour length in 1961.

"Tombstone, Arizona, the town too tough to die." Pat Conway as Sheriff Clay Hollister uses his boot to stop Rayford Barnes from firing his gun on Ziv Productions' *Tombstone Territory*, which debuts on ABC in 1957. Co-starring Richard Eastham as newspaper editor Harris Clayton, this western will last for two years. Among its assets is a catchy singing-whistling theme song.

Have Gun, Will Travel, the classiest western of all, has a theme song sung by Johnny Western that makes the Top Ten. Richard Boone plays the Shakespeare-quoting Paladin, a professional gun-for-hire, the TV western's first intellectual. The show is so popular that it will last from 1957 until 1963 on CBS, and Paladin will become a cult hero.

FAN FARE:
DEAR JOHNNY VALENTINE:

For the most part the heroes and villains of my youth are gone from the home screen. Where they have gone and how they might be found is a mystery to me. The great Antonino Rocca of the flying drop-kick is dead. This I know. So it is to you that I write, Johnny Valentine—you of the stunning peroxide locks—for you were wrestling's "TV Champion." It was never clear to me how you gained the title, and I don't recall you ever defending it. But you were six feet six and weighed two hundred and sixty pounds, and you could crack open a skull as easily as a cantaloupe with the "atomic skull crusher"—plus you were photogenic!

From the age of ten until I was fourteen, and already well along in a career of disrespect for my teachers and unfulfilled potential, I watched wrestling four and five nights a week. I'd fight my mother tooth and nail before yielding the second hour of *Live from Sunnyside Garden* so that she could watch *The Garry Moore Show*. *Sunnyside Garden* was a local wrestling show that came from Queens, New York and featured the dregs of the glamorous syndicated cards. Arnold "Golden Boy" Skaaland, Tomas Marin, Abe Jacobs ("The Jewish Champion"), Lou Albano—the hapless good guys and two-bit bad guys. But once in a while from out of the slag heap would come a surprise appearance by someone rare, like Ricki Starr, the undersized trickster, who danced around the ring like Nijinsky, making fools of hulks one hundred pounds heavier than himself. It was the fear of missing such a moment that kept me glued to the screen. At home my love of wrestling and disdain for homework led to my

---

> " . . . you could crack open a skull as easily as a cantaloupe with the "atomic skull crusher . . .' "

---

frequent visits to the principal's office at school. While all around people were trying to beat "sense" into me, I found comfort in the chaos and disorder of professional wrestling.

So, Johnny, if you know where they are, give my regards to those great champions of the past who came into my living room every night of the week. Tell Gorgeous George that he is still fondly remembered in his sequined robe and his ahead-of-its-time permanent, as he flies through the air, bouncing off the ropes and delivering a stylish knee to the groin. Pay homage from this poor commoner to those various kings of the ring, who ruled the world simultaneously in peace without ever having to go to war. There was something oddly egalitarian about having three world champions reigning at the same time. On Channel 5, from the Uline Arena in Washington, D.C., Ray Morgan would herald "Nature Boy" Buddy Rogers as the champ. In Boston on Channel 9, "Slammin' " Sammy Menaker swore up and down that the man with the cast-iron stomach and cauliflower ears, Pepper Gomez, wore the crown. And on Channel 13, on

Gene Barry, who had briefly played Eve Arden's romantic interest on *Our Miss Brooks*, is the stylishly dressed Bat Masterson. Wearing a cane, derby hat, and pearl-handled pistol, Barry will play the legendary law enforcer from 1957 until 1961.

Ex-movie musical lead John Payne (L) plays ex-gunfighter Vint Bonner in *The Restless Gun*, which debuts on NBC in 1957. Ex-schoolteacher Dan Blocker guest stars.

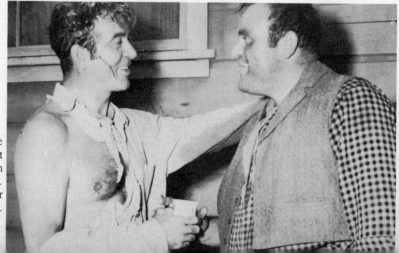

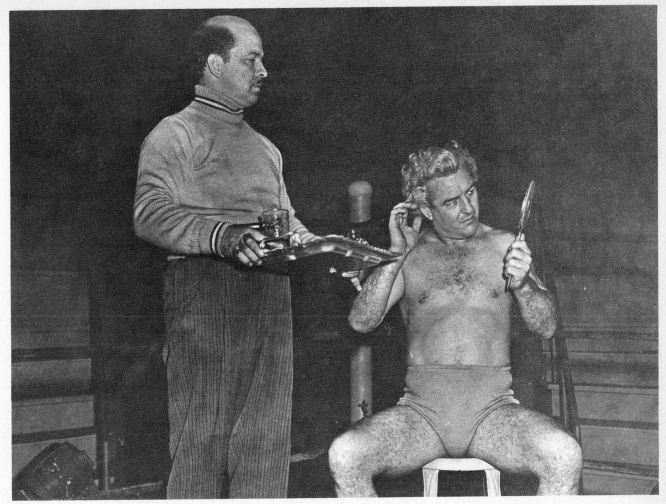

Gorgeous George, always meticulous, primps in the practice ring while one of his minions stands in attendance.

film, a nameless and unseen announcer from an unspecified location (probably Minneapolis), introduced long-time world champ Verne Gagne. The world was big enough for all these heroes.

Tell them all, Johnny, that they're still remembered, that it never really mattered to me when my wise-guy friends told me that the whole thing was fixed. It wasn't true. I didn't believe them. And anyway, I didn't care.

David Levine

David Levine is host of a sports talk show on radio in New York.

135

The success of *Cheyenne* causes Warner Brothers to begin churning out westerns. In 1957 likable Will Hutchins starts a three-year run as the sarsaparilla-drinking, lawbook-studying ''Sugarfoot'' Tom Brewster. Because of his shy manner, bad guys are unprepared for his quick gun. *Sugarfoot* alternates with *Cheyenne* on a bi-weekly basis.

Wayde Preston plays government agent Chris Colt in Warner Brothers' new series *Colt .45*, which debuts on ABC in 1957. Preston will leave the show before it goes off the air in 1962, and Donald May, playing Sam Colt, will replace him.

September 22, 1957. Warner Brothers' offbeat comedy-western *Maverick* debuts on ABC. James Garner and Jack Kelly star as brothers Bret and Bart Maverick, traveling gamblers, ladies' men, and television's first western cowardly heroes.

THE SPORTS AVOIDANCE RESPONSE
DEBBIE FLETCHER HART

What's your favorite sport?'' my husband says. ''Come on, come on, think fast.'' It's gotten to be a big joke with him, but I don't think it's very funny.

''What's your favorite sport?'' he wondered shyly on our first date. It was January, and there was snow on the ground.

''I don't know,'' I replied, because I wanted to say the right thing, but I didn't really have a favorite sport. ''Baseball?'' I wondered at last, with a faint smile. He nodded and shrugged as if that wasn't quite what he wanted to hear. I thought, *Oh boy, now I'll never see him again,* but I did.

Now and then he talked about sports. He wasn't crazy about them the way some men are, but he was interested. Contrary to my first impression, baseball turned out to be a game of particular attraction for him. He looked forward to spring and the start of the season and assumed I did too. I just nodded. ''Hey, you know what let's do this afternoon?'' he said. It was sunny, hot, and clear, early in June. ''Let's go out to the ball park. There's a doubleheader on.''

''A what?'' I asked.

''Two games. Yanks and Boston,'' he clarified.

''But it's such a beautiful day. Who wants to waste it inside?''

''Yankee Stadium isn't inside,'' he said, his expression clouding with doubt. ''It's open air.''

''Even so,'' I hedged. ''Do we have to go?''

He fixed me with a serious look. ''Hey, I thought you told me baseball was your favorite sport?''

''I did?'' I really had forgotten.

''Before long television will be . . . wall-to-wall sports!''

''Right after we met!''

''No,'' I insisted.

''Then what is your favorite sport?'' he demanded to know.

I thought about it for a second, and then a great big smile broke across my face. ''Football!'' I declared.

''Football!'' he repeated with contempt.

''What's wrong with that?'' I wondered.

''Nothing,'' he shrugged a little harder than he had when I said baseball in January. And we didn't have to go to Yankee Stadium either.

In August we got married. In September he told me he would get some pro football tickets for October. He was sure I'd want to go.

''Do I have to?'' I pleaded.

''Wait a minute,'' he insisted. ''Last June you told me football was your favorite sport!''

''No,'' I proclaimed innocently. ''You heard me wrong. It's basketball.''

We kept this up through the first year of our marriage. Every time my husband challenged me to name my favorite sport, I carefully selected one that was out of season. I even read the sports pages of the newspaper just to find out what they weren't playing at any

---

In 1958, seven of the top ten programs on TV are westerns. *The Rifleman,* starring former pro baseball player Chuck Connors as Lucas McCain, a peace-loving rancher who is forced to shoot his rifle week after week, is the most popular western to debut in 1958. Co-starring Johnny Crawford as McCain's son Mark, *The Rifleman* will be a top ABC program until 1963. Robert Altman will direct several episodes.

The Lawman is Warner Brothers' western entry for 1958. Co-starring John Russell (L) as Marshal Dan Troop and Peter Brown as Deputy Johnny McKay, this half-hour western will remain on ABC's schedule until 1962. Here Russell and Brown pose with guests, Andrea Martin (L) and Olive Sturgess.

Free-style skiing in the CBS Challenge of the Sexes, *1976.*

given time. Eventually he got the idea. "You hate sports!" he accused me when I told him in July my favorite was hockey. "Admit it, sports make you sick!"

"No," I lied sweetly. But he understood me perfectly by then.

I understood him too. That mild fan I thought I was marrying was in fact a wild fanatic, a lunatic, a sports freak. If they kick it, hit it, punch it, putt it, bang it, or run after it, my husband follows it. If I was guilty of selling myself under false pretenses, so was he. Fortunately we were compatible in other areas, or this sports problem could have destroyed our marriage before the first year was out.

The truth is I resent my husband's addiction to games. When I want to talk, or see a show, or go dancing, he wants to sit and stare at sports. When he can't get to the actual event, he watches on television instead. I beg him, "Please, please, at least turn off the sound! I can't bear to hear the voices of those awful announcers!"

But he just replies, "What? Two more innings, all right?" Or, "Only eight minutes to go! Geez, what a game!" I can't stand it. I have to leave the room.

"What's your favorite sport?" my husband says. "Come on, come on, think fast."

I wrack my brain to think of a safe one. "Soccer!" I blurt out.

"Better be careful," my husband warns me. "Soccer is getting very big. The season starts in two weeks. Say soccer two weeks from now and you'll have to watch! That's your jackpot!"

"My punishment, you mean," I correct him.

"Have it your way," he grins. "But be careful!"

Lately my husband has developed the look of a man who knows that eventually he is going to win, if only he will be patient a little while longer. And I'm afraid he's right, because the seasons for all sports are getting longer and longer, until pretty soon there will never be a time when all sports aren't being played all the time.

"That's right!" crowed my husband when I challenged him with this horrifying vision.

"But why?" I wailed. "It's unnatural! It's monstrous!"

"It's television!" he replied. "TV is a big business and big business needs more and more games to sell. Before long television will be one hundred percent wall-to-wall sports! You wait! You'll have to watch no matter what you say your favorite sport is! You won't have any choice!"

Maybe he's right. But until then I plan to keep shutting my eyes, blocking my ears, and trying to stay at least a week ahead of the seasons.

Debbie Fletcher Hart prefers Baryshnikov to basketball.

137

Rory Calhoun, star of "B" movies, explains the rudiments of his six-shooter to the fascinated Stephen Hammer in *The Texan*, which debuts on CBS in 1958. In 1960, ABC will pick up the program for two years.

Buckskin is one of the few westerns appearing in 1958 that doesn't catch on. It only lasts the summer season on NBC. It stars Tommy Nolan (R), Mike Road, and Sallie Brophie as a Montana widow trying to raise her son in a hostile environment.

X Brands, playing Pahoo-Ka-Ta-Wah, exits quickly after conferring with captive Paula Raymond in *Yancy Derringer*, which debuts on CBS in 1958. The series, starring Jock Mahoney as a New Orleans gambler in the 1880's, will run for one year.

WOMEN IN TV SPORTS
ELEANOR RIGER

I guess I've come a long way. I know at least that it seems to have taken forever, and *I'm* not there yet. On reflection I'll have to admit the achievements are real, but I know the women who are coming up in television sports after me will have a better chance to reach the goal I have set for myself—to produce live sports events on network television, including the Kentucky Derby and the 1980 Olympics at Lake Placid. The times are a'changin'.

Four years ago, in March 1973, when I rejoined ABC Sports as a full producer—the first and only woman staff sports producer on network television, as I was billed—I was amused and sometimes flattered by the newspaper articles that resulted from interviews of me. "A woman enters sports sanctum," was one lead from the Chicago *Sun-Times*. Although the piece by Ron Powers was fair and friendly, it was right about the "sanctum." Obviously, it is one thing to gain admittance, quite another to receive the full rights and privileges to perform the mysteries.

Why was I the first? Why was it such a rare thing—a news item—when I got the appointment? Why was television sports such an exclusively male area? Network news had a handful of women producers and writers and reporters in early 1973. Sports, none. Was it because only male sports were salable on televison? Because women were not interested in or had no feeling for sports? Because women could not be expected to have the intelligence or dedication or stamina required for the admittedly demanding routine at ABC Sports (or the other networks, for that matter)? Because no one thought

women could cope with travel and work in foreign countries and the interior of the USA? The influence of all these myths has limited the rise of women in TV sports, as has the very important fact that too many women themselves believe that being interested in sports or participating in sports is the exceptional and not-quite-accepted thing to do.

But things had already, in fact, begun to change in the late sixties and early seventies with the burgeoning of the women's movement. The new casual outdoor leisure life and informality of relationships between the sexes made it more and more acceptable for women to be athletic and to use their bodies in other than sexual ways. Participation in sports grew, and the pressure increased for athletic opportunities for women. And more women than anyone had ever dreamed were watching male sports events on television. Although fully a third of the audience for pro football in the late sixties were women, they were not even counted when pitches were made by the networks to advertisers, since it was assumed that only male-oriented products would be sold with football. In 1973 the audience for the Kentucky Derby was 55 percent female; 42 percent women watched *Wide World of Sports;* 49 percent looked at bowling, and 40 percent watched baseball. And the 1972 Olympics had almost as many women as men viewers in prime time. Television, however, is the least innovative and the most mass of the mass media, and exhibits a severe cultural lag. So in 1973 it was news when ABC hired me.

It was not "news," but it was significant when the first woman production assistant at ABC Sports

138

Bit movie actor Clint Eastwood, here with guest Debra Paget, plays ramrod Rowdy Yates on a new hour-long adult western, *Rawhide,* which begins an eight-year run on CBS in 1958. After *Rawhide's* cancellation, Eastwood will return to pictures and become the world's number-one box office star. Co-star Eric Fleming (trail boss, Gil Favor) will drown while filming a low-budget film in South America.

September 6, 1958. Steve McQueen, whose main claim to fame has been a starring role in the sci-fi movie thriller *The Blob,* stars as bounty hunter Josh Randall in *Wanted – Dead or Alive,* which debuts on CBS. By the time the popular show goes off in 1961, McQueen is a well-known actor. He will become a superstar in films.

Buddy Ebsen (L), Keith Larsen (as Robert Rogers), and Don Burnett star in MGM-TV's new all-color adventure series, *Northwest Passage,* which plays on NBC from 1958 to 1959.

Paula Sperber, a star in women's bowling and owner of a chain of bowling alleys, has done a lot to popularize the sport.

was sent out on the road on a regular basis in the fall of 1973—first on college football remotes, then to auto racing and boxing and all of the sports covered by ABC. The production assistant job is the entry job at ABC Sports, the basis for promotion to associate producer, associate director, and eventually producer. Our PAs have to deal tactfully with organizers of sports events from Don King, the boxing promoter, to the Soviet Gymnastics Federation; cue football players to take the field; corral race car drivers in Gasoline Alley at the Indy 500 for interviews; keep crowds from blocking cameras on a World Cup downhill course; stay awake and alert on round-the-clock editing sessions; and never take no for an answer when something needs to be done for a show.

The thorough, demanding, and exciting ABC Sports training is invaluable for any career in television production, and when it was opened up to women it signaled that eventual meaningful participation of women in sports production was possible. ABC leads the league in this statistic. As of today, there are three out of ten sports production assistants who are women. The work of the women who have held this job and of the two women associate directors and one associate producer (this job opened up to women in 1977) has given the lie to the myths and has finally proved that women can play on this team.

But becoming the coach is another matter. In effect, the producer is responsible for the creative content of the show, the appropriateness and accuracy of the reporting of the announcers and commentators, the personalization of the athletes with feature stories, the clarification of the event with instructional pieces, and isolation and replays of significant plays. In other words, the producer is responsible for the best possible coverage of the event, and just as important, the proper and timely insertion of commercials and of promos for upcoming ABC sports programs. In a show that is pretaped or prefilmed the responsibility is great, but the coordination of all these elements is not required as quickly as it is in a live program. When the show is live, you don't have a second chance; everything must be done correctly the first time. It's a job that can only be learned by doing, and it can only be perfected with experience. The exhilaration is incomparable when the associate director cues you, and you know you're "on"; you're communicating directly to millions of people, and you're responsible for using each of your precious minutes right the first time.

In 1958, *Disneyland* changes its name to *Walt Disney Presents* and broadcasts three rotating adventure series, based on the lives of Elfego Baca, Francis Marion ("The Swamp Fox"), and Texas John Slaughter. Here, in an episode of "The Swamp Fox" series, veteran movie villain Henry Daniell (R) threatens to torture Tim Considine (L), unless he reveals the location of Marion's headquarters. James Anderson plays Tim's Tory captor in this drama about the American Revolution.

Tom Tryon (C) plays the title role in the "Texas John Slaughter" episodes on *Walt Disney Presents* in 1958 and 1959. Here he is with his TV family, Brian Corcoran (Willie) and Betty Lynn (Viola). Tryon will later star in the Otto Preminger epic movie, *The Cardinal*, and go on to be a best-selling author.

". . . there should be more work in sports production and sports announcing for women."

I've produced many films and pretaped shows in four years, but I'm a novice at live. I've produced five live shows and want to do more, but I suspect that uncertainty about whether a woman is up to the pressures of the live telecast and the lingering myth of emotional instability from hormonal differences might be hindering my progress. It was a struggle to get to produce regional college football games. But I had a great technical and production crew and good announcers, who helped and encouraged me tremendously on my first two games. The telephone company kept the lines up and unmixed. (Sometimes on a regional telecast week when ABC has four or more games being fed at the same time to different regions of the country, a viewer can suddenly get the sound from the Colorado State versus Wyoming game, and the picture from Arkansas versus Alabama, or no picture or sound at all!) I was happy to receive commendations on the professionalism of the telecasts from the athletic directors and coaches of the teams involved and, most treasured of all, a letter from the NCAA liaison official, whom I consult about appropriate times for commercial breaks during the game and who can also hear on the internal production headset what I am saying to the director and crew. To my delight he wrote, "It was kind a nice to go through a game without the air turning blue with 'expletives.'"

Certainly, with the fabulous growth of sports programming on all three networks, there should be more work in sports production and sports announcing for women, as well as more coverage of women's sports. The amount of sports broadcasting has almost doubled in the last ten years. In 1967 about seven hundred hours of sports were telecast; four years later just under a thousand hours of network time were devoted to sports; and in 1977 there will be more than thirteen hundred hours of sports on network television. The proportion of women in the sports television audience has risen from one-third in 1967 to an average of 40 percent for all sports watched on television in 1976. But the most important factor for the future involvement of women in sports on television is the accelerating growth of college sports for women.

Men's college sports have been the backbone of both the amateur Olympic sports and the major professional sports which make up 99 percent of the sports television programming. Women's sports will receive more exposure on television as college programs increase. In the academic year 1974–75 there were 556 colleges with athletic programs for women; in 1975–76 the number had risen to 802. In the same period, financial aid for specific women's sports jumped dramatically. For instance, the number of schools giving women scholarships for basketball rose from 48 to 175, an increase of 265 percent; for volleyball the total went from 34 to 143, a 321 percent rise; and in track and field, from 17 to 73, up 329 percent. In the 1977–78 academic year there will be one hundred thousand women participating in intercollegiate athletics—"big time" programs and not just intramural pickup sports. This is just the very beginning. Already I see the influence of the growing participation of women in sports in the increasing numbers of women who want to *work* in television sports. And now, finally, they have a real chance of making a career of it, just like men!

Eleanor Riger is a producer for ABC Sports.

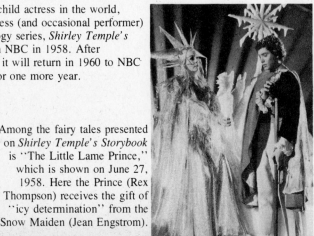

Formerly the most famous child actress in the world, Shirley Temple acts as hostess (and occasional performer) on a new children's anthology series, *Shirley Temple's Storybook,* which debuts on NBC in 1958. After switching to ABC in 1959, it will return in 1960 to NBC for one more year.

Among the fairy tales presented on *Shirley Temple's Storybook* is "The Little Lame Prince," which is shown on June 27, 1958. Here the Prince (Rex Thompson) receives the gift of "icy determination" from the Snow Maiden (Jean Engstrom).

Although cartoons had been made especially for television as far back as 1950, it is in 1958 — with the success of Hanna-Barbera's *The Huckleberry Hound Show, The Yogi Bear Show,* and *Ruff and Ready* (which first appeared in NBC's Saturday morning schedule in December 1957) — that networks start actively looking for more low-budget, quickly-made cartoons to fill children's viewing hours.

REMEMBERING MEL ALLEN

NED SWEET

In 1964, Mel Allen stepped down—somewhat reluctantly—as the announcer for the New York Yankees baseball games. During the previous twenty-five years he had broadcast Yankees baseball into living rooms across New York, New Jersey, and Connecticut. When the Yankees were in the World Series, which was more often than not in those days, he could be heard across the whole nation on the NBC network.

Much of the time he worked on the radio, of course, but some of it was also on television. And it was while on television, between Ballantine beer and White Owl cigar commercials, that he had more fun than anybody. He didn't work the games alone, and his colleagues were competent, professional broadcasters who managed to let everyone know what was going on. Mel wasn't a broadcaster, he was a fan. He was a fan with the second greatest job in the world, topped only by those fortunate few on the field.

Being a fan was easy for him in one sense. During his years in the booth, the Yankees seemed to win every game they played. But that alone doesn't make a person a fan, and it didn't make Mel Allen one either. It was his ability to see the fun and excitement generated by every game and situation that made him a fan.

Who else but a fan could turn a simple home run into a "Ballantine Blast"? Who else referred to ballplayers as "Ol' Reliable," "Scooter," and "Big Number 7"? Professional broadcasters were satisfied with reflecting excitement; they rarely added to it. Mel would never describe a home run by saying something like, "There's a long fly ball . . ." It was always, "Going . . . going . . . gone! Another Ballantine Blast!!" And you could picture him jumping out of his chair, waving his arms, and trying to control himself as yet another ball flew off yet another Yankee bat into the outstretched hands of yet another band of fans.

After the glory years, he announced games in another city, did some commercials, and tried his hand at a radio show. He still comes back to act as master of ceremonies for the Yankees' annual Old Timer's game, but it isn't the same anymore.

I still have a letter written by Mel Allen and addressed to my father, who, after several innings and several beers at Yankee Stadium, decided it would be a good idea to visit Mel while he was on the air. Two security guards convinced my father it wouldn't be such a good idea after all. A few days later that letter arrived. It's a very nice letter, too. Not only for its content, but for the fact that it was written at all. The real message lies between the lines, though. It was something like, "Hell, if they didn't let me in here, I'd probably try and force my way in once, too."

Well, that's what Mel Allen would have to do now. And listening to the Yankees games just hasn't been the same in more than thirteen years. Maybe they should let him in the booth just one more time. Let him roll up his sleeves, light up a White Owl, crack open a Ballantine, say "Hello there, everybody," and describe just one more Ballantine Blast. Just the way a fan would do it.

Ned Sweet never misses a World Series.

141

In 1958, Red Skelton celebrates his fifth year on CBS. He had left NBC in 1953.

In 1958, *The Lucille Ball-Desi Arnaz Show*, a series of hour-long monthly specials with the "I Love Lucy" gang continuing in their old parts, moves into its second year. This 1958 episode features Danny Thomas and his TV family. (L–R) Lucille Ball, Desi Arnaz, Marjorie Lord, Danny Thomas, Vivian Vance, and William Frawley.

Mel Allen announced the Yankees baseball games for twenty-five years of Ballantine Blasts.

Ann Sothern, who had guested on the first *Lucille Ball-Desi Arnaz Show* on November 6, 1957, stars in the Desilu Production's comedy series, *The Ann Sothern Show,* which debuts on CBS in 1958. It will last three years. Here young Barry Gordon gets a whack.

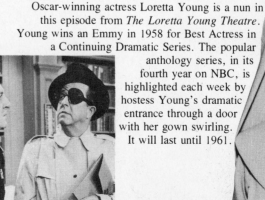

In 1958, *The Phil Silvers Show* (previously titled *You'll Never Get Rich*) moves into its fourth year on CBS. Here Bilko hoodwinks Howard St. John.

Oscar-winning actress Loretta Young is a nun in this episode from *The Loretta Young Theatre*. Young wins an Emmy in 1958 for Best Actress in a Continuing Dramatic Series. The popular anthology series, in its fourth year on NBC, is highlighted each week by hostess Young's dramatic entrance through a door with her gown swirling. It will last until 1961.

THE DRAMA OF SPORTS
HEYWOOD HALE BROUN

All the industrial arts," said Jean Renoir, "have been great at the beginning, and have been debased as they perfected themselves." Expanding on this bleak pronouncement, the French director went on to say that the desperate shifts of early filmmakers, who often could not achieve the effects they wanted, had a creative flair that the seamless perfection achievable through modern technology cannot equal. I don't know that I would go so far as "debased" to describe modern TV sportscasting, possibly because I do some of it myself, but I am not at all sure that the split screens, replays, zoom lenses, and freeze-frame time stoppages have not taken away from sport the primal excitement that is its heritage.

After all, most of us who watch are not students of sport, but fans. If I want something dissected, I'll put on a white coat and enter a laboratory. I am not all that anxious to know how the thing was done. Simply, I want to know that "we" did it, to cheer the fact, catch my breath, and watch the next moment of action.

Let me bring another distinguished scholar to my aid, even though TV executives seem to think distinguished scholars should only be heard early on Sunday mornings. Johan Huizinga, the great Dutch scholar, was fascinated by the ritual element in sport and pointed out that in common with all major rituals, sport has the unquestioned character common where reverence rules. "It creates order, *is* order. Into an imperfect world and into the confusion of life, it brings a temporary, a limited perfection."

If Huizinga is right, and those of us who have

George Halas and his 1946 Champion Chicago Bears.

read *The Waning of the Middle Ages* and *In the Shadow of Tomorrow* are not inclined to doubt this sport-loving sage, why, during a football game on television, are we suddenly looking at still pictures of football players, pictures with curiously red eyes and thick necks and costumes confusingly different from those of this occasion? Why are we looking at girls in the stands, small boys waving at us, and the last play twice repeated during the time when we and the quarterback should be thinking of the next play? Why, when watching a baseball game, do we first see the unbelievable fastball fly batwards, then, physics obeyed, fly outward with redoubled force—only to see the whole thing repeated in slow motion, the ball moving as slowly as a teacher's chalk line on a spring morning, the bat swinging as if the game were being

143

Keenan Wynn guest stars with Betty White on *The Betty White Show*, a half-hour variety show appearing on ABC in 1958. As did White's 1954 NBC variety show, it runs for only one year. In 1957, White had co-starred with Bill Williams in *A Date with the Angels*, a short-lived sitcom.

January 31, 1958. Hope Emerson guests on *Mr. Adams and Eve*, which is completing its three-year run on CBS in 1958. It stars Ida Lupino and Howard Duff as a husband-wife theatrical couple. Movie star Lupino, the only American woman feature film director in the forties and fifties, had co-starred with Dick Powell, David Niven, and Charles Boyer in CBS's *Four Star Playhouse* anthology series from 1953 to 1955.

Close-ups of action-filled moments are TV's genius.

played on the ocean floor? This undoubtedly teaches batting technique, but the long, slow rhythm of opposing forces in a baseball game has, at that moment, been as irretrievably shattered as a dropped egg. Television has again demonstrated its ability to interpret, but should games be interpreted?

If there is a rhythm to individual games, so there is a rhythm to the seasons of games, from the first calisthenics to the frenzies of the championship, an occasion when a city, a state (or rarely and wildly a nation of the world) lives in the exciting delusion that nothing more important is ever going to happen. In order for this overpowering delusion to reach full flower there must be a long stretch of increasing heat, the ever-more stifling pressure of the hothouse. Impatient at the small number of championships, television has tried to create its own with large sums of money on the one hand and new games on the other. Unhappily, as Huizinga reminds us, "In the faculty of repetition lies one of the most essential characteristics of play," and karate championships on roller skates somehow lack the tradition that gives even an old high school rivalry an undertone of bugles and drums.

The drama of a sport is built into the sport just as the emotional grip of a ritual is strengthened down the years in which it is, with loving precision, repeated. The pulse of the sporting year has been beating for a long time, and every schoolboy knows when it rises to a rattle, when it falls off to the widely spaced thumps of the restful doldrums. He cannot be cozened into interest by the distinctions of the players, or the stakes for which they play. I suspect that one of the reasons TV executives believe that money and fame create instant interest is that most of them come from a background of movies and theatrical television where indeed the right marquee names and the right sums of money can, from time to time, create The Big One, the blockbuster that leads on to sequels and "novelizations" and records of the sound track and trading cards. But then, however exciting, movies have never been part of a rhythm of life—a rite of spring, summer, autumn, or winter—a place and time of escape from the confusions of the great game of Life, that chaotic contest that one may play for a quarter of a century believing that it is croquet and one is winning, only to discover that life has been playing Parcheesi and one has lost.

Television does a marvelous job of giving us an eye that reaches round the world. It will do even better when it remembers that the essence of sport is immutable, unchangeable rules, not only about how sport is played, but also about why and where it is played. We would all do well to refresh our innocence and our excitement with the words of Paul Valéry, "No skepticism is possible where the rules of a game are concerned, for the principle underlying them is an unshakeable truth."

Heywood Hale Broun has been a newspaper writer, an actor, and a television sports correspondent.

144

After three years on NBC, *Father Knows Best* returns to CBS in 1958, where it will remain until 1962. Of all the families portrayed on television in the fifties and sixties, none will be remembered more than the Andersons: Betty, Bud, Kathy, Margaret, and Jim.

September 24, 1958. *The Donna Reed Show,* ABC's answer to *Father Knows Best,* debuts. It will gain a huge viewership and last until 1966. The Stone family is (L–R): Donna Reed (who won an Oscar for Best Supporting Actress in *From Here to Eternity*), Shelley Fabares, Carl Betz, and Paul Peterson. For a brief time, Fabares, with her song "Johnny Angel," and Peterson, with his "My Dad," will have modest success as recording artists.

THE TV PREACHERS
WAYNE ELZEY

The television evangelist exudes the same folksy lushness that inspires mother pillows and paintings of bullfighters on velvet. Blending a slightly countrified, Jesus-centered religion with a good deal of showmanship, the nationally syndicated television preachers are the superstars of popular religion.

One Sunday in 1974 Rex Humbard reported that God had licked the financial problems threatening his *Outreach World-Wide Ministry*. Flanked by wife Maude Aimee in a beehive hairdo, Reverend Humbard stood on a plushly-curtained stage overlooking an audience of five thousand people seated in cushy velveteen chairs under a one hundred foot red, white, and blue lighted cross suspended from the roof of the $3.5 million Cathedral of Tomorrow in Akron, Ohio. He thanked the child who had sent in twenty-five pennies taped to the back of a postcard. "Brother, that really charged my batteries," he told the congregation. "Now let's give the Lord the biggest hand you ever gave for answering prayer."

"Rubber City religion!" snort the critics. But Rex Humbard's hour-long program reached ten million viewers through 400 syndicated stations, well over half the commercial stations in the United States.

Billy Graham pioneered "televangelism" in the early 1950's with the *Hour of Decision* and Oral Roberts followed with *Contact!* Today, the super-ministers of Sunday morning TV spend up to $150,000 each week to carry a renovated version of the old American revival meeting throughout the United States and to many other countries.

A large audience is a diverse audience, and the

"... television preachers are the superstars ..."

successful preachers pattern their television ministries more along the lines of Merv Griffin than John the Baptist. The old-style revival preacher—flamboyant, strident, apocalyptic—seldom attracts a national following. The successful TV evangelist is a less abrasive personality—homespun Jerry Falwell, mod-young-contemporary LeRoy Jenkins, Reverend "Bob" Harrington (The Champlain of Bourbon Street) or the late Kathryn Kuhlman, who was ushered in each week as an internationally-recognized Beam of Light radiating divine power throughout the universe.

An attractive personality must be marketed, and the modern evangelists are skilled at turning worldly forms of programming to religious ends. The preachers appear on talk shows and telethons, produce travelogues and documentaries of "crusades" from the Holy Land to Honolulu, support the Christian Broadcasting Network (an association of stations owned by evangelists), and run prime time variety shows and vaguely religious "specials" with comedy skits and guest appearances by Dale Evans and Graham Kerr. "I'm selling the greatest product in the world," bragged Billy Graham. "Why shouldn't it be promoted as well as soap?" Something less than the gift of prophecy is needed to foresee an annual televised Oral Roberts Open.

145

George and Gracie kiss in front of "The Beverly Hills Uplift Society." *The George Burns and Gracie Allen Show* completes its eight-year run on CBS in 1958, when Gracie Allen retires from show business. "Say good night, Gracie." "Good night, Gracie."

Throughout the fifties, CBS has dominated afternoon TV with its soap operas, establishing such fixtures as *Love of Life* (1951), *Search for Tomorrow* (1951), *The Guiding Light* (1952), *The Secret Storm* (1954), *The Edge of Night* (1956), and *As the World Turns* (1956). In 1958, NBC counters with *Kitty Foyle* starring (L–R) William Redfield, Kathleen Murray as Kitty, Ralph Dunne, and Ginger MacManus. It lasts six months.

Despite the quiz show scandals, "small change" game programs thrive and often compete with soap operas. Former *Tonight Show* announcer Gene Rayburn is host of *Dough Re Mi*, a song-identification show, which begins a three-year stint on NBC in 1958. Rayburn will begin hosting *The Match Game* on NBC in 1962. In 1973, he will host a nighttime version.

An inspirational portrait of Reverend Billy Graham.

With success comes optimism. Increasingly, the old message of sin and salvation has been laced with a strong dose of mind cure. "Turn your problems into opportunities!" popular Robert Schuller challenges "possibility thinkers" on the *Hour of Power*. The *Campmeeting Hour* features singing evangelist Jimmy Swaggart delivering instructions on "God's cure for worry," and on "Revival in America" LeRoy Jenkins proclaims that "the greatest sin in the world today is depression."

The revival preachers always stressed "faith,"

"Billy Graham pioneered 'televangelism . . .'"

but ten years ago when Oral Roberts exhorted the crowds to "Expect a miracle!" the result was apt to be a cure for blindness or an outburst of religious ecstacy. Today, when he promises "Something *good* is going to happen to *you!*," the result is apt to be an outburst of positive thinking. The old command to "Let God transform your life!" is updated to "Let God rebuild your image!"

According to the preachers, the modern television ministries are dedicated efforts to revive a lifeless and unfeeling world with an unaffected spiritual vitality. At the center of the preacher's message is always the preacher, a visible link with the homely virtues of small town and rural America who has ascended rapidly (indeed, miraculously) to fame in a powerful but dispirited urban world of corporations and technologies.

Ranging from an Oral Roberts to a Reverend Ike, the preachers symbolize the best of both worlds. Theatrical, turned out in the latest fashions, presiding over a corporate empire of Christian colleges, retirement villages, vacation retreats, and television stations—and housed in the lushest of "cathedrals" —the preachers preserve a down-home unpretentiousness and folksy sense of perspective.

"Don't call me 'Reverend,'" an evangelist corrected a caller on a recent telethon. "I'm not reverend. God is."

Wayne Elzey teaches religion at Miami University in Oxford, Ohio.

MC Merv Griffin watches contestant Tad Tadlock do something with an egg on *Play Your Hunch*, a CBS game show which debuts in 1958. It will last four years, during which time a nighttime version will be added.

What's My Line moves into its eighth season on CBS in 1958. It is still going strong in its Sunday night slot.

IV. THE ENTERTAINMENT MACHINE

Henny Youngman will appear with Buddy Lester and Sid Gould on the premiere of ABC's new nighttime *Make Me Laugh* program on March 20, 1958. Contestants get a dollar for each second they can resist laughing at the comics' antics.

Edgar Allan Jones, Jr., a professor of law at U.C.L.A., presides over ABC's *Day In Court* three times a week. The show, which depicts reenactments of civil and criminal proceedings, will continue daily from 1958 to 1965.

October 26, 1958. Pablo Casals makes his first appearance in America in thirty years on CBS's *U.N. in Action* series.

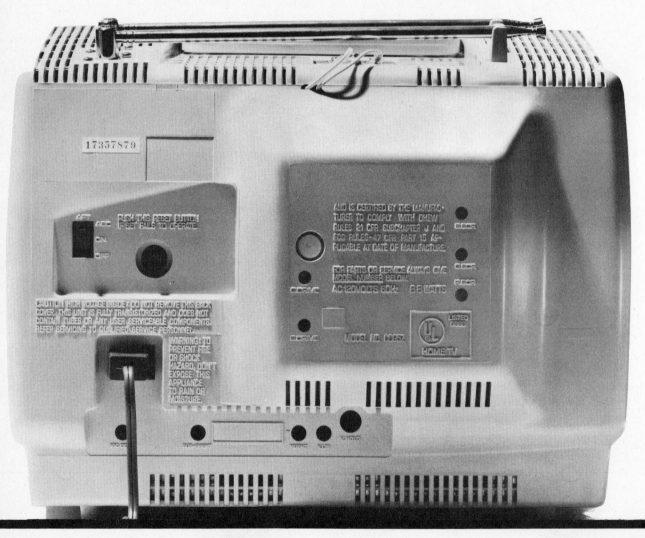

Because of TV's move toward action-adventure, *See It Now,* goes off the air in 1958. Here Edward R. Murrow goes to Florida for an interview with ex-President Harry Truman on February 14, 1958.

Warner Brothers expands its TV fare from westerns to private-eye shows. *77 Sunset Strip* debuts in 1958. Efrem Zimbalist, Jr. is private detective Stuart Bailey. Co-starring is Roger Smith as Bailey's partner, Jeff Spencer. The show will last until 1964, and will serve as the model for several Warner Brothers detective shows.

Ed "Kookie" Byrnes, forever combing his hair on *77 Sunset Strip,* begins the series as a carhop; when his popularity grows with viewers, he is made a full-fledged private eye. In the pilot for the show, Byrnes had been the villain.

"SAY GOOD NIGHT, GRACIE."
EUGENE SLAFER

GRACIE: *I'll never forget the night I had to call the doctor for my cousin Marie.*

GEORGE: *Your cousin Marie?*

GRACIE: *Yes. She's the one who laughs when she eats spaghetti.*

GEORGE: *She laughs when she eats spaghetti?*

GRACIE: *Yes. She takes a fork and winds it in a little ball and swallows it. And when it unravels it tickles her.*

GEORGE: *She's the one you had to call the doctor for.*

GRACIE: *Yes, she got up in the middle of the night and gave the biggest scream you ever heard.*

GEORGE: *What happened?*

GRACIE: *We looked down and her feet had turned black.*

GEORGE: *What did you do?*

GRACIE: *We sent for the doctor.*

GEORGE: *What did the doctor do?*

GRACIE: *He took off her stockings and we all went back to sleep again.*

The Palace Theatre closed to two-a-day vaudeville in 1932. Escaping just before they locked the doors was the comedy team of Burns and Allen. They had gone into the new medium, radio. Headliners in vaudeville, Burns and Allen were a hit in radio. So naturally, it was a piece of cake when, in 1950, George Burns and Gracie Allen soft-shoed their way into television.

> "Burns and Allen softshoed their way into television."

GRACIE: *You know George, it was a terrific social my grandparents had last night. The children were there, and the grandchildren, and the great-grandchildren. I can still see little baby Oscar sitting in his high chair chewing on lobster.*

GEORGE: *The baby had lobster?*

GRACIE: *Oscar was too young to hold onto his food so they gave him food that could hold onto him.*

The team's low-key, underplayed comedy was as attractive on television as it had been on radio. Television proved to be a personal medium. George could do a turn, hold a pause, work his cigar, and do takes for Gracie, with even more intimate audience contact than before.

GRACIE: *Did you know my uncle Harry was a holdup man?*

GEORGE: *Oh?*

GRACIE: *Yeah, but his gang was just getting started and couldn't afford a getaway car so my uncle used to meet them outside the bank with bus fare.*

In radio, actors played whole scenes gathered at a microphone while listeners had to imagine entrances and exits. It was little trouble to translate what was

149

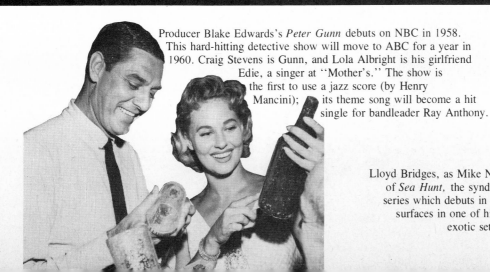

Producer Blake Edwards's *Peter Gunn* debuts on NBC in 1958. This hard-hitting detective show will move to ABC for a year in 1960. Craig Stevens is Gunn, and Lola Albright is his girlfriend Edie, a singer at "Mother's." The show is the first to use a jazz score (by Henry Mancini); its theme song will become a hit single for bandleader Ray Anthony.

Lloyd Bridges, as Mike Nelson of *Sea Hunt,* the syndicated series which debuts in 1958, surfaces in one of his less exotic settings.

already an aural transcription of a stage presentation back to a visual representation of the same on television.

GRACIE: *Say George, did I ever tell you about my cousin, P. T. Allen, the press agent?*

GEORGE: *No. Don't you mean P. T. Barnum? Well,* out how things would end as the audience.

GRACIE: *Well, for instance, one of his clients was an actress, and he thought he could get her picture in the paper if she just wore a few doves.*

GEORGE: *You mean . . . doves like birds?*

GRACIE: *Yes, doves like birds. But they like worms better.*

GEORGE: *I know . . . anyway, he was going to get her picture in the paper by posing her with a few doves.*

GRACIE: *Yes. The only trouble was, she didn't have a very good figure, but P. T. took care of that.*

GEORGE: *What did he do?*

GRACIE: *Simple, instead of doves, he used turkeys.*

GEORGE: *Did they use her picture?*

GRACIE: *Yes, but only on Thanksgiving.*

Their art was presentational. Laurel and Hardy, Charlie Chaplin, and W. C. Fields depended upon a grimacing comic delivery and physical jokes for their humor. George would just light up his cigar, and with a studied nonchalance, talk to the audience.

In the early shows, George would step out in front of the curtain and do a monologue.

GEORGE: *For the benefit of those who have never seen me, I am what is known in the business as a straight man. If you don't know what a straight man does, I'll tell you. The comedian gets a laugh. Then I look at the comedian. Then I look at the audience—like this.* [Looks.] *That is known as a pause. And when I'm really rolling, this is one of my ad libs.* [Surprised look with mouth open.]

Another duty of a straight man is to repeat what the comedian says. For example, if Gracie should say: "A funny thing happened on the streetcar today." Then I say, "A funny thing happened on the streetcar today?" And naturally her answer gets a scream. Then I throw in one of my famous pauses. [Looks.]

I've been a straight man for so many years that from force of habit I repeat everything. I went out fishing with a fellow the other day and he fell overboard. He yelled, "Help! Help! Help!" so I said, "Help, Help, Help?" And while I was waiting for him to get his laugh, he drowned.

And then the scene would cut to the Burns's house, where Gracie would be up to some improbable scheme, such as trying to prevent her son's friend from failing college and becoming a cattle inspector, or dressing up Harry Von Zell as an African witch doctor to chase away unwanted guests.

As the show continued a few seasons, the presentations became more complex. The next-door neighbors, Blanche and Harry Morton (Bea Benederet and Larry Keating), and the ubiquitous Harry Von Zell, would drop in and become enmeshed in the day's episode. The action would even spill over into the Mortons' house. But it didn't matter where the action took place, because in his den George had his all-seeing television set, on which he could follow the action and make the appropriate remarks. In the role of a modern-day Mr. Interlocutor, George would turn from his TV set, face the camera and say, "According to my calculations, Gracie should be over at Blanche's, and by now she should be mixed up in this problem too . . . let's take a look. . . ." And then back to George's TV set. It didn't seem to matter that George knew the plot, he was just as anxious to find out how things would end as the audience.

The Further Adventures of Ellery Queen premieres "live" and in color on NBC in 1958. George Nader is the fourth actor to play the sophisticated detective and writer on TV. Angela Austin guest stars.

Television looks everywhere for subjects to entertain viewers. In 1958, brave cameramen don surgical masks to televise an operation. Over three million people tune in.

March 9, 1958. Helen Hayes re-creates the title role in "Mrs. McThing" on *Omnibus*, now on NBC.

Gracie Allen confuses husband George Burns with her hilarious, cockeyed explanations.

March 12, 1958. Earl Holliman and Sessue Hayakawa battle for possession of a knife in this scene from the two-man survival drama, "The Sea is Boiling Hot," on *Kraft Television Theatre,* the earliest live TV anthology series. In 1958, it will end its eleven-year run.

Leon Ames, Frances Farmer, and James MacArthur (Helen Hayes's son) star in "Tongue of Angels." The story of a young boy afflicted with a serious speech impediment is one of the last episodes of *Studio One,* which goes off the air in 1958 after nine years on CBS.

Bea Benaderet and Larry Keating join Burns and Allen.

The later scripts were less set-piece routines and more screwball-story oriented. Running dialogue gags were set up early and topped and topped, just in time for Harry Von Zell to enter and make a fool of himself. But comedy dialogue was still the drawing card of the show, and in subsequent years audiences demanded that George and Gracie end each show with an "afterpiece" of comedy banter.

GEORGE: *Well Gracie, which one of your brilliant relatives shall we talk about tonight?*

GRACIE: *The one we're most proud of is Mozart Allen the famous composer and conductor.*

GEORGE: *Mozart Allen? . . . Is he living yet?*

GRACIE: *Not yet.*

GEORGE: *That's good. . . . What kind of music did Moe write?*

GRACIE: *Well, the first thing he wrote was his Symphony Number Ninety-seven.*

GEORGE: *That was the first thing?*

GRACIE: *Yes. He figured he'd have a better chance if people didn't think he was just a beginner.*

No, vaudeville didn't die, the little mahogany box just sent it out to a larger audience. Burns and Allen still packed 'em in for eight years on television. True, the dancing Masconi Brothers are no longer with us, and Dr. Rockwell's Bird Act has gone back to the roost, and who will ever replace Joe Cook and his imaginary Four Hawaiians? But at least, for awhile, we had George and Gracie.

GRACIE: *Remember I was telling you about my well-known cousin Mozart Allen?*

GEORGE: *Wait a minute Gracie, I remember your cousin, but if he's so well known, what's the most famous composition he ever wrote?*

GRACIE: *George, everybody knows it. "The Chihuahua Serenade."*

GEORGE: *Oh, a Mexican tune.*

GRACIE: *In a way. You see, Mozart couldn't afford a metronome so he had his little dog sit on the piano and wag its tail to give him the beat.*

GEORGE: *That must have been a ridiculous sight.*

GRACIE: *No, the dog was looking the other way.*

GEORGE: *Gracie . . . you made everything clear except one thing: when I asked you if your cousin was living yet, you said, not yet. Does that mean he's alive or dead?*

GRACIE: *George, of course, who isn't?*

GEORGE: *Gracie . . . say good night.*

GRACIE: *Good night.*

Eugene Slafer is a young vaudevillian and filmwriter living in Hollywood.

152

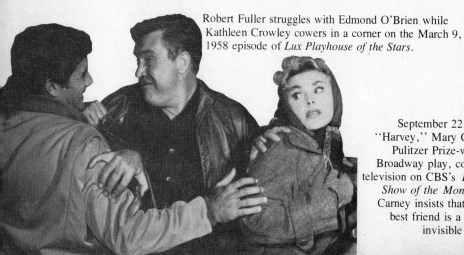

Robert Fuller struggles with Edmond O'Brien while Kathleen Crowley cowers in a corner on the March 9, 1958 episode of *Lux Playhouse of the Stars.*

September 22, 1958. "Harvey," Mary Chase's Pulitzer Prize-winning Broadway play, comes to television on CBS's *Dupont Show of the Month.* Art Carney insists that man's best friend is a 6'1½" invisible rabbit.

FAN FARE:
DEAR GRACIE ALLEN:

Why do you think the life in my house is nothing like yours? I watch your show every day and wish I could live with you instead. Your friends are always coming over; they're laughing and talking and getting into scrapes. We rarely have any company at all. My father says, "A quiet house is a house at rest."

Occasionally my Uncle Jack stops in on his way from visiting a patient, but he just sits in a chair and falls asleep.

We don't have an upstairs TV like yours, and though I've tried everything with the knobs, I can't make our downstairs set show pictures of anyone in the house the way George can. I wish I could watch my brother talk to his friend Walter, or spy on my parents when they're talking about me, but our television doesn't work that way and my father says it's not old enough to get another one. He doesn't understand me when I say I want to watch him on it, and tells me to go read the encyclopedia. No one in your house ever reads the encyclopedia. Even Ronnie, who goes upstairs to study all the time, calls his girfriend instead.

I tried spying on the neighbors yesterday in the bushes the way you and Blanche do, but they were only watching TV for hours and I couldn't see their picture very well through the window, so I went home. I wish I could live at your house instead, Gracie. Do you think when Ronnie goes to college you'll want someone else to come and stay with you?

I have followed the advice you give on all your shows. I made iced coffee by putting the can in the refrigerator (although I didn't know what to do with the can when it got cold), and I painted my nails with

Gracie's ingenuous twinkle shines through a glamour shot.

lipstick to match my lips perfectly. My mother's hairdresser, Helen, gave me a Gracie Allen hairdo (her specialty is Elizabeth Taylor, but the customer is always right), and I think I look a little like you from the side. My brother says I look like Sky King.

Please let me know how to make my family more like yours. The only excitement that ever happens here is when the fuse blows.

Your fan,
Esther Cohen

Esther Cohen still talks like Gracie Allen.

153

October 9, 1958. Jackie Gleason stars as Joe, "a young loafer with money and a good heart," in William Saroyan's Pulitzer Prize-winning comedy, "The Time of Your Life," on *Playhouse 90*. James Barton co-stars as Kit Carson; Betsy Palmer, Jack Klugman and Bobby Van also star.

"Little Moon of Alban," starring Julie Harris and Christopher Plummer, is presented on *The Hallmark Hall of Fame* in 1958. It wins the Emmy as 1958's Best Special Dramatic Program. Harris, writer James Costigan, and director George Schaefer also win awards. Julie Harris will play Brigid Mary Managan once more, when *Hallmark* redoes "Little Moon" in 1964.

October 17, 1958. *An Evening with Fred Astaire* wins eight Emmy Awards. In 1958, in spite of a growing trend toward videotape, this "Most Outstanding Program of the Year" is done live on NBC.

STAR TALK:
BERLE ON BERLE
AS TOLD TO LINDA GUTSTEIN

The contract given me by NBC is still in force; it's the only contract that ever was and ever will be that kind of contract. How I got it, I think, is a very interesting story. Everybody was going on film; the shows on film would be getting residuals and going into reruns, and I said to NBC, "Where will I be in the seventies?" and they said, "We'll take care of you." So they gave me the exclusive contract. Now Sid Caesar, if I recall, and Jackie Gleason, and a few other people had exclusive contracts with the networks, too, and when they went off the air, they were still under the contracts and couldn't appear for any other network. They started to get fidgety, as most actors do, and were told, "That's the way it is; that's why we're paying you." So I think both Caesar and Gleason got out of their contracts, tore them up. But my attorney advised me differently, because when I finally went off NBC with the series, I had offers from CBS and ABC, and finally, I made a deal with NBC. In fact, I said to General Sarnoff, "Look, I'm in jail. I'm not working. I live for work. An actor has to work; he needs it for his health." Sarnoff said, "I'll tell you what; let's see what we can do with the renegotiation of the contract." Now they could just as well have said, "Forget it. Let's cancel the contract." And they would have saved a lot of money, but they didn't. So we renegotiated, and I took a 40 percent decrease; and with that 40 percent less a year from NBC, I gained about 80 percent more by working nonexclusively.

Now, about our show: It originally started off as *The Texaco Star Theatre Vaudeville Show.* Nobody knows this, but we handed out programs. The program was called *The Texaco Star Vaudeville Revue,* and we handed them out to the studio audience. We started in a radio studio in Rockefeller Center in New York. In the early days we had parallel risers [portable platforms] with cameras, and the studio audience couldn't even see the stage. We didn't have monitors in the studio. After a few seasons I said, "Let's get rid of the parallels so the audience can see." So we made them put a break in the center aisle—like the Carson show has now—and the break was for the number one crane camera. That's the design I brought out to the Burbank studio. Then, in 1952 I suggested hanging the monitors in the studio, so that those in the audience who couldn't see the stage could see the show on the set. It was in 1954 that I devised the Berlite; it's for the non-audience show. If you want laughter or applause, the light blinks. The sound comes through the camera. They work it in the audio room as a laugh machine and applause machine.

But my anticipation of these things only goes back to my days of doing vaudeville shows, staging them myself, contributing the songs, the pace, and the speed. I had to learn, from scratch, what not to do and what to do on television. For instance, we had no clock in the studio. There wasn't anyone standing under a camera going, "Your three minutes are up!" I

Jonah Jones and the Jonah Jones Quartet provide music on *An Evening with Fred Astaire.*

For five months in 1958, Imogene Coca and Sid Caesar do the thirty-minute *The Sid Caesar Show* for ABC. Carl Reiner and Howard Morris are also program regulars, but the show does not catch on.

The Arthur Godfrey Show debuts on CBS in 1958, less than three months after the cancellation of the ten-year-old *Arthur Godfrey's Talent Scouts,* and two years after the cancellation of *Arthur Godfrey and His Friends,* which had lasted seven years. Godfrey's new show lasts only six months. In early 1959, both it and the seven-year-old *Arthur Godfrey Time* will be dropped. But Godfrey will be back in 1960 as host of *Candid Camera.*

Berle is "Mr. Television" on both sides of camera.

"Songwriters on Parade," and Hoagy Carmichael and Sammy Kahn would play their pianos on stage and sing their songs. Well, today these things would be done as specials. Almost all of those finales that I have in the files of the Texaco show have since been elongated and done as specials.

The thing is, the audience got what it saw. You only had one chance. It was always new material, and you never got a chance to break it in. If I told a joke and it bombed, that's where I ad-libbed. I'd stare at the audience and count, "Two, three," or I'd say, "What a night!" And if something happened, someone made a mistake verbally, or a piece of scenery fell down, well, I'd get more laughs ad-libbing than with the story line of the sketch. There was nothing funnier than Ted Lewis's toupee rolling down his arm when he took a bow. Or, when I was dressed up as a bride, the train of my gown got caught in the roller drop, and the next thing I knew I was hanging from the ceiling. Fatso Marco, who was the groom, was standing there looking up at me; I felt like a dummy.

In those sketches, when I dressed up as a woman, I did it as a camp. I didn't play it as a girl; I played it as a put-on. You see, now Flip Wilson—whom I enjoy tremendously, and who is a very talented comedian—plays it as a girl, Geraldine.

In those days, our writers had to write specifically for television, because there were so many no-nos. I couldn't say "I sold you a helicopter; I'd have to say 'heckicopter.'" I did it as a joke. Right now, you can get away with everything. I will say that television today is doing some fine things. I think that PBS now is sensational. They ran a program, "The Naked Civil Servant," which was excellent. Television's getting some very adult shows, and it's growing up.

Linda Gutstein is an associate editor at Parade *magazine, where she writes a weekly column on comedy.*

used to have to have a watch in my brain like a jockey who is riding a horse, timing the horse on the first quarter.

Because I belonged to all the unions (I had permission to run the camera, and would set up shots for the show), I even struck against my show. But that was later when I did the show from the Hollywood Palace for ABC. I remember I came to work one morning, and I saw my cameramen and everybody walking around with picket signs. They were putting in an unmanned camera. So I grabbed a picket sign and walked around with them.

On the Texaco show we did thirty-nine shows a year. Our finales ran about sixteen minutes with the cooperation of the performers and the guest stars. Let's say we had Rosemary Clooney or Tony Bennett; we'd do a medley of songs. Or I did a finale called

Ted Mack and the Original Amateur Hour moves to CBS in 1958. It will remain on the air for thirteen more years.

CBS's *Garry Moore Show* premieres on prime time in 1958. Regulars include comedienne Carol Burnett and Durwood Kirby.

REMEMBERING JACK BENNY

BRUCE KITZMEYER

Benny wasn't a stand-up comic telling jokes; *he* was the joke. He constructed the Jack Benny character over the years with great deliberation. He even chose three fingers on the cheek because they were "funnier" than four. By the time he reached TV his character was as polished as his bank vault; each word and gesture was a studied sure fire laugh. The magic in the formula was that the more familiar the mannerisms became, the funnier they were.

The Benny character was petty, self-centered, and hilariously cheap. To Jack's mortification, his cast and guests were forever exposing him. And just as Jack was humiliated by Rochester's sarcasm at home, so too was he besieged at work. Don Wilson, the announcer, and Dennis Day, the resident Irish singer, were demanding children yelling, "more money, more show time, more *me*." Don, peevish and overweight, was forever dragging out his dimwitted son from the wings for a whiny recitation. Dennis, who made a fetish out of his song, was forever nagging Jack about it: "Why not *two* songs this week, Mr. Benny?"

Because of the lack of respect Jack engendered, confusion reigned. Any member of the cast would storm out onstage to air a petty complaint. The stagehands would think nothing of wandering out to change a light bulb just as Jack would be coming down the stretch of a long joke. Jack would be incredulous. "Can't you see I'm doing the show?" he would shout. "Don't you know this is *my show?*"

And Jack's vanity was always coming face to face with another's indifference:

"Who should I say is calling?" asks the receptionist.

Jack smiles, rocks back on his heels, and answers slowly, "Just say [chuckle] *Jack Benny.*"

"He says he's 'out to lunch.' Call tomorrow."

Before the TV executives had locked into the formats of situation comedy and variety show, Benny's show was free to be experimental. He would come out onstage in front of a drawn curtain for the introduction. From there the show took off in any number of directions: from dreamy flashback to Jack's childhood, to Jack's trip to Italy one summer, to Jack's living room in Beverly Hills. Or Jack might do the whole show in front of the curtain. Usually there was "time-out" from the developing situation for a musical number from the Four Sportsmen or Dennis Day.

Among the regulars were Mel Blanc, who played a sleepy Mexican, and Professor LeBlanc, Jack's violin instructor. If Jack went to a store—and this was a surrealistic touch—the clerk was *always* Frank Nelson. Jack's call "Oh Mister . . . Mister," was the opening strain of that routine. Nelson would turn around and answer, "Yehhhhs?" the embodiment of obsequiousness and a parody of politeness.

The Jack Benny show consisted of a series of running gags. It was testimony to the fact that a thing done well was worth doing again and again. And Jack, a master of timing with his tried-and-true material, never grew stale.

Bruce Kitzmeyer is a free-lance writer in New York.

The Steve Lawrence and Eydie Gorme Show, a sixty-minute musical-variety show starring the married duo, plays on NBC in the summer of 1958. Lawrence and Gorme had been regulars on Steve Allen's *Tonight Show.*

Your Hit Parade tries again in 1958. The four new singers performing the nation's top tunes are Alan Copeland, Jill Corey, Virginia Gibson and Tommy Leonetti. They will soon be dropped.

Dorothy Collins, alone, returns to *Your Hit Parade* on October 10, 1958 in a CBS version. After seven months, the show is canceled. Collins will become a semiregular on *Candid Camera.*

REMEMBERING ERNIE KOVACS

JERRY BOWLES

The inscription on Ernie Kovacs's tombstone reads Nothing in Moderation. There is no better characterization of the brilliant pioneer of television comedy who died in a freakish car accident in January, 1962, a week before his forty-third birthday. Kovacs worked compulsively, smoked twenty two-dollar cigars a day, seldom slept, stayed late at card games he should have left early, and created television the likes of which has not been seen since. He left behind a half million dollars in gambling debts and a legend. His wife, Edie Adams, paid off the debts. The legend grows larger with each passing year.

It is an ironic thing, too, because Kovacs was never a giant hit in the ratings during his brief and furious career. He did shows for ABC, CBS, NBC, and Dumont, as well as local stations in New York and Philadelphia, but was always considered by many a specialized or acquired taste. One thing for sure, he was not your "but seriously, folks" kind of comedian. Unlike Bob Hope or Jack Benny, who said things that were funny, Kovacs' orientation was visual. He thought it would be funny to saw through the tripod of a camera while a show was on the air live and he did it. When a local show was canceled in Philadelphia, he spent the last program chopping down the set with an ax.

In the final year of his life, at a time when he was also trying to make a mark in the movies, Kovacs did a series of monthly specials for ABC. He spent so much of the show's budget on visual effects that he couldn't afford a band. That was his style.

Kovacs walks past a statue of *The Thinker* and

"He left behind a half-million dollars in gambling debts and a legend."

does a double take when he hears the statue mumbling "Hmmmmmm. Hmmmmmm." Kovacs stands looking at the *Mona Lisa;* the camera pans down and the good lady has legs that are dangling about a foot from the floor. He scratches a spot on an impressionist seascape and before your eyes the painting's sea drains, leaving a pile of sand and driftwood. There is the wonderful bit in which a lady is happily taking a bubble bath; suddenly, all sorts of people and dogs emerge from the tub, one at a time, while the startled lady looks on.

There was the famous show in which not a word of dialogue was spoken and an equally well-remembered one in which he used a tilted set to turn gravity into a comedy foil. That particular show completely upstaged a Jerry Lewis special that followed. He did the *1812 Overture* using slamming drawers and snapping celery stalks as percussion instruments.

He was not incapable of the devastating one-liner. "Thank you for inviting me into your home," he once said, "but couldn't you have cleaned it up a little?"

He created memorable characters like Percy Dovetonsils, a lisping poet, who read such wonderful nonsense as "Ode to Stanley's Pussycat," a sad la-

157

In 1958, the first of Leonard Bernstein's *Young People's Concerts* is broadcast on CBS. Bernstein conducts The New York Philharmonic Orchestra.

In 1959, Nikita Khrushchev's thirteen-day tour of the United States receives widespread television coverage. Here the Soviet premier is accompanied by Henry Cabot Lodge, Jr., U.S. ambassador to the U.N., and CBS News correspondent Harry Reasoner.

Ernie Kovacs with his ever-present cigar.

ment about a cat driven crazy by psychoanalysis. Another work was called simply "Ode to an Emotional Knight Who Once Wore the Suit of Medieval Armor Now in the Metropolitan Museum of Art While Engaged to One of Botticelli's Models." That one went: "Even though you may have grown to love it/There must have been times when you were aware/Of the inconvenience of it."

There was Pierre Ragout, ze French fairy tale teller. (When the evil queen's guard invites Snow White to go for a walk in the woods, Snow White responds, "Je wasn't born yesterday.")

And there was Wolfgang Sauerbraten, the Bavarian disk jockey (he dropped the "von" because Wolfgang wasn't that prosperous), J. Walter Puppybreath, and Irving Wong, Chinese songwriter and proprietor of the Square Wheel Rickshaw Company.

He interviewed "Harold, the world's strongest ant" and did bits like "Strangely Believe It." (Example: "Mrs. Arnold Frumkin of Liver Bile, Arkansas, raised a cat, a rat, a rattlesnake, and a raccoon as pets in an apartment only ten feet square. Oddly enough, the animals got along very well, and shared Mrs. Frumkin equally.")

There was a cutting edge to Kovacs's humor, a kind of uncompromising, no apologies cynicism. He refused to pay homage to the clichés of his day. Children were a favorite target. Thus, you might have "Uncle Buddy" encouraging two of his obnoxious charges to walk on the railing of the Staten Island Ferry ("Uncle Buddy used to wear a blindfold and then he would turn around three times real quick") or Miklos Molman, a drunken Hungarian chef, terrorizing kiddies in the peanut gallery with a whip, swilling wine from a bottle, cutting the strings of a loud puppet with scissors and sweeping the lifeless hulk into a garbage can. This was the 1950's, remember, and "black" comedy was the exception, not the rule.

Kovacs's greatest contribution was his innovative spirit. Somebody forgot to tell him that television had inherent limitations and he played with the medium like an overgrown kid with a marvelous new toy. It has become fashionable recently to call Kovacs a genius. Perhaps he was. One thing for sure, he was a consummate artist who spoke with an individual voice. That, in itself, is rare in television.

Jerry Bowles, the author of The Gong Show Book, *has written a book about the old Mickey Mouse Club, and is currently working on one about Ed Sullivan.*

158

February 6, 1959. Edward R. Murrow interviews Fidel Castro on *Person to Person*.

In 1959, Person to Person will go off CBS. During its six years on television, host Murrow had interviewed many historical figures. Among his most interesting subjects was Eleanor Roosevelt, with whom he spoke in 1954.

In 1959, *The Today Show* moves into its eighth year. Florence Henderson, seen here with Jack Lescoulie and Dave Garroway, is now a regular on the show. In 1961, Garroway will be replaced by John Chancellor.

STAR TALK:
LUCY ON LUCY
AS TOLD TO CECIL SMITH

When I heard one day that *I Love Lucy* was rerun seven times a day in some areas, I didn't like it —every time you turn on the water tap, you get me. You can have too much of anything, you know. But when I hear four generations are watching Lucy at the same time, it stops me. What makes her so universal?

Two things I think were always part of Lucy's character, whatever series she was doing. She always had financial problems. God knows, that's universal! And she always had a domineering figure over her, whether it was Ricky or Mr. Mooney or Uncle Harry. She was always knocking his silk hat off.

The financial situation was very important. If she needed a fur collar—a little ratty fur collar—we made a story out of it. Half the trouble she got into over the years was because of the need to make some extra money for something—a dress for Kim for a dance, a new kitchen gadget.

When CBS asked me to do television I was doing *My Favorite Husband* on radio. But I did want something Desi and I could do together. They wanted us to do a script about a Hollywood couple, two movie stars. I said, "Where's the conflict?" To the rest of the world, a Hollywood couple has no problems. (We do, but they don't believe it.) Two cars and a swimming pool; what the hell kind of problems could we have? But everybody has money problems. Lucy always had to bake something, borrow something, sell something, steal something; she always had to tell those white lies because of what she did. And she was

always getting Viv into trouble with her. That's why the show is universal. It's real.

Also we had wonderful writers. They wrote understandable comedy that you could follow even if you didn't know the language. They were not gag writers. They wrote structured plays, with a beginning, middle and end—the entire circle. Anytime we didn't have that, we were in trouble.

You must remember that we did stunts—wild, wonderful stunts and dangerous stunts. But there's where our writers were so great: Madelyn Martin Davis and Bob Carroll, Jr. When they wrote a stunt for me to do they went down on the stage and did it. Walking on stilts or roller-skating or doing a flip on skis or anything. Madelyn did every stunt first to make sure it could be done. Catch writers doing that these days! They turn in a script saying you fall in a parachute through a greenhouse roof and they take off, and then leave it up to you to figure out if it can be done.

God, I was lucky with my writers: Madelyn and Bob and the other Bobs—Bob Weiskopf, Bob Schiller, Bobby O'Brien. My writers always come up with the right stoppers for me. They stretched me further than I thought I could go. Many times I said, "I can't do that," and Madelyn would show me I could.

They had it rough; they couldn't use topical things—politics, social issues—like Norman Lear does. We weren't allowed. Hell, there's nothing new about topical humor. It goes back to Aristophanes. But

159

Groucho Marx visits Jack Paar on *The Tonight Show* in 1959 in order to promote his new book, *Groucho and Me*. More and more, talk shows are coveted by authors. In 1959, *The Tonight Show* switches from live to videotape.

Frequent *Tonight Show* guest Cliff Arquette sets up his weekly shop in 1959 on ABC with *Charley Weaver's Hobby Lobby*.

The queen of comedy, Lucille Ball.

we didn't do it. Maybe that's what makes Lucy so durable—she's never dated. We couldn't use the penny laughs they use today. Cheap jokes. Say a four-letter word and get a laugh. Suggest some sexual act and get a laugh. We were never allowed to resort to that. They say television is growing up, that this shock-value stuff is more mature or something. Thank God we didn't have it.

One thing we had: we knew when we were well off. I see these young people walk off shows. Kids not dry behind the ears, just learning their craft, and they walk away from a successful show. Okay, some are on booze or something else, but most of them are just

ill-advised, and dumb to take the advice. The way I look at it, they don't know when they're well off. As long as they've got their faces up there in front of the people, they're very lucky.

They say they're leaving for greener pastures. What greener pastures? I'm not talking about a great actor like Carroll O'Connor. He's a writer, a teacher; he knew where he was long before *All in the Family* came along. That cannot be said for most of us in this business. We didn't have that background. Take our shows away and the best we could do is be door-to-door salesmen. That's what a lot of these kids who walk away from lucrative shows will wind up doing—it's all they're qualified for.

And young people are so choosy about what they do. My kids are not like that. I told my daughter Lucie: "Turn down nothing. Everything you do, someday you can use. Maybe it's just someone you meet who later can do something for you. From my own experience, no matter how lowly a part seemed at the time, I always found it was worth doing."

"GET THAT GIRL'S NAME"

When Lucille Ball came to Hollywood as a Goldwyn Girl in Roman Scandals *with Eddie Cantor, director Busby Berkeley invented a stunt whereby a villain threw a handful of mud at Cantor. Just then Cantor bent over and the mud smashed square into the beautiful puss of one of the Goldwyn Girls. When Berkeley asked which of the girls wanted to take the mud in the face, all backed away except one–Lucille Ball. Cantor told Berkeley: "Get that girl's name. That's the one who will make it."*

Cecil Smith is the TV critic for the L.A. Times.

160

Keep Talking, a furiously paced game show on which players continue stories begun by others, moves into its second year on CBS in 1959.
Regulars are Morey Amsterdam, Cara Williams, host Carl Reiner, Paul Winchell, Danny Dayton, Pat Carroll, and Joey Bishop.

"The Gene Kelly Show" is presented as one of *The Pontiac Star Parade* specials on NBC in 1959.

FAN FARE:
DEAR LUCY:

I remember the time you accompanied Ricky to Hollywood for his big screen test. You even con- shot. But then you often did not get what you the camera,'' he warned. You squirmed and shifted in your seat, making faces at the director, until Ricky was finally forced to tie you to the bench. Undaunted, you wiggled around, bench and all, until you, not Ricky, sat full-face before the camera. However, the director filmed the whole sequence in close-up on Ricky, so you never even got in the shot. But then you often did not get what you wanted.

Lucy, you were like a kid who refused to go to bed when company came. You would hang about and poke your nose in where it didn't belong until—trouble! Your head would get stuck between the banister rails. Remember your first driving lesson? You disobeyed Ricky, took the shiny new convertible out before you were ready, and smashed it. Remember the trip when Ricky sped through a sleepy southern town run by a sheriff meaner than a rattlesnake? Ricky warned you not to argue with the sheriff, but your efforts landed the whole party in jail, and it took a wild square dance to get you out.

You misbehaved magnificently, Lucy. For you, it was all right to be crazy; chaos was the key to survival. Ethel was your partner in crime. Sometimes you fought, but battles made you a worthier pair, closer than ever. It was to Ethel you fled when you thought your mother-in-law despised you (''Wanna run away?''). When Mrs. Ricardo arrived

'' . . . you spoke a lunatic language of female discontent . . .''

from Cuba earlier than expected, you hid all the mess in the closet. And of course Mrs. Ricardo opened the door and got swamped by an avalanche of junk. But the Spanish-speaking woman learned to love you just as much as we did when you paraded around clucking like a chicken just to let her know what was cooking for dinner. She didn't even mind when you forgot her on the subway.

Lucy, you were a voice of rebellion for a pre-liberation, pre-Maude group of women. You shared a big secret with us: that women do not necessarily want neat, orderly homes and spic 'n' span lives, quietly serving their husbands. You rejected the expected, Lucy, and refused to behave correctly. You spoke a lunatic language of female discontent—you were an inspired feminist clown in the dog days before feminist consciousness. Now, with your reruns on four times a day, I remain faithful.

As the program says, I love Lucy.

Karyn Kay

Karyn Kay is co-editor of Women and the Cinema: A Critical Anthology.

161

Joining Kelly on *The Pontiac Star Parade* are Carol Lawrence and Donald O'Connor, Kelly's co-star in the classic film musical *Singin' in the Rain.*

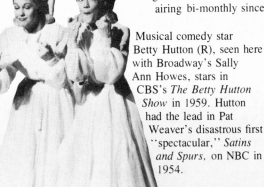

Milton Berle, no longer under an exclusive contract with NBC, guests on CBS' *Lucille Ball-Desi Arnaz Show,* which has been airing bi-monthly since late 1958 as part of *Desilu* Playhouse.

Musical comedy star Betty Hutton (R), seen here with Broadway's Sally Ann Howes, stars in CBS's *The Betty Hutton Show* in 1959. Hutton had the lead in Pat Weaver's disastrous first ''spectacular,'' *Satins and Spurs,* on NBC in 1954.

THE KRAMDENS, THE BUNKERS, AND THE FLINTSTONES

PERRY MEISEL

Who says there are no traditions on TV? Even though network programmers like to tell us how new this season's shows are supposed to be, every viewer knows that television's past is always a part of its present. Where would Phyllis or Rhoda be without Lucy and Gracie? And where does *Kojak* come from if not *Naked City, M Squad,* and *The Detectives?*

Television's lines of descent are probably easiest to see, though, in the story of the American workingman told by three classic shows in the history of situation comedy—*The Honeymooners, The Flintstones,* and *All in the Family.* Jackie Gleason's Ralph Kramden is the prototype for Fred Flintstone and Archie Bunker both, and Ralph's character and style of life constantly define and direct the temperaments of his successors, and the predicaments in which they are embroiled.

Ralph's famous rage has no clearer reflection in subsequent television history than Archie's famous ranting, while the Bunker racism and ultraconservative politics simply make overt what you might have expected from Ralph all along. It's one thing to share life at 328 Chauncey Street with the Mullinses and the Manicottis, but what would happen if a black or a gay tried to move in downstairs? If Ralph is so ready to send Alice to the moon, can you imagine the fate of such aliens in the confined world of Bensonhurst? Even a suave dance instructor gets booted from the building by Ralph and Ed Norton.

The Flintstones *are* The Honeymooners' *cartoon doubles.*

Norton's heir, of course, is Barney Rubble, Fred Flintstone's best friend and neighbor. In fact, the team of Fred and Barney is really an instant replay of Ralph's and Ed's legendary banter and mutual browbeating—just listen to the way the voices match up. If that's not enough, watch the way Fred lords it over poor Barney ("You're the stupidest man I ever knew," says Ralph to Norton), even when Fred concocts the world's dumbest schemes. Remember Fred's doomed attempts to sneak out on Wilma for some bowling? How many times has that bowling ball given Ralph away when he tries to slip out on Alice?

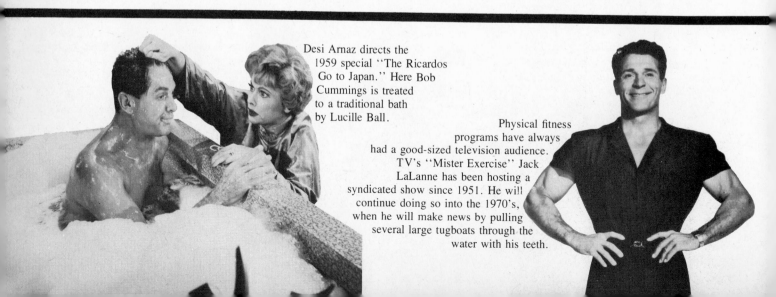

Desi Arnaz directs the 1959 special "The Ricardos Go to Japan." Here Bob Cummings is treated to a traditional bath by Lucille Ball.

Physical fitness programs have always had a good-sized television audience. TV's "Mister Exercise" Jack LaLanne has been hosting a syndicated show since 1951. He will continue doing so into the 1970's, when he will make news by pulling several large tugboats through the water with his teeth.

"Who says there are no traditions on TV?"

If the shows have common characters and situations, they also have common themes and a common vision of America. Ralph, Fred, and Archie are all working-class heroes, of course, but even more than that they tend to be schemers and dreamers hoping to get rich quick. Each is intoxicated with faith in himself, and each thereby underestimates what kind of world he is up against. "I got him just where I want him," says Fred when he thinks he has Mr. Safestone, the supermarket king, up against a wall in a deal to buy truckloads of Wilma's homemade pies. Fred's scheme does not only rely thoughtlessly on working Wilma to the bone. ("Go home and start cooking," Ralph commands Alice in a similar gesture when he tries to win a bet on his prowess as master of the house.) Fred's scheme also relies on his general unawareness of the social and economic realities that make his pies cost more to produce than they will yield in profit. Like the old squeeze play that Ralph so cavalierly tries to pull on his boss for a raise in pay and a promotion, Fred's estimation of Mr. Safestone precludes any realization that power here rests solely in the buyer's hands. So too Fred is unwittingly exploited as a stunt man in the movies for no pay, just as Archie is totally ignorant of the blatant rip-off scheme behind the local undertaker's obeisances. Archie's prejudices are particularly self-defeating, since they seal him off from sympathy with those other parts of society used and discarded like his own.

Such delusion, however, is usually the source of the shows' uniform brand of humor. But at what a price! Day after day, episode after episode, all three of our heroes are subject to the grossest humiliations and defeats imaginable. We laugh when Ralph and Archie hit the ceiling at the slightest challenge to their authority but that happens precisely because both are sensitive to their peripheral position in society and the powerlessness that accompanies it. Thanks to the resources of cartoon, Fred Flintstone literally finds the ceiling hitting *him*, at least when the script calls for some concrete expression of his victimization. Even Fred's intermittent torpor manages to represent the defeated cast of mind that seems to underlie both Ralph's and Archie's excessively combative (read defensive) attitude toward life. There's such trouble, such striving, such *pain* in Ralph's face when he starts screaming. And no wonder. "My whole life's been a struggle," says Ralph, "ever since I was a kid." It's a miracle he doesn't have a stroke right there on the set, a fear that may even connect Ralph and Archie medically when the Bunkers conspire to keep their breadwinner on a strict regimen to control his blood pressure and diet.

Sadness and despair, of course, wouldn't seem to rank high among comedy's attributes, but there they are, informing and directing the humor every step of the way. What's more, the workingman's submerged grief is a clue to the understanding of society that lies behind the shows' humorous exteriors, but which still seems to escape the consciousness of the major characters. Norton's job in the sewer, Ralph's on the bus, Fred's in the granite pits, Archie's in the warehouse loading room—all these jobs are basic functions in the economic system, and place the characters in each show at the center of society. This economic centrality is, of course, hidden, or at least made ironic, by the peripheral position the characters occupy from the point of view of status and upward mobility. But by placing such characters in the role of stars—that is, by making stars out of working-class

Nat Hiken's classic TV comedy, *The Phil Silvers Show,* goes off the air in 1959. Here Sergeant Bilko, pretending to be a member of the "top brass," tells a group of officers how he would run the war games. At his side is Al Hodge, formerly TV's Captain Video.

Just as the army goes off the air, the navy arrives. *Hennesey,* a naval comedy, debuts in 1959 and will remain on CBS for three years. Its cast members are Roscoe Karns, star Jackie Cooper as Chick Hennesey, Abby Dalton, and Henry Kulky.

In 1959, *Dennis the Menace* appears on CBS. Jay North plays the rascal created in the comics by Hank Ketchum. Herb Anderson portrays Dennis's father Henry Mitchell.

All in the Family's *Archie Bunker (Carroll O'Connor) has a tantrum as wife Edith (Jean Stapleton) calls for help.*

characters—American television really affirms this centrality after all, and renders the worker, with all his disappointments and defeats, the real hero of the society in which he lives.

Neither characters nor viewers, though, are allowed to tender such an insight for very long, since our blindness to it is what sustains the humor of all three shows and guarantees their success as entertainment. This fine tension or balance between facts and funnies, however, is what makes these programs as powerful—and as powerfully funny—as they are. It's also what succeeds in giving them the authority of a tradition on American television. Even though we like to think it's just the commercials that intrude on our entertainment viewing, there is more than a share of the realities they represent right at the heart of TV's funniest shows.

Perry Meisel teaches English at New York University and writes on a variety of topics for the Village Voice *and other publications.*

The brightest new comedy of 1959 is CBS's *The Many Loves of Dobie Gillis,* based on the novel by Max Shulman. Dwayne Hickman plays the dumb, love-struck Dobie, and Tuesday Weld is the spoiled Thalia Menninger who continually frustrates Dobie with her impossible demands.

Child star Patty McCormack plays Torey Peck in *Peck's Bad Girl,* which premieres on CBS in 1959. Marsha Hunt plays the mother of the mercurial tomboy.

FAN FARE:
DEAR HONEYMOONERS:

How did you do it? Do you remember? Did you know with the first few episodes that a legend was in the making? Or was it one of those things that developed as it went along—so natural that it came out perfect, and so filled with magic that each repeated viewing reveals new magic?

Jackie Gleason and production crew watch rehearsal of a scene from The Honeymooners.

Dennis O'Keefe bemoans the head of a fellow space traveler on *The Dennis O'Keefe Show*, a situation comedy that appears on CBS in 1959. It will last two seasons.

William Lundigan is a more serious space traveler on *Men into Space*, which debuts on CBS in 1959.

George Nader is the star of *Man and the Challenge*, which begins on NBC in 1959. Nader plays Glenn Barton, a scientist who studies man's endurance.

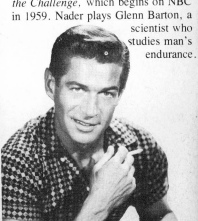

Perhaps, despite the quarter of a century that you have been on the air, you don't feel like legends. But you are, because you were so good. TV viewers will always take seemingly effortless perfection for granted. We can't see Jackie Gleason without thinking of Ralph Kramden, Art Carney without thinking of Ed Norton; ditto Audrey Meadows, ditto Joyce Randolph. For that matter, I can't see a Pat Perkins dress without thinking of Alice's wardrobe. (What ever became of that apron? I bet it would bring a fortune at auction today.)

In fact, I cannot see one of your episodes without feeling awe for the actors and writers who created the show. Twenty-five years ago, when situation comedies had to be described as "zany" and "madcap" and "scatterbrained" to get an audience, you found a subtler and more universal humor in genuinely hilarious situations that grew out of human nature and daily life. You didn't need a judge like Bradley Stevens, or a nightclub entertainer like Ricky Ricardo, as a springboard for comic situations. You gave us a bus driver, someone everyone could identify with, someone who got himself into one scrape after another because he was a well-meaning jerk, an exaggerated Everyman whose bungling struck close to home.

You gave us a product of the fifties that was ahead of its time, yet as timeless as the American Dream. As long as Ralph Kramden could hope and scheme for his pot of gold—no-cal pizza or wallpaper that glowed in the dark or the KranMar Mystery Appetizer (dog food) that he fed his boss—he was willing to fail, and bounce back, and try again. As long as he had his dreams, and his wife's love, and his best pal's friendship, his life was an adventure that was worth living. He never stopped scheming, but I don't remember that he ever really complained. He was a happy man.

On top of that, *The Honeymooners* is probably

Ralph and Ed register shock at a girlie magazine.

still the funniest show on TV.

For the lines and gestures and characterizations and situations and the magic that is too full of real life to ever be forgotten, there can be no question of the genius of *all* the creators of *The Honeymooners*.

That is why you are legends.

That is why I am a honeymoonie, and why the honeymoon will never be over.

Donna McCrohan

Donna McCrohan is a writer whose parents had the first TV on the block.

166

Former beauty queen Cloris Leachman screams and screams on "The Dark Room," an episode of the eerie ABC anthology series *Alcoa Presents: One Step Beyond*. Host John Newland will introduce strange tales based on actual case histories during the show's run from 1959 to 1961. Leachman had played Timmy's first mother on *Lassie*, before turning over the role to June Lockhart.

"It is the middle ground between light and shadow, between science and superstition." Writer Rod Serling is creator, host, and chief writer on CBS's *The Twilight Zone*, an anthology series that proves fiction, after all, is stranger than fact. *Twilight Zone* is exceptional for its imaginative stories, blending horror and wit; brilliant, memorable "twist" endings; intelligent performances by top actors; and thoughtful, tasteful productions. It will win Emmy Awards and become a cult favorite during its five-year run. Serling will host a less successful horror series, *Rod Serling's Night Gallery*, from 1970 to 1972.

STAR TALK:
EVE ARDEN ON EVE ARDEN
AS TOLD TO LINDA GUTSTEIN

I have thought about why Miss Brooks was so popular. I grew up in a small town, and my aunt had a lot of young friends who were teachers. So I got to know them on a social basis, and I never had any awe or dislike of teachers. I knew them from both sides of the fence and could identify with their problems, and I think that gave my performance a certain authenticity, perhaps. I tried to play Miss Brooks as a loving person who cared about the kids and kept trying to keep them out of trouble, but kept getting herself in trouble and looking for Mr. Boynton all the time. A young man came backstage the other night with his wife, and he pointed at my husband and said, "That's the man I'm jealous of. I became a biology teacher because I was looking for Miss Brooks."

Actually, on radio Mr. Boynton, the biology teacher, was Jeff Chandler. And it was very funny because Jeff was such a macho guy, but vocally he played Mr. Boynton very well. We always had a Christmas show when he would finally get to kiss Miss Brooks. It was supposed to be a rather shy kiss, but Jeff took it very seriously and ruined it—for the studio audience, at least. So when we went to TV, we knew he wouldn't be right. He was beginning to be a big film star then, you know, and so we persuaded him that was where his future lay. And then we were lucky to find Bob Rockwell, who was right for Mr. Boynton, who understood frogs better than women.

I think the role of Miss Brooks was closer to me than most of my film characters, where I got to be a wisecracking lady, you know; but never a mean, wisecracking lady. Even in *Mildred Pierce*—where I was acting in defense of Crawford and I made kind of nasty remarks to the villain—I always played it with, I guess, a heart of gold. You know, to give it some dimension. But, as I say, Miss Brooks was closer to me; she was a reactor.

To me that is the great part of acting, *reacting*. If you just act, and you don't react, you're kind of half a person standing there—because our lives are spent reacting to other people, right? So I guess that part of the character is like me. I think I have a pretty good sense of humor, maybe a little kookier than hers—Miss Brooks kind of followed a pattern—but I haven't seen it in so long. I have a hundred and fifty of the shows sitting in my basement, and I always figure if I can get someone to take out all the commercials, I'll look at them again.

Doing the show was maybe the easiest and most pleasant job I've had. I had done it for four years on radio before I started on television, and the fifth year of radio overlapped the first year of television, so I was pretty busy. But it got to be so easy to do that we would walk in and read two scripts practically cold, with the audience there. The cast was wonderful. We used no canned laughter, and the only time we dubbed any was when we had a sight gag that the audience couldn't see because of the cameras.

167

An early episode of *The Twilight Zone* is "The Hitchhiker." Inger Stevens's vacation turns into a nightmare when she keeps seeing Leonard Strong along the side of the road.

Keenan Wynn and two-time Olympic decathlon champion Bob Mathias star in the syndicated *The Troubleshooters* in 1959. It lasts one season.

Dane Clark stars in the syndicated series *Bold Venture*. Based on a radio program, it tells the story of Slate Shannon, his ward Sailor Duval (played by Joan Marshall), and the people who charter their boat.

Eve Arden will always be "Our Miss Brooks" for many nostalgic TV viewers.

My own children were too young to be aware of the show. We lived on a farm, and they went to a little country school. I don't think the boys saw it at all until it went into reruns. But occasionally one of the kids would come home and say, "Mommy, so-and-so says you're Miss Brooks. You're not, are you?"

Then I did *The Mothers-in-law* on TV, and I've always gone back to the stage. I did "Let's Face It," with Danny Kaye, and a picture with Bob Hope. So television was kind of an on and off project for me.

I've evolved a way of life that pleases us, my husband and me, because we work together and do plays that are right for us. We take them out for eight weeks at a time. And I'm going to go back to do the first picture I've done in a long time, *Grease*. They're writing in a part, and I'm playing—of all things—the *principal*.

Linda Gutstein is an associate editor of Parade *magazine, where she writes a weekly column on comedy.*

168

Warner Brothers, thrilled by the success of *77 Sunset Strip*, moves from Los Angeles to Honolulu for its newest private detective series, *Hawaiian Eye*. It will play on ABC from 1959 to 1963. Here Anthony Eisley, as Tracy Steele, shields guest Julie Adams. Also starring are Robert Conrad as Tom Lopaka, Grant Williams as Greg MacKenzie, and Connie Stevens as singer Cricket Blake.

Warner Brothers takes us to New Orleans for *Bourbon Street Beat* which also debuts on ABC in 1959. Starring are Andrew Duggan, Arlene Howell, Van Williams, and Richard Long. This detective series will be canceled in 1960 and Long will take his character Rex Randolph to *77 Sunset Strip*.

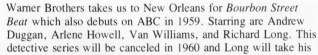

FAN FARE:
DEAR "YOUR SHOW OF SHOWS":

Has there ever been a funnier, more sophisticated, more beloved television variety program than you? From February, 1950 to June, 1954, with a hiatus every summer, you offered viewers ninety minutes of brilliant entertainment every Saturday night—*live* from New York City. Without the benefit of tape or canned laughter, you presented sketches, songs, and dances performed by a talented group of performers, all under the guiding hand of brilliant producer-director Max Liebman. You gave us some ''firsts'' as well: the first variety program with a full theater audience; the first with a regular stock company of players; the first with its own exclusive scenery and props.

And your stars! Who can forget that supremely talented duo, Sid Caesar and Imogene Coca? These two gifted clowns, supported by ''second bananas'' Carl Reiner and Howard Morris, appeared in a series of superbly written sketches that poked fun at human foibles and pretensions, or mocked the popular movies of the day. Alone onstage, Caesar would depict a befuddled Everyman trying to cope with life, or a blustering Germanic ''professor'' being interviewed at an airport and vainly trying to conceal his abysmal stupidity. Alone onstage (or with a partner), Imogene Coca would make us laugh at a passion-ridden torch singer, or a daffy ballerina, or a sweet, wistful tramp. Together, Caesar and Coca would take us through the hilarious marital tribulations of Doris and Charlie Hickenlooper, or show us two strangers exchanging clichés when they meet for the first time.

Every one of your fans remembers the great sat-ires of silent movies, or of popular movies of the day. We all laughed uproariously at Coca's version of a Theda Bara vamp, or Caesar's rendition of Rudolph Valentino. We cherished their versions of *A Streetcar Named Desire, A Place in the Sun, Shane, High Noon,* and *Breaking Through the Sound Barrier.* The old movie musicals or gangster films or hospital dramas were never the same after you took them on. And fans remember the skillful takeoffs of foreign movies, in which the performers actually seemed to be speaking Italian, German, or French. (Caesar was a master at imitating foreign languages, but didn't speak any of them!)

The comedy segments were unforgettable, but so were the musical interludes, which brought so many great artists to television for the first time. You showcased Robert Merrill, Marguerite Piazza, Lily Pons, Alicia Markova, Anton Dolin, Maria Tallchief, and many other great figures in beautifully staged musical numbers. And your regular singing and dancing performers were a weekly delight. We loved watching or listening to Bill Hayes, Judy Johnson, the Hamilton Trio, Mata and Hari, and the Billy Williams Quartet.

There have been many television variety shows since you left us. But none can match your wit and style—or the comic genius of the unforgettable Sid and Imogene.

Ted Sennett

Ted Sennett is the author of a book on Your Show of Shows *and of other books on the performing arts.*

169

Mike ''Touch''' Connors teaches waitress Carol Kelly how to use a police .38 on CBS's new action series *Tightrope* which appears in 1959 for one season. Connors's character, Nick Stone, an undercover agent, distinctively carries his gun strapped to his back.

The old movie classic *Mr. Lucky* comes to CBS in 1959 with John Vivyan (R) playing the Cary Grant role. Here Lucky, his sidekick Andamo (Ross Martin) and sultry Kitten Conner (Nita Talbot) attend the fights. *Mr. Lucky* is highlighted by the music of Henry Mancini.

Sebastian Cabot stars as criminologist Carl Hyatt in *Checkmate*, which premieres on CBS in 1959. This unusual crime detection series, created by Eric Ambler, also stars Doug McClure and Anthony George. Here Cabot helps a grown-up Margaret O'Brien track down the person trying to kill her.

STAR TALK:
COCA ON COCA
AS TOLD TO LINDA GUTSTEIN

It's most unfortunate *Your Show of Shows* can't be put out in its original form, because it was truly a review. There was fantastic talent on that show—dancers, singers. Max Liebman would bring in guest stars such as Lily Pons, Gertrude Lawrence. Now, if you see some of the syndicated things, or *Ten from Your Show of Shows,* the movie, you just see the sketches; so everyone's under the impression that it was just comedy.

But it was wonderful doing comedy on the show. If I'm not mistaken, I worked on the show for almost twenty weeks before Sid Caesar and I worked together. I had done a lot of New York reviews and nightclubs, so I had a lot of my own material, plus having worked for Max Liebman, our producer. I worked for Max for five summers in an adult camp up in the Poconos—Tamiment, it was called. So when I first went on *The Admiral Review* with Max, he, of course, knew everything I had done by that time. On *The Admiral Review* I was strictly on my own; the writers weren't writing for me.

I only started working with Sid because I went to Max one day and said, "Max I'm out of material. I don't know what I can do next week." Max said, "Why don't you do, 'You'd Better Go Now'—the popular song—followed with a pantomime." I thought that was a good idea. I'd done it first with my then-husband, Robert Burton, in *New Faces of 1937,* and I thought Max would engage Bob too, because it

> "I never expressed myself because Sid always said what I was thinking anyhow."

was more or less our creation. To my amazement Max said, "Do it with Sid." Well, I thought that was odd. I mean, we hadn't gotten to know each other because in a review people work in different rooms—dancers in one room, sketch people in another, and so forth. Anyhow, I told Sid the story of the pantomime—we weren't going to do the song—and to my delight, that's all I had to tell him. We just automatically did it, and it turned out most successfully.

Then, the next week, I said to Max, "Again I have nothing to do." So we decided on a burlesque sketch called "Slowly I Turn." Every burlesque comic has his own version of it. So Sid and I were again put in a cubicle to rehearse, and Sid asked, "Do you really want to do this old burlesque sketch?" And I said, "Well, it's Rags Ragman's version; it isn't the usual one, and, yes, I want to do it"—thinking, again, if he didn't want to do it, my husband could. But he said all right, and it was a smash. From then on, Sid said he wanted to work with me. And he carried much more weight on this show than I did. He had come to it fresh from a Broadway success and a movie career,

Johnny Staccato features John Cassavetes in an interesting portrayal of an Italian ex-musician turned private eye, on NBC in 1959. It will last one year.

October 1959. *The Untouchables* debuts on ABC. Robert Stack seen here with guest Thomas Mitchell, is FBI Agent Elliott Ness. Walter Winchell narrates. The show had originally been broadcast as a two-part episode on *Westinghouse Desilu Playhouse* earlier in 1959. From 1959 to 1963, there will be complaints from antiviolence groups about the show. Also Italians protest that the program blames them for all gangland crime during Prohibition. Nevertheless, *The Untouchables* will consistently have high ratings.

Sid and Imogene, always a zany team!

the material. I never expressed myself, because Sid always said what I was thinking anyhow.

Usually, the thing I like to do best is satire. For instance, when I saw "Afternoon of A Fawn" for the first time, I almost had to leave the theater, I got so hysterical. I thought, someday I must do this ballet. For two years up at Tamiment, I harassed Max. Finally, a musician up there thought of a way of orchestrating it so that ten musicians could play it—it calls for fifty or eighty in the original. Jerry Robbins and David Lichine were at Tamiment. They knew the Nijinsky choreography, and that's what we used. The only variation was, instead of taking off two scarves, I took off about thirty. But the steps and the movement were Nijinsky. And there was not one twist, except at the end of the thing, when the nymph goes up on the rock. What I thought was so funny about the ballet is that he [the hero] is really crazy about the scarves, not the nymph. He doesn't really dig *her*, because in the Nijinsky ballet he takes her long scarf, picks it up, throws it on the rock, and it was obvious how he felt about the scarf. So when we did it, there wasn't a scarf on the rock. *I* got up on the rock.

What we were doing was satire, not burlesque. In burlesque it would have been—let's say for *Swan Lake*—forget the idea; somebody's trying to kill a swan, and you'd take it from there. You'd have a rifle, the feathers falling off, from the shooting. We didn't do that. We did the choreography. You can't satirize something unless it's very good.

What I liked satirizing best on *Your Show of Shows* were the movies, when they weren't too long. It was such fun pretending to be somebody else. The first movie satire we did I almost think was the best, *A Place in the Sun*. It was just Sid, myself, and Carl Reiner as his alter ego. You just heard Carl's voice; you didn't see him. He was voicing what Sid was supposed to be thinking. We're in the rowboat and

and the writers were primarily writing for him. From then on, they wrote for both of us. It became a set thing that Sid and I would do four items together, and one on our own, so we always made five appearances in the show. And we usually had the same reaction to

Movie idol Robert Taylor comes to television in 1959 to star as Matt Holbrook in *The Detectives*. During its three-year stay on ABC, *The Detectives* will expand from thirty minutes to an hour.

Audrey Peters and Ron Tommee join the cast of *Love of Life* in 1959 to play Vanessa and Bruce Sterling; CBS's popular daytime serial is in its eighth season.

April 2, 1959. "Judgment at Nuremberg" is presented on *Playhouse 90*. Here witness Marketa Kimbrell is questioned by defense counsel Maximilian Schell, who repeats his role in the film adaptation. Also starring are Claude Rains, Melvyn Douglas, and Paul Lukas. George Roy Hill is the director of the Abby Mann story.

Sid's trying to get up enough nerve to murder me. It's the story of *The American Tragedy*. The satire was written by Lucille Kallen. She was one of the very good writers on the show, and I think it was the most perfectly written one. It only lasted eight minutes, but it was spooky. I really felt it; I remember having chills. I really don't know if it was nerves, or if I was really scared of being killed. See, Sid was contemplating killing me, and he's really a fantastic actor.

We used to get so involved in those things, we forgot we were doing comedy; we were playing them for real. The reason I remember *A Place in The Sun* so much is that when we did it in run-through not one person laughed. It was unusual too see a satire such as that. When they were announcing it, I looked at Sid and sweat was pouring down his face, and I was shaking. We had no idea what the audience would do. I can't tell you if the people laughed or not; but they must have, because it was a hit.

We had a wonderful working atmosphere on the show. Sometimes things came about in funny ways. One day Max said, "Somebody come up with an idea." Nobody could think of anything. So I said, "What about Sid, Carl, Howie [Howard Morris] and myself just standing and staring at the audience, not doing anything, then walking off." Well, Max got so mad, but all of a sudden, Mel [Brooks] jumped up and was at the door. Then Sid, Karl, Howie and I walked out, and without one word of conversation, Mel opened the door and said, "Lord So-and-so," and Sid entered and sat on the couch facing Max. Then Mel announced, "Lady So-and-so," and I came in and sat down too, the same with Karl and Howie. We just stared at Max and started to laugh. And every week at rehearsal we'd do this crazy piece of business. Finally, we convinced Max it should be done on the show. When I thought about what had made me suggest it, I remembered what I had done in the first

New Faces. We came out in single file, stood and faced the audience, did nothing, then turned around and exited four times during the show. So I was stealing from myself.

There was a special chemistry to *Your Show of Shows*, I think, because Max wasn't afraid to throw out material at the last minute. And I think when you do live television—well, we stopped for nothing. We had no cue cards, no TelePrompTers, and no ad-libbing on the air, because Max would have died if anybody had ad-libbed. It would have been utter disgrace, and you would have been drummed right out of the corps—like the British Army in India or something. Nobody ever forgot a line, and that was the amazing part of it.

I remember once we had a whole day's discussion; we were doing a marital sketch. In the sketch I went to a restaurant, and I thought everyone was looking at me. Of course, they didn't even know I was there. I kept saying to Sid, "See that man, the way he's looking at me." And he'd say, "Stop it, he's not looking at you." "Yes, he is. His eyes are undressing me." Well, he was to say: "Just because you have a new $220 dress . . ." Well, Sid balked at that; he felt nobody buys a $220 dress. So people went out to shop, and it was thoroughly investigated to the point where you'd think it was a drama. Finally, an amount was settled on that Sid thought was right for this man to have spent on his wife.

An awful lot of people forget that Max Liebman was the moving force of *Your Show of Shows*. How Max sensed the chemistry to have Sid and I work together, or why, I don't know. He's the one who put us together. Everything goes back to Max, you know.

Linda Gustein is an associate editor of Parade *magazine, where she writes a weekly column on comedy.*

October 14, 1959. Jack Hawkins plays a butler in love with a younger woman, and Jessica Tandy plays his unhappy wife in "The Fallen Idol." The Graham Greene thriller is presented on *The Dupont Show of the Month*.

October 30, 1959. Laurence Olivier makes his American television debut on NBC in Somerset Maugham's *The Moon and Sixpence*. He will win the Emmy for the year's Outstanding Performance by an Actor. Also starring are Geraldine Fitzgerald, Judith Anderson, Jessica Tandy, and Hume Cronyn. Richard Mulligan directs the $500,000 production.

June Allyson and husband Dick Powell co-star in "A Summer Ending," the story of a short-lived friendship, on *The Dupont Show with June Allyson*. This CBS anthology series, often titled *The June Allyson Theatre*, will last from 1959 to 1961. Powell is the host of *Dick Powell's Zane Grey Theatre*, which debuted in 1956 on CBS.

REMEMBERING "FATHER KNOWS BEST"

DANNY PEARY

There were many family comedies on television during the fifties and early sixties which depicted how middle-class WASP parents raised their children. *Leave It to Beaver, Bachelor Father, The Adventures of Ozzie and Harriet, The Donna Reed Show,* and *My Three Sons* all presented model families with whom we could compare our own, but none of these had the impact of *Father Knows Best.* It was the most popular of the family comedies, and today, ironically, it is the program most often cited to criticize what was wrong with the entire genre.

This is unfair criticism. *Father Knows Best,* week after week—from 1954 to 1960— was much better than the other family comedies: its characters were more mature; its women were more intelligent and capable; its situations were more dramatic.

Family life in *Father Knows Best* was more appealing than that displayed in other family comedies. It was the only show on which the children looked comfortable touching their parents. There was genuine warmth between the Andersons. In all the other shows, the children would stand stiffly in a row while talking with their parents who would face them, standing, from the opposite side of the room, ready to accuse or lecture. And during these conversations, the kids rarely exchanged words amongst themselves; they could only talk to their parents. In *Father Knows Best,* the parents and the kids mingled; the children talked to each other while the parents waited patiently

> "... it is the program most often cited to criticize what was wrong with the entire genre."

for their turn to speak. In some shows, the house seemed divided into two arenas. The children had sanctuary in their bedrooms, but they looked as if they were trespassing if the wandered into their parents' territory. In *Father Knows Best,* Betty, Bud, and Kathy knew they had the run of the house.

The critics of *Father Knows Best* protest that parents who watched this program expected their children to be as cooperative as the Anderson kids, and children expected their parents to be as understanding as Jim and Margaret. Since no one could live up to these TV role models, viewers would naturally consider each member of their family a disappointment and the family itself a failure. Even Billy Gray, who played Bud, has chastised the program for doing "everybody a disservice [by giving us characters and a family] that were all totally false."

But *Father Knows Best* did not try to present the Andersons as a typical American family. They were an ideal family for viewers at home and were even more so for the characters they made contact with on the show. It was more than coincidence that so many

173

Even Jose Ferrer plays a cowhand in the western-crazy television of 1959. Here the distinguished actor gets ready to battle an Apache in "Survival" on *The General Electric Theatre,* a Ronald Reagan–hosted anthology series in its sixth year on CBS. In 1949, Ferrer had played his "classic" Cyrano de Bergerac on *The Philco Playhouse.*

Riverboat, an adventure series starring Darren McGavin (R) and Burt Reynolds (not seen) begins a three-year run on NBC in 1959. Here the guest is Hugh Downs. McGavin had starred as Mickey Spillane's tough-guy private eye, *Mike Hammer,* on NBC in 1958.

On Father Knows Best *kids felt free to touch their parents.*

people, and an animal or two, gravitated toward the Anderson home. Into the lives of the Andersons would come an orphan, or a boy whose father was always too busy to spend time with him, confused newlyweds, Jim's lonely bachelor friend, Jim's unmarried, unfulfilled lady friend, a lonely aunt, or an absolute stranger. The Andersons welcomed people who had an unstable or non-existent family situation.

We admired the Andersons because they would help or defend those people less fortunate or with less clout than themselves. On one occasion, a friend of Betty's made fun of a defenseless orphan boy who was staying in their home by telling the family that he had been freeloading all over town. The boy hung his head in shame. All at once, all five Andersons rose to his defense, and Betty informed her ex-girlfriend that while the boy was an invited guest, she would no longer be considered one. For their part, Jim and Margaret found the boy some parents. Then there was the time the Andersons adopted and fell in love with a stray dog, not realizing it belonged to an elderly transient medicine peddler who had been thrown in jail. The man and the dog were reunited when he was released, but he needed a recommendation of a prominent citizen in order to avoid further trouble with the law. Although they had never met the man, the Andersons vouched for him. Since a friend of theirs—the dog—thought highly of him, they did too.

Because the Andersons never abused power or privileges, they could live together in relative har-

When Clint Walker walks out on *Cheyenne,* Warner Brothers tries to scare him into returning by signing Ty Hardin to play Bronco Layne, the new lead character on *Cheyenne.* When Walker returns to his role after Warners has renegotiated his contract, Hardin's series is retitled *Bronco.* It lasts from 1959 to 1960.

Two Warner Brothers contract players, Dorothy Provine (Rocky Shaw) and Roger Moore (Silky Harris), star in *The Alaskans,* an adventure series that runs on ABC in 1959 for a year. Here guest Everett Sloane goes over the script with the leads. Provine had starred in the movie *The Bonnie Parker Story.*

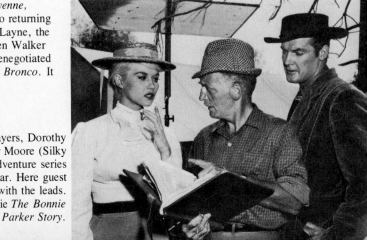

mony. But they did have problems. *Father Knows Best* was, in fact, a show which dealt primarily with strains on family ties. Almost every episode had a falling out between family members caused either by a misunderstanding or by the yearning of one to be independent of the others. At the end of the show, everything would be cleared up in a tearful reunion. It was the Christian way: a lamb would go astray, but open arms would await his return to the fold.

Jim was certainly very intelligent, but so was everyone else in the Anderson family; so it was never taken for granted that he "knew best." He made his share of poor decisions and mistakes. He was aware of his fallibility, and he did not really give a lot of advice. His role as father was to be a model whose fine values his kids could learn. Once Jim promised Kathy he would help her put together a leaf display for her Indian scout group by taking her on a long trip out into the wilderness. While he did this good deed, Bud and Betty fought over favors they wanted from each other but were unwilling to provide. Jim and Kathy returned from their journey only to discover that Kathy had forgotten her notebook in the woods. Jim went back into the wilderness, despite the late hour and the storm brewing. When he returned the following morning, he collapsed on the couch, and the grateful Kathy cuddled up with him. Bud and Betty witnessed this scene, forgot their petty selfishness, and immediately did favors for each other. Jim had not said a word to them, but they had learned by his example.

The three Anderson females were impressive. They were capable of doing anything the Anderson males could do. They were intelligent, proud, and resourceful. Margaret was Jim's equal, loved and respected for her wisdom. Usually she seemed contented being a housewife, but at times she rebelled. Once she walked out on her dishes for a few hours to take a jaunt down to the wild part of town. It wasn't much of an event, but the members of her family were outraged by her strange behavior and started questioning her motives. She was furious with them and defended her right to do atypical things without being criticized. She made it clear that she didn't want to be taken for granted. At the end of the show, the family understood that should she decide to leave her dishes again, she would not be questioned.

Kathy was a tomboy more interested in playing ball than in flirting with boys. If the dreadful *Father Knows Best Reunion* did anything worthwhile, it was to make the 1977 Kathy an unmarried gym teacher. Her fans were gratified to find her independence maintained and intact.

And Betty was certainly not the giddy, naïve teenage girl found in most sitcoms. She was the most intelligent person in her class, and was highly competitive—with girls or boys. When Betty entered college, she did not start seeking a husband. But at one point, she almost decided to marry her long-time boyfriend Ralph. In one episode Betty and Ralph visited the little house they would live in, once married. It looked awful to them, and they realized that if they were really meant for each other any house would look good. They decided to cancel the wedding and remain friends. Minutes later, Jim and Margaret entered the same house. It reminded them of their first house. It was heaven to them then, and this place was like heaven to them now. They hugged and kissed as they did twenty-five years earlier.

Father Knows Best showed us that not everyone, in fact hardly anyone, could have lived so happily together or raised such a nice family. That was exactly the point: the Andersons were not typical; they were among the best. They were nice people to visit.

Danny Peary has written on television, film, sports, and music for various publications.

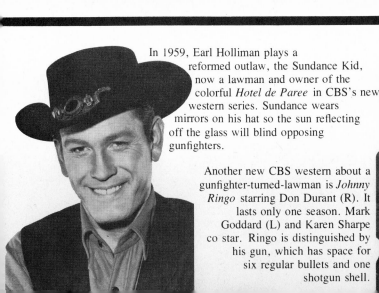

In 1959, Earl Holliman plays a reformed outlaw, the Sundance Kid, now a lawman and owner of the colorful *Hotel de Paree* in CBS's new western series. Sundance wears mirrors on his hat so the sun reflecting off the glass will blind opposing gunfighters.

Another new CBS western about a gunfighter-turned-lawman is *Johnny Ringo* starring Don Durant (R). It lasts only one season. Mark Goddard (L) and Karen Sharpe co star. Ringo is distinguished by his gun, which has space for six regular bullets and one shotgun shell.

Michael Ansara stars in *Tales of the Plainsman*, which begins a three-year stint on NBC in 1959. He plays Sam Buckhart, an Indian appointed U.S. marshal in the 1870's.

FAN FARE:
DEAR RICKY NELSON:

My name is Debbie Wiley and I live on a farm near Harrisburg, Illinois. I watch you and your mom and dad and brother *every* week, just to hear you sing at the end of the program. You're real good. Don't tell *anyone* because my mother doesn't know that is why I watch. And my little brother thinks you're creepy.

Some of the situations you and David get into are pretty funny. But your dad always seems to be around to smooth things over. (Does he have a job? He never seems to be rushing off to work!)

Well, the reason I am writing to you is because last week was my birthday, November 5, and I had a birthday party. I got lots of presents. *but* I got one *real neat* present. Jane Reed, she's in my Girl Scout troop, gave me a 45-rpm record. Guess what record it is? You! Ricky Nelson singing "Lonesome Town"!

When I listen to it I think about you singing at those dances at your high school. And the way your hair has that big wave that sometimes drops a curl across your forehead. And your lips, sort of curling as you sing about Mary Lou or crying all your troubles away. I'm sure *all* the girls in your school want a date with you!

By the way, if you send me a photograph, I'll put it in my new pink plastic wallet that I got for my birthday. It has a large photo section in it and I'm saving the first slot for Y-O-U.

Your fan,
Debbie Wiley

When Ricky turned twenty-one, he asked to be called Rick. Debbie Wiley became Debrah and sat through The Ed Sullivan Show *just to hear the Beatles.*

Black Saddle debuts on ABC in 1959. It will only last one season. Peter Breck (L) is Clay Culhane, an ex-gunslinger turned lawyer and Russell Johnson is Gib Scott, the marshal who never learns to trust Culhane. Both are after the affections of Anna-Lisa.

Texas Rangers Jace Pearson (Willard Parker) and Clay Morgan (Harry Lauter) are surrounded by gunmen in ABC's western series *Tales of the Texas Rangers*. The show tries to tell all the stories of the famous law agency covering two centuries, but it goes off in 1959 after a two-year run.

I REMEMBER ME
ROBIN MORGAN

When I think back to my childhood, I remember quipping answers on *Juvenile Jury,* floating down a special-effects rabbit hole as Alice, disproving the theory of relativity as a mutant baby genius on *Tales of Tomorrow,* receiving my first kiss as Corliss Archer, and playing a psychotic adolescent on *Robert Montgomery Presents.* When I recall those days, I think of all the other juicy starring parts in dramas written by the likes of Chayefsky and Serling; I think of certain directors who treated me like the professional I was—John Frankenheimer, Ralph Nelson, and especially dear Sidney Lumet, who had been a child actor himself. When I remember my childhood, I recollect costume fittings, and hard leather dressing room sofas on which I took much-detested naps; and how could I forget the sweet wild adrenaline panic exhilarating through me as the floor manager whispered fiercely, "Stand by!" But most of all, when I think back to those days when I was a child, most of all, I remember *Mama.*

This is hardly surprising, since that series—based on John Van Druten's stage adaptation, *I Remember Mama,* of Kathryn Forbes's book, *Mama's Bank Account*—ran from 1949 to 1956, and all that time I played Mama's youngest daughter Dagmar every Friday evening on CBS, *live.* That last little word has a meaning all its own, one which I now realize wrought a considerable effect on my own growth and development.

When, for example, despite the perfectionism of our set designer Jac Venza (now a distinguished producer of drama on public television), the antique

Robin Morgan as a child star.

player piano went mechanically berserk, snapping its rolls like a Kabuki dancer his fans, there was no reshooting for any such linguistic contradiction as "live-on-tape": we ad–libbed, live on the air. When one of my wobbly baby teeth fell out in the middle of a show, I worked its loss into the plot. When an adult colleague's eyes glazed over with dialogue amnesia (no TelePrompTers for *us*), one had to rescue the victim and save the continuity. Children, of course, are crazy enough to relish this sort of challenge, and I admit that it does develop a pride in craft which has subsequently served me well as a writer and feminist activist.

Yet those years were not all work and responsibility. I was more fortunate than many child

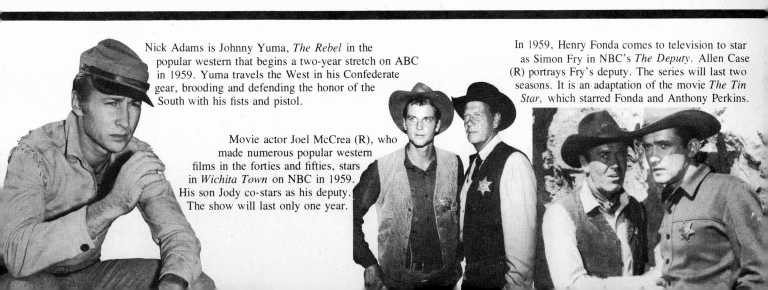

Nick Adams is Johnny Yuma, *The Rebel* in the popular western that begins a two-year stretch on ABC in 1959. Yuma travels the West in his Confederate gear, brooding and defending the honor of the South with his fists and pistol.

Movie actor Joel McCrea (R), who made numerous popular western films in the forties and fifties, stars in *Wichita Town* on NBC in 1959. His son Jody co-stars as his deputy. The show will last only one year.

In 1959, Henry Fonda comes to television to star as Simon Fry in NBC's *The Deputy.* Allen Case (R) portrays Fry's deputy. The series will last two seasons. It is an adaptation of the movie *The Tin Star,* which starred Fonda and Anthony Perkins.

actors, because the series' duration gave me an emotional security denied most of my contemporaries, who were being schlepped from audition to audition. And if *Mama* gave me less financial security than commonly assumed (there was then no "Coogan Law" in New York protecting a minor's earnings), it certainly accustomed me young to the privilege—and price—of celebrity, and brought me early to a mature perspective on such superficiality. It gave me a second family, too: Peggy Wood (Mama), Judson Laire (Papa), Rosemary Rice and Dick Van Patten (my sister Katrin and brother Nels), and Ruth Gates (the unforgettable Aunt Jenny). I learned how to play Parcheesi and wear a middy blouse from Rosie, and I was flower girl at Dickie's real-life wedding; Jud took me regularly to the opera and ballet, and Peggy kept me spellbound with tales of the Lunts and Noel Coward, taught me how to knit, and firmly discouraged my singing. Ruthie, Jud, and Peggy all read my poetry and took seriously my literary aspirations.

I learned to roller-skate hopping about the maze of cables on a studio floor, and my initial encounter with a bicycle had me careening into the canvas backdrop of 118 Steiner Street, San Francisco (circa 1910). The first cow-milking I ever saw took place fifteen floors above Manhattan—a crisis of nature which interrupted the dress rehearsal one year of our traditional Christmas show, "The Night the Animals Talked." In a sense, Dagmar and I grew up together, although her fictional naïveté diverged from my occupational sophistication, and many of our experiences and tastes differed dramatically: I think Dagmar at age eleven was reading Louisa May Alcott, while I was perusing the Brontës, Dickinson, and Kafka. Still, we did share an attitude of insouciance and a certain quality of sturdiness, and the blur of those characteristics lent realism to her personality and normalcy to mine.

For a long time after I extricated myself from the

Robin Morgan is now a writer and a feminist.

show and eventually from "the business" itself to pursue my first love, writing, I avoided discussion of my childhood. Only now, albeit with ambivalence, can I begin to contemplate that rich subject matter. "I disown none of my transformations," I wrote once in a poem. Indeed. Those years taught me, among other lessons, the discipline required of an artist—but what of the influence on me as a feminist? Well, Dagmar did routinely thrash the neighborhood bully whenever he tried to cramp her assertive style. Not coincidentally, the Hansen family was matriarchal less in structure than in affirming that its primary source of wisdom and strength was the title character—and after all, the name of the program was nothing so puerile as *Father Knows Best*. It was, let us remember, *Mama*.

Robin Morgan is a poet and the author of Going Too Far: The Personal Chronicle of a Feminist.

As TV westerns become more civilized, the newer cowboy heroes tend to be ranchers rather than drifters or lawmen. On September 12, 1959, *Bonanza* comes to television, ushering in NBC's all-color schedule. It stars Dan Blocker, Lorne Greene, Pernell Roberts, and Michael Landon as the Cartwrights — Hoss, Ben, Adam, and Little Joe — who live on the massive Ponderosa ranch.

Four days later, *Laramie* debuts on NBC. Robert Fuller is Jess Harper, who runs a combination ranch and stage depot with his partner Slim Sherman, played by John Smith.

INSTANT TV STARS
MICHAEL TOLKIN

A television star is a stereotype—a collection of always predictable gestures employed in a futile struggle with repetition and bewilderment. A television star inhabits an assembly-line world which he or she transcends only by tactless and often bumbling grace under pressure.

Television has no A pictures and B pictures; its spectrum fits in a much tighter band. Television lacks the tacky grandeur of even the crummiest movies, and its stars never seem so important or great. The real true movie stars, like Jack Nicholson, act with high energy and obviously have plenty of extra power in reserve. True television stars, like Farrah Fawcett-Majors, counter with the reassurance of their reduced energies, and their imitations of intelligence, sexuality, and action, proving that one can still find acceptance and adulation, even as a total ninny.

Farrah Fawcett-Majors comes to mind because she has recently seized the public's attention, but she has no more chance of remaining America's sweetheart forever than did John Travolta before her, or Henry Winkler before him. These instant stars are reductions. Farrah Fawcett-Majors is a Playmate with modesty. John Travolta is a diminished Sylvester Stallone, not so threatening, not so courageous. Henry Winkler is to James Dean what Count Chokulas is to monsters, a terror made palpable and smaller by television. He is as far removed from real delinquency as cereal is from Bela Lugosi. There are no tragic loners on television. It is a corporation, a family.

Since a television star's self-display must be diffused over the run of a series, a softer androgyny

Farrah Fawcett-Majors looking like an angel.

179

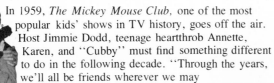

In 1959, *The Mickey Mouse Club,* one of the most popular kids' shows in TV history, goes off the air. Host Jimmie Dodd, teenage heartthrob Annette, Karen, and "Cubby" must find something different to do in the following decade. "Through the years, we'll all be friends wherever we may be, M-I-C-K-E-Y M-O-U-S-E. . . ."

In 1950, Milton Berle was the most popular entertainer on television and host of TV's most-watched program, *Texaco Star Theatre.* In 1960, Milton Berle hosts *Jackpot Bowling* on NBC.

Although Sid Caesar no longer has his own weekly TV show in 1960, he makes frequent appearances. Here he is off to woo an innocent and happily married housewife in "The Devil You Say" on *The General Electric Theatre.*

"The instant stars succeed because they play parts that match some obsession of the day . . ."

replaces the intensified character forged between love and death in the movies—the kind of character seen in Jack Nicholson's killer smile. Winkler, Travolta, and Fawcett-Majors have amiable, even embarrassed smiles which invite without seducing. In the burning bush that is a television set, they are not consumed by their own fires, but are extinguished by the flood of mass attention.

Television is a business, with too many people for too few jobs. The most important thing for an actor to do is just to hold on to that job, and the best way to manage that is just to do the job well and not gather inordinate attention. A handful of actors and actresses have survived their series with the equanimity of Shamu the killer whale in *Seaworld*'s "Salute to the Bicentennial." Next year he'll perform the same tricks in a "Salute to Sherman's March to the Sea." In the hierarchy of television, I count the following as the all-time true television stars, the models for longevity:

Martin Milner—the fair-haired boy. He entered television as William Bendix's son-in-law in *The Life of Reilly,* was in *Route 66,* and then *Adam-12.* His greatest expression is one of concern.

David Janssen and Robert Stack—the stiff necks. Fameless martyrs on their way to Golgotha, they are television's wounded wanderers for whom personal pleasure is brief and never satisfying.

Raymond Burr—here's Poppa. *Perry Mason; Ironsides; Kingston: Confidential.* The television star

as corporate-family hero-father surrounded by a competent if somewhat difficult staff.

Michael Landon—the kid. From Little Joe on *Bonanza* to the *Little House on the Prairie,* he is a model for never getting over the rites of passage.

Lucille Ball—all TV women, the dame who gets in trouble while her man throws his arms skyward in exasperation. This applies as much to Maude as to Angie Dickinson's policewoman, with Earl Holliman sweating in the background. *Charlie's Angels* discovered that the man need only be implied.

"Farrah Fawcett-Majors is a Playmate with modesty."

Rose Marie and Charles Nelson Reilly—the drones of television, celebrities without portfolio. Rose Marie's last prime time series was *The Dick Van Dyke Show.* Charles Nelson Reilly's last series was *Laugh-In.* Yet both of these people appear regularly on the tube, as guests of Mike Douglas or Merv Griffin, as "celebrities" on game shows, answering simple questions, all with a slightly ragged gloss of wit and charm.

These stars are perennials. Having preceded Henry Winkler on television, they will outlast him. The instant stars succeed because they play parts that match some obsession of the day, but the mainstays of television succeed from that quality of agelessness that is not a function of role but of actor. They offer the real moral lesson of television: life is mostly doing the same thing over and over again, and never really getting that much better at it.

Michael Tolkin was a Bachelor #2 on The Dating Game. *He lost a chaperoned trip to Catalina.*

Caesar stars in several specials on CBS in 1960. His fourth special of the season features a skit called "Bat Masterson Drops In," which pictures the total befuddlement of a suburban couple (Sid Caesar and Audrey Meadows) when they receive a visit from celebrity Gene Barry.

What's My Line? celebrates its tenth anniversary as the new decade begins. Here Debbie Reynolds joins regular panelists Arlene Francis, Dorothy Kilgallen, and Bennett Cerf.

CONFESSIONS OF AN EX-PAGE

Pete Hamilton

A lot of famous television stars and business executives started their careers in odd-looking "monkey suits"—as network pages. Eva Marie Saint, Kate Jackson, and Peter Marshall broke into TV as pages for various guest relations departments, as did Efrem Zimbalist, Jr. and Dave Garroway, not to mention an important executive, Ray Timothy, executive vice-president, affiliate relations, NBC-TV.

Pages have always served two functions: they usher eager audiences to their studio destinations, and they conduct large public tours of broadcast facilities. Pages, for the most part, are enthusiastic. Pages respond proudly to such questions as, "What is John Chancellor *really* like?" The page escorting singer Art Garfunkel's party to specially reserved seats in the *Saturday Night* audience feels like part of the show; another page was particularly honored to lead a private studio tour for actress Anne Francis and her daughter. I was once a page myself, and no matter how extraordinary or exciting the occurrence, I always tried to act nonchalant. But in fact I was always fighting back an overwhelming and sincere feeling of "gee whiz!"

All pages want to make careers for themselves in broadcasting. Those pages not lucky enough to ascend the corporate heights are invariably attracted to the performing side of the business. One wrote comedy for Joan Rivers, while many try stand-up comedy themselves,

Pages inclined toward the business end of broadcasting must also perfect their acts. The most enterprising ones spend all their free time poking around the studio, control room, or office getting to know the people whose business is broadcasting. Many a sharp page gets promoted this way. So, though the pay isn't much, the page's job is a foot in the network door.

A page always feels part of the action, but at NBC, those not lucky enough to find further employment in the company within eighteen months usually seek employment elsewhere. Thus, the staff remains fresh and enthusiastic. Young people in school and working with advanced communications equipment might be tempted to scoff at the idea of becoming an usher or tour guide for a network after graduation, because the job appears to have no relation to what the network actually does. While this may be true on paper, in reality a great many people have used the page's job as a first step to bigger things. The successful pages have long since forgotten the momentary discomfort of their "monkey suits."

Pete Hamilton is Associate Editor of NBC Newsline, *the network's in-house publication, and retired his "monkey suit" years ago.*

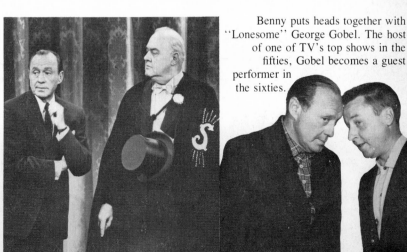

In 1960, *The Paul Winchell Show* goes off ABC after a three-year run. Winchell and Jerry Mahoney have hosted one show or another since television's early days. It will take them three years to get another show.

Ten years after it came to CBS in 1950, *The Jack Benny Program* is still a top-rated show. Here Benny does his famous "Well!" when announcer Don Wilson comes on stage wearing an outlandish outfit.

Benny puts heads together with "Lonesome" George Gobel. The host of one of TV's top shows in the fifties, Gobel becomes a guest performer in the sixties.

STAR TALK:
WINKLER ON WINKLER
AS TOLD TO CECIL SMITH

I look on a career the way a forest ranger looks at a tree—it doesn't grow overnight, it takes seventy-five years. I don't want to be a flash in the pan. I want people to know Henry Winkler after the Fonz is forgotten.

Right at the beginning, I started a national campaign to remind people that Henry Winkler was the reality and Fonzie the fantasy. I would go on talk shows, but only as Winkler, never Fonzie; I made personal appearances as Winkler, not Fonzie. I wouldn't even read a script for an outside show that called for me to play a part like the Fonz. I'm not cool like he is! When people yell, "Hi, Fonzie," at me, I correct them; I say: "Excuse me, but my name is Henry Winkler." Even little kids I correct. They call me Fonz; I tell them, "Call me Henry."

I know the terrible time Carroll O'Connor, a very intellectual man and a playwright, has had being identified with Archie Bunker. It hasn't happened with me. I went to New Orleans for Mardi Gras—that's when you know you're a star. It was too much. They told me they recorded the biggest crowd that they ever had for any event in the history of the Mardi Gras. I love to be in the center of a crowd. I'm not nervous. It doesn't scare me. But this was too much. I had more security than the President. But the point is that these thousands of people had signs and banners that said: "Welcome, Henry Winkler" and "Hello, Henry." Few even mentioned Fonzie. The people screamed

---

"I didn't know the Fonz was inside me until I did him."

"Henry," not "Fonzie." It's exhilarating, but it's too much.

I went on in Detroit in front of a hundred seventy-five thousand people. We outdrew The Who. And I didn't even have an act. I just stood there and said: "My name is Henry Winkler and I'm glad to be here." I went to Australia to accept the Logie Award, their Emmy. Afterward, I wanted to get completely away from everything to rest, and I went to this primitive island at the absolute end of the earth, Bora Bora. On this island, a lady came running across the sand for an autograph. She said she had seen *Happy Days* the night before in Tokyo. It blows your mind!

I didn't know the Fonz was inside me until I did him. It was just a small part, a bit—the contrast of this hard-eyed tough on his motorcycle among these clean-cut kids dancing to Chubby Checker records in their saddle shoes and cashmere sweaters. Nobody knew he would take off the way he did, not Paramount, not ABC. It surprised me. He's so different from me. When people ask about that, I always tell them that the distance between doing and not doing something is the "yes-no" in your own brain—yes, you must know your limitations, but no, do not let

---

In 1960, Red Skelton is more popular than ever. Here guest Sir Cedric Hardwicke, playing a Johnson's Wax executive, cracks down on "Clem Kadiddlehopper" when *The Red Skelton Show* visits its sponsor's Racine, Wisconsin plant.

Finally, in 1960, CBS takes *The Lone Ranger* rebroadcasts off its schedule. The reruns will play endlessly in syndication.

Horror-movie king Boris Karloff, who acted in and hosted *Starring Boris Karloff* back in 1949 on ABC, repeats his role when the frightening *Thriller* comes to NBC in 1960. It will last two seasons. Here Karloff appears in "The Strange Door" episode.

Henry Winkler, flashing a Fonzie grin, zoomed to TV stardom on Happy Days.

others impose them on you. If you know your limitations, you can break through.

When Fonzie took off and they made me costar of the show with Ron Howard, I told them at Paramount I had to be more than a guy walking around in a leather jacket. When I'm hired, it's for more than filling time and space. I must say they trusted me. I've worked with the Fonz. Every season he's changed. His attitudes and the attitudes about him have changed; there's been genuine growth. There had to be; otherwise, playing him would be too boring.

With the Fonz there is also an area of responsibility. Kids adore him. When I did the CBS special introducing Shakespeare to kids, I told Danny Wilson, the producer, that we had to be very careful. Alcoholism is a terrible problem for kids. We couldn't show Falstaff as a funny old drunk; we couldn't glorify alcohol. Suicide is another terrible problem for kids. I said if we do a speech from *Hamlet,* it can't be "to be or not to be." That's negative; that's about suicide. That was a terrifying experience—Henry Winkler on television in Shakespeare!

The movies came afterward. Now I'm starring in *Heroes* in a part as far from Fonzie as you can get. From the time I was seven or eight and saw Jimmy Stewart do *Rear Window,* my dream was that one day I'd be up on the screen. I am living my dream!

Cecil Smith is the TV critic for the L.A. Times.

January 7, 1960. Maureen O'Hara and Keir Dullea star in the CBS special, *Mrs. Miniver,* a ninety-minute adaptation of the Oscar-winning Greer Garson movie.

January 12, 1960. Joan Crawford plays twin sisters in "And One Must Die" on *Dick Powell's Zane Grey Theatre.* Although there are no women leads in TV westerns of 1960, many famous actresses star in single episodes of western anthology series.

FAN FARE:
DEAR FONZ:

Where did we go wrong? We should have been an item. The perfect pair. We could have met on my thirtieth birthday. A date with you would have been the dreamiest gift. That was my wish. A wish so secret I only shared it with my most intimate friends. To make it all come true, each and every one wrote inviting you to come and get me. I'm not going to go into each letter. There were eighty-three. But surely you must remember some.

Like the one from Tony. He's from Verona. He sent you a postcard with a picture of Juliet's balcony on it. Maybe you didn't think it was meant for you because it began: "Henry Winkler. Henry Winkler! Wherefore art thou, Henry Winkler."

Then there was George. Another Romeo, of sorts. We had just one date. He flipped. But he couldn't stand commitment. So he pleaded with you to take me out. To take me off his hands. Being a one-woman-man cramps his style. Yours, too?

Another who begged you to make my dreams come true was my best friend. She thought if there were something deep and meaningful between us, I would toss my Fonzie knee socks and T-shirts. I have such a nice wardrobe in a rainbow of day-glo.

The grand gesture came from my lawyer. His letter began: "We, the undersigned, hereby request the honor of the aforementioned addressee's presence on the above-mentioned date whereby he will be petitioned to participate in the celebration marking the thirtieth aniversary of the subject's date of birth." God bless. In addition to his own, he sent sixty-seven bonafide signatures.

Even my mother wrote. If you don't remember what she said, I promise I won't either.

Then a fatherly fellow named Chuck insisted on writing. Because he believes that couples should be properly introduced, he wrote a formal introduction. Did he address you as "Mr. Fonzie" or as "Arthur"?

My sweet friend Ting Ling sent you two giant fortune cookies. Cookie Number One promised good luck, inner peace, love, prosperity, happiness, and joy with a dark-haired woman who celebrates her thirtieth birthday. Cookie Number Two offered my name, address, and telephone number.

While the guy who owns the Baskin-Robbins on the corner tempted you with a rocky-road-strawberry-mint-chocolate-chip birthday cake for two, my dear Uncle John sent you one pressed rose. He guaranteed that if you took me out the sweet smell of success would be yours.

There were many, many more.

As the big day approached, everyone waited. Each phone was manned around the clock. Every mailbox checked twice daily. Well. My birthday came. My birthday went. And there was not one note. Not one call. Not even an autopenned photograph.

Sorry, Fonz. You had your chance. I could never fall for a guy with such bad manners.

Sincerely,
Marcia Lazar

Marcia Lazar has her own advertising agency in Chicago and is a charter member of a Fonzie fan club.

184

Claudette Colbert stars in "So Young the Savage Land" with Chris Robinson on *Dick Powell's Zane Grey Theatre.*

April 1, 1960. The final *The Lucille Ball-Desi Arnaz Show* special, "Lucy Meets the Moustache," with Ernie Kovacs, is broadcast on CBS. A month earlier, Ball and Arnaz, television's most beloved husband and wife team, were divorced, but the taped show goes on as scheduled. *The Desilu Playhouse* will go off in 1961.

STAR TALK:
MTM ON MTM
AS TOLD TO CECIL SMITH

We were lucky that our creative people were so tuned-in to what was happening in the world. It wasn't that Jim Brooks and Allan Burns created *The Mary Tyler Moore Show* because they were interested in polemics for women's rights—it wasn't that kind of program. But they *were* interested in what was happening to women in our society and, like all good writers, they wrote about what was foremost in their minds.

Remember that when our show went on, we were considered very radical—so radical that there were prophecies of instant disaster. Mary Richards was not a widow. She'd never been married. She even hinted at having an affair! She was a mature woman in her thirties, not a young girl having a fling before marriage. She wasn't even hunting for a husband! She was an ambitious career woman interested in her work and making it on her own. Nothing like Mary Richards had happened in television before.

The original writers were eventually joined by people like David Lloyd, Ed Weinberg and Stan Daniels—as well as by such first-rate women writers as Charlotte Brown and Tricia Silverman. (Women like Joan Darling got their first chance to direct on our show too.) Well, in devising situations for Mary— problems out of which the comedy could develop— these writers looked naturally to the basic issues of the women's movement: unequal opportunity, unequal pay, chauvinistic attitudes. We were lucky because all our creative people were so aware and understood so

> **". . . the success of our show opened the way for other television shows about women."**

clearly what was going on in the world and because they had such a sense of personal responsibility toward the subjects they wrote about.

There is no doubt that the success of our show opened the way for other television shows about women. Our own spin-offs *Rhoda* and *Phyllis*, for instance, are proof of this, as are some of Norman Lear's shows like *Maude* and *One Day at a Time*. But I had nothing to do with it. I'm always annoyed when people give me the credit for developing our company, MTM Enterprises, and when they talk of my business acumen. I'm married to a very intelligent and perceptive producer, Grant Tinker, and he built the company and he runs it. I don't. I have no more to do with it than any other wife who might offer a suggestion about her husband's business. My primary interest is in developing my new series for 1978—I wish some new direction could be found, perhaps using music and dance within a comedic format.

I was never a militant women's libber—though I have been very vocal about some of the inequities we

During the six years since Fess Parker became a national hero playing Davy Crockett, he has appeared in several films for Walt Disney. Trying to shake his Disney image, Parker stars in "Aftermath," an episode of *G.E. Theatre* in 1960. He plays Jonathan West, a Confederate Army captain.

A month later, Van Johnson plays an American running a tourist service in Paris in "At Your Service" on *G.E. Theatre*.

April 22, 1960. Mary Astor and young Peter Votrian star in "Journey to the Day" on *Playhouse 90*. They portray patients participating in group psychotherapy in a state mental hospital. Mike Nichols and Elaine May also star in Fred Coe's production; John Frankenheimer is the director.

Mary Tyler Moore sings about women's rights on a 1969 CBS Special, "Dick Van Dyke and the Other Woman."

still have. There's a lot of Mary Richards in me—but there's also a lot of Laurie Petrie, the housewife I played on the *Dick Van Dyke Show*.

Television is my medium—I'm convinced of that. I'm no longer concerned with doing a great movie, a great Broadway show. Of course, if a great part came along, I'd take it, but how many great women's parts have you seen in movies lately? Or on the stage? As Shirley MacLaine said: "Television is the only medium that takes women seriously, that treats them as intelligent, functioning human beings."

My first series was *Richard Diamond, Private Eye* with David Janssen. I played Sam, the answering-service girl. All you ever saw of me was a pair of legs. And you heard my voice—low and husky and sexy. Talk about your sex object! We've come a long way from that. I have. All women have. I like to think Mary Richards was in some way responsible.

Cecil Smith is the TV critic for the L.A. Times.

186

May 4, 1960. Game show host Johnny Carson appears as an ad man in "The Girl in the Gold Bathtub" on *The United States Steel Hour*. Also starring in this comedy are Marisa Pavan (with the book) and Jessie Royce Landis.

May 7, 1960. Jack Benny guest stars in Phil Silvers's CBS special "The Slowest Gun in the West." Silvers plays the "Silver Dollar Kid," and Benny is the biggest coward in the Arizona Territory. Nat Hiken, creator of Sergeant Bilko, is the producer and writer of this sixty-minute program.

TO RHODA MORGENSTERN
JANICE CRANE

Mary Richards, Edith, Gloria,
Major Hot Lips, Maude and Florida.
Wry and funny women, all,
Tread the small screen spring and fall;
But Rhoda, kid, you stand apart,
And being like me, touch my heart.

When you were fat and cracking wise
About your width of hips and thighs,
You had a friend in me who'd wail
At every visit to the scale;
You'd come on just a little strong,
You'd never know quite what went wrong,
You'd wonder—what would Mary do?
But I saw answers come to you.
Misfits who longed not to be,
(A million girls, including me).
Were you not trying to suppress
The painful truths of loneliness?

Hey, I don't mean to get intense—
I watched you grow in confidence;
You took some care, you took some steps,
And—gloriosky—gave up schlepps.
And those of us from sea to sea
Who measure real life by TV
Were given some small share of hope
When you began to really cope.
Brenda represents us now
In terms of wanting to learn how
To handle life while jokes fly fast
About the ghosts of blind dates past.
Still, when you finally found a man

According to your long-dreamt plan,
Your wondering disbelief, to me,
Was sheer believability.

The airwaves deal with—no, abound—
With friends and lovers lost and found.
You're no exception, as you've come
Full circle since your Season One.
Alone again and facing up
To challenges marriage interrupts,
You brave what you once left behind,
That not-so-swinging singles grind.
But we've all watched you grow so much,
We know you haven't lost your touch.
In fact you keep on every fall—
An inspiration to us all.

Show us new ways to be ourselves
When times would keep us on our shelves.
For we consider you a sister,
Looking for that just-right mister.

*Janice Crane, M.D., is single and lives in
Marina del Rey.*

187

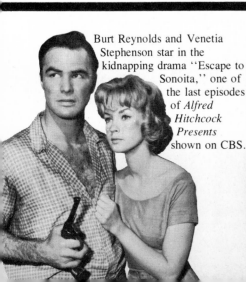

Burt Reynolds and Venetia
Stephenson star in the
kidnapping drama "Escape to
Sonoita," one of
the last episodes
of *Alfred
Hitchcock
Presents*
shown on CBS.

Jack Klugman tries to hit a note never reached
before in "A Passage for Trumpet" on *The
Twilight Zone*. Mary Webster offers encouragement.

May 18, 1960. Rod
Serling's "In the
Presence of Mine
Enemies" is presented on
Playhouse 90. George
Macready(L), as a Nazi
officer, and Sam Jaffe, as
a Jewish fugitive in
Warsaw, co-star with
Charles Laughton, Arthur
Kennedy, Susan Kohner,
Oscar Homolka, and
Robert Redford.

STAR TALK:
JEAN MARSH ON
"UPSTAIRS, DOWNSTAIRS"
AS TOLD TO STEPHEN SCHAEFER

While audiences may be angry or sad or both that the show is ending, I feel very good that we ended it when it still was so very fine. I remember we were shooting the last block of episodes and had gotten about one-third of the way through when I realized I didn't want to go on anymore. There didn't seem to be much for me to do as Rose; I thought the writers must have gotten bored with her. At that time I'd been offered a play in New York (*Habeus Corpus,* a farce) and I thought, *This is a perfect time to go.* As it were, I gave them my notice but said, "You go on with it."

They began mapping out the next season's scripts and, deciding that it wasn't working without me, asked me to come back. But I didn't want to. The writers then thought of alternatives—you know, things with people spinning off upstairs or sideways with Hudson and Andrew—things like that. But again they asked, "Will you come back?" By this time I had already signed the contract to do a Broadway show, which was something I had wanted so much to do, something I would love to do again, so I couldn't. And they thought, *She's right. Oh, let's end it.*

It *was* wonderful, and it seems so much better to stop at a peak and not drag it out. I don't think it's good to do seven or eight years and bore the public; it seems quite sensible for everyone to go their own different ways.

People will ask us what the series, a British production, gave to American television. I think it's the best series that's ever been done. I don't think there ever has been a series better. I'm not speaking of my contribution particularly, *everything* about it is superb. It's amazing, you know, to have people comment about the *sound quality!* The show wouldn't have worked if there were only three wonderful actors on it, or one wonderful writer, or a great producer—everything's wonderful all 'round. That's why on one level, it works.

In today's terms *Upstairs, Downstairs* is the way people—like Dickens—used to write in the last century. They would write serially in magazines and never know how it was going to come out, particularly. And it was extremely good writing; good enough to eventually make books out of the magazine pieces. I think *Upstairs, Downstairs* is that today—almost a book being written over a period of time.

I do find it absolutely ludicrous when people try to compare *Upstairs, Downstairs* with American soap operas. It's not the same! There is a huge difference in time and production and content. Here soap operas are done daily, while it took two weeks to shoot each episode of our show. Where soap operas here have an evolving story line that may go on for months, each chapter of *Upstairs, Downstairs* is complete unto

May 19, 1960. Eleanor Parker stars as Sister Cecilia and Richard Conte is the gambler, Cayetano, in "The Gambler, the Nun, and the Radio." This is the last of a series of Hemingway adaptations being presented this season on CBS's *The Buick Electra Playhouse.*

May 23, 1960. Distinguished Irish actress Siobhan McKenna stars with Walter Slezak in Wilkie Collins's classic mystery "The Woman in White" on *The Dow Hour of Great Mysteries.* This NBC series is hosted by Joseph Welch, the lawyer who gained national recognition battling Joe McCarthy in the Army-McCarthy hearings.

Bright young TV stars Warren Beatty and Tuesday Weld are regulars on CBS's *The Many Loves of Dobie Gillis.*

THE EATON PLACE PHENOMENON

In its four seasons on the Public Broadcasting Service (PBS) network, the British series *Up-stairs, Downstairs* took root and bloomed on the nation's cultural landscape. The Bellamy mansion in Eaton Place became as real and vital to audiences as Tara, the Old South plantation of Scarlett O'Hara, or the Minneapolis newsroom of Mary Tyler Moore. Jean Marsh and Eileen Atkins, two actresses who each had had a parent "in service," conceived *Up-stairs, Downstairs* as an illustration of class consciousness and English life in the post-Victorian era. Though it arrived in the midst of a virtual British invasion of American television, it is still hard to account for the show's remarkable popularity—broadcast in fifty countries, seen by nearly a billion people. *Up-stairs, Downstairs,* with its impeccable production quality, assured ensemble performance, and remarkable scripting, gave renewed impetus to high quality programming on the American commercial networks, and also helped to firmly establish the popularity of the concept of the "mini-series."

Angela Baddeley and Jean Marsh talk downstairs.

itself—there's no Friday cliff-hanger to make everyone tune in on Monday to see what happens. The basis of the soap operas seems to be guilt and trauma, and the characters are often more stereotypical than ours. *Upstairs, Downstairs* exhibits a solid appreciation for the minutiae of a lifestyle, yes, but from the perspective of social history. We were accurate about everything from what constitutes the proper menu with tea to the Victorian principles of managing a personal fortune. The content is totally different from soap operas.

As for playing Rose for sixty-eight episodes over five seasons [broadcast in the U.S. in four], I saw changes, but few fundamental ones. The series began in 1910 at a time in Rose's life when she wasn't going to change really; she was set in her ways. The younger ones on staff would change a bit. Rose was affected by outside events—the War, the twenties, but she adjusted to them more than she changed. As you see her at the end of the series, she's still a servant . . . still doing what she was bred to do.

Stephen Schaefer frequently writes about films and celebrities.

189

Ronnie Burns, the son of George Burns and Gracie Allen, and Yvonne Lime star in the innocuous domestic comedy *Happy,* which NBC broadcasts as a summer replacement in 1960. The baby, "Happy," is played alternately by twins, David and Steven Born.

Directly following *Happy* on NBC's summer schedule in 1960 is the western *Tate* with David McLean as an ex-soldier distinguished by a crushed left arm that he straps in a leather casing.

REMEMBERING ANDY GRIFFITH

MARK ANDERSON

The Andy Griffith Show had a flair for the ordinary. It dealt with the small concerns of simple people. It did not reach for the spectacular; it was content to explore the more amusing aspects of the dilemmas of being human.

The setting was the perfect "down-home" place, and the characters were so simple in their ways that they seemed peculiar. I grew up in a small town and knew the same kind of shady side streets, the sleepy center of town, and the dusty lanes that were in and around Mayberry. In fact, a good part of my formative years were spent hanging out at a gas station much like Wally's filling station in Mayberry.

Moving around in that quaint setting were Deputy Barney Fife and his truly odd string of friends and neighbors. They were essential to the show as much for their humor as for their innocent ways. Barney carried his only bullet in his shirt pocket. Floyd the barber was always in proper awe of the world that swirled around him. Goober could often as not be found sitting in front of Floyd's, reading comics and sniffing the customers as they emerged all spruced up.

But all the Mayberry characters were realistic enough to make them believable and capable of real emotion, no matter how trivial the concern. Trust in humankind tied all these characters together. This led to dilemmas that were often so subtle or delicate that a truly ingenious and sensitive solution would be needed.

Most often, the situation to be righted was a violation of someone's trust, either by a stranger coming into town, or by a neighbor. Innocence is the key, and

---

"Good old Andy Taylor. He was mellow before the word was in vogue."

---

invariably the insight of Sheriff Andy would satisfy people and get them back to their settled ways.

Good old Andy Taylor. He was mellow before the word was in vogue. He could amble better than anyone in my hometown. He was real home-grown. His drawl and country expressions always rang true. He played guitar, loved home cooking, and eschewed modern technology in his police work.

His methods of bringing his friends through troubled times were steady and deliberate. He would do only as much as was called for, whether it meant arranging for two people to have a quiet talk on the front porch, or nabbing bank robbers who wanted to take advantage of Mayberry's usual 9:30 PM bedtime.

Barney Fife was quite often central to the show's situations. It seemed that Andy always had his hands full protecting Barney's fragile ego or helping him save face in front of friends. Andy would often lay the groundwork for an arrest and then let Barney accept the accolades.

Andy and Barney were always at odds about police methods. Barney wanted dearly to be like the occasional state trooper who would come to Mayberry; Andy didn't even carry a gun. Barney was all for third-degree techniques, even on Otis, the

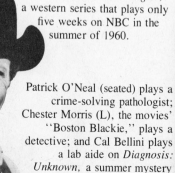

Jason Evers stars in *Wrangler*, a western series that plays only five weeks on NBC in the summer of 1960.

Patrick O'Neal (seated) plays a crime-solving pathologist; Chester Morris (L), the movies' "Boston Blackie," plays a detective; and Cal Bellini plays a lab aide on *Diagnosis: Unknown*, a summer mystery series on CBS in 1960.

Andy Griffith looks comfortable in the role of peacemaker, a role he played with simple charm on The Andy Griffith Show.

town drunk, whereas Andy never took a fingerprint and left the jail keys hanging on the wall within easy reach of the cell. Once while Barney was trying to swagger with the state police, Andy was busy cornering a fugitive, using the irrefutable country logic that no one, not even a fugitive, could resist the smell of a pie cooling on a windowsill. It had the makings of a story Floyd the barber would tell for years to come.

Mark Anderson's family did not get a TV set until he was sixteen years old. He has since been making up for lost time.

191

The 1960 Democratic and Republican political conventions are held in Los Angeles and Chicago. John Kennedy and Richard Nixon receive their parties' presidential nominations amid the most extensive television coverage ever given to the conventions. Twenty-five CBS news correspondents compete with Huntley-Brinkley and NBC for viewers. Here are ten of them.

Nancy Hanschman and CBS's top newscaster Douglas Edwards are among those who report on the convention from the CBS News Central desk.

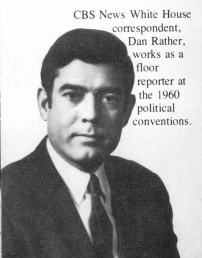

CBS News White House correspondent, Dan Rather, works as a floor reporter at the 1960 political conventions.

HOMAGE TO DAVID JANSSEN
DAVID THORBURN

The actor has always been the essential artistic resource of American commercial television, and the history of that medium is, at the very least, a history of exceptional artistic accomplishment by actors. All the good TV series have been centered on fine acting, and all the great shows—the classic texts that will one day be valued as highly as the best Hollywood movies—have depended on superior, memorably intense performances from two, three, or even four recurring roles.

One explanation—there are many others—for the lack of esteem in which television is held is that we have not yet begun to speak or write carefully about the art of performance, and especially about the complex modulated drama enacted by the faces and voices of the best TV actors. David Janssen's increasingly intelligent and subtle work as a series leading man is a good example of the actor's art on television and also an example of how television in general has matured.

Janssen's first series was a version of *Richard Diamond—Private Eye*, a character who had appeared earlier in books and radio. This late-fifties series was typical of television in that decade, which mechanically repeated stories and characters from other media. But in his next series, *The Fugitive,* one of the strongest and most popular shows of the 1960's, Janssen began to develop a whole range of facial gestures and vocal inflections that had a distinctive authority on the small screen. *The Fugitive* was a bold fable on injustice and flight whose ambivalent attitudes toward legal authority and middle-class life accurately reflected American cultural anxieties. But its

> ## "All the good TV series have been centered on fine acting . . ."

chief artistic distinction was Janssen's performance, which repeatedly turned the show away from the muscle-flexing violence of the plot and toward scenes of intimacy and emotional nuance.

In his four seasons (1963–1967) as *The Fugitive,* Janssen grew remarkably as an actor. The very premise of the series, conceived by Quinn Martin, made demands upon Janssen that were peculiarly congenial to an actor of his unflamboyant physical presence and restricted vocal range. The smoldering physical authority of most film stars would have been an impediment in this role, which required a hero of modest dimensions, an ordinary fellow able to lose himself in crowds and able to move and speak inconspicuously. Not physical energy or size, then, but pyschological subtlety was what the role demanded: an actor able to create a sense of character through the rhythms of his speech, the way he cocked his head or shrugged his shoulders; an actor alert to all the minute physical and vocal gestures that define our ordinary individuality.

The vulnerable, almost self-deprecating decency of Janssen's character in *The Fugitive* was refined and wonderfully complicated in *Harry-O,* a private-eye series which ran for two seasons (1974–1976). The difference between *Richard Diamond* and *Harry-O* is

192

Betty Furness reports from the floor of the 1960 Democratic Convention for CBS.

August 25, 1960. Vice-President Richard Nixon, the Republican contender for President, visits Jack Paar. A strong Kennedy supporter, Paar will later express sympathy for Nixon's uneasy television manner, explaining that Nixon's gestures and expressions never seem to be synchronized with what he is saying. Here, for instance, Nixon, with one hand open and the other clenched, appears to be smiling rather tensely.

David Janssen in trouble on Richard Diamond—Private Eye.

the difference between an apprentice art and a mature art; between a dramatic text, blind or indifferent to the special limitations and opportunities inherent in television, and a text that fully understands and exploits the distinctive features of that intimate medium. Even in *The Fugitive* Janssen's gentleness, his pained reluctance to impose himself on others, the singular tentativeness he brought to the act of speaking—all this came through only fitfully and was often submerged by tides of melodramatic violence or sentimentality. But in *Harry-O* these and other qualities were given prominence by writers and directors who clearly understood how to use story lines, interior spaces, close-ups, and voice-over narration so as to respect the principle of the actor's primacy on the small screen.

A sensitive, reluctant hero, Janssen's Harry Orwell was one of the great television characters, more

credibly and richly imagined than nearly all the TV detectives who preceded him, a true successor to the classic private eyes in the novels of Dashiell Hammett and Raymond Chandler and in the movies that grew out of those books. Unlike *Richard Diamond,* which merely repeated an earlier story, *Harry-O* drew creatively on this popular mythology, and the pleasure of watching the show partly consisted in one's repeated recognition of the variations and shadings the series introduced into this fertile American tradition. There were many explicit allusions to the older detectives in *Harry-O,* and Janssen's gently hoarse voice-over, used with great economy in every episode, seemed an aptly restrained echo of Hammett's narrators and of the movie detectives who also often told their own stories. There was no trace, though, of swagger or self-display in Janssen's weary voice, and his attitude toward the world was correspondingly unassertive.

Janssen's own previous work conferred an even more complex authority on the series. He was twenty-seven and looked younger when he did *Richard Diamond;* he was forty-four and looked older when he began *Harry-O.* As with other memorable television actors (James Arness, for instance, who did *Gunsmoke* for eighteen uninterrupted years; or James Garner, whose version of the hero as silver-tongued coward has grown richer with each series he has done), Janssen's aging was a lovely drama in itself, his quick, familiar face growing more expressive as it matured.

In his first season Harry Orwell hobbled through

193

August 26 to September 12, 1960. CBS provides eighteen hours of coverage of the Summer Olympic Games in Rome. American swimmers Lynn Burke (L) and Chris von Saltza capture gold medals.

September 10, 1960. "There she is . . . Miss America." Host Bert Parks poses with Lynda Lee Mead who will relinquish her title tonight to Nancy Fleming, the new winner. The Miss America Pageant was first televised in 1954.

Thirteen years after the first televised World Series between the Joe Dimaggio-led Yankees and Jackie Robinson-led Dodgers, weekly network baseball telecasts have still not caught on because of technical inadequacies. CBS's play-by-play sportscasting team in 1960 is Dizzy Dean and "Pee Wee" Reese. Dean had earlier worked with Billy Blattner.

Early in his career Janssen appears as a gunslinger in "Trial By Fear," a 1958 episode of Zane Grey Theatre.

194

General Electric College Bowl, the much-heralded quiz show that features opposing teams representing American colleges, moves from CBS to NBC in 1960. Robert Earle replaces look-alike Allen Ludden as moderator.

FRANK WOOD   D. GILLILAND   J. SHERTZER

CAPTAIN

KE FOREST COLLEGE

September 26, 1960. The first of the four "Great Debates" takes place in Chicago. Seventy-five million people tune in CBS. Senator John F. Kennedy of Massachusetts impresses as much with his charisma as with his arguments.

Richard Nixon's gray suit blends into the background during the first debate and he looks like he needs a shave. It is generally recognized that these disadvantages contribute to Kennedy's popularity.

Harry O with guest star Felicia Farr in 1975.

violent tasks to perform on the screen. But he never became much of an acrobat and retained his shambling awkwardness throughout his second season. Fitting himself with rueful slowness into his broken-down toy of a sports car, middle-aged and sagging like its owner, or stiffly climbing the wooden steps of his house on the beach, he seemed a subversively modest hero, the fugitive grown older and wiser.

He moved to Los Angeles in his second season, and into a recurring entanglement with Lieutenant K. C. Trench (brilliantly played by Anthony Zerbe), a meticulous, intelligent cop who respected Harry's honesty but was continually outraged by his habitual disorderliness and casual style. Harry's manner with Trench, as with clients and suspects, always registered a special sensitivity; he put questions to people with great hesitancy as if embarrassed to be violating their privacy. Like Garner's Jim Rockford, who also appeared in 1974, Janssen-Orwell was a great wheedler, more likely to coddle or flatter information out of his sources than to threaten them. "Why should I answer you?" asked an officious bureaucrat in one episode. Janssen's answer was characteristic, a half-audible mumble, delayed for a long moment as he settled on the edge of the bureaucrat's desk: "Because my feet hurt?"

Of course Harry Orwell was a figure of fantasy like all heroes. But he was a fine and healthy fantasy, an admirable dream of integrity and decency. And although his adventures were canceled prematurely, he and the gifted actor who brought him so vividly to life will be remembered fondly by tens of millions of Americans.

David Thorburn, a professor of literature at the Massachusetts Institute of Technology, is the author of Conrad's Romanticism *and many articles on literary subjects. He is writing a book about television.*

a brilliantly-photographed San Diego with a bullet in his spine, retired on a disability pension from the police force. Late in the season the writers allowed Harry an operation which removed the bullet, perhaps to stimulate ratings by giving him more strenuous and

195

Three more presidential debates follow in the next month. Although Nixon better coordinates his wardrobe with the set and comes off as Kennedy's equal in contesting the issues, the "Great Debates" are more beneficial to Kennedy, who gains the national exposure he needs to compete with the well-known vice-president.

September 27, 1960. *Alfred Hitchcock Presents* moves to NBC after four years on CBS. Here Hitchcock receives a kiss from Audrey Meadows, who stars in the premiere episode, "Mrs. Bixby and the Colonel's Coat."

REMEMBERING "CAR 54, WHERE ARE YOU?"

GERALD PEARY

As a rule, I detest trivia buffs. There occurs, however, one key suspension of my animosity: whenever, once in five stale years, I encounter that very *special* person—that delirious and *committed* person—who recalls, with the crystal clarity of a Proust, the golden, empyrean age when *Car 54, Where Are You?* rode the television waves.

"Didn't you love *Car 54?*" I squeal with delight. "Wasn't it the *greatest?*" bellows the other. We are soulmates. "Did you see when the precinct entered the barbershop quartet contest?" "Do you remember the captain's surprise present—orthopedic shoes?" We nod, we chortle, we double over with laughter. And some time on that sublime and sunny day, we pause and, with the solemnity of British war veterans singing "Tipperary," raise our voices in unison to energize that immortal theme song:

> There's a holdup in the Bronx,
> Brooklyn's broken out in fights,
> There's a traffic jam in Harlem
> That's backed up to Jackson Heights.
> There's a scout troop short a child
> Khrushchev's due at Idlewild.
> CAR 54, WHERE A-A-A-A-RE YOU???

Khrushchev? Does anyone remember him in this age of sorry revisionism Idlewild Airport? It exists today only in the world of Platonic Forms, where Toody and Muldoon fly forever through the streets in their indubitably wingéd patrol car.

Since few recall, here are the bare facts. *Car 54* was the 1960's brainchild of Nat Hiken, *farceur par excellence,* earlier responsible for *Sergeant Bilko.* Hiken's simple but genius idea was to take the fast-talking eccentrics, the nuts, the wallet-swipers, the inner city ethnics who populated Bilko's Kansas army base, and discharge them into their natural habitat, the streets of New York, swapping baggy army outfits for baggy police uniforms. The switch worked like a charm.

Leading the *Car 54* pack were a kind of white Amos 'n' Andy team of New York's Finest: Toody (Joe E. Ross), squat and lovably stupid, with the diction of Yogi Berra and the face of a cherub, including cheeks to pinch; Muldoon (Fred Gwynne), a long, tall, sad body and face, intelligent and urbane, and what was he doing in a police car? But they got along swell. Muldoon would drive about in a dreamlike stupor and Toody would go into his daily neo-Shakespearean soliloquy: "Ted Williams is nonchalant. Stan Musial is nonchalant. But do you know who is *really* nonchalant? Mickey Mantle. Now *he* is nonchalant!

The only threat to the partnership came when a third man was assigned to the patrol car, a Harvard man, who conversed about intellectual matters with Muldoon while poor Toody just sat there. Toody's solution: to memorize the encyclopedia, beginning with the letter A. The next day Toody was ready and

196

Jayne Meadows and husband Steve Allen star in the comedy, "The Man Who Thought for Himself," on *G.E. Theatre* in 1960. This is the first year since 1952 in which Allen doesn't host a show. In 1961, he will host a variety show on ABC, but it will be canceled after a few months.

September 28, 1960, Fred Astaire wins another Emmy for "Astaire Time," his third special on NBC. Once again Barrie Chase is his partner.

Fred Gwynne (L) and Joe E. Ross are the zany partners on Nat Hiken's creation, Car 54, Where Are You?

alert: "Did someone mention 'aardvark'?"

Car 54 had been off the air about seven years when an eerie, but wonderful, incident occurred in my life. I walked into a New York subway car with my brother, another *Car 54* zealot, and we saw a vision.

This subway car was bursting with zanies. An enormous black man sat next to a teensy, epicene white man. The white man had powdered his face to make it all the whiter. And these men, strangers, wore identical hats with identical feathers in them. Another person sported a Mickey Mouse mask. Elsewhere, a sailor was doing somersaults, high in the air around the hand grips near the ceiling. Across the way, a young couple was deep in an R-rated embrace. And amidst all this sat two New York City policemen with benign grins on their faces—relaxed, uncaring, for they'd seen such craziness on other occasions. And those policemen were—my brother and I both gasped—spitting real-life images of Toody and Muldoon.

CAR 54, WHERE A-A-A-RE YOU?

Gerald Peary teaches film at Livingston College, Rutgers University.

197

September 29, 1960. Telly Savalas plays gang lord "Lucky" Luciano in the premiere of *Witness*. This sixty-minute series presents simulated courtroom investigations of criminals and controversial figures of the past. Despite fine reviews, this CBS show will last only one year.

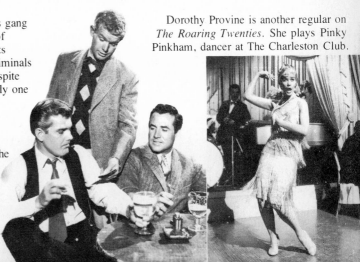

Because of viewer interest in the twenties generated by *The Untouchables*, Warner Brothers produces *The Roaring Twenties* for ABC. It will play from 1960 to 1962. Starring are (L–R): Donald May, Gary Vinson, and Rex Reason as reporters.

Dorothy Provine is another regular on *The Roaring Twenties*. She plays Pinky Pinkham, dancer at The Charleston Club.

POLITICS IN "THE DEFENDERS"

IDA JETER

In the early sixties the networks were still embarrassed by the quiz show scandals and looked for other types of entertainment. *The Defenders* was in the vanguard of a general trend (i.e., *Ben Casey; Mr. Novak; East Side, West Side*) toward serious drama as a counterbalance to action adventure, and as an adjunct to network interest in contemporary subjects. It was also a show with which CBS hoped to increase viewing by urban residents, who were assumed to be more liberal than many rural viewers.

The drama in *The Defenders* usually revolved around the technicalities of the legal profession. *The Defenders* attempted to inform the viewers about the law and judicial procedures. What we saw each week were established professionals, attorneys Lawrence Preston (E. G. Marshall) and son Kenneth (Robert Reed), functioning within the machinery established by jurisprudence. On this program, which was an obvious alternative to the *Perry Mason*–formula courtroom dramas, working with existing evidence was more important than uncovering clues. Moreover, *The Defenders* rarely allowed the sensational last-minute courtroom confession. Violence was restricted to the depiction of the crime. These lawyers never chased a suspect, dodged bullets, or defended themselves physically.

The law provided writer/editor Reginald Rose and producer Herbert Brodkin with a significant vehicle for the exploration of American values and contemporary issues. Yet despite its commendable examination of issues and overtly liberal ethic, *The Defenders'* overriding message seems to have been one

> "... this program ... was an obvious alternative to the 'Perry Mason' formula ..."

of accommodation to the realities of life. A common shortcoming of television social drama is its failure to define appropriate courses of action toward the solution of a problem once it is defined. Actual involvement in political movements tends to remain an unstated option, or, at least, takes a back seat to the exhortation to be informed. *The Defenders'* ideology was based primarily on a belief that men and women, once they are fully aware, once they replace blind passion with enlightened compassion, will do the right thing. Each week on *The Defenders,* Lawrence represented an individual in a particular legal dispute. Though the Prestons always examined the broader issues, their primary function remained apolitical. Kenneth's zeal for reform was generally tempered by his father's careful, practical approach to the immediate problem. Kenneth wanted to treat the social ill; Lawrence treated the individual. Like other broadcast social dramas, *The Defenders* could not transcend the realm of liberal platitude to encourage us to turn off the television and become involved—to intervene as organized, committed citizens in the political process.

The nature of the offenses for which Preston clients were charged varied considerably, and frequently concerned topical subjects and controversies.

Surfside Six, a new Warner Brothers private-eye show, based in Miami, debuts in 1960 on ABC. It will last two years. Starring are (L–R): Troy Donahue, Lee Patterson, and Van Williams who brought his "Kenny Madison" character from the defunct *Bourbon Street Beat*. Also appearing in *Surfside Six* is Diane McBain.

James Philbrook (L) and William Reynolds star as pilots in the ABC adventure series *The Islanders*, which appears in 1960. lasts for only three months.

Jan Murray (L) testifies on an episode of The Defenders *as E. G. Marshall listens intently.*

Lawrence and Ken handled their share of murder cases; but they also defended an accused arsonist, bigamist, abortionist, kleptomaniac, and even a traitor. Other crimes were vehicular homicide, euthanasia, manslaughter, fraud, child beating, criminal negligence, violation of federal selective service laws, distributing obscene literature, and dispensing illegal birth control information.

The legal and, thus, dramatic conflict also evolved out of situations other than a criminal trial. Divorce and child custody suits comprised one small aspect of the Preston's professional work. The Prestons unsuccessfully represented a blacklisted actor in his efforts to keep a job in his profession. They became involved in an arbitration between a private school and the atheistic teacher whom it had fired. A spy exchange found them in West Germany. They represented a reporter in his attempt to recover his passport, revoked because he illegally entered Communist China. Their affiliation with the civil rights movement as lawyers for a young protester prompted them to mount a defense based on a new conception of free speech then currently being developed by Freedom Rider attorney William Kunstler. Lawrence and Kenneth Preston tried to obtain a second trial for a convicted murderer, and clemency for several men on

Keith Larsen helps guest Leslie Parrish with her robe in *The Aquanauts,* which comes to NBC in 1960. Larsen, Jeremy Slate, and Ron Ely star as professional divers. The show will run for one season.

October 2, 1960. Alice Ghostley and Jane Powell, Tony Randall, Janis Paige, and Art Carney star in the hour-long ''Hooray for Love'' variety special on CBS.

October 3, 1960. Bob Hope dances with guest Patti Page on *The Bob Hope Buick Show*. Bobby Darin, Joan Crawford, and the Hollywood Deb Stars also appear.

" 'The Defenders' taught us that we are all morally culpable . . ."

death row. Indeed, *The Defenders* consistently spoke out against capital punishment.

Because *The Defenders* questioned existing laws and the Prestons frequently asked for mercy from the jury, the writers needed a device whereby Lawrence and Ken could interrogate witnesses about the effectiveness of the law in dispute, or introduce evidence about the defendant that would impress the jury with the need for compassion in a specific case. According to the strict rules of evidence, this information would have normally been inadmissible. Thus, the series' legal adviser Jerome Leitner invented a device—the court as a forum for discussion—to surmount these difficulties. With the consent of the district attorney and judge, Lawrence and Ken were allowed to introduce questionable evidence, or call witnesses who examined the issues. Without this procedure there could have been no programs that presented pro and con arguments about birth control, abortion, a merciful approach to drug addiction, or the legal definition of insanity. Nor could the defense of two teenage thieves have depended on Lawrence's attack against the materialistic, corrupt society that spawned them.

Though the law was the principal catalyst for dramatic tension, other sources of conflict were evident. Frequently, Lawrence, Ken, or a client had to make a decision which compelled him to examine his own values and ethics. In resolving their personal dilemmas, clients often learned about human responsibility. Some recognized their obligations to other human beings and learned to base decisions on the needs of their friends and families. Others were edu-

cated in their responsibility for a social organism, either their community or country. The most common manifestation of this awareness was patriotism, defined as the active participation in the preservation of democratic freedom for ourselves and others. The maxim that all human beings are interdependent was evident in *The Defenders'* conception of criminals as products of an ethnic or racial ghetto, poverty, loveless homes, or an affluent, acquisitive society. We were told that we are all responsible for the creation and care of America's victims. The most demanding form of responsibility derived from the Nuremberg principles. *The Defenders* taught us that we are all morally culpable when our nation uses force to achieve its ends. The primary application of this tenet was the proposition that every citizen is guilty when a human being is executed by the state.

Trials did not necessarily conclude with a not-guilty verdict. The Prestons frequently lost. There was an occasional hung jury. Sometimes the episode ended before the verdict was given. These last two conclusions generally occurred when an issue unresolved at the time was examined, or when the principal source of the drama was a moral or political conflict between characters. In such cases, the resolution of this conflict was of paramount concern, not the outcome of the trial. And, in those episodes in which a criminal case was not prosecuted, the Prestons failed nearly as often as they succeeded in achieving their goals. What was essential was that they express their ideas to the viewer at home.

The Defenders, a social drama about the law, was aired on the Columbia Broadcasting System television network from September 16, 1961 through September 9, 1965.

Ida Jeter is a Ph.D. candidate in broadcasting and film at the University of Wisconsin.

October 3, 1960. On CBS, *The Andy Griffith Show* debuts. Griffith plays the sheriff of Mayberry, North Carolina, and Ronny Howard plays his son Opie. The show is an immediate success, and CBS realizes that there is a market for "rural" comedies.

Guestward Ho! premieres on ABC. This comedy about a family moving to the country will last one year. Starring are (L–R): Mark Miller, Joanne Dru, J. Carroll Naish (as Chief Hawkeye, a local businessman), and young Flip Mark. Veteran actor Naish had starred in *Life with Luigi* when the radio program came to TV in 1952.

REMEMBERING "ROUTE 66"

BIFF ROSENSTOCK

I really went gaga over *77 Sunset Strip.* My friend Horatio would come over on Friday nights and we'd watch it on TV. We drank Pepsis out of old-fashioned glasses and wrestled. Sometimes I'd go to his house. His mother always had large tins of pretzels. *77* was his favorite show too. We liked Stu Baily (Efrem Zimbalist, Jr.) better than Jeff Spencer (Roger Smith), thought Roscoe was funny, and dug Kookie. They were real classy private eyes. We spent our Friday nights like that for a couple of years. Somewhere in the back of my mind I knew that there were other things doing on Friday nights, but as yet I didn't have any idea what.

Horatio and I had been in the sixth grade together, but in the seventh we went to different schools. There seemed to be a heightened social awareness in my new school. It was an all-boys school, but guys dressed up in ties and jackets and had silver-link identification bracelets. There were even guys in my class who went on dates and talked about them without embarrassment. Horatio and I had always worn blue jeans. We knew girls from the neighborhood but rarely spoke to them. Occasionally there was a party, and we watched them dance with each other. There was a pretty girl named Eva whom I once, for no functional reason, asked the time of day. I never heard the end of it from my friends. When I told Horatio about all the guys in my new school, he said they were idiots. He said there were kids like that at his school but he never hung out with them. I liked these new kids and didn't know what to do. I certainly didn't want to desert Horatio.

One Monday morning a kid named Stein, who

> ## ". . . the sixties were born in the backseat of a convertible headed west."

always wore a double-breasted blazer and loafers with tassels, came up to my locker. He asked me if I'd seen *Route 66* the previous Friday. I told him I watched *77 Sunset Strip,* which was on at the same time. He couldn't believe it. He said, "What are you, a retard?" He laughed.

The next day I asked Horatio if he'd ever seen *Route 66.* I don't know how he could ever have seen it because he was always with me watching *77,* but he said, "Yeah, I've seen it. It stinks."

"Well, I've never seen it," I said, "And I'd like to catch a little of it . . . just to see what it's like." Horatio informed me that if I wanted to watch any part of *Route 66,* he was going home. I let the matter drop. The subsequent Monday I listened to Stein and his friends talk about how cool the show had been. Hard as it was to believe, it sounded like there were no bad guys. I wondered what kind of show had no bad guys.

Friday nights stopped being as much fun as they had been. Horatio and I both had new friends. He did imitations of teachers I'd never seen. One week I called him to find out when he was coming over, and he said he'd been invited out to a party and was leaving right away. It was at the house of someone I'd never met for people I didn't know, and he didn't ask

A big comedy breakthrough for ABC is *My Three Sons,* which debuts in 1960. It will remain on ABC until 1965 when it will switch to CBS for an additional seven years. Fred MacMurray plays Steve Douglas, a widower who raises three sons played by Tim Considine (top), Don Grady (L), and Barry Livingston. William Frawley plays the grandfather.

October 5, 1960. Shirley Bonne (L) is Eileen; Elaine Stritch is her sister Ruth; and Leon Belasco is their landlord Mr. Appopolous in "The Photography Mixup," the premiere episode of *My Sister Eileen.* Adapted from the movie, this CBS comedy will only last one year.

Annie Fargé stars in *Angel,* a CBS comedy in 1960. She plays a Frenchwoman recently married to an American played by Marshall Thompson.

77 Sunset Strip *private eyes Jeff Spencer (L) and Kookie plan strategy against* Route 66 *in competing time slot.*

me to go with him. I was all alone.

I decided to try *Route 66* just once. From the moment I heard the jazzy piano riffs in the theme song and saw two cool guys bombing down the highway in a Corvette I knew I would never watch *77* again. It was at that exact moment that my adolescence began. Martin Milner and George Maharis led me away from the television set and articulated a thirst for independence I've yet to satisfy. For me that was where the fifties ended and the sixties were born—in the backseat of a convertible headed west.

I never questioned the boys' magic ability to get jobs wherever they went. They worked on oil rigs, drove bulldozers, or ran ferryboats. It didn't seem to matter that they weren't in any unions. None of that bothered me. I believed it all. They also had terrific love affairs. They didn't solve mysteries, they dealt with problems, and at the end of the show there were never four people sitting around laughing. The two boys drove into the sunset, one of them wondering if he should have stayed in the last town with the girl he felt so much for. That's what really got to me. Those guys got the blues.

The show crystallized all the sad feelings I'd ever had into one gloriously adolescent concept: depression. I hadn't yet discovered Jack Kerouac, but even if I had, being depressed in a sports car was better than being depressed hitchhiking. Especially to a kid who didn't yet have his driver's license. *Route 66* altered my fantasies, and maybe the best thing about it was that I began to miss it once in a while when I went out on Friday nights.

Biff Rosenstock is the fencing and baseball coach at The Huart Academy for Boys in Wormsey, Massachusetts.

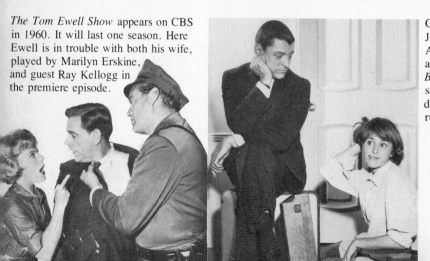

The Tom Ewell Show appears on CBS in 1960. It will last one season. Here Ewell is in trouble with both his wife, played by Marilyn Erskine, and guest Ray Kellogg in the premiere episode.

Guest Portland Mason, daughter of James and Pamela Mason, visits Frank Aletter and his aunts, Enid Markey and Doro Merande, in an episode of *Bringing Up Buddy*. It is one of several CBS comedies that debuts in 1960 and only runs for one year.

Cara Williams and Harry Morgan play the title roles in *Pete and Gladys*, a comedy which uses characters from *December Bride*.

REMEMBERING PALADIN
MICHAEL LAULETTA

Paladin was the last great man of television. During those long-ago years when the cowboy was king and western meant ratings, Paladin stood head and shoulders above them all.

Who else could quote the classics with such aplomb, sniff a vial of perfume and name its ingredients, read a Chinese newspaper, play masterful chess . . . and make his living as a gunfighter? All one had to do was wire Paladin, San Francisco—and be in the right in any feud—for the man in the black suit and chesspiece-decorated holster to be there.

Of course others will argue for the likes of Bat Masterson and Wyatt Earp, but I dismiss them as romanticized figurines strictly for viewing by my younger brother. Matt Dillon? Basically just a good old boy. A good old boy with the self-discipline of a Tibetan monk when you consider his relationship with Miss Kitty over two decades.

But Paladin. Now there was a man of intelligence, perception, ingenuity. Who can ever forget the time he was stranded in the Canadian Rockies, unarmed and defenseless? A lesser man would have succumbed. Only Paladin would have the presence of mind to fashion a deadly weapon based on a design used by eighteenth-century Eskimos and finally capture his would-be killers and still make it back for opening night at the San Francisco Opera House, a beautiful woman at his side.

After his initial success, it became fashionable to accuse Paladin of being pedantic and pompous. Perhaps. He was a bit overbearing at times, a bit superior in nature. He had a tendency to ride a high

"Paladin was the last great man of television."

horse. But who else in that cardboard period between *Amos 'n' Andy* and *Sanford and Son* ever came to the aid of an Indian marshal, sided with a Chinese detective, defended a woman doctor, or shot a black *bad guy?* Only one man would do such things, and do them with the self-assured air of someone who could only answer the questioning glances of those around him with a question of his own: "Doesn't everyone?"

Yes, Paladin was a violent man. He was in a violent profession. Yet, here too, Paladin knew the limits. A no-nonsense man of conviction, he shot to kill. He left the "just wing him" and "shoot the gun out of his hand" approach to fops like Yancy Derringer and nice guys like The Virginian.

One can still see Paladin crouched low, a scowl on his face, a piercing look of hatred in his eyes. But the hatred was not for his enemy; it was for the act of having to kill. Paladin's enemies always died quickly, pitching almost somnambulantly to the ground, often winding up cradled in Paladin's arms, the words of Horace or Shakespeare barely reaching their ears before they slipped peacefully into the next world. Paladin's victims died with dignity. There were no exploding shirtfronts, no splatterings of blood, no unearthly screams. They seemed to realize in those final few moments from the time Paladin took a final tug on his

The first prime time cartoon series, *The Flintstones*, debuts on ABC in 1960. It is produced by Hanna-Barbera. A stone-age version of "The Honeymooners," this will be the most successful cartoon series ever to appear on TV. It will spawn several spin-off cartoon series and be revived repeatedly with slightly different formats.

Petite Lori Martin takes the old Elizabeth Taylor movie role when *National Velvet* comes to NBC in 1960 for two years. With Martin are James McCallion and the horse Blaze King.

Richard Boone's debonair Paladin duels with a formidable opponent on Have Gun, Will Travel.

hat brim to the split second when he drew his specially designed handgun that indeed they were the bad guys, that Paladin was the good guy, and that this is the way it should end.

Paladin, Paladin, where do you roam? You roam quietly—and safely—wherever you are. There you will always be a great man, my first mentor. Only you could have gotten me to the library on a Saturday afternoon, only you could have gotten me to think conjugating verbs was a worthwhile pursuit, only you could have gotten me to open a book of poetry.

Would I like to see Paladin ride back again? No. I'm not fourteen years old anymore and his return would be too risky. Stay where you are, Paladin.

Michael Lauletta is a free-lance writer who is fortunate enough to remember radio as well as television.

204

Barry Sullivan as Pat Garrett and Clu Gulager as Billy the Kid star in *The Tall Man,* one of the few western series debuting in 1960. It will last on NBC's schedule for two years.

The Westerner, a series directed by Sam Peckinpah, lasts only thirteen weeks on NBC in 1960. Nevertheless, this unusual western will earn a reputation among western devotees as being one of the best of the genre ever to appear on TV. Brian Keith stars as Dave Blasingame. Brown is Blasingame's disloyal dog.

Horace McMahon (L) and Paul Burke (R) replace John McIntire and James Franciscus as the stars of ABC's hard-hitting police series *Naked City* when the show expands to an hour. They continue for three years in their roles. Here Eli Wallach is the guest star.

FAN FARE:
DEAR BRET MAVERICK:

Thx for yrs of May 7, 1958. My apologies for the delay in this reply, but I have been busy with my reading. I am embarrassed to report that the photo you kindly enclosed has somehow been misplaced. When last seen, it had become dog-eared, and then it must have evaporated or something. This carelessness, however, does not imply a waning enthusiasm for the slick-tongued, chickenhearted values you espoused. If anything, the opposite is true. I realize now that you were the true prophet of the sixties, and constitute a lost ideal for the seventies.

Maverick was a western that avoided violence. It was a tale of criminals whose comeuppance was never wrought by bald and pushy peace officers given to bullying. The western shows of that era—and there were more of them than hairs on a heifer—seldom batted an eye when it came to blood. But *Maverick* was different, since it portrayed a con man and card shark who openly preached the doctrine of flight from danger. Vengeance was to be reaped by trickery and confidence games. Years later *The Sting,* with Paul Newman and Robert Redford, stole the formula and, of course, made a fortune.

The plot of the great "Shady Deal at Sunny Acres" episode was typical. There was a crooked banker whose pitch was, "If you can't trust your banker, who can you trust?" You soon fell afoul of him and sought to settle the score, but characteristically you avoided the complications of violence. Instead you sat on a porch and let your friends prepare a great land swindle. While you whittled, townsfolk snickered and asked what you were going to do to get your money back? Your reply was always, "I'm working on it." Your partners worked their con and, sure enough, by the end of the hour the banker was tricked, you—Bret Maverick—were avenged, and no violence had been necessary.

I can think of no other program or episode in television history which better combined the ideals being promoted by the conflicting voices of the seventies. It had the rich entertainment value sought by network executives, avoided the blood and gore so offensive to social critics, and still was able to disregard the niceties of law in ways that audiences have loved since long before Homer.

It was also a program that well prepared me for the national traumas of the late sixties. In the years after you left, people began to say things like, "If you can't trust your President, who can you trust?" and they argued that violence was the only way to treat some situations. But you had taught me better and I was never completely unprepared for the disillusionment that followed. The John Wayne fans, on the other hand, have never recovered.

Your eternal fan,
Edmund Blair Bolles

Edmund Blair Bolles has watched television on three continents in the hope of seeing a Maverick *rerun.*

Former Warner Brothers movie star Pat O'Brien comes to television in 1960 as an attorney on *Harrigan and Son.* Roger Perry plays O'Brien's lawyer son and Georgine Darcy is Gypsy, O'Brien's secretary. This series will last only one season on ABC.

The Third Man, the Orson Welles–Joseph Cotten film classic, comes to TV, with nothing intact, in 1960 as a syndicated series. Michael Rennie plays Harry Lime and Jonathan Harris is his sidekick Bradford Denner.

REMEMBERING BEN CARTWRIGHT

ANDI LERNER

The first television series that really had an impact on me was *Bonanza*. I remember eagerly looking forward to Sunday nights, when my little brother and I could watch our favorite show together. In retrospect, it is not difficult to discover *Bonanza*'s appeal for us, even though we were not otherwise great fans of the western genre. In fact, despite the setting, *Bonanza* was much less a western than it appeared to be. Although the Cartwrights rode horses, and were quite handy with their guns, the series was more like a *Ben Cartwright Knows Best*. It was a family show, the story of a man and his sons achieving the American dream.

Bonanza was always carefully, and tastefully, done—right up to the beautiful watercolors in the opening and closing credits. There was a certain pattern of the story lines, although each episode was varied in setting and in tone. Some were true comedies, others left the viewer in tears. The main characters rotated with each episode, and only rarely did the whole company of actors appear as an ensemble. Along with the regulars, there were always one or two headlined guest stars as well.

Great care was taken to explain the relationships among the four Cartwrights, and how, with the same name, the three boys could turn out so differently. Each son had a different mother, who had imbued her son with those special characteristics that made him different from the others.

Adam, played by Pernell Roberts, was the intellectual. He always wore black, was somewhat mysterious and slow to anger. When Ben was not around,

> " 'Bonanza' was much less a western than it appeared to be."

Adam could serve as the surrogate father. Hoss, who was the middle son, was a typical gentle giant. He was kind, easily flattered, extremely strong, and eager to please. He was often the object of *Bonanza*'s comic side, either because of his gargantuan appetite or large frame. Little Joe was the baby of the family. By far the most impetuous, and also generally regarded as the most handsome, Joe was continually extricating himself from fights or love affairs.

The Cartwrights lived insular, yet exemplary lives. The Ponderosa was an idyllic setting for an extraordinary family relationship. As different as each of the characters were, they were devoted to each other. The Cartwrights were bound together by an overriding sense of family loyalty, and a desire for justice and truth.

The *Bonanza* story lines were always careful to stress moral choices rather than particular lessons. There was rarely one apparent answer to any problem: but Ben Cartwright was always there as a firm, loving, and effective parent to reinforce the best choice.

Bonanza's resiliency was challenged many times throughout the life of the show due to a changing cast. After Pernell Roberts left the series, the writers managed quite well with only the two sons. In order to inject new blood, David Canary entered the family as

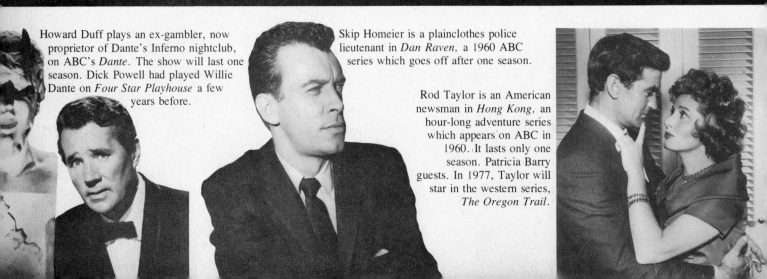

Howard Duff plays an ex-gambler, now proprietor of Dante's Inferno nightclub, on ABC's *Dante*. The show will last one season. Dick Powell had played Willie Dante on *Four Star Playhouse* a few years before.

Skip Homeier is a plainclothes police lieutenant in *Dan Raven*, a 1960 ABC series which goes off after one season.

Rod Taylor is an American newsman in *Hong Kong*, an hour-long adventure series which appears on ABC in 1960. It lasts only one season. Patricia Barry guests. In 1977, Taylor will star in the western series, *The Oregon Trail*.

The Cartwright men perch on a Bonanza corral (L-R): Ben, Hoss, Little Joe, and Adam.

a ranch-hand, with the same quiet, thoughtful manner Adam had demonstrated. By the time Canary departed, Little Joe had grown up and toned down. He took over the ''big brother'' role, and Mitch Vogel came on in the capacity of youngest adopted son.

One obvious move would have been to marry off one of the sons as a means of adding new characters. However, women in the Cartwright family were apparently unacceptable for longer than two episodes. Perhaps this was due to the stereotype of women's roles on the frontier as everywhere else. What could be done with a woman in the cast? In *The Big Valley*, this problem was solved by having Audra send up periodic ''damsel in distress'' signals while each of the brothers took turns rescuing her. While this strategy would not have interfered with the Cartwrights' attitudes toward women, it would not have fit in well with their ideas about self-sufficiency.

In the end, it was decided to keep the Ponderosa a male preserve, and not to risk the show's steady appeal. *Bonanza* had many magic qualities. The Cartwrights were the object of many children's fantasies, including my own. They lived in a beautiful house in handsome country. They were warm, caring, humorous, honorable people. They lived adventurous lives, and had the perfect parent. And because *Bonanza* was really a family show, the Cartwrights became one of the most ''identified with'' and well-known families on TV.

Andi Lerner has always considered television to be the greatest mediocre miracle in American history.

207

October 7, 1960. Route 66 debuts. George Maharis (Buzz Murdock) and Martin Milner (Tod Stiles) star as two twentieth-century wanderers in the popular CBS series.

October 28 and October 29, 1960. Zachary Scott, Barbara Robbins, and Suzanne Storrs star in ''The Scarlet Pimpernel,'' the premiere production on CBS's *Family Classics*. Also starring are Michael Rennie, Maureen O'Hara, and William Shatner.

FAN FARE:
DEAR MICHAEL ANTHONY:

I love you. I love you more and more each time I see you week after week on *The Millionaire*. I could love you much more if you personally brought me a million-dollar check—I don't care, I'll even pay taxes on it. I promise not to tell anyone about the money, Girl Scouts' honor.

Mike, you can get me that check. Just tell what's his name—John Beresford Tipton—that you know of a worthy case that he should look into; you can talk to him. How come he is always sitting in that big chair with his back to us? He has such a booming voice; he must have gone to broadcasting school in the Holland Tunnel! Mike, I know the answer—you're a ventriloquist and John Beresford Tipton is the dummy; if not, you're the dummy.

Mike, you're always getting punched in the mouth or a door slammed in your face when you hand those ingrates with their ridiculous problems a million-dollar check. Mike, maybe if you improved your entrance, they would like you. Why don't you watch Loretta Young?

Why do you always let JBT tell you what to do? He's always moralizing and doing good. Why don't you poison his fish? Mike, I hate to do this to you, but if you don't bring me the check, I'm going to reveal the identity of John Beresford Tipton. And I know.

Waiting with open palm,
Betty Odabashian

While waiting for her million, Betty Odabashian does research for documentaries at ABC.

Michael Anthony (R) and stunned millionaire.

208

Maximilian Schell (D'Artagnan) and Felicia Farr star in ''The Three Musketeers,'' a two-part episode of *Family Classics*.

November 8, 1960. Election Night. Correspondents Walter Cronkite and Howard K. Smith stand above a scale model of CBS headquarters for coverage of ''Election Night 1960.'' Returns come in late into the night. Finally, Nixon loses Illinois and concedes that John Kennedy will be the next President.

REMEMBERING EMMA PEEL

JOSEPH KOCH

When I was fifteen, just about the time I realized that the discrepancies between myself and Agent 007 would not be resolved by further growth, I discovered *The Avengers,* a British second-season import. In the proverbial nick of time. Instead of obliging me to fight through the hordes of S.M.E.R.S.H. to rescue the woman of my dreams, *The Avengers* presented me with the pleasant alternative of laying back and being rescued *by* the woman of my dreams.

The Avengers had many good qualities. Patrick MacNee was the 1960's best incarnation of the non–working–class hero. The writing was excellent: each script was populated by a host of semi-satiric villains, victims, and vaguely innocent bystanders designed to give all those wonderful British character actors work. And there were the plots, which blithely ignored all traditions of credibility; they cleverly juggled parody and suspense without ever degenerating into camp.

But most of all there was Diana Rigg, a Shakespearian actress in a black leather jumpsuit. Male viewers lusted after Emma Peel, and female viewers understood why. Emma Peel turned television's feminine mystique on its head. She rescued lots of men, and more importantly, she rescued women from their usual thriller roles of clumsy hostages, hysterical victims, and untrustworthy witnesses. She was capable, self-reliant, and intelligent.

In one episode, Steed and Mrs. Peel have to infiltrate a high IQ society which is being used by the enemy to design clever assassination plots. Steed can't pass the admissions test, but Mrs. Peel passes with flying colors. In another show, the British Ministry is

being depopulated by an evil genius who discovers and then uses the most irrational fears of high government officials to drive them insane. Finding Mrs. Peel on his trail, the villain captures and then subjects her to the same treatment, only to find that none of the conventional feminine fears seem to apply.

All this is not to imply that Mrs. Peel never needed rescuing, but rather that when she got into trouble, it was not because she was *out* of her element. She was an exemplary, if unconventional, damsel in distress. In fact, after watching Steed rescue her a few times, I began to reconsider the benefits of being the rescuer. The payoff in saving your usual TV woman seemed somehow dubious. How much honest reward is there in the gratitude of an over-reacting, generally incompetent female? None. The woman offers sex, but it is the men who provide the respect. Not so with Mrs. Peel. In rescuing her, I could find all my satisfactions in one person.

Joseph Koch is a comic book dealer in New York City.

209

November 18, 1960. William Shatner and Patricia Breslin star in "Nick of Time," an episode of *The Twilight Zone* about a fortune-telling machine with strange powers.

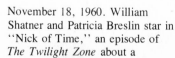

November 20, 1960. Director George Schaefer and actors Maurice Evans and Judith Anderson went on location in Scotland to shoot the two-hour *Hallmark Hall of Fame* production of "Macbeth." All three will win Emmys and "Macbeth" will win as "Program of the Year." Evans and Anderson also played together in Hallmark's 1954 production of the play.

November 24, 1960. Dick Van Dyke, Rosemary Clooney, and Carol Burnett star in the NBC Thanksgiving special "No Place Like Home."

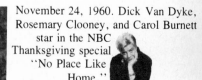

REMEMBERING "TWILIGHT ZONE"

HENRY BLINDER

Each *Twilight Zone* had a gimmick or a plot twist. What kept me tuning in each week was the fun of trying to outguess the show before the trick was sprung on you; it was the same sort of game that we all played watching *Perry Mason*.

There is an episode called "A Stop at Willoughby," in which James Daly plays a company man who has been stepped on, pushed and pulled to the limits by his wife and by his boss. One night as he rides his crowded, smoke-filled commuter train home he looks out the window as the conductor calls out, "Willoughby. This stop Willoughby." It is a charming 1890's town in the summertime, complete with horse-drawn carriages, women in hoopskirts, and men with handlebar mustaches. The man has been traveling this rail line for years and has never seen this town before. Townspeople beckon him off the train but he remains on. As his stop is called he is jolted awake, and realizes he has been dreaming.

The next day at the office, his boss bellows at him and his wife calls to remind him of their loveless marriage. That night on the train, the camera moves in for a close-up on his lined, careworn face which seems to beg for sleep. And again the train stops at Willoughby and again the townspeople beckon. This time he gets off the train. It is a wonderful, peaceful world. He watches as the train pulls away and decides this is where he will stay. (I had by now guessed the ending and was telling everyone in the room excitedly.) There is a cutback to reality. The businessman has jumped off the speeding commuter train and now lies dead in the snow. In a close-up we see a look of complete

"It was a remarkable show based on a gimmick."

peace on his face for the first time. It was a remarkable show based on a gimmick.

The *Twilight Zone* gimmicks that I tuned in for as a kid have since disappeared from the screen, but the emotions, the feelings, and the fears that those episodes tapped have remained with me. The late Rod Serling's genius created *Twilight Zone,* an indelible moment in television history. He wrote most of the shows and was the executive producer of all of them—an incredible output. There were 151 episodes, five seasons of the most consistently imaginative and affecting television ever created. Serling used to describe himself as a hardworking Hollywood hack writer. But I don't believe this any more than I believe that *Twilight Zone* was about the gimmicks the show was built around each week. Serling knew exactly what he was doing. We may have guessed the ending but Serling was still way ahead of us, translating our private thoughts and feelings, too dark to articulate, into weekly mass entertainment.

Now, when I'm riding on a train, sometimes I think of James Daly's exhausted businessman and I wonder at what point in one's life one decides to step off into the quaint 1890's town outside the window.

Henry Blinder is a filmmaker in New York.

210

November 30, 1960. Actress Anne Bancroft guests on Perry Como's *Kraft Music Hall*. Como will host this variety show until 1963.

December 11, 1960. Jack Benny and Barbara Nichols are the uninvited guests of Mr. and Mrs. Jimmy Stewart on *The Jack Benny Program*.

Benny's penny-pinching, wishy-washy shopping methods drive salesman Mel Blanc to contemplate suicide in an often-repeated routine on *The Jack Benny Program*. Blanc, the voice of Bugs Bunny, Porky Pig, Daffy Duck, and *The Flintstones's* Barney Rubble, plays many parts for Benny.

MY LIFE WITH SPOCK

LEONARD NIMOY

For three years, twelve hours a day, five days a week, approximately ten months of each year, I functioned as an extraterrestrial.

Many people have had some experience role playing. Some people have had more experience than I; some people have played a particular role longer than I. But given my intense commitment to the identification with this role, and given the unique nature of this extraterrestrial, there may be some value in reassembling the experience.

Six years after having completed the role, I am still affected by the character of Spock, the Vulcan first officer and science officer of the Starship *Enterprise*. Of course, the role changed my career. Or rather, gave me one. It made me wealthy by most standards and opened up vast opportunities. It also affected me very deeply and personally—socially, psychologically, emotionally. To this day I sense Vulcan speech patterns, Vulcan social attitudes and even Vulcan patterns of logic and emotional suppression in my behavior.

What started out as a welcome job to a hungry actor has become a constant and ongoing influence in my thinking and lifestyle.

In 1965, Gene Roddenberry was producing a TV series for NBC titled *The Lieutenant*. It starred Gary Lockwood and had to do with his adventures as a marine corps officer. My agent at that time, Alex Brewis, had submitted me for a guest-starring role. . . .

When the episode was finished, Gene Roddenberry commented to my agent that he was writing a script for a science fiction TV series and he had a role that he wanted me to play. My agent reported this to me but I didn't pay much attention, assuming it would be some time before the script reached the production stage and it was silly to raise my hopes.

However, several months later Gene did call and a meeting was arranged. At that first meeting it was my assumption that I was being interviewed for the role. Gene's conversation threw me off balance because he seemed to be selling me on the idea of working in his series. He took the trouble to walk me through the prop department and the scenic design shop to show me the nature of the work that was being done for the series. Above all he seemed to be trying to impress upon me the fact that this series was being very carefully prepared and that it indeed would be something special to television.

I was so excited at the prospect of getting a steady job on a television series that I tried very hard to keep my mouth shut. I felt that the more I talked the more chance there was of talking myself out of what could be steady work. I left Gene's office very excited and expected negotiations to begin. . . .

So in fact the die was cast and I was to become Mr. Spock, son of Sarek, the Vulcan, and Amanda, the Earth scientist, in the science fiction adventure called *Star Trek*.

Roddenberry and I had numerous meetings to discuss the nature of the character and his background. The Vulcans had been a violent and emotional people, which almost led to their destruction. They made a decision. Thenceforth emotion was to be foreign to the

December 22, 1960. In one of his rare TV appearances, Harpo Marx plays a "mechanical dummy" in a store window in "Silent Panic" on *The Dupont Show with June Allyson* in 1960. Next to him is Benny the Monkey.

Rod Serling wrote his "Night of the Meek" episode of *The Twilight Zone* especially for the 1960 Christmas season. Art Carney plays a drunk who is hired to play Santa Claus and discovers that he really is Santa Claus. Here Carney sings with Meg Wyllie.

Leonard Nimoy's famous Mr. Spock.

were Lon Chaney and Paul Muni, both great character actors of the past, but I had mixed feelings about it. At this point my career wasn't exactly what one would call extraordinary, but I was making a living as an actor and as a teacher. Most important, I took great pride in my reputation as a solid character actor. I had reached the point where I was able to be somewhat selective about the roles I played, accepting only those which I thought had merit and offered opportunities to play dimensional people. As yet, I had not read a *Star Trek* script. I was very much concerned about the possibility of getting involved in what might turn out to be a ''mickey mouse'' character. I felt it could be a ludicrous adventure, possibly leading to embarrassment for myself and the other people involved.

I discussed the problems with Vic Morrow, an actor whose talent and judgment I respected. Vic and I went through the pros and cons of the situation and even at one point touched on the possibility of devising a makeup that would be so complete that Leonard Nimoy would be totally unrecognizable. In this way I could do the job, earn the money, and avoid the dangers of being connected with a ludicrous character.

Of course, it didn't work out that way and I am very happy with the way the matter resolved itself. But, to this day, I still think it might have been fun to have played that character totally hidden and be totally mysterious and unavailable in my private life. It could have been the put-on of the century. Just imagine the headlines in the newspapers and magazines: ACTUAL ALIEN AGREES TO APPEAR IN SCIENCE FICTION TV SERIES.

So it began. I went to work and played the scenes, said the lines. Groping and learning to walk, talk, function as an alien. Putting out the sounds and motions and watching, recording the feedback of my fellow actors, crew personnel, and visitors. It was difficult for a long time. The total understanding of the

Vulcan nature. Logic would rule. Vulcans would be distinguished in appearance by their skin color, hairstyle, and pointed ears—a race concerned with dignity and progress, incorporating the culture and ritual of the past with the best of what the future could offer. In Spock there would be a special mixture of tensions. The logic and emotional suppression of the Vulcan people through the father, Sarek, pitted against the emotional and humanistic traits inherited from the human mother, Amanda.

These were rich beginnings for a TV character and especially challenging for an actor whose idols

212

January 15, 1961. Ethel Merman, ''The Queen of the Broadway Musical,'' is one of many big-name celebrities who appears in ''The Gershwin Year'' on CBS. In 1953, Merman sang medleys with Mary Martin on Leland Hayward's mammoth ''Ford Fiftieth Anniversary Show,'' TV's first major special, on both CBS and NBC.

January 18, 1961. Christopher Plummer plays a dual role in ''The Prisoner of Zenda'' on the *Dupont Show of the Month*. Farley Granger and Inger Stevens also star.

January 20, 1961. John Kennedy is sworn in as President of the United States by Chief Justice Earl Warren. Behind Kennedy are Vice-President Lyndon Johnson and Richard Nixon. Behind Warren are (L-R): Jacqueline Kennedy, Mamie Eisenhower, and Dwight D. Eisenhower, who, eight years ago to the day, was the first President sworn in on national television.

character would only be found in the total context. This rigid pointed-eared creature was only a visual gimmick until perceived as a part of a whole: the particular story we were filming, the ship, the crew, the antagonists, the entire buildup of another world, another time. Taken alone, in bits and pieces, out of context, it was still dangerously close to a joke.

Nevertheless, I began to feel more comfortable. I could understand my place, my function in the stories, my relationship to the other characters. A sense of dignity began to evolve. I took pride in being different and unique.

Above all, I began to study human behavior from an alien point of view. I began to enjoy the Vulcan position. "These humans are interesting, at times a sad lot, at times foolish, but worthy of study."

The scripts, particularly the character of Dr. McCoy, offered opportunities to deal with the human need to see everything and others only in relation to oneself. "Anybody who isn't like us is strange. Anybody who doesn't want to be like us is a fool."

I was becoming alienated and didn't realize it. My attitude toward the humans around me became quite paternal. In some respects I assumed the position of teacher, or role model. My hope was that we could reduce the inefficiency and silly emotionalism if I set examples through my higher standards of discipline and precision.

Nature abhors a vacuum. I showed little or no emotional response, so my co-workers and associates projected responses for me. For example, this quote from a co-worker passed along to me by a friend at the studio: "I see [in Nimoy] a growing image of a shrewd, ambition-dominated man, probing, waiting *with emotions and feelings masked,* ready to leap at the right moment and send others reeling. . . ."

At the onset, the actor felt protective of the character, much as a parent tries to protect a develop-

ing child. Certainly my ego was involved and was bruised. But it seemed important to help the character come to life. When he did, he protected the actor. He became an ever-present friend who could be called upon as an ally in adverse circumstances. Nimoy could submerge himself and let Spock take over.

Eventually, the show went on the air (Setpember 8, 1966). The reaction was immediate and multiplied at an astounding rate. The magic of Spock became quickly apparent. I was mobbed at personal appearances, and security measures were necessary to get me into and out of crowded situations. *Security* and *privacy* suddenly became important words to me and to my family. The mail and phone calls and in general the intense activity that I suddenly experienced made it obvious that we were involved in something that was "happening." Before too long even NBC became actively involved in the "Spock phenomenon."

I discovered later through Gene Roddenberry and Herb Solow that NBC had been very negative about the character and in fact wanted the character removed from the series before the shooting started. Where they had originally felt that "no one would want to identify with the Spock character," they now decided that everyone was identifying. Therefore they wanted Spock more actively involved in the stories that would be shot in the future.

Since the whole thing started I had felt a wide range of emotional reaction to my identification with Spock. The range has included at various times a total embracing and a total rejection of the character.

Spock was quickly becoming a pop-culture hero. I didn't set out to be a pop-culture hero. The simple truth is that I set out to be a craftsmanlike actor, a professional and possibly someday even an artist.

This article is excerpted from I Am Not Spock *by Leonard Nimoy (Celestial Arts, 1975).*

213

President Kennedy delivers a stirring inaugural address, including his famous admonition, "Ask not what your country can do for you; ask what you can do for your country."

John Kennedy escorts Jacqueline Kennedy to the inaugural ball. Jacqueline Kennedy will quickly become one of the most photographed women in the world and the subject of articles in women's publications and gossip magazines. Her "Tour of the White House" on CBS will be one of the most publicized shows of the 1961–62 season.

"STAR TREK": SPACE POLITICS

RUTH McCORMICK

No television program has been more successful in capturing the imaginations of its fans than Star Trek. With each new wave of reruns it wins new adherents of all ages—including adults who might have avoided it originally as a kids' program.

What is the extraordinary appeal of *Star Trek?* Why has it turned on a mass audience in a way that other shows of its kind, like *Lost in Space* and *Space, 1999,* were unable to do? Perhaps *Lost in Space* really was a kids' show, with its ''Swiss Family Robinson'' theme, while *Space, 1999* sacrificed whimsy in an attempt at authenticity. *Star Trek* combines the genuine awesomeness of *2001, A Space Odyssey,* with an appeal to our scientific curiosity, our most optimistic hopes for the world, and our desire to have our most cherished myths reenacted. It borrows themes from the greatest sci-fi writers, Isaac Asimov, Arthur C. Clarke, J. G. Ballard, A. E. Van Vogt, and Ursula Le Guin, and has even employed the talents of Robert Bloch, Harlan Ellison, Theodore Sturgeon, and Richard Matheson for some of its most challenging episodes. However, in *Star Trek* questions posed in the manner of the best science fiction are often resolved in a fashion more in keeping with *Flash Gordon,* thus assuring an appeal to the widest possible cross section of viewers. In addition, the production values of the show are consistently high, the situations, whether serious or silly, are colorful and well written, the acting is generally on a high level, and the main characters have great mass appeal.

But perhaps most important of all, *Star Trek* is a testament to the liberal optimism of the 1960's. Imag-ine a world free of wars and want, in which science and technology are employed for the fulfillment of human needs, and where national, religious, and racial conflicts have been eliminated. Having reached this level of enlightenment, we humans have become eligible for membership in the Galactic Federation, an association of planets civilized enough to have overcome irrationality, poverty, and hatred. Desirable as such a society might be, however, it is lacking in the kind of conflict that makes for good TV, so it is necessary dramatically that humans, along with the other races of the federation, seek further frontiers in space. This is the world of *Star Trek.*

We are never told how the earth ''grew up,'' although references are made to a nuclear holocaust having finally convinced people that they must learn to live together in peace. There is no more cold war, no more imperialism, but certainly more than a hint that the ''American way'' has prevailed. In several episodes it is mentioned that on earth, all are equal and powerful leaders are no longer needed.

The ''ideological'' struggle being waged by the federation is with the aggressive and authoritarian Klingon Empire. If the warlike and irrational Klingons are the Fascists of the galaxy, the ultrarational Vulcans, with their scientific objectivity, disdain for private property, and lack of emotionality, would seem to be the ''Communists,' neutralized in the interests of détente—friends, but oh-so-different from us. In fact, although we never see the utopia that earth has become, it is reflected to a degree on the starship *Enterprise.* Captain Kirk is friendly and egalitarian, except

214

In the sixties all three networks begin to emphasize documentaries. *David Brinkley's Journal* appears on NBC in 1961. Newsman Brinkley will take the cameras around the world for two years on this Emmy-winning public affairs show.

In 1961, ABC concludes its acclaimed twenty-six-episode documentary series *Winston Churchill: The Valiant Years.* Gary Merrill narrates, and Richard Burton reads from Churchill's writings. Richard Rodgers will win an Emmy for his original score. In 1952, he composed the rousing music for another documentary series, *Victory at Sea.*

Captain Kirk contributing to universal peace.

bring their superior technology to bear on the side of the leaders of the opposition, thus overthrowing tyranny. Once the planet is safely in the hands of the forces of liberation, our heroes wend their way back to the *Enterprise,* having served as "advisers" in the cause of human rights.

Star Trek had its heyday (1966–1969) before the full impact of the women's movement was felt, which may account for its not having stronger female characters. For its time, the show wasn't actually very bad. There were several intelligent women in the series—usually scientists or "alien" leaders who were not treated in tongue-in-cheek fashion. But sometimes even *Star Trek* sinned, and the show managed to have its share of stereotyped intergalactic sexpots. It would seem from many passing remarks that on the liberated earth, the nuclear family and marriage remained intact.

In the tumultuous 1960's, before the comparative outrages of *All in the Family, Saturday Night,* and *Mary Hartman, Mary Hartman* hit the TV screens, *Star Trek,* with its repudiation of cold war ideology, its espousal of the theory of evolution, its antiracism, and its flirtation with socialist ideas, was the closest thing to a progressive program to be seen on network television. If it basically left the ideals of God, Family and Leadership unquestioned, it offered, at its best, a vision of an egalitarian and humanist world and did so with wit, style, and imagination. Escapist fantasy has always expressed, in its way, a utopian vision, and much science fiction has now become fact, for better or worse. *Star Trek* expresses the aspirations of a liberalism that still believes that peaceful change within the system is possible, but that there will always be more worlds to conquer.

Ruth McCormick writes about film and the media for various publications.

in a crisis where he must assume command; the second officer is an alien; the fourth officer is a black woman. Multiracial and ethnic peace on earth is a basic assumption; the battleground is elsewhere.

The Other is now identified as outside our world and our federation, and the Klingons themselves are often portrayed, like movie Nazis, as slightly ridiculous and highly vulnerable to our superior rationality. The Bad is also represented by underdevelopment; planets still controlled by superstition and authoritarian elites, where effete intellectuals live in a cloud world while the workers—dehumanized mutants—grub around in the lower world. Or some variation of German Fascists, Roman emperors, or Chicago mobsters dominate and terrorize subservient populations. In such cases, the *Enterprise*'s heroes do not force change through colonization, but merely

215

Major live-news events receive maximum coverage by the networks. Television is there for all the early space launchings, including Alan Shephard's brief flight beyond the earth's atmosphere and John Glenn's trip around the earth.

John Kennedy is the first President to permit live TV coverage of his news conferences. Despite such new television offerings, Kennedy's chairman of the FCC, Newton Minow, tells the National Association of Broadcasters that they have created "a vast wasteland."

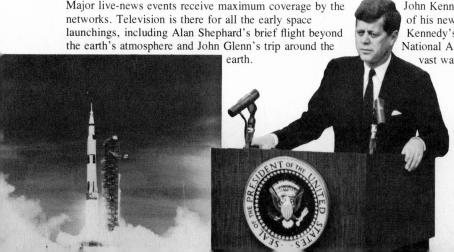

Jackie Gleason changes his style in 1961, when he hosts a prime time game show, *You're In the Picture.* It will be Gleason's first television failure, and will go off CBS after only a few weeks.

THE TALK SHOW HABIT
CHARLES SALZBERG

Back when television was in its "dark ages," someone came up with the bright idea of packaging conversation, and calling it a talk show. After all, people had long entertained themselves with snappy patter, so why not air conversation in the very place where it was supposed to be taking place—the family living room? The idea was to anoint a host and get a bunch of celebrities together, all of whom would then invite themselves into people's homes for a couple of hours of light conversation. It couldn't miss, because as one astute wag wryly observed, "Everybody has two businesses—his own and show business."

Of course the formula proved to be a great success, but there has been some unexpected fallout. Ironically, the talk show has contributed greatly to the decline of the art of conversation, and has substituted instead an electronic hodgepodge of gossip and meaningless gibberish, punctuated by an occasional song and dance. Now, instead of engaging in their own brand of conversation, calling for a certain amount of articulation and imagination, people let Johnny or Merv do it for them. Like voyeurs, they eavesdrop as these consummate hosts exchange inanities with a coterie of show biz folk who seem to be on a never-ending carrousel ride from one show to the next. Michael Arlen, of *The New Yorker,* characterizes them as "an endless parade of celebs and semi-celebs, prattling away about their agents, or Mexican vacations, or new bookings—sometimes joined by, say, a glamorous heart surgeon who has written a new book, and who in a matter of moments is grinning inanely and talking about his Mexican vacation like the rest."

"... the talk show has contributed greatly to the decline of the art of conversation."

Which is the way it is supposed to be, for what the viewer has come to cherish is the rhythm of conversation more than the actual substance of what is being said. As long as the host and his guests keep talking, people are happy. They can sit in the comfort of their homes doing none of the "work," and providing none of the heat of true conversation. They are passive observers who retain only the illusion of being active participants. The medium is cool, and the viewing is easy.

The inexpensive and immensely popular talk show has given rise to a new American folk hero—the talk show host. The first of this breed was the multi-talented Steve Allen, whose show was more akin to the controlled hysteria of a three-ring circus than to what we've come to know as the present talk show. Allen, who possessed dazzling talents as a songwriter, musician, comic actor and all-around madman, also introduced the public to such splendid comedians as Louis Nye, Don Knotts, Gabe Dell, Tom Poston, Dayton Allen, Gypsy Boots, and Professor Irwin Sumner Miller, whose instructive physics experiments provided an excellent target for Allen's humor. The show was a hybrid of talk, skits, music, and general zaniness that reflected the host's tastes.

216

Tony Young plays Cord, a U.S. agent posing as a gunfighter, in *Gunslinger.* This CBS western will disappear after several months.

March 20, 1961. Ingrid Bergman stars with Rip Torn in CBS's lush special "Twenty-Four Hours in a Woman's Life." Bergman had made her American television debut in 1959 in Henry James's chiller "The Turn of the Screw," for which she won an Emmy.

February 13, 1961. Julie Harris is Catherine Sloper in the live presentation of "The Heiress," adapted from Henry James's novel *Washington Square,* on *Family Classics.*

Jack Paar and Dave Garroway, tired of talking.

Leonard (who once wrote TV criticism under the name "Cyclops" for *Life* magazine), Carson became a "legitimizing agency, taking up where Ed Sullivan left off, defining the permissible in humor and music, conferring status." At the same time, the show became more of a stage for Carson than for his guests. The host was the message. People always knew exactly what to expect with Johnny. His show fell into a comforting, never-changing pattern: first came the monologue, then a few jokes with the hired help, and finally the guests trooped in for fifteen minute segments each. When a guest's time was up he was exiled from the chair to the couch, and each time a new fifteen minute segment began, he'd move farther away from Carson, out of the limelight. Everything was handled smoothly and Carson was the master of it all.

The success of his show and others like it brought a flurry of activity in television land. The powers that be decided that talk could sell during the day, too. For all those homebound souls bored with game shows and soap operas, TV produced people like Mike Douglas, whose style could best be described as apple-pie bland, and then women like Virginia Graham and Dinah Shore. These shows in turn spawned a rash of local talk shows, and now almost every city or locality has its own Johnny Carson. The big difference between these shows and their late night network models is that, if possible, the daytime talk is even lighter and less offensive. But talk it is, and it makes the daytime viewer feel that he or she has company during those long hours between breakfast and dinner.

In 1969, after failing in the talk show sweepstakes with the excessively ingratiating Joey Bishop, ABC came up with Dick Cavett, a literate, witty, urbane fellow who had gotten his TV start on the Carson show, first as a writer, then a performer.

Cavett got his shot at the "big league" after

In his day, Jack Paar was a household name. He wore his heart on his sleeve and told personal stories about himself, his wife, and his daughter—thus making them a kind of extended family for the viewer. Late each night millions of people tuned in to see whom Paar would rail against next, his targets ranging from Dorothy Kilgallen to Walter Winchell. Paar walked a tightrope and, like him or not, people watched if only to see whether he could keep from toppling off. Paar was still at the top of the heap when he abdicated in 1962.

Johnny Carson, the self-proclaimed "king" of late night TV, marked a distinct change of style. He was cool, detached, ironic, and showed very little of himself other than a quick, sharp wit. To John

217

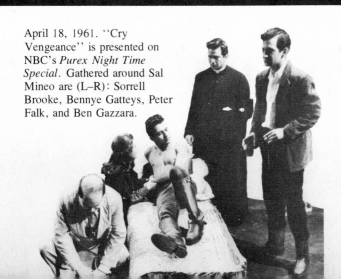

April 18, 1961. "Cry Vengeance" is presented on NBC's *Purex Night Time Special*. Gathered around Sal Mineo are (L–R): Sorrell Brooke, Bennye Gatteys, Peter Falk, and Ben Gazzara.

April 29, 1961. ". . . the thrill of victory, the agony of defeat." Former CBS sportscaster Jim McKay is on ABC's sports team for the premiere of *ABC's Wide World of Sports*. Everything that can possibly be called a sports event will be shown live, on tape or on film during the Saturday afternoon extravaganzas. Producer Roone Arledge's concept will become so popular in the seventies that it will expand to Sundays as well.

Talk show host Mike Douglas, smiling "no matter what."

Cavett was a TV schizo. He wanted things both ways. He hankered to entertain but also to inform, and at times, sitting beside so many of his own heroes, he became more a fan than a host. Yet, he also presented audiences with something they couldn't get from the usual TV talk show—a sense of spontaneity and topicality. One night he had introduced Gore Vidal and Janet Flanner, when in walked his next guest, Norman Mailer, angry at something Vidal had written about his work. Mailer proceeded to attack Vidal, igniting a verbal free-for-all that provided viewers with an unexpected moment of heated drama.

But TV viewers have proved over and over again that they don't want the unexpected, and ultimately Cavett failed. Viewers prefer good old predictable Johnny, or Merv, or Mike, and all the other interchangeable hosts. Recently Mort Sahl, a satirist-comedian and a veteran of many talk shows, told this story: On the air one night Mike Douglas asked him why he hadn't appeared on as many talk shows of late as he had in the past? Sahl answered that he was tired of them. Every one was the same. The host was always bland and had a glazed look in his eyes to go with a perpetual, painted-on smile. The host always asked the same inane questions without ever listening to the answers, and introduced totally different subjects after each commercial. Suddenly, as Sahl was in the midst of his tirade, he realized that he was describing the very host he was addressing. But Douglas, completely unaware, noticed nothing. They cut to a commercial. When the show resumed, Mike was still smiling as he brought on his next guest.

Nevertheless, Sahl continues to appear on talk shows and we continue to watch them. After all, we have to get our conversation somewhere.

warming up in the bullpen of daytime talk show television. But at night, Cavett gave his audience something they didn't expect. Once, when asked who his ideal male guest might be, he replied, "A combination of John Wayne and Oscar Wilde—a man who could kill Apaches with epigrams." And this is just what Cavett tried to provide. Rather than serving up a Zsa Zsa Gabor spinning warmed-over stories about her seventeenth husband, Cavett presented people like think-tanker Herman Kahn, philosopher Paul Weiss, and artist Salvador Dali, as well as big box-office stars. Sometimes Cavett's guests even stayed for longer than fifteen minutes.

Charles Salzberg is a writer who likes to eavesdrop.

218

The Bob Newhart Show, starring the young stand-up comic in a variety format, debuts on NBC. Although it will win the Emmy as the Best Comedy of the 1961–62 season, it will not be renewed for a second year.

The Ernie Kovacs Show debuts on ABC in 1961. Here director Kovacs and his associate director Ken Herman (L) rehearse with "ballerina" Muriel Landers.

REMEMBERING "THE TONIGHT SHOW"

JOHN BUSKIN

I used to tend bar at an establishment that had a beautiful twenty-six-inch color TV. The TV was always on but so was the jukebox so no one got to hear too much of either. Sports took precedence over all other viewing which was okay because you didn't have to hear commentary to follow the action. Cartoons were always a big favorite. As a matter of fact it was a wine drinking stonemason who explained Popeye's girl friend to me. I had remarked to him early one evening that I didn't understand what Popeye and his rival Bluto saw in the skinny Olive Oyl. The stonemason winked at me and said, "The closer the bone, the sweeter the meat."

The most consistently popular program was *The Tonight Show* with Johnny Carson. I never realized the power of the show until I was exposed to the regulars who watched it every night without the sound. (By the time Johnny came on, jukebox revelers had usually taken over and TV noise was totally obliterated.) The regulars were the five guys on the late shift at the corner Sinclair station, a couple of house painters and an aluminum siding salesman named Shorty. There was also a woman named Red who sometimes brought her cousin.

These regulars were a stern panel of judges; a kind of *Gong Show* in reverse. They judged Johnny's guests on poise, visual appeal, wardrobe, and whether or not they were heterosexual. The comments were generally predictable. If the guest were Rock Hudson,

Burt Reynolds or Rossano Brazzi, Red would say, "He can put his shoes under my bed anytime." If Johnny had either Fernando Lamas or Ricardo Montalban on, he would be referred to as "that coffee bean." Leslie Uggams, Mitzi Gaynor, and Charo always drew finger snapping and hooting. Paul Williams elicited snickering and words like, "would you take a look at that guy." My favorites were always the stand-up comics. If a comedian can make you laugh when you can't hear his jokes he's very good.

Johnny himself was charming with or without sound, a universally likable presence. One snowbound winter's night there were only about three people in the bar. A man walked in and ordered a beer. He had a southern accent. He turned out to be a truck driver from Texas on his way to Vermont. (The bar was in upstate New York.) I gave him a beer and we both turned toward the television. Joey Bishop was sitting in Johnny's chair talking to Ed MacMahon. The man turned back to me and in his Texas drawl said, "Johnny must be sick tonight."

"Maybe he's on vacation," I answered. "He goes on vacation a lot." I realized that this man from Texas and I had a mutual friend. Everyone across the country was on a first name basis with Johnny Carson and worried about his health as well. I was amazed. We agreed that though Joey was all right, he couldn't hold a candle to Johnny. (I've since realized that statements to that effect have become ritual accolades

219

Jolene Brand is a regular on *The Ernie Kovacs Show*. Her most famous bit on the show is playing "the girl in the bathtub."

In 1961, Durwood Kirby joins Allen Funt as cohost of *Candid Camera*, CBS's popular Sunday night snoopfest. Kirby, who replaces Arthur Godfrey, will remain with the show until 1966 when he will be replaced, in turn, by Bess Myerson for the show's final season.

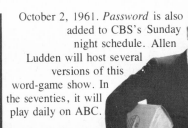

October 2, 1961. *Password* is also added to CBS's Sunday night schedule. Allen Ludden will host several versions of this word-game show. In the seventies, it will play daily on ABC.

Johnny Carson cracks up the monumental Orson Welles on The Tonight Show *in 1976.*

spoken by guests to Johnny himself.) The truck driver went on his way saying, ''I hope he's back tomorrow.''

Some time later when I was in the army I found myself in the Greensboro, North Carolina, airport one night at about midnight. I had an hour to kill before making a connection to Columbus, Georgia. Viet Nam was going on and I was in the infantry. The waiting room was a limbo of sorts, like a highway rest stop. There was a row of five or six chairs that had televisions attached to them. I sat in the chair on the end, plunked a quarter into the slot and on came Johnny. For that hour I was alone in that small southern airport waiting room watching *The Tonight Show.* I thought about my truck driver friend of one night and wondered if he were watching too somewhere.

It wasn't that the show was so good, it was just that it was so familiar. It was a show you watched at the end of the day when it was too late to worry about anything. Well, it wasn't the end of the day for me and I had plenty to worry about. It didn't matter. As I watched the show, with the same aging nymphet plugging her latest dramatic opus and the same author in his good suit making an impassioned plea for the vanishing foxbat, I began to cry. It was so familiar I felt like I was home. As my plane took off, I saw lights going out in peaceful looking suburban houses. I knew Johnny had just said good-night.

Since reaching his majority, John Buskin has enjoyed watching television in bars; he especially likes sports, which he thinks can't be beat.

220

The show with the most unusual title in TV history is *The Case of the Dangerous Robin.* This syndicated series stars Rick Jason (L) and Jean Blake as insurance investigators. Under their scrutiny in this episode is Royal Dano.

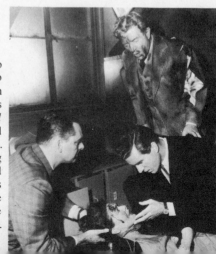

Guest Shirley Ballard tries to tell star Mark Richman who is responsible for an explosion on NBC's powerful *Cain's Hundred* series. Harlan Ward and Frank McHugh look on. Although Cain vows to bring America's top one hundred criminals to trial, the show's cancellation after only one year makes this impossible to accomplish.

DAVID BRENNER'S STAR RISES
ELEANOR LERMAN

It's eleven o'clock on a rainy weekday evening in New York. At Catch a Rising Star, the preeminent showcase club in the city and probably the entire country, David Brenner, a popular comedian well known for his frequent appearances and guest-host stints on *The Tonight Show,* is onstage, beguiling the audience. His unbilled appearance is a surprise treat for the customers so the management is only too happy to let him stay onstage as long as he likes, and stay onstage he will, although tonight he's not doing his act because he's a talented comedian who enjoys his work, but because he's a smart man who knows that talent is only part of the reason for his continued success.

Showcase clubs such as Catch a Rising Star and the Improvisation in New York, and the Comedy Store in Los Angeles, are both popular and profitable. The original intent of such places was to give newcomers to show business, particularly singers and comedians who are the perennial cabaret performers, a place to play to live audiences while honing their skills. The audience pays plenty, in cover charges and liquor bills, to see performers who are rarely paid anything, but the mutual rewards seem satisfactory: the audience usually enjoys an entertaining show and sometimes gets a first glimpse of a performer who may turn out to be a genuine star, while the performers, good or bad, at least get in a lot of practice.

But there is another category of performers who make use of showcase clubs: these are established comedians—like David Brenner—whose main livelihood is television and who use club audiences all over the country as sounding boards for the material they

will do on TV. David Brenner is a master at readying comedy routines in this fashion, so when he seeks out a live audience at a showcase club, it's only because he's preparing himself for the next guest shot on Merv, the next co-hosting stint with Mike, or the next guest-hosting job for Johnny. David Brenner knows full well that his star has risen because of television, and he's always practicing to keep it as high above his contemporaries as he can.

This night, when Brenner finally finishes his set and departs the stage, he leaves behind the boyish, enthusiastic charmer that is his performing personality, because for the rest of the night, and well into the morning, the disciplined and practical David Brenner will devote himself strictly to the exacting business of putting together the kind of short, powerful comedy routine that an upcoming guest-host spot on *The Tonight Show* demands. To extract the best lines for television from a live performance of well over an hour, Brenner depends on the tape recorder with which he tapes almost every live performance he gives: it is the only professional companion or critic he needs to tell him how funny he is.

At home, relaxing with a diet soda, Brenner listens to the tape, making note of ad libs that seem

221

Robert Blake tries to get Keir Dullea to throw a game on *Cain's Hundred*.

The Dick Powell Theatre debuts on NBC in 1961. This anthology series will last two years, ending with Powell's death. Here the suavely dressed Powell confronts Edward Platt. Powell's other series, *Dick Powell's Zane Grey Theatre,* will go off CBS in 1962 after a six-year run.

Raymond Burr has still not lost a case on *Perry Mason* after four years on CBS.

David Brenner. ''There isn't a comedian who works harder or who takes the business of comedy more seriously. . . .''

promising, of good lines, medium lines, and poor lines that will be upgraded if possible, discarded if not. Brenner will go through this process of performing, taping, and editing night after night, gleaning the best lines until he has a fairly solid routine of about twenty minutes. That twenty minutes of material might be fine as the basis of a live nightclub performance, but Brenner will take it back to ''Catch'' for another week until he's got it boiled down to a near perfect seven minutes of comedy, because an average of seven minutes of his own material is what he'll get to do on *The Tonight Show,* and *The Tonight Show,* Brenner readily admits, has made his career.

As of April of 1977, Brenner had appeared on *The Tonight Show* sixty-nine times and hosted it

twenty-two times. This has led to a standing joke among comedians that even Johnny himself has been known to repeat: David Brenner, they say, has done the Carson show more times than Carson. This kind of enormous public exposure, though desired by every stand-up comic with a joke to tell, has its own peculiar perils: ''Television,'' Brenner says, ''is a monster. It eats up your material. A comic used to be able to take a twenty-five minute act around the country for ten years. Now your material has to be fresh all the time.''

One of Brenner's personal triumphs is that he did *The Tonight Show* twenty-three times without repeating a line, but even he had to give in finally and reintroduce a few familiar jokes. Still, Brenner is keenly aware of how quickly the public can get used

Robert Reed (L) and E. G. Marshall play more realistic, socially committed attorneys on Reginald Rose's *The Defenders,* which debuts on CBS in 1961. The Prestons here defending Lee Grant, will lose several cases during the next four years, while the show wins several Emmys. *The Defenders'* 1958 pilot was a two-part *Studio One* program, starring Ralph Bellamy and William Shatner.

There is a definite trend on television in 1961 to present realistic urban drama. Cops and doctors replace all but the strongest western heroes. *Ben Casey* debuts on ABC with Vince Edwards (R) playing Casey, a resident doctor, and Sam Jaffe playing his mentor. This James Moser–created series will play five years.

"... for comedians, television is 'The Tonight Show.'"

to—and bored by—the routines of a comic they constantly see on TV. To defend himself against even the possibility of this kind of rejection, Brenner makes sure that at least 50 percent of the material he presents during any television appearance is new. Keeping up this pace isn't easy: it means that even when he goes on the road to play the important rooms in Las Vegas and other prestigious nightclubs, he's still taping himself, still gathering material for those all-important guest spots on the tube.

The road, for comedians like David Brenner, is much shorter than it was in days gone by. "The old timers spent twenty years on the road," Brenner says. "We spend two." The reason this distance has been so compressed is, of course, the immediacy of television, and for comedians television is *The Tonight Show* which, on an average evening, has the power to introduce an up-and-coming comic to approximately nine million potential fans.

Not many people know the date of their own personal Judgment Day, but a new comic with a first guest shot scheduled on *The Tonight Show* surely does, because if he's well received he may be on his way to creating a lasting and financially rewarding career, but if he does poorly, he may never be heard from again. On January 8, 1971, David Brenner made his first appearance on *The Tonight Show,* and did so well that Carson walked over to him, center stage, to shake his hand. Up until that appearance, Brenner had been making a maximum of $500 per week; two days after *The Tonight Show* spot he had received $10,000 worth of offers, including one to play one of the main

rooms in Las Vegas. "But on the other hand," Brenner says, "if you bomb on *The Tonight Show*, you're going to have to wait at least a year to get back on, so you've got a year of hard times ahead of you." That's a year many shattered comedians never survive.

Brenner remembers Carson shaking his hand in congratulations with a great deal of justifiable pride because few comedians get that kind of personal recognition from the old master on their first appearance. There is a kind of unspoken code on *The Tonight Show*—new comedians have to prove their worth over a series of appearances before Johnny will formally acknowledge them. Brenner broke that rule but, even more spectacularly, so did Freddie Prinze, who was so good that Carson called him over to sit on the couch next to Sammy Davis, Jr., and tell the world a little bit about himself. "That," Brenner says, "was a shocker," because very rarely if ever, before or since, has a comedian been invited over to sit on the panel on his first *Tonight Show* appearance.

Although it took David Brenner two appearances to be asked to join the panel, it wasn't much longer before he was sitting in Carson's own personal chair, behind Carson's own personal desk, and kidding with Carson's own personal sidekick, but if, by now, he seems comfortably entrenched as America's favorite guest-host, it can hardly be attributed to luck. Night after night, in club after club, David Brenner is telling jokes, taping himself telling jokes, listening to himself telling jokes, and it's all to find those seven minutes of great material that will keep you tuned in to *The Tonight Show*—and to him. There isn't a comedian who works harder or who takes the business of comedy more seriously, and that is precisely what keeps David Brenner in the chair behind the desk on the TV.

Eleanor Lerman, who lives in New York, is a poet and a collector of comedians.

Blair General Hospital is the setting for *Dr. Kildare,* which debuts on NBC in 1961. Richard Chamberlain (L) assumes the title role Lew Ayres played in several films and Raymond Massey (R) takes over Lionel Barrymore's Dr. Gillespie part. During the show's six-year run, James Kildare will progress from intern to resident. Here Claude Rains guest stars.

Some adult westerns continue to thrive. *Gunsmoke,* with Dennis Weaver (L), Amanda Blake, and Milburn Stone as James Arness's co-stars, is still TV's top-rated program for much of 1961.

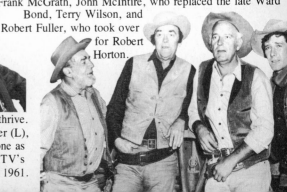

Wagon Train replaces *Gunsmoke* as TV's most watched program in the 1961–62 season. In September 1962, it will switch from NBC to ABC. It will complete its eight-year TV stretch in 1965 as a ninety-minute program. Starring are (L–R): Frank McGrath, John McIntire, who replaced the late Ward Bond, Terry Wilson, and Robert Fuller, who took over for Robert Horton.

REMEMBERING "THE DICK CAVETT SHOW"

EILEEN McGUIRE

I always wanted to be a guest on *The Dick Cavett Show*. What sort of career would propel me into sufficient celebrity was unclear. But my guest appearance was imagined in great detail:

Dick would be having one of those nights when he rebelled against his J. Press wardrobe and turned up in jeans, work shirt, and John Lennon cap. His hair would be just-washed and cowlicky (it was never the same from one night to the next) and he would make a self-conscious joke about it. As a newcomer I would probably be allotted a ten- or fifteen-minute segment in the first half hour. We would discuss my novel/film/play/achievement with displays of great wit on both sides. Perhaps Truman Capote would come on later to discuss his brush with death on the highway near Palm Springs. We would get along famously.

Dick's guests were all the right people, the people I wanted to know. When the network periodically threatened to cancel his show, we, his fans, would defend him hotly. Dick deserved to be on television; in a profession rife with quarter-wits, he had a mind and a conscience. He was "one of us."

In retrospect I think that what Cavett's following really yearned for was not the guest spot, but the job itself. Cover stories in *Time* and *Life* showed a fascination with the details of Dick's daily routine, his preparation and interview techniques. "It's Not as Easy as It Looks" was *Life*'s headline, and *Time* set up a mock *Cavett Show* during which the reporter played

"Dick deserved to be on television . . . ."

host and Dick played guest. And who wouldn't want the chance to chat with the likes of Marlon Brando, Janis Joplin, Fred Astaire, and Katharine Hepburn—the chance for a little fame-by-association?

Dick would be the first to understand. "Television," he told an interviewer, "used to be the biggest, most wonderful, most glamorous thing I could imagine; . . . and I thought, 'If I ever become famous, I'll talk to everybody who wants to talk to me; I'll be nice to people; I'll drop in at little houses on side streets where they don't expect me and dazzle and thrill them; and that'll be the fun of being famous.' "

The fun of being famous, vicariously, was what kept us up all those nights. The fun of being there the night Lester Maddox walked off stage in a racist huff, or Lily Tomlin walked off in a feminist huff; when Barbara Hershey Seagull breast-fed her son on the air, or Norman Mailer and Gore Vidal fed on each other.

Life has been a little ordinary since Dick disappeared.

Eileen McGuire used to dream that Dick Cavett was her English teacher.

224

Because of James Garner's contract dispute with Warner Brothers, Roger Moore joins *Maverick* as the brothers' British cousin Beau. In 1962, Warner Brothers will further attempt to make the audience forget the departed Garner by adding Robert Colbert to the cast as another brother, Brent, who wears Bret's garb. The ploy will not work, and *Maverick* will go off shortly after.

October 3, 1961. *The Dick Van Dyke Show* debuts on CBS. This fresh adult comedy conceived by Carl Reiner will be both an Emmy winner and a top-rated show for five years. Starring are (L–R): Mary Tyler Moore, Morey Amsterdam, Dick Van Dyke, and Rose Marie.

Dick Cavett was always being embarrassed by his guests' jokes. Here Flip Wilson makes Dick blush and duck.

The Lucy Show debuts on CBS. It will last seven years, during which time it will reaffirm Lucille Ball's position as queen of television. Ball's co-stars are Gale Gordon and Vivian Vance (not seen), who will leave the comedy in 1965.

Shirley Booth, who won an Oscar in 1952 for her strong dramatic portrayal in *Come Back Little Sheba,* will win Emmys playing the meddlesome maid *Hazel.* This new comedy series will play from 1961 to 1965 on NBC before moving to CBS for its final season.

The Marquis Chimps, Enoch, Charlie, and Candy, are featured in *The Hathaways,* which debuts in 1961 on ABC. Also starring Jack Weston and Peggy Cass, this comedy series will play for a year.

CONFESSIONS OF A TALK SHOW HOST
LARRY ANGELO

I have always wanted to be on television—especially on a talk show. To have a chance to be with the big shots, to use the dumb, corny lines I torture my friends with, and to meet a few girls.

Well, I got that chance.

Not long ago, I had a lot of free time. I was a part-time actor and temporary comedian living in New York City and browsing through the want ads when I found the following:

Can you see yourself as a talk show host?
Neither Can We!

I figured I had all the important qualifications—a sense of insecurity, underlying hostility, and an insatiable need for love—so I decided to give it a shot. I wrote and told them about myself, how I thought doing a TV show would be good therapy for me, and might give me a chance to straighten myself out on the air because I couldn't afford analysis.

They liked the idea. They said, "You sound just like our audience—alienated, bored, shiftless, and unemployed. We love you already!"

The initial interview was in New York. I had prepared a little opening speech, but before I could even say hello, a man with a weird squint from watching five TV sets at once shouted, "How would you do the show?"

I stayed calm. "Well, I'd like a warm homey set so the guests would be comfortable, maybe have some coffee for them because it's in the morning and—"

"Yes, but how would you do the show?!" the Squinting Man insisted.

Drunk? In the nude? I tried a couple of different suggestions until the squint became a huge crease running from ear to ear. Finally the man leaned back in his chair, pulled a little bottle out of his pocket, and quietly put drops in his eyes. Eleven in each.

"Thank you," said his assistant. As I went out I heard her say, "He's good."

"Yes," agreed the squinting man, "but how would he do the show?"

Well, I was sore. What kind of interview was that? *Beat the Clock?* I mailed a protest letter to them condemning their "cold insensitivity which is characteristic of ruthless commercial television."

An hour later I got a call from them. They said I was warm and intelligent, not to mention attractive, and would I tape an interview for them?

A few days later, I did. I wasn't nervous at all. What did I have to worry about? I knew I didn't have the slightest chance of getting the job. In TV you have to be cunning, quick-witted, well-groomed, and cool. Everybody knows that. Their reaction? "This guy's terrific! He's cute, he's sloppy, he doesn't know what the hell he's saying! Sign him up!"

I got the job.

The preparations began as soon as I arrived at the station. I got a crash course in the fine art of interview-

226

Several made-for-TV cartoons debut in 1961. *Top Cat* appears on ABC where it will play one year. Arnold Stang supplies the voice of T. C., a character based on Sergeant Bilko. Maurice Gosfield of *You'll Never Get Rich* does the voice of "Benny the Ball."

Calvin and the Colonel is a 1961 cartoon series voiced and created by Freeman Gosden and Charles Correll. It is based on their *Amos 'n' Andy* Show.

A very unusual cartoon series that debuts in 1961 is *The Beany and Cecil Show.* Using puns and topical references, the wild adventures of a boy and his daffy sea serpent are enjoyed as much by adults and kids. This Bob Clampett series is a spin-off from his old daily puppet series *A Time for Beany* (1949–54), which won several Emmys and listed among its devotees John Barrymore and Albert Einstein.

Angelo practices his kick with gymnast Judy Wolfe.

Inquisitor. We'd sit with a tape recorder and he would play roles:

"Okay. I'm a hundred-year-old-man. Go!"

"Okay. Now I'm Liberace. Go!"

And so forth. After a few hours, an interesting thing happens—you lose the power of speech. Then D-Day arrived. I was ready. I had my new suit, my new hairdo, my new identity, and my instructions. "Be yourself. Stay away from controversy. Don't interrupt. Keep it moving. Smile. Don't squirm in your seat, keep your tie on straight, and enjoy yourself."

Amazingly, I didn't lose my power of speech on the air. I mislaid it now and then, mind you, but I never lost it. It was a strange show. I did calesthenics with a city official. I bounced a Playboy Bunny in my lap. And I interviewed a monkey.

This is show business? I asked myself as I wrung the perspiration out of my suit.

The critics hated me. I was crushed, I was mortified. They called me "Another nice guy!" But what was worse, I was popular! I had started in the last weeks of a rating period, and the ratings went up. Were people that sadistic? Or were they curious? I decided that people were watching for the same reason you stop at the scene of an accident—to see something really horrible for a change!

Still, doing a talk show you have to be positive, optimistic. At least I do. I read an article that stated that most women commit suicide at 10:00 A.M.—the time my show goes off the air. Imagine being the last straw! Who wants negative stuff anyway? My defenses are down in the morning. Anybody can be witty, incisive, and authoritative at a party after a few drinks. But in the morning, the natural thing is to want to sit quietly, with some good coffee, and speak softly to a sympathetic fellow creature. But probe? Expose? Charm? With the dew still lingering in the bushes? So it's true, I tend to be nice to my guests.

ing. There I was, doing mock interviews, surrounded by an army of two station executives who shouted encouragement:

"Don't stop talking!"

"Ask him something!"

"Why are you stammering?"

"Ask him something!"

"Don't pause!"

"Stop rushing—why is he rushing?!!"

Then I'd have private sessions with the Grand

227

October 22, 1961. "The Twist" is an enormous dance craze in 1961 and Chubby Checker, its champion, appears on many TV shows to show how it is done. Here he dances and sings his million-selling record "The Twist" on *The Ed Sullivan Show*.

November 30, 1961. Julie Harris has the title role in "Victoria Regina" on *Hallmark Hall of Fame*. Harris will win an Emmy for her performance and the presentation will be designated "The Program of the Year." George Schaefer is the director.

It's harder to be "nice" off the air. You're really put to the test when you're recognized on the street. Talk show hosts are a new minority group. People love to tell you how much they hate talk shows. "Hey! Aren't you . . . how are you? Boy, I'm so glad that bum Frost is off. Well, you know, these talk shows are dying."

Now what do you say to that? "Yeah, well I hope you'll keep watching." It's usually easier to talk to my guests.

Though not always. Take for instance the break, that magic time when the audience is away for a commercial. I used to think that the best part of any talk show was never seen because the host and guest always seemed to be secretly laughing about something after the commercial. Even now *I* seem to be secretly laughing about something after the commercial. But most of the time, very little is said until the show resumes, when the cardinal rule is simply, "Keep it moving!" If you can't get any voltage out of the interview, the least you can do is don't stop. So there's rarely even a *hmmm* in the conversation. There's no time for one.

Or maybe there is, if you're a secure person. I'm not. One lull and I begin to perspire. Sweatiest damn host around. I thought this would be good analysis for me, and it is.

I've learned a lot about myself on television. For instance, I never realized how sincere I am. Profoundly sincere. I'm attentive to everybody. Dummies I can take. Inane celebrities I can take. But you know what really bugs me? Authors who won't talk about their books on the air. I hate it when the answer to every question is, "Ah yes! I deal with that problem in Chapter Four." I beg, I plead, but from some authors, the answers are always in Chapter Four!

Most authors, however, are good guests. If they've written a good book and you've read it, they love you. You've shown your good taste! If they've written a bad book and you've read it, they're amazed! I read them all—about six books a week. But my respect and feeling for literature is shot to hell. My producer has encouraged me to do terrible things to save time, so now I cut, slash and mark books, but rarely do I digest them.

And now I think of authors only as guests, which is depressing. I only want to read living authors. Shakespeare? Who cares! He's dead! He won't appear on our show so the hell with him!

Finally, my integrity is disintegrating. I always told myself that if I ever got into TV, I'd do everything in my power to get rid of all those awful old movies that were originally awful new movies. Stations love them because they can buy two thousand hours of such film art for $19.99. Well, now I close the show with the introduction to the morning movie. I've got no choice. It comes on next.

Also, now I look at the nighttime talk shows differently. They all seem to operate on the idea that *something will be coming up*. The chesty starlet may be boring you to death now, but an eminent psychiatrist will be on in a little while to tell you how you can become a creative genius! Meanwhile you watch, and nothing happens. You reach the point when the chitchat becomes mind boggling, and you feel yourself becoming psychotic. *Dear God, I'd like to kill them with their stupid anecdotes! If I can just hold on!*

So that's it. I've become a member of the ridiculously tiny community of TV people. I still say it's good analysis. And it's great preparation for my true calling. Someday, I'll make a terrific guest!

Larry Angelo, formerly the host of Angelo Live *at WJZ-TV Baltimore, is now the host of* Evening Magazine *which originates from KYW-TV in Philadelphia.*

In 1961, with CBS's James Aubrey — programming chief since 1959 — emphasizing situation comedies, *Playhouse 90,* the most prestigious program on the network, is canceled. During its six years on CBS, it showcased some of the finest productions and performances ever seen on television. Sterling Hayden made an appearance in "A Sound of Different Drummers" on *Playhouse 90* in 1957.

In 1962, *The Adventures of Ozzie and Harriet* celebrates its tenth anniversary on ABC. This underplayed situation comedy stars the real-life Nelson family: David; former singer Harriet Hilliard; Ozzie, a former bandleader and all-American quarterback; and Ricky, who has become a rock music idol. It will continue until 1966.

FAN FARE:
DEAR "SATURDAY NIGHT LIVE":

See, it isn't that I don't have anything better to do on Saturday evenings or anything. It's that you are sometimes very funny.

Why else would I be laughing out loud to an empty room in the middle of the night when I could be feeling sorry for myself, getting a head start on the Sunday *Times,* or resting up for a dawnlight jog?

I ask you. Was Don Pardo so amusing on *Jeopardy?* Not that I remember. Does Candice Bergen look as lovely in the Polaroid commercials as she does when she is the guest host? Not in my opinion. Can Cronkite do the job of "weekend update"? Never.

Something is going on over there in Studio 8H at "30 Rock," NBC headquarters, live from New York. You are writing well and acting well and playing good music and being stupid and scathing and very funny indeed. After all, it was you who thought up Baba Wawa, and that was used so much it's almost a tired joke by now. One thing is, you've got a great cast. John Belushi is a funny actor. (I especially liked Samurai Big Man on Campus.) Garrett Morris and Dan Aykroyd are funny too. (Remember your sketch about the Natural Causes Health Food Restaurant?) Sometimes I get the feeling Dan Aykroyd is the head of it all, sort of the father or some such to the not-ready-for-prime-time players, the person who has taken up the mantle Chevy laid down. But I don't want to start any trouble.

That is especially because I am personally in love with Bill Murray, the new one who keeps forgetting his lines, but who cares? When he plays a singing tour director or master of ceremonies, or when he takes a

Buck Henry and Chevy Chase on the loneliest night of the week.

shower and uses his soap as a microphone, I am his.

Not that it's just your men who are funny. Gilda Radner sure is. And Jane Curtin, who can be a priss or a bimbo. And Laraine Newman with that voice!

Mostly I would like to say hello to your writers, though. Once Michael O'Donoghue told me on the telephone—he probably doesn't remember this, but I wrote it down—that he is "America's leading foremost humor writer." I took it on faith.

I think you're a funny show, and I hope you can continue to come up with material for at least another season. That way you will all have had the chance to waste several years of your lives and grow old before your time. (Lorne Michaels, your producer said that—I read it someplace.) Don't split up too soon. Look at Martin and Lewis.

Jennifer Carden

Jennifer Carden watches TV in the dead of night.

229

Peggy McCay and Andrew Duggan head a made-for-TV family in *Room for One More.* This series, based on a Cary Grant movie about a real-life couple who keeps adopting kids, will only play for a few months on ABC.

In 1962, the popular NBC morning game show *Concentration* moves into the fourth year of its fifteen-year run. In addition to his duties here, host Hugh Downs replaces John Chancellor in 1962 as host of *The Today Show.* He will continue in that position until 1971.

In 1962, Barbara Walters of *The Today Show* reports on Jacqueline Kennedy's goodwill tour of India. It is Walters's first major on-the-air assignment.

REMEMBERING "THE ACADEMY AWARDS"

SUZANNE WEAVER

This is the truth: Dracula rises once a year, resurrected in the form of the Academy Awards program, a show long dead and dry as dust. It is a corpse that drains my blood and transforms me into a zombie.

We have a strange relationship, me and that show. I am, according to friends, an embarrassment on the subject. I leave the entire late winter and early spring open until I know which night the AAs will be televised. I wait anxiously for the big night in constant fear that it will somehow sneak by and I'll miss it.

While waiting, no moss grows on me. I'm out there rolling: I wait in long lines to see all the movies, pay lots of money to see all the movies, spend lots of time seeing all the movies. I am convinced that no academy member sees any of the movies.

I make notes on all the nominated performances using my own system: Could I have played that part as well or even better? Do I deserve the award more than the professional? This tells me plenty.

I listen carefully to background music and theme songs, because when these tunes are played on the AAs, they will be unrecognizable.

Comes the night and I sit transfixed, the vampire's fangs embedded firmly in my eyeballs, my mind blank—an obvious reflection of the program's content. There are no highs, no lows, no original ideas, no entertainment. I don't move.

Two and a half hours later I am released, and for a brief moment my brain is wracked by a series of

> "Dracula rises once a year, resurrected in the form of the Academy Awards . . . ."

distressing questions:

How come all those alleged talents, who memorize thousands of lines in order to entertain us, suddenly can't be trusted to remember the names of five nominated candidates (more or less) without the help of prompters and eyeglasses which magically appear from outfits that can't possibly conceal them?

What would happen if someone who got seated in the fifteenth balcony won an award?

If a presenter read off the wrong winning name, would that person have to be given an award, or is that too capricious even for a show that excels in capricious decisions?

Do the winners ever feel guilty about boring the viewers with long discourses on who they couldn't have done it without? Do they ever think afterwards, "I don't believe I ran down the whole list"?

How come the Oscar statuettes resemble bowling trophies, and do you think everyone on the Oscar factory assembly line owns at least one?

Why are the film segments shown always the

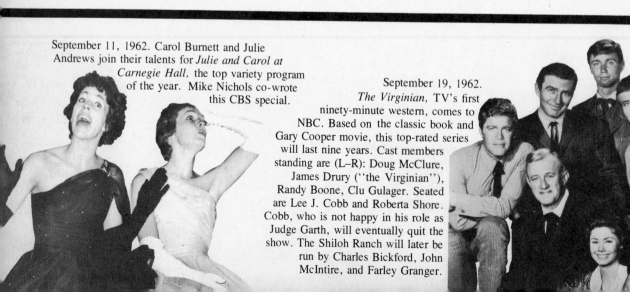

September 11, 1962. Carol Burnett and Julie Andrews join their talents for *Julie and Carol at Carnegie Hall*, the top variety program of the year. Mike Nichols co-wrote this CBS special.

September 19, 1962. *The Virginian*, TV's first ninety-minute western, comes to NBC. Based on the classic book and Gary Cooper movie, this top-rated series will last nine years. Cast members standing are (L–R): Doug McClure, James Drury ("the Virginian"), Randy Boone, Clu Gulager. Seated are Lee J. Cobb and Roberta Shore. Cobb, who is not happy in his role as Judge Garth, will eventually quit the show. The Shiloh Ranch will later be run by Charles Bickford, John McIntire, and Farley Granger.

At the Bicentennial Academy Awards ceremony in 1976, Elizabeth Taylor led us all in the singing of "America the Beautiful."

most uninteresting two minutes in the entire movie and, when out of context, make no sense?

What is the point of the opening number, and is it an honor to be asked to perform it?

What's the rate of no-shows, and are the people who accept awards for unable-to-attend-winners hired from a special service? Might I have a future as a professional acceptee?

These questions, the same one's each year, settle unpleasantly on the otherwise discriminating good-taste area of my brain. Dracula sleeps once again, satiated and safe, until we begin the cycle again next year.

Suzanne Weaver is an editor who thought Sylvester Stallone deserved to win best actor in 1977.

231

Charles Bronson and Ryan O'Neal work on the Garrett Ranch as regulars on *Empire,* a modern-day western on NBC in 1962. It will last one season, but in 1964 star Richard Egan will revive his Jim Redigo character for several months in ABC's spin-off series *Redigo.*

Walter Cronkite replaces Douglas Edwards on CBS's *Evening News* in 1962.

September 12, 1962. *The Beverly Hillbillies* debuts on CBS. Although critics attack this silly show about a backwoods family discovering oil and moving to Hollywood, it immediately becomes the number one-rated program in America, the first comedy since *I Love Lucy* to hold that position. Starring are (L–R): Buddy Ebsen (Jed Clampett), Max Baer, Jr. (cousin Jethro Bodine), Donna Douglas (daughter Elly May), and Irene Ryan (Granny).

REMEMBERING "ROOTS"

ALAN CARTER

Just as a tree has roots, so do races of people. Although these roots are sometimes buried, they can be dug up to find one's past just as one can tell the years of a tree by its rings. *Roots* is the story of all people: not just black and white, rich or poor, young or old. It is the story of people living, loving, laughing, and sharing in the pain, tragedy, and suffering of a decadent society where people were judged as chattel.

Roots surprised me. I didn't expect television, where profit is primary and educating people is secondary, to take a serious subject and manage to move so many people. TV took Alex Haley's 688-page manuscript and made a monster—a good monster. For eight consecutive nights, millions of Americans adjusted their entire lives to *Roots*. Phones sat unanswered, movies lost money, bars and restaurants sat silent—while the other networks were left fuming.

Roots and all the people involved in its production deserve a big thank you. Thank you for not being a situation comedy about a divorced mother or father with two kids. Thank you for not being a cop show where every criminal is captured. Thank you for not being a medical show where the doctor systematically falls in love with and cures every patient. Thank you for not being a tiresome game show.

We as TV viewers wanted something new, fresh, and exciting. And finally we got it. *Roots* did for prime time what *The Gong Show* did for daytime. It is no surprise that *Roots* became the most-watched TV program in history. We all anxiously await *Roots 2* or *Son of Roots,* but only if the sequel can capture the brilliance of its predecessor. Some shows get even

better, like *Family;* this is what I hope for *Roots.*

The mere fact that *Roots* appeared on TV at all is a good indication that race relations in the United States are changing. An estimated eighty-five million people, almost two-thirds of the nation, saw some of or all of *Roots.* These ratings are phenomenal, particularly because there are only twenty-five million black people in the country. *Roots* was the biggest thing to hit TV since Rhoda's wedding, the first episode of *All in the Family,* or Lucy's baby.

Roots gave us the unique chance to be educated, informed, and entertained, all at the same time. It gave us a chance to know its characters and grow with them. It made us laugh, shed a tear or two, and get angry. And *Roots* also made us aware, proud, ashamed, determined, and helpless. It made us feel, it made us pity, it made us hurt, and it made us think.

Alan Carter is a high school intern with ABC in New York. He plans to study communications in college and hopes someday to work on a TV show about a black lawyer or doctor.

John Astin and Marty Ingels star in *I'm Dickens, He's Fenster* on ABC in 1962. Despite good reviews, this comedy series is dropped after one season.

Oscar-winner Ernest Borgnine is Lieutenant Quinton McHale and Tim Conway is Ensign Charles Pulver in *McHale's Navy,* an outlandish war comedy that debuts on ABC in 1962. The series, a sort of naval version of *You'll Never Get Rich,* will play until 1966. Joe Flynn (not seen) co-stars as Captain Wallace B. Binghamton.

A more serious WW II series is the action-packed *Combat*, which debuts in 1962 on ABC. *The Gallant Men,* another 1962 war show on ABC, will be dropped after one season but *Combat* will continue until 1967, establishing itself as the first successful TV war series. Starring with Rick Jason (not seen) are (L–R): Jack Hogan, Vic Morrow, and Pierre Jalbert.

TV TRIVIA
DANNY PEARY AND HENRY BLINDER

Truth Or Consequences

1. Who donates all fur products to the *Hollywood Squares* game?

2. Fill in the Blank: On *Leave It to Beaver,* one of Beaver's favorite phrases was, "Cross my heart and hope to _____."

3. How did the audience participate on the old *The Price Is Right?*

4. In *The Real McCoys,* what did Pepino call Walter Brennan?

5. What was the sign-off of *The Arthur Murray Dance Party?*

6. What was the name of the frog belonging to Mr. Boynton on *Our Miss Brooks?*

7. Who was Jeff's best friend in the original Lassie series?

8. Every day on *The Mickey Mouse Club* had a special name. Name all five days.

9. What was the name of the group in residence on *Shindig?*

10. What was the name of the communications channel Napoleon Solo and Illya Kuryakin used on *The Man From U.N.C.L.E.?*

11. What was the weekly feature of *People Are Funny?*

12. What mythical magazine provided a format for a Jackie Gleason series?

13. Who were the two Marilyns on *The Munsters?*

14. What did Chatworth call Dobie on *The Many Loves of Dobie Gillis?*

15. What two people, later to become famous, were a team on *Name That Tune?*

16. Where is Rocket J. Squirrell from?

17. Where did Adam Cartwright go, and why did he go there?

18. What is the name of Daniel Boone's rifle?

19. Who is Helen Hayes's son?

20. On television in what apartment building did Clark Kent of *The Adventures of Superman* live?

21. Where did contestants stand in Jan Murray's *Treasure Hunt?*

22. On *My Little Margie,* what was the name of the woman who lived across the hall from Gale Storm?

23. What was it that *The Girl with Something Extra* had?

24. What did Raquel Welch do on *The Hollywood Palace?*

25. What was the name of the buzzer on *Truth or Consequences?*

26. What was the perfume they used to give as a consolation prize on *Truth or Consequences?*

27. Who played *The Ugliest Girl in Town?*

In 1962, CBS schedules its own hospital drama *The Nurses* to compete with ABC's *Ben Casey* and NBC's *Dr. Kildare.* Zina Bethune and Shirl Conway star.

In England in 1962, a cult begins to form around a bizarre, cleverly written crime series called *The Avengers.* Patrick MacNee stars as the sophisticated solver of supercrimes, John Steed, whose deadly derby is lined with metal. When the series began in 1961, MacNee alternated weekly with Ian Hendry (as Dr. David Keel).

28. How many times does the hammer strike at the end of *Dragnet?*

29. What was the name of the mayor on *People's Choice?*

30. In what club did Danny Williams work on *Make Room for Daddy?*

31. In what clubs did Ricky Ricardo work?

32. Who is the ABC science editor?

33. On what subject did Joyce Brothers answer questions to win the limit on *The $64,000 Question?*

34. Where did Howdy Doody live?

35. Who was Paladin's valet?

36. What three actresses at different times played the starring role on *Beulah?*

37. Who trained Lassie?

38. Who failed in a try-out as replacement for Don Meredith on *ABC Monday Night Football?*

39. Mary Tyler Moore played Sam on what show?

40. What TV show featured Hedda Hopper's son and in what role?

The Match Game

1. Match the game show with its host:
   a. *The Who, What or Where Game*
   b. *G.E. College Bowl*
   c. *Supermarket Sweep*
   d. *Video Village*
   e. *It Could Be You*
   f. *The Newlywed Game*

   1. Jack Narz, Monty Hall
   2. Art James
   3. Allen Ludden, Robert Earle
   4. Bill Malone
   5. Bob Eubanks
   6. Bill Leyden

2. Match the school with the show:
   a. S. Peter Pryor Junior College
   b. Jefferson High School
   c. Walt Whitman High School
   d. Harry S. Truman High School
   e. Jefferson Junior High
   f. Western State University

   1. *Mr. Peepers*
   2. *Lucas Tanner*
   3. *Room 222*
   4. *Hank*
   5. *The Many Loves of Dobie Gillis*
   6. *Mr. Novak* and *Happy Days*

3. Match the place to the show:
   a. 485 Bonnie Meadow Road, New Rochelle, N.Y.
   b. The Fabulous Moulin Rouge
   c. 90 Bristol Court
   d. Springfield
   e. The Treasure House
   f. 12th Precinct, Greenwich Village

   1. *Captain Kangaroo*
   2. *The Dick Van Dyke Show*
   3. *Queen for a Day*
   4. *Barney Miller*
   5. *Father Knows Best*
   6. *Ninety Bristol Court*

4. Match the boat to the show:
   a. Narcissus
   b. S.S. Minnow
   c. Tiki
   d. U.S. Kiwi
   e. P.T. 73
   f. The Enterprise
   g. S.S. Ocean Queen

   1. *Gilligan's Island*
   2. *Adventures in Paradise*
   3. *The Gale Storm Show*
   4. *Tugboat Annie*
   5. *McHale's Navy*
   6. *Riverboat*
   7. *The Wackiest Ship in the Navy*

Beginning in 1962, Honor Blackman plays John Steed's assistant, Mrs. Catherine Gale, a widow. Here Blackman, wearing a black leather evening dress, talks to Paul Whitsun-Jones. *The Avengers* will be in time accused of catering to "leather freaks."

Movie star Edmond O'Brien has the title role of attorney *Sam Benedict* on NBC in 1962.

Wendell Corey treats his patient Vera Miles on the psychiatric drama *The Eleventh Hour*, which debuts on NBC in 1962. Corey will be replaced by Ralph Bellamy in 1963. Because of the initial success of this program, ABC will counter with *Breaking Point* in 1963. Both shows will go off in 1964.

5. Match the everyday name to the famous name:
   a. Simon Templar   1. Captain Nice
   b. Don Diego de   2. The Lone Ranger
      la Vega   3. The Saint
   c. Jamie Sommers   4. The Bionic Woman
   d. John Reid   5. Zorro
   e. Carter Nash

6. Match the characters to the show:
   a. Pete Cochran, Julie   1. *Hawaiian Eye*
      Barnes, Linc Hayes   2. *Rawhide*
   b. Alexander Mundy,   3. *I Spy*
      Noah Bain   4. *It Takes a Thief*
   c. Tom Lopaka, Tracy   5. *F Troop*
      Steele, Cricket Blake 6. *The Farmer's*
   d. Kelly Robinson,   *Daughter*
      Alexander Scott   7. *The Mod Squad*
   e. Gil Favor, Rowdy Yates
   f. Katy Holstrum,
      Congressman Glen
      Morley
   g. Sgt. Morgan
      O'Rourke, Cpl. Ran-
      dolph Agarn, Capt.
      Wilton Parmenter

7. Match the animal to the owner:
   a. Neil   1. Jungle Jim
   b. Astro   2. Sock Miller
   c. Tamba   3. Honey West
   d. King   4. George Jetson
   e. Fred   5. George and
   f. Bruce the ocelot   Marian Kirby
   g. Cleo   6. Tony Baretta
   h. Minerva   7. Steve Douglas
   i. Tramp   and Sons
                        8. Mrs. Davis
                        9. Sgt. Preston of
                           the Yukon

TV Trivia Test Answers

Truth or Consequences 1. Dicker & Dicker of Beverly Hills; 2. "spit"; 3. By yelling "higher, higher," and "freeze, freeze"; 4. Señor Grampa; 5. Kathryn Murray said, "America, keep dancing"; 6. MacDougall; 7. Porky; 8. Monday: Fun with Music Day; Tuesday: Gest Star Day; Wednesday: Anything Can Happen Day; Thursday: Circus Day; Friday: Talent Round-Up Day; 9. The Shindogs; 10. "Open Channel D"; 11. A long distance phone call made by a contestant, the object of which was to keep the party on the phone for three minutes; 12. Jackie Gleason's *American Scene* magazine; 13. Beverly Owen (first) and Pat Priest (daughter of Ivy Baker Priest, treasurer of the U.S. under Eisenhower); 14. Dobie-Doo; 15. Eddie Hodges, John Glenn; 16. Frost Bite Falls, Minn.; 17. Europe to attend college; 18. Tick Licker; 19. James McArthur, co-star of *Hawaii Five-O;* 20. The Standish Arms; 21. In carved out replicas of Spanish galleon hulls; 22. Mrs. Odetts; 23. ESP; 24. She carried the card announcing guests; 25. Beulah; 26. Jungle Gardenia by Tuvache; 27. Peter Kastner; 28. twice; 29. Mayor Peoples, played by Paul Maxey; 30. Copy Club; 31. Tropicana and the Ricky Ricardo Babalu Club; 32. Jules Bergman; 33. Boxing; 34. Doodyville; 35. Hey Boy; 36. Ethel Waters, Hattie McDaniel, Louise Beavers; 37. Rudd Weatherwax; 38. Fred Williamson; 39. *Richard Diamond, Private Detective*; 40. Paul Drake on *Perry Mason.*

1. a-2; b-3; c-4; d-1; e-6; f-5. 2. a-5; b-6; c-3; d-2; e-1; f-4. 3. a-2; b-3; c-6; d-5; e-1; f-4. 4. a-4; b-1; c-2; d-7; e-5; f-6; g-3. 5. a-3; b-5; c-4; d-2; e-1. 6. a-7; b-4; c-1; d-3; e-2; f-6; g-5. 7. a-5; b-4; c-1; d-9; e-6; f-3; g-2; h-8; i-f.

235

Jack Lord (C) stars as a rodeo cowboy in *Stoney Burke*, which premieres on ABC in 1962. NBC counters with its own rodeo series *Wide Country*. Both shows will go off in 1963.

Jackie Gleason brings back his old character "Joe the Bartender" for his *Jackie Gleason and the American Scene Magazine* variety series. It will play on CBS from 1962 to 1966. Among the show's regulars is Frank Fontaine, who plays "Crazy Guggenheimer."

TV CROSSWORD PUZZLE
BOB FITZPATRICK

Across

1 Enterprising officer?
5 Boobs
9 Recent TV series
13 Bread spread
14 Reinforce
16 *Baretta* forerunner
17 Old sitcom
20 African antelope
21 Focal points
22 Baseball stat.
23 *I Spy* star, for short
25 Celtic language
26 Snakes
29 Makes a mistake
31 Peter Lawford's TV dog
35 Formerly
36 See 52 down
37 Chester Goode's boss
39 Old sitcom
42 Tempt
43 Gumbo
44 Singer Starr
45 For fear that
46 Co-star of *MASH*
47 Snake-like fishes
48 Bedtime for Bilko
50 Thither
52 Plant
55 Bedouin, e.g.
56 _____ *with Judy*
60 Game show
64 Verdi opera
65 Props for *Room 222*
66 Like Felix Unger
67 He was Artemus on *Wild Wild West*
68 Roberta's group on *MHMH*
69 Host of the *Match Game*

Down

1 Kind of nut or tree
2 _____ *Three Lives*
3 Peruse
4 Late TV comedian and director
5 Sash for Mrs. Livingston
6 Host of *Jeopardy*
7 Old TV series
8 Scrubs
9 TV chan.

10 Entwined
11 Alistaire Cooke series (abbr.)
12 Character on *The Avengers*
15 Abates
18 Outer (prefix)
19 Compass point
24 Twilled fabric
26 Annie Farge series
27 Fisherman's net
28 Beats incessantly
30 Certain R.R. shippers
31 _____ *My Children*
32 Satisfy; quench

33 Of a sound
34 _____ *Gang*
36 _____ *Tac Dough*
37 _____ *Sally*
38 *Love* _____ *Many Splendored Thing*
40 Ignited
41 Snow runner
46 Intervals
47 Cessation
48 McHale, e.g.
49 Climate in *Rat Patrol*, e.g.
51 Rower

52 TV series, with 36 across
53 Fernwood's state
54 Unites
57 Omnibus's "Mr. Lincoln" playwright
58 ". . . _____ a breadbox?"
59 Female (suffix)
61 Dance movement
62 First President to be inaugurated on TV
63 Fast plane

See page 402 for solution.

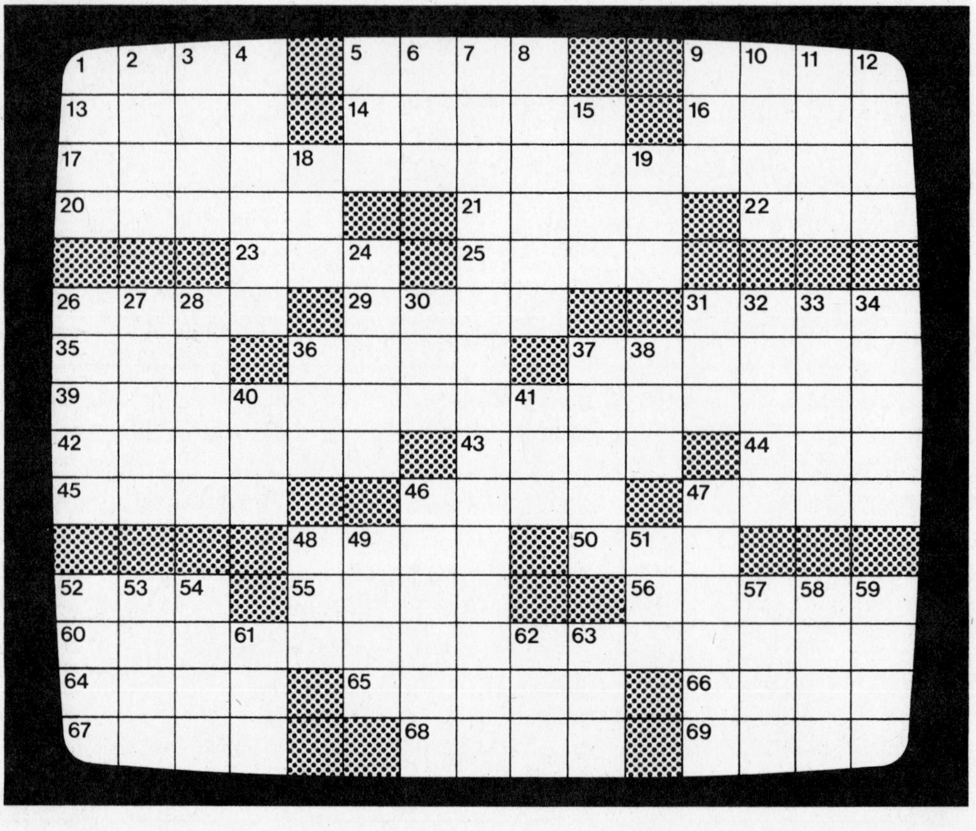

236

Andy Williams, who has hosted a short-lived variety series on each network, finds success on NBC in 1962 with *The Andy Williams Show*. It as Best Variety Program before going off in 1967. Williams will have another series on NBC from 1969 to 1971. Williams got his "break" on *The Tonight Show* with Steve Allen.

October 1, 1962. *The Tonight Show with Johnny Carson* premieres, and Carson's show quickly surpasses the departed Jack Paar's in popularity. Meanwhile, Paar moves into prime time with an hour-long talk show that will last until 1965. Here Doc Severenson and Skitch Henderson pose with Johnny Carson.

Sing Along With Mitch debuts on NBC in 1962. It will last two years. Here Mitch Miller (L) speaks with singer Bob McGrath, a regular on the show.

V. THE INFORMATION MACHINE

Skitch Henderson tries to convince Mitch Miller to sing along with (L–R). Burl Ives, Commander Whitehead, and Rex Stout.

October 22, 1962. President John Kennedy interrupts regular programming. He tells terrified viewers that he has just commanded Russia to turn back ships transporting missiles to Cuba and to retrieve all their missiles already in Cuba. Kennedy's critics claim that the "Cuban missile crisis" had been cleared up earlier and that Kennedy has no reason to panic the country.

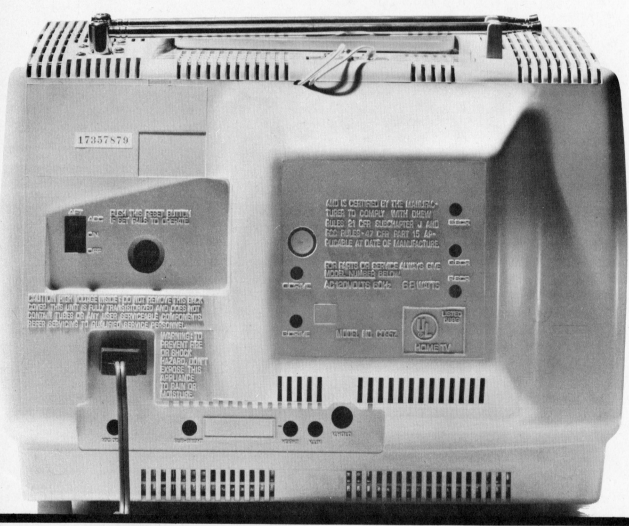

In 1962, Ernie Kovacs, one of television's great innovators, is killed in a car crash.

Host John Daly and hostess Arlene Francis, both of *What's My Line?*, pose with Norma Nolan, the current Miss Universe, prior to the 1963 *Miss Universe Beauty Pageant* on CBS.

TELEVISION LANGUAGE

EDWIN NEWMAN

I am, in the language of the trade, a "commentator." Every so often a letter arrives asking when, as a commentator, I commentate, and whether I couldn't simply comment instead? It is probably too late. Commentator is a word that radio and television have fixed in American English. It is unlikely ever to be dislodged.

Television's effect on language is not all that it should be. There is the evasion implicit in "We'll be back after this message," when the "message" ought, more forthrightly, to be called a commercial. There is the unthinking habit of saying, "We'll be back in a moment," although a moment is a brief and indefinite period of time, and it is actually a minute we're talking about, sometimes more. There are the sports broadcasters who tell us that a player's future is before him, or that they cannot "visually see" something, or pronounce the United States "in good shape Davis Cupwise," or begin comment after comment with "Y'know?"

But more generally, the state of a language to some extent reflects the condition of society, and also to some degree shapes it, and television is perhaps the chief influence on language today. It does not follow from this that television language ought to be self-consciously grand and artificially elevated. There is, however, some obligation to show what language can be, and to get all the fun, excitement, color and satisfaction we can from it. We live in a big and marvelously varied world. Television ought to reflect that, and the language can help.

I must confess that I am not invariably guiltless

of offenses against American English. On the dustcover of one of my books, it was stated that I had "anchored" NBC's coverage of various events. This soon prompted letters asking me to make a diagram showing precisely how I had performed this task, and suggesting that it must have been a weighty assignment. I understood the objection, for I dislike hearing that somebody hosted a program, and I detest hearing that somebody authored a book. Still, anchored is now a common term, like it or not. It had been used occasionally before, of course, as when ships anchored in harbors, or when a football player, performing heroically, was said to have anchored his team's defense. But television made it an everyday word.

Some words are used because nothing else will serve. Think of "moderator." It is an assignment I have often had, and I know that most debates don't need the toning down that moderating implies; if anything, they need the opposite. But the term is universally understood. "Host," as used on television, isn't quite right either. But "master of ceremonies" is long and clumsy, and the French word "compère" has never caught on with us. Therefore, host.

At that, I find "host" less troubling on talk shows than the loose use of "great," for appearing on a talk

Television in 1963 is dominated by half-hour comedy series. Paul Henning, who created *The Beverly Hillbillies,* gives CBS another popular comedy in 1963, *Petticoat Junction.* Pat Woodell, Jeannine Riley, and Linda Kaye Henning play the daughters of star Bea Benaderet. Edgar Buchanan helps Benaderet run the Shady Rest Hotel.

In 1963, Bill Dana brings his famous Jose Jimenez character to *The Bill Dana Show* on NBC. Jimenez is a bumbling bellhop in a Miami hotel run by Jonathan Harris (R). Don Adams plays a house detective in this comedy that will run two years.

My Favorite Martian debuts on CBS in 1963. Ray Walston (R) plays a conceited, highly advanced alien who pretends to be the uncle of earthling Bill Bixby. This is one of the first comedies in which a character has "special powers."

Edwin Newman, NBC correspondent and commentator, is revered by TV watchers for his intelligence and acerbic wit.

show does not automatically confer greatness on those who do it. The result was predictable: being called great nowadays means little. One must be very great, or really great, or truly great, if one hopes to be set

Inger Stevens plays Loretta Young's Oscar-winning character Katy Holstrum in ABC's adaptation of *The Farmer's Daughter* which debuts in 1963. Kathy is the live-in housekeeper of Congressman Glen Marley (William Windom), a widower with two children. In 1962, Stevens had played opposite Peter Falk in the acclaimed ''The Price of Tomatoes'' on *The Dick Powell Theatre*.

Young Patty Duke, who won an Oscar for playing Helen Keller in *The Miracle Worker*, stars in her own ABC comedy series in 1963, *The Patty Duke Show*, playing look-alike cousins Patty and Cathy Lane. Jean Byron and William Schallert, both formerly on *The Many Loves of Dobie Gillis*, play Patty's parents, and Paul O'Keefe is her brother. The show will run three years.

The Many Loves of Dobie Gillis is one of the few comedies to go off in 1963. Here Dobie looks on while his good buddy, Maynard G. Krebs, played by Bob Denver, conducts an odd experiment. Several episodes of this critically lauded series were surrealistic in nature.

"... it is not what's up front, but what can be implied, that counts."

apart. Nor would anyone new aspire to be a mere star. It is now necessary to be a superstar.

The most memorably pleasing language on television is usually found in commercials: "You've Come a Long Way, Baby," "If You've Got It, Flaunt It," "Leave the Driving to Us," "We Try Harder," "It's the Real Thing," "Try It, You'll Like It," "Fly Me," "We Must Be Doing Something Right," and "It's What's Up Front That Counts" are examples.

The reasons these slogans catch on are clear. They are repeated often, but more important, they are succinct, pithy, and usually rhythmic. Also, they can be used in situations in which they have no reference to the products they advertise. In these cases, it is not what's up front, but what can be implied, that counts.

Until these phrases wear out their welcome through overuse, they make our lives more cheerful. At any rate, some do. But it is difficult to be cheerful about commercials in which the model, advertising women's underclothing, looks naughtily into the camera and proclaims, "It makes me feel like I'm not wearing nothing." That is the opposite of what she means. Moreover, enough Americans already use "like" when they should say "as though," and there are enough double negatives in American speech without advertisers promoting more. "Winston tastes good like a cigarette should" all but killed one use of the word "as." And commercials that begin chummily with "Y'know" are perpetuating a habit of American speech that is not only tiresome but also an enemy of thought. "Y'know" is a surrender. It suggests that there is no need to frame a thought.

Entertainment shows also create and quickly wear out popular phrases. Does anybody now remember "Would you believe?" In its heyday, would you have believed that "Would you believe?" would fade so fast? On the other hand, some cue lines from television news resound good-naturedly through many business meetings: "Now, here with a report is our treasurer . . ." and "Now, with a report on last quarter's sales, here is . . ." and "Over to you . . ." and "Back to . . ." and "I'm afraid we've lost audio on that, folks . . ." and, a popular concluding phrase, "That's the way it looks from here," are all common.

Among current phrases, "prime time" is pure television, and it may survive. "Instant replay" surely will; think of the many possible applications of "I'd like an instant replay of that." The outlook for "live" is less certain, for we now hear about programs that are "live on tape" or were "taped before a live audience," and both of these amount to saying that live is what the program is not.

It is probably misleading to speak of television language. There are many television languages or, more precisely, there is a wide variety in the competence with which the language is used on television. Some of what we hear is crisp and direct; some is imaginative; some is deplorable. Yet on the whole, television language does not compare unfavorably with language in most other parts of society, and in some areas—this is certainly true of network news and public affairs programs, among others—every effort is made to be grammatical and, where appropriate, eloquent. Occasionally, we even succeed.

Edwin Newman is a correspondent and commentator for NBC News, and the author of Strictly Speaking *and* A Civil Tongue.

241

Since the mid-fifties, viewers have been fascinated by TV cowboys and their weapons, but in 1963 the TV western craze is almost over. Long one of TV's most popular westerns, *The Rifleman* goes off the air in 1963. Later in the year, Chuck Connors, seen here with a group of *Rifleman* fans, will co-star with Ben Gazzara in the ninety-minute *Arrest and Trial* on ABC.

The Travels of Jamie McPheeters, based on Robert Lewis Taylor's Pulitzer Prize–winning novel, debuts on ABC in 1963, one of only three westerns to appear this year. It will last one season.
Here Charles Bronson, Henry Hull, and Mariette Hartley appear with stars Dan O'Herlihy and young Kurt Russell (Jamie).

NEWS MANIPULATION

ROBERT SOBEL

Approximately 70 percent of all Americans cite television as their prime source for news, and the figure is rising. Some television newspeople are considered to be as influential as senators and congressmen, while a small handful may be even more powerful when it comes to shaping opinions. It is due primarily to television that the media are looked upon as a fourth branch of government.

Some critics charge that television news has much power but little by way of responsibility. Protected by the First Amendment, regulated by an often-timid Federal Communications Commission, un-elected by its viewers, and as much or more dependent upon the personality of the newscaster as upon the information and ideas disseminated, television news is a curious hybrid of old-fashioned journalism and a new variety of entertainment.

The news one gets from newspapers and magazines can be manipulated. Editors bury stories they don't want the public to see, or create news by featuring others. Writers use catch phrases and slogans so as to sway their readers. Columnists may distort issues, vent biases, and even try to make or break politicians. But newspapers have been around for a long time, and readers have come to expect this from them. In addition, the printed word is geared to the brain, where it can be analyzed and pondered—or simply ignored. Words can be used to convey abstractions and philosophies; readers understand and can deal with this.

Television is quite different. Whereas the reader knows that the print reporter is describing what he sees

in a selective fashion, the television viewer assumes the camera is showing all—the raw material from which a story could be written, if one were of a mind to do so. The newspaper story is an image of reality; the television picture comes across as reality itself.

Furthermore, there is a marked difference between the reporter and the newscaster. The former is a disembodied collection of words and ideas, the latter a flesh-and-blood human, looking straight at the viewer through the tube. While it is possible to develop empathy and trust in newsprint, this is much easier to accomplish on television, especially if the newscaster is warm, outgoing, and convincing. In a cynical period like the 1970's, Walter Cronkite is one of the most respected Americans in public life. At a time when few institutions inspire confidence, only two out of every ten readers believe in the fairness and accuracy of their newspapers. In contrast, half again as many viewers say they trust television news.

Yet seldom is a major story broken on television. Newspaper journalists uncovered the Watergate scandal and exposed inaccuracies in official news releases during the Viet Nam War. All that television could do was report on these developments. But television did show the actual horrors of war—while print could only analyze situations and explore alternatives. The

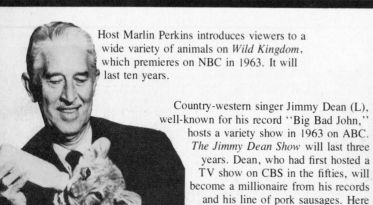

Host Marlin Perkins introduces viewers to a wide variety of animals on *Wild Kingdom*, which premieres on NBC in 1963. It will last ten years.

Country-western singer Jimmy Dean (L), well-known for his record "Big Bad John," hosts a variety show in 1963 on ABC. *The Jimmy Dean Show* will last three years. Dean, who had first hosted a TV show on CBS in the fifties, will become a millionaire from his records and his line of pork sausages. Here Sheb Wooley makes a guest appearance.

An American soldier sets fire to a house in Viet Nam. TV viewers numbly watched the horrors of war nightly in the 1960's.

former appealed to the emotions, the latter to intellect. Most people are capable of strong feelings; fewer have the capacity for sustained analysis. Thus, TV often has a greater impact on many people.

During the Viet Nam War, newspaper journalists learned the subtle power of television. While the print journalist appeared contentious when he openly criticized American policy, the television newsperson, in contrast, could select the right pictures and simply let them do the job. On the other hand, the Watergate affair required analysis, investigation, and reason, and most important, could not easily be pictorialized. It was a story best reported upon in print, and so it was.

Television newspersons are both the beneficiaries and victims of technology and tradition, neither of which they can control. The tradition was established in the early 1950's, when the first television newscasts were created. These were fifteen minute programs,

243

The Danny Kaye Show premieres on CBS in 1963. It will win an Emmy as the season's Best Variety Show. Here Kaye is at his best, talking with a little child.

"There is nothing wrong with your television set. Do not attempt to adjust the picture. We are controlling transmission." *The Outer Limits* debuts on ABC in 1963. This sixty-minute science fiction series will last two years. Here Harry Guardino appears in "The Human Factor" episode.

The Sid Caesar Show appears on ABC in 1963. Gisele MacKenzie is the fourth female partner for Caesar. This half-hour series will last only one year.

"Cronkite does not mean what he says literally . . ."

consisting of a former radio broadcaster reading news reports while seated at a desk. Occasionally he would employ visuals in the form of still photos, and he might point to a map. This could not disguise the fact that such programs were just radio shows on a cathode-ray tube.

After a while this radio format was wedded to newsreels, similar to those shown in motion picture theaters, and always outdated. Thus, breaking news was read, and background material was gleaned from the film file.

To differentiate one newscast from another, the stations tried to make "personalities" of their reporters. The most prominent of these was John Cameron Swayze, who dressed splendidly, and so was deemed more videogenic than his competition on the other channels.

Finally, television had to worry about regulation by the FCC. In theory the airwaves belong to the public, and the stations are trustees. In contrast, newspapers and magazines have always been completely free of government controls of this kind. Thus politicians can threaten the existence of television stations, but cannot do the same to newspapers. This threat encouraged the development of a tradition of blandness in newscasts.

The technical situation changed somewhat with the arrival of videotape in the late 1950's, which enabled the networks to combine pictures and words in breaking stories. The flexibility provided by tape meant that pictures took precedence over words, while the growth of color and the development of satellite communications added to a heightened sense of immediacy. But this development also meant that more than ever, sensation would take precedence over ideas and analysis. The unspoken assumption was that television provided the sights and sounds, which the viewer then put together to form ideas. This is equivalent to the difference between *The New York Times*'s claim that it contains "All the News that's Fit to Print," and Walter Cronkite's sign-off, "That's the way it is." The former indicates editing and selection, the latter implies an accurate presentation.

Of course, Cronkite does not mean what he says literally, and he himself has complained about and criticized television news. Still, polls indicate that a goodly number of his followers accept the thought behind the closing.

Television news can run into difficulties in a number of different ways when it attempts to manipulate perceptions. Edward R. Murrow's famous report on Senator Joe McCarthy, shown in 1954, was criticized as a subtle hatchet job. The editors had selected footage showing McCarthy at his worst, and he appeared unattractive and coarse when set beside the videogenic Murrow. The senator was given an opportunity to respond to the report and he did a sorry job of it—he was not of the stuff needed for the television age. But in general, despite criticisms, such presentations as Murrow's have always been considered acceptable, and even illuminating; they derive from the print medium and its traditions.

Less acceptable was the editing of tape for a subsequent program called *The Selling of the Pentagon,* in which an interview was manipulated so as to show an officer answering questions he hadn't been asked. Another of these special news programs dealt with hunger in America, and it ended with the commentator holding what seemed to be a malnourished baby and stating that the child was dying of starvation.

244

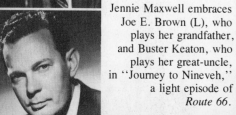

September 9, 1963. *The Huntley-Brinkley Report* expands from fifteen minutes to a half hour.

Jennie Maxwell embraces Joe E. Brown (L), who plays her grandfather, and Buster Keaton, who plays her great-uncle, in "Journey to Nineveh," a light episode of *Route 66.*

Gary Lockwood (L) plays marine Lieutenant William Rice, and Robert Vaughn is Captain Ray Rambridge in *The Lieutenant,* which debuts on ABC in 1963. This sixty-minute series will last one season. Gene Roddenberry is producer-writer.

The baby did die, but doctors declared he was not malnourished or underfed. Later the network conceded as much, and said the picture had been shown for impact, in order to make the point. Indeed babies may have been dying of starvation somewhere but deception had been employed in this particular case. And the public believed it—after all, the viewer had seen it, with his own eyes.

No respectable print journalist would have resorted to such a device, because of established ethics, tradition, and the nature of print technology. But television news has little by way of tradition (and some that it does have derives from show business), no clear code of ethics, and is bound to utilize visuals as effectively as possible. That network news specials would utilize dramatic devices like the dying baby is not surprising. The technology existed, and so did the audience, and the temptation to employ the former to sway the latter was irresistible. Furthermore, it was what viewers has learned to expect from the medium.

Most television fare is drama and comedy, which by the 1970's was taped live so as to give the impression of immediacy, but which can also be edited and augmented with necessary. Television actors become stars in less than a season while appearing in ongoing series in which they play the same character. Tape permitted television news to put the same emphasis on immediacy and stars. In the early 1970's, many local stations went over to the concept of "action news," which employed a team of reporters and anchor persons. The former went into the community with cameramen to "bring back the story," which was then presented by the anchor person. In conclusion, the reporter and newscaster might enter into a short conversation about what they had seen. Frank N. Magid Associates surveyed the field and noted that action news reports "what people *want* to know" rather than what is truly important. Thus, action news teams have developed stories on prostitution, child abuse, and similar subjects that aren't really news, but are sufficiently sensational—pictorially—to draw a large audience.

The action reporter actually enters the story, so he/she has to be appealing, glib, and at times humorous. In other words, the newsperson has become an actor, and indeed the line between the two has tended to vanish by the late 1970's. John Lindsay went from being mayor of New York to playing a senator in a motion picture, and finally emerged as a television news interviewer. The actor who portrayed a newscaster on *The Mary Tyler Moore Show* seemed more true-to-life than most of the people he was supposed to lampoon. If Edward R. Morrow was the past of television news and Walter Cronkite is its present, Ted Baxter is a portent of the future.

Television news has drifted further into show business than anyone anticipated it would. Visuals continue to take precedence over ideas, and blandness reigns with the FCC ever watchful. That news broadcasting will continue to evolve in this general direction seems beyond doubt. Despite outcries from critics, the public, and even the medium itself, there appears no way of altering the situation. Experienced viewers know they are being manipulated in a subtle fashion, but most seem to enjoy the experience, which offers the impression of knowledge and insight without the hard work that goes into obtaining both. We are heading from Cronkite's "That's the way it is" to the eyewitness news "happy talk" slogan, "You'll like them because they like each other." And the public—audience might be a better word—apparently does.

Robert Sobel teaches at New College of Hofstra and is the author of The Manipulators: America in the Media Age.

September 17, 1963. Desilu Productions' *Greatest Show on Earth* premieres on ABC. It stars Jack Palance (C) and Stu Erwin (R). Palance had won an Emmy in 1956 as the star of "Requiem for a Heavyweight"; Erwin starred in *Trouble with Father*, a comedy series, from 1950–55. Here Dorothy Malone guests.

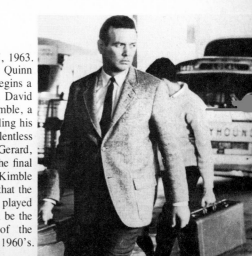

September 17, 1963. *The Fugitive*, a Quinn Martin Production, begins a four-year run on ABC. David Janssen plays Dr. Richard Kimble, a man wrongly accused of killing his wife; he must constantly flee relentless pursuer Lieutenant Philip Gerard, played by Barry Morse. In the final episode of this popular series, Kimble will finally convince Gerard that the true killer is a one-armed man, played by Bill Raisch. That episode will be the most-watched single program of the 1960's.

THE MINICAM REVOLUTION

JORDAN GOODMAN

It is 10:30 P.M. in Indianapolis. All of a sudden, the three local television stations break away from their network programming to show a crazy man named Anthony Kiritsis holding a sawed-off shotgun to the head of Richard Hall, a mortgage company president-turned-hostage.

Kiritsis has been holding Hall for sixty-two hours, and now he is threatening to blow his head off if the media don't cover his demands live. "Get those goddamned cameras on!" he keeps yelling at the cameramen. The three stations comply.

Satisfied that he is on live TV, Kiritsis starts a twenty-six minute harangue against the mortgage company in religious and sexual obscenities that probably have never before been heard over the airwaves. ABC affiliate WTHR pulls the plug on their coverage soon after their news director sees that he is losing control of what is going on his station's air. But the other two stations stick it out until the bitter end, risking the possibility that their audiences will witness a live murder.

The next day WTHR is showered with phone calls and mail complimenting their decision to bail out. The other two stations are flooded with angry objections to the live broadcasting of so much obscenity and potential bloodshed.

Decisions about whether or not to broadcast events at the moment they occur have become increasingly common since the introduction of the latest technological advance in TV newsgathering, the Electronic News Gathering System (ENG)—or the minicam as it is commonly known. This device can

> " . . . the urgency of a dramatic moment can overwhelm balanced news judgment."

either shoot action live or record it on videotape. It has the potential to revolutionize both the form and substance of television news.

Ever since Jack Ruby shot Lee Harvey Oswald in Dallas in front of a live national audience, the dramatic impact of live news coverage has been apparent. Each viewer feels that he has witnessed such an event for himself, free of the biases of a reporter or editor. The impact is greater and the event is probably remembered longer and more vividly than when the transmission is delayed.

On May 17, 1974, one of the most dramatic events of the year—a shoot-out between the Symbionese Liberation Army and the Los Angeles police—was broadcast live by minicam from coast to coast for two hours. Previously, unpredictable events like this one never could have been covered live, in the way space lift-offs and political conventions had been, because of the enormous technical preparations that were necessary.

Possibly the most controversial use of the minicam to date occurred on June 24, 1975. An Eastern Airlines jet had crashed at Kennedy Airport, killing 113 passengers in the worst single-plane disaster

246

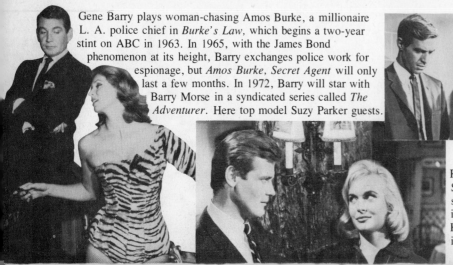

Gene Barry plays woman-chasing Amos Burke, a millionaire L. A. police chief in *Burke's Law*, which begins a two-year stint on ABC in 1963. In 1965, with the James Bond phenomenon at its height, Barry exchanges police work for espionage, but *Amos Burke, Secret Agent* will only last a few months. In 1972, Barry will star with Barry Morse in a syndicated series called *The Adventurer*. Here top model Suzy Parker guests.

James Franciscus (L) becomes a favorite of teenage girls in 1963 when he stars in *Mr. Novak* as a high school English teacher. Co-starring Dean Jagger, the show will last two years on NBC. ABC's "schoolteacher" series of 1963, *Channing* (starring Jason Evers), will only last one year. Here Steve Franken, a regular on *The Lieutenant*, guest stars.

Roger Moore stars in 1963 as the dashing ex-thief Simon Templar in *The Saint*, a popular syndicated series being filmed in England. Several actors — including George Sanders, Tom Conway, and Louis Hayward — had played Leslie Charteris's character in the movies. Here Shirley Eaton guest stars.

In 1937, RCA's first mobile TV unit, including a huge truck, accomplished a remote broadcast from a New York street.

In 1976, cameramen carrying minicams broadcast live from the floor of the Republican convention in Kansas City.

George C. Scott (standing with guest Joanna Merlin) stars as a social worker in *East Side/West Side,* which debuts on CBS in 1963. More than any fictional series to date, this controversial show explores the problems of the indigent. The grim, realistic drama wins critical acclaim but few viewers and goes off after just one year. Cicely Tyson co-stars with Scott and Elizabeth Wilson, making it one of the first TV shows to have an integrated cast.

November 22, 1963. The world is stunned. President John F. Kennedy is shot in Dallas, Texas, as his motorcade passes a book depository. He dies several hours later. Lyndon Johnson becomes President. Lee Harvey Oswald is arrested as the lone gunman responsible for the assassination.

in American history. WNBC in New York quickly reassigned a minicam crew to the scene from Shea Stadium, where it was shooting a baseball game. Almost as soon as the crew arrived, it started to send back live pictures of the carnage at the crash site. The camerman showed priests performing last rites over bodies covered by white sheets. Some people say too much gory detail of bloody limbs and burned flesh was fed live to the public. The next day criticism was severe. Many complained that WNBC had abused journalistic discretion in its rush to beat the competition to this shocking story.

As minicams have become more portable, more events ranging from disasters, holdups, and criminal trials to strikes, political speeches, and presidential inaugurations have been covered live. The trials of Patty Hearst and Samuel Bronfman, Jr., two millionaire kidnap victims, were subjects of extensive minicam coverage; KDKA in Pittsburgh offered live coverage when local public school teachers voted to strike, and again when they ratified the decision to return to work eight weeks later; KPRC in Houston sent a minicam reporter to the site where an ammonia-laden truck had overturned and exploded, spilling its lethal contents onto a busy highway and into the air. Most stations equipped to do so cover election night events live from the headquarters of various candidates. Minicams are even used for live reports from weathermen in the field, and from film and play reviewers at the theater.

The most serious problem with live reporting is the tendency of the minicam to attract crowds, and sometimes to incite them. The option of walking away from a story until a crowd has dispersed or calmed down, once available to film-equipped crews, is lost when the story is being transmitted live. Raymond Smith, news director at WKYC in Cleveland, warns reporters: "In covering news stories, news people either go to crowds or they draw crowds. In any crowd there will usually be someone who will try to mess up your story with antics or obscenities. Keep in mind you cannot edit live feeds . . . yet the FCC holds you responsible."

Problems start as soon as the brightly painted vans, each mounted with a distinctive microwave dish, arrive at a scene that may already be chaotic. In a dramatic situation like the SLA shoot-out, people are drawn to the area, and potentially into danger, as they try to get a glimpse of the action. When a reporter starts to transmit his story live, he attracts another crowd of his own. Police often have to be called in to protect him. If residents of the area see the story on TV, they often come out of their homes to survey the situation for themselves, further adding to the chaos.

News judgment and good taste must be exercised with special care at tragic events. Larry Connors, a reporter for KMOX-TV in St. Louis, commented: "You have to remember when you show gore that people who are watching might be at the dinner table. You have more difficult decisions to make when you're live at the scene of a car accident. If you know the name of the dead victim, you feel terrible being the first one to release that information over the air. But if you don't release it, all the housewives who are watching will start to worry about their husbands driving home."

For those in the newsroom, ENG's live capability offers other challenges to news judgment. The temptation to cover sensational or trivial stories at the expense of more important, but less visually exciting developments can be powerful. *Newsweek* reports that "the competitiveness of live coverage has caused a glut of gimmicky minicam coverage regardless of news value. WRC-TV in Washington, which last year promised a live feature every night, resorted at one point to interviewing a Taiwanese acrobat who

Regular TV programs and commercials are canceled and all channels broadcast reports on the Kennedy assassination around the clock. Millions of viewers sit glued to their sets. They are shocked to see on their screens — "live" on NBC — Lee Harvey Oswald gunned down and killed by Jack Ruby, a Dallas striptease-joint owner. Here Oswald lies fatally injured in the background while police try to wrestle the gun away from Ruby.

John Kennedy's funeral is the culmination of the most tragic series of events ever covered by television, and ever endured by American viewers.

Marina Oswald, the widow of Lee Harvey Oswald, another victim.

couldn't speak English. Last month Detroit's WJBK-TV sent its electronic unit to a downtown tree to cover the rescue of a Siamese cat.''

Although news directors and anchor men continually warn of the danger of using too much live material, the urgency of a dramatic moment can overwhelm balanced news judgment. *The Wall Street Journal* reports that when a gunman was holding some hostages in a Cleveland office building, the WEWS news department got so carried away that it allotted six minutes to the event in the eleven o'clock report, while providing only six and a half minutes total coverage to eight other important stories. If this kind of distortion were to become widespread, the public's perception of the news could become seriously jaded.

Live coverage that interrupts regular programming has to be used even more sparingly. Soon after KMOX had converted to ENG, it interrupted a children's program to cover a battle over the opening of a pornographic movie house in East St. Louis, prompting calls from many outraged parents. In other situations where criminals are surrounded by police, stations have to be careful not to reveal law enforcement strategies to criminals who might be watching the TV program.

Technological developments will allow the minicam of the future to be miniaturized even further. Already the Thomson Microcam weighs eleven pounds, compared to the fifty-pound minicams first used in the 1960's. If the charge-coupled device (a component that translates images onto videotape) now used in security cameras is perfected, pocket-sized minicams could weigh as little as three pounds. Newsmen look forward to the time when such cameras could be used in the halls of Congress where TV is now banned, or for investigative purposes where present equipment is too awkward.

Viewers who are now only vaguely aware that

"The minicam should allow more and better investigative reporting . . .''

news is being covered live and on videotape will grow accustomed to it. The extensive promotion of ENG equipment that labels the minicam system everything from "Newscam" and "Instacam" to "Electracam" and "Instant Eye" will seem as passé as the boast that a station broadcasts in color today. In every area of news broadcasting, the conversion from film to videotape seems inevitable.

As further developments refine the minicam, its uses will broaden. News coverage will be more immediate; so will the need for more responsible news judgment. Immense restraint will have to be shown by news directors if the nightly news is not to become merely a headline service with live and taped inserts of crimes, fires, crashes, and other disasters. A finely tuned sense of taste and timing will be required to give viewers the news they want without subjecting them to unruly crowds, and unnecessary blood and sensationalism. The minicam should allow more and better investigative reporting, and provide greater access to television by alternative production groups. Like any technology, electronic news gathering offers possibilities for excellence. It also provides dangerous opportunities for the unwary journalist. Ultimately, the people running the machines will have the hard choices to make.

Jordan Goodman wrote his master's thesis on electronic news gathering while at the Columbia University Graduate School of Journalism.

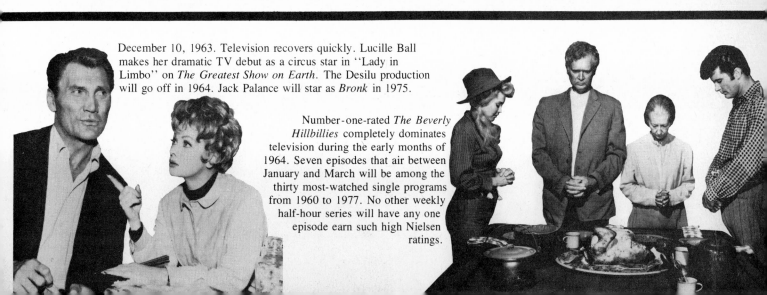

December 10, 1963. Television recovers quickly. Lucille Ball makes her dramatic TV debut as a circus star in "Lady in Limbo" on *The Greatest Show on Earth*. The Desilu production will go off in 1964. Jack Palance will star as *Bronk* in 1975.

Number-one-rated *The Beverly Hillbillies* completely dominates television during the early months of 1964. Seven episodes that air between January and March will be among the thirty most-watched single programs from 1960 to 1977. No other weekly half-hour series will have any one episode earn such high Nielsen ratings.

TV INVESTIGATIONS: "SAFE" NEWS

BERNARD GAVZER

One of the most glamorous phases of news journalism in any medium is investigative reporting. Many of the most remarkable revelations of the Watergate era were due to the persistence of reporters Bob Woodward and Carl Bernstein of the Washington *Post*. But television contributed an urgency and immediacy to their disclosures, by disseminating them widely to the American public. What television could do *better* than any newspaper was illustrated by its coverage of the Senate Watergate hearings. The home viewer became an eyewitness to history-in-the-making. Participants in the hearings were revealed by the camera in intimate and often naked ways. There is admittedly disagreement about the effect of television coverage on any event. TV equipment and crews can hardly be expected to blend into a scene and remain invisible. Some people feel that this presence influences events, while others argue that television has become so much a part of the everyday environment that it no more intrudes on what is happening than would a chair or a table. Nevertheless, these and other problems make it difficult for television to produce detailed, in-depth inquiries into certain kinds of stories. As a result, television "investigations" often prove to be shallow and superficial. Indeed, some investigative reports resemble nothing so much as non-fiction versions of prime-time adventure series. The viewer is merely titillated, while the subject remains unillumined and obscure.

Very often these stories focus almost brainlessly upon tired, stereotypical problems such as narcotics peddling, junkies and their dreadful lives, the horrors

Daniel Schorr left CBS over the issue of reporting methods.

of abortion in old-style abortion mills, juvenile delinquency, conflict of interest in greedy politicians, the Mafia, all varieties of prison abuse, arson, rape and alcoholism. Long ago these topics and others like them were established as staples of the newspaper journalist's police beat. Television merely employed its sophisticated technology to cover them in a more exciting way. Still, the stories were and are essentially exposés, that seldom manage to reveal anything new or different. In fact, they often seem to be resounding discoveries of the painfully obvious. But because television coverage of *anything* possesses an inherent urgency and immediacy, these hackneyed vacuous reports often manage to conceal their poverty of content.

What the subjects of these unoriginal investigations have in common is an inability to strike back.

250

TV sports finally come of age in 1964. Instant replay, slow motion, and other sophisticated technical advancements make coverage of basketball, baseball, and particularly football so spectacular that many people stay home to watch an event rather than see it in person. Networks raise their advertising rates for sports shows. CBS buys the New York Yankees.

Instant replay makes it possible to see events such as this over and over again.

Lucille Ball, Jack Benny, and Bob Hope, television's three top comedians, appear together in 1964 on *The Lucy Show*.

". . . television 'investigations' often prove to be shallow . . ."

Teenaged criminals, drug addicts, prostitutes and the Mafia seldom have public relations directors to complain about the media's almost unnatural interest in their activities. Unlike big labor, big business, big medicine, big government, and big wealth, they have no clout. The great powers in American society employ immense skill to invent self-serving images, and prevent them from being tarnished.

Television documentaries looking into the actions, responsibilities, and influences of such powers have tended for the most part to be superficial or bland. Not always, of course. There have been some notable exceptions, earning deserved kudos for all the networks and public TV. In fact, one network financed a brave and costly investigation—one which it conceived of as having the impact of Watergate—which had to be abandoned because the investigators simply could not produce an airtight case.

But the fact remains that investigations often cover what appear to be safe areas. These stories can be depended upon to attract public attention and sympathy. They generally uphold the established myth about the subject. If such stories appear critical, the criticism is often regarded by the subjects as within acceptable bounds, giving the story a quality of being "objective," and "not one-sided." This is best illustrated by the stories that are regularly done about narcotics, almost all of which are labeled "investigative." Who knows how many dozens of reports have been aired about drug laws, drug treatment, drug operators, drug users, alleged attendant crime, et cetera, et cetera? Much of what has been done reflects the attitudes and approaches of agencies and individuals with a vested interest in narcotics: federal, state and municipal law enforcement agencies; federal, state and municipal drug treatment, education, and eradication programs. American television viewers, it would seem, could qualify for Ph.D.'s on the drug world if they've been even remotely attentive.

But a truly revealing investigation of drugs would be one which showed the raising of opium in Turkey; its processing into morphine base in Lebanon; its processing into heroin in Marseilles; its smuggling into America; and only finally its injection into the vein of a Harlem junkie. Yet, precious little has been done to show the varied vested interests which depend for their existence upon the narcotic addict.

It took years for anyone—TV or print—to do the sort of investigative reporting which asked whether the venerable Harry J. Anslinger, powerful head of the Federal Bureau of Narcotics, knew what he was talking about when he insisted that one puff on a sinister marijuana reefer led invariably to the ravishments of heroin. A whole scenario of law enforcement control of drug trafficking was based on Anslinger's say-so.

In the same manner, the pronouncements and conclusions of J. Edgar Hoover and the FBI were treated as scripture and it was only belatedly, in the post-Watergate period, that TV attempted in-depth investigative reports on the FBI.

The investigative report, ideally, aims not merely to reveal but to explain the essence of the revelation. It explains the environment in which a situation arose, the conditions which acted to encourage its growth, and what it means. That is a very tough order in a medium that has developed inordinate skill at being able to titillate viewers without truly informing them.

Bernard Gavzer is the investigative producer of NBC-TV for the local New York evening news.

February 9, 1964. "I Want to Hold Your Hand. . . ." England's popular new singing sensation The Beatles come to America for three appearances on *The Ed Sullivan Show*. The first show is the most-watched single program in the show's history. (L–R) Ringo Starr, George Harrison, John Lennon, and Paul McCartney make their American TV debuts.

After only one year, the much-praised *Judy Garland Show* is dropped by CBS. What Garland had expected to be a wonderful experience has turned out to be a period of turmoil and disappointment. However, Garland's last few programs in 1964 are among the best of the year. She does several one-woman shows, a blockbuster hour with Barbra Streisand (who is about to star in Broadway's *Funny Girl*), and this program with Liza Minnelli.

CONFESSIONS OF AN INVESTIGATIVE REPORTER

WAYNE SATZ

Most investigative reporters on local TV are trite, voice-conscious drama majors who do simplistic, illustrated versions of stories they clipped from the morning paper. My station has permitted me to step out of that stereotype. Ironically, my employer is a network-owned station in Los Angeles that is associated with the birth of "happy talk," unbelievably attractive anchor people, and ninety second "action film" stories. To the company's credit, it found time in the format for inquiries by a less-than-perfect face who turns out longish, "talking head" stories looking skeptically at local institutions. It found room on the news set for a journalist who seeks—and occasionally, gets—information that the power structure doesn't want revealed. I am its "investigative reporter."

Perhaps I'm merely tolerated in this role because it is good public relations—a symbol of the station's commitment to news. Or maybe we actually pick up viewers (ratings) when I appear with an "exclusive" slide across my chest. I'd like to think I'm aboard for both reasons, and maybe even because—who knows?—the audience is hungering for something more than fast-moving pictures. In any case, the reporter who goes digging for *television* news faces a special set of barriers, and thrills, that newspaper journalists can only wonder about.

An investigative reporter on the tube, like reporters in any medium, needs a source. But potential sources are often put off by the reputation we broad-

" . . . I occasionally use tricks to overcome these barriers . . ."

cast newsmen have for being superficial. The fellow who's hidden away in some bureaucracy where he sees evil going on is uncomfortable about calling the video reporter. He assumes first of all, that TV newsmen only want to cover events—news conferences and fires and retirement parties for lovable school janitors. The source figures he ought to take his information to a "real" reporter on the *Times*. Or the guy worries that, if he does come forward, the television reporter won't go to the mat to keep his source's identity a secret (as a newspaper reporter surely would). Or the insider reckons that his information is useless to broadcasters unless he's willing to put his face on television, which he is usually reluctant to do. All these are false notions from where I sit, but they are reminders of how novel it is to see TV reporters really dig for the truth.

Interestingly, once I'm on the trail of something, I am suddenly awash with sources. After I've hit the air with my first installment on, say, an ugly little conspiracy inside a government office, I know that by the time I walk from the news set to the newsroom the switchboard will be lit up with callers who invariably

252

The Garry Moore Show goes off CBS in 1964 after a successful six-year run. Here guests Patti Page and Tony Randall flank regulars (L–R) Marion Lorne, Garry Moore, Durwood Kirby, and Carol Burnett. In 1966, Moore will have another variety show on CBS for a year. In 1969, he will begin hosting the syndicated *To Tell the Truth*.

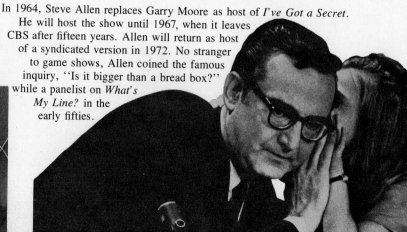

In 1964, Steve Allen replaces Garry Moore as host of *I've Got a Secret*. He will host the show until 1967, when it leaves CBS after fifteen years. Allen will return as host of a syndicated version in 1972. No stranger to game shows, Allen coined the famous inquiry, "Is it bigger than a bread box?" while a panelist on *What's My Line?* in the early fifties.

Wayne Satz: "The reporter who goes digging for television news faces a special set of barriers, and thrills . . ."

say, "Hell, if you think *that's* a story, listen to *this!*" I do, and what I hear often leads to bolder revelations of misconduct than I'd foreseen when I began. "Ah," I think, "so there *are* people at the other end of that camera lens I stare at, and they do want to help the truth come out." Suddenly I'm involved in a sort of participatory journalism that, I'm fairly sure, print journalists rarely experience.

The difficulty for all video newsmen is that we have to record our conversations in order to fully share them with the viewers. And filming (or taping) tends

to make conversations a big deal. I often have to bring several technicians to an interview. There are bright lights and intruding microphones. Given these trappings, it's very tough to elicit anything other than guarded and self-laudatory remarks from people.

I admit with no shame that I occasionally use tricks to overcome these barriers that my equipment creates. There are times when I'll walk up to my subject unannounced, camera rolling. He is without the benefit of a prepared spiel, and yet knows that dodging me will not look flattering on the evening news. In

253

Bill Cullen continues to be a panelist on *I've Got a Secret* in 1964, but *The Price Is Right,* which he hosts, goes off television after nine seasons on NBC and ABC. In the 1970's, Cullen will be a panelist on the syndicated *To Tell the Truth* and host several game shows, including *Three on a Match.*

April 30, 1964. *Jeopardy* premieres on NBC. Hosted by gentlemanly Art Fleming, this intelligent daily quiz show will last until 1975.

Alumni Fun, a 1964 CBS version of *G.E. College Bowl,* pits celebrity college alumni teams against one another. Hosted by Peter Lind Hayes, this quiz show will go off after one year.

other situations I'll ask my camerman to lay down his camera, creating the impression that the conversation of my reluctant subject could never be televised. When the camera-shy interviewee gets to matters of public interest, I subtly signal the cameraman to start recording the sound portion of the dialogue.

Being discreet can also be difficult when I've left the camera crew behind, and I'm out foraging for background information. As a news reporter, I have got a face that simply won't blend into the environment. I remember well a visit to a Hollywood massage parlor, back in the days when we were all still wondering if they offered more than massages. I was disguised with glasses, a cap, and tinted hair. It was nighttime, and the Palace of Love was lit only with small red bulbs. But Bernadette and I had only begun discussing my ''pleasure centers'' when she observed that I looked ''A lot like that guy that does the news, you know, whatshisname . . .'' Within moments, Bernadette was quite sure I *was* whatshisname, and was wondering why someone in my position couldn't get unpaid companionship.

The great satisfaction from my work comes when I perceive something awry in our system, figure out what's going on, and then tell that story with smartly edited film in the community's homes. It is a very personal kind of communication, in a world that seems to have little place for that these days. And my version is much more powerful than the fifteen column inches of black ink on newsprint that my counterpart on the major daily would crank out on the same story. Walter Lippman declared that the job of the journalist is to take ''pictures of reality on which people can act.'' We TV reporters can do that better than anyone.

For example, when I got word that some local doctors were writing prescriptions for dangerous drugs to any teenage ''patient'' who could pay the fee, I hooked up ''patients'' of my own with wireless mikes,

"Newspaper reporters are often envious of my medium."

sent them to alleged ''drug doctors,'' and later played for the world the fifteen-second conversations in which my helpers easily scored barbiturates from M.D.'s. The series that developed from this and other surveillance stands up as pretty good journalism—investigative journalism—and it was undoubtedly good television as well.

Newspaper reporters are often envious of my medium. Many are the print journalists, for example, who've tagged a revealing story with a denial from a shadowy figure, and wished they could show that denial as only TV can—with the tightness in the voice, the unsteadiness in the eyes, and the faltering response to the follow-up question. No typeface, of any size, can compete with the immediacy of television.

Part of journalism's job is to take an adversary stance to government, and that's a role well suited to television news. In a long series on the Los Angeles Police Department's secrecy about those it has killed in action, my hallway confrontations with the chief of police became a staple. I was comfortable with my stance as a challenging reporter, and secure in the knowledge that these encounters were evidence for viewers of their chief's good or bad faith, and his confidence in them. This was not investigative reporting made palatable by theatrics. It was simply investigative reporting on television—a marriage that just happens to make for interesting viewing with surprising frequency. I think the marriage will last.

Wayne Satz, an attorney, is an investigative reporter for KABC-TV, Los Angeles.

The Danny Thomas Show, previously called *Make Room for Daddy,* goes off television in 1964. It has been on ABC and CBS for eleven years. In 1967, Thomas will host *The Danny Thomas Hour,* a variety show on NBC. It will last one season.

George Maharis leaves *Route 66* in 1964 to pursue film acting and singing. He will never regain the immense popularity he acquired while making this series. *Route 66* will last one more year with Glenn Corbett, late of NBC's excellent, but short-lived *It's a Man's World* series. In the final episode Martin Milner will marry Barbara Eden and settle down.

TV ACTION REPORTING
CHRISTOPHER JONES

The action reporter is a concept in television news based on the following assumptions: that ordinary people make good news if their stories are told well; that journalism is the voice of ordinary people; that people in general, and Americans in particular, empathize with the underdog; and that good journalism will lead to worthwhile reform in a democratic society.

The front page of The New York *Times* rarely concerns itself with "ordinary" people. That may be one reason why "ordinary" people rarely concern themselves with The New York *Times*. On the other hand, local newspapers are beginning to show the giant metropolitan dailies that the road to journalistic riches is not necessarily paved with international celebrities. Everyone has a problem—the garbageman who can't get a bank loan, the banker who can't get his garbage picked up—and we all have a mutual interest in the resolution of the problems of others. This is the principle behind the popularity and the power of the action reporter.

He or she is a kind of electronic ombudsman dedicated to solving a wide range of problems sent in by viewers. Twenty years ago, the action reporter could not have existed. Television, although not in its infancy, was still a toddler, unwilling or unable to incur the wrath of even its smallest sponsors. Today, television is a sellers' market, and, while that may be bad news for corporations and advertising agencies, it is very good news for the viewing public.

Television can work for you. It can represent your interests remarkably well. But most of us still

> ## "The action reporter focuses public power."

don't fully appreciate television's capabilities for assisting people with their problems. We see "exposés" of major offenders on various newscasts (although even now it is no mere coincidence that few of these "exposés" attack corporations with large television advertising budgets), but how often does television recount the problem Aunt Tillie had when her local furniture store sold her a table without legs and refused to listen to her protests when she discovered the mistake? In a major market, the argument against reporting this kind of problem has been traditional and self-serving. It goes something like this: "We have thirty million potential viewers in the New York City television audience. Who gives a damn about Aunt Tillie's table?"

The answer to the question as posed is simple. Nobody gives a damn about Aunt Tillie's table, but *everyone* cares about what happens when Aunt Tillie gets ripped off and can't do a thing about it. If it can happen to her, it can happen to us, and probably already has.

The concept of the action reporter is simple, but it works. It has proved that your problem can be solved through the intervention of television and the power of the press; and that your problem and its solution, if it is televised, will interest others.

255

Lyndon Johnson wins the Democratic nomination for president at the 1964 convention. Having succeeded the late John Kennedy, Johnson will have the opportunity to be elected president for the first time in November. Daughter Luci, wife Lady Bird, and daughter Lynda surround him.

Conservative Barry Goldwater wins the Republican presidential nomination in 1964. To his left is his vice-presidential choice, William E. Miller. The inner workings of the convention are hidden behind a wall of secrecy, and news correspondents are not allowed much freedom. NBC newsman John Chancellor is arrested on camera. He calls out: "This is John Chancellor, somewhere in custody."

September 5, 1964. *Peyton Place* debuts on ABC. Playing twice a week, the adaptation of the once-scandalous Grace Metalious novel about a small New England town full of sin, is television's first prime time soap opera. Mia Farrow, as Allison MacKenzie, and Ryan O'Neal, as Rodney Harrington, become fan magazine favorites.

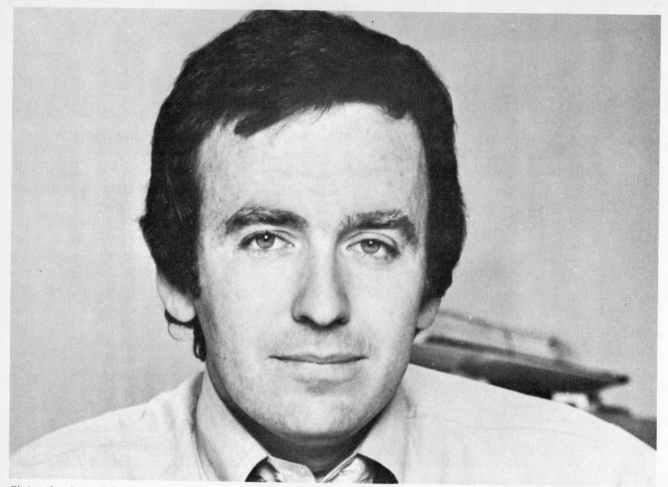

Christopher Jones defines the action reporter as ''a kind of electronic ombudsman'' dedicated to solving viewer problems.

The ''power elite'' is accustomed to lawsuits—if a member gets sued, he employs a good lawyer and forgets about it until the bill comes. The action reporter cuts through this impersonal response and gets back to the basics. The president of Corporation X and Bureaucracy Z can have a staff member handle a lawsuit, but who's going to explain to his golf partners, or his wife, why he is victimizing consumers?

The public is the forum for the resolution of any dispute: judgment is in the hands of the people through their opinion. The action reporter focuses public power. And like democracy, the action reporter gets results.

Christopher Jones, an attorney, is the action reporter for WNEW-TV News in New York City.

256

September 17, 1964. Elizabeth Montgomery, who had made several appearances in the 1950's on her father's anthology series *Robert Montgomery Presents,* stars as a good witch, Samantha, in the comedy *Bewitched* on ABC. Dick York is her mortal husband.

September 18, 1964. *The Addams Family,* a zany comedy series based on Charles Addams's weird cartoons, debuts on ABC. It will last two seasons. Starring are: (L–R, front row) Lisa Loring, Carolyn Jones, John Astin, Ken Weatherwax, and (L–R, back row) Jackie Coogan, Blossom Rock, and Ted Cassidy.

THE INVISIBLE NEWS SHOW

CHARLES NOVITZ

Seven days a week the news show "no one" sees is broadcast nationwide for at least half an hour to an audience of 162 people. These select "viewers" are the producers and editors of the news programs televised by all the local stations affiliated with the American Broadcasting Company.

At ABC, the name of the show that "no one" sees is abbreviated DEF, which stands for Daily Electronic Feed. This means that each day (hence "Daily") ABC News transmits along its network lines (hence "Electronic") a score of news items (hence a news "Feed"). Each affiliated station records these items on videotape, and later chooses those it wants to play back in part or in full on the local news broadcast.

What do stations get during a typical half-hour feed?

First and foremost is the top news of the day. Among twenty or more DEF items, or "spots" as they are sometimes called, there may be half a dozen stories from Washington. The activities of the President are documented, as are the doings of Congress and its committees. There are also stories about the bureaucracy, and seasonal items about such events as the blossoming of the cherry trees around the Tidal Basin every spring. ABC collects news material from all over the world by way of feed lines and satellites, and when there is a particularly urgent story, it can be "turned around" and sent out to all the affiliated stations within five minutes of its receipt in New York.

There are also DEF spots of a less somber nature than politics. Usually up to half a dozen items in a typical DEF will concern sports. Depending on the season, athletes will be shown shooting basketballs, kicking footballs, or smashing baseballs over fences. A filmstrip of composite photographs, taken from a satellite with optical and infrared cameras, is provided daily by an agency of the government. This filmstrip shows storm clouds and clear weather over the country, and can be used to illustrate the predictions of the local weather person.

On any given day there may be one or more features on such things as a record litter of twenty-seven live piglets born in Hungary, or a pregnant whale in Brooklyn, or hot-dog ski antics in the Yugoslavian Alps. If a new feature movie has just been released, a scene may be provided by the producer, or a review will be sent out. The Sunday network talk shows are excerpted when these newsmaker interviews make news.

Anything that can be captured on film or tape anywhere in the world, whether it be funny or tragic or merely serious, can be transmitted quickly by ABC/DEF to a national television audience. The 162 "viewers" in ABC stations around the United States are the "gatekeepers" who decide which of the many news items offered each day by the network will be seen by the millions of people who make up the nation's TV news audience.

Charles Novitz, manager of ABC's Syndicated News Service, knows his p's and q's about ABC/DEF.

257

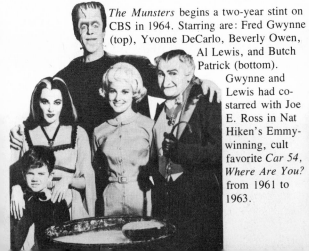

The Munsters begins a two-year stint on CBS in 1964. Starring are: Fred Gwynne (top), Yvonne DeCarlo, Beverly Owen, Al Lewis, and Butch Patrick (bottom). Gwynne and Lewis had co-starred with Joe E. Ross in Nat Hiken's Emmy-winning, cult favorite *Car 54, Where Are You?* from 1961 to 1963.

Bob Cummings returns to TV in 1964 to star in CBS's *My Living Doll* on which statuesque Julie Newmar plays a robot. The comedy series will last one year.

CBS's *The Cara Williams Show* in 1964 casts Cara Williams and Frank Aletter as newlyweds who work at a firm that prohibits the employment of married couples. This comedy series will only last one year.

TV NEWS STARS
WILLIAM A. WOOD

Television news has stars too, and often the brightest of these are the anchor men and women whose popularity largely determines which programs people want to watch. Nationally-known newscasters such as Walter Cronkite and Barbara Walters have local equivalents: Fahey Flynn in Chicago, Jim Mitchell in Louisville, and Tim Baldridge in Dayton. It is these celebrities and others like them who gather large personal followings, build audiences and ratings, and therefore generate advertising and profits for their stations and networks. Throughout the nation there is fierce competition for popular and successful anchor people, and there are never enough of the best ones to go around.

A first-rate newscaster must also be an entertaining showman. Anchors are successful primarily because they are good communicators, and only secondarily because they are good journalists. Sherlee Barish, a New York agent who finds anchors for local stations, says, "What they want is a big, sexy stud with youth, charisma, and credibility." Anchor people must be both attractive and authoritative. Those who have little or no journalistic experience can get by as long as they are supplied with good copy written by competent news people. But when there is a fast-breaking or unexpected story and the newscaster is forced to extemporize, then the mere "communicator" who is not also an experienced journalist is betrayed by his emptiness even if he is glib.

Occasionally newscasters are discovered in beauty contests, modeling schools, or in the theater. However, these people are exceptions, and rarely go

"A first-rate newscaster must also be . . . a showman."

far. Television's ancestor, radio, used to supply many anchors, as did the print media. Walter Cronkite, John Chancellor, and David Brinkley all used to work for newspapers before they went into television, but now anchor people have increasingly varied backgrounds. Some begin as TV newsroom assistants, or graduate from journalism schools. Many anchors begin as street reporters, where they get initial camera exposure. Ellen Fleischer, Frank Reynolds, and David Schoumacher started this way. In small cities, some future anchors simply walk in off the street. After successful apprenticeships in other newsroom jobs, a promising candidate may get a chance to become the on-camera centerpiece.

Successful anchor people possess considerable upward mobility. Popularity in a small city will usually lead to work in a larger one. Big broadcast organizations often shift anchors from one station to another looking for the perfect chemistry, or use stations in small markets as farm clubs where apprentice anchors can gain experience. A news director on the prowl will come into a town, lock himself in a motel room with a television set, and assess the local talent. When NBC was casting its new two-hour news program in New York, this evaluative technique was carried to extraordinary extremes. Videotape recordings

258

Bob Denver plays Gilligan, the first mate of the shipwrecked S.S. Minnow, on *Gilligan's Island,* which begins a three-year run on CBS in 1964. Co-starring in this comedy series are Tina Louise (R), Alan Hale, Jr., Jim Backus, Natalie Schaefer, Dawn Wells, and Russell Johnson.

September 2, 1964. Richard Crenna fights for justice as politician James Slattery in the CBS dramatic series *Slattery's People.* This unusual series will receive acclaim, but will go off after one season.

September 22, 1964. Robert Vaughn is superagent Napoleon Solo on the fast-paced James Bond parody *The Man from U.N.C.L.E.,* which debuts on NBC. Although most women on the show chase Vaughn, more around America favor unknown David McCallum, who, as Illya Kuryakin, helps Solo battle Thrush. Leo G. Carroll co-stars.

Walter Cronkite, perhaps the most trusted man in America, covers the Project Mercury space shot in 1962.

As the careers of countless anchors demonstrate, the smaller markets feed the larger ones, and at the head of the line beckons New York, and network television. Roger Grimsby was kidnapped from KGO, San Francisco, by WABC, New York. He was joined there by two Boston anchormen, Tom Ellis and Bill Bonds. Tom Snyder of NBC came to New York from Los Angeles after starting his career in Savannah, Georgia, and then returned to Los Angeles. Another New York anchor, Chuck Scarborough, began in Biloxi, Mississippi. Minneapolis, Buffalo, Miami, Tulsa, and Houston have launched anchors to national stardom; both Jim Hartz and the late Frank McGee got their starts in Oklahoma City.

Every anchor who moves up leaves a vacuum in his or her wake. When Tom Ellis left Boston, his replacement was found in Denver. In turn, the Denver station had to raid somewhere else. The competition for talent intensifies as the financial stakes increase. Many anchors employ agents to negotiate more and more lucrative contracts as they rise through the system. When a station finds a good anchor, it will pay handsomely. In the littlest markets, salaries are quite modest, but even in small cities salaries range upward from twenty thousand dollars a year. Salaries of forty to fifty thousand dollars are likely in the top fifty markets, while in the ten largest cities, anchor salaries reach one hundred thousand and beyond. At the national networks, multi-year contracts are in seven figures. Barbara Walters at ABC News makes one million dollars a year.

259

were made of anchors in action at every station in the country's top forty markets. Six finalists were presented to test audiences in a TV van at shopping centers and over selected cable TV outlets. These tests determined the ultimate choices.

The Rogues, a stylish comedy-caper show about a group of cultured con artists, debuts on NBC in 1964. It will last one year. Starring are Gig Young, Charles Boyer, David Niven, and (not shown) Robert Coote and Gladys Cooper. Boyer and Niven co-starred in *Four Star Playhouse* in the mid-fifties.

Dennis Weaver leaves *Gunsmoke* and his limp when he stars as a veterinarian in *Kentucky Jones.* NBC will cancel this half-hour drama after one season. Harry Morgan co-stars.

Tom Brokaw moved up through the ranks to anchor on Today.

Anchor people are valuable because they give a news program its image and style. Chet Huntley and David Brinkley were the most famous anchor team at NBC. Because of their great success, most station managements now try to combine two or three anchors on teams they hope will achieve equivalent rapport and appeal. But the most recent innovation in newscast personnel casting is the rapid emergence of blacks and women as anchor stars. In responding to pressures for equal opportunity of employment, broadcasters have also discovered that they can attract a broader spectrum of viewers than they have in the past. There are now close to a thousand television stations in the country, employing approximately one anchor woman for every four anchor men. Chinese-American Connie Chung co-anchors on KNXT, Los Angeles; Cassie Mackin of NBC anchors a weekend network news program. More and more stations also employ at least one black or Hispanic anchor. Max Robinson, a black, is at WTOP, Washington, Jack Jones co-anchors at KYW, Philadelphia, and CBS White House correspondent Ed Bradley anchors a weekend network news program as well.

The best-known anchor men, like Walter Cronkite, have been around longest and achieved the status of father figures. The next generation of anchors will be different. At age twenty-six, Jane Pauley of the *Today Show* won't become a father figure any time soon. Depending upon the talent of these new, increasingly young, female, and black anchors, they will be either cosmetic figures who are merely pleasing on-camera performers, or they will become a good deal more. By the time most anchor men and women begin to reach large audiences, they will have worked their way up through the small and medium-sized markets, and should have learned the trade of journalism in the process.

William A. Wood is a broadcaster for CBS Radio, teaches at the School of Journalism, Columbia University, and is the author of Electronic Journalism.

260

September 25, 1964. Jim Nabors takes the dim-witted Gomer Pyle character he created on *The Andy Griffith Show* out of Mayberry and into the service on CBS's *Gomer Pyle, U.S.M.C.* Frank Sutton co-stars in this hit comedy series.

Broadside, a comedy spin-off from *McHale's Navy* featuring Waves at war, debuts on ABC. It will last only one season. Starring are Kathy Nolan, Sheila James, Joan Staley, and Lois Roberts. In the 1970's, Nolan will become president of the Screen Actor's Guild.

DOROTHY SARNOFF: STAR MAKER

DEBRA WEINER

Dorothy Sarnoff is an ex-opera singer and actress who makes her living creating good-news faces. She teaches television journalists, talk show hosts and guests, business executives, and politicians how to make-the-most-of-their-best. Since she began her practice thirteen years ago, she has personally revamped more than twenty-seven thousand personalities, and for $1,500 she will spend six hours training any enthusiast how to evince I-care-about-you feelings.

"A gourmet chef can take a piece of raw meat and with a little bit of this and that make you start drooling," she says. "Well, I do the same thing with personalities. I teach people how to serve up their best selves." Sarnoff teaches her students to look as if they love what they are doing, and because most news and talk shows are shot in closeup, she concentrates on creating an animated face. Particular care is taken to develop "talking eyes" that say, "Oh, Fascinating," or "Fabulous," or "Yes, I'm Listening," or "Prove It." She encourages students to make eye-to-eye contact 90 percent of the time they are on television. Newsmen frequently develop glazed looks and start to drone when they speak. Sarnoff suggests that newscasters pretend they are actually inside a viewer's home, and make eye-to-eye contact with the imagined host.

Even commanding eyes are useless, however, if partnered with lazy cheek muscles, so Sarnoff reminds her students to lift up their cheeks at all times. She guarantees that the resulting love-apples will bring variety to the most static of one-face faces.

"If you can physically convey a message, then

"Most of Sarnoff's advice is top secret."

the message will be accepted that much better," she says. "Even if the news is disastrous, it doesn't mean you have to tell it with a long, noncommittal face. An 'up' face, a feeling face, is much more consoling."

Sarnoff's office resembles a television studio. Lighting and camera equipment are at one end of the room and a video playback is at the other. Each new client plays his or her role opposite Sarnoff in front of the camera. Then the client views the tape and studies the problems it reveals. Slouching, nail-picking and foot-tapping might not be picked up on a real television screen, yet these are just the kinds of sloppy and nervous habits that can affect voice quality.

Sarnoff's operation is titled Speech Dynamics Inc. She was a speech major at Cornell University, so lessons in how to cosmetize the voice are, of course, part of her service. Sarnoff claims to have rid several newscasters of their singsong phrasing, and would like to rid one Hollywood interviewer of her high-pitched, little-girl elocution.

Yet the author of *Speech Can Change Your Life* dislikes being considered a glorified speech teacher. Sarnoff prefers to be thought of as a plastic surgeon specializing in personae. Thus she may advise a client to switch hairstyles, wear different makeup or clothes, or even improve his or her emotional manners.

A television interviewer must never seem to be

261

Twelve O'Clock High comes to ABC in 1964. It is produced by Twentieth Century-Fox and based on its movie classic starring Gregory Peck. Robert Lansing plays Frank Savage, general of the World War II bomber squadron, during the show's first year. After Savage is killed in action, Paul Burke becomes the series's star.

Twentieth Century-Fox's *Voyage to the Bottom of the Sea* comes to ABC in 1964. Richard Basehart and David Hedison star in this science fiction adventure series produced by Irwin Allen.

Lassie gets her third owner in 1964. Robert Bray will star as Forest Ranger Corey Stuart for the next four years on *Lassie*.

Dorothy Sarnoff in the well-equipped office where she trains people to make-the-most-of-their-best for television.

"... she will spend six hours training any enthusiast how to evince I-care-about-you feelings."

persecuting a guest, insists Sarnoff. But he or she mustn't seem to champion a guest either. In both cases the interviewer will lose the audience. A talk show guest, on the other hand, must exude an I've-been-there-before, I-know-all confidence without sounding pompous. Should the guest be a state official on a program like *Meet the Press,* he has to know how to "protect his country as well as his personal integrity."

Most of Sarnoff's advice is top secret. There is one important lesson, however, about which she is totally candid. In fact, it is printed on the red and white button each pupil receives upon graduation. It reads: I'm Glad I'm Here, I'm Glad You're Here. Sarnoff wears her button all the time.

Debra Weiner is a correspondent for New Times *magazine.*

In its fifth year *Bonanza* usurps *The Beverly Hillbillies* as America's most popular show during the 1964–65 season. Although Pernell Roberts (R) will leave the show in 1965, *Bonanza* will retain its number-one position until the 1967–68 season and continue to be enormously popular for several years after that.

TV's first dolphin comes to NBC in 1964 in *Flipper.* Luke Halpin and Tommy Norden are Flipper's pals in this MGM production. Brian Kelly and Andy Devine also have starring roles.

PERFORMING INSTRUCTIONS IN THE EARLY DAYS

These instructions were handed to performers when they entered a New York TV studio in 1938. Nobody had conceived of personality coaches in the early days of commercial broadcasting.

1. Arrive at the studio in time for adequate rehearsal, at least one hour before the television program goes on the air.

2. Explain special aspects of your program to the television producer; secure any special instructions from him.

3. Present yourself for the application of make-up. If you apply your own make-up, use broad strokes and remember that red lips do not televise as such; lips must be made up in violet or brown.

4. When you are in front of the camera, make no unusual motions. Look pleasant. If it is necessary to go off the air for any emergency, walk or move to one side of the scene.

5. Speak loudly and project your voice as on the legitimate stage, particularly if you are in a play and are several feet from the microphone.

6. Watch the signals of the television producer. He will raise his arm for you to begin. Start gracefully after he has given his signal. He will raise his arm again when you must cease your production, or at the natural end of your production. In case you are requested in such manner to conclude your program, you may always have a few seconds longer to place a pleasant ending to your presentation.

7. Do not give evidence of discomfort because of heat or other factors.

8. Do not start talking or come out of the character until you are sure that you are not being picked up both orally and visually.

9. In close-ups, do not move to and from the camera any more than necessary. Moves to the side or up and down are preferable. This also applies to gestures with the hands, which should be held near your body and not placed in front of you toward the camera.

10. Do not hesitate to gesture or emphasize your presentation in any manner that you desire in keeping with the above rule.

11. Look directly into the camera as often as possible. Smile and otherwise conduct yourself as though there was a whole audience inside the camera lens.

Once again, Fess Parker becomes a frontiersman on *Daniel Boone*, which begins a six-year run on NBC in 1964. Parker, who got only a small salary from *Davy Crockett*, will get rich from this popular series.

Fess Parker and Buddy Ebsen, who had co-starred in "Davy Crockett," are reunited on *The Danny Kaye Show*. Also joining them and Kaye in song is Clint Eastwood of *Rawhide*.

October 5, 1964. Debbie Watson, in the middy blouse, plays the title role in the comedy "Karen," one of three half-hour segments running back-to-back on NBC's *90 Bristol Court*. Mary La Roche (L), Richard Denning, and Gina Gillespie co-star. When the show is canceled in January, *Karen* will become a separate series. It will only last a few months.

TV HEARINGS: McCARTHY AND WATERGATE

SIDNEY KLINE

Television is the most powerful means of communication ever devised by man. At public hearings, when conditions are at their best, its power can be awesome. The main characters are in fixed positions, where the camera can capture them in unguarded moments. Asides and unexpected outbursts enrich and reveal the meaning behind prepared statements. Drama unfolds with the sudden force of life, and the impact on the viewer can be enormous. The Army-McCarthy hearings and the Watergate hearings are two cases in point.

In 1954, Senator Joseph McCarthy was riding high on ruthless demagoguery. The cold war, the Korean War, the Alger Hiss case, the Russian acquisition of the atom bomb—all contributed to an atmosphere of fear in America. McCarthy capitalized on this fear as he attempted to smear those whom he considered to be America's internal enemies, but his accusations were rarely founded on fact. His victims were random targets, and he tainted the nation. Few newspapers and magazines dared to challenge the powerful senator. The first major counterattack came in Edward R. Murrow's *See It Now* broadcast on CBS in March 1954. "This is no time," Murrow said, "for men who oppose Senator McCarthy's methods to keep silent. We can deny our heritage and our history, but we cannot escape responsibility for the result."

The Army-McCarthy hearings began in late April 1954, and concerned the senator's charges that there

> " . . . the power of television . . . showed the American public the truth as no other medium could."

was subversion in the American military. The counsel-without-fee for the U.S. Army was Joseph Welch, a tall, balding, sixty-three-year-old lifelong Republican who was the senior partner in a prominent Boston law firm. Welch was integrity personified. Throughout the hearings—which were televised by the American Broadcasting Company, because it was the smallest network at the time and had no regularly scheduled programming to offer its affiliates— McCarthy interrupted the proceedings again and again with the cry: "Point of order, Mr. Chairman!" Whereupon, he would digress into unrelated areas of what he called "the Communist conspiracy." His great error occurred when he charged that the conspiracy had even spread to Welch's law firm.

McCarthy charged that a young associate in the firm, Frederick Fisher, had been a member of the Lawyers Guild, which McCarthy characterized as "the legal bulwark for the Communist party." When the senator finally concluded his long, imprecise, and haranguing accusation, Welch attempted to reply.

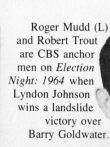

October 13, 1964. Ed Wynn (R) visits CBS's popular *The Red Skelton Hour*. Skelton is interested in harem girl Sandy Wirth in this sketch.

Roger Mudd (L) and Robert Trout are CBS anchor men on *Election Night: 1964* when Lyndon Johnson wins a landslide victory over Barry Goldwater.

NBC's *Hollywood and the Stars* shows a segment called "Hollywood Goes to War." In an early film clip, Bob Hope entertains World War II troops. Joining him are Jerry Colonna, and Frances Langford.

The Army-McCarthy Hearings made dramatic television viewing in 1954. The nation sat transfixed as the workings of government appeared live in their living rooms. Public exposure on TV contributed significantly to McCarthy's ultimate downfall.

Among TV's most popular annual Christmas shows since 1952 have been Bob Hope's Yuletide visits to Armed Forces bases around the world. Here Hope visits troops in South Viet Nam. Although news coverage of the war in Southeast Asia will expand in 1965 with the escalation of the fighting under Lyndon Johnson, much early reportage will be similar to Hope's films, which show united, happy, healthy, determined American soldiers.

December 30, 1964. *Let's Make a Deal* debuts. Host Monty Hall asks a conservatively dressed contestant if she will exchange her contraption for either the table, the package, or the smiling man. In 1968, the show will move from NBC to ABC. Enormously popular, an evening version will be added in 1969.

"And the public made judgments."

When at last he could, the attorney said, "Until this moment, Senator, I think I never really gauged your cruelty or your recklessness." Welch then proceeded to explain simply and straightforwardly the case of Frederick Fisher, concluding to the senator: "If it were in my power to forgive you for your reckless cruelty, I would do so. I like to think I am a gentle man, but your forgiveness will have to come from someone other than me." As McCarthy continued his tirade against Fisher, Welch cried, "Have you no sense of decency, sir, at long last? Have you left no sense of decency?" When the exchange was concluded and Welch finally called the next witness, there was applause from the committee room. A brave man had dueled openly with a vicious demagogue and clearly defeated him—on television, for all the nation to see.

The hearings continued through the middle of June, but everything after Welch's outburst was anticlimactic. In early December, the Senate censured McCarthy and stripped him of power. Always a heavy drinker, McCarthy drank even more than usual and died, a discredited man, in May 1957, leaving the term "McCarthyism" as his heritage.

In June 1972, a group of burglars were caught in the Democratic National Committee headquarters in Washington, D.C., and touched off the massive national political scandal known as Watergate. A year later, the Senate elected to hold open hearings on the charges that were shaking the administration of President Richard Nixon to its very foundations. Nineteen years after the Army-McCarthy hearings, the Watergate hearings were held in the very same caucus room. All three major networks provided rotating coverage of the proceedings, while public television carried all the hearings in full and rebroadcast them at night. Thus, heroes were made and villains felled in a continuing drama watched by hundreds of millions of people in America and around the world. Day after day, viewers saw Senator Sam Ervin of North Carolina cut through the defenses and rhetoric of unhappy witnesses with his earthy, Bible-quoting wisdom. They saw John Dean, President Nixon's counsel, expose his boss. They saw arrogant John Ehrlichman, cold-as-ice H. R. Haldeman, brazen John Mitchell, loyal but unconvincing Rose Mary Woods, and many others. And the public made judgments.

President Nixon did not appear at the Senate Watergate hearings, but, in turn, the House Judiciary Committee opened its doors to television for the deliberations on whether or not to impeach the President. Viewers were able to watch their elected representatives wrestling openly with the hardest decision of their political careers. Ultimately, the viewers were there when impeachment was voted. Nixon resigned, and television captured his rambling, almost incoherent farewell to the White House staff in August 1974, before he flew off to exile at his estate in San Clemente, California.

The Army-McCarthy hearings were a unique event on television in 1954. In 1973, the power of television to expose those involved in Watergate again showed the American public the truth as no other medium could. In both cases, television helped shape the events of history it was recording.

Sidney Kline, a veteran newspaper and television journalist, has been at ABC network news for the last twelve years.

266

What's My Line? moves into its fifteenth season in 1965. It is the year of controversial panelist-columnist Dorothy Kilgallen's death. The program will continue until 1967. The first mystery guest was Phil Rizzuto. The last will be host John Daly.

Bill Leydon, who had reunited a lot of people with long-lost relatives on *It Could Be You* in 1956, is host of *Call My Bluff*, a word game that makes its debut and exit in 1965. Peggy Cass and Abe Burrows are celebrity guest panelists.

STAR TALK:
JOHN RANDOLPH ON THE BLACKLISTINGS

AS TOLD TO DAVID LEVINE

It was about 1951 that we became aware of the existence of the "graylist." That was a list of one hundred and fifty-one names that Procter & Gamble and Borden's had that was used in the beginning to "blacklist" actors. It contained the names of actors who couldn't remember lines, who were obstreperous, actors who were radical, even actors whose names were being mixed up with other actors' names. It was that horrible.

In my own case, I was doing a show with Anthony Quinn on CBS; Sidney Lumet was directing. Suddenly one day, I was called in by the producer, who said, "Sidney doesn't want to talk about it; he's very upset. He was called up to CBS and told that the network had been contacted by a Mr. Johnson of Syracuse, who owns several supermarkets up there." Johnson had contacted *Amm-i-dent* toothpaste, which was the sponsor of the show, and told them that he was going to put up signs in the windows of three supermarkets he owned that would read: "*Amm-i-dent* toothpaste hired an actor named John Randolph, who is a Communist. Don't buy *Amm-i-dent* toothpaste!" The producer didn't know anything about this; but advertising agencies are very sensitive, and they had ordered CBS to knock me off the show. Sidney had said to them, "Look, you can't do that. John's costing us five hundred dollars (which was a lot of money at the

> "... I was the first actor to get a job on Broadway who had been a hostile witness before the House Committee on Un-American Activities."

time). There's not enough time to break in another actor. They told him all right, "But you don't work again for CBS if you ever hire him again."

I really didn't work in films, television, commercials, or radio from 1951 to 1965. Fortunately, I was able to work on the stage. I had to "read" for every job. No one gave me jobs easily. I found out I was considered a particularly dangerous person because I was the first actor to get a job on Broadway who had been a hostile witness before the House Committee on Un-American Activities. I was doing a show called *The Wooden Dish*, and I was picketed on opening night by the Committee Against Communism led by Roy Cohn. Although Charlie Chaplin's movies had also been picketed, I was the first actor to be picketed "in the flesh."

I finally made my initial break into television in

Art James, who had moderated a New York quiz program for teenagers, *It's Academic,* for several years, is host of NBC's audience-participation game show, *Fractured Phrases*, in 1965. It will go off after one season. James will host other game shows, including *The Who, What, or Where Game*, from 1969 to 1974.

January 23, 1965. *The King Family Show* debuts on ABC. It will last one season. ABC will give them another variety show in 1969. It will last six months.

January, 1965. Joseph Campanella, seen here with Zina Bethune, joins the cast of *The Nurses* which, under a revised format, becomes *The Doctors and the Nurses*. This show will go off in September. ABC will quickly bring back *The Nurses*, with a new cast, as a daytime serial that will play for two years.

John Randolph, a hostile witness before HUAC, was blacklisted from TV, film, and radio work from 1951 to 1965.

Ginger Rogers makes her first TV dramatic appearance in five years in "Terror Island" on *Bob Hope Presents the Chrysler Theatre*, an anthology series that began its four-year run on NBC in 1963. Donnelly Rhodes, Katharine Ross, and Carol Lawrence (not shown) co-star.

April, 1965. *Secret Agent*, a high-class British-made spy thriller, comes to CBS in 1965. Patrick McGoohan plays John Drake, who he had created on *Danger Man* in 1961. Here Dawn Addams guests stars.

" 'No, no, John Randolph can't work; he's on the list.' "

1963 while I was appearing in *A Case of Libel* on Broadway. I had had several bad experiences in which TV parts were offered and then withdrawn. I had sneaked through on one show, but I was afraid that I was going to be blacklisted completely. One afternoon, I got a call from my agent, who said, "Johnny, they want you on *The Defenders,* but are you clear?" Those words, "Are you clear?" aroused all kinds of feelings that I had tried for years to suppress. I had gone through experience after experience in which I got calls for jobs and the term was, "Are you available?" Then they would send the list down to Vincent Hartnett, who had a list of one hundred and fifty "unclear" actors. He charged the networks seven dollars for each actor they wanted "cleared." Next to the name of each actor he would indicate "politically acceptable" or "not acceptable." If Hartnett marked you off, they'd call back and say, "Well listen, John, we changed the part to a midget"; or, "We changed it to a woman"; or, "We cut the part out." I used to smash my fist against the wall at those times, it was so frustrating. So I knew I wasn't going to work, and tried to put the hope of work out of my mind.

When my agent asked me if I was "clear," I said, "I don't know what you mean by that. I haven't heard that term in a long time, but I did work on *East Side, West Side* with George C. Scott for CBS. My agent said, "Good, this is CBS, too. Everything will be all right. I'll call you back right away." I waited as long as I could. No call. I left my apartment and went to the theater.

A Case of Libel was an interesting show about

Westbrook Pegler and Quentin Reynolds, both great sportswriters and correspondents. Pegler had become a reactionary, and because Reynolds had advocated a second front while he was covering World War II in Europe, he was accused by Pegler of being in the pay of the Communist party. Louis Nizer defended Reynolds in the famous case. In the play, Van Heflin took the role of Nizer, and I played Quentin Reynolds. In the opening scene, I asked him to take my case and he hemmed and hawed, and finally I said, "Well, you've gotten rich; you've sold out; you've got no guts anymore." At the end of the scene, I stalked out of the office, and he would decide finally to take my case. We did this scene every night.

The night after I had gotten the call from my agent, I walked on the stage, not as John Randolph or Quentin Reynolds, but as a fiery combination of both. In that first scene, I blasted Van Heflin so hard that he didn't know what hit him; I was so emotionally charged that I actually scared him with my anger. At

JOHN RANDOLPH'S CAREER

For over thirty years John Randolph has been one of America's finest character actors. On Broadway, he was featured in *Come Back Little Sheba, Our Town, The Visit, The Sound of Music,* and many others. Recently, he appeared in the films *Earthquake, King Kong,* and *Serpico.* On television, Randolph has appeared in numerous commercials and on such shows as *Hawaii Five-O, Columbo, All in the Family,* and *The Bob Newhart Show.* He is on the board of the Screen Actors Guild.

Dorothy Malone (L) plays Constance MacKenzie, the mother of Mia Farrow (Allison) on *Peyton Place.* When Farrow cuts off most of her hair, teenage girls all over America contemplate doing the same thing.

April 28, 1965. Barbra Streisand's first CBS special, *My Name is Barbra,* gets rave reviews and wins several Emmys. Among the many highlights is Streisand's medley from her Broadway smash, *Funny Girl.*

Eventually Streisand will sign a million-dollar contract with CBS for exclusive right to her specials.

John Houseman and William Devane star in Fear on Trial, *a 1975 TV movie about John Henry Faulk, a blacklisted radio star.*

the end of the first act, Van asked me what had made me so angry. I told him what had happened with my agent that day, and because his sister and brother-in-law had also been blacklisted, he understood.

After the show, I picked up *The New York Times* and read that *The Defenders* had just bought a script about a Hollywood actor who'd been a hostile witness before the HUAC and hadn't worked in ten years. Jack Klugman was to play the lead. I couldn't believe they were going to shoot a script on that subject but wouldn't hire an actor who had actually been blacklisted. But I hadn't heard from them all day, and so I figured I was out. When I got home, my agent called and told me I'd gotten the part. He said, "Don't ask questions. Just go there."

When I arrived on the set, I said to E. G. Mar-shall, Jack Klugman, and some of the other actors in a very loud voice, "I'm glad that I have a chance to work again after being blacklisted for ten years." Nobody said anything. I never knew why they decided to use me until many years later. The author of the script, Ernest Kinoy, told me that they were sitting in conference, casting, when my name came up. On of the vice-presidents immediately said, "No, no, John Randolph can't work; he's on the list." Kinoy then said, "How can we do a show on blacklisting with our left hand and with our right hand, the very next day, blacklist?" That was the reason I was hired.

It wasn't until 1965, when John Frankenheimer cast me with Rock Hudson in the movie *Seconds*, that things really began to change. Once I broke through in Hollywood, I began to work in television again.

In 1965, *The Alfred Hitchcock Hour*, previously *Alfred Hitchcock Presents*, goes off the air. Geraldine Fitzgerald appeared in "A Woman's Help" on this popular anthology series that lasted ten years on CBS and NBC.

Among the show's spookiest episodes was an adaptation of Ray Bradbury's "The Jar." Pat Buttram and Collin Wilcox starred.

THE PRESIDENTIAL DEBATES

R. JEFFREY SMITH

On the last day of the 1976 Republican National convention, Jim Karayn, a television producer employed by the League of Women Voters, called a press conference in a large room of the Muehlbach Hotel in Kansas City. Karayn, a large man who paces compulsively, had summoned newsmen to announce that the League had sent telegrams to the newly chosen Republican presidential nominee, Gerald Ford, and to the Democrats' choice, Jimmy Carter, offering a forum for public debate.

Only eight of the several hundred reporters attending the convention came to Karayn's press conference. "I showed them the telegrams and they yawned," Karayn said. "It was like handing out religious tracts at a party." Later that same evening, however, when Ford made his challenge to Carter for a debate under the League's supervision, Karayn's efforts prompted a different reaction. "All of a sudden, the League and I were very, very popular," he said. Officials of the television networks in particular became friendly. ABC chairman Leonard Goldenson offered Karayn his chair in the network's convention booth, after an earlier brush-off.

Reporters and network officials had not expected presidential debates to occur in 1976, because conventional political wisdom dictated that an incumbent president such as Ford would lose natural advantages in prestige and the power to attract public attention by appearing on the same platform with an opponent. When Richard Nixon and John Kennedy debated in 1960 for one hundred thousand television viewers, neither candidate was the incumbent.

> "The candidates . . . sought to impose restrictions and uniformity on the coverage."

Karayn, who had produced a series of similar debates for PBS television during the presidential primaries, realized that Ford technically was not an elected incumbent and that Carter was likely to be considerably ahead in the public opinion polls after Ford's battle with Reagan. Karayn persuaded the League to pledge its sponsorship of the debates, and after considerable pressure from the league, including a national petition drive, letter-writing campaign, and endorsement efforts, both Ford and Carter had come to believe the debates would be in their own best interest.

Once the candidates had agreed to debate, though, details of the broadcasting had to be thrashed out with network representatives of the networks, whose friendship with Karayn quickly evaporated over disagreements on how the debates should be run. The broadcasters, especially Richard Salant, the president of C.B.S. television news, wanted Ford and Carter thrust into challenging roles before the cameras to heighten interest and drama. Salant also urged that each network be allowed to employ its own cameras (instead of pooled cameras) and to use audience reaction shots during the debates. The candidates, on the other hand, sought to impose restrictions and uniformity on the coverage in order to minimize the polit-

Westerns have a slight resurgence in 1965. *Laredo,* an hour-long comedy-western starring William Smith, Peter Brown, and Neville Brand begins a two-year stint on NBC.

September 13, 1965. Robert Horton returns to TV to star in *A Man Called Shenandoah* on ABC. Horton plays an amnesiac roaming the West in search of his identity. This series will go off in 1966, before his task is over.

Christopher Jones (R), a James Dean look-alike, plays western outlaw Jesse James in *The Legend of Jesse James.* Allen Case (not shown) plays brother Frank James in this series that will go off in 1966. Here John Cassavetes guests.

ical risks inherent in the journalistic discretion so prized by the networks.

Negotiations between the networks and the candidates over such matters took up fifteen sessions in 1960, and wrangling eventually killed the possibility of a debate between the vice-presidential candidates. Only two negotiating sessions were needed in 1976, however, primarily because nearly every request made by representatives of Ford and Carter was accepted by the independent sponsor, the League of Women Voters, acting out of concern that the candidates might decide to back out. Each concession infuriated the networks. Both candidates, for example, wanted to exercise private control over the choice of panelists for the debates. The League offered them the opportunity to submit long lists of suggested names, which would be added to master lists compiled by the League for the ultimate choice by the League's coordinating committee. Karayn claimed that at least four of the twenty selected panelists did not appear on either of the lists, but another League director said that Karayn got approval for virtually every choice.

Whether or not Ford and Carter actually were able to choose their questioners, the networks were aghast at even the appearance of candidate control. When Richard Salant protested vehemently during a discussion of the panelist selection, he was told by a director of the League's debate committee to ''shut up.'' Enraged at what he considered to be a serious affront to himself and to the integrity of his network, Salant stalked out of the meeting. Subsequently, several CBS reporters declined invitations to participate as panelists.

There was little else that Salant could do, because the networks are prohibited by law from organizing debates between just two candidates. Under a 1975 interpretation by the Federal Communications Commission of a law written in 1959, broadcasters are forbidden to provide air time only to the major party candidates, unless the broadcasters themselves exert no control over the manner in which the debates are organized and run. In 1960, Congress had suspended the basic law temporarily for the Nixon-Kennedy debates, but sixteen years later the networks could not organize the debates without allowing every presidential candidate to participate.

Eugene McCarthy, hoping to be included in the debates as an independent candidate, accused the networks of controlling the debates through the League, but Karayn said, ''If we really cooperated with the networks, it was the most sadomasochistic marriage in history.'' Indeed, the networks remain bitter about the way the debates were run by the League. Salant recently said, ''The joint appearances—they were not debates—were better than nothing,'' but he referred sneeringly to the League's coordinating committee as ''two lawyers and a banker'' who knew nothing about journalism, and to Karayn as a ''hustler.'' Reuven Frank, of NBC, also said that the League was ''way out of its depth, dazzled by national attention.''

Still, the debates could not have been broadcast without the League's supervision. They were viewed by 250 million people in 113 nations throughout the world, at a cost to the League of $275,000 and to each of the three networks of two million dollars in lost advertising revenues. Ruth Clusen, president of the League, said that she is convinced they were worthwhile, and she would like her organization to sponsor the debates every four years as a regular political event. ''But we probably won't get the chance,'' she said. ''The networks will probably get the law that required our participation repealed during the next three years.''

R. Jeffrey Smith is a free-lance writer who specializes in sorting out the FCC.

Gunsmoke is still a top-rated show in 1965, its tenth year on CBS. Starring are James Arness, Burt Reynolds, Milburn Stone, Amanda Blake, and Ken Curtis who plays Festus Haggen.

September 14, 1965. *F Troop*, a slapstick western comedy, begins a two-year run on NBC. Larry Storch, Forrest Tucker, Frank deKova, and Don Diamond star. Storch was host of his own variety show on CBS in 1952.

Ronald Reagan fights Jack Lambert in a scene from ''A City is Born'' on *Death Valley Days*. Reagan will host this western anthology for three years. Robert Taylor and Dale Robertson will succeed him.

THE FEDERAL COMMUNICATIONS COMMISSION

R. Jeffrey Smith

When U.S. Secretary of Commerce Herbert Hoover ordered his department inspectors to shut down the illegal radio station owned by Aimee Semple McPherson, a Los Angeles evangelist, in 1925, she telegraphed Hoover: PLEASE ORDER YOUR MINIONS OF SATAN TO LEAVE MY STATION ALONE STOP YOU CANNOT EXPECT THE ALMIGHTY TO ABIDE BY YOUR WAVE LENGTH NONSENSE STOP WHEN I OFFER MY PRAYERS TO HIM I MUST FIT INTO HIS WAVE RECEPTION STOP OPEN THIS STATION AT ONCE

Other efforts to control the chaotic system of broadcasting in the early 1920's were met by similar resistance. By 1927, 732 stations were competing noisily for 96 legal radio channels; as a result, nearly 200 of the stations broadcast off their assigned frequencies. Hoover demanded and finally received from Congress legislation that established the Federal Radio Commission in 1927—a regulatory agency that generally was welcomed by the industry.

The FRC was replaced in 1934 by the Federal Communications Commission, but most of the provisions of that first regulatory act remain in effect today, as the pillars of government control of television.

The FCC, which also regulates the telephone and telegraph industries, is still responsible for minimizing broadcast station interference. Toward that end, the seven members of the commission—appointed by the President for seven-year terms—and their fifteen-hundred-member staff allocate television broadcasting licenses, channels, and signal strengths. Technological innovations in the industry—such as cable television—also are regulated by the commission, often harshly and in favor of well-established broadcast interests.

In addition to this technical responsibility, the FCC in 1934 was charged with a social responsibility. Because the number of radio channels was scarce, Congress reasoned, license recipients were to be chosen according to "public interest, convenience or necessity." The concept of scarcity and the ambiguity of the public interest standard pervade FCC regulation of television today, even though the industry now claims that channel scarcity has been wiped out by new technology. The standard has been the legal basis for substantial FCC control of program content—especially public affairs programming—of television advertising, and of television station ownership.

Television stations, for example, are "required to make a diligent, positive, and continuing effort to discover and fulfill the problems, needs, and interests of the communities they serve," according to the FCC. Any citizen may complain to the FCC if he or she feels a local TV station is not fulfilling this responsibility. Information about the procedure is available from the FCC, Washington, D.C. 20554, or in *How to Talk Back to Your Television Set,* by Nicholas Johnson, a former member of the commission.

273

September 15, 1965. *The Big Valley* begins a four-year run on ABC. Movie star Barbara Stanwyck (L) heads the Barkley clan just as her male counterpart Lorne Greene does the Cartwrights on *Bonanza*. Her adult children are played by Richard Long, Peter Breck, Lee Majors, and Linda Evans. Here Colleen Dewhurst and Michael Burns guest.

September 15, 1965. Comedian Bill Cosby is the first black to have star billing in a TV dramatic series when he co-stars with Robert Culp in *I Spy*. The Sheldon Leonard production, filmed all over the world, will go off in 1968.

TV WAR COVERAGE: THE VIEW FROM HIGHWAY 1

MICHAEL ARLEN

Viet Nam scenes from the past merge in one's memory—a more than ten-year-long television serial. There were a number of rotten stories: for years, until the mood of the country turned, or became ambivalent, the network news programs went out of their way, or so it seemed, to portray the air war—the heavy bombing, the light bombing, the deadly "gunships"—as romantic and ennobling. I remember one hour-long special, "Vietnam Perspective: Air War in the North," that consisted largely of film provided by the Air Force, extolling its exciting planes, and of straight-faced, R.A.F.-beer-hall-type interviews with several pilots, who chatted of "strikes" and "missions," and one of whom, I recall, spoke heartily of gunning down "gooks" and "suspected Cong" as they ran across an open field. There were also some examples of first-rate combat journalism. I think of John Laurence reporting for CBS from Con Thien; of the coverage by all three networks of the Tet offensive; and of various, seemingly isolated moments of actuality which broke through, as it were, the generally impersonal, unquestioning ritual of network Viet Nam coverage.

However, the natural bias of television news is for action and immediacy. At its most professional, television covers fast-breaking news more vividly than any other form of journalism. It is even widely understood that this single-track ability of television to communicate objective events directly has served al-

> " . . . network television news—as a voice—almost never reported the true, full story . . ."

most to heighten an instinctive public tendency to associate "news" only with objectified happenings. But the question is, to what degree is it excessive and willful to find fault with such a system, inasmuch as this system surely reflects human nature—or, at least, the traditional difficulty that men and women experience when they try to focus on something other than objective action?

One must be wary of blaming television for too much. For sometimes in recent years it has become a kind of badge of embattled individualism to blame commercial television—or "the mass media"—for the flaws and errors and imperfections of our society. If it weren't for television—so various arguments run—our children would be more responsible; our minorities would be less demanding; our middle class would be more serious; our politicians would pay more attention to issues; our popular values would be somehow higher; and, as a nation, we would not have been so sadly and unsuccessfully involved in Indochina.

The truth is obviously that the audience shapes its

Ben Gazzara plays incurably ill attorney Paul Bryan on *Run for Your Life,* which debuts on NBC in 1965. Although Bryan is given two years to live at the most, this adventure series lasts three.

Anne Francis stars as TV's first female private detective in *Honey West,* which appears on ABC in 1965. John Ericson plays her partner Sam Bolt.

Diana Rigg replaces Honor Blackman in *The Avengers.* She plays brilliant amateur sleuth Mrs. Emma Peel, a widow who becomes John Steed's partner because of her love for adventure. Her part was originally conceived for a man.

Direct reports from combat zones were a commonplace in TV war coverage, which only increased the unreality of the horror.

television and television also shapes its audience; but this kind of unmeasurable truth becomes murkier than usual in the matter of telelvision and its audience and the Viet Nam war, because for all concerned it was an entirely novel experience. By a number of standards of comparison, American television's coverage of Indochina was fairly good. The network camera crews did not go everywhere, or even vary far from officially certified events; still, they pushed their way into an astonishing number and variety of places—the more surprising when one considers the number of persons (three) and the amount of equipment they needed in order to work. And if the articulate, politically liberal element in the nation has often been impatient at commercial television's timidities—notably in waiting so long to report even skeptical opinions about the

September 17, 1965. John Gavin stars in *Convoy* on NBC. This World War II drama goes off in December. In 1964 Gavin had starred in the TV version of *Destry*, which lasted only three months on ABC.

September 17, 1965. Another World War II series debuting on NBC is *The Wackiest Ship in the Army*, an adaptation of a Jack Lemmon–Ricky Nelson movie. Gary Collins (R) and Jack Warden (not shown) co-star in this comedy-drama which will go off in 1966. Here Ruta Lee plays a stowaway. Collins will star in *The Sixth Sense* in 1972. Lee will be a regular on several 1970's game shows, including *High Rollers*.

". . . the audience shapes its television and television shapes its audience . . ."

conduct of the Viet Nam war—one should keep it in mind that during most of that time the majority of the nation (and of the audience) actively favored, or clung to, the government's consistently confident and optimistic pronouncements. But questions about television's coverage of the Viet Nam war go deeper than this, and it seems to me that the reason they remain important is that they still don't appear to be admitted, even as questions, by the persons who are most concerned: the public and the broadcasting establishment.

In fact, American television is at present largely defined by various quasi rules, which are determined not by the actual, evolving, functional relationship of broadcasting organizations to their audience but by superficial considerations of marketing and, even in the matter of news, by the rigid and anachronistic profit-and-loss conventions of the industry.

In a typical few weeks of crisis in Viet Nam and Cambodia, for example, *The New York Times* supplied an average of twenty-five thousand words of information each day about the military, political, and human situation there, together with continued commentary on related developments in Washington. The *Times* is owned by the New York Times Company, which last year had sales of $390 million and a net income of over $20 million. In these same weeks, each of the major networks presented a maximum of around three thousand words each day on the Indochina situation. The networks also—as the main feature of their news reports—presented numerous brief news film accounts, of which some were dramatic and immediate and others disjointed and routine. They also (as a group total) presented two or three "special reports." NBC presented a thirty-minute "special report" on Cambodia, which consisted mainly of a wrap-up of NBC's regular news footage of the previous week by the New York commentator and was shown on Saturday afternoon. CBS presented an hour-long, altogether conventional "special report" titled "Indochina 1975: The End of the Road?" which featured a narration by Charles Collingwood (about four thousand words) and was shown at ten o'clock in the evening, in competition with the Academy Awards ceremonies. The point is that CBS Television, whose news division produced fifty-three minutes on the Indochina crisis on the night of the Academy Awards, is a part of CBS, Inc., which last year had sales of $1.75 billion and a net income of $108 million. The question that, it seems, no one will yet attend to, because it is not yet real, is: To what extent is it important, or even necessary, in a communications society—in which citizens-as-businessmen receive a constant stream of telephoned or Telexed "news" throughout the day as an accepted function of their business role—for citizens-as-citizens to receive information of a similar quality and texture as a function of their perhaps more important role?

I have sometimes written to a similar point: namely, the question of the responsibility of television news organizations to communicate information more seriously than they have in the past. And each time, invariably, I have received letters in reply accusing me of being "unrealistic" in these criticisms—one correspondent lately finding me "dishonest" for talking of television news in terms of possibilities that do not exist. The reason I bring up this subject once again is that it strikes me that—with the fact of the collapse of our Indochinese position—the question of what is "realistic" or "unrealistic" in television news

276

A third World War II series premieres on September 17, 1965 on NBC. *Mr. Roberts* is an adaptation of the Henry Fonda–Jimmy Cagney movie classic. This Warner Brothers comedy–drama series starring Roger Smith (L) and Richard X. Slattery (R) will last one year.

September 17, 1965. Bing Crosby Productions' *Hogan's Heroes,* starring Bob Crane, premieres on CBS. The show—sort of a comedic version of *Stalag 17*—about antics in a German P.O.W. camp during World War II, raises questions about what viewers think is funny. The show is an immediate hit.

War was glorified on TV before the Viet Nam War. In footage from Winston Churchill: The Valiant Years, *soldiers were filmed against the open sky to create heroic sentiments. War coverage in the 1960's largely abandoned such cliches.*

could perhaps begin to be glimpsed in a new light.

At the time of President Thieu's angry resignation speech, I read in the paper that since the beginning of our involvement in Viet Nam 56,000 of our own men had been killed; 156,000 of them had been gravely wounded (which is to say, often maimed for life); and we had spent roughly $155 billion of our national treasure. I said earlier that I think television often did an extremely competent job in reporting scenes of immediate combat. But I think, too, that network television news—as a voice—almost never reported the true, full story of what at any given time was happening either to the Vietnamese or to us in

Indochina. In the beginning, this voice talked to us about the brave South Vietnamese government—when reporters knew of its corruption and weakness, and knew that the point, anyway, was not its virtues or lack of them but our government's strategic ambitions. The voice told us about the "military advisers"— when reporters knew that the advisers' efforts were being devoted largely to turning the South Vietnamese into a conventional army with which to fight what was then a guerilla war. The voice told us of 150,000 soldiers, and then our 300,000 soldiers, and about their "sweeps" and "missions" and "patrols" and "reconnoiters" and "air aupport" and "captured

277

Irwin Allen's *Lost in Space* debuts on CBS in 1965. The show about a space-age Swiss Family Robinson stars ex-*Lassie* mother June Lockhart and ex-*Zorro* hero Guy Williams.

September 17, 1965. Robert Conrad (R) is secret agent James West and Ross Martin is his partner Artemus Gordon, a master of disguises, on *The Wild, Wild West* which premieres on CBS. This western parody series features science fiction gimmickry and evil villains.

September 18, 1965. "Would you believe?" Don Adams is the unbelievably stupid secret agent Maxwell Smart and Barbara Feldon is "99" on *Get Smart,* a zany spy spoof which debuts on NBC. Together they help C.O.N.T.R.O.L. Chief Edward Platt fight K.A.O.S. Feldon first gained TV viewers' attention in 5-Day Deodorant Pad commercials.

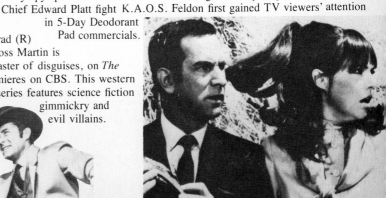

"Each night, the great orchestration of the evening news went on. . ."

ammo dumps" and "reinforced perimeters"—when the story was what these young soldiers could not do, what could not be done. Our troops played touch football at Thanksgiving. President Johnson put his arm around President Thieu. President Nixon put his arm around President Thieu. Toward the end of the story, the voice announced to us that there was peace—when all too many knew that there could be no real peace, and that it existed under a South Vietnamese government all too many knew could not govern for long.

All of us in this country, to say nothing of the citizens of Indochina, have lost a great deal in the course of the narration of these false—or, at least, surreal—stories. And yet the real stories were no great secret. There were reporters who knew about them —many of them reporters working for television. I have several times heard network executives remark on the considerable government pressures that were brought to bear on their companies as a result of the few critical news reports they did present in the Viet Nam period. There is no denying that Presidents Kennedy and Johnson (to say nothing of President Nixon) were congenitally unpleased by journalistic criticism and often tried to throw their weight around with company officials. But one wonders what might have happened—not just in terms of the nation's understanding and support of the war but in terms of the public's long-term respect for television news, for "the mass media"—if the networks had chosen to seriously acknowledge their role as journalists, as something more than transmitters of certified events,

and had given their correspondents honest reportorial missions and then had stood behind them. After all, was Lyndon Johnson's hold on the warrior spirit of the nation so secure that he would finally have compelled a network *not* to report, say, the chaotic forced uprootings of Vietnamese that so disastrously occurred from 1966 to 1969? Did the businessmen of the nation (who are still reeling from the effects of our Vietnam-inspired inflation) have such an irrational stake in our Indochina adventure that if NBC, CBS, and ABC had said, "Look, it is different from what the politicians and generals say, and from what you think or hope; technology will not win this war; more often, too, we are destroying rather than creating," they would have ceased to sponsor network programs?

Such might-have-beens! The networks never stood up, at least not for long, and, for all their billion-dollar resources, almost never gave their reporters honest, enterprising reportorial missions—except into direct combat, which was mostly a false story. Each night, the great orchestration of the evening news went on, with its parade of surreal or superficial stories, and the vast audience traveled through time in its strange company. I think it is wrong or foolish to imagine that television news in some idealized form could have somehow "solved" the problem of Viet Nam for us. But I think it is evasive and disingenuous to suppose that, in its unwillingness over a space of ten years to assign a true information-gathering function to its news operations in Washington and Viet Nam, American network news did much beyond contribute to the unreality, and thus the dysfunction, of American life.

Michael Arlen is the television critic for The New Yorker. *This article is excerpted from the title essay in his book* The View From Highway 1 *(Farrar, Straus & Giroux, 1976).*

278

Green Acres, a rural comedy starring Eva Gabor and Eddie Albert, debuts on CBS in 1965. An immediate smash, it will play until 1971.

Barbara Eden plays a genie in the NBC comedy *I Dream of Jeannie.* She will fall in love with her "master," astronaut Anthony Nelson, played by Larry Hagman.

Efrem Zimbalist, Jr., plays Inspector Lew Erskine on Quinn Martin's *The F.B.I.,* which begins a nine-year run on ABC in 1965. F.B.I. director J. Edgar Hoover will announce his personal endorsement of this series.

CBS NEWS GUIDELINES: COVERAGE OF TERRORISTS

RICHARD S. SALANT

The following CBS News guidelines governing the CBS News reporting of events involving terrorist/hostage stories were issued on April 14, 1977, in the light of the increasing incidence of terrorist activities. The guidelines were issued by CBS News in the basic conviction that terrorist activities are newsworthy events which news organizations must be free to report, but that at the same time such events impose special obligations upon news organizations in order to minimize, as far as possible, the dangers of contagion, the dangers of oversensationalism, and, above all, the dangers to the innocent hostages.

Because terrorist/hostage events in the United States are of rather recent origin, the guidelines are new in that they deal specifically with such incidents. But generally they are simply applications of longstanding CBS News policies concerning inflammatory of dangerous events such as riots and demonstrations.

RICHARD S. SALANT *President, CBS News*

These guidelines, now included as part of CBS News standards, are as follows:

Coverage of Terrorists

Because the facts and circumstances of each case vary, there can be no specific self-executing rules for the handling of terrorist/hostage stories. CBS News will continue to apply the normal tests of news judgment and if, as so often they are, these stories are newsworthy, we must continue to give them coverage despite the dangers of "contagion." The disadvantages of suppression are, among other things, (1) adversely affecting our credibility ("What else are the news people keeping from us?"); (2) giving free rein to sensationalized and erroneous word-of-mouth rumors; and (3) distorting our news judgments for some extraneous judgmental purpose. These disadvantages compel us to continue to provide coverage.

Nevertheless, in providing for such coverage there must be thoughtful, conscientious care and restraint. Obviously, the story should not be sensationalized beyond the actual fact of its being sensational. We should exercise particular care in how we treat the terrorist/kidnapper. More specifically:

1. An essential component of the story is the demands of the terrorist/kidnapper and we must report those demands. But we should avoid providing an excessive platform for the terrorist/kidnapper. Thus, unless such demands are succinctly stated and free of rhetoric and propaganda, it may be better to paraphrase the demands instead of presenting them directly through the voice or picture of the terrorist/kidnapper.

2. Except in the most compelling circumstances, and then only with the approval of the president of CBS News, or in his absence, the senior vice-president of News, there should be no live coverage of

October 21, 1965. Former movie goddess Hedy Lamarr makes an off-beat TV appearance as the hostess of a segment of *Shindig*. This rock show, featuring such singers as Glen Campbell and Sonny and Cher, debuted in 1964. Both *Shindig* and NBC's teenage music show *Hullabaloo* will go off in 1966.

November 26, 1965. NBC's *The Julie Andrews Show* will win an Emmy as the season's top variety special. Because of *Sound of Music* and *Mary Poppins*, Andrews has become a top television attraction.

The "Peanuts" gang comes to television in 1965 for the special "Charlie Brown's Christmas." This popular show will be repeated yearly and many more Charles M. Schulz "Peanuts" specials will follow.

© 1969 by United Feature Syndicate, Inc.

Irish Protestant partisans appeared on a CBS documentary in 1975 to present their side of the Irish question.

the terrorist/kidnapper since we may fall into the trap of providing an unedited platform for him. (This does *not* limit live on-the-spot reporting by CBS News reporters, but care should be exercised to assure restraint and context.)

3. News personnel should be mindful of the probable need by the authorities who are dealing with the terrorist for communication by telephone and hence should endeavor to ascertain, wherever feasible, whether our own use of such lines would be likely to interfere with the authorities' communications.

4. Responsible CBS News representatives should endeavor to contact experts dealing with the hostage situation to determine whether they have any guidance on such questions as phraseology to be avoided, what kinds of questions or reports might tend to exacerbate the situation, etc. Any such recommendations by established authorities on the scene should be carefully considered as guidance (but not as instruction) by CBS

News personnel.

5. Local authorities should also be given the name or names of CBS personnel whom they can contact should they have further guidance or wish to deal with such delicate questions as a newsman's call to the terrorists or other matters which might interfere with authorities dealing with the terrorists.

6. Guidelines affecting our coverage of civil disturbances are also applicable here, especially those which relate to avoiding the use of inflammatory catchwords or phrases, the reporting of rumors, etc. As in the case of policy dealing with civil disturbances, in dealing with a hostage story reporters should obey all police instructions but report immediately to their superiors any such instructions that seem to be intended to manage or suppress the news.

7. Coverage of this kind of story should be in such over-all balance as to length, that it does not unduly crowd out other important news of the day.

In 1966, Walt Disney dies at the age of sixty-five. This cartoonist, producer, master showman, and businessman knew more than anyone else how to create family entertainment. Despite his death, his studio will continue to turn out successful projects and his TV show, which began in 1954, will continue long after his death. Nature films and old Disney movies will be featured in the 1970's.

January 11, 1966. Marshall Thompson plays Dr. Marsh Tracy, here examining Judy, the chimp, on *Daktari* which debuts on CBS. Set on an African game preserve, this adventure series will play two years. It is based on the movie *Clarence, the Cross-Eyed Lion*.

Danny Kaye and Liberace appear in a sketch about secret agent "James Blonde" on *The Danny Kaye Show*.

VI. THE SELLING MACHINE

January 12, 1965. *Batman,* an intentionally campy crime series about the famous comic book superhero, appears on ABC. Aired twice a week, the series immediately creates a sensation around the country. Unknowns Adam West (R), who plays Batman/Bruce Wayne, and Bert Ward, who plays Robin/Dick Grayson, becomes instant celebrities. When the Batman fad fades out in two years, their careers evaporate.

Martha Raye dons Batman garb for this sketch on Bob Hope's NBC special. One of the first women to make it big on television, comedienne Raye in 1951 preceded Groucho Marx as alternating host with Jimmy Durante on *All Star Reveue.* From 1953 to 1956 she was hostess of the popular variety hour *The Martha Raye Show.*

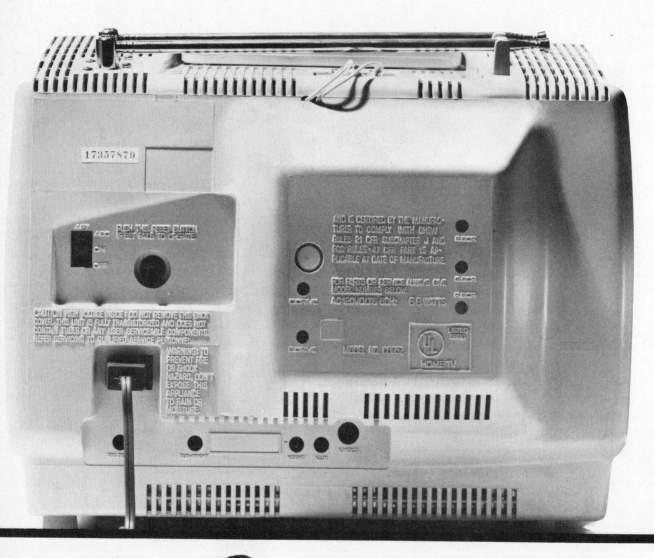

Soupy Sales, who has been on network or local television since 1953, becomes host of *The Soupy Sales Show* in 1966. Originally a local New York program, it will be syndicated and play nationally until 1968. Featuring puppets White Fang and Pookie and a lot of pie throwing, this children's program becomes popular with loony adults. Here Sales does his hit song "The Mouse."

Mary Ann Mobley is April Dancer and Norman Fell is Mark Slate, both agents on *The Man from U.N.C.L.E.* Although the characters will be used in a spin-off, neither Mobley or Fell will keep their parts.

David McCallum as Illya Kuryakin leads bit player Sharon Tate by the hand in "The Girls from Nazarone Affair" on *The Man from U.N.C.L.E.*

DIARY OF A COMMERCIAL: SOVIET GEORGIANS EAT YOGURT

PETER LUBALIN

June 1975: Our assignment is to film a new TV commercial for Dannon yogurt. The art director Joe Goldberg and I approach the assignment in the usual way. We take out a map of the world and decide where we'd like to shoot. We also read practically every word that's ever been written on yogurt. The research turns up something interesting. In certain parts of Bulgaria and Soviet Georgia, the people consume enormous quantities of yogurt. They eat it at almost every meal. There's another curious thing about these people. They live to be well over one hundred years old. Yogurt and long life. In a moment of unsurpassed brilliance, we conclude that perhaps there's an idea in this.

We keep reading. Scientists think many things contribute to longevity, but they're especially interested in yogurt. Experiments show that yogurt cultures kill harmful bacteria in the intestines. The scientists aren't sure if this can make you live longer. We decide that it couldn't hurt.

We create a simple commercial. We show people in their nineties and hundreds working in fields, chopping wood, riding horses. The copy talks about yogurt. We end with a close-up of a 90-year-old man thoroughly enjoying a cup of Dannon. The scene widens to reveal the 90-year-old man's mother, delighted that her little boy is eating his nice yogurt. To sell this thirty-second spot to our client takes exactly thirty seconds. We're a step closer to filming what we

> "The second day of shooting. We film a 'backup' mother and son. He's 85. She's 114."

believe is the first commercial ever shot in the Soviet Union.

July–August 1975: Preparations begin. Arlene Hoffman, Marsteller TV producer, calls Dr. Alexander Leaf in Boston. Dr. Leaf has written a book on the centenarians of Abkhazia in Soviet Georgia, and has published an article on the subject in *National Geographic*. He's very cooperative, and gives us names of people and places. Then he advises us to forget the whole thing because the Russians will never let us do it in a million years. Eleven months later we will send him a postcard from Sukhumi in Soviet Georgia. Next, Arlene contacts our connection in Moscow, who will coordinate things on the Russian end. This won't be an easy job. We're asking to go to a place where foreigners aren't usually allowed to go. We're asking to go to a place where even Russians aren't usually allowed to go.

September 1975–May 1976: We decide to wait for warmer weather. The job goes into hibernation for the winter.

March 28, 1966. "We're needed, Mrs. Peel." *The Avengers,* starring Patrick MacNee and Diana Rigg, comes to American television on ABC. Although critics initially give it mixed reviews, the show attracts a fanatical following. Later many critics will themselves become devoted fans.

In March, 1966, Julian Goodman becomes president of NBC. He will have to answer questions about news coverage of the Viet Nam war, student riots, civil rights demonstrations, and violence on television during his hectic reign that runs until 1974.

The Story Board is prepared by the agency to suggest ideas and sequence for the proposed commercial to the client.

In Soviet Georgia, there are two curious things about the people.

And we're not saying Dannon Yogurt will help you live longer.

Only that Dannon is a wholesome, natural food that does supply many nutrients.

284

Under the Johnson administration, civil rights becomes a major political issue. Dr. Martin Luther King appears on several talk shows to discuss the goals of black Americans. In 1963, King led a march on Washington and delivered his famous ''I Have a Dream'' speech. In 1968, he will announce a Poor People's March against Johnson's war policies.

Hal Holbrook does his famous interpretation of Abraham Lincoln on *The Ed Sullivan Show*. This gifted actor will make his mark on TV starring in the critically acclaimed ''The Senator'' episodes of *The Bold Ones* from 1969 to 1973 and the TV movie *That Certain Summer* (1972), the first TV drama that truly attempts to explore homosexuality in a thoughtful manner.

A large part of their diet is yogurt. And a large number of them live past 100.

Of course, many things affect longevity.

By the way, 102-year-old Ludmilla Petrova liked Dannon so much, she ate two cups.

That pleased her mother very much.

April 2, 1966. Mildred Dunnock and Lee J. Cobb re-create their original 1949 Broadway roles in Arthur Miller's play, *Death of a Salesman*. This CBS special will win the Emmy as the Outstanding Dramatic Program of the Year.

George Segal plays Willy Loman's son Biff in *Death of a Salesman*. CBS will rebroadcast the two-hour special in 1973.

April 11, 1966. Barbara Parkins (Betty Anderson) marries Steven Cord (James Douglas) on *Peyton Place*. Previously she had been married to Ryan O'Neal's Rodney Harrington. Neither marriage was made in heaven.

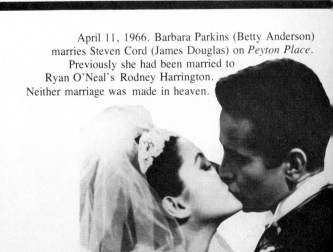

June 1976: It's time to crank things up again. A pleasant surprise: We learn the Russians are enthusiastic about our project and anxious to cooperate. Why not? We are going to film Soviet citizens who live, in vigorous health, to be 120. The visas, which can take months, come through in two weeks.

July 10, 1976: Arlene Hoffman leaves for Russia to find a 90-year-old man with a mother. Two days later she calls to ask if an 89-year-old man with a mother is okay.

July 17, 1976: Bob Gaffney, cameraman/ director; John Knoop, assistant director; Joe Goldberg and I leave for Russia.

July 18, 1976: We arrive at Moscow airport. A young man approaches and calls me by name. I ask him how he knew who I was. He explains that he has had my photograph for two weeks. I'm thinking ''welcome to Russia.''

We change planes and fly to Sukhumi, 800 miles south of Moscow. Our hotel rooms overlook the Black Sea which is actually a lovely turquoise. The rooms are surprisingly luxurious except for the bathrooms, which look like the public washrooms in New York subway stations. When it comes to bathrooms America has nothing to worry about. Russia is still about two centuries behind us.

At our first dinner in the Soviet Union, four full bottles of vodka are brought to the table. There are only seven people. We are introduced to the Russian custom of marathon toasting.

July 20, 1976: The first day of shooting. We're in our rented bus, heading for the village of Kutol, in the Caucasus, a drive of an hour and a half from the hotel. The crew consists of five Americans, five Russians and a Canadian. Gaffney is playing a tape of Irish love ballads on his cassette deck. By the end of the third day, the Russians will know the words to ''Danny Boy'' by heart. We arrive at the first home and do three shots: a 96-year-old man chopping wood, a 98-year-old man hoeing in a vineyard, and a 107-year-old woman feeding chickens. She doesn't look a day over 80.

We arrive at the second home, where we will film the 89-year-old man and his mother. The man is still out working in the fields. The women are preparing a banquet for us (the first of five we will have during the next three days). They suggest we eat first. As we sit down, we notice that the head of the collective farm is lining up eight shot glasses in front of him and filling them with vodka. He's going to perform eight consecutive toasts, downing a glass of vodka with each toast. We're getting very concerned, because we realize that each time he downs a glass, we're expected to do the same. Just as we finish our toasts, the 89-year-old son arrives. Quickly we set up the shot. I notice that Gaffney is a little wobbly; I begin praying that he can focus the camera.

July 21, 1976: The second day of shooting. We film a ''backup'' mother and son. He's 85. She's 114. Then we sit down to the first banquet of the second day. Immediately, the head of the collective raises a glass of vodka and begins talking about Americanskis and Russkis, peace and friendship. Lined up in front of him are five more glasses of vodka. Behind us, the women of the village stand waiting to fill our glasses after each toast. Here we go again.

On maybe the ninth or tenth toast, Joe Goldberg glances around the table. Nobody is looking. Instead of tossing the vodka down his throat, he tosses it over his shoulder. Unfortunately, someone is looking. Joe gets to do the next toast by himself.

Later, our bus driver, the only person to be excused from the toasting, takes us to the second location. We are going to shoot the village elder. She is at least 130. Maybe 140. Before we roll film, she asks to have her picture taken with the Polaroid SX-70. You

286

June 27, 1966. *Dark Shadows,* the most unusual daytime serial in television history, debuts on ABC. Jonathan Frid will become popular playing vampire Barnabas Collins in this gothic chiller. Joan Bennett, Alexandra Molka, Lara Parker, Anthony George, and Donna McKechnie also star. Two movies will be made from this series.

Perry Mason, television's most popular courtroom drama, goes off the air in 1966 after nine years on CBS.

Ralph Bellamy (L) and John Ireland guest star on *Rawhide,* which goes off the air in 1966 after eight years on CBS. Bellamy had starred as private eye Mike Barnett on *Man Against Crime,* a very popular show on CBS from 1949 to 1953.

haven't seen anything until you've seen the face of a 140-year-old woman as she watches herself come to life on a piece of SX-70 film.

We sit down to the second banquet of the day. The food is always the same. Tomatoes, cucumbers, buffalo cheese, a cornmeal mush called *mammaliga*, and a couple of chickens. And, of course, there's the vodka.

July 22, 1976: The third day of shooting. We film a 79-year-old woman and her mother in the village of Duripshi. Inside the house, they are preparing the first banquet of the third day. Today we will be ready for their vodka. We sneak behind the house and wolf down cups of Dannon yogurt to line our stomachs. Now they can bring on the vodka. Only this time, instead of vodka, they bring on fruit juice.

At the final location, they have painted the entire outside of a farmhouse for us. Once again, these people have gone to great lengths to please their guests. We're not used to this kind of cooperation even when we pay for it. More important, we've been overwhelmed by the openness and warmth of the Georgian people. They seem to have no hang-ups or inhibitions. Everywhere, we've been taken in as friends. We're filled with our own feelings of affection and gratitude, which we express at each banquet in our toasts to them.

We film the Abkhazian Senior Men's Choir. They range in age from 80 to 105, yet their voices are remarkably rich and powerful. We also shoot a 98-year-old man chopping wood, a 105-year-old man picking tobacco, and a 95-year-old man riding a horse. The commercial is now in the can. We begin our fifth banquet in three days.

Sitting at the long table eating and drinking and joking and feeling terrific, you forget for a moment that you are in the State of Abkhazia in the Republic of Georgia in the U.S.S.R. hoisting vodka with

hundred-year-old men who are enjoying themselves as much as you are. And when it hits you, it all seems a little unreal.

The party goes on until one in the morning. When the sun sets, they string lights from the trees. The old men ask us to join in their folk dances. We tire before they do. Before we leave, we pin American flags on their uniforms. I say to Joe and Arlene: "If somebody asks you what you did today, what are you going to say?"

July 23, 1976: We spend a beautiful day on a beach near Sukhumi. We don't think about vodka or tomatoes or *mammaliga*. In the evening, we meet with our friends in the Russian film crew. We drink one champagne toast and exchange gifts. They give us Russian patriotic pins and recordings of Abkhazian folk songs. We give them Mark Cross pen and pencil sets and denim work shirts. They're thrilled with the shirts. Denim is hard to come by in Russia. John Knoop goes to his room and returns with two pairs of broken-in Levi's which he gives to the men in the Russian crew.

July 26, 1976: We're in London screening the dailies. We've invited the general manager and the creative director of our London office to the viewing. While they're watching pretty film of some rather remarkable old people, we're silently reliving the most memorable week we've ever had.

August 2, 1976: Back to work. An account executive is waiting for me in my office. It seems that a client has rejected a perfectly fine headline because it ended with a preposition. He needs a new line in two hours. I am back in the real world.

Peter Lubalin is vice-president and creative director at Marsteller, Inc.

287

The Dick Van Dyke Show, with Dick Van Dyke and Mary Tyler Moore, goes off the air in 1966 after five years on CBS. It is still a high-rated program, but producer Carl Reiner announces that everyone wants to quit while they're still on top.

Katy Holstrum and Glen Morley marry on *The Farmer's Daughter,* which goes off in 1966 after three years on ABC. William Windom will star as a James Thurber-inspired character in *My World . . . and Welcome to It* on NBC in 1969. Inger Stevens will commit suicide in 1970.

CONFESSIONS OF AN AD MAN

PETER WISEBRAND

Commercial. Everybody hates that awful word, particularly when it's a noun. Sometimes it's called a "message" instead. Other times a "spot." Some announcers say, "We'll be back in a minute," but they don't say where they are going, or what will happen while they're gone. Others say, "And now this." And now what? One pictures an announcer with his head turned away, his arm outstretched, and in his hand an old brown paper bag with a terrible odor coming from it. Everybody, it seems, is embarrassed by commercials. Yet television is a huge business that depends for its profits, and by extension for its very existence, on commercial revenues. Talk show hosts apologize profusely for each inconvenient "interruption," but when the interruptions stop, or even decline, the fastidious host can be sure that his days on the air are numbered. Notice how even the Super Bowl game is halted by officials when the time arrives to "come back in a moment." Quite simply, there wouldn't *be* any Super Bowl—or any television at all, for that matter—without commercials. So let's take a look at what goes into one of these embarrassing, revolting, and inconvenient little unmentionables.

A client is any person or company with a product to sell. An advertising agency is an organization that creates and places commercials for clients. A television show is an entertainment vehicle that carries commercials. And *you* are the viewer who watches the show and sees the commercial created by the ad agency to sell the client's product. It sounds simple enough, doesn't it? Let's take a closer look behind the scenes.

"Everybody, it seems, is embarrassed by commercials."

Boomer's Beefless Burgers is a client. John Boomer had a diner in Indiana, and when beef shortages occurred during the Second World War, he developed a hamburger without meat. After the war he started to branch out, and before long had a huge chain of hamburger places. When another beef shortage occurred a few years ago, he got out his old recipe for beefless burgers. It caught on. He got into franchising, and the rest is history.

Boomer's Beefless Burgers has an advertising agency named Burton, Barton, and Boller (or BBB to the trade). This agency/client relationship has lasted an astonishing eighteen years (most such relationships are lucky to last six months), and the two companies have grown and prospered together. But last year Boomer's Beefless's sales dropped off unaccountably in the second quarter. The trend was confirmed in the third quarter. By the end of the year, John Boomer was convinced that a tough new ad campaign was in order to beef up sales.

Even before this momentous decision was reached, however, the people on the Boomer's account at BBB were in a state of nervous alert. They could read the sales reports as accurately as old John Boomer. And they were scared to death—because what if wily John decided that *they* were to blame for

288

September 6, 1966. Peter Duel and Judy Carne star as young marrieds with little money but a lot of love on *Love on a Rooftop,* a comedy which debuts on ABC.

September 8, 1966. *That Girl,* a comedy series starring Marlo Thomas and Ted Bessell, begins a five-year run on ABC. It is one of the first TV programs about a career girl who lives alone.

his poor sales? He might conveniently forget his astonishing eighteen-year relationship with BBB and jump to another agency. Such catastrophes had occurred with much less cause before. When a client's wife doesn't like the casting in a commercial—contracts are canceled. When a company gets two letters of criticism about an ad—contracts are canceled. The people at BBB were uncomfortably aware of the old advertising maxim: "When in doubt, blame the agency." So just to be on the safe side, people employed exclusively on the Boomer account at BBB started writing and updating résumés even as they began making mental notes for copy for the new campaign they hoped would be upcoming at any time. Visions of unpaid mortgages and even unemployment lines danced in the heads of more than a few poor defenseless copywriters. But when the decision finally came down to launch the new campaign; the folks at BBB did not bother to relax; they just transferred all their anxiety to other, more complex concerns.

Simply put, the problem before BBB was how to sell more Beefless Burgers to more people. Newspaper ads were a possibility. So were magazine ads, and radio spots. But after much careful thought (lasting about thirty seconds) it was decided to create yet another great TV commercial like the one that had launched the Beefless boom in the first place.

Air time was bought, and copywriters were given their assignment: Create a series of TV commercials for Boomer's Beefless Burgers with a brand-new theme line and copy. The objective was to gain a two percent share of the fast food business. Note: Copywriters remember—we want to attract the family trade but not risk losing the teenage crowd we now have. Be sure to mention the fresh buns, and the 100 percent beef-free hamburgers. Also how about something on the summer special—a colorful Boomer's hat free with every twelve-dollar purchase! The copywriters manned their typewriters. The battle began!

One would think that all the creative people should have been working together for the common good of Boomer's burgers. Wrong. Good theory, but wrong. A successful copywriter is one who has a successful campaign to his credit. That is to say, *not* a shared credit. Isolated, individual originality counts. So it's every copywriter for himself. The combat rules for the Boomer's job were the same as for every other: (1) Never leave an idea in the typewriter when you go to the lavatory. (2) Do not crumple any rejected copy and toss it in the wastebasket. (3) Never put finished copy in an unlocked desk drawer. (4) Never ask another writer what he thinks of a line you just wrote. (5) Do not present any copy to a superior unless there are others present to witness the act, or else you may see your idea with another person's name on it in the final presentation. Yes, stealing ideas is a way of life at BBB and at every other agency. It is spawned by the demand for a sale, and for success. A successful campaign assures respect and sometimes even awe for its creator. But the day any campaign starts to falter, copywriter beware!

As it turned out, the new Boomer's commercials were pretty good. Sales are already up 8 percent over the final quarter last year. Boomer's has in fact gained 2.2 percent of the market shares of the fast food business. These figures translate into increased revenues of $7 million projected through the second quarter of next year—when it will be just about time to gear up for yet another new campaign.

In the face of all this success, perhaps it is still not clear where all the embarrassment comes in. It is caused, quite simply, by the word *commercial,* not by the thing itself. The word *commercial* acknowledges openly and squarely that television is not primarily an art form, or a news forum, but rather a business enterprise whose purpose is to make a profit for all

289

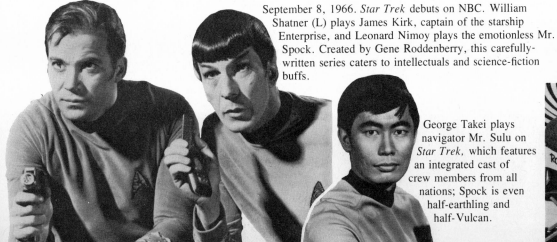

September 8, 1966. *Star Trek* debuts on NBC. William Shatner (L) plays James Kirk, captain of the starship Enterprise, and Leonard Nimoy plays the emotionless Mr. Spock. Created by Gene Roddenberry, this carefully-written series caters to intellectuals and science-fiction buffs.

George Takei plays navigator Mr. Sulu on *Star Trek,* which features an integrated cast of crew members from all nations; Spock is even half-earthling and half-Vulcan.

Irwin Allen's *The Time Tunnel,* a sci-fi adventure series in which Robert Colbert and James Darren travel into the past and future, comes to ABC in 1966. It will last one season. Lee Meriwether plays an engineer.

ROBERT COLBERT

LEE MERIWETHER

JAMES DA

A LITTLE MUSIC HELPS

Tami Crystal

From "See the USA in Your Chevrolet" to "Have It Your Way at Burger King," commercials have provided television with its most memorable music. And that's because the aim of commercial music is to be remembered. What you go around humming during the day is usually the last catchy thing you heard the night before. And so, although music is used in a wide range of ways in advertising, most of the time it intends to be catchy, to get you to remember the name and try the product.

In the old days, jingles weren't as a rule very sophisticated. Tommy Hamm, who produces a lot of advertising music, remembers those early spots as "simplistic, uncomplicated nursery rhymes." But over the years, the quality and complexity of advertising music has increased a great deal. Top writers and performers, from jazz, rock, films, and Broadway have become interested in the challenge of getting something into twenty-eight seconds that's both musical and technically right.

Commercial music is greatly influenced by the innovation, excitement and drive of pop music. Composer/producer Tom Dawes, with a very successful rock background, notes that "Pop music is free to experiment— they've got the time on an album you don't have on a commercial. But as pop music opens up and uses new musical ideas and gets them accepted by the public, it opens up ad music too." The result is commercial music that is not just catchy—it is good. In fact, this music even influences popular music, because the people who shape the music scene are constantly picking up ideas wherever they hear them. And, like us, they watch TV and remember commercials.

Tami Crystal is associated with the Society of Advertising Music Producers, Arrangers and Composers (SAMPAC).

concerned—for old John Boomer out in Indiana; for all the creative types cutting each other's throats at BBB; and for the stations and networks that sell their air time to sponsors. In fact, the only person who doesn't make any money in this arrangement is you, the viewer. But you've got no complaint either. After all, you get to see a free show, in color, in your living room. And all you have to do in return is buy, buy, buy all the Beefless Burgers you can eat, and more. That's not such a bad deal, is it?

Peter Wisebrand is an account executive with a large New York advertising agency.

Hoping to duplicate the excitement caused by its *Batman* series ABC brings ex-radio superhero *The Green Hornet* to TV in 1966. This program will only last one year. Van Williams plays the fugitive crime fighter and unknown Bruce Lee plays his trusted aide Kato. Martial arts-expert Lee will become the top international movie star in the 1970's, and a legend after his mysterious death in 1975.

Ron Ely (R), seen here with Lloyd Haynes, becomes television's first *Tarzan* in 1966. He will continue to play Edgar Rice Burroughs's lord of the jungle until 1968 on NBC.

It's About Time debuts on CBS in 1966. It will go off in a year. Joe E. Ross (Gronk) and Imogene Coca (Shad) are prehistoric cave dwellers discovered by astronauts Frank Aletter and Jack Mullaney when they crash through the time barrier. In April Coca will co-star in ABC's Emmy-winning "The Sid Caesar, Imogene Coca, Carl Reiner, Howard Morris Special."

COMPARATIVE ADVERTISING: KNOCKING THE OTHER GUY

JACK ROBERTS

Coca-Cola drinkers prefer Pepsi. American Express comes in second to Carte Blanche. Behold polish outshines best-selling Pledge. Ultraban deodorant wins by a nose over all six named competitors. Wait a minute, now Pepsi drinkers pick Fresca? Three-to-one? And here's another Coke-Pepsi blindfold test, where the winner is . . . tennis ball fuzz? Suffering Nielsens! Suddenly the commercial break is a free-for-all. Our favorite brands look good one minute, and are shot down the next. If you can't believe in someone's Pledge, what *can* you believe in?

Well, you might place your faith in the persuasive power of the Federal Trade Commission. In 1972, The Consumer Protection Department of the FTC issued a memo urging the networks to discontinue potentially-misleading "brand X" and "leading brand" comparisons. Naming names, the memo pointed out, would enable the consumer to make an informed choice. And the advertising industry's polite tradition of not using competitive brand names in their sales pitch went, appropriately, down the tube.

The FTC's innocence of comparative techniques, and of the advertisers' relentless search for agreeable statistics, has generated claims, counterclaims, and confusion. The resultant barrage of "I'm O.K, he's not O.K." commercials is hardly informative. After all, no advertiser pays a bundle for prime time to do his competitors any favors. All advertising is comparative to some degree, but when the FTC opened the

> "... when the FTC opened the door to naming ... competitive brands, TV advertising became a brand name shooting gallery."

door to naming, and showing, competitive brands, TV advertising became a brand name shooting gallery. Sharpshooting copywriters easily knocked over the competition. Like ducks in a barrel.

Flattening the competition with a comparative zinger is very effective. Viewers believe the comparison must be valid or the sponsors would be sued or the station wouldn't allow it on the air. What the viewers don't know is that advertisers *are* being sued, that competitors are meeting in the courts instead of the marketplace, and that TV stations have neither the technical staff nor the means to handle the validation problems of comparative advertising.

The National Association of Broadcasters does attempt to exercise some control over these commercials through its Acceptance Code which is concerned with the accuracy and honesty of identifying competitors and is strictly opposed to disparagement. Other bodies such as the National Advertising Review Board and the American Association of Advertising Agencies also deplore disparagement; the network legal de-

The Jean Arthur Show debuts on CBS in 1966. Movie star Arthur plays an attorney in this comedy series which co-stars Ron Harper (L) and Leonard Stone. The show will last three months.

September 12, 1966. Mike Nesmith, Mickey Dolenz, Davy Jones, and Peter Tork, an incredibly successful media-created pop singing group, star in *The Monkees,* which begins a two-year run on NBC. Featuring slapstick humor, snappy dialogue, trick photography, and hit songs, this wild program will win an Emmy as the year's Outstanding Comedy Series. It is produced by Bert Schneider and Bob Rafelson.

"Pepsi drinkers pick Fresca?"

partments flatly reject it. However, the interpretation of "disparagement" is open to debate.

To disparage is defined as "to lower in rank or estimation, to depreciate by subtle methods." This, of course, is the not-so-subtle intent of most comparative advertising. Advertisers are not exactly interested in *raising* the rank or estimation of their competition, not at prime-time TV prices. So it appears that "disparagement" needs to be redefined as "getting caught" while knocking the other guy. Since the air is filled with disparaging comparatives, there seem to be a number of ways of getting away with it.

The *isolated comparative,* which points out some danger or drawback in the competitor's product, overlooks the same feature in the sponsor's product. The *consumer comparative* is another means of getting-away-with-it. It utilizes everyday people making sponsor-favoring comparisons between competing products, and relies on finding folks anxious to please.

The *test comparative* is based on the grandeur of agreeable statistics. Look long enough and hard enough, and you'll find some. "Independent laboratory tests prove. . ." that independent laboratories are successfully doing just that. And then there's the *brand leader comparative* which trades on the name of a leading brand for associative recognition, for a pot shot, or just for the hell of it.

The technique of comparative advertising is hardly the most wicked thing happening in television. Many comparisons are honest, useful and informative. A few have resulted in competitive product improvement. Yet the opportunity for abuse and for unfair comparison remains. Certainly the FTC's goal of providing relevant product information has led, instead, to irrelevant comparisons and product misinformation. The viewer cannot be expected to distinguish between the fair comparison and all the others.

While the FTC ponders its good intentions, and the advertising industry discovers the credibility problems this technique has caused, the abuses of comparative advertising continue. The practice of naming competitors unfavorably is increasing, and will continue to do so until advertisers recognize their latent public responsibility, reject this damaging technique, and return to advertising products or services on their merits. Knocking the competition may be profitable (it's surely keeping the lawyers busy), but it's really not very much fun.

Jack Roberts is with Ogilvy & Mather, Los Angeles.

Christopher George (L) fights Rommel in Africa on *The Rat Patrol,* which comes to ABC for two years. Also starring in this World War II action series are Gary Raymond, Justin Tarr, and Larry Casey.

Twentieth Century-Fox TV's police drama *The Felony Squad* premieres on ABC in 1966. It will last three years. Howard Duff plays Detective Sam Stone in this hard-hitting crime series.

MGM-TV's World War II series *Jericho* comes to CBS in 1966. John Leyton, Marino Mase, and Don Francks play Allied agents. The show will last four months.

IMAGES OF WOMEN IN TV COMMERCIALS

JEAN KILBOURNE

Television is the most influential medium of communication in American society and it is primarily an advertising medium. The average viewer sees over five hundred commercials a week; by the time a person graduates from high school, he or she has seen 350,000 commercials. Since the commercials themselves are trivial and superficial, they often are not considered worthy of serious analysis and their cumulative impact is ignored. Most of us know that advertisements perpetuate stereotypes and peddle goals, values, and correct behavior along with products, and we know that advertisers spend about $20 billion a year controlling our responses, arousing our anxiety, and stimulating our needs; yet we often avoid examining the implications and effects. By remaining unaware of the profound seriousness of the ubiquitous influence, the redundant message, and the subliminal impact of advertisements, we ignore one of the most powerful "educational" forces in the culture, one that greatly affects our self-images, our ability to relate to each other, and our concepts of success and worth, love and sexuality, popularity and normalcy.

The aspect of advertising most in need of analysis and change is the portrayal of women. Scientific studies and the most casual viewing yield the same conclusion: women are shown almost exclusively as sex objects or housewives.

The sex object is a mannequin, a shell. Conventional beauty is her only attribute. She has no lines

> "The average viewer sees over five hundred commercials a week . . ."

or wrinkles (which are, after all, signs of maturity, of expression and experience), no scars or blemishes—indeed, she has no pores. She is thin, generally tall and long-legged, and, above all, she is young. All "beautiful" women in advertisements (including minority women), regardless of product or audience, conform to this norm. Women are constantly exhorted to emulate this ideal, to feel ashamed and guilty if they fail, and to feel that their desirability and lovability are contingent upon physical perfection.

The image is artificial and can only be achieved artificially (even the "natural look" requires much preparation and expense). Beauty is something that comes from without; more than half a million dollars is spent every hour on cosmetics. Desperate to conform to an ideal and impossible standard, many women go to great lengths to manipulate and change their faces and bodies. A woman is conditioned to view her face as a mask and her body as an object, as *things* separate from and more important than her real self, constantly in need of alteration, improvement, and disguise. She is made to feel dissatisfied with and

293

September 12, 1966. Dale Robertson returns to television in ABC's new western series *The Iron Horse*. This hour-long series will play two years. Here Robertson poses with Ellen McRae, who will win an Oscar for *Alice Doesn't Live Here Anymore* in 1974 as Ellen Burstyn.

The Monroes, about five orphans who must fend for themselves in the Wyoming wilderness, appears on ABC in 1966. Starring in this hour-long western are Michael Anderson, Jr. (with rifle), Barbara Hershey, twins Keith and Kevin Schultz, and little Tammy Locke. The show will last one season.

ashamed of herself, whether she tries to achieve "the look" or not. Objectified constantly by others, she learns to objectify herself.

Women are dismembered in commercials, their bodies separated into parts in need of change or improvement. If a woman has "acceptable" breasts, then she must also be sure that her legs are worth watching, her hips slim, her feet sexy, and that her buttocks look nude under her clothes ("like I'm not wearin' nothin' "). The mannequin has no depth, no totality; she is an aggregate of parts that have been made acceptable.

The image is difficult and costly to achieve and impossible to maintain—no one is flawless and everyone ages. Growing older is the great taboo. Women are encouraged to remain little girls ("because innocence is sexier than you think"), to be passive and dependent, never to mature. The contradictory message—"sensual, but not too far from innocence"—places women in a double bind; somehow we are supposed to be both sexy and virginal, experienced and naïve, seductive and chaste. The disparagement of maturity is, of course, insulting and frustrating to adult women, and the implication that little girls are seductive is dangerous to real children.

Women are told from their teens on to use moisturizers, to cover wrinkles and preserve their youth—their desirability—at all costs. Old women are treated with contempt and derision. Men can grow old, can show signs of maturity (such as gray hair), but women cannot. If women do have the bad taste and poor judgment to grow older than thirty, they are transformed into moronic, asexual housewives.

A National Organization for Women survey of television commercials found that 37.5 percent of the women shown were unpaid household workers. Housekeeping and mothering are constantly devalued and degraded, and other career options are narrow and

"Women are shown almost exclusively as sex objects or housewives."

limited (less than one percent of the women in the NOW survey were in traditional "male" professional roles). Housewives are stereotyped as stupid and obsessive (Mary Hartman is the satirical epitome) and are shown needing male advice (about 90 percent of all voice-overs are male) and magical male helpers, such as Mr. Muscle, Mr. Clean, and the Man from Glad. Women use products, whereas men demonstrate and advocate them. The female voice-over is a rarity.

The sex object is young, flawless, and narcissistic; she buys beauty products and worries about attracting men. The housewife, pathologically obsessed by cleanliness, buys cleaning products and worries about "ring around the collar" (which is, after all, *his* problem). She feels guilt for not being more beautiful, for not being a better wife and mother.

Some of the advertisers' attempts to reach the "liberated woman" market only exacerbate this feeling of inadequacy. It doesn't help to give housewives irrelevant degrees in astrophysics, to put a briefcase in the hand of a sex object or to show her changing a tire without so much as chipping a nail. The superwoman is a no less damaging stereotype than any other.

In many commercials, the female body is used merely to attract attention or is offered as a reward to men for buying the product (yes, the girl comes with it). The advertiser is America's real pornographer. A commercial for deodorant shows some women grouped around the phallic-shaped product; when the male voice-over asks, "What do you like about Tickle?" the women giggle. An ad for a razor has a

294

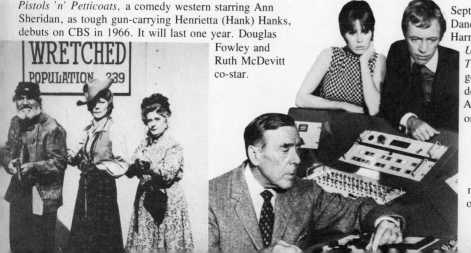

Pistols 'n' Petticoats, a comedy western starring Ann Sheridan, as tough gun-carrying Henrietta (Hank) Hanks, debuts on CBS in 1966. It will last one year. Douglas Fowley and Ruth McDevitt co-star.

September 13, 1966. Stefanie Powers is April Dancer and Noel Harrison (R), the son of Rex Harrison, is Mark Slate on NBC's *The Girl from U.N.C.L.E.* It will not have the same success as *The Man from U.N.C.L.E.*, and will go off in a year. Leo G. Carroll does double duty, playing Alexander Waverly on both shows.

Burt Reynolds is part-Iroquois Indian in *Hawk,* which plays for three months on ABC in 1966. In the *Naked City* tradition, this modern police drama benefits from its on-location shooting in New York City. Reynolds will play another cop, *Dan August* on ABC in 1970.

NBC used Inga Nielsen to advertise its 1970 sports season.

man smugly announce to the mailman, "Boy, did I get stroked this morning" and another deodorant ad has a woman inform us, "I like to start my day with a couple of soft strokes."

The reduction of sexuality to a dirty joke and of people to objects is the real obscenity of the culture. Although the sexual sell, overt and subliminal, is at a fever pitch in most commercials, there is at the same time a notable absence of sex as an important and profound human activity. Sex in commercials is narcissistic and autoerotic and exists apart from relationships. Identical models parade alone through the commercials, caressing their own soft skin, stroking and hugging their bodies, shaking their long silky manes, sensually bathing and applying powders and lotions, and then admiring themselves at length in the mirror. Commercials depict a world in which there is pervasive sexual innuendo but no love, and in which passion is reserved solely for products.

This curious sterility is due mainly to the stereotypes, which reduce variation and individuality, mock the process of self-realization, and make empathy impossible. When the goal is to embody the stereotype (which is by definition shallow and uniform), depth, passion, and uniqueness are inevitably lost. Men lose, of course, as well as women. Although not as subject to the tyranny of the aesthetic ideal themselves, men are made to feel inadequate if their women—that is, their property—don't measure up ("My wife, I think I'll keep her"). Women are portrayed as sexually desirable *only* if they are young, thin, carefully polished and groomed, made up, depilated, sprayed and scented—rendered quite unerotic in fact—and men are conditioned to seek such partners and to feel disappointed if they fail.

Women are stereotyped by their absence in commercials as well as their presence. Commercials for products involving complex decisions or expense (as cars, banks, insurance) generally feature men; 75 percent of ads using women are for products in the bathroom or kitchen. Little boys are shown far more often than little girls and usually in more active circumstances, such as getting dirty while playing

September 16, 1966. Robert Loggia (L), who had starred in "The Nine Lives of Elfego Baca" on *Walt Disney Presents* in 1958–59, stars as ex-sneak thief *T.H.E. Cat* on NBC in 1966. It will last one year. Here Don "Red" Berry (R), of "B" western fame, guest stars.

September 17, 1966. Suspense thriller *Mission: Impossible* premieres on CBS. Here special U.S. agents Barbara Bain and Martin Landau wear their weekly disguises. Also starring as members of the Impossible Missions Force are Steven Hill, who will leave in 1967, Greg Morris, and Peter Lupus.

Morgan Fairchild of Search for Tomorrow *plays the kind of stereotyped beautiful woman TV viewers are asked to emulate.*

baseball. Action and serious business are left to men; women of all ages are relentlessly trivialized, condescended to, and overlooked and, as a result, often find it difficult to take themselves seriously.

This is the real tragedy, that many women internalize the stereotype and learn their "limitations," thus establishing a self-fulfilling prophecy. If one accepts this mythical and degrading image, to some extent one actualizes it. Some women project their self-hatred onto other women, and this too is exploited by advertisers. Again and again in commercials, women are alienated from other women who are presented as enemies in the constant competition for male attention and approval (as in the stockings campaign in which

"The advertiser is America's real pornographer."

"gentlemen prefer Hanes").

Commercials didn't exclusively create the stereotypes, but they play a larger role in perpetuating them than any other single influence (a report by the United Nations Commission on the Status of Women claims that "advertising is the worst offender in perpetuating the image of women as sex symbols and an inferior class of human being"). Even the relatively innocuous ones carry the insidious message via sheer repetition and cumulation. It is essential that we struggle to change these stereotypes and to examine honestly the damage that has been done. The latest trend in advertising is violence against women, often presented in the guise of sadomasochism. This is a logical but frightening result of the portrayal of women as objects, of the linking of sex with violence, and of hostility (both overt and unconscious) to the messages, discoveries and demands of the women's movement. Battered, mutilated, and murdered women are showing up in magazines, store windows, and on record album covers. Inevitably this violence will find its way into television commercials; it already exists in the shows. Left unchecked, this reduction of human beings to types, this dehumanization and objectification will undoubtedly increase, with grave consequences for everyone in the society.

Jean Kilbourne, assistant director of the New England Screen Education Association, is a teacher and media consultant who presents her slide show, The Naked Truth: The Cultural Conditioning of Women Via Advertising, *nationally.*

296

September 17, 1966. "The Honeymooners" return as an hour-long musical on *The Jackie Gleason Show,* which begins a four-year run on CBS. Sheila MacRae (R) replaces Audrey Meadows as Alice Kramden and Jane Kean replaces Joyce Randolph. Art Carney returns as Ed Norton.

October, 1966. Anthony Franciosa and Jill St. John in the ninety-minute "Fame is the Name of the Game," which starts networks executives thinking that made-for-television movies have a big future. This will be the first of many made-for-TV movies in the late 1960's and 1970's that serve as a pilot. *The Name of the Game,* a ninety-minute weekly series starring Franciosa, Robert Stack, Gene Barry, and Susan St. James, will appear on NBC from 1968 to 1972.

THE TV COMMERCIAL AUDITION

SUSAN BARRISTER

So you want to perform in television commercials? Stars, or perhaps cash registers, gleam in your eyes! After all, selling cars, detergents, and hair spray—the things that make our lives, our homes, and ourselves more fragrant and delightful—should be easy enough to do.

There are certain catches however. For one thing, if you tend to sneer and point at people who seem ludicrous, you'll have to learn to control yourself in the presence of certain commercial producers and directors whose behavior will amaze you. These supposed artists may refer to their so-called script in hushed, passionate tones reminiscent of Kazan or Strasberg. And this may seem bizarre, since the material is clearly authored by neither Tennessee Williams nor Arthur Miller, but calls for you to punch the stomach of a genderless, animated little person who is exclaiming about the softness of a particular toilet paper or a special kind of dinner roll.

For another thing, you will have to learn to deal with a phenomenon known to the commercial actor as "humiliating yourself." For example, my agent called one afternoon to ask if I could sing.

"Yes," I replied, "if need be, I can sing. A Streisand or Sills I am not, but I can carry a tune."

"Fine," said my agent, "that's all that's needed. Just look all-American, sultry, Sandy Duncan, red-lipped. It's for a bank commercial."

Many responses came to mind, some less charming than others, but I kept my mouth shut and applied red lipstick.

Several actors were waiting in the lobby of the

> "... you will have to learn to deal with a phenomenon known ... as 'humiliating yourself.' "

commercial producer's office, and after ten minutes or so, the receptionist remembered to give us each a set of lyrics. She then turned on a tape recorder which played the song we were to sing, rendered by a tenor. It played over and over. The song had an Italian flavor. It was a short but passionate ode to a loved one—in this case a car for which the bank had agreed to lend money. We all hummed to ourselves, attempting to learn the tune and lyrics. When it was my turn to enter the audition room, the director explained that actual singing was of little import. It was the sensuality, the passion with which I related to the car standing before me now, that was important. It was, she said, the car of my dreams, and it was a Pinto. As a matter of fact, the car in this case was portrayed by a bicycle exerciser, the kind you sit on and pedal.

I knelt upstage of the apparatus, preparing to relate sensually. Happily, the machine was equipped with a long neck and handlebars, so I could easily imagine all sorts of sensual things to do with this particular love object. I wondered what my voice would sound like with the tape of the tenor to accompany me. The camera rolled; the tape was turned on, and I began to sing and seduce the exerciser.

297

October 15, 1966. Lerner and Loewe's *Brigadoon* is the Outstanding Musical Program of the Year. Peter Falk, Sally Ann Howes, and Robert Goulet star. Falk had won an Emmy in 1962 for his role in "The Price of Tomatoes" on *The Dick Powell Theatre*. Early in 1966, Goulet had failed to attract viewers with his *Blue Light* espionage thriller.

November 16, 1966. Louis Armstrong appears on *The Danny Kaye Show*. In 1960, Armstrong was special guest star on the acclaimed special "An Hour with Danny Kaye" on CBS. Armstrong also appeared in the Danny Kaye movie *The Five Pennies*.

December 6, 1966. Allen Funt and Abbe Lane join Red Skelton in a "Candid Camera" sketch on *The Red Skelton Hour*.

Susan Barrister, exuberant at the prospect of an audition.

"I could easily imagine all sorts of sensual things to do with this particular love object."

Unfortunately, I quickly realized that I was singing in the same key as the tenor—a key lower than my normal register. As a result, I did not sound lyrical but rasping, rather like the voice of the possessed child in *The Exorcist*. I was appalled, but also unable to stop, and equally incapable of switching octaves in mid-stanza, so I rolled on like a German tank. I tried desperately to make up in gesture and feeling what I lacked in vocal quality. By the end of the song I was no longer visible to the camera; I was cowering behind the bicycle, and only my hands could be seen clutching at handlebars and wheel spokes.

It ended. A pause followed. I stood up in shock while the director—not one to be intentionally cruel—called out phrases of thanks and goodwill, attempting to fill the space between me and the door. I collected my things and departed without uttering a further sound.

All the way home I thought about ways to commit suicide. Then I caught myself and remembered the punch line of a seedy old borscht belt joke: "What? And quit show biz?"

Susan Barrister is an actress who needs work.

Psychiatrist Vincent Price tries to convince Skelton that he isn't a butterfly on *The Red Skelton Hour*.

December 21, 1966. Geraldine Page will win an Emmy for her portrayal of Miss Sookie in Truman Capote's "A Christmas Memory" on *ABC Stage '67*. Donnie Melvin plays her young cousin Buddy in this production that will also win Emmys for author Capote and Eleanor Perry for screen adaptation.

December 25, 1966, *The Ed Sullivan Show* has long featured acts for the entire family. Here the Mascotts perform for everyone's pleasure.

THE NIELSEN RATINGS

BILL BEHANNA

For many people, the Nielsen ratings are one of the great, powerful mysteries of television. But when the mystery is removed, what remains is easily understood and not particularly exotic. A Nielsen rating is in fact nothing more than an estimate of the size of a television audience. It tells "how many were watching." The term "rating" is something of a misnomer because it implies something that is subjective, which Nielsen ratings are not. They are strictly quantitative.

Currently there are about 71,200,000 homes in the continental United States that have at least one television set. Nielsen ratings for network programs indicate audience size as a percentage of all TV homes in the U.S. Audience size is also given in terms of people in different age/sex categories, but the basic and most commonly used unit of measurement is the household. For example, you might read in a paper or magazine that the ABC program *Happy Days* had a rating of 31.8 and it was the top program for the week. This means that 31.8 percent of all TV-equipped homes in the U.S., or approximately 22,640,000 households, were tuned to *Happy Days* when it was telecast that week (31.8 percent of 71,200,000 equals 22,640,000). The program was the "top" program of the week when all programs were placed in rank order based on audience size.

"Share" (share of audience), is another term used with ratings and is also an expression of audience size. At any given time of the day, it is unlikely that all 71,200,000 television-equipped households will have at least one set on. At best, perhaps 75 percent will be using their TVs. Share is the size of the audience

> " . . . the Nielsen ratings are one of the great, powerful mysteries of television."

expressed as a percentage of all homes actually using TV. In the *Happy Days* example, suppose at the time the show was on the air, 63.6 percent of all TV homes actually had a set on and were watching something. We know that 31.8 percent were tuned to *Happy Days*. The 31.8 percent also represents 50 percent of those actually using TV at that time. The share of a program indicates how competitive a program is in its time period.

All network programs each day of the year are rated in the same manner. The A. C. Nielsen Company does not go from house to house throughout the land making note of what is being viewed on TV. As a practical matter it would be impossible to take a census of viewers every day of the year. Giving all known households an equal chance of being selected, Nielsen has chosen at random 1,200 homes as a sample on which the ratings are based. A random sample is called a probability sample by statisticians, and among its attributes is its ability to provide in proper proportion the same characteristics as the larger group from which it was selected. In effect, the sample used by Nielsen is a scale model of our population. Its size in, relation to our population is, to say the least, very small. However, generally speaking, the size of a ran-

299

In 1966, ABC viewers are offered *The Dating Game*, which will play until 1973, *The Newlywed Game*, which will play until 1974, and *Supermarket Sweep* (1965–67). At the end of the year, a daily beauty pageant show, *Dream Girl of '67*, hosted by Dick Stewart, is added to ABC's schedule and Annie Hayes is the first winner. It will last one year. In 1967, ABC will unveil *The Honeymoon Race*, which will last a few months.

In 1967, the nighttime version of *To Tell the Truth* goes off the air after eleven years on CBS. The daily show, which premiered in 1962, will go off in 1968. Here host Bud Collyer stands behind panelists Tom Poston, Peggy Cass, Orson Bean, and Kitty Carlisle.

The famous Nielsen "black box," which is actually brown.

ter sample, though selected in the same manner. The people in about 2,300 households are asked to keep a record of their viewing in diaries supplied by Nielsen. Each diary covers one week and entries indicate the age and sex of all family members watching the various programs turned on during the week. A diary is provided for each set in the home and at the end of the week the diaries are mailed to Nielsen where the viewing information is extracted and meshed with household ratings produced from the Audimeter sample.

dom sample is not dependent on the size of the group from which it is selected.

With the consent of the owners, all TV usage in the sample homes is monitored by Nielsen using an electronic device called a Storage Instantaneous Audimeter. This is the famous "black box" you may have heard about, which is actually brown and about the size of a cigar box. It can be located almost anywhere in the house, but it is not actually bolted to the TV sets, as some people imagine. Associated equipment is physically attached to the tuning mechanism inside the set cover and then connected to the audimeter by a wire much like a phone cord. A complete record of TV usage, indicating off/on status and channel selection, is made twenty-four hours daily and stored by the device. This record is fed daily through the meter's private phone line to Nielsen's computers for the computation of ratings. Greatly simplified, Nielsen is saying that if 31.8 percent of its sample tuned to *Happy Days*, then 31.8 percent of all TV homes in the U.S. were tuned to *Happy Days*.

The Audimeter is great for collecting information on a household basis, but does not have the ability to gather people information. There is no formula that can be used to translate "households tuned" to "people viewing" a particular program.

To produce "people" ratings Nielsen uses another sample completely separate from the Audime-

The millions of ratings produced annually by the A. C. Nielsen Company, in a sense, belong to the networks, advertisers, and advertising agencies that have hired the Nielsen Company to produce these ratings. Ratings function as a business tool used in buying and selling commercial time, which is in part dependent on the size of the audience. In this respect TV is much like magazines and newspapers, which base their rates for ad space on circulation.

The networks also use Nielsen ratings in the process of deciding what programs will be taken off their schedules. A program's Nielsen rating by itself is not a judgment of the program. Networks evaluate ratings, as well as other factors, in deciding what programs will be canceled. There is no question that rating estimates are a valid and reliable measurement of television audiences and as such objectively document which programs were viewed the most. The odds are twenty to one against an average prime time program's rating differing more than 10 percent from the results of an actual census. If broadcasters wish to provide programs appealing to the largest possible audience, ratings are a logical and justifiable tool for them to use in determining which programs will be continued and which will be canceled. It is for this reason that ratings usually play a decisive role in programming decisions.

Bill Behanna works for the A. C. Nielsen Company.

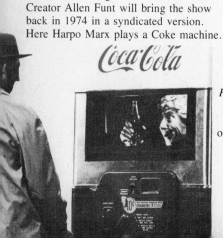

Candid Camera goes off CBS in 1967. Creator Allen Funt will bring the show back in 1974 in a syndicated version. Here Harpo Marx plays a Coke machine.

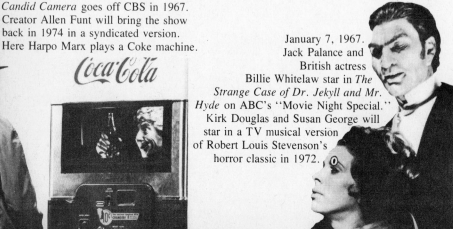

January 7, 1967. Jack Palance and British actress Billie Whitelaw star in *The Strange Case of Dr. Jekyll and Mr. Hyde* on ABC's "Movie Night Special." Kirk Douglas and Susan George will star in a TV musical version of Robert Louis Stevenson's horror classic in 1972.

The Invaders, a science-fiction entry from Quinn Martin, appears on ABC in 1967. Roy Thinnes (L) stars as a man who tries to convince authorities that the earth is being infiltrated by aliens in human form. Although this unusual show develops a small loyal following, it will go off in a year and a half. Here William Windom guests.

THE NETWORK RATINGS BUSINESS

ARNOLD BECKER

If you are reading a book like this one, you are interested in television. And the odds are that if you have read other articles on television, you probably think ratings are magic—black magic. After all, they are often portrayed as the nasty little fellows that canceled your favorite show. But to me, a network ratings analyst, they are "a thing of beauty . . . a joy forever." Obviously, there is a lot of distance between these two attitudes, so let's try to reduce some of the spread.

Television is a business. The product is entertainment and information. But television is a unique business—it gives its wares away at no charge. Well, at almost no charge. Television does not ask the viewer to spend any money, but it does ask you to spend some time watching commercials. In turn, television sells this time to advertisers. And that is the way television makes its money. There is no source of income other than the money that sponsors are willing to pay in order to get their message to you, the viewer.

Well, it doesn't take any great sophistication to figure out that the more people who watch an advertiser's message, the more money he is willing to pay, and that is our selfish reason for wanting to please you, our audience. The more you watch, the more money we make. The more money we make, the more we can afford to spend on programs. Everybody comes out ahead. However, there is one catch to this system. How do we know, or, more important, how does the advertiser know you are watching? You don't have to buy a ticket so we can't count the stubs. You don't have to buy a subscription so we can't count the checks. Yet, the communications industry has to have some way to count the house, and ratings are a convenient, economic way to do so.

> "It is, perhaps, a more democratic system than exists anywhere else in American society."

Now, let's put aside these business aspects and pretend that we have, Lord forbid, a government-run system—that television is not a business and that prices do not have to be established because no sales have to be made. Instead, you the viewer would pay for television, not with the time that you spend watching commercials, but with your tax dollars or a license fee or some such device. And let's also pretend you are the lucky bureaucrat who is in charge. There is only one limitation on your power: Periodically, you must stand for election and if the audience doesn't like the job you're doing, you are out! Even without advertising, you would have to know which programs are more popular and which less. Thus an audience measurement system (ratings) would still be absolutely necessary. It is simply unthinkable that one person or small group of people could possibly know the tastes of the television audience without some measurement system. So unless you were content to say, "Damn the people, I will put on those programs that *I* think

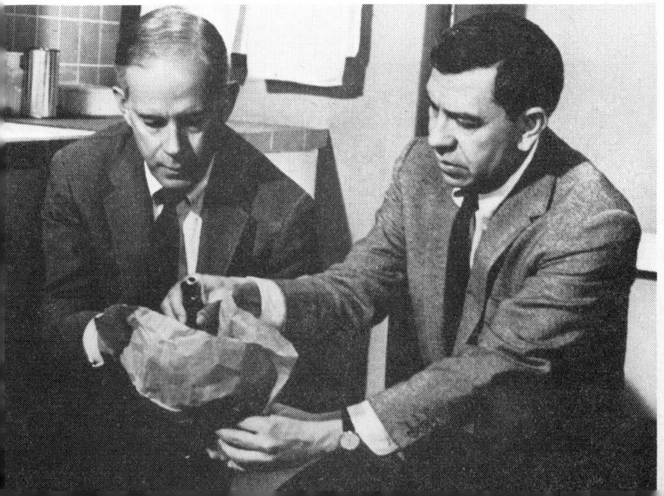

January 12, 1967. *Dragnet* returns to television after seven and a half years. Producer Jack Webb (R) once again is Sergeant Joe Friday and carries badge 714. Harry Morgan debuts as Officer Bill Gannon. This series, which emphasizes the professional aspects of police work, will go off in 1970.

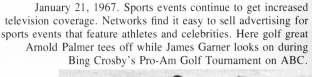

January 21, 1967. Sports events continue to get increased television coverage. Networks find it easy to sell advertising for sports events that feature athletes and celebrities. Here golf great Arnold Palmer tees off while James Garner looks on during Bing Crosby's Pro-Am Golf Tournament on ABC.

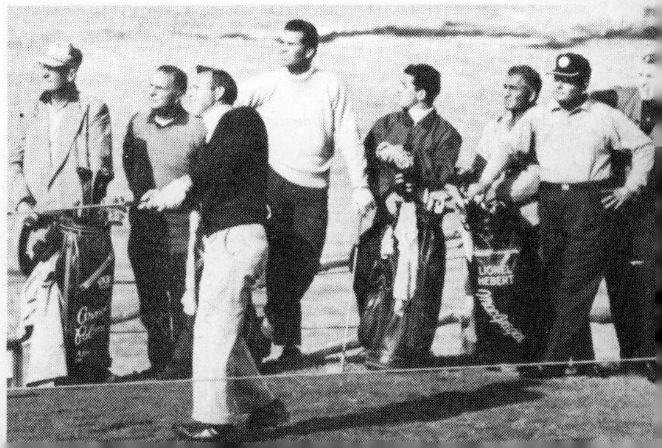

Patients in Fernwood Receiving Psychiatric Ward watch TV attentively. They are proud of their newest family member, Mary Hartman, and they are particularly happy at being made a Nielsen family, part of the national TV rating service.

Diana Rigg rehearses a scene on the "Never, Never Say Die" episode of *The Avengers,* in which movie villain Christopher Lee (R) co-stars.

February 5, 1967. "Mother always liked you best." Tommy and Dick Smothers bring their unique brand of verbal and visual wit to CBS in *The Smothers Brothers Comedy Hour*. Because many sketches deal with topical political issues, CBS censors will constantly threaten the duo with cancelation, unless their humor becomes less pointed.

The Saint is picked up by NBC. Here guest Jennie Linden follows Roger Moore.

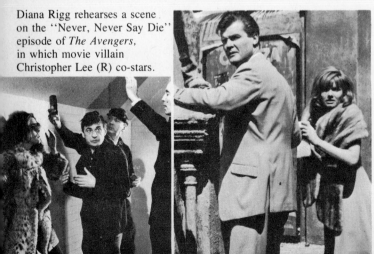

"... essentially untouched by human hands, ratings are produced. ... it's neat, and best of all, it's accurate."

are good for them," you would need ratings. Hence it is unreasoning to be opposed to them, but it is not unreasonable to question their accuracy, and so a word about that.

Ratings are based on sampling procedures, and laymen often do not understand sampling. Consequently, ratings take on an air of mystery and magic. But, the fact of the matter is, all of us are very familiar with sampling procedures. When Mama takes a drop of soup from the kettle to see if she has put in enough salt, she's sampling the soup. She doesn't have to consume the whole kettle to know if there is enough salt. When your doctor wants to know if your blood is of the right color and consistency he takes a tiny drop. He doesn't have to drain it all. Numbers that you read about every day concerning the cost of living, the gross national product, even the temperature of the air, are all based on sampling. All sampling means as far as audience surveys are concerned is that you do not have to ask everyone what programs they are watching in order to determine what programs are being watched!

The three commercial television networks pay the A. C. Nielsen Company a king's ransom each year to perform the service of supplying television ratings. The Nielsen Company draws a sample of approximately twelve hundred households. The sample is drawn so that each household in the United States has an equal opportunity of being selected—which is the mark of a well-drawn sample. Because 97 percent of all households in the United States own television sets, 1,164 of the twelve hundred sample households own a television set. In each of these 1,164 television households, the Nielsen Company installs a meter. The meter registers when the set is on and to what station it is tuned. The meter does not record what program is on the station at that time, but the networks supply this information to the Nielsen Company. In the middle of the night, a computer automatically dials a telephone number connected to each meter, and each meter discharges its stored information into the computer. The computer now knows at what times and to what stations each of the sample homes was tuned. The computer also knows, because it has been told in advance, what programs were on each station. It marries the tuning information with the program information and, essentially untouched by human hands, ratings are produced. The system is clean, it's neat, and best of all it's accurate.

These ratings represent a continuous voting by the American people as to what programs they like and what programs they do not like. It is an ongoing, highly competitive election. It is, perhaps, a more democratic system than exists anywhere else in American society. Without this system, television as we know it could not exist. And, if you think you have troubles now, just imagine what the programs would be like if they were chosen by a committee of politicians tucked away in some office building in Washington, D.C.

So, the next time you hear someone curse a rating, remember that it is one of the best friends you have.

Arnold Becker is the director of Television Network Research for the CBS Broadcast Group.

In 1967, *The Andy Griffith Show* replaces *Bonanza* as the Nielsens top-rated television program. Don Knotts, who left the show as a regular, will win his fourth Emmy as Deputy Barney Fife guesting in 1967 in the "Barney Comes to Mayberry" episode. Griffith will leave the series in 1968, its eighth season.

The Beverly Hillbillies continues to be one of television's most popular programs in 1967. It will go off in 1971. Here Max Baer, Jr., son of the former heavyweight boxing champ, is no match for co-star Donna Douglas in a wrestling match. In the 1970's Baer will become a successful movie producer.

TOP-RATED SHOWS

What follows is a listing of the top-rated shows in television history as compiled by the A. C. Nielsen Company. The average audience percentage rankings are based on Nielsen reports dating from July, 1960 through January, 1977. The listings represent only sponsored programs telecast on individual networks; no unsponsored or joint network telecasts are represented.

RANK	PROGRAM NAME	TELECAST DATE	NETWORK	AVERAGE AUDIENCE %
1	Roots	Jan. 30, 1977	ABC	51.1
2	Gone With The Wind, Part 1	Nov. 7, 1976	NBC	47.7
3	Gone With The Wind, Part 2	Nov. 8, 1976	NBC	47.4
4	Bob Hope Christmas Show	Jan. 15, 1970	NBC	46.6
5	Roots	Jan. 28, 1977	ABC	45.9
5	The Fugitive	Aug. 29, 1967	ABC	45.9
7	Roots	Jan. 27, 1977	ABC	45.7
8	Bob Hope Christmas Show	Jan. 14, 1971	NBC	45.0
9	Roots	Jan. 25, 1977	ABC	44.8
10	Ed Sullivan	Feb. 9, 1964	CBS	44.6
11	Super Bowl XI	Jan. 9, 1977	NBC	44.4
12	Super Bowl VI	Jan. 16, 1972	CBS	44.2
13	Roots	Jan. 24, 1977	ABC	44.1
14	Beverly Hillbillies	Jan. 8, 1964	CBS	44.0
15	Roots	Jan. 26, 1977	ABC	43.8
16	Academy Awards	Apr. 7, 1970	ABC	43.4
17	Ed Sullivan	Feb. 16, 1964	CBS	43.2
18	Beverly Hillbillies	Jan. 15, 1964	CBS	42.8
19	Super Bowl VII	Jan. 14, 1973	NBC	42.7
20	Super Bowl IX	Jan. 12, 1975	NBC	42.4
20	Beverly Hillbillies	Feb. 26, 1964	CBS	42.4
22	Roots	Jan. 29, 1977	ABC	42.3
22	Super Bowl X	Jan. 18, 1976	CBS	42.3

Bewitched continues to be ABC's top comedy series in 1967. Here Agnes Moorehead (as Samantha's mother, Endora), Elizabeth Montgomery, Dick York, and Erin Murphy as the Stevens's witch-daughter Tabitha, star in the "Allergic to Ancient Macedonian Dodo Birds" episode. York will be replaced by Dick Sargent in this series that will go off in 1972.

Husband and wife Richard Benjamin and Paula Prentiss star as Richard and Paula Hollister in *He and She* on CBS in 1967. Although this witty comedy series will win an Emmy, it will go off after one year.

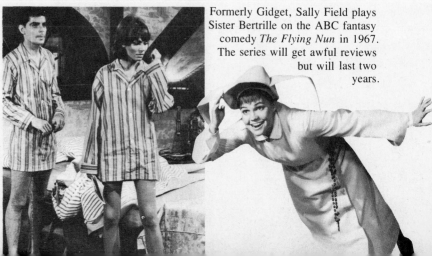

Formerly Gidget, Sally Field plays Sister Bertrille on the ABC fantasy comedy *The Flying Nun* in 1967. The series will get awful reviews but will last two years.

RANK	PROGRAM NAME	TELECAST DATE	NETWORK	AVERAGE AUDIENCE %
22	ABC Sunday Movie (Love Story)	Oct. 1, 1972	ABC	42.3
22	Airport (Movie Special)	Nov. 11, 1973	ABC	42.3
22	Cinderella	Feb. 22, 1965	CBS	42.3
27	Beverly Hillbillies	Mar. 25, 1964	CBS	42.2
28	Beverly Hillbillies	Feb. 5, 1964	CBS	42.0
29	Beverly Hillbillies	Jan. 29, 1964	CBS	41.9
30	Beverly Hillbillies	Jan. 1, 1964	CBS	41.8
30	Miss America Pageant	Sept. 9, 1964	CBS	41.8
32	Super Bowl VIII	Jan. 13, 1974	CBS	41.6
32	Bonanza	Mar. 8, 1964	NBC	41.6
34	Beverly Hillbillies	Jan. 22, 1964	CBS	41.5
35	Bonanza	Feb. 16, 1964	NBC	41.4
36	Academy Awards	Apr. 10, 1967	ABC	41.2
37	Gunsmoke	Jan. 28, 1961	CBS	40.9
38	Bonanza	Mar. 28, 1965	NBC	40.8
39	Bonanza	Mar. 7, 1965	NBC	40.7
39	All In The Family	Jan. 8, 1972	CBS	40.7
41	Roots	Jan. 23, 1977	ABC	40.5
41	Beverly Hillbillies	May 1, 1963	CBS	40.5
41	Bonanza	Feb. 2, 1964	NBC	40.5
41	Gunsmoke	Feb. 25, 1961	CBS	40.5
45	Gunsmoke	Dec. 17, 1960	CBS	40.4
45	Bonanza	Feb. 21, 1965	NBC	40.4
47	Beverly Hillbillies	Jan. 23, 1963	CBS	40.3
47	Miss America Pageant	Sept. 12, 1964	CBS	40.3
49	Beverly Hillbillies	Feb. 13, 1963	CBS	40.1
49	Bonanza	Feb. 14, 1965	NBC	40.1
49	Beverly Hillbillies	Apr. 8, 1964	CBS	40.1
49	Gunsmoke	Feb. 4, 1961	CBS	40.1
49	Gunsmoke	Feb. 11, 1961	CBS	40.1

Eve Arden (R) returns to television in 1967 as the star of *The Mothers-in-Law* on NBC. Co-starring are Kaye Ballard, Roger Carmel, and Herbert Rudley; this comedy will play two years. Richard Deacon, formerly of *Leave It to Beaver* and *The Dick Van Dyke Show*, will replace Carmel.

Saturday morning, September 9, 1967. Comic book super-heroes become stars of poorly-animated Saturday morning cartoons for children. Hanna-Barbera produces *The Fantastic Four* for ABC. The four Marvel comic book characters making their TV debuts are Mr. Fantastic, the Invisible Girl, the Human Torch, and the Thing.

TV PROGRAMMING RESEARCH

NEIL SHISTER

There was a time when television programmers, the people in New York responsible for deciding what gets broadcast on the national airwaves, prided themselves on their show business instincts. Foremost among these powerful impresarios was William Paley, the suave chairman of CBS who consistently led his network to the top of the heap through shrewd hunches about what the folks out there wanted to watch. In the 1950's this usually meant quiz programs and variety reviews, in the 1960's the *Beverly Hillbillies* and adult westerns, and in the early 1970's spy thrillers and cop shows. But Paley is retired now, and for the first time in modern memory, CBS is having trouble in the ratings derby. Paley's retirement from the scene and his network's gradual decline seem appropriate symbols for what is happening these days in television as the programming showmen are being replaced by research scientists. Sometimes it is hard to believe, but most of what you see on your screen is there because advance audience research predicted that each show would be a success.

Audience research has become increasingly important as production costs soar and network competition for rating points—each of which is worth over a million dollars in advertising revenues over the course of a season—grows more intense. Every season each network will air between five and ten new series selected from approximately two thousand proposals, one hundred twenty-five trial scripts, and forty taped pilots. Mistakes in this business are costly. In designing their season's offerings, the networks want to attract an audience that is demographically pleasing to

"Mistakes in this business are costly."

advertisers (surburban, under-forty, mean income twenty-thousand-plus) with programs that can be pre-sold. To do this they rely on elaborate research.

CBS first began testing radio shows in the 1930's, and now a large part of the third floor at its Manhattan headquarters is taken up by the Viewer Session Room (VSR). Almost every day CBS representatives scour midtown Manhattan inviting people off the street to screen programs and register their opinions. These shows are usually pilots. Inside the VSR the panel sits around a long oval table facing a color television set. Each viewer holds two push buttons, one green and one red, one or the other of which he or she presses continually to register pleasure or displeasure with what is shown. As many as one hundred fifty people will screen a program, and the responses of all the viewers are then collated to produce a wavelike chart, similar to a polygraph, which plots a moment-by-moment summary of the high points and low points of the sampled show.

ABC and NBC use a Los Angeles-based service, Audience Studies Incorporated (ASI), to test their pilots. The procedure is similar to that pioneered by CBS although different in detail. Told by their network clients what kind of audience (social class and income) to test, ASI finds a suitable sample and in-

September 9, 1967. Marvel Comics' top attraction *Spider Man* comes to ABC on Saturday morning. Congress and citizen groups will start examining the violence and the quality of programs designed for kids.

September 9, 1967. Jay Ward Productions, which produced the adult cult cartoon series *Rocky and His Friends* (1959) and its spin-off *Bullwinkle*, gives ABC *George of the Jungle*. As it was with its predecessors, it overcomes animation handicaps with clever, genuinely witty scripts and great characters. It will play until 1970.

The Beverly Hillbillies *was an immediate smash success in the ratings when it began on CBS in 1962. The critics abhorred it, but this trite sitcom about country bumpkins in the big city was a programming coup.*

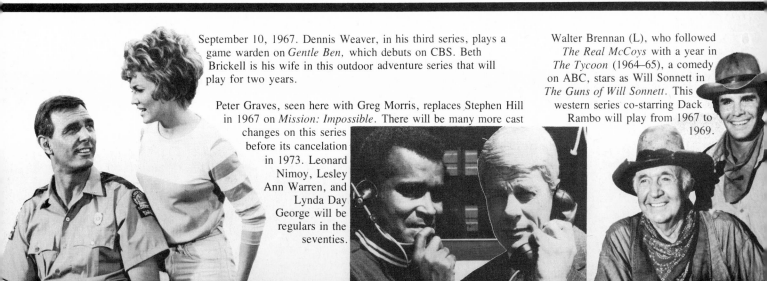

September 10, 1967. Dennis Weaver, in his third series, plays a game warden on *Gentle Ben*, which debuts on CBS. Beth Brickell is his wife in this outdoor adventure series that will play for two years.

Peter Graves, seen here with Greg Morris, replaces Stephen Hill in 1967 on *Mission: Impossible*. There will be many more cast changes on this series before its cancelation in 1973. Leonard Nimoy, Lesley Ann Warren, and Lynda Day George will be regulars in the seventies.

Walter Brennan (L), who followed *The Real McCoys* with a year in *The Tycoon* (1964–65), a comedy on ABC, stars as Will Sonnett in *The Guns of Will Sonnett*. This western series co-starring Dack Rambo will play from 1967 to 1969.

vites them to a Sunset Boulevard theater. There the audience sits in seats equipped with a rheostat dial marked "very dull, dull, normal, good, very good" and evaluates the offered program.

How accurate are research results? That is a tightly guarded trade secret which none of the network research vice-presidents is willing to disclose. They do agree, however, that testing can usually identify and weed out likely bombs. "We're better as a negative than a positive indicator," says NBC research chief William Rubens. Arnold Becker of CBS directs a department of over fifty people, and claims that predictions of how a show will do are accurate about 85 percent of the time. "But," admits Becker candidly, "if it were up to research, *All in the Family* would never have gotten on the air." If research is so revealing, why do most new series fail? "Well," says one seasoned veteran of the broadcasting wars, "sometimes what research tells you is that what you got ain't so good, but that it's better than anything else you got."

The research executives, while quick to point out that they don't originate programs but simply test those produced by the creative types, feel they have a fix on what pleases the public. "The crucial element," thinks Becker, "is an effective hero. The lawyer has to save his client, the cop has to catch the criminal. Then the story line is vital—a problem must be posed and resolved during the course of each show. The mass audience likes endings." Marvin Mord, ABC research vice-president who has a ouija board conspicuously displayed in his thirty-first-floor office, considers "upbeat" tone very important. "The public wants humorous, friendly, courteous, virtuous characters with whom they feel comfortable establishing a personal relationship."

To help measure viewer involvement in a test pilot, the latest development in research technology is a procedure known in the testing trade as the Galvanic Skin Response, or GSR. Physiologists know that when a person is emotionally excited, the electric voltage charge of the skin changes. Broadcast researchers, building on this insight, have developed a method whereby electrodes are attached to the fingers of viewers who are then exposed to a program being tested. The electrodes measure any change in GSR, which then serves as an index of viewer emotional involvement. Although the networks haven't yet included GSR in their battery of data gathering techniques, some local stations are already using it to rate the effectiveness of their newscasters.

Broadcasters know that the personal relationship created between an on-screen character and the audience ultimately determines the success of a show. Until now, however, it has been nearly impossible to get a reliable fix on the emotional chemistry that occurs when a stranger is projected into somebody's living room and temporarily becomes a member of the family. The ability to measure in advance the probable warmth of the viewer's response obviously tantalizes researchers. But the GSR technique is controversial because it scares some others, who see it as a first step toward the brave new world of mass mind-control since it operates entirely on the subliminal level and does not require the subject to register any conscious choices. Nevertheless, GSR represents the next logical step in programming research, and one executive, intent on improving his department's forecasting record, summed up the feelings of his industry colleagues generally when he declared, "Why would one hundred percent predictive accuracy be bad? I consider it a goal."

Neil Shister is a correspondent for Time *magazine and has had a long-time love-hate relationship with TV.*

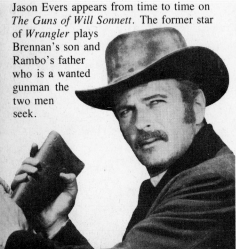

Jason Evers appears from time to time on *The Guns of Will Sonnett.* The former star of *Wrangler* plays Brennan's son and Rambo's father who is a wanted gunman the two men seek.

The Legend of Custer debuts on ABC in 1967. This fabricated historical distortion almost makes Custer friends with Crazy Horse and all Indians. An embarrassment, this series will go off after three months. Starring are (L–R, top) Peter Palmer, Robert Simon, Wayne Maunder (as Custer), Grant Woods; (L–R, bottom) Slim Pickens and Michael Dante (as Crazy Horse).

Four years after *Dennis the Menace,* Jay North (L) stars with Sajid Khan in *Maya* on NBC. This show about two boys and their pet elephant, Maya, in India will last one year.

THE RATINGS CONTROVERSY

MICHAEL WEISS

Television is a business, and a big one at that. Though people speak glowingly of the golden age in terms they would never use to describe General Motors, GM and TV share a number of similarities. Neither will continue to manufacture products that do not sell, and both do a lot of research to determine what will succeed. They talk of the public good, but usually the term is synonymous with the bottom line on a dividend statement.

The ratings are at once an indicator of bottom-line corporate health and a selling tool. They plot the assumed popularity of programming, and the results are passed on to advertisers wanting to purchase com-metered set is tuned to), not viewing, is the basis of the household sample. Watching a game at the corner bar won't figure into a Nielsen rating, since few bars can be considered households. Similarly, among households, the Nielsen gauge tells little about the attention paid to programming on the set—how intently a show is watched.

Indeed, the Nielsen meter can easily lead to overstating audience size, since tuning (what station the metered set is tuned to), not viewing, is the basis of measurement.

One media time buyer notes the kinds of problems inherent in a system that measures the wrong thing: "Older people feel that their eight-year-old dog is lonely, so they leave the television on. In urban areas they leave the set on so that it seems like someone is home." But the Nielsen meter says the set is on, period, and that is all that counts.

The concept of "public good" is beside the

"The ratings are . . . a selling tool."

point. The marketplace is what matters. Broadcasters pay nearly 90 percent of the cost of ratings, so the most important viewing measurement is controlled by the people who want the information for a single narrow purpose. One NBC researcher notes the consequences: "Since the research is paid for by broadcasters, advertising agencies, and their clients, it only provides the information they need and only with the degree of accuracy which they consider economical . . . methods are improved and methodological studies are undertaken usually only to improve the competitive position of a rating service, or because a client is willing to pay for it."

There was a time when the customer was not the judge of rating accuracy. It was a time broadcast executives like to forget. A 1963 House of Representatives investigation of the ratings industry alleged gross improprieties in operations, including the unauthorized disclosure of where a number of Nielsen meters were located. Since the Nielsen meters are in relatively few homes, such information could easily have been used by an enterprising individual to alter ratings figures and the advertising structure based on them.

A result of this investigation was the creation of the Broadcast Ratings Council, an industry watchdog funded by ratings companies and broadcasters. The BRC's main tool is the audit. Two firms do the work at

September 11, 1967. *The Carol Burnett Show* premieres on CBS. Featuring regulars Harvey Korman, Lyle Waggoner, and Vicki Lawrence, this hour-long variety show will win many Emmys and become one of TV's top all-time variety programs. Here Lucille Ball, TV's top female comedienne, makes one of four visits with her heir apparent.

September 12, 1967. *The Jonathan Winters Show* begins a two-year run on ABC. For Winters, here as Maude Frickett, one of his most popular characters, this is his first show in ten years and his first hour-long program. In 1972, he will host the syndicated *The Wacky World of Jonathan Winters*, which will emphasize his improvisational skills.

He and She, with Paula Prentiss and Richard Benjamin, was a hit with the critics and a failure in the ratings in 1967.

a reported cost of over $225,000 a year. The audits are said to cover all areas of methodology.

Yet many critics contend that the BRC and its audits are just a paper tiger. One advertising time buyer says, "The audits just confirm what the ratings companies say they are doing. If they [the ratings companies] say, 'We are lying, cheating, and stealing,' the auditors will say, 'Yes, that's what you're doing.' The Broadcast Ratings Council is a perfect example of a case in which the people doing the examining are paid for by the examined."

Both ratings of established shows and tests of new programs before they go on the air are similar to a doctor testing reflexes by hitting a patient's knee with a rubber mallet. The doctor sees a reaction, but can't tell by the test why there is one. Similarly, the ratings and program tests indicate, at best, what America wants, given the existing choice, but do little to show what America is potentially capable of enjoying.

All In The Family, innovative in its time, failed CBS testing. "It was so different from what they [the

"The marketplace is what matters."

test audiences] had seen, they didn't think it was socially acceptable to find the show funny," notes one CBS official. "Testing tends to be conservative. But innovation, by definition, tends to be a rarity."

A communications consultant puts it into dollars-and-cents terms. "If you can make fifty dollars on Shakespeare, and you can make a hundred and fifty dollars on a western, you'll have westerns. Commercial television will react to audience preferences. Advertisers say, 'I need this consumer; whatever he'll view, I'll give him.' "

Says an official of RKO television, pointing to the high ratings of professional wrestling opposite the news in Atlanta, "Who can determine what is best for the public?"

In recent years there has been a new recognition of the influence of television on the American way of life. Various groups have begun exerting pressure on broadcasters of violent programming, because of its perceived effects. The ratings and program tests are part of the system that resists innovation and looks for appeal to the lowest commercially and economically acceptable common denominator. It is a system in which broadcasters and the ratings companies are the prosecution, judge, and jury, because they pay for the trial. Those without commercial influence have no chance in the video courtroom.

Michael Weiss is a journalist who did research on the ratings controversy at the School of Journalism, Columbia University.

310

September 12, 1967. *The Jerry Lewis Show* debuts on NBC. This sixty-minute variety series will last two years. In 1963, Lewis, seen here with Anne Baxter, hosted a disastrous two-hour talk show on ABC. His former comic partner Dean Martin continues to have television success as host of a top-rated variety series, *The Dean Martin Show*, which began in 1965 and will play nine years on NBC, Lewis's main television fame will come as host on an annual Labor Day telethon for muscular dystrophy.

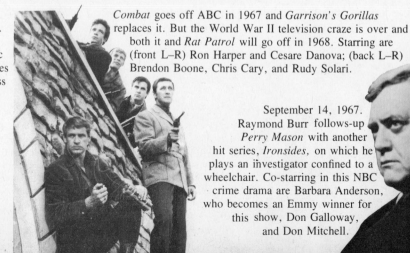

Combat goes off ABC in 1967 and *Garrison's Gorillas* replaces it. But the World War II television craze is over and both it and *Rat Patrol* will go off in 1968. Starring are (front L–R) Ron Harper and Cesare Danova; (back L–R) Brendon Boone, Chris Cary, and Rudy Solari.

September 14, 1967. Raymond Burr follows-up *Perry Mason* with another hit series, *Ironsides*, on which he plays an investigator confined to a wheelchair. Co-starring in this NBC crime drama are Barbara Anderson, who becomes an Emmy winner for this show, Don Galloway, and Don Mitchell.

TV INDUSTRY AWARDS
EUGENE MATALENE, JR.

When people discover that the three major television networks have departments called "Awards" their immediate reaction is one of disbelief, followed by amusement. The television industry is constantly bombarded by accusations that all its programming is without merit. It must constantly justify itself in the face of critical media coverage, and turns to outside plaudits as one legitimate form of self-defense. The Awards Department's raison d'etre is simply to see that television's good programming gets as much recognition as the bad. Television does provide many hours of excellent broadcasts, and just the way Ford wants you to remember the Model T and forget the Edsel, we want the public to forgive us our *S.W.A.T.*s and keep in mind our better work, like *Eleanor and Franklin, Roots,* and *Mary Tyler Moore*. To this end, the Awards Department constantly appraises upcoming awards competitions and seeks to find appropriate network broadcasts as entries.

The job of finding an appropriate broadcast begins with an assessment of the types of awards contests that are upcoming. Many competitions are very specific as to what programming they wish to honor. What is a good entry to the Aviation-Space Writers is out of place at the Mortgage Bankers Awards. Even so, the decision of what to enter is not reached simply. Each department and, moreover, each producer naturally wants to see his programs submitted to as many competitions as possible. The crucial factor, as always, is money, and since preparing an entry can sometimes run into the thousands of dollars, not all acceptable shows can be submitted. The awards manager

> "... we want the public to forgive us our *S.W.A.T.s* and keep in mind our better work ..."

must make the choices, based on a number of factors. First, the entries must be very good. Every producer thinks his work is great. Some of it is, some of it isn't. In the end, it is the awards manager's opinion that counts. Second, the awards manager is often familiar with the contest in question. He knows what has won in the past, what types of programs have been honored before. This intangible "feel" for a competition can mean the difference between first place and honorable mention. Third, the manager must be aware of programs that the network is pushing, and other programs that perhaps could be called "hot." All these things, along with the limitations of budget, are considered by the awards manager.

When an appropriate entry is decided upon, several steps must be taken according to the requirements of the contest. Most want a copy of the program to view. This request, though simple on the surface, is the most difficult to fulfill. Copies of programs come in all different shapes and sizes. Do they want a film? Sixteen or 35 millimeter? Or a videotape? ¾-inch videocassette, or two-inch standard? Will they return the material? If so, when? A large part of the Awards Department's time is spent searching for a copy of the entry, and then converting it to the proper form and

Carl Betz stars as attorney Clinton Judd in *Judd, for the Defense* which begins a two-year run on ABC in 1967. Here Lee Grant guests on the Emmy-winning drama as a film producer who attempts to expose conditions in a mental hospital.

Sharp editing, bizarre camera angles, gritty scripts, and New York locales highlight *N.Y.P.D.,* a realistic police drama that begins a two-year run on ABC in 1967. Frank Converse (L), who had starred as an amnesia victim in the acclaimed *Coronet Blue,* a summer series on CBS in 1967, co-stars with Robert Hooks and Jack Warden (not shown).

An Emmy Awards banquet with Dick Van Dyke and his party in the lower right. Everyone in the industry wants an Emmy.

David Susskind, the producer of such TV programs as *N.Y.P.D.*, *East Side, West Side*, and *The Dupont Show of the Month*, is host of a syndicated two-hour talk show featuring controversial guests. In 1967, *Open End*, which debuted in 1958, becomes *The David Susskind Show*. Although he gets his share of hate mail, Susskind is not as unpopular as either Joe Pyne or Alan Burke, hosts of syndicated talk shows begun in 1966.

October 11, 1967. Jason Robards, Jr. makes his musical comedy debut on Barbra Streisand's third CBS special ''Belle of Fourteenth Street.''

October 12, 1967. Host and attorney F. Lee Bailey (C) visits the London home of actress Patricia Neal and her husband, writer Roald Dahl, on ABC's *Good Company*. This interview series will go off in December. Bailey will become a celebrated TV news figure in the seventies as lawyer for Patricia Hearst. In the summer of 1961, Dahl was host of *Way Out*, considered by many the best series about the supernatural ever to appear on TV.

"Every producer thinks his work is great."

oftentimes a script will be requested too. Finally, of course, there are the inevitable papers to be filled out. Once the entry is completed and delivered, then comes the wait.

Some contests are entered because they honor a very specific type of work for which we may have an excellent entry, like the Aviation-Space Writers Awards I mentioned earlier. Usually, in a case like this, we know if we have a winning entry because the area of consideration is very small. Other competitions honor excellence in general, and though our entries may be good, the categories cover a broad range, and so the outcome is in doubt right up to the day awards are announced. When the competition is as prestigious as the George Foster Peabody Awards, the day of the announcement can be a time for nail biting. If we do well, it can mean lots of coverage on various media, and very good publicity for the network. It is impossible to say what effects this beneficial exposure has. Whether enough new people tune in to raise the ratings would be hard to determine, and unfortunately, most people outside the industry do not realize the stature of some awards for which the networks compete. Besides the Emmys, there are none that are household names. But rest assured that they are out there: the Clarions, the Gavels, the Teddys, and many more. And while they may not increase viewership, they do encourage healthy rivalry and pride—which, after all, is what makes people strive for excellence in the first place. And that is really what awards are all about.

Eugene Matalene, Jr. is the awards manager at ABC.

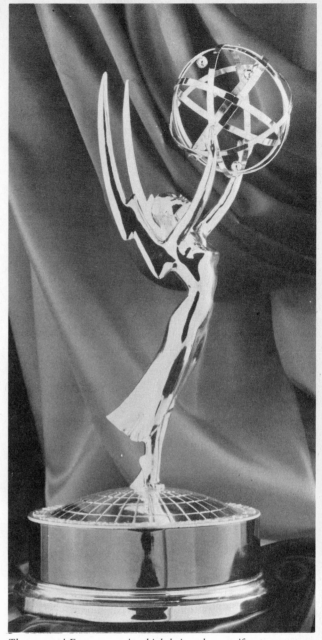

The coveted Emmy award, which brings honor, if not revenue.

313

November 26, 1967. *The Diary of Anne Frank* is presented on ABC. Peter Beiger, Viveca Lindfors, Theodore Bikel, Donald Pleasance (on stairs), Diane Davila, Marisa Pavan, Lilli Palmer, and Max Von Sydow play Jewish refugees hiding out from Nazis in a tiny Amsterdam flat.

Fred Rogers educates children using a variety of methods on *Mr. Rogers' Neighborhood*, which is broadcast in 1967 on NET (National Educational Television). Though it started in 1952, public television, of which NET is a part, actually took hold in 1962 with the purchase of Channel 13 in New York. In 1967 the Carnegie Commission on Education drafts its blueprint for public TV. The Public Broadcasting Act of 1967 formally initiates public television for the coming years. In addition to educational programs, there will be documentaries and more high-quality entertainment. PBS stations spring up around the country.

TV COMMERCIAL QUIZ

VINCENT TERRACE

The T.V. Commercial Quiz is designed to elicit the important facts of the TV media, the facts you should have been listening to instead of the programs.

1. Lori Saunders, of *Petticoat Junction* fame, was the star of which commercial?
    a. Silva Thins Cigarettes; b. Playtex; c. Salem Cigarettes; d. Drano.

2. Who was the "Brylcream" girl who made her TV series debut as a spy?
    a. Lola Falana; b. Barbara Feldon; c. Joyce Bulifant; d. Ruth Buzzi.

3. Who advertised and wore socks costing over $2.98 per pair?
    a. Captain Kangaroo; b. Gene Autry; c. Willie Mays; d. Frank Perdue.

4. Remember Bert and Harry Piel? Who did their voices?
    a. Bob and Ray; b. Rowan and Martin; c. The Smothers Brothers; d. Mel Blanc.

5. Who was the first to advertise Lay's Potato Chips?
    a. Jack Carter; b. Hoot Gibson; c. Buddy Hackett; d. Gabby Hayes.

6. Who sang the old Pepsi Cola jingle, "Be sociable, have a Pepsi"?
    a. Doris Day; b. Polly Bergen; c. Debbie Reynolds; d. Linda Ronson.

7. Mr. America had his first TV contest against a woman. What did she use as her defense?
    a. Lestoil; b. Mr. Clean; c. Scope; d. Sure.

8. Which cigarette had the thinking man's filter with the smoking man's taste?
    a. Camel; b. Dutch Master; c. Pall Mall; d. Viceroy.

9. Who used to advertise Dr. Pepper?
    a. Dick Clark; b. Ozzie & Harriet; c. Annette Funicello; d. Frankie Avalon.

10. What does Joey Heatherton currently advertise?
    a. Perfect Sleeper mattresses; b. Playtex bras; c. Prell Shampoo; d. Gravy Train Dog Food.

Scoring: Give yourself 10 points for each correct answer. If you happen to miss a question, score one point for trying hard.

Your Commercial Rating

0–20: You're a real genius, nothing can brainwash you.

21–50: You've been in the bathroom and refrigerator too much during program breaks.

51–80: You find more entertainment in the commercials than the shows they sponsor.

81–100: Bravo. You have a keen insight into what TV is really all about.

Answers: 1c; 2b; 3c; 4a; 5c; 6b; 7a; 8d; 9a; 10a.

Vincent Terrace is the author of The Complete Encyclopedia of Television Programs, 1947–1976.

314

January 8, 1968. Underwater explorer and conservationist Jacques Yves Cousteau, the inventor of the aqualung, presents a documentary on sharks as the first episode of *The Undersea World of Jacques Cousteau*. On this series of ABC specials that continues well into the seventies, Cousteau and Rod Serling narrate films of Cousteau's expeditions aboard the *Calypso*.

Journey to the Unknown, an anthology series dealing with the supernatural, appears on ABC in 1968. This hour–long series made at Hammer Studios in England will last just one year. Here Julie Harris, Tom Adams (L), and Marne Maitland star in "Indian Spirit Guide."

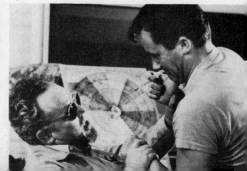

Robert Vaughn (R) struggles with a fanatic brain doctor played by Carroll O'Connor on *The Man from U.N.C.L.E.*, which leaves the air in 1968. Vaughn will star in the syndicated *The Protectors* in 1972.

VII. THE CONTROVERSIAL MACHINE

Robert Wagner plays Alexander Mundy, an ex-thief turned American spy, on *It Takes a Thief,* which debuts on ABC in 1968. Fred Astaire co-stars in this adventure series. Here Bette Davis guests in a rare TV appearance.

January 22, 1968. *Rowan and Martin's Laugh-In,* featuring wild satirical humor, becomes an NBC series and television's top-rated program simultaneously. The comedy team of Dan Rowan (L) and Dick Martin hosts this hour-long variety show, which had debuted as a special in September 1967. Judy Carne (C) has a bucket of water thrown on her each week.

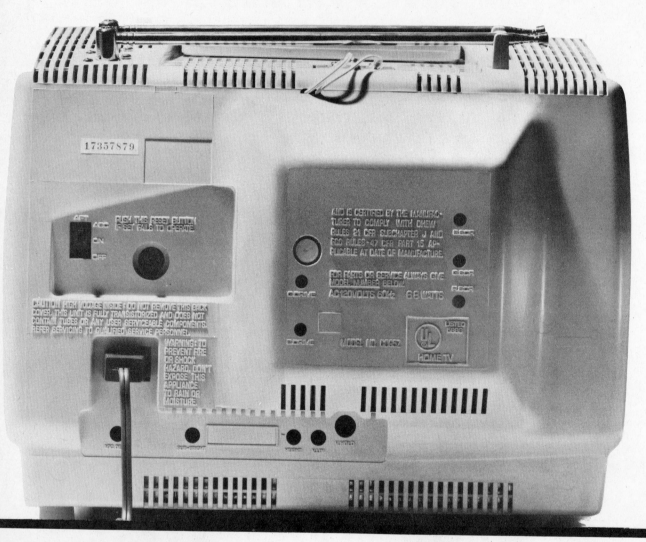

Goldie Hawn is one of many performers who get their "big break" on *Rowan and Martin's Laugh-In* during its five-year run. After leaving the series, she will become a top movie actress, playing the lead in both comedies and dramas.

Steve Allen, seen here interviewing "the 200-year-old man" created by Mel Brooks, is host of the ninety-minute variety show, *The New Steve Allen Show*.

THE PRINTED WORD

C.P. SNOW

Imagine that the world is going to end in three weeks' time. Some unlooked for cosmic disaster is coming unstoppably toward this planet. The first intimation has been picked up by the Armenian observatory near Yerevan. How does the news break? Nothing can ever stop scientists talking, and the rumor has spread within days, or hours, to astrophysics departments everywhere.

Governments don't know how to tell their people. The Soviet government has imposed a clamp down on all statements of any kind. The British government is conferring with the Royal Society; one of the prime minister's civil service secretaries observes impassively that this will at least diminish the urgency of the economic problem. But the news breaks here. In New York. On TV.

A TV journalist isn't going to wait. Nor is his program. The news goes out. The TV circuits become full of nothing else—except, rather oddly, for exhortations to buy new cars and after-shave lotions. The message, also on TV, flashes across to Europe and the world.

Of course, newsprint carries the message almost simultaneously. There are thoughtful analyses in *The New York Times* of the causes of this cosmic event. Crowds flock into churches, even in secular countries such as England. Wall Street goes down. Gamblers like J. M. Keynes buy and buy—on the principle acted on in London in 1940, if the worst happens, it doesn't matter a damn, if the imponderable takes care of us, the stock will be worth having. But most people aren't reading thoughtful analyses in newspapers. They are

spending hour after hour looking at the faces, listening to the voices, on the television screen.

By the way, this particular incident will not happen. We have plenty to worry about, but not that. The parable is intended to suggest how TV has taken over as the main means of communication. I don't think it is grossly unfair. It applies all over the Western society, and increasingly elsewhere. The spread of TV is the greatest revolution in human interchange since the invention of printing. Far more than radio, since most people, though not all, are more deeply affected by what they see than what they hear, and most of all by what they see-and-hear.

This has had an immediate, an increasing, a corroding effect upon the printed word. Let me say at once that I have a lot of use for TV. I am not one of those lofty English persons who say, as one of my dearest friends once said to me, "Of course, I never think of watching it, dear boy. I believe the servants have one of those machines somewhere." Myself, I watch for an hour or two most nights if I am home. English TV is rather good, and there is some of the best acting on earth. I am not concerned with the social effects of TV, which are complex, pervading, both positive and negative. But I am concerned with

317

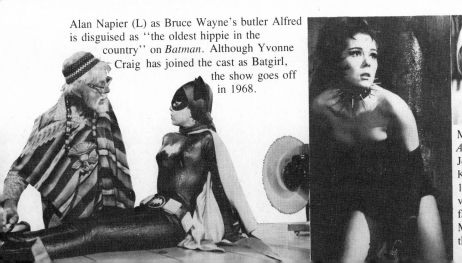

Alan Napier (L) as Bruce Wayne's butler Alfred is disguised as "the oldest hippie in the country" on *Batman*. Although Yvonne Craig has joined the cast as Batgirl, the show goes off in 1968.

March 20, 1968. Diana Rigg leaves *The Avengers*. Linda Thorson replaces her as John Steed's third female partner, Tara King. Although the series will go off in 1969, reruns of the Rigg and Thorson versions will keep the show a cult favorite. A new *Avengers* with Patrick MacNee will be produced in England in the late seventies.

Bill Burrud is host of NBC's *Animal Kingdom* nature series which debuts in 1968.

its effects on the printed word.

If we are going to preserve the reflective intelligence or the rational soul of man at all, there is no substitute for the printed word. It was, I suppose, at its most dominating in the nineteenth century and just before and just after the First World War. In America and England a large literate public had appeared for the first time in history. A successful writer could hope to reach, through books and journals of opinion—there were far more of them than there are now—a sizable proportion of this public.

We have to keep our heads. A successful writer today can, mainly through paperbacks, reach quantitatively a larger public than our nineteenth-century predecessors ever did. But he won't be taken as seriously as they were, because literature in any shape or form isn't taken as seriously. His sizable public is bombarded with so many messages in so many guises, and he is one court jester among many. He can't hope to make any genuine impact on people's thought, or scarcely any impact whatever. In my country, there are periodical honors lists, awards from the State. No English writer living, if he got such an award, which isn't very frequent, would receive attention on our news programs. That attention is devoted to awards to TV comedians. They are often called celebrities. It is they who receive the public veneration.

Does this mean that the rational soul of man has had its day? In dark moments I am inclined to think so. To train and employ the rational soul needs discipline and work. It even means a bit of intelligence. It means reading books, and that often takes time and effort. Our societies aren't much disposed to that kind of effort.

Sometimes it seems that the range of stimuli which hit us take away from any desire to think. Thinking has gone out of fashion. When I was a young man, visual stimuli were nothing like as pressing as they are now. Visual taste has improved out of knowledge and visual interest. Exhibitions of painting attract large followings. The pressure of aural stimuli is an order of magnitude more pressing still. Among many, musical taste has developed. Among far more, one feels that they have become totally immune from all effects of noise. The brute noise level has gone up as though we were living in a country of the deaf. English pubs used to be places where one could hear one's companions talk. Now, with a jukebox shattering the air, those placid evenings have gone.

Our sensuous life has changed. Some of the results are benevolent, some aren't. Too many of these results are enemies of the rational soul.

That applies to some of the results of TV. We can become punch-drunk with mindless pictures and mindless sound. We needn't remember anything. The week is a long time in politics, said one of our recent prime ministers. The week is a long time in today's culture. The printed word—including those obsolescent objects, books—is the collective memory of the human race. Books don't fade with last night's show. Maybe that is why they are ceasing to be read.

But again, we ought to keep our heads. We have all learned that major changes have unexpected consequences. Sometimes changes brought about by men of sincere goodwill have wretched consequences. That has happened in my country over education, though we may be waking up in time. The enormous technological pervasion of TV has had some entirely amiable consequences which no one could foresee. There is a trivial one which gives me mild pleasure almost every day in London. If you travel by underground, which is the most sensible way of getting about London, you will notice an extremely curious transformation. Twenty years ago you would never see anyone reading a book. Newspapers yes, no books. Now the exact opposite is beginning to take

Darren McGavin and Barbara Luna guest on *Cimarron Strip*, a ninety-minute western series that stars Stuart Whitman. It will go off in 1968 after only a year on CBS. One of television's most prolific actors, McGavin will star on *The Outsider* in 1968, and the vampire thriller, *The Night Stalker* in 1971, which will be one of the most-watched made-for-TV movies of all time. In 1974, it will be turned into a series, *Kolchak: The Night Stalker*.

Bea Benaderet, seen here with a selection of her *Petticoat Junction* daughters, dies in 1968, four years after the death of Gracie Allen with whom she co-starred on *The George Burns and Gracie Allen Show*. June Lockhart replaces Benaderet on *Petticoat Junction*, which will last until 1970.

A family portrait of the Rostov family from the 1972 BBC twenty-part production of Tolstoy's War and Peace.

over. Apparently many people are getting their news from TV, and don't want any more. The circulation of newspapers is going steadily and calamitously down, which of course is another defeat for the printed word. But underground journeys can be long and boring. So a good many resort to those old-fashioned articles called books. Not new books, but as a rule books collected from the public library. There they sit, reading steadily away. It is an unexpected sight.

There has been a much more important consequence of TV, and a totally admirable one. It has given another lease on life to some fine works of literature. It happens that TV is specially adapted to reproducing some of the very best novels. Much more so than the theater. The theater is a medium addressed to a collective audience. TV is an intimate medium addressed to one person by himself.

TV can cope and does cope with all the intricacies, the twists and turns of personality, of the great realistic novels. It is merciless to fancy. It shows up the falsity of decorative literary art or of literary parlor games. It doesn't like symbols unless they are embedded as deep as Ibsen's. But anyone who saw the TV serial of *War and Peace* realized how splendidly it conveyed the greatest realistic novel ever written. In England there was another consequence. A surprisingly large number of people read *War and Peace*—and even bought the book—who would never have thought of doing so.

There are plenty of similar successes. A few weeks ago, I watched a beautiful version of *The Ambassadors*. Paul Scofield did an almost perfect Lambert Strether—except for one or two false notes with American speech, which is always a difficulty for En-

319

April 4, 1968. Martin Luther King is killed by a sniper in Memphis, Tennessee. Two hundred thousand people attend his funeral, which is telecast around the world.

June 5, 1968. "Not again!" Robert Kennedy is assassinated in Los Angeles moments after delivering a speech declaring victory over Eugene McCarthy in the California Democratic primary. Since Johnson's withdrawal from the race on national television on March 31, Kennedy had been expected to win his party's presidential nomination.

July 1, 1968. Patrick McGoohan stars in *The Prisoner*, a seventeen-episode series about an ex-secret agent who is confined to a mysterious underground community called The Village. Although he is called "Number Six" in this series, it is probable that McGoohan is once more John Drake of *Secret Agent*. *The Prisoner*, the most complicated series ever to appear on television, will become a minor cult classic.

glish actors. It is a singular irony after James's long, dogged, pathetic, completely futile attempts to write stage plays, but his novels work wonderfully on TV. It sharpens them just a little. Which in the case of *The Ambassadors* is not, shall we say with suitable circumlocution, altogether an unmixed disadvantage.

That TV production lasted about an hour and three quarters. It was put out on the second BBC channel, which has usually slightly fewer watchers than the other one. Our population is about a quarter of America's, so *The Ambassadors* was probably seen by only five or six million people. However, that is almost certainly more people than have read a James novel from his own lifetime up to the present day.

That is a strange reflection. And yet one has to remind oneself that TV has no memory. Probably the experience, to almost all those watchers, has already passed out of mind, and maybe did so within days. Whereas the Henry James books exist in some sense as part of the collective literary memory, and a relatively small number of people still read them.

Which brings me to something of a puzzle. Which would a writer choose—a gigantic audience, many millions, for a few nights, immediate impact, gone like yesterday's news—or a trickle of an audience, not in a hundred years anything like what can be reached in one night, but with a few readers each year still picking up a book. Nearly all the writers I have known would opt for the second. It may be a sentimental choice, and difficult to justify in cool intellectual terms. Yet great masters like Dostoevski and Trollope would have made it, and in fact did say something like it. Dickens probably wouldn't have. But Dickens was the most histrionic of very great writers, and was all for the immediate impact wherever he could make it. Most writers have a pathetic hope for what used to be called immortality, which is both sentimental and quite unrealistic. It is almost un-imaginable that any living writer will be read—read that is as living literature, not just for scholarly or historical purposes in, say, five hundred years. And even five hundred years is a very short time on the historical scale. Immortality is considerably longer.

Of course, a good many writers, being both rapacious and optimistic, would like both blessings—millions watching them on the screen today, a few sympathetic persons understanding the books next century. Well, we mustn't take those hopes away. Writers don't have much to comfort them.

I have said that for purposes very close to my own literary interests I gain much from TV. But, at the end of it all, the message is as plain as a platitude. The printed word must not surrender. It is very easy—we have seen it in other contexts—for sensible persons to lose their nerve in the face of what seems irreversible change, above all technological change.

The literary mind might even help to cut its own throat—which sounds somewhat of a physiological oddity—mainly by escaping, as it has often escaped all through our century, into sheer silliness. Nevertheless, what little we can, we ought to do.

The most useful thing is, I think increasingly, not to be frightened into conformity. We are all much more conformist than we think. I hate to recall the amount of nonsense I have listened to in my time, and have, by silence, tacitly associated myself with. Each of us has his own word, as a great Russian used to say. It may not be an important word, but it is ours. If we say it, and print it, we shan't be giving up the game. We might even seduce some young person into reading an occasional line of print.

C. P. Snow is an internationally-known novelist, scientist and civil servant. Lord Snow delivered this address at the 1977 National Book Awards ceremony in New York City.

July 8, 1968. Mike Douglas poses with Barbara Walters, *The Today Show*'s top personality, when she co-hosts the *Mike Douglas Show* for a week. Originating from Philadelphia, the syndicated afternoon talk-variety show came on the air in 1966.

July 17, 1968. *One Life to Live* debuts. It will be one of ABC's first successful soap operas. Starring are Lillian Hayman, Justin McDonough, Jan Chasmar, Anthony Ponzini, Gillian Spencer, Lynn Benish, and Michael Storm.

THE EFFECTS OF TELEVISION

GEORGE COMSTOCK

Television has not escaped the inquiry of social and behavioral scientists. Psychologists, sociologists, pollsters, and others of about every disciplinary stripe have given some attention to television's influence on people. But for most viewers, the effects of television amount to their immediate reactions to what they see, which vary from absorbed attention to sufficient outrage to write the President protesting disregard for public morality. One effect television does not seem to have is an impulse to switch off the set.

Since the mid-1950's when television began to join the refrigerator as a principal appliance in American homes, television viewing has steadily increased. In the winter of 1977, it reached an all-time high of an average of more than seven hours a day for every individual in the 71 million households with television in the United States—which is almost every household there is. This increasing consumption of the medium is testimony to the effectiveness of the cyberneticlike relationship that has evolved between the medium and mass taste, which through continual, up-to-the-minute ratings of audience attention, permits the immediate discarding of programs of less than optimal appeal.

The incursion of television on time and therefore on other activities has revolutionized the leisure of Americans. Studies of urban dwellers in the United States, western Europe, and Latin America indicate that television has reduced sleeping time by about thirteen minutes. It has also reduced the amount of time spent in housework, conversation, use of many other media, and in leisure other than television viewing. Television has increased the amount of time spent

> ## "One effect television does not seem to have is an impulse to switch off the set."

with the mass media by about 40 percent, with three-fourths of all time spent on the media devoted to television. As a consumer of time, television ranks third behind work and sleep. Americans spend about 40 percent of all their leisure time with television—which has also affected the availability of other options. Television reduced the audience for movies, and the competition between the two has probably contributed to the level of violence in each. Television brought about the demise of mass circulation general audience magazines such as the *Saturday Evening Post, Collier's, Life,* and *Look,* by providing advertisers with a superior means of reaching consumers. Comic books decreased in sale from about 600 million in the early 1950's to about 300 million in 1970. In book publishing during the same period, fiction, poetry, and drama titles declined from 22 to 13 percent of all books published. To the extent that these shifts in comics and books are attributable to television, they reflect the medium's assumption of the role of bringing fantasy to the public. Television converted radio from a national medium, with the major outlets in each community delivering a full spectrum of network-disseminated entertainment and news to a heterogeneous audience, to a largely local medium where each station caters to a

Dean Martin Presents the Golddiggers plays on NBC during the summer of 1968. The singing and dancing Golddiggers, known as much for their looks as their talent, will appear many times during the next few years.

America's Peggy Fleming wins the Women's Figure Skating Gold Medal at the 1968 Winter Olympic Games in Grenoble, France. One of the few bright spots on the American team, Fleming will return to the U.S. as a celebrity. She will host several variety specials during the next decade; one will co-star Frenchman Jean-Claude Killy, who wins two skiing Gold Medals at the Grenoble Olympics.

Kip Keino of Kenya upsets American Jim Ryun in the 1,500-meter race of the 1968 Summer Olympics held in Mexico City. This run and Bob Beamon's electrifying 29′ 2½″ long jump (almost two feet farther than anyone else has ever jumped), called by many the greatest individual feat in sports history, highlight the Olympic Games. Black power protests by several victorious American athletes on international television become the talk of the entire world.

"Americans spend about 40 percent of all their leisure time with television. . ."

demographically distinct audience, and the principal communication is the playing and promotion of recorded music.

Television brings a common set of images and experiences to the heterogeneous population of the United States. The eventual consequences are a matter for speculation. The predominance of middle class values on television may increase their adoption by blue-collar and lower socioeconomic strata. The treatment of topics in comedy and drama such as homosexuality, abortion, adultery, and sexual relationships outside of marriage, probably reduces the control of parents over what their children may know. Heavy viewers of television have been found to perceive a greater likelihood of falling victim to a crime, for example, than do lighter viewers. The heavy television viewer has a vision of life closer to the violence-filled world of television drama than to the statistics of real life, suggesting that television may instill fear and, conceivably, arouse support for stricter and more punitive law enforcement.

Television's influence on presidential politics has been the subject of extensive investigation and debate. Television has become the medium of principal focus among politicians; nominating conventions increasingly have become show business, and television increasingly absorbs campaign funds and preoccupies candidates. Because each election is a special case in a context of gradual change, general rules are hard to formulate. Typically, voter choice has not been found to be affected by exposure to television news because of the self-canceling nature of roughly balanced coverage, and the tendency for most voters to reach a decision based on party preference before the national campaign begins. An additional factor has been the emphasis of television news on events and visual coverage rather than on issues; recent studies have found voter knowledge unaffected by viewing of news but, ironically, increased by viewing of political commercials, which sometimes do emphasize stands on issues, if one-sidedly. The most common conclusion has been that television, along with other mass media, "reinforces" voters because their eventual vote has been in line with predispositions regardless of attention to the media. However, over the past decade and a half, party alignment among the public has been decreasing, thus reducing the number of predisposed voters who can be reinforced, and opening the way toward other effects. In certain cases, such as the 1976 election when there was an extraordinary number of uncommitted and wavering voters throughout the campaign—as many as half in some polls shortly before the election—television has the opportunity for considerable influence, particularly when it provides a media event such as the Ford-Carter debates that penetrates far beyond the usual audience for political coverage. Available evidence from 1976 suggests that viewing of the debates affected the decision of many voters, and that the viewing of television news in this unusual campaign assisted still others in reaching a decision.

Slightly less than half of the more than two thousand experiments and surveys concerned with television and behavior that have been reported since the mid-1950's are concerned with children and adolescents. It is true that at any given moment the average American child will always have spent more time in his life watching television than in a classroom. It is not true that young viewers are a homogeneous audi-

Walter Cronkite anchors CBS's *Campaign '68* coverage at the national political conventions. At the Republican convention in Miami Beach, Richard M. Nixon is nominated for President. He chooses Spiro T. Agnew as his running mate.

August 25–29, 1968. "The whole world is watching." Hubert Humphrey wins the Democratic nomination in Chicago. Meanwhile, throughout the city, television cameras cover protests and capture furious confrontations between police and demonstrators. Newsmen, including Dan Rather who is assaulted on camera by security officers, are among those arrested or beaten. Walter Cronkite makes his outrage public.

Presidential candidates Jimmy Carter and Gerald Ford square off in one of three debates in Fall 1976.

ence. Viewing often begins as early as the first year of life, although it is not until between the second and third years that the child begins to think of himself as viewing television; before that, it is simply one among many not clearly differentiated experiences. Amount of viewing typically increases through elementary school, then declines with the increased social life and greater freedom from the home of adolescence.

Throughout there is considerable individual variation, with the average child viewing several hours a day while some children view not at all, and others view such extraordinary amounts as to total forty or fifty hours a week—well above the national average of 27 hours a week for elementary school age children.

A series of ingenious experiments has demonstrated that very young children will imitate be-

In 1968, *Lassie* changes its format. For the next four years, the capable collie, seen here with guest Kathy Martinez, will have no master. In 1971, after seventeen years on CBS, the show will become a syndicated series. In 1972 Lassie will settle down at the Holden Ranch with Larry Pennell, Larry Wilcox, and Skip Burton.

Jack Lord stars as police chief Steve McGarrett in *Hawaii Five-O,* which premieres on CBS in 1968.

This show will be repeatedly criticized for using too much violence. Nevertheless, it will become one of television's most popular programs.

September 14, 1968. *Fantastic Voyage,* a Saturday morning cartoon adaptation of the movie, debuts on ABC. It will last two years. Marvin Miller, Jane Webb, and Ted Knight supply the voices.

havior they see performed on television immediately after viewing, and that observed behavior may be added to their repertoire of possible acts for display in some future circumstance. These experiments have most often measured the influence of violent portrayals on subsequent aggressiveness, and thus suggest that television violence may increase the likelihood of aggressive behavior by young viewers. Other experiments have demonstrated that adolescents who view a violent portrayal are more likely to act with greater vigor when subsequently engaged in aggressive behavior. The various aspects of the televised portrayals that appear to enhance the likelihood of aggressive behavior are: the depiction of the aggressor as gaining a reward, the inclusion of cues also present in real-life, the motivation of the violence by malevolence or intent to do injury, the justification of the in-inflicted violence as just punishment, and the presentation of the violence as real rather than made-up fantasy. The implied conclusion that violence in entertainment increases the likelihood of aggressive behavior on the part of young viewers is strengthened greatly by surveys that demonstrate a positive correlation between prior amount of viewing of violent television drama and everyday aggression against friends and classmates.

Television also appears to join such traditional influences as parents and teachers in affecting beliefs and perceptions. Like adults, young people who are heavy viewers of television are more likely to believe in a greater degree of personal danger when outside the home. Television appears to have its greatest influence when real-life experience is lacking; thus, children's perceptions of occupations have been found to adhere to the portrayal of these occupations on television when the children have had no real-life experience with persons in the portrayed activities. Television is a major source of children's knowledge about public affairs. However, a variety of studies make it very clear that when parents or other influential adults express an opinion, whether it is on the justifiability of a national entanglement, such as the Viet Nam War, or on the advisability of turning to aggression or violence to resolve a conflict with others, the adult perspective is likely to be decisive in the attitude or behavior of the child. Thus, the increase in vicarious as contrasted to real-life socialization that some psychologists attribute to television should be seen in part as the result of nonintervention by parents and other adults.

There is even some question as to precisely what constitutes "watching" television. From mobile units parked in the subjects' yards, a group of investigators filmed the behavior of twenty Kansas and Missouri families during a typical week of television watching. The films depict a wide variety of behavior associated with an operating television set, including a great deal of disinterest and involvement in other activities. Television "viewing" was probably an absorbing activity for most people when the medium was a novelty, but as it has become a commonplace, viewing has become a disconnected, often-interrupted activity with "viewers" oscillating constantly between attention and inattention. The proper definition of "viewing" is not "watching television" but "conducting life before an operating television set that often holds the attention of those present." Among the most frequent activities occurring in conjunction with viewing are housework and eating. This does not bode well for the boeuf Bourguignonne, but it has done wonders for brand names.

George Comstock is a social psychologist and the senior author of Television and Human Behavior *to be published early in 1978.*

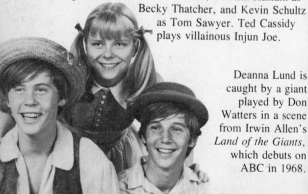

September 15, 1968. *The New Adventures of Huckleberry Finn*, which cleverly mixes live action and animation, debuts on NBC. Starring are Michael Shea as Huck, Lu Ann Haslam as Becky Thatcher, and Kevin Schultz as Tom Sawyer. Ted Cassidy plays villainous Injun Joe.

Deanna Lund is caught by a giant played by Don Watters in a scene from Irwin Allen's *Land of the Giants*, which debuts on ABC in 1968.

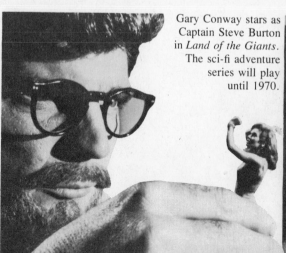

Gary Conway stars as Captain Steve Burton in *Land of the Giants*. The sci-fi adventure series will play until 1970.

TV: THE CHILDREN'S DRUG

MARIE WINN

Concern about the effects of television on children has centered almost exclusively upon the *contents* of the programs children watch. Social scientists and researchers devise complex and ingenious experiments to determine whether watching violent programs makes children behave more aggressively or, conversely, whether watching exemplary programs encourages ''pro-social'' behavior in children. Studies are conducted to discover whether television commercials make children greedy and materialistic, or, as some have suggested, generous and spiritual.

Yet the very nature of the television experience, as opposed to the contents of the programs, is rarely considered. Perhaps the ever-changing array of sights and sounds coming out of the machine fosters the illusion of a varied experience for the viewer, allowing him to overlook a deceptively simple fact: one is always *watching television* when one is watching television, rather than having any other experience.

Regardless of program content there is a similarity of experience about all television watching. Certain specific mechanisms of the eyes, ears, and brain respond to the television stimuli regardless of the cognitive content of the programs. It is a one-way transaction that requires the taking in of particular sensory material in a particular way. There is, in fact, no other experience in a child's life that permits quite so much intake while demanding so little outflow.

Preschool children are the single largest television audience in America, spending a greater number of total hours and a greater proportion of their waking day watching television than any other age group.

> ''. . . preschool children . . . spend more than a third of their waking hours watching television.''

Even the most conservative estimates indicate that preschool children in the United States spend more than a third of their waking hours watching television.

What are the effects upon the vulnerable and developing human organism of spending such a significant proportion of each day engaged in this particular experience? How does television viewing affect a child's language development, for instance, or his developing imagination, his creativity? Is the child's perception of reality subtly altered by a steady exposure to television unrealities? How does the *availability* of television affect the ways parents bring up their children? Does it cause them to discard certain child-rearing strategies and adopt new ones? How does watching television for several hours each day affect the child's abilities to form human relationships? What happens to family life as a result of family members' involvement with television?

The fact that these questions are rarely raised signals the distorted view American parents take of the role of television in their children's lives. For while parents are often deeply troubled about television and its effects on children, their concern remains centered

September 21, 1968. *Adam-12* starring Kent McCord (R) and Martin Milner as Los Angeles police officers premieres on ABC. Producer Jack Webb of *Dragnet* once more pays a personal tribute to the modern policeman in this fast-moving, half-hour crime series. *Adam-12* will last seven years.

The Mod Squad debuts on ABC. Three hip anti-establishment youths, played by Peggy Lipton, Michael Cole, and Clarence Williams III, become undercover police agents as an alternative to going to prison for committing petty crimes. Tige Andrews plays the Los Angeles police officer who befriends Julie, Pete, and Linc.

on the actual programs that their children watch. They join organizations that work to improve those programs to meet the needs of young children.

But is it the needs of *children* that are at stake when parents demand better programming? Surely the fact that young children watch so much television reflects the needs of *parents* to find a convenient source of amusement for their children while easing their own child-care burdens.

The needs of young children are quite different.

The developing child needs opportunities to work out his basic family relationships, thereby coming to understand himself. The television experience reduces these opportunities.

The child needs to develop a capacity for self-direction in order to liberate himself from the dependency which the television experience helps to perpetuate.

The child needs to acquire fundamental skills in communication—to learn to read, write, and express himself flexibly and clearly—in order to function as a social creature. The passive television experience does not further his verbal development because it does not require any verbal participation on his part.

The child needs to discover his own strengths and weaknesses in order to find fulfillment as an adult. Watching television does not lead him to such discoveries; indeed, it only limits his involvement with those real-life activities that might offer his abilities a genuine testing ground.

The young child's need for fantasy is gratified far better by his own make-believe activities than by

"But is it the needs of children that are at stake . . . ?"

". . . television has a destructive effect upon family life. . ."

adult-made fantasies he is offered on television.

The young child's need for intellectual stimulation is met infinitely better when he can learn by manipulating, touching, *doing,* than by watching.

Finally, the television experience must be considered in relation to the child's need to develop those family skills he will need in order to become a successful parent himself someday. These skills are a product of his present participation in family life, of his everyday experiences as a family member. There is every indication that television has a destructive effect upon family life, diminishing its richness and variety.

Thus it begins to appear that the television experience is at best irrelevant and at worst detrimental to children's needs. Efforts to make television more attractive to parents and children by improving programming can only lead to the increased reliance of parents upon television as a baby-sitter, and the increased bondage of children to television as a time-filler. Sometimes it even appears that the television industry's cool indifference to the quality of children's programs may be more beneficial for children than the activities of those who insist that fine children's programs be available at all times, since conscientious parents are more likely to limit their children's television intake if nothing besides unsavory programs is available much of the time.

Parents may overemphasize the importance of content in considering the effects of television on their children because they assume that their children's television experience is the same as their own. But there is an essential difference between the two: the

Mike Connors is a Los Angeles detective in the revised *Mannix,* which premieres on CBS in 1968. Gail Fisher is his secretary on the popular series that will play seven years. An earlier version co-starring Joe Campanella had been on CBS in 1967.

first series since *Beulah,* sixteen years before, to star a black woman in the title role. Here she tells her son, played by Mark Copage, that she expects him to be more than a shoeshine man. Lloyd Nolan, as her boss, and Michael Link co-star. The comedy will play from 1968 to 1971.

Mayberry R.F.D., appears on CBS in 1968 soon after the final episode of *The Andy Griffith Show* (1960-1968). This spin-off comedy series will be very popular during its three-year run. Ken Berry, formerly of *F Troop,* and Arlene Golonka star.

Diahann Carroll plays a registered nurse in NBC's *Julia,* the

CBS's Saturday morning Shazam! *is the adventures of Billy Batson (R) who becomes Captain Marvel, crime fighter.*

September 23, 1968. *Here's Lucy* begins a very successful six-year run on CBS. Co-starring with Lucille Ball in this wild comedy are Lucie Arnaz, Desi Arnaz, Jr., and Gale Gordon. Beginning in 1974, Lucille Ball will confine herself to television specials and guest appearances. Reruns of *I Love Lucy*, *The Lucy Show*, and *Here's Lucy* will dominate their time periods for years to come, and strengthen Lucille Ball's position as television's all-time star.

September 24, 1968. Doris Day, the top female movie attraction a few years ago when "bedroom" comedies were in vogue, finally comes to television for *The Doris Day Show*. Although there will be a new format almost every year, her popular CBS comedy will last until 1973.

adult has a vast backlog of real-life experiences; the child does not. As the adult watches television his own present and past relationships, experiences, dreams and fantasies may come into play, transforming the material he sees into something reflecting his own inner needs. The young child's life experiences are limited. He has barely emerged from the preverbal fog of infancy. It is disquieting to consider that hour after hour of television watching constitutes a *primary* activity for him. His subsequent real-life activities will stir up memories of television experiences, not, as for the adult watcher, the other way around. For the child, real events will always carry echoes of television.

Inevitably parents of young children turn their attention to the content of programs their children watch because they have come to believe that television is an important source of learning. But the television-based learning of the preschool child brings to mind the *idiot savant,* a profoundly retarded person who exhibits some remarkable mental abilities—one who can, for instance, multiply five-digit numbers in his head. The television-educated child can spout words and ideas that he does not comprehend and "facts" that he doesn't have the experience or knowledge to assimilate. The small child mimicking television commercials or babbling words and phrases learned from programs, the young *television savant,* has no more ability to use his television-acquired material for his own human purposes than the defective pseudo-genius has of using his amazing mathematical manipulations.

Because television is so available a child-amuser and defuser, capable of rendering harmless at the flick of a switch a volatile three-year-old, parents grow to depend on it in the course of their daily lives. As they continue to utilize it day after day, its importance in their children's lives increases. But despite their increasing resentment of television's intrusions into their

"For the child, real events will always carry echoes of television"

family life and despite their considerable guilt at not being able to control their children's viewing, parents do not take steps to extricate themselves from television's domination. They cannot cope without it.

In 1948 Jack Gould, the first television critic of The New York *Times,* wrote: "Children's hours on television are admittedly an insidious narcotic for the parent. With the tots fanned out on the floor in front of the receiver, a strange if wonderful quiet seems at hand. . . ."

At first it appears that Gould's pen has slipped. Surely it is the strangely quiet tots who are narcotized by the television set, not the parents. But indeed he had penetrated to the heart of the problem before anyone dreamed that children would one day spend more of their waking hours watching television than doing anything else. It is, in fact, the parents for whom television is an irresistible narcotic, not through their own viewing (although frequently this too is the case) but through their children, fanned out in front of the receiver, strangely quiet. Surely there can be no more insidious a drug than one you must administer to others in order to achieve an effect for yourself.

Marie Winn is the author of ten books for parents, the parent of two school-age sons, and the owner of one carefully-controlled television set. This article is adapted from The Plug-In Drug *by Marie Winn. Copyright © Marie Winn Miller, 1977. By permission of the Viking Press.*

In 1968, *The Ghost and Mrs. Muir* moves from NBC to ABC for its second season. Here Hope Lange and Edward Mulhare, as the spirit living in her nineteenth-century seaside cottage, give testimony in front of judges Bluebeard, Nero, and Jesse James in the "Not So Faust" episode. Lange will win an Emmy for Best Actress in a Comedy Series, but the show will go off in 1969.

Family Affair moves into its second season on CBS in 1968. Guests David Livingston, George Ostos, and Scott Garrett visit regulars Johnnie Whitaker and Anissa Jones. Brian Keith, Sebastian Cabot, and Kathy Garver co-star in this comedy series.

THE ELECTRONIC FIREPLACE
PETER CROWN

The flickering presence of television has become part of our environment. The countless hours viewers spend before the screen constitute a relationship that is not well understood, but which is beginning to be explored by scientists.

Most research on television and viewers has asked questions related to content: What effect does televised violence have on children? Do political debates influence voters? Did an advertising campaign increase sales? More recently researchers are asking a different type of question, exploring the viewer-screen relationship apart from content: What perceptual characteristics of video and audio increase viewer attention to the screen? To what extent do people use television for relaxation, as a sleeping pill, or just for background? Does television influence brain psychology?

I am intrigued and concerned by the notion that the state of the television viewer might be characterized as a passive captive of the flickering images, like the moth to the candle. Or, in the extreme instance, imagine the TV addict as a compulsive consumer/ abuser of the tube as a form of passive stimulation.

My interest in these questions began in 1973. While research coordinator and an artist-in-residence at WNET/13's Television Laboratory in New York City, I reviewed a wide range of research publications and kept in touch with the people doing the research. Some of the research findings were presented in "The Tube and Eye," an experimental documentary that I coproduced with Bill Etra for the lab's VTR series, shown on many PBS stations.

> "... about 20 percent of the time the set is on, no one is in front of it."

For part of the show we videotaped interviews with people on the street regarding their TV viewing habits. Some of the responses applied directly to the "relationship" question. For example, one man said, "At the end of a busy day I like to watch the light flicker [from the screen] and let anxieties drain away." Another said, "As soon as I get home I turn on the TV and then do something else." One interviewee was a graduate student who said, "Television is something I watch either because I want to learn about what's on, or it's something to turn me off and take me over." Finally, one of the responses was so extreme that several people asked whether it was a setup (it wasn't). This person said, "I used to come home from school every day, get into bed, and lie there like a zombie until I fell asleep. After several years of this I realized that I had no other life and I finally threw away my TV."

I began to develop the notion that television, in addition to being a source of information and entertainment, had taken on the role of the "electronic fireplace" of our time. Just as gazing into a campfire can be absorbing and hypnotic, so can gazing at the TV screen. It doesn't matter what's on, it only matters that there is something emitting light patterns.

329

September 25, 1968. Bob Denver (R), Herb Edelman, and Joyce Van Patten run a diner in *The Good Guys,* which debuts on CBS. It will go off in 1970. Van Patten was a regular on *The Danny Kaye Show,* which went off CBS in 1967.

In 1968, *Blondie* returns to television after a fourteen-year absence. Patricia Hardy (Blondie), Will Hutchins (Dagwood), Peter Robbins (Alexander), and Pamela Ferdin (Cookie) star. Jim Backus plays Mr. Dithers. This CBS comedy will go off in a year.

Robert Brown (R) plays lumberman Jason Bolt who, on ABC's *Here Come the Brides,* recruits one hundred refined eastern ladies and brings them to wild Seattle in the 1890's. This adventure series, which co-stars David Soul, Bobby Sherman, Joan Blondell, and Henry Beckman (L), will play from 1968 to 1970. Brown will star in 1971 as an oceanographer in the syndicated *Primus.*

David Niven demonstrates one way to break television's hypnotic hold on its viewers.

Some of the research studies do seem to point to this. Dr. John Robinson of the University of Michigan published a study in which he asked a national sample: "Were there any times yesterday that you would have liked to watch TV but didn't because there weren't any programs worth watching at that time?" Only 10 percent answered yes. Robinson interprets this as meaning that once someone decides to watch TV, he or she will find the least objectionable program and stay tuned whether they enjoy the show or not. He also noted that from one-third to one-half of all TV viewing is done as a secondary activity, that is, to the accompaniment of a primary activity such as reading or doing housework. In discussing electronic rating devices he noted that observational studies indicate that about 20 percent of the time the set is on, no one is in front of it. Perhaps most intriguing was his finding that television set owners sleep less than nonowners. Since sleep is a physiological function, this suggests that there might be a trade-off between television

Christmas Eve, 1968. Appolo 8 carries astronauts Frank Borman, James Lovell, Jr., and William Anders around the moon. Viewers thrill to majestic photos sent back to earth. Here the rising earth is about five degrees above the lunar horizon in this breathtaking telephoto shot from the Apollo 8 spacecraft. Borman, Lovell, and Anders will return from their monumental journey on December 27, 1968.

In 1969, *Star Trek* completes a four-year run on NBC. William Shatner, DeForest Kelley, and Leonard Nimoy are the stars of what will become TV's all-time cult favorite. Reruns will be shown around the world, and the show's popularity will grow. Fan clubs will form and annual *Star Trek* conventions will be held in many cities. In 1978, creator Gene Roddenberry will revise the program in a syndicated version.

January 20, 1969. Richard Nixon, who won a narrow victory over Hubert Humphrey in the November presidential election, is inaugurated.

watching and sleeping. In other words, television may fulfill some of the same needs that sleep provides.

What are the factors, both video and audio, that increase or decrease the viewer's attention? This question is being addressed by two researchers, Dr. Dan Anderson and Dr. Steve Levin. Their recent studies contain "the first formal descriptions of the development of visual attention to television based on direct observations of children." Their technique involves careful analysis of a Sesame Street test program. Knowing what was happening on the screen and on audio at every moment, they videotaped each child watching the show. The tape was analyzed so that attention or nonattention to the screen could be correlated with the attributes of the show by computer. As an example of their many findings, they reported that all children in the experiment paid less attention if there was an adult male on the screen and more attention if there were child characters on the screen.

In a more informal part of the study they asked the children to name their favorite segment from the show and also asked the parents which segment they thought their kids would like best. A segment showing a gibbon swinging from jungle branches was rated number one by parents. Their kids rated it twenty-third on the list. This says something about the ability of adults to intuit what will capture the attention of children watching television.

Perhaps the most basic consideration in the "relationship" question is perceptual—how the image is formed on the screen and how we perceive it. I was reminded of this on my trip to the Vidcom convention in Cannes in 1976. Our minibus from the airport got stuck in traffic, quite by coincidence right outside a TV store with several sets on in the window. I thought they were flickering strongly. The others in the minibus, all just arrived from the States, saw the same thing. The flickering was caused by the fifty hertz line frequency in Europe as opposed to sixty hertz on this side of the Atlantic. Images in the U.S. flicker sixty times per second; they flicker in Europe at fifty. An informal survey revealed that Americans could easily see the flicker during the first few days they were in Europe, while Europeans who were acclimated to it could not.

The perception of television images has been considered by Julian Hochberg and Virginia Brooks of Columbia University. The noted that while the normal field of vision is about 180 degrees, and that in a typical movie theater it is about 25 to 45 degrees, a television screen subtends an angle of only 7 to 14 degrees (for a screen eighteen inches across viewed from six to twelve feet away). This means that when a viewer watches TV, his or her saccadic eye movements (the rapid, exploratory movements of the eyes) are restricted to a small "window." They remark that, "Not much is known about the behavior of the visuomotor system in such situations, but it is surely not safe to assume that it is the same as in free-gaze or even movie theater situation."

My own guess is that when the research is done it will show a significant relationship between the relatively small size of TV screens and the sometimes hypnotic effect of TV. It must work the way Hindu mandalas concentrate one's visual attention to a small area for the purpose of attaining meditative states. It may follow that the brightness and relatively small size of TV screens may have a similar effect. Future work in this area by students, other experimenters, and video artists should bring a new perspective and a new look to the video medium.

Peter Crown is a video consultant and a physiological psychologist at Hampshire College in Amherst, Massachusetts. This article appeared in a somewhat different version in Videography, *March 1977.*

James Stacy plays Johnny Madrid Lancer on the hour-long western *Lancer,* which begins a two-year run on CBS in 1968. Wayne Maunder plays his half-brother, Scott Lancer, and Andrew Duggan is their father, Murdoch Lancer, owner of a huge cattle spread. What is unique about this series is that the sons dislike their father and each other.

Because its demands for censorship have been ignored, CBS cancels the popular *Smothers Brothers Show* in 1969. Eventually, the comedy duo will win a money settlement from CBS for breaking their contract. They will have unsuccessful variety series on ABC (1970) and NBC (1975). Here the Smothers Brothers are with Glen Campbell, who was their summer replacement in 1968. From 1969 to 1972, he will host *The Glen Campbell Goodtime Hour* on CBS.

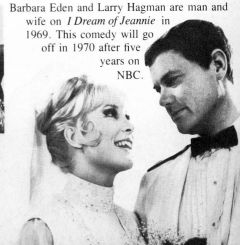

Barbara Eden and Larry Hagman are man and wife on *I Dream of Jeannie* in 1969. This comedy will go off in 1970 after five years on NBC.

NEW HOME TV SYSTEMS

LOUIS JAFFE

As crude phonographs of yesteryear evolved into the high fidelity systems of today, so television is maturing technically into a medium which will soon make today's TV seem like a toy. Free TV broadcasting will be joined by pay cable and disks where the mass audience will pay directly for entertainment or instructional value received, and this will profoundly alter the nature of programming. The media presence will be felt as never before; it will dominate the very walls of our homes.

By mid-1975, a first generation of equipment to provide wall-sized television pictures and record and playback programs in the home was put on the market. Media lovers in-the-know began buying the Advent Videobeam projection TV and a Sony U-Matic videocassette deck, subscribing to their local cable TV system, and recording and exchanging their own high-quality copies of movies and other programming. The Advent Corporation was the early winner in the giant-screen race with a projection unit using an optical system to throw the color video image across the room onto a seven-foot screen. Costing twenty-five hundred dollars, this video projector was at least fifteen times cheaper than previously available professional units, and its quality was excellent.

The home video projector demonstrated for the first time that a strong demand for wall-sized TV does exist, but it is only a crude forerunner of giant screens to come. Every major TV research lab is pursuing the ideal of a self-contained, hang-on-the-wall TV that could be built any size. Although working prototypes exist, such a TV set is still years away from the market. Early use of large-screen TV revealed that industry standards for broadcast picture quality, adequate for a small screen, are quite marginal when the image is enlarged. A future doubling or even quadrupling of the number of lines comprising the picture might be technically feasible, but would require broadcasters to rebuild their equipment from scratch.

As projection TV established itself on the market, Sony introduced Betamax, the first video recorder to be sold through such consumer outlets as audio and appliance stores. After the failure of earlier attempts to market a home video recorder, notably Avco's Cartrivision, the industry adopted a wait-and-see attitude, but this time Sony achieved a solid success. In 1977, an updated Betamax, with the capability of recording two hours of picture and sound on a fifteen dollar cassette the size of a small paperback book, has faced off against Matsushita's competing videocassette system with the same capabilities. Tapes recorded on one machine will not play on the other. With Zenith buying machines from Sony and RCA buying from Matsushita to sell under their own names, a major marketing battle is under way.

Repeatedly postponed, but still due for introduction in the next few years, are various disk systems for playing back video. These are playback-only systems, analagous to audio LP's. It would seem that disk and tape could coexist in tomorrow's home video systems, as they do in the audio systems of today. Videodisk could become a mass distribution medium like the audio LP, if manufacturers can agree on a format.

Video recording in the home by a potentially

Hee Haw, an hour variety show featuring country music and comedy, debuts on CBS as a summer series in 1969. A smash hit, it will become a regular series in December. When CBS cancels the popular show in 1971, *Hee Haw* is bought by numerous independent markets. As a syndicated series it will become a successful show. Buck Owens (L) and Roy Clark will host into the late seventies.

The Johnny Cash Show debuts on ABC in 1969 as a summer series. It will be a regular series beginning in January and run for more than a year. The country music superstar will host another musical variety show with his singer-wife June Carter in 1976.

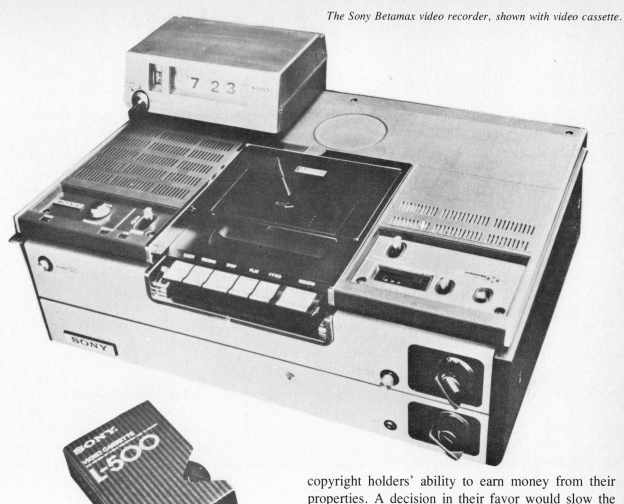

The Sony Betamax video recorder, shown with video cassette.

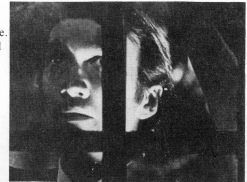

massive number of viewers is the issue behind a suit brought by Universal Studios and Walt Disney Productions against the Sony Corporation to restrain use of the Betamax. They argue that home recording of copyrighted shows is an infringement that harms the

copyright holders' ability to earn money from their properties. A decision in their favor would slow the progress of the videodisk system being readied by MCA Incorporated, owners of Universal. Sony's position is that home recording which does not involve resale of copyrighted material does not infringe copyright—that recording for personal use is a First Amendment right.

Louis Jaffe, a New York-based independent producer, works under the name ''Videotape Projects.''

333

July 20, 1969. Man walks on the moon! Astronaut Edwin E. Aldrin, Jr. poses beside the flag during Apollo II extravehicular activity on the lunar surface. The footprints of Aldrin and flight commander Neil Armstrong are clearly visible in the soil.

Cooking programs have been popular since the early days of television. In 1969 the entertaining Graham Kerr comes to television on the syndicated *The Galloping Gourmet*.

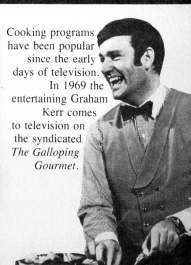

Strange Paradise debuts in 1969. This syndicated program starring Colin Fox as the haunted Jean Paul Desmond is television's second serial dealing with the supernatural. It will not have the popular or critical success of *Dark Shadows*.

CONFESSIONS OF A TV JUNKIE

DON AUSPITZ

One night a few months ago a close friend and I were very stoned on some exquisite grass and watching Joe Franklin, a preposterous, bloodcurdlingly gauche leprechaun of a talk show host on a local New York station. I was railing about how awful the whole thing was ("who the hell *are* these people anyway?") when my friend asked why we were watching.

"Everything else is worse," I said.

She said, "So why don't we just turn off the TV?"

My friend, who has known me for many years, turned to face me on the sofa. She took a long look, and then, verging on the giggles, said, "I just flashed on what they're going to choose for your purgatory. It's this other reality. . . . with only one channel, and it has a talk show—the same one playing over and over again, endlessly. The guests are always the same—Zsa Zsa Gabor, John Davidson, and Charo. And the host," she said, with a devilish gleam in her eye, "is Joe Garagiola."

How well she knows me. She devised one of the few examples of TV that would nearly drive me nuts. But even that—even the torture of those vacuities would probably be better than a dark television screen. I've heard that one of humanity's most laughable and frequent illusions is that we think we're in complete control of ourselves (heh! heh!) and the contents of our minds and psyches. For going on four decades I've been an obsessive compulsive who thought (heh! heh!) he was in control. Until recently, one of my standard fantasies was that I only watched as much TV as I

"I love it, hate it and do not choose to turn it off."

chose to watch. What makes my friend's vision of my purgatory particularly hellish is that I am also an intelligent and discerning fellow, often capable of good taste, at times even fastidious in my aesthetics. I guess I'd call myself an intellectual.

But the fact is that I'm completely hooked on TV. I love it, hate it and do not choose to turn it off. It's alive, it's entertaining as hell, and it's always there to keep me company. I am a TV junkie.

For a quarter of a century now I have watched as my reflection in the blank screen went from early adolescence to the onset of middle age while I waited for the set to warm up and show me *I Remember Mama; Your Show of Shows; Strike It Rich; The Monday/Wednesday/Friday/Saturday Night Fight(s); Mr. I-magination; Highway Patrol; The Late Show; Milton Berle's Texaco Star Theatre; Omnibus; The Millionaire; Ed Sullivan; Dragnet; Playhouse 90; The Early Movie; McGraw; Medic; Twilight Zone; Have Gun–Will Travel; Naked City; The Fugitive; Batman; Laugh-In; Mission Impossible; The Late Late Show; Star Trek; The Odd Couple; The Bionic Woman;* and *Hollywood Squares,* to say nothing of thousands of news stories on inaugurations, nominations, assassinations, resignations, Korea, Viet Nam, moon landings, and hostages. I'll watch anything.

334

In 1969, singer-actor Merv Griffin, who has hosted talk, variety, and game shows since the mid-fifties, is brought in by CBS to challenge Johnny Carson's late-night supremacy. But *The Merv Griffin Show* will only last three years. In 1972 Griffin, seen here with ex-boxing champs Gene Tunney and Jack Dempsey, will host a syndicated talk show that will become very popular.

The on-the-air wedding of singer Tiny Tim and Miss Vickie wins *The Johnny Carson Show* its highest rating in history. Here the bride and groom sing love songs on *The Ed Sullivan Show.*

In 1969, *Peyton Place* leaves the air after five years on ABC. Ex-regulars Ryan O'Neal and his wife Leigh Taylor Young star in a pilot for *Under the Yum Yum Tree.* It does not get picked up.

Phyllis Elizabeth Davis and Stuart Margolin in clinch on Love, American Style, *a popular, much—rerun comedy series.*

The Pink Panther Show debuts on NBC in 1969. This popular children's cartoon series features a theme song by Henry Mancini. Among those providing voices are Marvin Miller, Paul Frees, John Byner, and Rich Little. In 1969, TV censors will force many cartoon makers to edit violence out of their cartoons.

H. R. Pufnstuf debuts on NBC in 1969. It will switch to NBC in 1972 for its final season. Among the characters on this children's show are Raunchy Rabbit, Dr. Blinky, Hippy Boyd, Ludicrous Lion, and H. R. Pufnstuf.

September 4, 1969. *The Bill Cosby Show* begins a two-year run on NBC in 1969. Cosby plays Chet Kincaid, a high school gym teacher in this off-beat comedy. In 1972, Cosby will host *The New Bill Cosby Show,* a variety series that will play a year on CBS.

". . . the peak of my week was the day the new *TV Guide* came out."

I finally admitted my habit to myself one recent morning as I was having a late breakfast in a nearby coffee shop. Before me on the table were the *TV Guide, Cue, Cable TV Magazine,* and the week's television listings from *The New York Times,* the *Post,* and the *Daily News.* I was, as usual, checking out what was on. It suddenly struck me for the first time that food was beside the point; it was the week's TV glories I was devouring.

But there was a crisis. I had invited some people for dinner and on that same night CBS had decided to rerun, all in one night, the terrific three-part *Hawaii Five-O* show about the Vachon crime family, starring Luther Adler and Harold Gould. Not to be missed! I was sitting there, staring into space, slowing chewing on my fingernails, trying to figure a way out. Get them to cancel? Say I was sick? Maybe I could simply brazen it out and watch the show while they were in my apartment? Not a good idea. Although the mark of a lush is solitary drinking, and social drinking is considered okay, for a TV watcher the reverse is true. You're suspect when you have to keep watching, especially in the company of others. Of course, the *real* junkie never shows up when his favorite shows are on.

Madness. I asked myself, had it reached the point where the peak of my week was the day the new *TV Guide* came out? Yes, it had. I was watching TV all the time, all the time. And what was more, it had been going on for years.

I remembered moving into my new studio apartment and spending days shifting things around in a search for the perfect setup—I had to be able to see the television set equally well from any angle in the room. The last step was to fit the set onto a lazy Susan for easy swiveling—thus forming a tiny video shrine all my own, with the liturgical program listings in neat little piles around it. There were times when I was so intent on "worship" that I didn't take my coat off until two or three shows after I got home. Let me be perfectly clear. Even now, at this very moment, I am splitting my attention between writing this piece and a rerun of *Love, American Style.*

But look, don't get me wrong. Nothing is better than TV. Imagine drug addicts waltzing into a supermarket to pick from shelves crowded with a huge assortment of narcotics. Think of new drugs, ever more brightly packaged, appearing every few months or so. No, I wouldn't have it any other way. So what if I often find myself doing nothing but changing channels for fifteen minutes looking for something to watch? I cannot bring myself to turn it off.

Anti-TV snobs claim television is vapid, childish, simplistic, dangerous, corrupting, mind-destroying and crassly commercial. They only watch occasionally and then they only look at public television or things like Watergate or the Kennedy murders. But as a self-confessed TV junkie, I'll take *Starsky and Hutch* over any special on earthquakes, and give me *The Gong Show* instead of *Meet the Press.* As for the people who say TV is garbage, I refer them to Nietzsche who believed that we should not turn away from garbage, but embrace and contain it, like an ocean. No problem for me there. I read the *National Enquirer* every week too.

Don Auspitz is on the verge of deciding who or what he is.

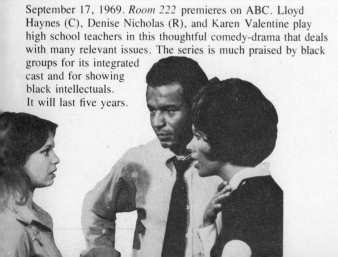

September 17, 1969. *Room 222* premieres on ABC. Lloyd Haynes (C), Denise Nicholas (R), and Karen Valentine play high school teachers in this thoughtful comedy-drama that deals with many relevant issues. The series is much praised by black groups for its integrated cast and for showing black intellectuals. It will last five years.

A quiet comedy, *The Courtship of Eddie's Father* begins a four-year run on ABC. Bill Bixby (R) stars as Tom Corbett, a widower for whom his son, played by Brandon Cruz, is seeking a mate.

THE HEALING POWERS OF TV

ROBERT BEDICK

Much has been written about the negative aspects of television. A number of years ago the public was warned about the dangerous levels of radiation emitted by color sets. More recently, attacks against TV have stressed its undesirable sociological impact. TV is held responsible for crime, wasteful consumption, illiteracy, and creeping idiocy. Whatever the point of view, the message seems to be clear: TV Is Dangerous To Your Health.

The truth, however, as anyone who has ever been sick well knows, is the exact opposite. TV can actually cure physical illness and is directly responsible for maintaining the mental well-being of millions of people since its invention. Except for the discovery of the modern wonder drugs, TV is probably *the* medical breakthrough of the twentieth century.

Children have known of the healing powers of TV for years. Think back to your own experiences. When you were sick as a child what would be the first thing plugged into your room after the vaporizer? The television set, of course. Immediately, the uninterrupted hours of cartoons, quiz shows, and ball games would begin. And during the hours of daytime TV shows, the mysterious curative powers of the cathode tube would be at work. It is no coincidence that you'd soon be feeling better. Scientists and doctors are baffled, but the statistics prove that children who watch TV while suffering from the mumps, measles, chicken pox, strep throat, and the flu return to school two to three days sooner than their counterparts who do not watch TV.

It is not merely to keep patients entertained that

> "TV is probably *the* medical breakthrough of the twentieth century."

hospitals across the country have placed TV's in almost all their rooms. Statistics on TV hospital room installations again support the healing value of TV. The fact that the sick are required to pay to watch the sets does not mean that hospitals don't realize that TV is a helpful cure, but is instead only another example of how in America you have to buy your good health.

The facts are clear. As TV ownership has increased, so has good health. Pick the ten countries with the best health-care statistics and you'll have picked the ten countries with the highest per capita television ownership. Pick households with more than one TV and chances are that these families will be healthier than those who own no TV set at all.

But getting away from numbers, I'd like to recount a personal experience that testifies to the healing power of TV. Recently I suffered from a case of mononucleosis complicated by hepatitis. My doctor could not offer any help with traditional drugs. He determined from extensive blood tests that two months of intensive bed rest was required.

Recalling how I had dealt with illness in my youth, I had a television rushed into my room. The fact that I used a Sony black-and-white nine-inch, the fact

337

Michael Parks gives up his meaningless nine-to-five lifestyle to wander the country on a motorcycle in *Then Came Bronson,* which plays on NBC in 1969. Among those who benefit from his presence are Akim Tamiroff and his three children.

Century Studios in Hollywood is the setting for *Bracken's World,* an NBC drama series that begins a two-year run in 1969. Laraine Stephens and Karen Jensen are among the show's beautiful starlets hoping for their "break" from producer Kevin Grant, played by Peter Haskell. Leslie Nielsen (not shown) stars as studio head John Bracken.

September 22, 1969. Harold Robbins created *The Survivors,* which begins a short run on ABC in 1969. Lana Turner and George Hamilton star in this lushly-produced serial. Also in the impressive cast are Ralph Bellamy, Jan-Michael Vincent, Rossano Brazzi, Kevin McCarthy, Louise Sorel, Louis Hayward, Diana Muldaur, and Pamela Tiffin.

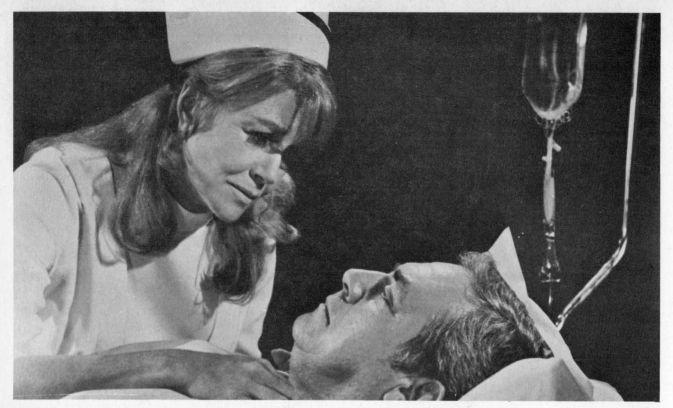

Raymond Burr and Dorothy Malone in scene from Ironside. *Maybe a strong dose of television would help.*

that I religiously watched *The Gong Show* and *The Match Game* (afternoon and evening versions)—these things were unimportant. What was important was that the TV was in my room and on. Often I was unaware of it. But it was on, and it stayed on. And because of that I quickly began to feel better. The TV was a supportive friend, a constant companion who wanted and urged me to get well. Soon, I was capable of changing the channel myself. Within a week I was switching around during commercials. In two weeks, the cure was complete; I was able to turn the set off and return to a normal life.

Like any drug, TV can be abused. Its critics have

their points concerning the detrimental effects it often has on the average healthy person. But for the ill, television—when properly used—undeniably has important therapeutic value. Aside from purely physical ailments, it is also helpful for such things as stress, depression, anxiety, and loneliness. It should be only a matter of time before the medical profession admits to what millions of people have known ever since they were little kids: TV Is Good For You!

Robert Bedick is currently seeking government funds to establish TV health-care clinics throughout the Sun Belt.

September 23, 1969. Robert Young stars in *Marcus Welby, M.D.*, which premieres on ABC. In 1971, it will replace *Rowan and Martin's Laugh-In* as television's most popular show. Television's most successful doctor series, *Marcus Welby, M.D.* will remain on the air until 1976. Here Jon Cypher guests.

September 24, 1969. *Medical Center* begins a seven-year stay on CBS. Chad Everett is Dr. Joe Gannon in this series that boasts of its medical accuracy. James Daly co-stars.

E. G. Marshall (R) stars as a neurosurgeon in ''The Doctors,'' one of four rotating series presented on *The Bold Ones*, which begins a four-year run on NBC in 1969. John Saxon, David Hartman, and Robert Walden co-star. Below, Burl Ives (C), Joseph Campanella (L), and James Farentino star in ''The Lawyers'' segment of *The Bold Ones*.

FAN FARE:
DEAR MISTER ROGERS:

Hello, neighbor. I want to explain why you have not found me waiting in front of the TV this week. Mr. Reitman, my boyfriend, doesn't want me to visit you anymore. But I didn't want you to think that I was sick or that I didn't like you anymore, and anyway I remembered you talking about how sometimes friends hurt each other without thinking and how it was important to be considerate of other people's feelings, and that's why I'm writing.

It all started that day I visited you and you showed me you drain—your kitchen drain. I love visiting you because your house is like a picture—everything is always in its place. I spend all my time picking up after Mr. Reitman, who isn't concerned with things looking pretty as a picture. I hope this doesn't embarrass you, but I also think you look as neat as your house; before we became friends, I never knew anyone who changed from his street clothes to his comfortable clothes at home.

Well, that day, after you had hung up your street jacket in your closet and taken off your street shoes and put on your comfortable sweater and sneakers, you walked into your kitchen and turned on the faucet in your sink. (Of course, there was not one dirty dish!) We both watched the water go down the drain; then you turned off the tap and turned to me and said, "Isn't that wonderful? Did you ever stop to think about what a drain does? You have at least two drains in your house—in the kitchen and in the bathroom. Perhaps you have some more. Do you?" Then you turned on the faucet again, and we watched the water swirl—sometimes swiftly, some-

times slowly—down the drain. I had never thought about the function of a drain before—not even when I was washing all of Mr. Reitman's dirty dishes. Without a drain, where would the water go? Drains are wonderful; life is wonderful! How could anyone be bored when life is filled with the wonder of the drain? As Henrietta would say, "Meow-meow drain, meow-meow wonderful!" That day, after you sang good-bye and put on your street jacket and street shoes and left your perfect house, I left the TV and went to the kitchen where I blissfully watched the water go down the drain.

For awhile my boyfriend didn't notice that something new and wonderful had entered my life. But one day he found me leaning blissfully over a clean sink. Well, as you can imagine (and no one can imagine better than you), that was the beginning of a steady deterioration of our relationship. Now there are more dirty dishes than ever. Finally, a week ago, Mr. Reitman dragged the truth out of me—that the first drain I had ever experienced was yours. I explained that we were just being neighborly, but he said that if I didn't want our relationship to go down the drain, I had to stop visiting you. And that's why you haven't found me in front of the TV. Good bye, neighbor.

Platonically yours,
Miss Odabashian

Miss (Barbara) Odabashian became a fan and neighbor of Mister Rogers during the Watergate Hearings when he and Senator Ervin became neighbors on NET.

339

Governor Winthrop Rockefeller (L) of Arkansas is guest on *The Governor and J.J.*, a comedy series that debuts on CBS in 1969. Julie Sommars (C) plays the daughter of Dan Dailey, who is Governor Drinkwater. Because of interest in the Nixon daughters, in 1970 NBC will debut *Nancy*, a sitcom about the newlywed daughter of a president. Both series will go off the air in January 1971.

September 26, 1969. Robert Reed (R), who has three boys, and Florence Henderson, who has three girls, get married and form *The Brady Bunch*. Playing the children in this ABC comedy are (L–R) Susan Olsen, Michael Lookinland, Eve Plumb, Christopher Knight, Maureen McCormick, and Barry Williams. Ann B. Davis (L), who was "Schultzy" on *Love That Bob*, plays the housekeeper.

IMAGINATION IN CHILDREN'S TELEVISION

JONATHAN LEVY

My daughter, who is almost four, prefers to watch her television alone. I am called in to locate a channel or fix a blurry picture and then am quickly banished. Sometimes I hear the sound through the walls, or catch part of a program from the doorway before my daughter senses my presence and turns on me in fury. I recognize the look. It is the look of disoriented rage she had as a baby drifting off to sleep when her pacifier dropped out of her mouth.

I am curious, professionally curious, about what mesmerizes her so. I write plays, some of which are for children, and have come to respect and cherish the quality of perfect attention children sometimes bring to the theater and which my daughter regularly brings to television. So I have taken to watching children's television (covertly and, like my daughter, alone) the way my wife watches her diet, trying to calculate what nourishment she is getting from it. And the more I watch, the more I worry.

At first I worried about the cartoons: the endless round of cat-and-mouse vendettas she watches when our will is weak on Saturday mornings. But soon I came to see them not so much as exercises in ingenious violence (which, of course, to some extent they are) as a kind of high-metabolism action painting, an almost abstract form, bloodless in every respect. They *are* addicting. They *do* create a craving. But, like a craving for pure glucose, it is one that is easy to recognize and easy to say no to, or at least control.

What has begun to worry me more is the "quality" programming that once so attracted and charmed me. I mean specifically the programs like *Sesame Street* and *The Electric Company,* which seek to educate my daughter. I worry because I wonder what it is she is *truly* learning from them.

Clearly she is learning her alphabet and her numbers. She is also learning a certain gentleness of attitude and behavior which I greatly admire. But what else, I wonder, is she learning—peripherally, unwittingly—along the way?

When a child learns the alphabet in a song, he is learning the song as well as the alphabet. When he learns his numbers in an animated film, he is learning about film along with his numbers. When he learns about the virtues of sharing in a skit, he is learning about the theater—about dialogue, acting and timing—as well as about sharing.

What I question are the *purely artistic* qualities of the songs, films, and skits my daughter sees and hears; the quality of the songs as music, of the animated films as film, of the skits as theater. For it is those qualities that are shaping her imagination and it is the development of her imagination, not her skill in arithmetic or her reading readiness, that most deeply interest me.

Lest it seem unfair of me to question the artistic quality of a program as meticulously put together as *Sesame Street,* let me give examples of what I mean in

Although NET has added such strong dramatic and educational programs as *Black Journal, NET Journal, NET Playhouse, PBL* (Public Broadcast Laboratory), and the enormously successful BBC serial *The Forsyte Saga* to its schedule, there is still time for Julia Child to prepare gourmet foods on *The French Chef.*

November, 1969. *Sesame Street* debuts on NET. Produced by the Children's Television Workshop and funded by the Office of Education, the Ford Foundation, and the Carnegie Corporation, this daily program will quickly establish itself as the most significant educational program in television history. Here Bob (McGrath) teaches reading skills to preschoolers, the show's target audience.

Bob McGrath (C) and Loretta Long (R) with children from the long-running, educational children's show, Sesame Street.

September 5, 1969. Frank Sinatra gives a dynamic performance in ''Sinatra,'' a one-man special, on CBS. In 1965 on NBC he had starred in another one-man special, ''Frank Sinatra—A Man and His Music,'' which was that year's Emmy-winning variety special.

Cab Calloway (L), portraying the angel Gabriel, sings a hymn to Johnnie Whitaker on his arrival in heaven in ''The Littlest Angel'' on NBC's *Hallmark Hall of Fame.*

Guy Lombardo and his Royal Canadians usher in the seventies with their annual *New Year's Eve Party.* Lombardo began this event on radio in the 1930's.

two specific areas: the treatment of fairy tales and the development of dramatic character.

The fairy tale is a profound genre. Traditional fairy tales embody important psychological truths and provide children with the imaginative latitude they need to explore questions central to their development. *Sesame Street* frequently produces playlets in fairy tale form. Recently, for example, it broadcast a puppet skit called "The King who banished the Letter P," in which a king forbade the presence of any object beginning with the letter P in his kingdom. When he discovered this would mean he would have to do without his palace, the princess, and even proclamations, he rescinded the edict.

The skit, which was done with considerable ingenuity and charm, looked on its surface like a fairy tale. Its setting was vaguely medieval, and its protagonist was a king with a problem. But the skit had none of the depth or resonance of a true fairy tale. Its substance was educational, not magical. What was memorable about it—and what I think was meant to be remembered—was that certain words begin with the letter P, nothing further and nothing more. It provided no space for the imagination at all; and the truths it embodied were the literal schoolroom truths of pronunciation and spelling.

The recurrent characters on *Sesame Street* have become part of the imaginary company of millions of American children. They pop up in children's conversations, occur regularly in their play, and perhaps even appear in their dreams. On the whole, the *Sesame Street* stock company is an appealing bunch—Oscar, the grouch with a good heart; Big Bird, the androgynous nebbish; Bert and Ernie, the odd couple; and all the rest. They are appealing, but viewed purely as dramatic creations, they are to a man (or puppet) flat characters, by which I mean they are simplistically conceived and barely developed past their premise.

The situations they are put into change. They, with the tiniest of variations, remain the same.

It is probably desirable that the characters in works for children be clearly drawn. But a character can be clear and also be complex. The White Knight and Toad of Toad Hall are clear in outline, but they are also interesting and various. They cannot be captured in a phrase or understood in a moment. Unlike Oscar or The Count, they have more than one note to play. They are characters worth knowing well. No matter how familiar they become, there is always something new to discover and relish about them.

The characters on *Sesame Street* are flat not because of a lack of imagination on the part of their creators, but because the nature of *Sesame Street* requires them to serve two functions. Because the program is *educational,* they are obliged to be not only dramatic characters but also instruments of instruction. And, in a profound way, these two functions are contradictory.

Fully realized dramatic characters have distinct lives of their own. These lives cannot be manipulated without injuring or destroying the truth of the character. The Red Queen could no more teach the alphabet or demonstrate the virtues of cooperation than Falstaff could host a telethon for muscular dystrophy. In neither case would it be in character for them to do so, no matter how worthy the cause. And therein lies the heart of my quarrel with *Sesame Street* and its offspring.

The more I reflect, the more certain I am that when art is used to teach, either the teaching or the art must suffer. The didactic imagination and the artistic imagination work in different ways. There is mutual respect between them and, from time to time, they have come to an uneasy truce. But in that truce, one must be dominant and the other subordinate. And when it is the artistic imagination that is subordinate,

In 1970, Dinah Shore returns to television with *Dinah's Place*. Her first show in eight years blends music, talk, and cooking hints from guest stars. Although this morning series will win Emmys and gain a huge following, surprisingly NBC will cancel it in 1974. Undaunted, Shore will then hostess a popular afternoon syndicated talk-variety show.

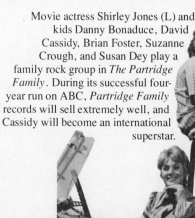

September 17, 1970. *The Flip Wilson Show* debuts in 1970 on NBC where it will be one of television's top-rated programs for four years. Here Wilson portrays his most famous character, Geraldine.

Movie actress Shirley Jones (L) and kids Danny Bonaduce, David Cassidy, Brian Foster, Suzanne Crough, and Susan Dey play a family rock group in *The Partridge Family*. During its successful four-year run on ABC, *Partridge Family* records will sell extremely well, and Cassidy will become an international superstar.

A much-beloved children's book comes to life in ''Dr. Seuss' The Cat and the Hat,'' an animated special on CBS.

when art is employed not for its own ends but to make some predetermined point, what you have is advertising, no matter how worthwhile the product or how well-meaning the sponsor.

I would not suggest that educational children's television is mere advertising. What it has set out to do it does marvelously well—always with skill and often with wit, charm and tenderness. I would only suggest that, whether it seeks to nor not, educational television is daily shaping millions of uncritical imaginations, and that, if the theory behind teaching on television is to sugarcoat the pill, a bit less attention be paid to the size of the pill and a bit more to the quality of the sugar.

Jonathan Levy is a playwright and a senior fellow at the Lincoln Center Institute for the Arts in Education in New York City.

September 19, 1970. Television sitcom reaches new heights when *The Mary Tyler Moore Show* premieres on CBS. This series, created by James Brooks and Allen Burns, has Moore playing Mary Richards, a single woman in her thirties who is assistant news producer at a Minneapolis TV station. The MTM ensemble: (top) Valerie Harper as neighbor Rhoda Morgenstern; Ed Asner as WJM news director Lou Grant; Cloris Leachman as landlady Phyllis Lindstrom; (bottom) Gavin MacLeod as newswriter Murray Slaughter; and Ted Knight as conceited TV reporter Ted Baxter. It is this show that paves the way for many untried female script writers such as Susan Silver and Charlotte Brown.

Neil Simon's *The Odd Couple*, previously a play and a film with Walter Matthau and Jack Lemmon, comes to television as a weekly series on ABC. Jack Klugman (L) plays the sloppy Oscar Madison who must live with perfectionist Felix Unger, played by Tony Randall, now that their wives have kicked them out. This series will last five years. In 1976, Randall will play a judge on *The Tony Randall Show* and Klugman will star as a coroner in the dramatic *Quincy*.

CHANGING CHILDREN'S TELEVISION

PEGGY CHARREN

The average American child watches over twenty-five hours of television per week, more time than she or he spends in the classroom or in any single activity except sleep.

Approximately 15 percent of a child's viewing takes place on Saturday morning, the period most often associated with "children's television." Saturday morning on commercial television stations has been referred to as the "Kidvid Ghetto," a home for animated and live-action moving pictures featuring monsters, superheroes, animated animals, and flying cars. All Saturday morning and weekday programming for children is filled with stereotypes. TV teaches that young, white, middle-class males rule society: women are usually inept, conniving, or frivolous; blacks, Hispanics and other minorities are rarely in positions of leadership; elderly persons are victims; disabled people are virtually nonexistent.

Mindless entertainment is a bait used to attract the attention of children. Once they have been caught, the Madison Avenue marketeers take over. Using fast action, slow motion, loud music, and distorting camera angles, advertisers take careful aim at their impressionable young audience and bombard them with ads for expensive toys, sticky candy, sugared cereal, amusements, and record offers. The commercials teach that food is fun, that owning toys brings friends, and that wearing a certain sneaker will mean "you'll never be lonely again." Over $400 million is spent

"Over $400 million is spent each year to advertise to children..."

each year to advertise to children, and it is obvious that advertisers have not made such a commitment in order to extract small change from a child's allowance. The child becomes a surrogate salesperson, the advertiser's personal representative in the home.

It was perhaps inevitable that such manipulative broadcast practices should result in consumer protest. In 1968, four Newton, Massachusetts women organized a national campaign called Action for Children's Television. Seeking change through a variety of means, ACT has formally petitioned the federal regulatory agencies who have responsibility in the area of children's broadcasting and has urged networks and advertisers to be responsive to the needs and interests of the children in the audience. Through legal action, education, and research, ACT is trying to reduce violence and commercialism and to encourage diversity in children's television.

The organization's program combines advocacy and education. ACT urges the reduction of violence during hours when children watch television, the elimination of sexual and racial stereotypes, and the elimination of commercials for expensive toys and

344

Danny Thomas's television family returns after six years in *Make Room for Granddaddy* on ABC. Starring are: Marjorie Lord; Angela Cartwright; Danny Thomas; Jana Taylor as Rusty's new wife; and Rusty Hamer. This series will last only one year. In 1975, Thomas will play a doctor on *The Practice*, a comedy that will rely heavily on vaudeville gags.

September 21, 1970. Roone Arledge initiates *ABC's Monday Night Football*, the first move of network sports into prime time. Its tremendous success will shake up the industry, and by the mid-seventies evening hours will be flooded with sports events. In the 1970's professional football will become an enormous attraction for TV advertisers. Sunday football doubleheaders become routine, and games are telecast on both Saturday and Sunday. The annual Super Bowl will become TV's top single attraction.

Lynn Redgrave and Sir John Gielgud cut up during The ABC Afterschool Special'*s children's show about Shakespeare.*

Talk shows continue to flourish in the early seventies. *The Phil Donahue Show* (top), a syndicated Chicago-based program, and PBS's *Firing Line* (below), hosted by arch-conservative William F. Buckley in New York, explore controversial topics with interesting guests such as Georgia politician Lester Maddox and novelist and social critic Mary McCarthy.

December 7, 1970. Julie Andrews and Carol Burnett are reunited for the "Julie and Carol at Lincoln Center" CBS special. Andrews will have her own variety show on ABC in 1972. Produced by her husband Blake Edwards, the high-class weekly series will last only one year. Burnett will join opera star Beverly Sills in a TV special in 1976.

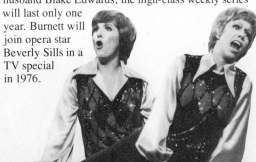

Paul Winchell and E. J. Peaker play practical jokers on ABC's Emmy-winning comedy anthology series, *Love, American Style*, which switches to an hour in 1971. The series will complete a four-and-a-half year run in 1974.

products harmful to children, such as highly sugared foods that cause tooth decay. ACT also publishes a variety of literature on children's television, maintains a reference library, and a speaker's bureau.

Pressure from ACT has already effected considerable change. The Federal Trade Commission has acted to eliminate the sale of vitamin pills directly to children, and House and Senate subcommittees on Communications have held hearings on television violence. As a consequence, the TV industry is beginning to tone down violence during hours when children are watching, and several leading companies that spend millions on television advertising are making it known that they will not sponsor violent programs. Furthermore, broadcasters have reduced advertising time during weekend children's programs by 40 percent, and "host selling" on children's programs has been eliminated, so that children's favorite performers can no longer be salespeople for a sponsor's product.

Through the Annual Achievement in Children's Television awards, ACT has recongnized the introduction of many delightful and creative children's programs: *The ABC Afterschool Special; Call It Macaroni; In the News; Special Treat;* and a number of excellent series on the Public Broadcasting System, including *Rebop* and *Once Upon a Classic.* These are TV alternatives for children and their families.

Changing television into a positive force in the lives of children is a dual responsibility, one which broadcasters share with adults in the home. Among the other steps which ought to be taken by the industry to improve children's viewing are: scheduling for diversity of viewer choice; airing public service announcements to inform children about good nutrition to promote good health and to help children develop a positive self-image; publicizing and recycling quality programs; developing programs for minority audiences and for children with special needs; encouraging the creative development of alternate technologies—pay cable, videodisks; and the elimination of commercial abuses directed toward children.

An equal responsibility rests with the adults in a child's life. It is the parent who can determine when, what, and how much a child will watch. We cannot make, nor would we want to make, every program on television appropriate for children. ACT does not advocate censorship. There must be room for serious and mature discussion of important issues and for drama and entertainment designed for adults.

Television has the power to enhance the wonder of words with the magic of pictures. It could be another type of *Whole Earth Catalogue,* a shopping list of creative strategies for coping with an increasingly complex world. One has merely to sit down in front of a television set any Saturday morning to realize how much more needs to be done.

Peggy Charren is the president of Action for Children's Television.

The Red Skelton Show goes off the air in 1971. Skelton, seen here with Connie Stevens, starred on NBC, CBS, and again on NBC for twenty years.

In 1971, *The Ed Sullivan Show* goes off the air after twenty-three years on CBS. Among his own most memorable moments from the show was this ballet performed by Margot Fonteyn and Rudolph Nureyev. Sullivan will pass away in 1974 at the age of 72.

The Huntley-Brinkley Report concludes in 1971 after fifteen years on NBC, ending the strange working alliance between conservative Chet Huntley and liberal David Brinkley. "David Brinkley's Journal" will become a regular feature of John Chancellor's evening report. Huntley will die in 1974 at the age of sixty-three.

THE TV SEX TABOO

EDWARD A. KEARNS

Matt Dillon, Mannix, Kojak, and Baretta are television's "real men." But none of them could ever have a mature relationship with a "real woman," and neither could their domestic counterparts, Stu Irwin, Robert Young, or Ozzie Nelson. The Ponderosa could never merge with the Big Valley. The space between the twin beds might just as well have been a moat.

Mrs. Muir was an image of real woman. Attractive, intelligent, blonde, but of proven fertility, she was simply too much for an Ozzie Nelson, or for any other domesticated man. She required a virile ghost—a sea captain—who would come to her in the night from the nineteenth century. The audience understood completely. No one believed that when the lights went off the ghost disappeared. After all, the Mrs. had moved into his house, his bedroom, and his bed. Yet whatever happened had to be immaculate, miraculous, and safe. There could be no Davids or Rickys or Beavers to complicate this relationship. Indeed, recalling other widows and widowers—Pa Cartwright, Barbara Stanwyck, Fred MacMurray—it is safe to conclude that on television, as a prophylactic, death is preferable to impotence.

Or to put it another way, familial bliss is purchased at the cost of potency. Harriet Nelson was hardly a real woman, but at least she kept busy making brownies. Ozzie, on the other hand, did nothing by way of work, and little on behalf of paternity. So where did David and Ricky come from? As likely as not, from Harriet's little Hotpoint. Kitchen power.

"Real sex is the forbidden fruit . . ."

Turn Lucille Ball loose in the kitchen and you had to scrape the batter off the walls. Ricky Ricardo got his kicks beating his drum and babbling Babba-Loooo. Only a miracle could provide these two with a child.

But set Samantha's nose twitching, and you might have a seven-course dinner. Since no one ever knew Donald-Darwin-Dummy-Dick York's name, his potency was never at issue. So Samantha transcended the dream of the push-button kitchen, twitched her nose, and produced Tabitha.

The newest version of amazing offspring is Steve and Jamie, the fantastic kids. Through them, the domestic man has trumped the kitchen with the computer room. What is a brownie compared to a printout? For every twitch of Samantha's nose, ol' Oscar can punch a button. Mucking about in his little room, fiddling with wires and plastic, circuits and tight connections, Oscar discovered that "We have the technology," and that therefore he can make all the decisions. Daddy incarnate! And since Oscar has no wife, the kids had to spring from his head—Greek-style, immaculate as Athena.

The kitchen is the key. On television, real men and real women manage to feed themselves. They don't need help. Cannon and Baretta cook their own

Alias Smith and Jones, a comedy-western in the *Butch Cassidy and the Sundance Kid* tradition, begins a two-year run on ABC. Ben Murphy (L) and Pete Duel play ex-bank robbers who try to go straight. The show will end prematurely a little after Duel's suicide. Murphy will star as the invisible *Gemini Man* on ABC in 1976.

The Selling of the Pentagon is telecast on CBS in January 1971. This documentary examines the tremendous buildup in arms by the U.S. and the link between big government and corporations who have military contracts. It will be praised by disarmament proponents and Nixon critics and damned by Vice-President Spiro Agnew. Television documentaries that investigate previously untouchable subjects have been more prevalent since the showings of Felix Greene's movie, *Inside North Vietnam*, on NET in 1967 and the highly controversial "Hunger in America" on CBS in 1968.

A passionate kiss like this from the movie The Jackals *would not be seen on shows made for TV.*

meals. Baretta might slop spaghetti sauce on his sweatshirt, but he's still got the power. Kojak and the rest eat out a lot—with clients and lovers—but they have the power. It's a matter of identity. Real men and women are self-sufficient, and resist sacrificing this aspect of their identity. They only flirt with domesticity.

It was all spelled out clearly on *Happy Days* recently. Fonzie, who eats at Arnold's or is occasionally served by his surrogate mother, fell for Pinky Tuscadero. Both could handle each other's horsepower. But it became clear that should the Fonz marry, he would become Mr. Pinky. (Pinky wasn't about to jeopardize her career by bending over a stove.) And Fonz, true to his identity, wouldn't trade his leather jacket for bridal veils, money, or love.

Given the same option, neither would Pathfinder, Lone Ranger, Range Rider, Superman, or Batman. Real men can never marry, or even grow up, which is another way of saying the same thing. Real sex is the forbidden fruit, the one frontier they cannot penetrate—at least not without a very rapid withdrawal so as not to become entangled in adulthood. Thus, the women these heroes meet are either two-dimensional cartoons, crippled, racially-taboo (recall the Indian Maiden here), or shot in the tummy before the end of the segment.

Lacking female companions, our heroes face a special problem. They can remain independent, or they can take up with a sidekick. In cop shows, the partner can be droll and dumb (Joe Friday's Bill on *Dragnet*); young, vigorous, but as yet unwise (as on

348

January 11, 1971. *All in the Family*, based on a British hit series, premieres on CBS. Created by Norman Lear, *All in the Family* will be the first of many seventies sitcoms to deal with topical issues. Carroll O'Connor's bigoted Archie Bunker will become a "cult hero" of sorts and TV's most controversial character. Jean Stapleton as Edith Bunker, Sally Struthers as their daughter Gloria, and Rob Reiner as her unemployed, left-wing husband Mike Stivic (called "Meathead" by Archie) also star in what will be television's top-rated show from 1971 to 1976.

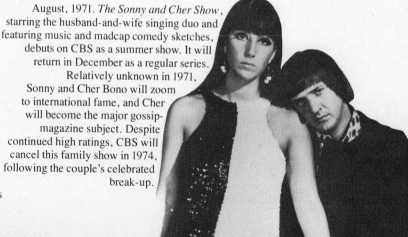

August, 1971. *The Sonny and Cher Show*, starring the husband-and-wife singing duo and featuring music and madcap comedy sketches, debuts on CBS as a summer show. It will return in December as a regular series.

Relatively unknown in 1971, Sonny and Cher Bono will zoom to international fame, and Cher will become the major gossip-magazine subject. Despite continued high ratings, CBS will cancel this family show in 1974, following the couple's celebrated break-up.

Blondie and Dagwood, a typical TV couple.

talk to his car, so he turns to his bird. Rockford tinkers endlessly with his job and women, but Father hovers over him. McCloud left his horse in New Mexico, went east to seek his fortune, but the captain hovers over him.

It is clear that the hero is eternally caught between youth and age, longing for what he was, and fearful of what he might become. He is the perpetual adolescent, powerless to do anything but beat up bad guys and tip his hat to the ladies. In the past, his place was the wide open spaces, beyond the frontier, where he could retreat for security from cities, civilization, and women. But now the frontier exists in the imagination of the adolescent who goes off to brood in his room. Batman and the Green Hornet had their mansions. Baretta has his flat, Fonzie his place over the garage. These symbolic refuges from maturity allow the hero to gird himself for his confrontation with life.

But there is reason for hope. Barney Miller is surrounded by a young dude, a young dope, an Oriental (inscrutable, but unable to make coffee), and an old man. And the station house is not a refuge—even from the implicit homosexuality. Indeed, when an overtly homosexual character appears, Wojo's heterosexual hang-ups can be a source of humor. In *Barney Miller*, television has miraculously conceived of human beings capable of acting like human beings.

Edward A. Kearns lives with his wife and children in Greeley, Colorado, where he teaches English at the University of Northern Colorado.

The Streets of San Francisco); or somewhat indistinguishable from the hero himself (*Adam-12; Starsky and Hutch*). Recently, Baretta has demonstrated that a sidekick can be a withered drunk or a parrot.

The marshall's deputy is often seedy and unshaven, crippled, mentally disturbed, or terminally young. Superman's Jimmy was hardly a sidekick, but he was youthful, stupid, and enthusiastic. The Green Hornet's Kato was Oriental (hence ageless) and dutiful. Batman tutored an adolescent.

A pattern emerges, but it's complicated. The homosexual tendency implicit in the hero's relationship with a young-man-sidekick is only part of the story. It doesn't explain Gabby Hayes or Baretta's parrot. On TV, real companionship can be found only with the young, the old, and animals. Baretta can't

349

August 1, 1971. Keith Michell stars in *The Six Wives of Henry VIII*, a six-part British production broadcast on CBS. One of the first successful television mini-series to play on a major network, it will be repeated on PBS's *Masterpiece Theatre*, which premieres in 1971.

Ian Carmichael plays Dorothy Sayers's urbane sleuth, Lord Peter Wimsey, in the five-part "Clouds of Witness" on PBS's critically acclaimed *Masterpiece Theatre*. Carmichael will repeat this part several times in future Sayers stories. Among other early *Masterpiece Theatre* offerings are the six-part "Elizabeth R," starring Glenda Jackson, and the twelve-part "The First Churchills," starring Susan Hampshire and John Neville.

The most innovative series of 1971 is PBS's controversial *The Great American Dream Machine*, a conglomeration of sketches and films that satirize America. Marshall Efron (L) and Lee Meredith are frequent participants on what will be a short-lived series. Chevy Chase, Nicholas Von Hoffman, and Andrew Rooney also appear with regularity.

TV'S SEXUAL LESSONS

ELIZABETH J. ROBERTS AND STEVEN A. HOLT

In recent years, the subject of sex has received increasing attention on television. Preliminary data from a survey of 1,400 midwestern parents indicates that most parents across all income levels believe that their children receive a substantial portion of their information about sexuality from television. Many of these parents voice deep concern about the accuracy of the information and appropriateness of the values conveyed. In response to this public concern, much Congressional energy, FCC attention, and press space has been devoted to the problems of "sex on television." However, the phrase remains an ambiguous one; issues are emotionally charged and confusing; and oversimplifications often cloud discussion on the topic.

Clearly, at the present time, discussion of sex on TV is an occasion for contention, strife, and conflict. Organized citizen and church groups are calling for the removal of "sex" from television, while advocacy groups such as the National Organization of Women and Gay Liberation are demanding more adult themes and more diversified portrayals of sex roles and relationships in the media. Many of these groups decry the emotional banality of television and what they see to be its conservative presentation of social/sexual relationships. In response to these conflicting pressures, government and industry executives are involved in an ongoing and abrasive struggle about the meaning and impact of television's sexual content, and the best means of responding to the public concern over this issue. For those in the television industry, a resolution of these conflicts is particularly urgent. Many believe that real inroads on the broadcasters' freedom of expression are occurring because of public criticism and confusion about the nature of sexuality on television. Yet many critics believe that the television industry is abusing its privileged access to public airwaves by careless and inappropriate portrayals of the behavior of men and women in general and the sexual relationships between them in particular. These individuals argue that external regulation of television programming is the only meaningful solution. But until "sex on television" is clearly defined, any action (voluntary or regulatory) that might be taken to control it is likely to be either too narrowly construed to be meaningful or too broadly stated to be useful.

In fact, televised sexuality is more than "sex." It is not simply a program on pregnancy, VD, or homosexuality. It is an ever-present and subtle part of each and every interaction that is woven into the full fabric of television programming through the characters that are scripted and the actions that are plotted.

When viewers see men respecting each other for being violent, controlling, or unemotional when we see women relate to each other only through men, when we see unmarried women primarily as victims and married men primarily as fools, when we see children with "asexual" parents, we are receiving messages that inform our notions about sexuality.

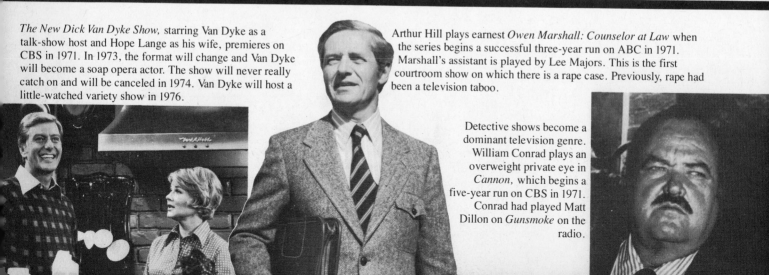

The New Dick Van Dyke Show, starring Van Dyke as a talk-show host and Hope Lange as his wife, premieres on CBS in 1971. In 1973, the format will change and Van Dyke will become a soap opera actor. The show will never really catch on and will be canceled in 1974. Van Dyke will host a little-watched variety show in 1976.

Arthur Hill plays earnest *Owen Marshall: Counselor at Law* when the series begins a successful three-year run on ABC in 1971. Marshall's assistant is played by Lee Majors. This is the first courtroom show on which there is a rape case. Previously, rape had been a television taboo.

Detective shows become a dominant television genre. William Conrad plays an overweight private eye in *Cannon,* which begins a five-year run on CBS in 1971. Conrad had played Matt Dillon on *Gunsmoke* on the radio.

Two out of every three female leads on TV are either married or expecting to get married. This wedding scene is from Nancy.

Sexual conduct does not begin and end with the laying on and taking off of hands. Human sexuality is not mere "organ grinding." It is expressed in a set of **human relationships, meanings, and feelings.** Therefore, television's focus on the relationships between people may be far more important and have far more potential impact on the sexual socialization of children and adults than the portrayal of any one particular nude scene, rape theme, or sexual act. We all spend far more time in the social relationships that lead to sexual expression than we do in sexual activity itself.

There is no one right way for television to handle a bedroom scene or a young boy's first love affair. A list of dos and don'ts might reassure public interest groups and seem to make life easier for industry executives. However, that kind of specificity would only perpetuate the public's misunderstanding of televised sexuality by suggesting that it can be conveniently compartmentalized, monitored, and regulated. To simplify either the meaning of sexuality in our lives or on television is only to add to the confusion and fall into the trap of equating sexuality with the number of kisses on prime time or orgasms in the bedroom.

Responsible television entertainment does and must deal with issues of sexuality. These issues are central to our humanity and the core of human drama. Through discussion and exploration about such issues as intimacy, love, relatedness, vulnerability, and affection, perhaps the public and the TV industry will come to understand the fullness of human sexuality and television's responsibility to present the diversity of this human experience with honesty and accuracy.

Elizabeth J. Roberts is assistant director and Steven A. Holt is executive director of the Project on Human Sexual Development in Cambridge, Massachusetts.

351

The NBC Mystery Movie, which rotates several two-hour detective series, makes its debut in 1971. Peter Falk is a bumbling, irritating master detective in *Columbo;* Rock Hudson is San Francisco's chief of police, the husband of wacky Susan St. James in *McMillan and Wife;* and Dennis Weaver is a New Mexico cop transferred to New York City on *McCloud.* All three segments will have tremendous success. In 1976, St. James will quit and Hudson's less-popular spin–off, *McMillan,* will be dropped the following season.

Dennis Weaver stars as a motorist who is terrorized by an unseen lunatic truck driver in *Duel,* a highly-rated TV movie. This Richard Matheson thriller will be shown as a feature film in Europe. Weaver will appear in several more popular TV films.

FIGHTING TV VIOLENCE

TED CARPENTER

Many viewers have come to think of television as a mystifying and formidable magic box. It informs us, entertains us, delights us, frustrates us, and when it comes to things like TV violence, concerns and troubles us. When we at the National Citizens Committee for Broadcasting, a consumer group that advocates television reform, decided that something more ought to be done to reflect the widespread concern over television violence, we concluded that we had to discover three things: what constituted violence; where violence occurred in prime time programming; and who supported it.

NCCB conducted a twelve-week study of the new fall 1976 programming in order to record all incidences of violence in prime time—the evening hours when most people watch television. The result was a report ranking not only programming from the least violent to most violent, but also ranking advertisers from the least to the most violent.

The response of the broadcasters to our study has been revealing and has begun to lead us down that demystifying yellow brick road to unravel the media mystery of television program practices. The broadcasters, of course, claimed that NCCB and the public did not understand TV, with its complex ratings points, audience shares, demographics, and production schedules, and insisted that we were irresponsible to meddle in their affairs. That Oh-we're-just-so-very-much-more-complex-than-you-can-ever-understand attitude was as familiar as it was misleading. I call that attitude the Media Wizard of Oz.

Remember when Dorothy, the Tin Man, the

> ## "Advertising today has the power to help shape the quality of life."

Scarecrow, and the Cowardly Lion finally reached their destination, an audience with the Great Wizard? Who was the Great Oz? No more than a mystifying and formidable figure on a TV screen who bellowed with absolute authority, "Who are you to challenge the Great Oz?"

How many of us have rattled and shaken like the Tin Man or put our tail between our legs like the Cowardly Lion in the face of the Great Broadcasting Industry when it claims to know full well what it can do for us already, thank you, and wonders who we are to challenge its authority or freedom to fill our television screen with whatever suits its purpose? Well, that is all very well and good, I say (which is sort of what Dorothy said), but I am another one of those people who expects something more.

Besides, I can't help remembering one of the most important principles from that fascinating old movie. Remember Toto, the little dog whose instinct for the jugular and unquenchable curiosity led him to pull back the curtain behind the big screen? What did he find? Who was the Great Oz? A simple huckster, an entrepreneur, a seller of patent medicines—to wit, an advertiser who was manipulating the magic screen for his own personal benefit.

Roger Moore and Tony Curtis are wealthy troubleshooters on *The Persuaders*, which appears on ABC in 1971. It will be a major flop and go off in a year. Curtis, who cannot duplicate his movie success on television, will later star as a con man on *McCoy*, another failure.

Glenn Ford comes to television in 1971 to play a modern–day sheriff in *Cade's County*. This CBS series co-stars Edgar Buchanan and features the music of Henry Mancini. It will last only one year. In 1977, Ford will play a Southern minister married to Julie Harris on *The Family Holvak*, a well-intentioned drama series that CBS will cancel after two months.

James Franciscus plays a blind insurance investigator in *Longstreet*. Bruce Lee plays his karate instructor. ABC will cancel this series after one year, but will offer Franciscus *Doc Elliot* in 1973, which will be canceled after one year.

Billie Burke is Glenda the Good Witch and Judy Garland is Dorothy in the film classic, The Wizard of Oz.

In 1972, four former stars of *Your Hit Parade* are reunited on ABC for "Zenith Presents a Salute to Television's 25th Anniversary." Waving good night are Russell Arms, Eileen Wilson, Gisele MacKenzie, and Snooky Lanson. In 1974, a summer version of *Your Hit Parade* will play on CBS. Kelly Garrett, Sheralee, and Chuck Woolery will star.

January 13, 1972. *Me and the Chimp,* a comedy starring Ted Bessell, Jackie (as Buttons), and Anita Gillette debuts on CBS. Critics suggest that this series may well have replaced *My Mother the Car,* which played on NBC in 1965-66, as the worst program ever to appear on television. It is axed in May.

Burt Reynolds often used brute force on Dan August.

354

And isn't that the point really of the NCCB violence rankings? In spite of all that the broadcasters have said about the unsolvable problem of television violence, NCCB's violence study simply pulled back the screen to reveal the advertisers who were manipulating the TV images, including violence, in order to promote and sell their products. The advertisers certainly have been as embarrassed and uncomfortable about this sudden exposure as that half-lovable old seller of patent medicines in the movie. And it is revealing that the limelight has forced the advertisers to confront the very human values that Dorothy and her friends represented to Oz.

The problem of violence on television teaches us a lot about actual programming practices. We conducted our fall study during the same period that the rating services were conducting theirs. We could compare our program rankings with their program ratings. We were shocked to discover that the ratings did not show violent shows to be that popular at all, in spite of what broadcasters say. During our twelve-week study period, of the twelve most violent shows on TV, only two were in the top twenty most popular shows—*Six Million Dollar Man* and *Charlie's Angels*, both of which have attractions beyond violence.

Networks sell time to advertisers on the basis of demographics—that part of ratings which tell what kind of viewer (age, sex, income) or potential buyer an advertiser can reach. For instance, if an advertiser sells a home product, he will want to find a program that attracts women ages eighteen to forty-nine, who do most of the buying.

The force of this principle was recently brought out when the Ford Motor Company wrote back to people who had written them criticizing their sponsorship of violent programs. Ford stated: "On many occasions we have refrained from placing our commer-

January 14, 1972. A year after *All in the Family* debuts on CBS, Norman Lear sells *Sanford and Son* to NBC. Also based on a British TV comedy, this stars former burlesque comic Redd Foxx and Demond Wilson as bickering junk dealers. *Sanford and Son* will be a tremendous hit for five years. In 1977, Foxx—who will have yearly contract hassles—will leave the network, forcing NBC to create a spin-off series, *Sanford Arms.*

January 22, 1972. *Emergency!*, a Jack Webb production about a medical team attached to the L.A. County Fire Department, premieres on NBC. Starring in this hour series are (L–R): Kevin Tighe, Robert Fuller, Julie London, Bobby Troup, and Randolph Mantooth.

Prime time broadcasts are often interrupted in 1972, with special reports of President Nixon's visits to China, Russia, and Poland. Here Richard and Pat Nixon are accompanied by Chou En-lai in Peking. A broadcast from the Great Wall thrills American viewers.

cials in such [violent] programs, even though they have been among the most efficient for reaching our best new car and truck prospects—young males who are naturally attracted to action programs on TV.''

What demographics means, therefore, is that programs for television don't have to be widely popular or get high ratings if they still attract certain kinds of buyers for certain kinds of advertisers. This use of buying power by advertisers and networks to determine programming is really a clear form of restriction that affects program design, distribution, content, and scheduling. Such practices really amount, in the extreme, to supermarket censorship—using the indirect product-buying behavior of viewers, instead of the direct viewing behavior of the audience, to influence programming decisions.

Although it is proper for the public to hold the advertiser accountable for abusive programming practices that are vehicles for presenting their products, it may also be fair to point out that the advertiser may get too much of a bum rap and that the broadcasters may be abusing both the advertiser interest and the public interest in the simplistic formulas and program practices that lead to things like excessive violence.

Most advertisers are content to stay out of the creative process of producing and scheduling programming. All they really ask is that the networks provide them with a good environment for their commercials, and they stand by their paid-for right to be sure it is a good environment. And it is curious, in this respect, that they seem far more open to the real interests and concerns of the viewers than the networks are.

While the public outcry and research findings on TV violence have gone on for years, the broadcasters have done little in response. However, within six months of our fall 1976 study, eleven of the twelve most violent sponsors named in our rankings had issued strong public statements, revised many of their guidelines on program sponsorship, and given specific instructions to their ad agencies and the TV networks to sever their association with unnecessary, gratuitous violence. Other advertisers have followed suit.

This bandwagon effect of advertiser influence combined with our research, broad public concern, and the concern of prestigious mainstream organizations like the AMA and the PTA, caused the networks to alter their behavior dramatically. There was a significant reduction in overall violent programming in the fall 1977 schedule. For once, the viewers were heard in a rare public interest victory over an unnecessarily abusive corporate practice.

A most revealing response to our advertiser rankings was recently given by Robert D. Lund, a vice president of General Motors and general manager of the Chevrolet Division. (Chevrolet was the most violent advertiser in our fall study.) He said, ''The time is at hand when society is beginning to demand higher standards from many of its institutions.'' Lund went on to say, ''We've got to go beyond ratings, beyond market share, beyond pragmatism. Advertising today has the power to help shape the quality of life. Our strategies of communications must put a tremendous emphasis on both integrity and innovation. The creation of powerful advertising is not an end in itself.''

Such a statement is a powerful admission from this nation's number two television advertiser and indicates clearly that corporate policy makers in television, or in any other industry, are finding it harder to divorce their profit maximization from more fundamental human, social, and community values at a time when our economic system and its resources are facing serious tests and fundamental changes.

Ted Carpenter is the executive director of the National Citizens Committee for Broadcasting in Washington, D.C.

May 3, 1972. "The Andersonville Trial" is presented on PBS's *Hollywood TV Theatre*. Richard Basehart, Jack Cassidy, Cameron Mitchell, George C. Scott, and William Shatner star in what will be an Emmy-winning production.

In the 1972 Munich Summer Olympics, American heavyweight boxer Duane Bobick is knocked out; American Dave Wottle (R) wins the 800 meters by the length of his cap; and American swimmer Mark Spitz becomes an international sensation by winning eight events. But none of this seems to matter. On September 5th, Arab terrorists invade the Israeli dormitory and kill two athletes. On September 6, there is a shootout at the Munich airport between Munich police and the terrorists. Five terrorists and nine Israeli hostages are killed. The Olympics continue.

NCCB VIOLENCE STUDY

The National Citizens Committee for Broadcasting violence study, which was funded jointly by the American Medical Association, NCCB, and contributing private foundations, utilized the definition of violence and incidents of violence developed by Dr. George Gerbner.

The Gerbner definition of a violent action as used in the NCCB study is: an overt expression of physical force (with or without weapon) against one's self or other; a compelling action against one's will on pain of being hurt or killed; and/or an actual hurting or killing. To be considered violent an action must be plausible and credible and must include human or humanlike characters. It may be an intentional or accidental action, humorous or serious, or a combination of both, as long as the previous conditions are satisfied.

Despite the careful research that went into the development of the Gerbner definition of violence, industry critics suggested that this definition was too broad. Therefore, for the fall 1977 ratings, NCCB conducted two parallel studies, one based on the Gerbner definition and one on an industry-suggested definition. The results showed no significant divergence in ratings.

The violence ratings were computed as follows: The combination of the number of violent incidents and the length of time of those incidents was expressed as a percentage of the total number of violent incidents and the total length of the incidents in all prime time. These figures were then computed on the basis of an average week for the total study period and that final figure is the rating figure shown in the following chart.

Advertiser Ranking

The rankings shown below list those advertisers who, during the study period, sponsored the least amount of violence in prime time and those who sponsored the most amount of violence in prime time.

Least violent sponsors

Rank	Sponsor	Rating
1	Peter Paul Candy	3
2	Hallmark	8
3	Texaco	10
4	Whirlpool Appliances	13
5	Prudential Insurance	17
6	Jean Nate	18
7	Schaper Toys	20
8	Green Giant Vegetables	30
8	Keebler Cookies	30
10	Carnation Dog Foods	32
11	Efferdent	34
11	Quasar Television	34

Most violent sponsors

Rank	Sponsor	Rating
1	Chevrolet Cars	751
2	Whitehall Labs—Anacin	596
3	American Motors Cars	498
4	Sears, Roebuck & Company	417
5	Eastman Kodak Products	363
6	Schlitz Beer	356
7	Procter & Gamble Soaps	353
8	General Foods Food Products Division	341
9	Burger King Corporation	315
10	Frito Lay Incorporated	303
11	Mr. Coffee Coffee Maker	
11	Campbell's Soup Company	300

Program Ranking

The following is a complete ranking of all prime time network programming from the least to the most violent shows during the monitoring period.

TV heroes still carry guns. Richard Boone stars in *Hec Ramsey,* which debuts in 1972 as a segment of the *NBC Sunday Mystery Movie.* Boone plays a law enforcer at the turn of the century who solves crimes through new scientific methods and captures villains in the old-fashioned way.

September 12, 1972. Bea Arthur (L) is the outspoken, strong-willed, but vulnerable *Maude,* a Norman Lear comedy premiering on CBS. Also starring in this *All in the Family* spin-off are Bill Macy as Maude's fourth husband, Adrienne Barbeau, Esther Rolle, Conrad Bain, and Rue McClanahan (seen here). This popular comedy will have several controversial episodes, including one in which Maude has an abortion.

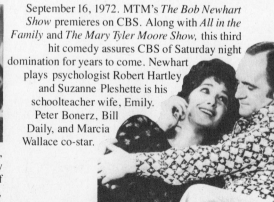

September 16, 1972. MTM's *The Bob Newhart Show* premieres on CBS. Along with *All in the Family* and *The Mary Tyler Moore Show,* this third hit comedy assures CBS of Saturday night domination for years to come. Newhart plays psychologist Robert Hartley and Suzanne Pleshette is his schoolteacher wife, Emily. Peter Bonerz, Bill Daily, and Marcia Wallace co-star.

	Network	Rating
CPO Sharkey	NBC	0
McLean Stevenson	NBC	0
Doc	CBS	0
Sirotas Court	NBC	0
Mr T & Tina	ABC	0
Ball Four	CBS	0
Phyllis	CBS	0
Mary Tyler Moore	CBS	0
Bob Newhart Show	CBS	0
Chico & the Man	NBC	0
All's Fair	CBS	0
Alice	CBS	1
Rhoda	CBS	1
The Tony Randall Show	ABC	1
Barney Miller	ABC	1
Welcome Back Kotter	ABC	1
What's Happening	ABC	1
Maude	CBS	2
The Practice	NBC	2
Sanford & Son	NBC	3
The Jeffersons	CBS	3
One Day At a Time	CBS	3
All in the Family	CBS	3
The Nancy Walker Show	ABC	4
Gibbsville	NBC	4
The Waltons	CBS	5
Good Times	CBS	5
Mash	CBS	7
Executive Suite	CBS	7
Happy Days	ABC	7
Tony Orlando & Dawn	CBS	7
Little House on the Prairie	NBC	8
Donny & Marie	ABC	9
Family	ABC	10
Laverne & Shirley	ABC	11
Once an Eagle	NBC	11
The Captain & Tenille	ABC	12
Rich Man, Poor Man	ABC	13
Sonny & Cher	CBS	16
Carol Burnett Show	CBS	17
Emergency	NBC	17
Wonder Woman	ABC	18
Blue Knight	CBS	18
Holmes & Yoho	ABC	20
Captain & the Kings	NBC	21
Gemini Man	NBC	25
Dick Van Dyke	NBC	26
Wonderful World of Disney	NBC	28

	Network	Rating
Spencers Pilots	CBS	29
Switch	CBS	30
McCld/Colum/Quincy/McMil	NBC	31
Bionic Woman	ABC	33
Streets of San Francisco	ABC	38
Barnaby Jones	CBS	38
Rockford Files	NBC	45
Police Woman	NBC	47
Charlie's Angels	ABC	48
Most Wanted	ABC	48
Serpico	NBC	51
Delvecchio	CBS	52
Police Story	NBC	52
Kojak	CBS	52
Six Million Dollar Man	ABC	54
Hawaii Five-O	CBS	60
Baa Baa Black Sheep	NBC	65
Baretta	ABC	65
Starsky & Hutch	ABC	69
Quest	NBC	86

Movie Ranking

Least to most violent

Rank	Network	Movie	Rating
1	CBS	Wednesday Movie	38
2	NBC	Wednesday Movie	48
3	NBC	Monday Movie	64
4	ABC	Friday Movie	67
5	NBC	Sunday Movie	71
6	CBS	Friday Movie	92
7	NBC	Saturday Movie	101
8	ABC	Sunday Movie	128

Network Ranking

The networks were ranked according to the total violence contained in their prime time programming during the study period. CBS is the least violent network with ABC second and NBC the most violent.

Network	Rating	Network
CBS	967	ABC

Rating	Network	Rating
1111	NBC	1419

September 14, 1972. *The Waltons*, a tasteful, often sentimental series about a poor, virtuous rural family during the Depression, debuts on CBS. Having little violence and a cast without celebrities, it will surprise the industry by moving to the top of the ratings. Starring are: (grandparents) Will Geer and Ellen Corby; (parents) Ralph Waite and Miss Michael Learned; and (children, L–R) Mary Elizabeth McDonough, Kami Cotler, Jon Walmsley, Judy Norton, Eric Scott, Richard Thomas (who plays John-Boy), and David Harper.

A rich Irish Catholic girl marries a poor Jewish boy and both their families go berserk on *Bridget Loves Bernie*, a comedy series that will be yanked off the air by CBS after one year because of protests from offended religious groups. Nevertheless, stars Meredith Baxter and David Birney will marry. In 1976, she will star in the hit *Family* and he in the flop *Serpico*.

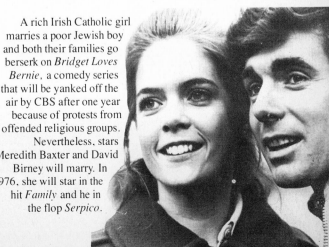

THE REAL THREAT OF TELEVISION VIOLENCE

GEORGE GERBNER

My research associates and I have been working on defining and measuring the nature and effects of violence on television for almost a decade. We believe that the problem has been greatly oversimplified and distorted on *both* sides of the issue. Test it yourself by considering the following common propositions:

1. The goal of violence is to hurt or kill.

2. All violence is basically alike.

3. Violence on television is like violence in movies and books.

4. Violence on television reflects a violent world.

5. The main danger of television violence is that it makes children (and perhaps other viewers) more aggressive and violent.

6. Scientists have no evidence so far that television viewing alone has any significant and systematic effect on behavior.

Do these propositions sound plausible? Of course they do. But they are all false.

Violence is the expression of force intended to hurt or kill if necessary to accomplish a given goal. Except in a relatively few pathological cases, the goal is to dominate, to conquer, to control. But violence need not actually hurt or kill in order to be effective; it needs only to generate enough *fear* of being hurt or killed so that people will obey or acquiesce to something they otherwise would not do. Most violence,

> ## ". . . television generates fear . . . as well as aggression."

from wars to muggings, is basically demonstration of power to compel action against the victim's will. Its immediate objective is fear and its more distant goal is power.

Telling the story of violence is not the same as committing it (although as a *show* of force, it may have the same end result). To strike out against brutality and injustice is not the same as to perpetrate them. When we see violence on television we do not call the police or an ambulance, but we absorb the *message* of the act. If the message helps us distinguish between just and unjust uses of power, the story of violence may be a legitimate dramatic element serving liberating ends. If the message is the gratuitous cultivation of prejudice and fear or of acquiescence to inhuman and unjust uses of power, or if it is a ritualistic and dramatically cheap solution to any conflict, it becomes a legitimate cause for serious concern.

Violence on television is *not* like that in movies or books because television is a very different medium. People don't have to know how to read or to go anywhere to see it. Television comes to the homes of all classes and groups, everywhere in the industrialized world. And it is used indiscriminately; most

In *Kung Fu*, David Carradine plays a Shaolin priest who wanders the American frontier muttering wise proverbs and disarming bad guys. This ABC series, which uses flashbacks and slow motion on its fight sequences, will play four years and make Carradine a star. He had appeared as TV's *Shane* in 1966.

September 16, 1972. Michael Douglas and Karl Malden are cops in *The Streets of San Francisco*, which begins a five-year run on ABC. Douglas will produce the Oscar-winning movie, *One Flew Over the Cuckoo's Nest*, and leave the show in 1976. Malden will make a series of American Express TV commercials. In the background are Alan Fudge and Clu Gulager.

ABC fills its schedule with action shows. *The Rookies* debuts in 1972. Starring are Gerald S. O'Loughlin and his "rookie" cops Georg Sanford Brown, Michael Ontkean, and Sam Melville (not shown). Kate Jackson co-stars. Brown will have a major part in *Roots* in 1977 and become an important TV director.

Agents with guns drawn on The FBI.

In demonstrating only selectively how power works and what types of people run what kinds of risks in life, television presents victims as well as victimizers, and generates fear, the real goal of violence, as well as aggression. Furthermore, in stereotyping people and their fates, television sets up a pattern of fear, so that some groups of people can exercise more power than others. Notions of fear, prejudice, and power are enhanced by violent television programming, and may have far-reaching consequences on the public's general thinking and behavior.

There *is* sufficient scientific evidence to conclude that television alone, as well as in combination with other social and cultural factors, makes a significant and systematic difference in the way viewers deal with reality. Such evidence comes from our long-range research project called Cultural Indicators, including the Violence Index and Profile, conducted for the Eisenhower Commission, the Surgeon General, the National Institute of Mental Health, and now also for the American Medical Association. The evidence shows that heavy viewing of television, independent of other facts of life, induces an exaggerated sense of danger, mistrust, and vulnerability. Irrationally fearful citizens may demand ever more protection and ultimately repression by the authorities as both a release from and a confirmation of their fears. Incitement of a small minority may be the price—a high price to be sure—we pay for the pacification of the vast majority through engendering a sense of fear and victimization. Symbolic violence achieves the purposes of real violence in setting up a scenario of domination and control through the manipulation of our fears. That is the ultimate menace of violence on television.

George Gerbner is the dean of the Annenberg School of Communications, University of Pennsylvania, and the country's leading authority on television violence.

people watch by the clock, not by the program, and the TV clock runs for over six hours a day in the average U.S. household. Therefore, TV *is* like the environment: it is everywhere; it is indivisible; it is inescapable. TV violence is but one consequence of the distribution of values and power in the world of television programming.

Ours may be a violent world, but television presents a distorted picture of its violence. The leading causes of injury and violent death are highway and industrial accidents, but we rarely see those on television. Rather, television presents such violence as can best serve its dramatic and social functions: to demonstrate how power works in society and show who can get away with what.

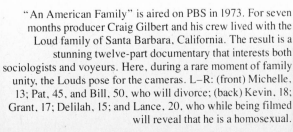

November 1972. Nixon and Agnew win a landslide victory over George McGovern (below) and Sargent Shriver in the presidential election. Little attention has been paid to the June 17th arrest of five men caught burglarizing the National Democratic Headquarters at Washington's Watergate complex.

"An American Family" is aired on PBS in 1973. For seven months producer Craig Gilbert and his crew lived with the Loud family of Santa Barbara, California. The result is a stunning twelve-part documentary that interests both sociologists and voyeurs. Here, during a rare moment of family unity, the Louds pose for the cameras. L–R: (front) Michelle, 13; Pat, 45, and Bill, 50, who will divorce; (back) Kevin, 18; Grant, 17; Delilah, 15; and Lance, 20, who while being filmed will reveal that he is a homosexual.

TV IN PRISON
CAROL MUSKE

In 1972, when I was teaching a regular creative writing class at the Women's House of Detention on Riker's Island in New York City, there was a woman who came to class very rarely and sat the entire time looking extremely bored, without saying anything.

If I had any illusions about her interest in the class (I thought for a while she was just too shy to admit her secret desire to write), they were shattered when another class member told me that she was a dayroom addict, a prison euphemism like "TV freak" for someone who watches the tube all day every day from about 7:00 A.M. till 11:00 P.M. "lock-in." During the count (when inmates are literally counted to verify their presence), at meals, and when the TV broke down were the only times she wasn't glued to the screen. Needless to say, she only came to writing class during viewing crises. Her name was Mildred and once she came up to me after class and told me she had enjoyed some of the poems read that evening, but that they didn't come close to the *I Love Lucy* reruns for entertainment.

In general, TV in prison is limited to one set per floor or cellblock area (servicing from twenty to a hundred inmates), although in some state and federal prisons, inmates can have television sets in their cells. There is no really significant difference between TV viewing on the "outside" and on the "inside"—except perhaps in the stakes involved in TV watching.

In prison, television takes on the power of "barter," as do all goods and services. Cigarettes, sex, and almost any item from the prison commissary—each acquires the conceptual muscle and purchasing power

I can't believe these commercials. The idea that there's this group of people sitting around seriously discussing toilet paper really blows me away. I don't feel I'm missing all that much out there when I watch them.

A Riker's Island inmate

of currency. It becomes a type of money. TV is used in a similar way, though not quite as dramatically. The more powerful inmates tend to control program choice, but only when something "hot" is on. The rest of the time the tube belongs to the TV freaks and the dayroom addicts. A heavy sense of resignation to one's fate prevails; what's on is on, and stays on.

The TV addicts in prison seem doubly incarcerated—in jail and in the idiot box. TV watchers look the same as their counterparts in the "free" world—glazed eyes, slumped posture. The mental imprisonment is the same as outside: a prehypnotic, pseudocatatonic state is induced in the viewer, resulting in anesthetization, distraction, alienation.

Still, the illusion is always one of escape. Just as it is outside. To sit and watch moving images on a screen as they dissolve into each other somehow is liberating; it gives a sense of being "connected" to some huge pleasurable source of energy.

At Riker's Island, the sense of "escape" is made even more poignant by the planes that roar overhead at

January 28, 1973. Buddy Ebsen becomes milk-drinking private detective *Barnaby Jones* on CBS. Lee Meriwether plays his assistant, the widow of his murdered son.

February 1, 1973. "LBJ: The Last Conversation" is presented on CBS. Walter Cronkite had spoken to Lyndon Johnson in January.

Famous disc jockey Wolfman Jack is the announcer of NBC's new rock 'n' roll show *The Midnight Special*, which plays Friday nights from 1:00 A.M. to 2:30 A.M. beginning in 1973. Its success will prompt NBC to fill up its other four weeknight 1:00 A.M.-to-2:00 A.M. slots with a talk show for adults. In October, *Tomorrow* with host Tom Snyder will debut as a follow-up to *The Johnny Carson Show*.

TV film, Women in Chains, *about women in prison.*

irony of that small hunched figure mesmerized by images of the world's playgrounds from her prison room lingered in my mind.

One day Mildred showed up in class looking dejected. The TV wasn't working and she was looking for something to do. I told her about the day I saw her watching the "getaway" commercial and I asked her if she could write about "escaping" and use some television imagery. It connected. She decided to use the language of a recent sexist ad for air travel and wrote this poem:

Fly Me, I'm Mildred

Finger my earring as I lean low
over your bomber cocktail
I've been known
to put you on a throne
send you off alone (not united)
through the tomb-boom roar
you get what you're asking for
when you fly me, honey,
I'm Mildred.

It was one of the most exciting poems we had heard in the writing class—but Mildred couldn't stay around to discuss it. She had to get back to the tube, because *Mary Tyler Moore* was on that night.

Carol Muske is a poet and the director of Art Without Walls/Free Space, an arts program for prison inmates in New York state.

regular intervals in their takeoff from nearby LaGuardia Airport. Every eight minutes or so, a jet shakes the Women's House of Detention as a powerful reminder of the possibilities of free passage.

Once I walked past the Dayroom on the floor where Mildred lives and observed her for a few minutes as she watched a commercial. It was one of those getaway types of hype, with the camera panning a luxury jetliner taking off and the voice-over urging the prospective customer to get away fast from the snow and drudgery of the N.Y.C. winter. The supreme

361

A Brand New Life, about a middle-aged couple expecting their first child, is one of the few ABC made-for-television movies that isn't in the action or suspense vein. Martin Balsam co-stars with Cloris Leachman, whose performance will win her an Emmy.

Bruce Jay Friedman's bizarre comedy "Steambath" is presented on PBS's *Hollywood Television Theatre.* Containing partial nudity, this often daring production about twelve dead characters in a steambath attracts an unusually high audience for PBS. Valerie Perrine and Bill Bixby head the cast.

Bobby Riggs, a tennis champion back in the forties, humiliates women's tennis star Margaret Court by winning straight sets on Mother's Day, 1973. In a match in the Houston Astrodome, in front of an enormous live audience and one of televised sports's largest audiences in history, Riggs will lose straight sets to Billie Jean King. These matches will stimulate many male vs. female televised sports contests.

TV CRITICS
CHRISTINE KRAUS

Television is not merely the sum of the individual programs that are broadcast; it is a subliminal force that consumes as much as half our waking lives. Television criticism has existed since the invention of the medium; yet by their own admission, critics are still groping for ways to address the whole television experience, and to assess its place in American life. There are as many approaches to this problem as there are writers on the subject.

Harriet Van Horne, former New York Post TV critic, built a distinguished reputation by simply reviewing the programs at hand, while trying "to entertain and inform." Though she recalls wracking her brain at times for a new angle on *I Love Lucy,* she has no regrets about the work she did. "Besides," she adds, "TV criticism is a good job for a woman."

John Leonard gave up in articulate despair. His farewell television column in *The New York Times* celebrated the schizophrenia of the TV critic's trade. He argued that to write about television is to write about life and death, politics, nature, the arts, black humor and romance; yet ultimately to write about TV means trying to grasp an experience that escapes us as soon as it is over. Television is an art form that embraces our entire culture and yet, Leonard confessed, the essence eludes us. According to Leonard, a television critic must become a pop anthropologist.

Michael Arlen has a profound understanding of our TV-oriented passivity. Writing for *The New Yorker* in the mid-sixties, during the undeclared "conflict" in Viet Nam, Arlen brilliantly dissected the distorted, fragmented view of war that filtered into

> ## " . . . critics are still groping for ways to address the whole television experience . . ."

American households between commercials. Since then he has written about family holidays spent between football games, television's version of Recession U.S.A., and about television criticism itself. Arlen is surprised that despite the amount of talk generated by critical writing, there is little real TV criticism being written in this country. Arlen believes that the task of the critic is to draw connections between the work and the world, and that this task is often hindered by television's lack of "formal aesthetics or intended seriousness." All other criticism, he says, is based on mere affection for the medium; yet he can feel little love for what he sees on TV: "A literary or art critic can articulate a relation to the work, bring his own principles to bear, and commune with the work. We have The Novel, The Play—there is no The Television. In popular culture it is difficult to feel so private . . . TV criticism requires a great deal of nerve, an acceptance of being lonely. Artists have always been willing to do this, but journalists have not."

Few critics have allowed themselves to be lonely enough to write the truth about television. Most see themselves not as adversaries of the medium, but as its interpreters to the public. Standing ready to aid this process are the network press departments, armed

Sam Ervin becomes a national hero when he stands up to powerful "Nixon men" who are called before the Ervin-chaired Senate Committee investigating the Watergate break-in. The live hearings are covered daily by each network on an alternating basis and attract a huge audience. PBS gains prestige and new followers by showing tapes of the hearings each night.

In 1973, Gene Wilder and Blythe Danner star in "The Scarecrow," a play by Percy MacKaye, on PBS's *Special of the Week,* about a scarecrow who is brought to life as an instrument of revenge, but softens when he falls in love. Also in 1973, Danner plays opposite Ken Howard in *Adam's Rib,* ABC's series based on the Spencer Tracy-Katharine Hepburn film classic. It will go off in December.

The final episode of The Mary Tyler Moore Show *that ended in March 1977 to the almost unanimous sorrow of the critics.*

Dom DeLuise (R) is stuck with the most unpleasant housemates ever to appear on TV in *Lotsa Luck,* a comedy which debuts on NBC in 1973. Kathleen Freeman (standing), Beverly Sanders, and Wynn Irwin will keep DeLuise's blood pressure up for one year.

Helen Hayes and Mildred Natwick are television's most unlikely crime solvers as *The Snoop Sisters.* This series appears as one of several rotating series on the *NBC Wednesday Mystery Movie.*

Burgess Meredith is the chief of Probe, a high-computerized detective agency on *Search,* which debuts on NBC in 1973. His three top agents are played by Hugh O'Brian, Tony Franciosa, and Doug McClure. This series, made confusing by the overuse of gimmickry, will last one year.

with information, interviews, and even gifts.

A CBS press liaison woman described the way in which she nurtures a symbiotic relationship with the press. Her days are spent on the phone planning tours, announcing schedules, and arranging interviews with CBS stars. She would never give two critics in the same city the same story, and learns to distinguish their different tastes. Like its sister networks, CBS constantly reminds critics of its existence. Hundreds of fourteen-inch trees were flown to critics announcing the ''Charlie Brown Arbor Day Special.'' Critics receive a daily press packet supplemented with books, magazines, records, and gadgets.

Networks provide junkets at least twice a year prior to each new season. Contact is sustained through special trips and national promotion tours sponsored by the network and affiliate stations. ''A star's visit to your city,'' a promotional guidebook promises, ''brings phenomenal return for the money.'' Indeed, for the cost of the tour, a network can transform local critics into enthusiastic publicists. The recent tour of *M*A*S*H* star Mike Farrell yielded such dazzling insights as: ''Mike Farrell has big teeth; at 38, he also has 190 lbs. arranged on a 6'3" frame like a 25-year-old mail order catalog model . . .'' ''Mike Farrell sports a newly acquired beard and deep blue eyes . . .'' ''This is a story about Mike Farrell, husband, father, self analyst and also star of *M*A*S*H* on CBS . . . it's a story of love and fear and courage and determination.''

Like most of his colleagues, William Henry III is aware of the seductive convenience of network publicity. Unlike most, he rejects it. Henry gave up covering electoral politics for the Boston *Globe* to write TV criticism, believing that television is a strong, but less evaluated, political force. ''Networks,'' he said, ''prefer to see critics as part of the TV industry. They have an almost obsequious approach. A lot of phone

''Television, as any veteran addict can testify, changes only slightly . . .''

calls go back and forth . . . one of the worst is the phone interview with The Celebrity, who is given a list of critics to talk to and points to cover. It's an easy format to use for projecting an image.''

Henry is sure that critics succumb to subtle, psychological pressure: ''A lot of critics can't make up their minds whether they're working from their own standards, or from some fixed moral standpoint, or from a sense of what the public will like. Most critics are sure that their tastes are different from average tastes, and operate from a kind of condescension. And the natural tendency is to assume that the networks know best what the public will like.''

According to Los Angeles *Times* critic Cecil Smith, scorn for writers who faithfully attend network junkets is malicious and unproductive. ''I cannot take the view,'' he said, ''that these things are evil or corrupt. Information is exchanged. . . . Intelligent questions are asked and intelligent answers are given. It is important for critics to know TV industry people on a personal basis if they are to do the job.''

Television, as any veteran addict can testify, changes only slightly, if at all. But perhaps our understanding of it can change. God knows there is nothing wrong with Mike Farrell's face. But hopefully a critical attitude toward television will evolve that encourages us to see behind the face.

Christine Kraus, a writer in New York, used to write television criticism in New Zealand.

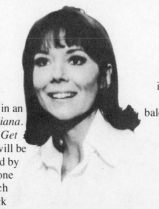

In 1973, movie star James Stewart plays an honest country lawyer who repeatedly out–thinks slick big city attorneys on *Hawkins,* a ninety-minute drama on CBS. This series will last only one year. In 1972, Stewart starred in the NBC comedy *The Jimmy Stewart Show.*

Amid much publicity, Diana Rigg stars in an American-made sitcom called *Diana.* Created by Leonard Stern, whose *Get Smart* series lasted five years, *Diana* will be a big disappointment and be dropped by NBC after several months. Its one highlight will be an episode in which Rigg and *Avengers* co-star Patrick MacNee are reunited.

October 24, 1973. *Kojak,* a police show that strives for realism, premieres on CBS and is an immediate hit. Telly Savalas plays the bald, tough, New York cop, who first appeared in Abby Mann's three-hour TV movie *The Marcus-Nelson Murders.*

REFLECTIONS OF A TV CRITIC

JOHN LEONARD

For seven years, I have been trying to compile a mobile history of the only American infinite, which is television. A grown man spends seven years tethered to a piece of noisy furniture, distinguishing between *Hawaii Five-O* and *Delvecchio*, discriminating among *Good Times, Happy Days,* and *The Partridge Family,* wondering whether Raymond Burr ever goes to the bathroom, pining for Blythe Danner.

I lasted as long as Mary Tyler Moore, and that's it. If she's going, I'm not sticking around. Let the gnomes of academe busy their decorous selves with monographs on the Golden Age of Situation Comedy. Let theoreticians of the car chase drink friction-proofing and break out in rivets. I'm taking my sordid nightmares elsewhere.

Dave Scherman at *Life* magazine in 1970 dreamed up the idea of paying me to watch television. Since TV was killing *Life's* advertising, he may have wanted a kamikaze. If so, I failed in my mission. For two years I signed my own name to those columns. Then *The New York Times,* which owned me, and *Life* magazine, which borrowed me, came to a kind of Vladivostok agreement, and I was henceforth "Cyclops" when sermonizing about television for the next four years. Half the readers who bothered to comment on this changing of nym congratulated *Life* for dumping me in favor of Cyclops; the other four denounced Cyclops, demanding my immediate return. So much for a distinctive prose style.

Either way, a certain schizophrenia was involved that had nothing to do with by-lines. On the one hand, to review TV programs is much of the time to experi-

ence the self as nugatory. You might as well be a weatherman, reporting a day late: a low-pressure Weltschmerz moved last night across the Waltons, unbunching at least one Brady and leaving thousands of Efrem Zimbalists without an excuse; meanwhile, drought continues in the mid-Kojak. But: everybody has already been weathered.

How can you be taken seriously if you are powerless to alter events or cloud men's minds? By the time your comment appears in print, the object of it will have vanished. Or, if it persists in a series, millions of other people will have seen it too, and made up their own minds. If your reviews are read at all, it is by those who seek a confirmation, either of their own gut reaction to a new program or of their suspicion that you are a jerk. You can no more review television according to agreed-upon criteria than you can review old girlfriends—or compile a mobile history of the infinite. The lout on the next barstool considers himself just as much an expert.

On the other hand, being paid to watch television means you don't have to apologize for doing what all your friends do secretly and feel guilty about. It is a way of spending time with your children, without having to read *Babar* aloud for the one hundred fifty-

365

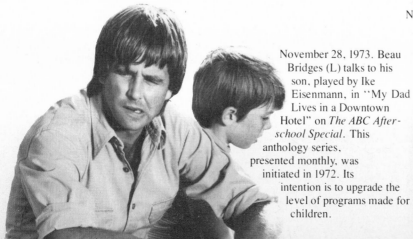

November 28, 1973. Beau Bridges (L) talks to his son, played by Ike Eisenmann, in "My Dad Lives in a Downtown Hotel" on *The ABC After-school Special.* This anthology series, presented monthly, was initiated in 1972. Its intention is to upgrade the level of programs made for children.

NBC newscaster Frank McGee, host of the *The Today Show* since 1971, dies in 1974. Jim Hartz becomes *The Today Show's* fifth host.

Redd Foxx (R) hypnotized on Sanford and Son.

seventh repeat or running a staple through your thumb. Your powerlessness itself is liberating: you can say what you want about the play and the actors; it won't close, and they won't be fired, on your account. And since television *is* an infinite, since it is *about* everything—politics, sex, sports, comedy, theater, the ordinary routine of buses and history—you can review everything. Vertigo of possibility!

It seemed to me that television, which grew up to be what it is today by accident, without long-range planning, had done something in the process, also by accident, to the nation. Just as our car culture, our restless motoring, required drive-in restaurants and fast-food franchises, filling stations of the stomach, so our developing TV culture required fast-food distraction, junk entertainment, psychic beef patties. The living room was converted into a kind of car; the TV screen was its windshield; every home was mobile, everybody was in the driver's seat, and we all saw the same sights simultaneously. If this was true—if, having always been tourists in our own country, now we didn't even have to leave the house to be alienated—it seemed worth writing about, maybe by taking an anthropological approach.

Besides, I was a fan. Like everybody else, I had my favorite programs. I liked watching television. I still like watching television. What I don't like is having to think about what I'm watching.

Television criticism, I thought, swells too much on the singular and the perishable. As a pop-anthropologist, I was drawn to the continuum, the gel, the security blanket that hums, the Muzak for the eyes,

366

January 6, 1974. *Upstairs, Downstairs,* destined to be PBS's most popular multi-part series and a favorite among sophisticated TV viewers, comes to television. It will play until 1977. The first year of this British-made series was not shown in America.

January 15, 1974. *Happy Days* debuts on ABC. This sitcom about teenagers in the fifties which stars (L–R) Donny Most, Henry Winkler (as "Fonzie"), Anson Williams, and Ron Howard, will have only modest success until the show is revamped to make Fonzie the major character. Winkler will become TV's biggest star, and *Happy Days* will replace *All in the Family* in late 1976 as America's number-one-rated show. The pilot show was a segment of *Love, American Style.*

Norman Lear continues to have unparalleled success with his sitcoms. *Good Times,* a 1974 spin-off of *Maude,* becomes an instant hit for CBS. This comedy, which often deals with social issues, stars (L–R): Ralph Carter, BerNadette Stanis, Jimmie Walker, Ester Rolle, and John Amos. When Amos's character is killed off, the show receives many complaints.

Blythe Danner (L), a favorite of critic Leonard's.

the convenience program around which we Americans, week after week, organize our dinner hours and our social lives. Repetition is what counts.

Yes, it might have been the golden age of situation comedy. At MTM and Tandem, the Mary Tyler Moore and Norman Lear organizations respectively, they let the writers out of their cages. Abortion, infidelity, homosexuality, impotence, and death came to television. And for a season or so, my columns wrote themselves.

But how many times can you get away with approving in print of *Mary Tyler Moore, M*A*S*H, The Carol Burnett Show, Sanford and Son,* and *Sesame Street?* As they recycle the actors, are you just recycling your opinions?

You resort to the standards: Every year there will be two football columns, one at the beginning of the season and the other at Super Bowl time; a baseball column; a basketball column; a column on the Emmy Awards and the Oscars; a column on reruns; a column on violence; a column on Johnny Carson and on children's programs. Election and Olympic years are nice, impeachment proceedings help, and somewhere there's always a war. A column on commercials, a column on trends, the obligatory "Was This the Worst Season Ever?" column, maybe something about cable technology, the fairness doctrine, whatever happened to live TV, disaster coverage . . .

Nobody ever told me I was going to have to think. I have written about the crybaby style on TV in the 1950's, from Richard Nixon to Jack Paar to Charles Van Doren, and I have written about the media-brat style on TV in the 1960's on to the 1970's, from Muhammad Ali to Abbie Hoffman to Mark Spitz to Mason Reese to Jimmy Connors. What was I saying, and why was I saying it?

I have written that network television covers the news better than most newspapers in this country. If

367

February 3, 1974. Tennessee Williams's "The Migrants" is presented on CBS's *Playhouse 90,* an infrequent revival of the classic program. Starring are (L–R): David Clennon, Lisa Lucas, Cloris Leachman, Dinah Englund, Sissy Spacek, and Ed Lauter.

Cicely Tyson will win an Emmy for her performance as a fictional 110-year-old former slave in *The Autobiography of Miss Jane Pittman,* which many critics hail as the finest TV movie ever made. Adapted from Ernest J. Gaines's novel, this CBS film uses flashbacks to show episodes in Pittman's life. It culminates in the sixties when she takes part in a civil rights demonstration, and later wins a climactic symbolic victory by using a "white only" drinking fountain.

"Nobody ever told me I was going to have to think."

this is so, and we consider how poorly television covered Vietnam and Watergate in their important early stages, what does it say about journalism, about our "information environment"? Who knows?

I have written of the situation comedy as a socializing agency, taking up where the family and the public school system failed. If this is so, if we are being advised on one hand that it's all right for career girls to think about sex, then, on the other hand, the continuing inability of the American father on sitcoms to lace up the shoes of his own mind without falling off his rocker must be of some cultural significance. But what?

I have written of Johnny Carson as a legitimizing agency, taking up where Ed Sullivan left off, defining the permissible in humor and music, conferring status. If this is so, if this crystallized cynic, this toad with the jewel in his brow sitting on our nights as though they were lily pads, croaking ad lib, is our authenticator of celebrity, what does that tell us about ourselves? I don't know.

I have written, like everybody else, of television's having taken over from the government as the agency to which we petition for redress of grievances; and of television's having taken over from organized religion as our agency of celebration, worship, mourning. If this is so—if television is both our court and our ceremony; if watching the political conventions, the Super Bowl, the moon landings, the Academy Awards, the Kennedy and King funeral corteges, a president resigning, Billie Jean King thrashing Bobby Riggs, is the way we participate with ourselves as a

368

nation, the glue that holds the mobile homes together—are we live or on tape?

I have blabbed these blabs in *Life,* until it folded; in *Newsweek* until *The New York Times* picked up my option, and then one Sunday morning put out the eye of the four-year-old Cyclops and gave me back my name. And I seem somehow to have missed the point. Or the point has shunned me. If I don't stop now, next week I will be writing about the trend in "mini-series." The mini-series may liberate television from its padded cell of formulas, alarm clocks, punch lines. Real people will be allowed to grow, experience love and disappointment, die in a mini-series, in prime time, not just during the sudsy serials of our blank and shining day. . . . Does this matter?

That, of course, is the trouble with concentrating on the writing, acting, and direction of the continuing and formula-ridden series; of going on at length about the style and personality of the news and sports. An essence eludes us. To write about style is to try to get by on style, theirs and mine. Why *are* we in this room? What do we take away?

Something is going on in the living room. Television assures us that the way people behave on television is the way we are. It assures us that the politics we see on television are the real politics. It tells us we are not alone, and tomorrow at work we will tell one another that this is true, because we all saw it last night at the same time on television, and what we saw is what we know.

I want to watch myself watching. To do so, it seems a good idea to stop writing about what I see—which doesn't change enough to make it of compelling interest—and think about the way we see.

John Leonard writes about books and private lives for The New York Times. *This article is excerpted from* The New York Times, *April 17, 1977.*

Television drama in the seventies has used the subject of rape to attract and titillate viewers. *A Case of Rape,* an NBC made-for-television movie, is one of the first efforts to treat rape honestly. Elizabeth Montgomery plays a rape victim who discovers that law and society have little compassion for those who suffer through the ordeal.

February 12, 1974. David Hartman plays an English teacher in the NBC movie drama *Lucas Tanner,* which will become a series in September. In November 1975, Hartman will be the surprise choice of ABC to host *Good Morning, America,* its early morning answer to NBC's *Today Show.*

The Brady Bunch goes off in 1974 after five years on ABC. In 1977, the cast will be reunited for a successful variety series.

THE PUBLIC TELEVISION GUILT COMPLEX

MARVIN KITMAN

Despite a number of urgent appeals, I have the feeling I won't get around to sending in my check. This will be the sixth year in a row that I will not have contributed to the support of my public television station, WNET/13 New York City, even though I could easily bury the fifteen dollars in my expense account. What's wrong with me? Why don't I rush out to support public TV, like every other pointy-headed intellectual? Isn't this the only way the system can work—partly subsidized by my tax dollars, partly by my donations?

The problem is that I resent the appeals for pledges and money because they tend to interrupt the programs a lot. In the beginning it was amusing the way my interruption-free public TV station would interrupt a fine movie like *The Lady Killers,* while viewers were informed that public television presents classics such as *The Lady Killers* uncut without commercial interruption.

Over the years I began to notice the curious fact that the more popular the show, the more it tended to be interrupted or delayed. *Masterpiece Theatre,* for example, became a cultural disaster area during pledge weeks. You could almost go to London yourself before they finished with the necessary business.

A primary reason for establishing the public television system in the first place, as I recall, was to eliminate the interruptions. But the current system of pledge days, pledge weeks, pledge months, pledges

"... on public television ... they are always trying to make you feel guilty ..."

before certain programs to help pay for the events, appeals for products to auction off, and even the auctions themselves, tends to increase interruptions.

Public television today suffers from *intellectualus interruptus,* a new disease it probably caught from proximity on the dial to commercial TV. In the cases of auctions, the disease is terminal—all programs can be interrupted for as long as two weeks.

The public TV commercials—and there is no other honest word for them—are generally speaking far more irritating than the ones on commercial television, which are often better than the programming that interrupts them. The finest creative minds that money can buy work on the commercial TV ads, which often cost more money to make per second than *Gone With the Wind.* On public TV, the spots tend to be unimaginatively conceived, have poor production values, and they are not very entertaining.

The worst thing about the commercials on public television is that they are always trying to make you feel guilty if you ignore them. Commercial television is much more tolerant. I never feel guilty about not

July 8, 1974. *Hollywood Squares,* which premiered in 1966, is still going strong after two thousand shows. On hand for the telecast are panelists Cliff Arquette, Rose Marie, John Davidson, George Gobel, Ruta Lee, Kent McCord, Sandy Duncan, host Peter Marshall, Vincent Price, and Paul Lynde, who sits in the center square.

House Judiciary Committee Chairman Peter Rodino presides over hearings to decide if President Nixon should be impeached because of Watergate revelations. The committee will decide that impeachment is in order.

Dizzie Gillespie solos on this segment of Evening at Pops *on PBS. Arthur Fiedler conducts.*

August 9, 1974. Richard Nixon says farewell at the White House, a day after his televised resignation. Gerald Ford, who was appointed Vice-President following Spiro Agnew's resignation, is the new President.

September 11, 1974. *Little House on the Prairie,* based on the books by Laura Ingalls Wilder about her family, which settled in Minnesota in 1878, debuts on NBC. Michael Landon, whose *Bonanza* series ended a fourteen-year-run in 1973 following Dan Blocker's untimely death, stars as Charlie Ingalls. Laura, in front, is played by Melissa Gilbert. Also starring are Lindsay or twin Sidney Greenbush, Karen Grassle, and Melissa Sue Anderson.

President Gerald Ford

supporting a dog food company or a new deodorant spray. But public TV can make me cringe.

Obviously there must be one thing faulty with the concept of the on-the-air begging. For one thing, they keep coming back for more money. In a sense they are like welfare recipients. In the old days, public journals like the New York *Daily Mirror* used to warn that once you gave "them" a handout, "they" expected it. But at least the so-called "welfare scroungers" did their thing in private.

What happens when one finally contributes to public TV? Do the stations tighten their belts, grateful to have met their contribution goals? Do they live more frugally so they won't have to beg in public again? On the contrary. They tend to think bigger. They become more ambitious. They find their inadequate quarters even more inadequate than before. As in the case of WNET/13, they hire famous architects and move into dilapidated midtown hotels that need to be remodeled at great expense. They hold press conferences explaining why they need such a grandiose building. Houston has one. Louisville has one. Should elevator operators wear gray or blue uniforms? Those are the important issues today.

Let this be Kitman's Law: the more money you give a public television station, the more it needs, and the more necessary it will be to interrupt the program to get it. As Sir Kenneth Clark might have put it, "another case of art imitating life."

A number of alternative plans have been advanced to finance the public television system without the constant begging, hustling, and interruptions. In Great Britain there is a licensing fee. The set owner pays once a year and that's it. But that would be a discriminatory tax here: it makes public TV's friends and enemies pay equally.

A fairer way to pay for public TV, it once seemed to me, is through such existing quasipublic agencies as the bridge and tunnel authorities. A toll booth on the George Washington Bridge and the Golden Gate Bridge would be marked Public Television. All tolls dropped in these booths would go for the support of public TV. I withdrew support for the plan when experts pointed out that the majority of motorists would avoid the booth, as they avoid public television on the dial.

I now think that commercial TV ought to pay for public TV. Don't just tax the successful networks across the board, as early broadcasting pioneers suggested, but tax them for specific crimes. Every time a network decided to rerun a show, for example, it would have to pay a fee to public TV. There could also be a rebate from game shows: something reasonable, like 3 percent from each show's total cash and prizes, would go the public TV kitty.

Here is a breakdown of how the "network creative tax" would run:

Tax Rates for Networks

Each police car light whirling: $100,000
Each gun being fired: $200,000
Each gun being fired in anger: $250,000
Each gun being fired in self-defense: $175,000
Each woman being raped: $300,000
Each use of canned laughter: $400,000

The good thing about this plan is that while it helps pay for public TV, it also helps improve the quality of programming on commercial television, which may be the real public television after all.

Marvin Kitman, a syndicated newspaper TV critic and author of The Marvin Kitman TV Show, *has another idea: Public TV could raise money by classifying itself as a disease.*

Paper Moon, based on the hit movie starring Tatum and Ryan O'Neal, appears on ABC in 1974. Jodie Foster and Chris Connelly, who played O'Neal's brother on *Peyton Place,* star in this comedy-drama set in the Depression. Although the series will get good reviews, it will go off in four months. Foster will become a major movie star.

Rhoda Morgenstern (Valerie Harper) marries Joe Gerard, played by David Groh on *Rhoda,* a spin-off of *The Mary Tyler Moore Show.* The hour-long wedding episode will be the top-rated show of its week, but the writers will have trouble developing original scripts for a married Rhoda. In 1976, the writers will put new life into the show by having Rhoda and Joe break up.

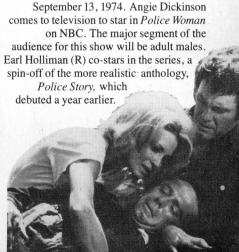

September 13, 1974. Angie Dickinson comes to television to star in *Police Woman* on NBC. The major segment of the audience for this show will be adult males. Earl Holliman (R) co-stars in the series, a spin-off of the more realistic anthology, *Police Story,* which debuted a year earlier.

TV FANS: SHORT OR LONG?

JOE BLADES

I have a theory that there are two kinds of television viewers—short-form and long-form fans; and three kinds of programming—short, long and cultural.

Within the short-form camp are devotees of approximately six or seven specific weekly shows—all either half an hour or sixty minutes in length. These viewers rarely invest more than one hour in a single program, although they may watch upward of three hours per evening. The viewers in the long-form and cultural camps are quite the opposite: They never warm to short-form shows. Instead, they choose among these alternatives: lengthy, at times evening-long specials (docu-dramas like "Tailgunner Joe" or "The Missiles of October," for instance); continuing series with open-ended episodes (*The Pallisers; The Forsyte Saga; Rich Man, Poor Man; A Family at War;* or *Executive Suite*); and the limited-run show (continuing six or seven weeks, one or two hours a week, or—like *Roots*—eight evenings in succession).

Why these extremes? It's basically a function of aesthetics. The crucial factors seem to be genre preference, attention span, and—most importantly—the individual's value of time. Let's examine each in turn.

The short-form regular is easy to peg. Nowadays, as situation comedies are the principal prime time half-hour form, the short-form viewer is, by necessity, a sitcom fancier. (Thirty-minute westerns, police shows and thrillers are practically history.) On occasion, the short-format aficionado will respond to a program sixty minutes in length; other genres then become accessible. His heart, though, is with the half-hour form.

ABC's Nanny and the Professor, *a short form.*

In contrast, fans of long and cultural formats regard half-hour programming as frivolous. Depending upon individual tastes, they can choose among cops, cowboys, bionic men and women, killer sharks, upstairs masters and downstairs domestics, captains and kings—whose stories all require, at bare minimum, a full hour to tell. And some people just do not want to invite certain genres into their living rooms. A person who hates sitcoms must watch longer shows. But a person who hates cowboys can always watch cops, or culture.

The long-form and cultural enthusiasts believe that substantial gifts do not arrive in tiny packages.

372

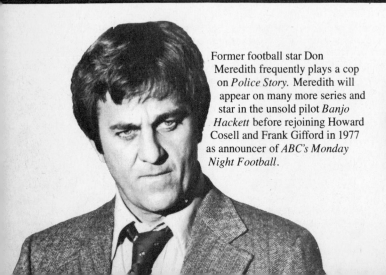

Former football star Don Meredith frequently plays a cop on *Police Story*. Meredith will appear on many more series and star in the unsold pilot *Banjo Hackett* before rejoining Howard Cosell and Frank Gifford in 1977 as announcer of *ABC's Monday Night Football*.

In 1974, David Janssen plays Harry Orwell, one of TV's first "classic" detectives on *Harry-O*. This series about a loner ex-cop with integrity and a bullet lodged in his back, will go off in 1976. One of TV's most used performers, Janssen had starred in *O'Hara, United States Treasury* on CBS in 1971.

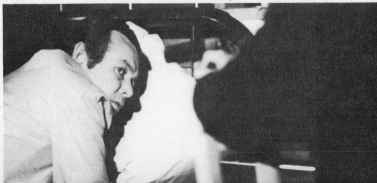

Masterpiece Theatre's "Vanity Fair," a long form.

Hence, the clock does not exist for these viewers, who will greet the dawn after a marathon telecast of *Rock Follies* or an all-night screening of *The Sorrow and the Pity*. They are long-distance runners, while short-form fans haven't the endurance. They reject programming served in large chunks. Their attention wanders.

This is not to label the short-form viewer a simpleton. We can just as legitimately attribute his brief attention span to the conviction that television, at root, is facile and a waste of time. The short-form fan only has patience for half-hour installments. He might enjoy some of those extended forms he shuns; but he prefers not to devote fifteen hours of his life to them. I know short-fans who ignore part one purely because they know ahead of time they'll be otherwise engaged the evenings of parts two through six. Rationale: Why start something you won't finish?

The long-form and culture addicts probably don't relish being prisoners of their TV sets either. In their eyes, however, it may be less troublesome to devote one week to *Roots* than be home every Saturday night of the season to watch the half-hour comedy lineup.

The short-form fan opts, for whatever reasons, to make small investments. He'll see three or four little clumps of programming in preference to one large clump. If you support the least-objectionable-program theory, preference for brevity or length can even indicate how much TV the consumer is willing to tolerate. Long-form and cultural viewers, if they endure to the finish, simply have more patience than their short-term counterparts. Ultimately, *chacun à son gout. Chacun à son enfer.*

Which kind of TV viewer are you?

Without Mary Tyler Moore, Saturday is the loneliest night of the week for media critic and short-format fanatic Joe Blades.

James Garner stars as a private detective in *The Rockford Files*, a drama with comedy overtones, which premieres on NBC in 1974. Here Rob Reiner guests. Garner returned to TV in 1971 as the star of the NBC comedy-western *Nichols*, a show distinguished by the fact that its main character was killed in the last episode.

Barry Newman plays an Italian lawyer in the Southwest in *Petrocelli*, which begins a two-year run on NBC. Albert Salmi (L) co-stars. Petrocelli is one of TV drama's few leads who is married; Susan Howard plays his wife.

Glynnis O'Connor co-stars with Gary Frank in *Sons and Daughters*, a venturesome drama series about high school students in the fifties, which plays briefly on CBS in 1974. In 1977, O'Connor will star in a major TV production of Thornton Wilder's *Our Town*. A musical version of the play, starring Paul Newman, Eva Marie Saint and Frank Sinatra had been presented on *Producer's Showcase* in 1955.

ANCIENT MYTHS ON TV

HAROLD SCHECHTER

To many people, a myth means something made-up—a fiction, a fable—but to primitive man, myths mean the very opposite: stories that have a special significance, that transmit eternal truths. And because these stories are so full of meaning and exert such a powerful hold on the human imagination, they are repeated over and over again, in one form or another, throughout history and in all societies. But if myths are so universal, then what has become of them in modern times, where do we find them today? Well, one answer is that these tales of wonder—of gods and romance and heroic adventure—form the basis of our popular culture. If we want to find the present-day versions of primitive myths, all we have to do is open a comic book, go to a movie, read a pulp novel—or best of all, switch on the television set. For in a sense, TV has taken on the role played in ancient cultures by the shaman; it has become the medicine man of the electronic age. Instead of huddling around a flickering firelight listening to a witch doctor chant the legends of the tribe, people now see them acted out on the flickering blue light of the tube.

Every season, the networks proudly unveil their new shows—but far from being new, most TV programs portray characters and plots that are as old as civilization itself, stories that can be traced all the way back to the myths of ancient Greece and Mesopotamia. Behind the cop and cowboy supermen of the "action-adventure" series, for example, stands the figure of the mythological hero, the stouthearted savior who does battle with the forces of darkness on behalf of a helpless society. The Six Million Dollar

Man, after all, is nothing more than the latest incarnation of Hercules, clothed in the garb of contemporary American society—his superior powers bestowed on him, not by the lords of Olympus, but by their late-twentieth-century counterpart, the great god Technology. And when the star of *Sea Hunt* dives to the ocean floor in search of sunken treasure, or the Bionic Woman descends into the depths of a military installation to defuse an atomic doomsday machine, or Captain Kirk and the crew of the *Enterprise* probe deep into space—the "final frontier"—what the viewer is really seeing is a modern-day rendition of the mythic hero quest—the voyage into the dark unknown—with Gilgamesh in a scuba suit and Odysseus in the uniform of a starship commander.

Did you know that when kids sit glued to the tube on Saturday mornings watching Bugs Bunny play prank after sadistic prank on that eternal sucker, Elmer Fudd, they are really enjoying the updated antics of a character whose mythological lineage dates back to the nineteenth-century folk figure Brer Rabbit and, beyond that, to a Winnebago Indian deity named Hare? This character is known to mythologists as the Trickster, and he appears on TV in various forms: not only as the anarchic animals of the kiddie shows (Road Runner, Heckle and Jeckle, Froggie the Gremlin, etc.) but as such human characters as Hogan's Heroes and Sergeant Bilko (a trickster-figure in the uniquely American form of the con artist).

Ben Cartwright, the Ponderosa Patriarch; Jim Anderson of *Father Knows Best* and Marcus Welby, M.D. (both played by actor Robert Young); Doctors

October 18, 1974. Richard Burton and Sophia Loren star in Noel Coward's "Brief Encounter" to open the twenty-fourth season of NBC's *Hallmark Hall of Fame.*

October 20, 1974. Lee Majors will become the idol of kids throughout America by playing Steve Austin in *The Six Million Dollar Man.* Majors first played the superhuman government agent, given bionic parts following a tragic accident, in a highly successful TV movie. Here Britt Ekland guests.

October 22, 1974. Fidel Castro gives his first in-depth interview to a U.S. newsman since 1968 when Dan Rather visits him for *CBS Reports:* "Castro, Cuba, and the U.S.A." In 1977, Castro will be interviewed again, by Barbara Walters of ABC.

Lee Majors, the Six Million Dollar Man, a modern Hercules.

Zorba (*Ben Casey*) and Gillespie (*Dr. Kildare*); Grandpa Walton; and the blind Shaolin priest of *Kung Fu* who offers endless bits of inscrutable Oriental wisdom to the young "grasshopper"—these characters are all video versions of the archetypal Wise Old Man: the sage, the master of knowledge, the hero's mentor.

And all of those Circes of the soap operas—those predatory females in the sinister guise of career women—are really modern-day manifestations of the mythological temptress, the *femme fatale*.

Even commercials contain mythic figures: Mother Tums ("Tell me where it hurts"), Borden's Elsie the Cow (a descendant of Nut, the heavenly cow goddess of the ancient Egyptians "who waters the earth with her rain-milk"), and Mother Nature of the margarine ads ("It's not nice to fool Mother Nature") are examples of the *magna mater* archetype, the Great Mother—the nourisher, protector, and comforter of mankind.

What conclusions can we draw from all this? Well, for one thing, we can say that, just like old soldiers, ancient myths never die—they just start popping up in unexpected places. If the old gods have disappeared from our religions, they can still be seen nightly on network TV. Humanity, it seems, just can't live without myths. Endlessly repeated in every possible variation, they're the most popular reruns of all.

Harold Schechter is an assistant professor of English at Queens College, City University of New York.

375

Jack Benny's death in 1974 saddens the world. Here the gifted entertainer appeared with singer-actor Bobby Darin (who died in 1973) in a 1964 segment of *The Jack Benny Program,* just prior to its move to NBC where it completed its fifteen-year run in 1965. Benny hosted many specials in the nine years that followed.

Barney Miller, which will become the first successful police comedy since *Car 54, Where are You?* (1961–1963), debuts on ABC. Hal Linden (R) stars as Miller, the chief of detectives in a Greenwich Village precinct. Abe Vigoda (L) plays sergeant Phil Fish, who will be the main character of a spin-off series *Fish,* beginning in 1977.

January 17, 1975. Still another Norman Lear sitcom comes to television when *The Jeffersons* joins CBS's powerful Saturday night schedule. This *All in the Family* spin-off stars Sherman Hemsley as snobbish, foolhardy George Jefferson and Isabel Sanford as his practical down-to-earth wife. The Jeffersons, former neighbors of the Bunkers, have moved to an elegant Manhattan apartment.

IN DEFENSE OF TELEVISION

ERNEST DICHTER

Ilike American TV! It has introduced me to many people whom I never would have met otherwise. Some of them have become familiar faces, and all of them have contributed to my knowledge of the varied and interesting, sometimes annoying, sometimes exciting human species. Television viewers know about the destinies of Mrs. Trudeau and Barbara Walters. We know entertainers who have grown shockingly old over the years, or remained unnaturally young. American TV personalities are much more human than those in most other countries—perhaps because Americans are generally more relaxed, but also because of the much more rigid rules for public behavior existing elsewhere. There are no John Chancellors or Walter Cronkites on German TV, nor can I imagine them. French newscasting is stiff and formal. In America, we know our celebrities intimately.

It would be interesting to study the number and the variety of people recognized by American TV viewers as compared to those in other countries, or to nonviewers. Television broadens our horizons and ought to make us more tolerant. We know what a murderer looks like, for example, as well as a person who insists on being shot for murder.

Though many explanations for human behavior are wrong or stereotyped on television, good shows have taught us to understand people like Isadora Duncan and John Adams, or the loyalty of an English butler and the deeper roots of Archie Bunker's prejudices. Television has made us better observers of body language and of human peculiarities, whether they be Rhoda's, Maude's, or Jimmy Carter's. Maybe one of these days some psychology professor will begin to study the extent to which we adapt our behavior from the various types of people we see on TV. The medium forms as well as informs us.

Television has transported us to remote villages in India and Africa, and showed us death and destruction in Vietnam until we could stand it no longer. It permits us to travel around the world without leaving our homes. When I took my children to Europe for the first time, they hardly looked up when we saw the Eiffel Tower. When I got mad, they stated in a blasé fashion, "We've seen it before, on TV." Armchair travel may make us jaded, but on the other hand it can increase our desire to visit the places we are most fascinated by.

Series such as *The Adams Chronicles, The Pallisers, The Johann Strauss Family,* and *Jesus of Nazareth* takes us backward in time, just as shows like *Star Trek* allow us to explore the future. Week after week television helps us grasp the lives of famous people and important eras in much more vivid detail and with much more psychological insight than any history teacher could make possible.

Television educates us many ways. Medical dramas that present correct facts in an entertaining and exciting form not only provide us with escape but also familiarize us with many medical procedures. *The Ascent of Man* has made us better understand our cultural development. *The Incredible Journey* helps us to learn some of the fundamentals of biological and medical science in a pleasant way. Today's child has a much better grasp of the animal world because of seeing

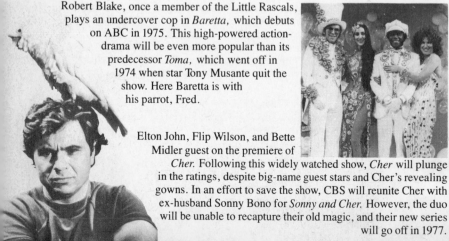

Robert Blake, once a member of the Little Rascals, plays an undercover cop in *Baretta,* which debuts on ABC in 1975. This high-powered action-drama will be even more popular than its predecessor *Toma,* which went off in 1974 when star Tony Musante quit the show. Here Baretta is with his parrot, Fred.

Elton John, Flip Wilson, and Bette Midler guest on the premiere of *Cher.* Following this widely watched show, *Cher* will plunge in the ratings, despite big-name guest stars and Cher's revealing gowns. In an effort to save the show, CBS will reunite Cher with ex-husband Sonny Bono for *Sonny and Cher.* However, the duo will be unable to recapture their old magic, and their new series will go off in 1977.

March 6, 1975. Katharine Hepburn ends her television boycott when she appears with Sir Laurence Olivier in "Love Among the Ruins." The teleplay was written by James Costigan especially for Hepburn's long-awaited TV debut.

George Grizzard and Leora Dana are John and Abigail Adams on PBS's top-rated The Adams Chronicles.

Animal Kingdom and *Survival. Sesame Street* is fortunately beginning to find imitators. The range of educational shows that could be devised is very wide.

Undue violence on TV is abhorrent, but a well-conceived crime show is often more like a satisfying chess game than a brutal slugfest. It is a challenge to your intellectual powers to be able to compete with Colombo or Kojak. And a crime story, if well done, usually leaves no loose ends. Everything adds up. In real life, things hardly ever come out just right. Thus a good detective program is at once relaxing and reassuring. Viewers can be more entertained by deep psychological insights into the motivations of real people than the gory details of bloody corpses.

Talk shows have helped us come to appreciate the lives and accomplishments of many of our contemporaries, both celebrated and obscure. We deplore the fact that TV destroys the ancient virtue of good conversation, but few cocktail parties or high teas offer the wealth of human insight of a good biography.

American TV is an important part of our culture, and we should not be ashamed of it. How good it is depends of course on our selectivity. We can watch junk and blame the medium, or we can learn to appreciate the shows of real excellence. I would like to see more international exchange of programs, not just the export of American westerns to other countries and the import of British shows to these shores. We have not even begun to utilize the potential for cultural exchange in the comfortable and inexpensive form that TV offers. It is a window on the world. Why not open it still wider?

Ernest Dichter is a cultural anthropologist and motivational researcher who is a critic of television and an avid viewer.

Burt Lancaster comes to television in the summer of 1975 in the heralded mini-series *Moses—The Lawgiver.* These six CBS specials receive surprisingly strong audiences and pave the way for a future mini-series on the life of Christ, once considered an impossible subject for television.

The two most popular, trend-setting soap operas to appear in the seventies, CBS's *The Young and the Restless* (below) and ABC's *Ryan's Hope* (R) deal with "touchy" subjects that the more established soap operas have been avoiding since the early fifties. In the seventies, the genre will mature, and its audience will consequently expand.

TV'S POWER AND RESPONSIBILITY

NICHOLAS JOHNSON

My principal complaint about television is not what it does (as destructive as that often is) but what it fails to do.

Historically, entertainment—drama and comedy—have often dealt with some of people's greatest problems: the political, economic, and social issues of the day and the personal, psychological, and emotional issues of the ages. Dramatists and balladeers have been guiding figures in men's and women's quest for understanding of the human condition.

Television is today the major American theater-lecture hall-nightclub-movie house-sports arena-newspaper. When the television industry takes over the power and profits that accompany its near-monopoly control of our culture, it acquires an enormous responsibility as well.

Charges have been made, and documentation has been provided, that corporate censorship of artistic freedom is rampant, that children's programming encourages poor nutrition and violent behavior, that there is little or no regularly scheduled prime time public affairs programming, and so forth.

The response of the broadcasters tends to be that they have to make a profit, they give the public what it wants, and that the cost of the occasional, fringe-time "quality programs" must be borne by the profits from the "popular programs" supplied by the television program manufacturing plants in Los Angeles.

Taking the broadcasters at their word, and accepting their own criteria for purposes of argument, the evidence is mounting that greater attention to the public interest may in fact be the road to greater profits.

"So much of 'television' is a waste of the medium."

There have always been exceptions to the broadcasters' arguments. NBC's *Today* program has done well for years and years in the ratings and the profit-and-loss statements.

And the ratings have also proven the truth of Mason Williams's aphoristic observation that "the best thing on television is a golf match because no script has been written for the ball." So much of "television" is a waste of the medium. It's motion pictures of radio programs. The "news" isn't even a picture of a radio program; it's pictures of a newspaper (Uncle Walter reads the funnies).

"Live" to most television executives means "live on tape"—as distinguished, presumably, from "dead on tape." But television's ability to transmit pictures of events around the world as they are happening is its unique quality, what it does best. And the audience knows it.

The highest ratings have not gone to *I Love Lucy* and *Perry Mason*. They have gone to live televised events: Tiny Tim's wedding on *The Tonight Show*, the walk on the moon, Kennedy's funeral, the Super Bowl and other sports events. Measured by the ratings it is simply not true that "what the public wants" is an unending grind of soap operas, game, and police series shows.

Beacon Hill, an American serial fashioned on *Upstairs, Downstairs,* premieres in prime time on CBS in 1975 and jumps into TV's top ten programs. But it will quickly drop into the bottom ten and be canceled. Edward Herrmann (standing third from right) will give stand-out performances opposite Jane Alexander in two heralded specials "Eleanor and Franklin," and its sequel, "Eleanor and Franklin: The White House Years." Linda Purl (front, center) will star in several top-rated TV movies in succession following this series' demise.

Barbara Bain and Martin Landau, who quit *Mission: Impossible* following contract disputes, are back together in *Space: 1999,* a science fiction adventure series that was rejected by all three networks. When this series receives tremendous audience share on independent channels, each network will regret its poor decision.

Apollo 12 astronauts Alan Bean and Charles Conrad, Jr. (reflected in Bean's visor), do experiments on moon in 1969.

Interns Beau Bridges (C) and Shelly Novack (L) try to save the life of burn victim Gene Woodbury in the two-hour pilot for *Medical Story*. This powerful, realistic anthology series, which was created by David Gerber of *Police Story* and Abby Mann, will only play on NBC for one season. Shirley Knight is the nurse in the background.

CBS Reports: "The Guns of Autumn," an uncompromising attack on hunting in America, is presented on September 5, 1975. This documentary receives unprecedented viewer response pro and con. Another documentary will follow on which hunters and members of the hunting lobby will express their outrage at what they consider to be CBS's misrepresentation of what "hunting" is really about; and conservationists will say CBS didn't go far enough in revealing crimes hunters commit against wildlife.

ABC Sports' *The American Sportsman* usually features celebrities with a rifle or fishing pole, but actress–photojournalist Candice Bergen carries neither during her trip to Kenya.

"It is possible to put useful information in an entertaining package."

Who could have convinced a network executive that live coverage of Congressional hearings would beat the soaps in the ratings? And yet the Army-McCarthy hearings and the Watergate hearings did it—while bringing to television an enormous number of viewers who normally don't watch TV at all.

Another broadcasters' myth that is being rebutted by ratings is the notion that the American people don't want controversy and serious issues thrown in with their "entertainment."

Norman Lear is now responsible for more top-rated television shows than any American network. And if there is any common theme that runs throughout his work it is his willingness to take on controversy with courage and compassion.

The two-part *Maude* episode on alcoholism won the praise of numerous alcoholism organizations, the Jaycees, doctors, and a U.S. senator. Similar praise has come his way for *All in the Family* episodes dealing with breast cancer, the elderly, the mentally retarded, and smoking. The American Heart Association reported that a *Good Times* episode on hypertension in blacks noticeably stimulated the demand for blood pressure checks in black clinics.

The list of subjects is virtually endless: homosexuality, jealousy, menopause, cheating on income taxes, gambling as a sickness, interracial marriage, unwed mothers, legalization of marijuana, abortion, and heart attacks are but a few additional examples.

These are not exceptions to the general pattern.

Such subject matter is the grist of Norman Lear's shows. Increasingly, his style is being copied by others. This is not to say that I personally agree with all the subjects selected or the way in which they have been treated. Various citizen groups would undoubtedly protest some of them—perhaps justifiably.

The point is simply that it can be done. It is possible to put useful information in an entertaining package. Not only is it possible, the ratings would seem to indicate that it is—commercially—a more successful way to operate the broadcasting business than the conventional wisdom dictates. That it is also more socially constructive seems obvious.

". . . corporate censorship of artistic freedom is rampant . . ."

No longer can broadcasters argue that pap, pabulum, and the product of censorship (what Mason Williams has called "a doily for your mind") are commercially compelled. From now on their commitment to perpetuating an uninformed public will be clearly seen by all as the ideological power play for establishment preservation that it has been all along.

Now that this issue is behind us, what other areas of seeming disagreement between citizen groups and broadcasters may there be where the best public service may also produce the highest profits? It's a matter well worth pursuing by both sides.

Nicholas Johnson, a former member of the FCC, is chairperson of the National Citizens Committee for Broadcasting, a consumer advocacy group.

380

Fay, a sitcom about a middle-aged divorcee, which lost its punch when rewritten to make it acceptable for the newly initiated "family viewing hour" (8:00 to 9:00 P.M.), goes off in less than two months. Its star, Lee Grant, will angrily blame the shows failure on the "mad programmer." Many TV personalities will join her to protest what they consider to be the curtailment of artistic freedom.

September 18, 1975. Cloris Leachman (R) begins a two-year run in *Phyllis,* a spin-off of *The Mary Tyler Moore Show.* Here Mary Richards makes one of her periodic visits to her friend, now widowed, who has moved from Minneapolis to San Francisco.

INDEX

Jack Albertson (L) and Freddie Prinze (R), seen here with Avery Schreiber, star in the hit comedy *Chico and the Man,* in its second year on NBC in 1975. This James Komack-created series about a cynical garage dealer and his happy-go-lucky Chicano apprentice will remain a top-rated show until 1977, when Prinze, a young stand-up comic who has risen quickly to stardom, will kill himself.

Welcome Back, Kotter, another James Komack comedy series premieres on ABC in 1975. Stand-up comic Gabe Kaplan plays a former pupil of a tough Brooklyn high school who returns ten years later to teach. Debralee Scott plays student "Hotsie" Totsie.

Milton Berle and Sid Caesar make a rare joint appearance when they parody "A Streetcar Named Desire" on *Tony Orlando and Dawn,* a hit CBS variety series hosted by the popular singing group.

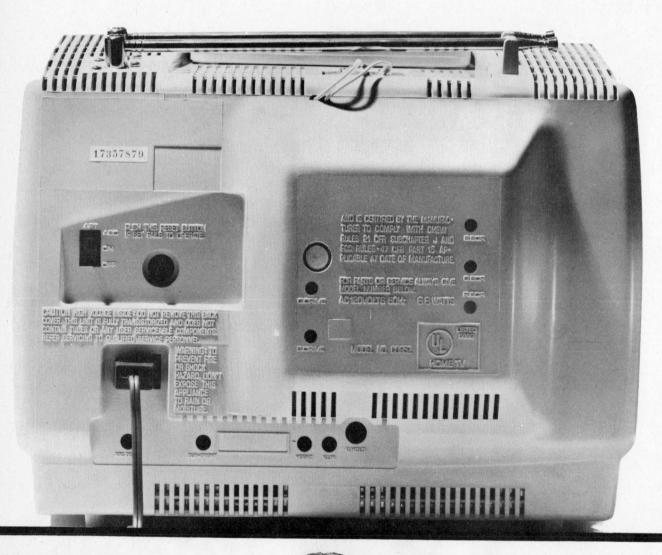

David Soul and Paul Michael Glazer will evolve from unknowns to television superstars, playing police buddies on *Starsky and Hutch*, a violent, simply written drama that debuts on ABC in 1975 and moves toward the top of the ratings.

Jessica Walter is the chief of detectives for San Francisco's police force on *Amy Prentiss*, which becomes a rotating series in 1974 on the *NBC Sunday Mystery Movie*. Art Metrano (L) plays Detective Roy Pena, who is happy to have a female boss.

Private eyes Eddie Albert and Robert Wagner are partners on *Switch*, which begins a two-year run on CBS in 1975. Each week ex-cop Albert and ex-con Wagner turn the tables on swindlers in this light drama.

After sixteen years, *Ellery Queen* returns to television in 1975. Jim Hutton (R) is the fifth actor to play the mystery writer-detective in a series. David Wayne plays Ellery's father, Inspector Richard Queen, in this NBC program that will be dropped after one year, despite moderate popularity. In this episode, George Burns, already a murder victim, talks on film about who might want to do him in.

September 20, 1975. *Saturday Night Live with Howard Cosell* debuts. The plans to make the controversial sportscaster into another Ed Sullivan, on the first prime time series in years that is done live, will go awry. ABC will cancel the experiment in four months.

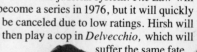

October 11, 1975. *NBC's Saturday Night*, a wild, irreverent comedy-variety show broadcast live from New York each Saturday from 11:30 P.M. to 1:00 A.M., debuts. The "Not Ready for Prime Time Players" are: (L–R) Chevy Chase, John Belushi, writer Michael O'Donoghue, Gilda Radner, Jane Curtin, Laraine Newman, and Garrett Morris. Chase will become a major star and leave the show in 1976, but the series will continue to have surprising popularity.

Lee Remick stars as *Jennie: Lady Randolph Churchill* in a critically acclaimed PBS mini-series in 1975. Paul Ambrose (L) plays young Winston Churchill, and Ronald Pickup is his father.

October 22, 1975. *The Law*, an NBC–TV film, stars Judd Hirsh (L) here with Gary Busey, as a rebellious public defender. Critics will rave about this program which presents a realistic behind-the-scenes look at the judicial system. *The Law* will become a series in 1976, but it will quickly be canceled due to low ratings. Hirsh will then play a cop in *Delvecchio*, which will suffer the same fate.

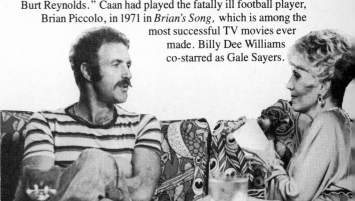

William Holden (R)
stars as Bumper Morgan
in The Blue Knight,
a mini-series adapted
from the novel of
policeman-writer
Joseph Wambaugh (L)
that is presented on
NBC on four
consecutive nights.
George Kennedy will
play Morgan in CBS's
The Blue Knight weekly
series in 1976.

December 11, 1975. James Caan is interviewed by Hollywood gossip columnist Rona Barrett on her second daytime special, "Rona Looks at James Caan, Michael Caine, Elliott Gould, and Burt Reynolds." Caan had played the fatally ill football player, Brian Piccolo, in 1971 in Brian's Song, which is among the most successful TV movies ever made. Billy Dee Williams co-starred as Gale Sayers.

Mike Wallace (R), who gained a reputation as a hard-hitting interviewer on his pioneer *Night Beat* series in the fifties, interviews former Nixon aide John Ehrlichman on *60 Minutes*. This investigative CBS magazine-format show, hosted by Wallace, Dan Rather, and Morley Safer, will shock everyone in the industry by becoming one of America's top ten shows. Imitations will result. Meanwhile, Ehrlichman will take his typewriter to prison. A major ABC six-part mini-series *Washington: Behind Closed Doors* will be adapted from his book.

One Day at a Time is a new Norman Lear comedy that premieres on CBS. Bonnie Franklin (L) plays a divorced mother and Richard Masur is her boyfriend who has the unique distinction (for television) of being younger than she. He will be written out of the hit series in its second season. MacKenzie Phillips and Valerie Bertinelli play the daughters Franklin must raise alone.

Norman Lear's *Mary Hartman, Mary Hartman* premieres on independent stations throughout the country in 1976. This ambitious nightly soap opera parody, which all three networks refused to buy, will become the talk of the nation. Louise Lasser, as Mary Hartman, and Greg Mullavey star as a much-troubled married couple in this show that will delight and offend viewers until the summer of 1977. It will spawn *Fernwood 2-Night*, a nightly talk show parody, hosted by Martin Mull.

Nick Nolte marries Kay Lenz in the conclusion of ABC's smash mini-series *Rich Man, Poor Man*. This adaptation of Irwin Shaw's best-seller will pave the way for many series based on popular novels. *Rich Man, Poor Man, Book II* will flop on ABC in the 1976–77 season.

Mary Kay Place plays country singer Loretta Haggers on *Mary Hartman, Mary Hartman*. A song she writes for the show, "Baby Boy," will actually go to the top of the country-and-western charts. Place wrote for some of TV's most popular comedies before hitting stardom as Mary Hartman's best friend.

April 5, 1976. Mae West makes a rare TV appearance on the CBS special "Dick Cavett's Backlot U.S.A." Cavett hosted several talk shows, including one on ABC that lasted four years opposite *The Johnny Carson Show.* He will host a talk show on PBS in 1977.

Game show producer Chuck Barris is host of *The Gong Show,* a wild daily show on which amateurs perform zany acts. If celebrity judges disapprove of an act, they bang on a gong and the contestant must leave the stage. This show will attract a huge following.

Women athletes become television celebrities during the 1976 Olympics. American figure skater Dorothy Hamill (L) captures Gold and hearts at the Innsbruck Winter Olympics. Rumania's twelve-year-old gymnast Nadia Comaneci (below) dazzles the world with several perfect performances at the Montreal Summer Olympics. ABC preempts its regular schedule to broadcast both Olympics in prime time.

Howard Cosell (C) and Frank Gifford (R), seen here with their *ABC Monday Night Football* co-host Alex Karras, are part of the huge team of ABC sportscasters who broadcast the 1976 Olympic Games. The nightly telecasts are so successful that NBC bids $100 million for rights to the 1980 Moscow Olympics.

Curt Gowdy and Tony Kubek broadcast NBC's Baseball *Game of the Week*. They are also the broadcasters of NBC's *Monday Night Baseball*, until 1976 when ABC outbides NBC for the rights to the Monday games, intensifying the sports rivalry between the two networks.

ABC charms Barbara Walters off NBC and *The Today Show* with a one-million-dollar-a-year contract and a promise that she will moderate several specials. Walters becomes Harry Reasoner's partner on the *ABC Evening News,* replacing Howard K. Smith.

Jimmy Carter wins the 1976 Democratic presidential nomination. Highlighting the campaign will be three televised debates between Carter and President Gerald Ford that are sponsored by the League of Women Voters. In November, Jimmy Carter will win the presidential election.

Fred Silverman, programming wizard who made CBS the top network in the early seventies, lifts his new network, ABC, into first place for the first time in its history in 1976.

Laverne and Shirley, an ABC comedy about two female roommates who work in a Milwaukee brewery during the fifties, is a spin-off from *Happy Days*, which it joins at the top of the ratings. Penny Marshall and Cindy Williams star.

Good, clean family entertainment is provided when the young singing sensations Donny and Marie Osmond join forces for ABC's *Donny and Marie*, a variety show that will surprise many by gaining high ratings.

Charlie's Angels, a tongue-in-cheek action-adventure about three beautiful female detectives who go braless, is added to ABC's schedule. It will quickly zoom to the top of the ratings, and its stars (L–R) Jaclyn Smith, Kate Jackson, and, particularly, Farrah Fawcett-Majors will become popular subjects of fan magazines. Fawcett-Majors, whose celebrated poster has sold several million copies, will quit the series in 1977 and be replaced by Cheryl Ladd.

The Bionic Woman, a spin-off of *The Six Million Dollar Man*, becomes a weekly ABC series. Lindsay Wagner stars as the superhuman government agent who must don various disguises in order to trap evil wrongdoers. *The Bionic Woman* will switch to NBC in 1977.

Wonder Woman, starring Lynda Carter, is another show that features a woman with superpowers. Based on the famous comic book heroine, it begins on a monthly basis but will become a weekly series in 1977. *Wonder Woman* will move from the forties to the seventies when it shifts from ABC to CBS later that year.

Versatile performers Shirley MacLaine (L), Mitzi Gaynor, (C) and Lily Tomlin (R) each hostess several popular specials in the seventies.

Alice, a straight comedy spawned from the film *Alice Doesn't Live Here Anymore*, a comedy-drama that starred Ellen Burstyn, appears on CBS in 1976 and is an immediate hit. Linda Lavin (front) plays a divorcee who works in a diner to support her son. Also starring are: (L–R) Polly Holliday, Vic Tayback, and Beth Howland.

October 22, 1976. CBS shows the taped replay of Muhammad Ali's controversial title defense against Ken Norton which was originally presented live on closed-circuit television. Heavyweight champion Ali has fought on television many times during his illustrious career; his bouts against both worthy opponents and hand-picked unknowns have always attracted a large audience.

November 7–8, 1976. At long last, the 1939 movie classic Gone With the Wind comes to television. Presented on NBC's Big Event on two successive nights, the Margaret Mitchell epic starring (L–R) Olivia DeHavilland, Vivian Leigh, and Clark Gable attracts the largest audience in the history of television. NBC makes plans to present The Godfather Saga in the 1977–78 season.

Natalie Wood and Robert Wagner star in Laurence Olivier's Tribute to American Theatre production of Tennessee Williams' "Cat on a Hot Tin Roof," in which Olivier plays Big Daddy. Wood and Wagner had appeared together in the TV movie Love Affair soon after their second marriage.

December 12, 1976. Mia Farrow is Peter Pan and Danny Kaye is Captain Hook in the new musical production of ''Peter Pan,'' the Silver Jubilee presentation of *The Hallmark Hall of Fame*, which is telecast as part of NBC's *The Big Event*. This production will get lukewarm reviews and little of the attention that the Mary Martin version received.

January 23–30, 1977. *Roots*, a mini-series adapted from Alex Haley's best selling novel about several generations of a black family in America, plays on ABC in prime time for a full week. *Roots* will draw the largest television audience in history. LeVar Burton plays Kunta Kinte, who is kidnapped in Africa in the seventeenth century and brought to America to be a slave. He and his ancestors are the subjects of the massive epic, which will probably be the most widely-discussed, influential program ever on TV. Plans are made for a continuation—*Roots II*.

William Paley retires as the active head of CBS in 1977, the network's fiftieth anniversary. Paley took over the infant Columbia Phonograph Broadcasting System (later CBS) in 1928. In the following year, he temporarily sold 49% of the company to powerful Paramount; this significant move strengthened the struggling network and made it a bona fide challenger to NBC.

The Mary Tyler Moore Show goes off the air after seven years on CBS. The final season's cast is: (top) Ted Knight, Gavin MacLeod, Ed Asner; (bottom) Betty White, Georgia Engel, and Mary Tyler Moore, who has called it quits while the show is still among the top-rated programs. White, McLeod, and Asner will get their own shows.

March 3, 1977. "Hot Lips" Houlihan gets married on *M.A.S.H.*, now in its fifth hit year on CBS. This black-comedy, based on the movie, stars (L–R) Mike Farrell, Alan Alda, Loretta Swit, and Harry Morgan as medics in Korea during the Korean War. Wayne Rogers and MacLean Stevenson left the show in 1975.

(L–R) Lauren Chapin, Elinor Donahue, Billy Gray, Robert Young, and Jane Wyatt are back together for the TV movie, *The Father Knows Best Reunion* in 1977. It will attract a tremendous audience and cause many to guess there will be future shows about the Anderson family.

In 1977, scandal hits televised sports. The FCC begins investigations of four tennis matches by Jimmy Connors on CBS that were billed as "winner-take-all" contests. It is revealed that in each case the loser was guaranteed a large sum of money and that CBS helped deceive the public. Meanwhile, another embarrassed network, ABC, withdraws Don King's *U.S. Boxing Championships* when it is revealed that false records and histories were provided for the participants.

One of tennis's most popular figures is Chris Evert (L), who is seen almost every week winning a televised tournament. But in 1977, England's Virginia Wade (R) briefly takes the spotlight away from Evert by taking her title at Wimbledon. Queen Elizabeth presents her with the victory trophy.

If Evert is the male fans' favorite woman tennis player in 1977, then young Bjorn Borg is certainly the most popular with female fans. In 1977, Borg becomes Jimmy Connors chief competition as the world's top tennis player by winning Wimbledon for the second straight year.

Televised golf tournaments receive more and more promotion, particularly on CBS. When five-time Masters Champion Jack Nicklaus challenges for a title, the network carrying the tournament is guaranteed a large audience. Since the mid-seventies, women's golf has been increasing in popularity, and the *Colgate-Dinah Shore Winners Circle Championship* has become a major sports event. It is expected that when golf glamour girl Laura Baugh, already famous from doing commercials, becomes a consistent winner, women's golf will have its first superstar and TV draw.

Roone Arledge becomes the head of ABC News. He is given the task of lifting the Reasoner-Walters *ABC Evening News* past CBS and NBC in the ratings. He is also expected to acquire prime time from the network for news programming, just as he did for sports programming while in charge of the ABC sports department.

Following the departure of co-hosts Barbara Walters and Jim Hartz, *The Today Show* has a new look. Former White House correspondent Tom Brokaw (seated) and Jane Pauley are hosts in 1977. Here they are joined by regulars (L–R) Gene Shalit, Lew Wood, and Floyd Kalber.

The Tonight Show with Johnny Carson continues to be an NBC late-night fixture in 1977, despite pressure from CBS which is showing reruns of several recent action series. Here Carson speaks with Ed McMahon, Carson's long-time announcer, who made the move with him to California in 1972.

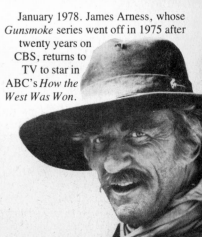

January 1978. James Arness, whose *Gunsmoke* series went off in 1975 after twenty years on CBS, returns to TV to star in ABC's *How the West Was Won.*

Answer to TV Crossword Puzzle on page 236.

Experimentation to improve television viewing is never-ending. Showcase 80 features four small black-and-white TV screens and a large color TV screen for simultaneous viewing. This is what RCA plans for the future.

And Vladimir Zworykin smiles.